John J. Gilligan

John J. Gilligan

THE POLITICS OF PRINCIPLE

Mark Bernstein

THE KENT STATE UNIVERSITY PRESS

KENT, OHIO

To David, my brother

Publisher's note: John J. Gilligan died on August 26, 2013.

© 2013 by The Gilligan Institute

ALL RIGHTS RESERVED

Library of Congress Catalog Card Number 2012048158

ISBN 978-1-60635-113-0

Manufactured in the United States of America

This publication is made possible in part through the support of The Gilligan Institute.

Every effort has been made to obtain permission from those persons interviewed by the author who are quoted in this book.

LIBRARY OF CONGRESS CATALOGING-IN-PUBLICATION DATA

Bernstein, Mark.

John J. Gilligan : the politics of principle / Mark Bernstein.

pages cm

Includes bibliographical references.

ISBN 978-1-60635-113-0 (hardcover) ∞

1. Gilligan, John J. (John Joyce), 1921– 2. Governors—Ohio—Biography. 3. Legislators—United States—Biography. 4. United States. Congress. House—Biography. 5. Ohio—Politics and government—1951– 6. Cincinnati (Ohio)—Biography. I. Title.

F496.4.G55B47 2013

977.1′043092—dc23

[B]

2012048158

17 16 15 14 13   5 4 3 2 1

Contents

	Acknowledgments	vii
1	Mr. Gilligan	1
2	Background	8
3	Jack's Family	18
4	Notre Dame	26
5	To D-Day	36
6	To Okinawa and Back	45
7	Xavier	54
8	Charter Politics	63
9	The First Election	70
10	The Democrats Stir	84
11	Urban Renewal	97
12	"The Miamis Are Everywhere"	110
13	The 1964 Campaign for Congress	122
14	The Great Society Congressman	127
15	Defeat	143
16	Frank Lausche	151
17	The Unbeatable Foe	155
18	The Summer of Discontent	170
19	"My Purpose Holds"	181
20	Setting Sail for Columbus	195
21	The 1970 Campaign	209
22	Ohio on the Verge	222
23	Setting Up Shop	231
24	Round 1: The House	241
25	Round 2: The Senate	259
26	The High Point	278

27 The Progressive Moment 302
28 The Humane Environment 306
29 The Physical Environment 317
30 The Economic Environment 330
31 The Political Environment 339
32 The Sure Thing 350
33 A Long Night, and the Morning After 379
34 Departure and the Next Step 388
35 Washington, Again 394
36 Notre Dame, Again 407
37 Cincinnati, Finally 417
   Afterword 430
   Notes 432
   A Note on Sources 479
   Bibliography 481
   Index 486

Acknowledgments

As will become apparent to the reader, my principal debt in this work is to John Joyce Gilligan, who was enormously generous with his time, even-handed thoughtfulness, candor, and humor. He always wished to press on with the project. I particularly recall three days of interviews conducted by candlelight in the governor's home after the remnants of a tropical storm had rendered Cincinnati free of electricity.

Perhaps next most intimately involved were James Friedman, Robert Daley, and William Chavanne, the three principals of the Gilligan Institute. They not only saw to the project's underwriting and were a continuing source of advice, but they were steadfastly clear that the work and the conclusions it carried were to be those of the author.

To have one's spouse or father made the subject of a book is perhaps an intrusive thing. I was therefore greatly pleased at the full cooperation of Susan Gilligan, the governor's wife, and of his four adult children: Donald Gilligan, Kathleen Sebelius, John Gilligan, and Ellen Gilligan.

The principal archive I used in researching this work was the Ohio Historical Society in Columbus. I owe an enormous debt of gratitude to Thomas Rieder, who as head archivist not only seemed to know everything but knew where it was shelved. The staff of the Ohio Historical Society, operating in somewhat straitened circumstances, was unfailingly competent, cooperative, and a pleasure to work with. Most of the day-to-day accounts of the Ohio General Assembly during Governor Gilligan's tenure come from Gongwer News Service, an invaluable newsletter published whenever the legislature is in session. As a great courtesy, Alan Miller, president of Gongwer, made freely available four years' worth of publications. I also acknowledge the assistance of Charles Lamb at the University of Notre Dame Archives, Father Thomas Kennealy at Xavier University in Cincinnati, and Mark Motz at Cincinnati's St. Xavier High School, each being an institution Jack Gilligan attended or at which he taught.

Though I lived in Ohio from 1973 to 2004, I was a resident of Maryland when this project began. An enormous amount of "on the ground" work needed to be done in Ohio, from searching out 500 newspaper clippings to securing copies of reports from the State Library of Ohio in Columbus. This project could not have been completed without research associate Mary Kay Mabe and her resourcefulness, her fundamental good sense, and her ability to draw others into the effort. These others included Christine Wolff, public affairs office of the Cincinnati Public Schools; Connie Ostrove, reference librarian at the State Library of Ohio; Melanie Chapleau, personal assistant to Father Theodore Hesburgh at the University of Notre Dame; and Carol Hester, chief public information officer at the Ohio Environmental Protection Agency. Led by Nancy Horlacher, local history specialist, the staff at the Dayton Metro Library was very helpful: Nicole Eby, government records reference librarian; Gregory Estes, interlibrary loan reference historian; and Jean Waselewski, interlibrary loan clerk. Additionally, thanks to Rhonda Wiseman, library specialist, and Shannon Keman, reference librarian, both at the University of Cincinnati Law Library, and to "everyone" in the periodicals department of the Cincinnati Public Library and microfilm department of the Columbus Public Library.

For their comments on the manuscript, I am particularly indebted to Dr. George Knepper of the University of Akron and to Michael Curtin, whose career at the *Columbus Dispatch* took him from reporter to associate publisher. They read and critiqued the manuscript in its entirety, discovering both virtues of which the author was unaware and matters that needed correction. The production of the book was ably executed by Kent State University Press, most notably Will Underwood, director; Christine Brooks, production manager; Joyce Harrison, acquiring editor; and Mary Young, managing editor.

Less formally, but no less important, was the advice and moral support received from Mark Stern, Mark Sondheim, Tony Dallas, Alan Loeb, Neil Shister, Jean Bernstein, Michael Derr, Tom Suddes, and doubtless others. Despite this, there were times when I seriously questioned the project's future. At those times, I was blessed to have near me someone of unwavering confidence in the successful completion of the task. To Susan Drake Swift, whose faith was the evidence of things unseen by the author, I am most deeply indebted.

1.

Mr. Gilligan

Wilbur Wright was once asked to name the prerequisites of success. Easy, he said, "Pick out a good father and mother and begin life in Ohio."[1] There was more than state (or family) pride in Wilbur's response; there was due appreciation of the Buckeye state's peculiar history. When Americans first spilled over the Appalachians, Ohio was the only contiguous free state on the other side. As such, it attracted all manner of groups—from the Mormons who settled in Kirtland to the German separatists who founded Zoar. Ohio was where the Yankee blacksmiths from New Hampshire and the mill workers from Massachusetts and the small farmers of Virginia mixed and mingled and where they created a population no longer tied to the Atlantic, a population that looked forward to the West rather than back to Europe. A population, for the lack of a better word, of Americans.

Ohio offered vast resources to a scattered population, an imbalance that rewarded inventiveness. Initially, these inventions were incidental things, like better ways to squeeze cider from an apple or extract honey from a hive. Eventually these inventions changed the world—the work of the Ohio-born Thomas Edison, of Ohio-born Charles Kettering, and of Wilbur and his Ohio-born brother Orville.

Ohio was patriotic to its fighting core. The state was home to the generals who won the Civil War—Grant, Sherman, and Sheridan—and home to most of the presidents who followed that conflict; between 1869, when Ulysses S. Grant took office, and 1923, when Warren G. Harding died, there was an Ohio-born president in the White House more than half the time.

With industrialization, Ohio offered location, mineral wealth, and deep reserves of water. Iron ore from Minnesota traveled by ponderous lake carriers to be made into steel in Cleveland, the city in which John D. Rockefeller built the very model of the modern monopoly. Ohio cities specialized. Akron had rubber; Toledo had glass; Dayton was second only to Detroit in the auto industry. Visiting northeastern Ohio in 1962, John Steinbeck wrote, "My eyes and mind were battered by the fantastic hugeness and energy of production, a complication that resembles chaos and cannot be."[2] That energy had been fueled by enormous investments in industrial plants made during the Second World War. Arguably, the immediate postwar years saw Ohio's industrial strength at its peak. From that peak, it is difficult to say with certainty when the state's decline began. Cleveland's manufacturing employment, for example, began to drop off in 1969. Historian George Knepper notes that in the 1950s Ohio's economy accounted for more than 6 percent of the nation's gross national product (GNP). Thereafter this percentage fell, slowly but steadily, to less than 5 percent by the century's close.

There are numerous reasons for this decline. Still, if the word is used broadly, the best explanation might be underinvestment. Knepper observes, "Too many of [the] industrial plants had been built fifty or sixty years earlier, when industries were first reaching giant size, and too little had been done to modernize these plants or to replace them with more efficient, competitive facilities."[3] Competitive, that is, with the newer and often union-free plants, first in the Carolinas and the Sunbelt and then later in Asia. But the shortchanging of investment was not simply of industrial capital. The state, generally, declined to invest in itself: Ohio did not boast of the quality of its public schools, its facilities for the disabled, its local government services; rather, it boasted of how little it spent on them. And there was a further underinvestment, which might be termed a lack of receptivity to ideas: the future could always be secured by patching the old ways together.

One day may be identified as the beginning of when things started to change: on January 10, 1971, John Joyce Gilligan was sworn in as Ohio's sixty-second governor. All but universally known as Jack, Gilligan had a political career short by the standards of major national politicians. He served a single term in the U.S. Congress and then a single term as governor of Ohio.

That term in the 89th Congress is, however, generally regarded as the most important since the early New Deal. It was the Congress that enacted Lyndon Johnson's Great Society legislation, landmark actions like the Voting Rights Bill, Medicare, the War on Poverty, the Model Cities program, the Elementary and Secondary Education Acts. And for these and other measures Jack Gilligan, then a forty-four-year-old congressman from Cincinnati, voted—and, in most cases, voted enthusiastically.

Gilligan's 1971–75 tenure in the Ohio Statehouse may be similarly viewed as the state's most important since the 1913–14 governorship of the business progressive James Cox. In Gilligan's four years, and very much under his leadership, Ohio enacted the state's first personal and business income tax, an act with multiple consequences. It not only established the wherewithal with which to reverse the history of underfunded services in the state, but it was a statement by the people of Ohio of what kind of state they wished to live in. It was a state which, among other things, would protect its environment, fund its schools, provide decent treatment to the mentally and physically disabled, and apply ethical standards to those who governed.

The establishment of the income tax is seen as a watershed in Ohio state politics; it was a measure that undergirded state government finances for ensuing decades. To hear Jack Gilligan tell it, the enacting of that tax was rather a simple matter. First, one had to establish the fairly simple proposition that Ohio needed the money. Second, one had to establish the fairly simple proposition that a progressive income tax was the fairest way to raise the funds needed. As it happened, the establishing of these two simple propositions involved ten months of siege warfare with a Republican-controlled legislature.

Jack Gilligan was a natural teacher drawn to the company of the young and open-minded, whom he did the service of taking seriously. Some of those who responded to his politics and his nature went on to highly notable political careers. Pollster Peter Hart joined Gilligan's 1968 Senate campaign at age twenty-six. Political analyst Mark Shields, then thirty-one, arrived a few months later as political director of the fall campaign. With them and with a good deal of others, Gilligan, despite the age difference, developed warm and lasting ties. Shields suggested that the basis of Gilligan's appeal was that "he could make people believe they were better than they were, and so they became so."[4]

This was part of a broader outlook. Jack Gilligan was an unlikely politician. In his various campaigns, Gilligan drew to his banner a fair number of individuals who in their adolescence or college years had imagined themselves as future senators or governors or congressman or campaign managers or, God forbid, press secretaries. But Gilligan was the only one engaged in the enterprise who, as an adolescent, saw himself becoming a Jesuit priest. Jack Gilligan was not Catholic by identification. His religion was more than a matter of habit and ritual; it was something by which he was informed, a body of social thought on which he reflected and from which he drew sustenance and direction—and this included politics. In one interview, Gilligan said:

> One of the basic things to answer is the question: what is politics all about? Is it a matter of a contest—like the American League—where the emphasis in on scoring points? That's the way the game had been played for a very long time by both the Democrats and the Republicans. Often, that was the end and the objective: capture office; hold office; reward the friends of the winning side. But there is an alternate notion, that of using political office primarily for changing the society, changing in substantive ways how we live together and work together.[5]

Jack Gilligan was a good-sized, good-looking man (despite what he termed his "banana nose") whose distinctive characteristic was his red hair. He was highly intelligent, a very quick study, and a sharp debater. He was a true son of Cincinnati,

a city that is a mélange of German, Irish, Jewish, African American, and Appalachians set on hills that make for curious intersections and wonderful views, and altogether Ohio's most interesting city. Cincinnati was a place Jack Gilligan loved. He
was a fourth-generation Cincinnatian and also the fourth generation in the family
business, which was funeral homes. It was a business which provided death's necessities, one that made the Gilligan family affluent and fairly prominent and one in
which Jack had no discernible desire to take part.

Between the time Gilligan gave up on the Jesuits and entered into his political
career, he spent some years teaching English at Xavier University in Cincinnati.
He had an English teacher's respect for the language and regard for the power of
words well chosen. This was evident when, in 1944, during his wartime navy service, he sat in the officers' quarters of the USS *Emmons* and carefully selected the
words he would write to Mary Kathryn Dixon in Cincinnati to propose marriage.
Due to the war, their courtship had occurred all but entirely by correspondence.
Katie was the daughter of longtime family friends. Well-educated in her own right
and a high school English teacher, she was a somewhat reticent woman, but she
was a lover of children. And, Gilligan said, "she was pretty."[6] Their marriage produced four children and lasted the half-century until her death.

The seat in Congress that Gilligan captured in 1964 had considerable pedigree.
Earlier in the century, it was held by Nicholas Longworth, known for his wealth, his
charm, his Speakership of the House, and his wife, Teddy Roosevelt's daughter Alice.
Alice Roosevelt Longworth, who survived her husband by half a century, became
something of a Washington institution and was known for her sharp but discerning
wit. In the days before women had the vote, Mrs. Longworth noted that politicians
were either men or boys. The boys, she said, went into politics to *be* something; the
men went into politics to *do* something. Gilligan was one of the latter.

What Gilligan shared with others was a vision of government as a kind of inter-
generation compact that knitted up the community. As Shields expressed it, "The
inescapable truth is that each of us has been warmed by fires we did not build; each
of us has drunk from wells we did not dig. We can do no less for those who come
after us."[7] Those words were spoken at a 2008 breakfast gathering in Columbus that
served as the kickoff event for the Gilligan Institute (one of whose projects is this
book. Gilligan engendered loyalty among those who had worked in his administration and elsewhere; the crowd on hand on that occasion numbered well over 300.

In political terms, Gilligan was something of a head turner. As a freshman
congressman, he was the subject of a cover story in the *New York Times Magazine*
written by David Broder. Broder said of Gilligan, "There are, God knows, plenty
of charming Irishmen in politics. He had that in spades. Aside from the charm
quotient, what was distinctive about him was that sense 'I know what is corrupt-
ing and distorting the politics here'—whether it was in the House or in Ohio—
'and that's my target.' He was very clear in his mind what he was fighting against."[8]

Indeed, in a 1997 interview, Gilligan said so with some eloquence:

It was not government that depressed wage scales and benefits to the point where it is almost impossible for middle class families to exist on the income of a single wage earner; it was not government that has outsourced work to take advantage of non-union wage rates; it was not government that ran the entire savings and loan industry [the then current financial catastrophe] into bankruptcy to the tune of a hundred billion of taxpayers' money; and, finally, it was not government that poisoned our rivers and lakes, polluted the air we breathe, pillaged our forests, and ravaged the countryside for private profit.[9]

Gilligan was, often enough, angry. He had an already-florid complexion that readily went red-faced. He thought of life in terms of purpose and was impatient with those who did not act accordingly. One of his children recalled:

We would often go to Mass together as a family on a Sunday. Pretty much every week, we'd get back in the car and my father would begin to redeliver the sermon. Because whatever it had been about—say, Jonah and the whale—Dad would start on what should have been said. We are in the middle of war in Vietnam, why are we not talking about that? Or something that might be happening in Cincinnati that he thought of in terms of right or wrong. He would start to redeliver the sermon that should have been given. He saw it as a missed opportunity to deliver a message.[10]

He was a very quick study, a possessor of a keen political intelligence, and a sharp-edged debater, one strongly disinclined to suffer fools gladly. One high school classmate said that as a young man Gilligan projected "hauteur—as though he imagined himself destined for big things."[11] Later, the pejorative most applied (rather frequently) to Gilligan by persons with a less delicate sense of language was "arrogant."

There is an alternate explanation. Gilligan was an extraordinarily self-directed individual; unusual for a politician, it was his own approval that chiefly concerned him, not the approval of others. One member of his gubernatorial circle said, "I think he felt he had a belief system of what needed to be done to accomplish his goals; therefore, as long as he was meeting his own expectations, he felt he was doing what was needed."[12] Another member of the inner circle agreed that Gilligan's most important contract was with himself but noted that this "might be a definition of arrogance."[13]

Leave the last word to a member of the loyal opposition. Charles Kurfess served as the Republican Speaker of the House during Gilligan's first two years as governor; as such, he was an indispensable ally in securing the state income tax.

Some years back, a reporter approached Kurfess and said he was writing something in connection with a forthcoming Gilligan birthday event. Would Kurfess, the reporter asked, say that Jack Gilligan was "arrogant"? Kurfess arched himself and replied, "I would never say that Jack Gilligan was arrogant on his birthday."[14]

Gilligan likely did not feel in large gatherings the comfortable ease that was his in smaller settings. He was a considerable raconteur, the story-telling voice on which the other dinner guests would focus. One advantage of hailing from Ohio is that the state is filled with implausible political figures who lend themselves to anecdote. Like "Jumping" Joe Ferguson, who, as a candidate in the 1950 U.S. Senate election, was asked what he thought about Quemoy and Matsu, two contested islands off the Chinese mainland. Ferguson replied, "I plan to carry both those towns."[15] Or U.S. senator Stephen Young, who responded to a critical letter from a constituent with the pithy note: "Sir: Some idiot has written me a letter and signed your name."[16] Or state senator Anthony Calabrese, who wore double-breasted suits and talked out of the side of his mouth in what was regarded as a fake-Mafia manner and who said, "Before we have drinks, let's have cocktails."[17]

In 1974 Gilligan's reelection to the Ohio governorship was broadly, if perhaps too nonchalantly, assumed. The tax increase was secured; large increases in funding for education and mental health were made; the EPA was established; and more. A survey of statehouse reporters that spring was unanimous: Gilligan would be returned to office.

So with that victory surely achieved, what was next? It is difficult to be the two-term governor of a major state without casting a more than curious eye in the direction of the White House (and, in truth, if a governor doesn't himself see visions of sugar plums dancing on Pennsylvania Avenue, his staff likely will). Had he been reelected, Gilligan would clearly have stood somewhere on that short list of eight or ten potential nominees. Gilligan's actual interest in the Presidency is a question that, for the moment, will be begged, as no campaign to that end was ever launched. But in what stands as evidence of life's disproportion, it was not the sea of national politics that drowned Gilligan but a puddle much closer to home. The certain reelection victory anticipated for 1974 did not occur.

Gilligan never again held a major elective office. He served two years as administrator of the Agency for International Development under President Jimmy Carter and then spent longer periods in academia, first at his alma mater, Notre Dame, and then returning to his home city and the University of Cincinnati. In 1996, his wife of half a century, Katie, died. Three years later, at age seventy-eight, Gilligan stood for election to the Cincinnati school board; someone, he said, must speak up for the children that system was ill-serving. He was elected, as the leading vote-getter on the ticket. The following year, he remarried, to a family practitioner, Dr. Susan Fremont. In 2003, he sought and secured reelection to the school board.

John Gilligan's career is difficult to summarize. One close associate stated, "There was steel in Jack's spine, but there was also an urbane and genteel quality. I never thought he was a good fit for Ohio."[18] Noting Gilligan's defeats in his reelection bids to Congress in 1966 and the governorship in 1974, David Broder said, "He was cut off by the voters at the very point at which he might otherwise have become even a historic figure. Had he been able to build some seniority in Congress, he would have been a force in the House; had he had a second term as governor, he could have changed Ohio politics fundamentally."[19]

In 1997, Jack Gilligan was associated with a public policy undertaking at the University of Cincinnati. Asked if his general perspective had changed in the two decades since he had left office in Columbus, he replied, "I think now what I thought then—government, at whatever level, is we the people working in concert to do what we cannot do as individuals. That is what government is or should be."[20]

2

Background

Cincinnati, like St. Louis and Chicago, was too peripheral and perhaps too important to be a state capital. Sitting on the northern bank of the Ohio River, Cincinnati was a triumph of commercial location in the nineteenth century. As early farmers and artisans unlocked the wealth of the Ohio Valley, they found that producing goods was rather less costly than moving those goods to market. Roads were few, dreadful, and long. Rivers not only moved; they moved goods downstream for free. A portion of the wealth that moved along the Ohio River rubbed off on Cincinnati as it passed—considerable fortunes that, several generations later, would underwrite a startling array of cultural facilities.

The city is splendidly set. Its flood plain is surrounded by an amphitheater of hills that rise at gasping angles. Charles Dickens, an early visitor, and one not always charmed with America, wrote, "Cincinnati is a beautiful city: cheerful, thriving and animated. I have not often seen a place that commends itself so favorably and pleasantly to a stranger at the first glance as this does: with its clean houses of red and white, its well-paved roads, and footways of bright tile."[1] In 1840, its population of 46,338 ranked it sixth in the nation and made it the largest city that was not an oceangoing port on the Atlantic or the Gulf of Mexico. Cincinnati was, effectively, the capital of the Old Northwest Territory—the biggest place west of Philadelphia and north of New Orleans—and by far the most sophisticated. River cities are places of variety—where merchants gather, travelers tarry, deals are struck, and the news arrives more quickly. By 1840, Cincinnati had not only eight brewers, but thirty-five physicians and sixty lawyers to sort whatever might be the injury and litigation the consequent drinking caused. To this, the city added "nine dry-goods dealers, sixteen booksellers, and nine printers and publishers."[2]

Along with attracting the region's largest number of professionals, Cincinnati welcomed in a great many hogs—half a million entered the city each year, only to depart as salt pork, hams, and bacon. One observer commented, "It is Cincinnati that perfected the system that packs fifteen bushels of corn in a hog, packs fifteen hogs into a barrel, and then sends the barrels down the Mississippi to feed the world."[3] The parts of the pig that stayed in town—the fat and the bristles—were bought up by two Britons, William Procter and James Gamble, who in 1837 founded the company that remains the city's largest employer.

Cincinnati was inclined to regard the praise it received from Dickens and others as only its due. As the Midwest's "Queen City," it felt a certain noblesse oblige—not merely to live well but to instruct others in doing likewise. It was home to William Holmes McGuffey, head of Cincinnati College, who in 1836 published his first *McGuffey's Eclectic Reader,* which, in its many editions, combined short readings with admonitions for traditional morality and became the core curriculum for most American schoolchildren. Over time, 122 million copies were sold. The *Columbia Encyclopedia* said of McGuffey's works: "Concerned with traditional morality as much as with reading, their influence on shaping the American mind in the mid–nineteenth century can scarcely be exaggerated."[4]

Not far from Cincinnati College, at 2950 Gilbert Avenue, lived the daughter of one minister and wife of another. Harriet Beecher Stowe spent eighteen years gathering observations on slavery. Cincinnati was a good place for such study. Perched on the northern side of the Ohio River, it looked across that boundary to the slave states and the South, across the Jordan that would-be runaway slaves hoped to cross. Cincinnati had the largest population of free blacks in the Midwest, and it had slave markets at which their enslaved brethren were quite literally sold down the river to the cotton lands to the south. In 1850, Stowe published her monumental best-seller *Uncle Tom's Cabin.* Between McGuffey and Stowe, Cincinnati can lay fair claim to America's two most influential writers.

Cincinnati was a boomtown. During the 1840s, the city's population more than doubled, bringing it to 115,435, nearly overtaking New Orleans's 116,375 and closing in on Philadelphia's 121,376. Cincinnati felt apart from Ohio. Northeastern Ohio drew its citizens from New England; the southeast part of the state was settled largely by families from Virginia and Kentucky. As a river city, Cincinnati was the port of entry for persons considerably more distant, including many from the German states. In 1851, 28 percent of Cincinnati's residents had been born in Germany. Under their influence, "the city began to lose its exclusively American character."[5] The city's Germans settled in two- and three-story brick-home neighborhoods on the flat land just north of the Miami-Erie Canal, in an area that for their presence came to be known as Over-the-Rhine. The city's German population was defined by the language many continued to speak and was joined together by the singing societies, schools, savings and loans, and sporting clubs that crossed the Atlantic along with the emigrants. At a time when agricultural Ohio was living on mostly pork and cornmeal, Cincinnati's Germans were dining on sauerkraut, apple dumplings, and a bonanza of sausages. Not least, the German influx made Cincinnati the first city in the Midwest to have a substantial Catholic population.

Of German Cincinnati, one local observer wrote in 1851: "Their presence has accelerated the execution of our public improvements, and given impulse to our great manufacturing operations, without which they could not have reached their present extent and importance."[6] Cincinnati's Germans were early for the Republican Party, strong for Lincoln, and solid for Union. Three days after Lincoln first called for volunteers to suppress the rebellion in 1861, the 9th Ohio Volunteer Infantry regiment was formed in the city—with 1,014 of its 1,155 members German immigrants.

In 1853, the city established the nation's first professional fire department, aided by two local inventors, Abel Shawk and Alexander Latta, who designed the "Uncle Joe Ross," the first successful steam-powered fire engine. In 1854, Rabbi Isaac Mayer Wise moved to the city that he would make the center of Reform Judaism, with its magnificent Plum Street Temple built in 1866 and Hebrew Union College opened in 1875. And in 1869, Cincinnati professionalized what for most of the next century would clearly be America's game: it fielded the Cincinnati Red Stockings, the nation's first professional baseball team, which, to local satisfaction, went undefeated in its first year.

But these innovations did not signal the city's continued rise. In 1850, Cincinnati had been perhaps a few uncounted heads shy of overtaking New Orleans and Philadelphia. That gap never closed. Economically, once the Civil War was declared, nothing ever went entirely right for the city. The Confederate citadel of Vicksburg, Mississippi, clamped down on the river traffic. The hog traffic moved to Chicago, which, serviced by rail, soon earned Carl Sandberg's encomium as "hog butcher to the world." By a painful irony, perhaps, the actor Junius Brutus Booth was in town for an engagement at Pike's Opera House on Fourth Street when word reached the city that Booth's younger brother had murdered the president.

Cincinnati, seemingly secure in its waterway, pretty much passed on the opportunity to take part in the next big thing: the railroads. Postwar, it lost out to St. Louis, which had a bigger river, and to Chicago, which was casting out a net of railway lines to capture the Midwest's trade. In his 1869 annual report, the city's mayor reported that St. Louis and Chicago were taking the lead. Several years later, a letter writer to a local newspaper suggested that Cincinnatians who had sent aid to Chicago following its great fire of 1871 had made the mistake in aiding their rival.[7]

In rough, Cincinnati prospered when the major paths of trade ran north and south and by river. When those paths were superseded by rails that ran east and west, Cincinnati's prominence waned. The *WPA Guide* to the city states that by the 1870s, "Cincinnati's commercial overlordship of the Midwest had ended."[8]

Historian Zane Miller noted that there have been phases to Cincinnati's boosterism. The first was that it was the most booming, most prosperous, most economically vibrant city west of Appalachians. When relative economic decline set, the city quickly advanced a second thesis of self-regard: if it could not dominate, it would enlighten. And it did so with some skill and considerable funds. The physical centerpiece of this effort was Music Hall. Opened in 1878 with a 3,500-seat auditorium, it provided the podium once graced by the reigning German composer Richard Strauss. Built without a proscenium or orchestra pit, Music Hall was intended to serve as well as a convention site. Shortly after Music Hall opened, Cincinnati had the satisfaction of winning out over Chicago and St. Louis in landing the 1880 Democratic Convention. (Winfield Hancock and William English, nominated at the Music Hall, lost narrowly to Ohio congressman James Garfield that November.)

To add to its great music and fine opera, Cincinnati in the next decade opened the first art museum west of the Appalachians that had been built expressly for that purpose. It established the city-chartered University of Cincinnati, the nation's second municipal university (after the City College of New York). It opened, and later expanded, the forty-five-acre zoological gardens. It was the birthplace of such notable turn-of-the-century painters as Robert Henri and John Henry Twachtman, with a third-ranking artist, Frank Duveneck, born in Covington, Kentucky, just opposite on the Ohio. And, subsidized by the immensely wealthy Longworth family, it was home to the Rookwood art pottery, whose works won a string of major international prizes beginning with the 1889 Paris exhibition. Ohio historian George Knepper summarized this effort: "The fact remains that Ohio could claim more accomplishments in the arts than most of its neighbors thanks to the cultural leadership of Cincinnati after the Civil War."[9]

Cincinnati's cultural blossoming reinforced the city's sense of being in Ohio but not of it. That sense of apartness remained the case for some time, as a bit of anecdotal evidence suggests. An official at Ohio State University noted that prior to the Second World War, Cincinnati's better high school graduates might enroll locally in the University of Cincinnati; they might go west to Indiana University or south to the University of Kentucky. Catholic students might attend Xavier University locally or else seek out Notre Dame in South Bend, Indiana. But very few of Cincinnati's high school graduates headed northeast, to the state's largest institution, Ohio State University in Columbus.

Cincinnati bore one further distinction. From the turn of the century, Cincinnati was a city whose politics were dominated by the Republican Party and by persons named Taft or Longworth. Indeed, the Democratic Party—in 1932, 1936, 1940, and 1944—offered Cincinnati four opportunities to vote for Franklin Delano Roosevelt, and Cincinnati rejected all of them. Two conclusions follow. The first is that in Ohio Cincinnati was something of a place apart. The second is that in Cincinnati a Democrat was something of a person apart—apart, that is, from the various Republican-controlled wheels and levers that ran the city. These factors combined to make Cincinnati a particularly unlikely place in which to hatch a liberal Democrat to lead the state.

The first Gilligan, Patrick of County Sligo, on the west central Irish coast, arrived in Cincinnati in the mid-1870s. That the city had passed its economic peak may not have concerned him; he did not come to Cincinnati to praise the city but to bury it. In 1877, Gilligan, apparently having secured the necessary capital working as a van driver in the city, established a funeral home downtown. Why he opted for the funeral home business is lost to history. The downtown location was dictated by topography: virtually all businesses first located there. Cincinnati's famous hills—Mount Auburn, Mount Adams, and the rest—rise sharply from the city floor just north of the Ohio River. Until the traction lines and other means came along in the late nineteenth century, the hills—too steep for the energy of a horse or, for that matter, most men—were only thinly populated.

The funeral business is one life's necessities. It is a general anthropological fact that people everywhere undertake some display to mark the transit of the dead from this world into whatever other world their belief prompts them to expect. These obsequies, wrote Thomas Lynch (author, poet, and funeral home director) are commonly characterized by "the food, the drink, the music, the shame and guilt, the kisses of aunts and distant cousins, the exaltation, the outfits, the heart's hunger for all homecomings."[10]

At the time Patrick Gilligan opened for business, and for the better part of a century thereafter, funeral homes were family-oriented undertakings. They operated at a time when families dealt with a short list of purveyors. A family had its particular grocer and butcher, a particular physician, and, on occasion, a particular attorney. These arrangements were part of a family's definition of itself. And along with these purveyors of goods and services, the family also had its funeral director, who "did for us" when the need and necessity arose.

A family saw its grocer and butcher perhaps every few days; it saw its physician on threatening occasions. But the need for an undertaker was once in a lifetime. The support of a funeral home, therefore, required that a considerable number of families grant it their allegiance. In the 1870s, and for many decades thereafter, Cincinnati families preferred that the ceremonies for their deceased be arranged by those who the recently departed might have found congenial had they met in the world of the living. Reflecting this, the Gilligan funeral home rather shortly became principally patronized by Cincinnati's community of Irish Catholics. (There was a second Irish Catholic funeral home in Cincinnati at the time, that of John T. Sullivant.)

The Irish reached Cincinnati later than the German immigrants and in lesser numbers. The 1851 census that placed the city's German population at 28 percent reckoned the Irish in Cincinnati at 12 percent. Of them, a visiting Charles Dickens wrote that the Irish "worked the hardest for their living, and doing any kind of sturdy labor, that came their way, [and] were the most independent fellows" in the city.[11] The Irish arrived as well with more limited resources. While the Germans arrived in organized waves, the Irish—at least initially—came in a clamoring panic, fleeing a land where survival depended on the potato and the potato had failed. Curiously, though the arriving Irish spoke English, they may have felt less at home in the Queen City than their German-speaking counterparts. They were, on arrival, less likely to be literate, less likely to have skills that traded for much in the marketplace. While the Germans had their language, saving and loans, oompah brass bands, and strings of sausages to support self-definition, the Irish arrived with only two strong social institutions to bind their new community: the church and the wake.

From its early days, the Gilligan Funeral Home recorded each service it performed and the associated arrangements and costs in a large ledger book produced by the W. H. Stange & Company, a printing establishment. There was, of course, always a casket—generally, of rosewood, costing $30–$35 (though one "casket, of 'extra size,' cost $90").[12] There was also a hearse to transport the body to the cemetery, some number of carriages to carry the mourners, candles, and whatever else the occasion required. Thus, the arrangements made for the Saturday, October 14, 1893, burial of Mrs. William Sutton, amounted to:

Rosewood coffin	$35.00
Hearse to St. Joseph's cemetery	$8.00
Five carriages	$25.00
Preserving body	$5.00
Crepe gloves and ribbon	$5.00
Door crepe	$1.50
1 Gents Black Wrapper	$15.00
Candles	$1.50
Grave	$7.25
Mass	$10.00
Advertisement	$0.60

The total charge of $113.85 was somewhat above the average of the time.

Burial was expensive. The sum might represent nearly two months' income of the average laborer, though a smaller share for the more affluent who were likelier to make use of the services. The address recorded in the ledger was that of the paying party, generally a relative. Thus, John Ladkin paid $109.20 for the burial of his father, James; Charles Belle paid $96.50 for the burial of his wife, Mollie; and Joseph Gray paid $29.50 for the burial of his three-month-old son, Edward. In the days before ready transportation and communication, business was highly localized. Addresses fell generally in the downtown near the funeral home itself—East Sixth, East Eighth, Broadway, East Pearl, Sycamore. Some stories may be inferred—like that of Miss Francine Blawn, whose address is given as the Merchants' Restaurant and who paid $9 for the burial of two-month-old Albert Perry.

What startles the modern eye is how short the spans of life were. Thomas Don-
nelley reached 60, but Alice Foley was 33, Mary Holoeher 37, Anne Sulligan 48,
Kate Jeffers 38, William Farley 21, James Farrell, 60, James Leonard 36, Mary Murray, 53. Indeed, of the thirty or so people the Gilligan funeral home buried in October 1893, only one lived to be 65; the average age at death appears to have been
the late 40s. Other sources suggest this was about average for the place and time.
Women died often in childbirth and men from harsh labor; and all suffered from
poor sanitation and the limits of medical expertise.

Funeral directors, with their ready familiarity with death, are to many a dis-
comforting lot; to some, theirs is an industry that preys financially on grief. And
some may do so. Thomas Lynch notes, however: "Most of the known world could
not be paid enough to . . . stand with an old widower at his wife's open casket or
talk with a leukemic mother about her fears for her children about to be mother-
less." Lynch adds, "Unless the novice mortician finds satisfaction in helping others
at time of need, or 'serving the living by caring for the dead,' as one of our slogans
goes, he or she will never stick it."[13]

Lynch's comments point to the social role of the funeral director. Indeed, though
perhaps not obviously, being a successful funeral director requires traits similar to
those required for success in politics. The funeral director cares for people in a period of their need, hears their concerns, and is sensitive to their wishes. It is a task
that calls for diplomacy, organizational skills, and attention to detail.

And like a successful politician, a funeral home director must also constantly
be proselytizing: holding the allegiance of those families which were within its
fold while at the same time adding others. Harry Gilligan, Jack's father, who entered the funeral business after the First World War, was in this mold—a gentleman, a hard worker, a deft public speaker, a patter of backs, and a teller of jokes.
He expanded his role of funeral director out into the community and took the
lead in such civic enterprises as the building of the new St. Xavier High School
and other undertakings. In an act that any ward politician would appreciate—
part legitimate charity, part legitimate promotion—the Gilligan family would at
Thanksgiving pack the family hearse with turkeys that were then delivered to the
poorer Irish families on Cincinnati's Mt. Adams and elsewhere in the city.

Founded as it was in 1877, the Gilligan funeral home went into business the
same year Tolstoy published *Anna Karenina* and Queen Victoria was proclaimed
Empress of India. Today in its fifth generation, the undertaking has outlived both
the Czarist and British empires. The Gilligan funeral business has five locations,
having spread its operations around Greater Cincinnati area as the city's population dispersed. The multiplicity of locations, Gilligan commented, means that "no
matter where you drop, we catch you on the first bounce."[14] It is a mildly cynical
comment, but then Jack Gilligan never much liked the funeral business.

Asked how Irish he felt in growing up, Gilligan answered, "Quite."[15] He grew up in proximity to all four of his grandparents, each of whom was Irish Catholic. Such things mattered considerably more then, than now; with and since the Second World War—and with, as well, the Civil Rights movement—the suspicions and suppositions that lay between races, ethnicities, and religions have lessened. In Cincinnati of the 1920s, not only were blacks separated from white and Protestant from Catholics, but German Catholics were separated from Irish Catholics. The social divide was considerable. Cincinnati historian Judith Spraul-Schmidt remembers "people saying, 'My late husband was a good man, even though he was German.'"[16] And Jack Gilligan recalled how when he was in high school "there was a real distinction made if you had an Irish background or a German background. They didn't talk to each other."[17]

The Catholic Church had a hand in sustaining this separation; until the 1920s, the Vatican insisted on separate churches for different language speakers. Thus, two Catholic churches might sit within several blocks of each other—one with an Irish priest and congregation and the other with a German priest and congregation. Separation applied as well to schooling. In the largely Catholic neighborhood of Mount Adams, the children of German Catholic families attended Immaculata; Irish Catholics went to Holy Cross. (In the event of a "mixed marriage"—that is, one between persons of German and Irish descent—matters were settled matrilineally: the offspring attended the school of their mother's church.)[18]

The Irish had been chased out by the impoverishment of their native land. They arrived in America largely insolvent and uncertain. They settled, worked and, for the most part, prospered, in no small measure due to an entrepreneurial success that had been unlikely in British-dominated Ireland. Jack Gilligan had entrepreneurs three generations back and on both sides of his family. His paternal great-grandfather, Patrick, founded the funeral home. When Patrick died in August 1903, following the death of his oldest son, Andrew, the previous February, the business then devolved on son John. John Gilligan was a small, mild man with a white moustache and considerable business judgment. Like most entrepreneurs of the time, he lived close to his business, which allowed him to keep an eye on operations and also make it home most days for lunch. Even when they traveled, they didn't go far. In 1909, John Gilligan bought an early automobile for both business and vacation use. The common vacation took the family only as far as the home of some friends in Cincinnati's Price Hill neighborhood, less than four miles away. But the success of the funeral home did take him into the larger world of Cincinnati business. He served on the original boards of directors of the Kroger Company and the Provident Bank. He also served for a time as president of the Friendly Sons of St. Patrick and was one of the five founding members of Cincinnati's Hyde Park Country Club, to which generations of his family would belong.

About the same time Patrick Gilligan opened his funeral home, Gilligan's maternal great-grandfather, Harry Cain, established a business selling game and fish; indeed, it is credited with being the first to sell fresh fish in the city's downtown. Harry Cain prospered, retired in 1902, and built a substantial home on Woodburn Avenue in the fashionable Walnut Hills neighborhood. John's wife, Mame, was a short, stocky woman about whom one Gilligan sibling said, "You tried to stay on her good side or you tried to stay clear."[19] She was a woman of strong opinions that were offered with no great anticipation of disagreement and expressed in a manner that suggested she was speaking not merely for herself but for the more reliable elements in the Catholic Church. Jack Gilligan said of his grandmother, "She was the Grande Dame. No one debated with her or argued with her; she just let it be known that this was right or wrong, or up or down, and had no particular reservations about saying so."[20] (One particular point of her adamancy was that her teenage grandchildren should not date persons of German descent. Gilligan recalled, "If I dated a girl in high school with a name like Ramaker or Hartken, my grandmother would say, 'What's the matter with you? What's the matter with Katie O'Donnell?' She really meant it."[21]) If anyone escaped Mame's criticism, it was her son, Harry. One of her grandchildren commented, "Grandma, of course, was convinced that Papa was the Prince of Wales."[22]

Harry Gilligan was born in 1895. The family then lived at 617 Mound Street on Cincinnati's West Side home, which had been presented as a wedding gift to John and Mame by the Gilligan and Cain families. Harry attended local elementary school, devoured the upwardly mobile exploits of Horatio Alger, and matriculated on to what was then called St. Jaeger College (later St. Xavier), a Jesuit institution from which he graduated in 1912. It was an association that strengthened two family allegiances: the first to Jesuit-directed education and the second to argumentativeness. Harry spent considerable time on debate and disputation. He later told an interviewer, "I found out that the old Jesuit system of when a person made a statement, the rule was you admit what is true, you deny what is false and what is not clear you question."[23] John Gilligan expected his son to enter the funeral business. But Harry—who a generation later would have bitter arguments with his son Jack over the same question—had little interest in doing so. His interest at the time was focused on driving the family Ford to the Latonia race track and watching the horses run. What changed Harry was his encounter with the future Mrs. Gilligan, Blanche.

Jack Gilligan's maternal grandparents had arrived separately from County Sligo, on the west central Irish coast. Gilligan's maternal grandfather, Patrick Joyce, settled in Youngstown, then a thriving steel center, where he founded a company that was claimed to have poured half the sidewalks in Youngstown. His maternal grandmother, Julia Branigan, came to this country with a sister, settling first in Cincinnati. When her sister married a man from Youngstown, Julia followed to her new brother-in-law's city of residence, living with her married sister. Several years later,

Patrick and Julia met. They married and settled in Youngstown, where Julia bore Patrick eleven children, of which the fifth, Blanche, would be Jack Gilligan's mother.

Blanche Joyce was a woman of exceptional beauty, the kind of beauty that sometimes expects to be pampered and which, a younger relative said, might prompt the unknowing to question whether she had grit or industriousness. Patrick Joyce died when Blanche was just eleven, and she shouldered much of the burden of raising her younger siblings. (She had a favorite sibling, Frank, who entered the priesthood and served as a pastor in Youngstown and Cleveland, a fact in which she took considerable pride.) While the fatherless family was hardly well off, five of the children completed some form of education beyond high school, with Blanche attending a business school. She was, however, reticent by nature, not one to put herself forward or to undertake responsibilities outside the home.

Harry and Blanche met at Cedar Point, a popular vacation resort on Lake Erie, in August 1916. Even though Cincinnati and Youngstown were 274 miles apart, connected by roads that were more intention than fact, for the better part of the next year Harry Gilligan "managed to get to Youngstown some way by hook or crook three or four times a month."[24] But war intervened. Harry entered the U.S. Army with the understanding that he had been promised a commission. When he arrived in camp to claim it, however, he learned that the system had been changed, that officer candidates were required to pass certain tests. Having told any number of people in Cincinnati that he would be serving as an officer, Harry was loathe to return home with no bars on his shoulder and campaigned unsuccessfully for a rank and, as a sergeant, left for France in August 1917, where he ended up helping run a mail unit. (By a further oddity, he got the post because the soldier who was to have been given it was named Schardt—a name that struck some British officials as too German to be trusted with the mail.)

In April 1919 Harry returned from France. He and Blanche were married in her parish church in Youngstown and then settled in Cincinnati, where Harry, aged twenty-four, made a slightly delayed entry into the family business.

3

Jack's Family

For many years, Jack Gilligan believed he was the oldest of his siblings, arriving at Cincinnati's Bethesda Hospital a few minutes before the appearance of his twin sister, Jeanne, on March 22, 1921. He may have been told this as fact; or he may simply have assumed that, by general prerogative, the male should be the older. He wasn't, as he was somewhat deflatingly told when he was enrolled in college. Rather remarkably, his younger siblings, born, his father carefully reckoned, three days shy of three years and three months later, were also twins. Blanche had planned to name the second set Pat and Mike, but when told that these were names used in numerous semi-derogatory jokes about the Irish, she reconsidered. The elder was named Frank, for her mother's favorite brother, Father Francis Joyce, and the younger Harry Jr., though he was all but universally known as Mike.

Harry had a simple enough explanation for the arrival of two sets of twins. It reflected the way his wife played bridge: she always doubled. Pushing unlikelihood a step further, three of the four children grew up redheads, with Frank being the exception. By family joke, the only way Blanche could get Frank to have his hair washed was to tell him that this time it would come out red.

Through the births of the four children, the Gilligans lived in a duplex apartment on Kleinview Avenue in the comfortable but not particularly upscale Walnut Hills section of Cincinnati, with a side yard hospitable to the outdoor play of young children. At one point, Jack, Jeanne, and Mike pitched a tent in that yard but tried to exclude Frank due to his lack of red hair. The Kleinview address was within walking distance from the rather grand home of Harry Gilligan's maternal grandfather, Harry Cain, at 2926 Woodburn Avenue. In 1924 the Gilligan family and Harry's Cain widow switched residences, and the Gilligan family moved into the larger home on Woodburn.[1]

In 1927, Jack and Jeanne were enrolled in Summit Country Day School. Summit was not a local parish school but a private, fee-charging Catholic school whose pupils came largely from fairly well-established families, particularly those more focused on their children's educations and with ambition for their futures. Gilligan recalled Summit as "an old, grand and very good school."[2] It was located on Grandin Road in Cincinnati's Madisonville neighborhood, well beyond walking distance from the Gilligan home, which meant that Jack and Jeanne rode the bus.

The family relocated one additional time. This, for the Gilligans, was a definite move up. In about 1930, John and Harry Gilligan, father and son, decided to tear down the home on Woodburn and replace it with the first structure in Cincinnati specifically designed as a funeral parlor. (Most funeral homes had been originally constructed as large residential properties.) With that, Harry and Blanche Gilligan built a new home at 2812 Ambleside Place in an upscale neighborhood. The land had once belonged to the first Nicholas Longworth, who had made a fortune speculating in early Cincinnati real estate and then lost a portion of that wealth in an extended attempt to raise grapes for making wine.

The home, located on land once cultivated for grapes, was impressive by any measure. Ambleside was a spacious setting—woods for roaming, paths for biking, space for baseball. Frank, in time, proved to be the best student; Mike, the best athlete. Occasionally, there were chores. Jeanne recalled, "Dad would try to con us into cleaning the weeds off the bank once in a while and we'd get ten cents a bushel but that usually petered out after the second bushel."[3] Whatever work there was rarely involved the funeral business. "The only thing we would do [with the family business]," Mike remembered, "is that at Christmas time we would help sort the bills into an accordion folder. That was a winter job intended to get us out of our mother's hair."[4]

The Gilligans' was a favored upbringing. Jack recalled shopping with his mother as a grade school student at a time before buying on credit had become common. It was "an astonishing feat to have a charge account. It was a mark of station: you could go into Pogues and identify yourself as a person who could sign a chit."[5] Affluence created possibilities. Years later, Harry Gilligan encouraged his daughter to pursue her interest in literature, telling her that "he was in a position that [she] didn't have to earn money."[6] The Gilligans had domestic help. When the children were young, on Woodburn, the family employed a nurse and a cook. For years, Mrs. Himmel, a laundress, came on Mondays. A succession of help followed. Blanche Gilligan was notably tolerant of their failings. Jeanne quoted her mother as saying of one cook, "Oh, yes, a miserable dinner, but she does get up in the morning on time to have the breakfast ready."[7] That assessment, Jeanne added, was in keeping with her mother's general influence: "tolerance, and an allowance for people's weaknesses."[8]

For the former Blanche Joyce, marriage into the Gilligan clan and the move to Ambleside represented a substantial jump in her economic well-being. Jack said that she "loved the middle-class life."[9] She had a substantial number of friends of her age and background; she belonged to various women's organizations, did charity work, and spent considerable time at the Hyde Park Country Club.

Blanche Gilligan was devout in her Catholicism. The family belonged to St. Francis de Sales on Woodburn Avenue, not far from the funeral home, even then a very old church. The family observed Holy Days; Good Friday meant three hours of devotions. Like most practicing Catholics of the day, she and her children would fast from midnight on if communion was to be taken. She was proud to be Irish Catholic; proud that her brother was a priest. It was so at a time when the divide between Catholic America and Protestant America was a good deal sharper than it is today. The 1928 presidential nomination of New York governor Al Smith, a Catholic Democrat, had sparked a rush of anti-Catholicism, particularly in the Midwest and South. Many Protestants believed that if Smith was victorious, the Pope would move the papacy to Washington, D.C. By one history, "Along byways of towns and villages, roadside signs—small, handwritten notices—appeared, reading: 'For [Herbert] Hoover and America, or For Smith and Rome. Which? Think it over Americans.'"[10] The Gilligan children remembered their growing up as all but entirely in the company of their fellow Catholics. Mike recalled, "We just really stayed with the Catholics. Frank and I had a number of fellows we palled around with in high school; most of them were Catholic. We just kind of stayed together."[11]

About their father, Jeanne noted that "he never used the expression 'Don't let me ever catch you . . . ,' because that implied to him that we could do it as long as he didn't catch us. We weren't to do it at all."[12] It was a matter of standards, setting and keeping to them. Jeanne saw parallels between father and eldest son. Her father, she said, had some quality of "intellectual arrogance. If he's going to do something, he's going to do it well." She recalled walking each day in the hallway of Summit Country Day past a sign that read, "To whom much is given, of them much is required."

Harry Gilligan worked hard, often returning to the funeral home in the evening after having had dinner with the family. And, like his father, he also served on the boards of directors of Kroger and Provident Bank. He was often in a public role and much enjoyed playing master of ceremonies; professionally, he served for several decades as secretary of National Funeral Directors Association. And he was athletic, having once played football for the local parish team; he was a regular golfer and enjoyed the distinction of being the first basketball coach at Xavier University. His tenure was brief; he stepped down from his coach's post after a single contest, retiring with a lifetime record of 0–1.

The Gilligan family was sports-minded, both playing and watching. Baseball, Jack Gilligan recalled, was a ritual almost as sacred as High Mass, which it frequently followed. Jack and his father's parents would attend Mass on Sundays at St. Francis de Sales's Church, have Sunday dinner at a downtown hotel, and then go see the Cincinnati Reds play at Redlands Field, where the elder Gilligans kept a box. At the intersection of Western Avenue and Findlay Street, Redlands Field was a sprawling expanse (420 feet to the center field fence) that opened in 1912 during the game's "dead ball" era; nine years passed before a Cincinnati outfielder, Pat Duncan, managed to hit one cleanly out of the park. Local baseball historians report that "the first player ever to hit a ball over the center field fence at Redlands Field did so in an exhibition game in the 1921 season. His name: Babe Ruth."[13] The Gilligan family outings must have afforded satisfactions other than victory; between 1929 and 1934 the Reds finished no better than seventh.

Both sets of twins grew up healthy, though Jack and Mike suffered seriously from hay fever, a common malady in Cincinnati and one they shared with their father. The sneezing, the restless breathlessness started in June and often lasted until the first frost, all but ruling out activity involving sustained exertion. Jack recalled how some nights the need for air would drive him gasping to an open window. (He never entirely overcame his hay fever, which did not add to his eagerness, as governor, to visit the show barns at the Ohio State Fair.) This shared affliction pushed the family north during summers. Initially, the Gilligans rented a cottage at Northport Point, near the northernmost tip of Michigan's Leelanau Peninsula, where a number of Catholic families rented cottages. However, one year, when the families tried to renew the rentals, they were refused, informed that there were too many Catholics in the area.

Rejected in Northport Point, Harry Gilligan looked a dozen miles to the southwest, where the unincorporated town of Leland sat on a narrow strip of land separating Lake Michigan from finger-shaped Lake Leelanau. The area's fishing grounds had first drawn white settlement in the 1830s; a sawmill built two decades later marked the start of timbering. Initially, the land was thought poorly fitted for agriculture; it proved, however, to be splendid for cherry trees, whose blossoms colored the region in their billions. Lake Leelanau ran generally north to south, twenty-one miles in length, though little more than a mile and a half across at its widest. Of importance, the site offered convenient rail service through Traverse City, twenty-five miles to the southeast.

Harry Gilligan acquired 200 feet of frontage on Lake Leelanau, part of a much larger parcel owned by two maiden sisters known as "the Brooks Brothers" for the hunting and fishing wear they favored. Without an architect, and using his own ideas and a complement of local carpenters and craftsmen, he built a large two-story house with a full finished basement. The second floor had four large bedrooms. The living room below had a ground-level attachment where the Gilligans slept; the basement in early years held the Gilligan children's bunk beds. When fully deployed, the home could accommodate twenty Gilligans and assorted friends in comfort.

Leland was a little more than 500 miles from Cincinnati; for the family, it was a full, hard day's drive. Harry generally followed by rail, taking the 5:00 P.M. club car from Cincinnati overnight to Traverse City. Even at that distance, he kept an eye on

the business; often, a telegram summoned him back to Cincinnati to attend to someone's funeral. And the trips back became more frequent with the declining health of
Harry's father, John, whose death in 1938 left Harry as sole head of the firm.

The free and easy breathing in Leland opened a range of outdoor pursuits for
Jack Gilligan—golf, tennis, and, best of all, sailing. The peninsula, Gilligan recalled, drew people from various midwestern cities, Milwaukee, Chicago, and
Cleveland. The thirty or forty families with an interest in sailing formed a "yacht
club." Harry Gilligan was the club's commodore, a title that fortunately required
no actual knowledge of sailing (Harry did not sail) but that allowed him to serve
as starter for the Wednesday and Saturday races on Lake Leelanau and to host the
Commodore's Ball that closed each season.

Jack Gilligan recalled, "I was enamored of small boat racing. We did a lot of it
up in Michigan. I liked the water and everything connected with it. We raced all
sorts of small boats—everything from snipes to star boats, which were the queen of
small boat racing. They had a keel and were twenty-two feet long; 280 square feet
of sail. Great boats. So with a friend I would sail in those, and every other waking
moment I'd be on a raft or something out in the water."[15] On those occasions when
no friend was available, Jack would impress his brothers Mike and Frank into seaman's service, occasionally inviting his sister along in the role, perhaps unknown to
her, of ballast. The younger twins did not greatly welcome the honor. Mike recalled
how, "being the older brother, Jack was naturally the skipper. He would holler nau-
tical terms at us—'something the jib' or whatever."[16] Mike perhaps imaginatively
likened his older brother's command style to that of Captain Bligh.

Leland became the family's second home. (The home remains in the family to
this day; at one point, Jack Gilligan bought out his siblings' interests; today, the
home is owned by his children.) Friends, including school friends, visited. Bill
Geoghegan, a classmate of Frank and Mike, recalled the water sports, the golf
and tennis, the evening parties, and the sessions in which he learned how to play
bridge. Jack and his siblings spent the full summer there: "As soon as school was
out in June, we took off," Jack said, and in September, "we had to be dragged kicking and screaming back to school."[17]

That school was St. Xavier High School, in which Jack enrolled in the fall of
1935 after graduating from Summit Country Day. St. Xavier was a well-established
Jesuit school, the city's only private Catholic high school, with about 300 young
male students. At the time, the school was located in the city's downtown, a five-
story brick building at Sycamore Avenue and Seventh Street, which most students
reached by streetcar.

A classmate of Gilligan's, now Father Jack Beckman, said of the school, "Without being snobbish, we had the view that the Jesuit education was a cut above."[18]
Indeed, the Jesuits were generally recognized for running first-class schools, offering an education superior to that available either in the city's parish-run parochial

schools or public high schools. St. Xavier required an entrance exam, and the rigorous curriculum included four years of Latin and two years of Greek. Teaching was largely by lecture, and most of the classroom staff were Jesuits. Particularly influential with the students were those known as Scholastics: younger men who taught at the school as part of their religious training. Father Beckman, who later served for ten years as principal of St. Xavier, recalled how

> the Jesuit influence was primarily in the atmosphere that was created. The theme of St. Ignatius was that the Jesuits should be men who were men for others. Their lives were going to be given to the service of other people. The spirit of the Jesuit philosophy was not something concrete but something that you lived. This is what we saw in the young Jesuits [Scholastics] who were teaching us. They were young men, good men, strong men—dedicated in a special way to the service of God.[19]

Gilligan's sophomore year at St. Xavier was interrupted by the 1937 Ohio River flood, when, following nearly a foot of late-January rain, the river rose to 79.9 feet, 28 feet above flood stage, its highest level ever. More than one-tenth of the city was submerged; 50,000 people were homeless. The Gilligan home, well up the hillside, was secure—a fact not known to their parents, who were in New York City on a business trip that had been extended to include some Broadway shows. When Harry and Blanche heard of the flood and tried to return to Cincinnati, they learned that flooded bridges had brought rail traffic to a halt. Worse, they were seeing press accounts of an enormous fire in Mill Creek Valley on the city's west side: floodwaters had ripped storage tanks from their moorings and sparks from downed utility lines ignited the spilled contents. The photographs of those flames, Jack Gilligan recalled, "made it look like the city of Cincinnati was on fire. My parents were frantic. They really had the impression that the whole town was going up in flames."[20] A long-distance phone call from New York—in those days a rarity—provided reassurance until their return was possible.

Natural disasters aside, the Gilligan family had a fairly set weekday routine. Mornings, their mother woke them, and they ate breakfast as a family. Then school and possibly football or basketball practices for the boys and then home. Often, the family listened to Lowell Thomas's 6:45 P.M. newscast, followed by *Amos and Andy* and then the family dinner. Michael Gilligan recalled the meals as "fairly plain—meat, potatoes, and vegetables. My mother had a rule: you had to eat the salad before you got anything else."[21] Recollections of dinner table conversation vary. Jeanne recalled how their father would discuss such aspects of the Jesuit philosophy as "'the end does not justify the means,' and we would nod wisely over our carrots and peas."[22] Mike's recollection was that the conversation was frequently dominated by Jack and their father, "the two politicians in the family."[23] On at least one occasion, Mike recalled, Frank was equally willing to join in.

I do recall one incident where the Archbishop and Bishop McCarthy were the dinner quests, and we anticipated them leading the conversation, and my brothers Jack and Frank got into a heated argument of a political nature. The two clergymen sat there in stunned silence. Instead of having the floor to themselves, they were busy listening to these two teenagers argue their points to no final conclusion. I think they were stunned because the two boys dominated the conversation, until my father put a stop to it.[24]

Gilligan's record at St. Xavier was typical for a busy high school student—academically, he took first or second honors; he appeared in the senior class play, *Room Service;* he joined the debate team; and he went out for basketball and football. He sometimes played basketball in a tiny gym in which any shot launched from a distance was in danger of hitting the ceiling. Football, Gilligan pursued with more zest than success. He played second string, as did his brothers Frank and Mike later. (Mike proved to be the best athlete in the family, being named an all-star guard on the basketball team.) Still, he earned his varsity letter, which gained him admission to St. Xavier's X Club.

Classes at St. Xavier let out at 2:30 P.M. This was convenient, because the Cincinnati Reds then played most of their baseball games in the afternoon. Gilligan and friends would take a dime streetcar ride to the stadium (renamed for the team's new owner, local industrialist Powel Crosley), where bleacher seats could be had for fifty cents or a quarter. Gilligan was then "a red hot fan," and he knew the names of the players: the Reds' light-hitting infield of Scarsella, Kampouris, Myers, and Riggs, with the outstanding Ernie Lombardi—a consistent .330 hitter in those years—behind the plate. Gilligan followed his Reds through the worst—only one first-division finish in a decade.[25] There were compensations: Gilligan claims to have been at Crosley Field on June 11, 1938, when Reds' pitcher Johnny Vander Meer threw the first of his two consecutive no-hitters, the only pitcher in baseball ever to do so, and he celebrated when Ernie Lombardi and Paul Derringer carried the Reds to win the 1939 National League pennant, a feat achieved shortly after Jack left for college.

At St. Xavier, Jack was a student of some standing. Father Jack Beckman, who shared various junior year classes with him, said, "He was probably highly regarded by all our classmates. There was a certain air about him that commanded respect. He wasn't stand-offish; he was congenial and friendly, but he showed signs of being a cut above—as though he was called for something special."[26] Possibly, that something was religious. Gilligan was conscientious about religion while at St. Xavier. Along with Mass, confession, and communion, he, for three years, participated in Sodality, a Bible study group. St. Xavier, Gilligan observed later, was not simply a school; it was also a common point of entry for young men into the Jesuit order and the Catholic clergy. No particular pressure was placed on students, he said, but, given that the Jesuits were "the role models in the school," the possibility of undertaking a religious life was a topic students often discussed.[27] Gilligan joined in that discussion. Four of those who graduated in Gilligan's 110-man class of 1939 soon thereafter joined the Jesuits; four more did so later. While Gilligan did not join them, the Jesuit priesthood was a possibility he did not rule out.

In the spring of 1939, John Gilligan was a senior at St. Xavier, with college beckoning. As a more than good student, he considered attending Xavier University, a Jesuit institution in Cincinnati, where his father earned his bachelor's in 1912 and, later, a master's degree. But events intervened. Gilligan was "president" of a group of St. Xavier students who called themselves the Mules and fancied themselves something of a fraternity, even though, Gilligan said, "we had no very clear notion of what a fraternity might be."[28] One weekend, various Mules—Gilligan not included—turned up at a house party held by a girl whose parents were out of town. A certain amount of damage was incurred. When the parents returned, they took the matter to officials at St. Xavier, possibly thinking that the Jesuit fathers would be more severe in their punishment than the police might be. The school suspended the group—Gilligan included—for ten days. That penalty, Gilligan recalled, "scorched" Xavier as an undergraduate option.[29]

Eventually, the school agreed to readmit the Mules on condition that entirely new officers be chosen. Here, ethnicity ruled. As Gilligan recalled it, those impeached carried surnames of Gilligan, O'Ryan, O'Donnell. Their replacements were Backmeyer, Bismeyer, Schotmir. However embarrassing the episode was at the time, Gilligan's suspension would prove to be a blessing in disguise.

4

Notre Dame

With Xavier University eliminated as an option, Harry Gilligan suggested his son consider two other well-regarded Catholic universities, Georgetown and Notre Dame. Jack wrote for the schools' respective catalogs but made his choice on a sartorial basis: Georgetown instructed incoming freshman to bring both black tie and white tie, as these were needed apparel. That, Gilligan said, decided him on Notre Dame.[1]

Notre Dame also offered a more familiar setting. Gilligan had been to the campus—the football stadium—a number of times, as his father held season tickets and, on occasion, took Jack with him on the drive to South Bend, Indiana, to watch the Fighting Irish play. Gilligan recalled: "So, I went to Notre Dame and had the very good fortune in my freshman year to be put in a freshman English class taught by a man named Frank O'Malley."[2]

Francis J. O'Malley was the strongest influence Jack Gilligan encountered in his thirty-nine months at the University of Notre Dame—indeed, the strongest nonfamily influence in his life. O'Malley was born in 1909 to Irish immigrant parents in Clinton, Massachusetts, where his father was a weaver in a cotton mill. Following high school, O'Malley worked for two years to gather the funds needed to enter Notre Dame, where he graduated as valedictorian in 1932. He continued at Notre Dame, where in 1936 he was charged with reorganizing the school's English program. A commonly shared sentiment on campus was that "there were only two people on campus who were genuinely interested in souls; one was Father Craddick, prefect of religion, who wondered whether your soul was soiled or clean; and the other was Frank O'Malley, who wondered whether your soul was alive or dead."[3]

Along with advanced classes such as Modern Catholic Writers and Catholic Philosophy in Literature, O'Malley each year taught one freshman-level class, Philosophy of Literature, in which Jack Gilligan enrolled in the fall of 1939. Gilligan recalled how O'Malley "would just walk into the classroom. He was physically small, unprepossessing. He'd walk up to the desk at the head of the room, lay down a book or some sheets of paper, and start talking. There was very little interaction with the students. Most of the time it was straight talking about what he was interested in at the time. He could keep a whole class utterly silent for an hour, and then walk out."[4]

For Gilligan, O'Malley revealed new, unsuspected worlds. A 1962 *TIME* magazine article spoke of how "O'Malley plumbs life's most basic emotions, using Charles Peguy to examine the virtue of hope, Claudel to plumb suffering, Kierkegaard to emphasize the shallowness of religion without love."[5] One former student said that O'Malley's aim was not at a student mastering the subject but at discovering his ultimate vocation.

But the study of literature was not what most people associated with Notre Dame. For much of the nation in 1939, Notre Dame meant football, first, and Catholic, second. That ranking owed largely to the spectacular success of the football teams coached by Knute Rockne. Unlike most colleges, Notre Dame was independent of any football conference. The Fighting Irish traveled the country, each season playing a game in California, a game in New York, a game against a military academy, and so forth. Besides giving Catholic fans in each locale the chance to see the Irish tar the daylights out of some local largely Protestant squad, this brought the team, and the school it represented, not only national recognition but a loyal national following.

Briefly, Jack Gilligan toyed with joining the team on the field. At the time, any student was welcome to try out. Gilligan and his first-year roommate, a young Chicagoan named Roger Sullivan Cummings, dared each other into making the attempt. Each was given a uniform, a helmet, a locker, and "the chance to bump heads."[6] Each lasted about a week.

As a freshman, Gilligan roomed in Zahm Hall, a four-story brick structure newly constructed in 1937 that housed 206 first-year students, two to a room. One of Notre Dame's then fourteen student residences, it was named for Father John Augustine Zahm, an 1871 graduate of the school and a former faculty member. It sat due east of the school administrative building, with its famed Golden Dome, and only a few rods from the Basilica of the Sacred Heart, the center of campus religious life.

In Gilligan's years there, Notre Dame may have been the major American university most restrictive of student conduct. As an example, not only were students forbidden to have automobiles on campus, they were forbidden to drive—an injunction that extended to any family car that a visiting parent might bring to campus for the weekend.

Gilligan's daily schedule, as given in the school's yearbook, had a firm precision: the "order of the day" began with rising at 6:00 A.M.; breakfast at 7:00; classes at 8:00; dinner at 12:00; supper at 6:00, and "lights out" at 10:00. Each hall had a live-in rector charged with "maintaining an easily accessible quality spiritual life and acceptable social behavior."[7] The rector was generally a Holy Cross priest and definitions of what was "acceptable" proceeded from that fact. Alcohol consumption was not acceptable, a rule doubtless flouted but stringently enforced when infractions came to light. (Gilligan's twin younger brothers, Michael and Frank, enrolled at Notre Dame in 1942. During a visit by a high school friend, Bill Geoghegan, they obtained some beer, which was then discovered by those in authority. Gilligan's brothers reasoned that discretion demanded they blame Bill, who, as a nonstudent, would be less compromised by the incident. Bill took the fall.)

In making his college choice, Gilligan had selected Notre Dame over Georgetown. Georgetown was then sometimes referred to as "small c" Catholic and Notre Dame as "large C"—meaning, that religion played a more prominent role at Notre Dame. Gilligan's class yearbook stated: "It is not only in the classroom, where the Commandments and Sacraments, Apologetics and Dogma, are formally expounded, but in the whole great variety of day-to-day activity, in study, and in recreation, that Religion, as a strong and forceful habit of mind, might be said to be gently evoked from the student."[8] The intended consequence was that religion was to be imparted to the student as something "he will never forget and never cease to live."[9]

With so much either required or proscribed, what did students do in such free time as they had? At the time, Gilligan said that Notre Dame was a "jock school." Foremost, that meant that students—Gilligan among them—were in the stands every Saturday afternoon for home football games. (The Irish posted a record of twenty-nine wins, six losses, and three ties during Gilligan's years as a student.) The school also had an extensive intramural sports program. Each of the fourteen residence halls on campus fielded a football team in the fall and a basketball team over the winter; the full roster of teams was divided into two leagues, and a championship game was played between the respective winners. Gilligan played both sports. At Notre Dame, even intramural sports were a serious undertaking. At one point, the basketball team Gilligan played for included one former All-State player from Illinois and another from New Jersey, and the postseason intramural football championship, played in the football arena, drew crowds upwards of 20,000.

Gilligan played intramurals partly out of interest and partly "because there wasn't anything else to do."[10] There were a few things—movies on Saturday night in nearby Washington Hall and milkshakes at the Huddle snack shop in the student union—but there were no girls. Notre Dame was an all-male school, and immediate social prospects were grim. What Gilligan termed "the nearest reserve of girls" was at St. Mary's, a Catholic women's college located nearby, where tea dances were sometimes held.[11] Rarely did Gilligan attend. There were also dances held in downtown South Bend at the Palais Royale dance hall, which he also rarely attended. On the whole, Gilligan, who had dated widely while in high school, had a limited social life at Notre Dame.

As student preoccupations, football ranked well ahead of world politics. Even though Jack Gilligan's matriculation at Notre Dame coincided closely with Germany's September 1, 1939, invasion of Poland, the war in Europe made little impression on the student body in Indiana. Gilligan recalled, "We read the news from Europe like we read the sports pages."[12]

Politically, the campus was conservative. In 1939 the institution enrolled just shy of 3,000 students—Catholic, predominantly middle class, and largely of Irish, German, or Italian heritage. Most of these students had fathers in business or law, and the fathers were generally Republican, so the sons generally followed suit. Gilligan recalled how the students would "talk about politics in the dining hall—they were viciously anti-Roosevelt in the most brutal way. They would talk about him as being a cripple, as though that was some disqualifying condition. I became an anti-anti-Roosevelt, stuck up for him because everybody seemed to be against him."[13]

But the rise of Hitler affected Notre Dame in an unforeseen way. Father John F. O'Hara, the university's president when Gilligan arrived, had been pushing to build the school academically. While the size of the student body remained the same through the 1930s, the faculty increased by 40 percent, with the share of those holding a doctorate rising appreciably. Father O'Hara extended his faculty recruitment to include scholars fleeing Nazi-dominated Europe, including physicist Arthur Haas and political scientists Ferdinand Alois Hermens and Waldemar Gurian. Combined, Gilligan said, they constituted a body of academic talent that, but for the crisis in Europe, would never have reached the flatlands of northeastern Indiana.

Gurian had been run out of Germany and Austria for authoring works that included *Hitler and the Christians, Bolshevism: Theory and Practice,* and *The Rise and Decline of Marxism.* Prior to coming to South Bend, he had been living stateless in Switzerland. While at Notre Dame, he completed *The Sources of Hitler's Power* and founded and edited *The Review of Politics,* a highly regarded journal that published such scholars as Jacques Maritain, Mortimer Adler, and Carl J. Friedrich, among others. Gurian, Gilligan said, "was an extraordinary man and an entirely new experience for the administration, faculty and students at Notre Dame. No one like him had ever lived and worked in the community before."[14] Gilligan commented that, for Gurian, coming to Notre Dame "must have been like going out to Aztec territory, or something."[15]

In his second semester, Gilligan enrolled in Gurian's Rise of the Dictatorships class. He recalled Gurian as "a great, large guy who wore a black vest, a black tie and a porkpie hat with a brim."[16] He would walk into the class and deliver his lecture in thickly accented English that devolved into German as he became caught up in his lecture. Part of the time, Gilligan acknowledged, he and other students "lacked the historical background to understand some of what he was talking about. He would refer to events in his country or in Europe. Generally, we were treading water."[17]

Indeed, most undergraduates' sense of history reflected the parochialism of prewar America. "What little we knew about politics and history and so forth," Gilligan commented, "was a pretty narrow point of view—the American legend of who we were and what we were and why we were better than anyone else in the world."[18] For Gilligan, though, Gurian offered a new model, one in which scholarship and activism combined. "It wasn't just an academic exercise for him," Gilligan said. "He was living the struggle."[19] In particular, Gilligan recalled the professor's entry into the classroom on June 14, 1940, the day Paris fell to the German army: "Gurian walked into the room; he came up the side aisle to the front of the room and the blackboard and stood there for a few minutes with his back to us. Then he turned around to face the class; it was evident that he was weeping. He said something like, 'Today, those bastards are standing in the streets of Paris, cheering.'"[20]

For Gilligan, there was a further education stemming from the fact that Gurian was a Jew. Cincinnati had a substantial Jewish population; the city was generally regarded as the center of American Reform Judaism. But Gurian was not a member of the synagogue on Plum Street; he was a refugee from a continent where the persecution of Jews was the forerunner to their intended extermination. It was something Gilligan had not previously imagined, "to have a whole people uprooted, torn out of their homes and fields, and slaughtered or chased into exile."[21]

While Gurian's may have been the most intellectual political voice on campus, his was not the dominant one. That standing fell to Father Jack A. O'Brien, author of the widely popular tract *The Faith of Millions*, who came to teach religion in 1940, the fall of Gilligan's sophomore year. Ignoring a university ban on faculty members engaging in public debate, O'Brien "quickly emerged as a strident critic of Roosevelt's foreign policy and as one of the most widely known Catholic isolationists in the country."[22] With the fall of France in June 1940, Germany's Luftwaffe was attacking Great Britain in what was widely believed to be a prelude to invasion. President Roosevelt favored major aid to the beleaguered British. O'Brien regarded Britain's fight as neither winnable nor worth winning—views he expressed from podiums across the country, eventually joining the national board of the America First Committee, the principal isolationist organization, whose best-known speaker was aviator Charles Lindbergh. Twice, O'Brien invited Gilligan to join a group he directed that made presentations on current events; both times Gilligan declined.

Some counterargument to O'Brien's isolationism emerged within the Notre Dame community. Philosophy professor Francis E. McMahon became statewide head of Fight for Freedom, which argued in support of Roosevelt's policy of "all aid to Britain short of war." Frank O'Malley was among those faculty members signing newspaper ads in support of FDR's position. (Once war came, the extremely nearsighted O'Malley twice secured letters from the Notre Dame president asking the navy to waive its vision requirement so that he could enlist. The requests were denied.) Isolationism, however, largely ruled—both on campus and in surrounding Indiana. In December 1940, forty local businessmen placed an ad in the *South Bend Tribune* demanding "no gas masks for America."[23] In spring 1941, the same newspaper published a petition opposing U.S. entry into the conflict. It was signed by 1,000 Notre Dame students, a third of those enrolled. Gilligan was not among the signatories.

By the close of his sophomore year, Gilligan was clearly fixed on English as his major. Years later the faculty members whom he clearly recalled—beyond O'Malley and Gurian—came from the English department, among them Richard Sullivan, who taught Chaucer. His recollection of science and math instructors, however, was dim—perhaps because, while Gilligan consistently got good grades in English and history, subjects such as chemistry, advanced math, and physics proved something of a chore.

At least one professor remembered Jack. When Michael Gilligan enrolled in Notre Dame in the fall of 1942, his first class was English, taught by Father Thomas Brown. Running through the cards students had filled out on reaching class and coming to the name Gilligan, Father Brown said, "From Cincinnati, Ohio?" Mike said, "Yes." "Brother named John?" "Yes." "Then get out of my class." Michael was readmitted the following day, but he never discovered from what presumably hereditary fault he suffered.[24]

It is common in interviews to ask about one's influences. The question suggests a certain passivity—as if, to a broad extent, people choose their influences. Gilligan, as noted, had rejected the prospective influence of the isolationist Father O'Brien. He was simply out of sympathy with O'Brien's politics and suspicious of his motives.

But it was Frank O'Malley who was the dominant influence on Jack Gilligan. O'Malley was for Gilligan a kindred spirit and a wise mentor. "We liked the same things in literature. The more we talked, the more I realized that his thinking and my thinking went on similar lines, only his went further. He read voraciously. If he was interested in a book he would talk about it. I'd get hold of that book and most often agreed with him."[25] Age may have been a factor. O'Malley was only thirty when Gilligan first enrolled in one of his classes; like the Scholastics at St. Xavier, O'Malley was younger and more enthusiastic than most members of the faculty.

O'Malley had other followers, too. When his lecture was complete, O'Malley would exit the classroom, trailing behind him a line of students with questions that urgently needed answering, Gilligan among them. O'Malley, who was unmarried, lived on campus as a proctor and encouraged students to visit his monk's cell of a room in Morrissey Hall for further conversation. (On one such visit, O'Malley complained to Gilligan of having trouble sleeping. O'Malley, as it happened, read in bed before retiring. Examining the bed—a standard, student cot—Gilligan discovered that "so many books had been stuffed under the mattress that it had become distended."[26])

O'Malley introduced students to a wide range of original texts, but he had his preferences in literature. He was, Gilligan said, "an unabashed admirer of Irish writing and Irish writers. He made the statement that the Irish had saved the English language and culture—the outstanding dramatist was George Bernard Shaw; the outstanding poet was William Butler Yeats; and so on."[27] Yet O'Malley's literary preferences did not obscure his deeper commitment; he was a deeply religious, as this passage in his journal demonstrates:

> Man is not a being sufficient unto himself who can acknowledge his relationship
> to God or reject it, precisely as he thinks and decides. The nature of man is essentially determined by his relationship to God. Man exists only as one related to
> God: Where there is no God there is no man. And the way in which he understands this relationship, how seriously he takes it, and the consequences he draws
> from it—all this determines the nature of his life, his work, his vocation.[28]

It was in his Modern Catholic Writers and Catholic Philosophy in Literature courses where Jack Gilligan was introduced to religious perspectives in literature. He took particular interest in the work associated with the French Renaissance, early-twentieth-century French writers who strove to close the gap that had existed between intellectuals and the Catholic Church. These included the eccentric Leon Bloy, an essayist, diarist, and the first Catholic writer to synergize creative expression with an absolute defense of the faith, and Charles Peguy, a one-time socialist who returned to the Church in 1908 and whose polemical writings were highly influential among intellectuals in the years before the First World War.

The writer whose work most influenced Gilligan was Jacques Maritain. Born a French Protestant, Maritain and his Russian-born Jewish wife converted to Catholicism under Bloy's influence in 1906. Maritain produced an extensive body of work and is regarded as a leading Catholic philosopher of the twentieth century. Maritain regarded secular humanism as antihuman in its exclusion of spirituality from consideration. He believed a broader humanism was needed so that Christianity could influence political thought and social action in a pluralistic age. Maritain's influence was enormous; he served on the commission that drafted the United Nations' Universal Declaration of Human Rights, and his social thought was an important source for the Christian Democratic political parties that flourished in Western Europe in the postwar era.

The thinking of Maritain and others he was reading at the time nudged Gilligan in a direction he had never entirely foresworn. At St. Xavier, he had been drawn to the energy and character of the Scholastics who comprised the younger

members of the teaching corps. At the time, he gave some consideration to entering the priesthood, a subject he then discussed with other students. Early in his
junior year at Notre Dame, he was again considering the possibility of entering
the priesthood, though this time it was a subject of considerable private reflection.
He did not even discuss his plans at any length with Frank O'Malley. His plan
was to withdraw from Notre Dame, with his degree incomplete, and enroll in the
Jesuit seminary outside Cincinnati in Milford, Ohio. He recognized that such a
decision would be a step through a one-way door—"the seminary isn't like joining
the army, where you serve your term and leave. If you join [a seminary], you ain't
coming back. I [knew I] would be cutting myself off from everything."[29] None of
the students from Gilligan's high school who became Jesuits ever left the order.

Founded in 1540 by St. Ignatius, the Jesuit Order—sometimes referred to as
the "shock troops" of Catholicism—is an organization of extraordinary history,
range, and consequence. Jesuit missionaries were active in Japan by 1580, founded
Sao Paulo and Rio de Janeiro in the sixteenth century, reached Lhasa in Tibet in
1661, and preached among the native peoples of Quebec. For Jesuits, proselytizing
is tied to learning. For instance, Jesuits introduced Western science and mathe-
matics to China; and in 1651 the French Jesuit Alexandre de Rhodes transliterated
the Vietnamese language into the form still used in that country today. The order
made important contributions to science; in the mid–seventeenth century, thirty
of the world's 130 astronomical observatories were run by Jesuit astronomers. By
the mid–twentieth century, the operation of secondary schools and colleges had
become the order's most distinctive activity worldwide.

Reflecting on the attraction he felt to the Jesuit order, Gilligan said, "I had thought
about a life like that for a long time; it had great appeal. The intellectual dimension
as well as the spiritual dimension was captivating. I just thought it would be great
to spend time with books and with teaching and with colleagues on the faculty.
Foregoing the normal attributes and attractions of civil life, that was okay with me.
That was a fine tradeoff; I did not regard it as a sacrifice at that time."[30] It was a prospect that he believed would, at minimum, be acceptable to his family. After all, his
mother's favorite brother was a priest, and it was no secret that she harbored hopes
that one of her sons would enter the priesthood. And so Gilligan prepared himself
for his family's reaction to the news. In November 1941, he recalled, "I decided that
I would go home at Christmas and tell my parents that I wasn't going to finish the
course at Notre Dame. Instead, I was going to go to Milford."[31]

Several weeks before his intended visit home, however, twenty-year-old Jack
was showering after an intramural basketball game at the Rockne Memorial athletic center when a fellow student burst in with the news that Pearl Harbor had
been bombed. He reacted, "How did the Germans ever get planes out to the Pacific?"[32] The prospect of war with Japan had been as distant from his mind as it was
from the minds of most Americans. But the bombing brought all other thoughts

to a halt. Gilligan, like most Americans, now looked out on an entirely new land-scape, and his plan to enter the seminary was replaced by an intention to join his nation's armed forces.

Within days, Notre Dame students began crowding the army, navy, and marines recruiting tables hastily set up on campus. Gilligan, a summer sailor in Michigan, got in line for the navy: "I thought I'd rather spend my time splashing about in the water than crawling around in the mud."[33] Initially, the navy thought otherwise. As evidence of the nation's general unpreparedness for war, the navy recruiters at Notre Dame were using a height/weight chart left over from the First World War. By its standards, Gilligan, then a shade over six feet and about 180 pounds, was too large to leave shore.

Undaunted, back home in Cincinnati over the Christmas break, Gilligan tried his luck at a local recruiting facility. By chance, his arrival there coincided with that of Lou Rymkus and Wally Zimba, two tackles from the Notre Dame football team, each of whom carried the then-extraordinary weight of 230 pounds. Gilligan posi-tioned himself between their bulk and emerged a naval recruit.

He was enrolled in the navy's V7 program, which provided college juniors and seniors an accelerated graduation followed by entrance into the service. While this allowed undergraduates to complete their educations, the more important reality was that the armed forces did not have the immediate means to train all those stepping forward to serve. For Gilligan, this meant graduating in Decem-ber 1942 rather than the following spring. Before beginning his military service, therefore, Gilligan had another eleven months at Notre Dame, into which a year-and-a-half of study would be compressed.

Notre Dame had been operating a small naval Reserve Officer Training Corps (ROTC) program, but after Pearl Harbor the program ballooned, with 800 midship-men moving into campus housing. One incidental consequence for Gilligan, then living in Dillon Hall, was that a third student was squeezed into all dorm rooms on campus. The crowding in the dorms was a minimal sacrifice students were making for the war effort. The presence of the midshipmen, the crowding, and each day's war-dominated news—early on, much of it bad—gave Gilligan and other students the sense that "real life" was taking place somewhere else. Gilligan's feeling at the time—doubtless common on campuses across the country—was that he "wanted to be in on that."[34]

But for the time being, Jack Gilligan was nowhere near the war; rather, he was a prize student in English. Early in his junior year, he fell into ready company with the two reigning stars of the English program, seniors Donald Dennis Conners and Charles John Kirby. Conners, a big guy, and Kirby, a little guy, were both redheads. Their shared hair color, and perhaps a measure of literary pretension, led to the trio being dubbed "the Three Sun Gods." Kirby and Conners were editors of the campus literary magazine, *Scrip*; when they graduated, Gilligan took the helm.

As editor, Gilligan secured work from a larger number of contributors—essays, poems, reviews, and short stories. His statement of editorial mission sounded rather strongly influenced by Frank O'Malley: "Intellectual honesty among college men, first trying the steel of their intellects and emotions on a fresh, wide world, is a delicate and sometimes elusive thing."[35] Editor Gilligan strayed near the pretentious. Too many young writers, he wrote, adopted pseudo-intellectuality as a protection against less sophisticated minds; in doing so, they produced "fraudulent, formalized, synthetic" writing. He added, "The refusal of *Scrip* to be taken in by routine and hollowness has sometimes incurred the displeasure of the more thoughtless of its readers; but has at the same time earned the esteem of many others, on and off the campus, including several nationally known arbiters."[36]

By general consent, among the best things *Scrip* published were two short stories by Gilligan himself, "Who Has Tasted Bread" and "Inherit the Earth." The first, published in May 1942, presents a wandering laborer who progressively impresses on others the awareness that they are not able to experience life directly or represent it in its essence.[37] The second, and better, story, "Inherit the Earth," published in August 1942, again presents a roving character, one who wanders in an elegiac mood through the shops and taverns of a working-class neighborhood without directly engaging with its occupants. The character intervenes on behalf of a middle-aged Jewish shopkeeper being taunted by two men in a crowd. The tormentors turn on him, attacking him and leaving him lying unconscious in the street. The police, thinking him simply passed out, roust him off to jail as drunk and disorderly. He tries to explain, saying, "He was just a little guy, ya see, don'cha? Just a little Jew." Plausibly, the story traces to Waldemar Gurian's influence on Gilligan.[38]

Still, a student life focused on a literary magazine was some considerable distance from the struggle proceeding elsewhere. About the time "Inherit the Earth" was published, German and Russian armies were locked in combat at Stalingrad; the British, under General Bernard Law Montgomery, were taking the offensive against General Erwin Rommel's Afrika Korps in Egypt; and U.S. Marines clung to their positions on Guadalcanal.

Perhaps as a reaction to feeling they were adrift in one of the day's backwaters, some at the university asserted a special wartime role for Notre Dame: "America will never fall by the method of 'divide and conquer' as long as there are universities like Notre Dame to which young men may bring the gifts of their imaginations and the experiences of their religions."[39] That task was centrally spiritual: "With the advent of war and its trail of destruction and death, the popular intelligence tends to give way to emotions of hate, revenge and despondency. It is against such intellectual and spiritual confusion that Notre Dame stands firmly to oppose."[40]

It was perhaps a statement of the young who, thus far, knew only peace. In the very near future, however, the young men of many places, including Notre Dame and Jack Gilligan, would face the greater confusion of warfare.

5

To D-Day

John Gilligan graduated from the University of Notre Dame on December 10, 1942. Though wartime travel restrictions were in place, Harry and Blanche Gilligan were present as the first of their children received a degree. Gilligan then returned briefly to Cincinnati; less than a week later, he reported to Chicago for active duty.

During those few days in Cincinnati, Gilligan spent final time with family and a few friends, and he took a young woman he had known for much of his life, Mary Kathryn Dixon, downtown to see a movie. Katie Dixon was the daughter of Edward T. Dixon, an attorney and former judge who was active in Cincinnati reform politics.[1] Within the settled and established world of Eastside Catholics, the Gilligans and the Dixons were particularly well-known to each other. Indeed, Katie Dixon had also attended grade school at Summit Country Day, though a year ahead of Jack. Before he departed for Chicago, the pair agreed to correspond.[2]

In Chicago, Gilligan spent thirty days as an apprentice seaman and then three more months in midshipman training. He learned close-order drill in a field house just off Michigan Avenue and received classroom training in buildings near Chicago's Water Tower in the near-north downtown. Prospective junior officers such as Gilligan were being instructed in droves. "We were landlubbers," he recalled. "We didn't know anything about ships or the ocean and the people who were teaching us didn't know much more."[3] By way of example, Gilligan and his fellow recruits were taught how to do celestial navigation by a method that even then was no longer in use, along with more pertinent training in gunnery.

Military life proved less restrictive than life at Notre Dame. One of Gilligan's college roommates, Roger Sullivan Cummings, was being trained in the same unit. Cummings was a Chicago native, and his mother, who was from a politically prominent family, maintained a very large upscale apartment at 3400 North Sheridan. Mrs. Cummings welcomed her son, his friends, and various others on the sole, never-to-be-violated condition that no one ever set foot in her bedroom. Gilligan recalled that it was rather like having one's own private USO outpost. The first dozen people who got into the apartment got beds; the rest slept on the floor. One night Gilligan entered the apartment awhile after midnight and heard what he took to be the voice of Bing Crosby coming from a record player. Wandering into the kitchen, he encountered the elevator operator having a beer with several others—one of whom was Bing Crosby, who, it turned out, was a friend of Mrs. Cummings.[4]

Gilligan's hope was that when he completed his training he would be assigned to a destroyer—"somehow, that seemed dashing."[5] Instead, he was sent to sub-chaser school in Miami. The school had been established during the worst of the German U-boat attacks in 1942. However, with the advent of radar and sonar and other countermeasures, that danger greatly diminished, and so Gilligan's training in Miami was cut short and he was sent to Norfolk, Virginia, for duty on a destroyer.

On August 10, 1943, Gilligan stepped onto the USS *Emmons,* where each day started with the sounding of the ship's bell and the boson's whistle. Despite its size, the *Emmons,* a 348-foot vessel that displaced 1,630 tons, was a graceful, highly maneuverable craft capable of a top speed of 37.5 knots (about 42 miles per hour). It had been built at the Bath Iron Works in Bath, Maine, at a cost of $4.9 million. Commissioned on December 5, 1941, the *Emmons* was the final American warship put into service prior to Pearl Harbor. Its original armament included five 5-inch 38-caliber dual-purpose guns for use against surface and air targets, six 50-caliber machine guns, five torpedoes, and two tracks on its fantail, from which 600-pound barrel-shaped depth charges could be dropped into the ocean. "Unlike later ships her superstructure was neatly faired and deck edges gracefully rounded to lessen resistance to wind and water."[6]

Gilligan included, the *Emmons* carried a crew of about 240. He came aboard as an assistant gunnery officer. All on board had assigned spots to go to for general quarters, battle stations. As an assistant gunnery officer, Gilligan's post was in the gunnery director, the topmost station on the ship. Gilligan acknowledges that when he started out he did not know much about gunnery; however, "the posting put me in a position where I could learn something; and perhaps be of some use on the ship. Generally, you learned from the guys already on the ship."[7] As Gilligan years later told a novice and nervous campaign volunteer, when he came on board the *Emmons,* he had thought he was the new kid surrounded by sailors with ten or fifteen years of experience. But what he realized was that experience wasn't about longevity—most of those on board had never seen combat either. The new guys, he noticed, picked up the manner of veterans in a few weeks.[8] In time, Gilligan qualified as a watch officer, and he served his rotation on the helm, generally at night. The ship's captain slept separate from the rest of the officers, in a small cabin just aft of the bridge. If anything turned up on the radar, the watch officer's prime charge was to awaken the captain.

When deployed, destroyers were most commonly used to escort much larger ships—cruisers, carriers, or battleships—or to protect merchant fleets against submarines. They operated in divisions of two to six ships. For most of its time at sea, the *Emmons* was paired with the USS *Rodman*. As a consequence, in the words of one seaman, "The crews of the two destroyers formed an affection for each other similar to that between two brothers."[9]

Bonds formed among the *Emmons's* crew. Gilligan's best shipboard friend was Tom Menaugh, a fellow junior officer, a fellow Irishman, and the son of a Chicago newspaperman. The pair had met in Chicago in midshipman school. As Menaugh later told an interviewer, "We stood watches together. We had a great mutual respect for each others' confidence at what we were doing. Gilligan was a good officer, very popular with the enlisted men."[10] One of Menaugh's favorite recollections of Gilligan was seeing him scaling a ladder with a copy of *The Skeleton Key to Finnegan's Wake* sticking out of his back pocket.

On October 24, 1943, the *Emmons* arrived at Norfolk, Virginia, to join what seemed like an unusually large number of destroyers assigned to escort the battleship *Iowa* across the Atlantic. At sea, a member of the *Emmons* crew reported that, while in Norfolk, he had learned from a seaman on the *Iowa* that the larger ship had received an unusual alteration: a passenger elevator. To Gilligan, this suggested a single conclusion: the only passenger who could both need and rate an elevator was President Franklin Roosevelt, crippled with polio. To Gilligan's considerable surprise, many crewmen hotly contested Gilligan's speculation: so carefully was Roosevelt's disability hidden from public view that "many abroad simply did not believe the president was wheelchair-bound."[11]

Gilligan was right—and his inference unintentionally constituted something of a security breach. Roosevelt's presence was secret; he had boarded the *Iowa* directly from what was "ostensibly a short cruise for relaxation" on the presidential yacht near the mouth of the Potomac.[12] FDR's destination was the Teheran Conference, where he would meet with British prime minister Winston Churchill and Soviet leader Joseph Stalin. The *Iowa* and its escorts reached Gibraltar on November 19. The Teheran Conference, held in Teheran, Iran, from November 28 to December 1, was the first great wartime meeting attended by all three Allied leaders. There, Roosevelt and Churchill committed their armies to a 1944 invasion of France, and Stalin agreed the Soviet Union would enter the war against Japan following Germany's surrender. After the conference, the *Emmons* helped provided antisubmarine protection and escort duty for the *Iowa* on the first leg of its homeward voyage.

That task completed, the *Emmons* headed back across the Atlantic, refueled at Bermuda, and then sailed north to Casco Bay, Maine, from which it then operated in the chilly, choppy waters of the North Atlantic. The *Emmons* had been built before the war, before the danger aircraft posed to ships at sea was realized. Mindful of this risk, the *Emmons* was retrofitted with 20mm and 40mm antiaircraft guns. But the weight of the ammunition lockers for these guns made the ship top heavy. As a result, in heavy North Atlantic seas the ship rolled sufficiently to allow seawater to be sucked into its ventilating system, which would then spray near-freezing droplets into every compartment of the ship and onto the faces of everyone there. To contend with this icy spray, many on board decided to grow beards, an effort to which ginger-haired Gilligan could manage only a somewhat scraggly contribution.[13]

During these months at sea, Gilligan continued his correspondence with Katie Dixon. They wrote back and forth at two- or three-week intervals: one would write, and once that letter had made its slow wartime way to its recipient, the other would reply. Gilligan was forbidden from letting her know his whereabouts, so the pair developed something of a code to identify his location. She then shared this information with Gilligan's family. The code—or perhaps it was Katie's sense of direction—may have been deficient, for at one point Gilligan received a letter from his father asking how his son had managed "to maneuver a U.S. destroyer into the Gobi Desert."[14]

Initially, the letters were fairly humdrum—reports on her doings that might interest him, and reports on his doings that would escape censorship. And the pair did see each other briefly whenever Gilligan had shore leave of sufficient duration to allow him to return to Cincinnati. But sometime in 1944, Gilligan, in his letter writing, shifted from informing his correspondent to wooing her. By his own count, in the twelfth letter he wrote Katie, Gilligan asked her to marry him. She accepted, an acceptance both knew was conditional on his safe return from the war. She, by that time, had completed her course of studies at the University of Cincinnati, where she majored in English, and was working as a classroom teacher at Cincinnati's Walnut Hills High School.

One mission remained. Gilligan was resolved to ask his future father-in-law for Katie's hand. So in April 1944, when the *Emmons* returned to Boston Navy Yard for refitting, Gilligan made his way to Cincinnati and presented himself in the small study in which Edward Dixon was listening to a Reds game. They spoke for some while on a whole range of subjects before Gilligan summoned himself and made his intentions clear. Dixon immediately gave his blessing, but added, "What took you so long? I missed three innings."[15] Word of the engagement, Gilligan recalled, sent a double "whew" of relief through his family: "Not only had I decided against becoming a Jesuit, I was getting married. And not only married, but married to Katie."[16]

Gilligan returned to the *Emmons,* which in April 1944 was dispatched to the Mediterranean, reaching port at Mers-el-Kebir, a tiny fishing harbor in Algeria. After the hostile seas of the North Atlantic, Gilligan found the Mediterranean almost as smooth and easy as Lake Leelanau. The *Emmons* and *Rodman* were in the four-destroyer division posted there for antisubmarine duty. Gilligan recalled how "the alarm bell would go off—like in a firehouse—and the destroyers would go streaking out, trying to locate the submarine that had attacked one of our vessels."[17] The unit was credited with eliminating the *U-616,* which surfaced and scuttled itself while being pursued.

By that point in the war, the fighting in the Mediterranean was pretty much a sideshow. In mid-May the *Emmons,* the *Rodman,* and the two other destroyers in its division received orders summoning them to England. Arriving in Plymouth on May 22, they saw the vast gathering of ships, landing craft, barrage balloons. No official announcement was needed to tell them that the invasion of France was at hand. Until this point, the *Emmons* had not once been under enemy fire during the time Gilligan had been on board.

After reaching Plymouth, the *Emmons* several times went into the Irish Sea on escort duty. One night, a ship they were escorting was sunk. Gilligan recalled, "The captain got on the intercom and said: 'Guys, the war has just started. The ultimate outrage has been perpetrated by the Germans. That ship had sixty thousand cases of Irish whiskey on board. They will pay for that.'"[18]

The Germans would pay, though not for the whiskey. The exact timing and target of the invasion of Europe were among the war's best-kept secrets. For weeks following the *Emmons*'s arrival, Gilligan watched from the deck as the landing craft slowly moved out of the harbor to practice the formation maneuvering the invasion would require and then return to port. "One night, everybody was whistled back from shore leave to the ships. As they got back on the ships, you could see the landing craft in the open river coming down to the sea heading for France."[19]

But all were called back. On the night of June 4, 1944, General Dwight Eisenhower, Supreme Allied Commander in Europe, made the decision that the storm on the English Channel was too severe to permit the invasion fleet to cross and ordered a twenty-four-hour postponement. In the Channel, the *Emmons* "helped gather landing craft up like so many ducks and bring them back to England." Gilligan recalled, "By the time they got back and were refueled, it was just about time to head back out to sea again on their way to France—this time for real."[20]

Around midnight of June 5–6, Gilligan was called to the radar room. Instead of a usual scattering of dots, the screen displayed an unbroken white line running north to south. One officer asked, "What the hell is that?" Nothing seaworthy could create any such image. Gilligan and others realized that the unbroken line was caused by the stream of hundreds of troop-carrying aircraft and gliders that would drop U.S. paratroops landward of German coastal defenses in the prelude to the invasion. At that point, they knew the invasion was on. For Americans, D-Day was the hoped-for beginning of the end. In his broadcast of the day, Edward R. Murrow, the voice to which the nation listened for war news, caught that spirit.

> Early this morning we heard the bombers going out. It was the sound of a giant factory in the sky. It seemed to shake the old gray stone buildings in this bruised and battered city beside the Thames. The sound was heavier, more triumphant than ever before. Those who knew what was coming could imagine that they

heard great guns and strains of the Battle Hymn of the Republic well above the roar of the motors.[21]

When June 6 dawned, military historian John Keegan wrote:

> The spectacle that confronted those embarked—and those ashore—was perhaps more dramatic than any soldiers, sailors or airmen had ever seen at the beginning of any battle. On the Normandy coast the sea from east to west and as far north as the seaward horizon was filled with ships, literally by the thousand; the sky thundered with the passage of aircraft; and the coastline had begun to disappear in gouts of smoke and dust as the bombardment bit into it.[22]

Murrow and Keegan give panoramic views of the conflict. For the common sol-dier—and the junior navy officer named Gilligan—those involved in the fight, few had much of a sense of what was going on beyond the gaze of their own units. For Gilligan, D-Day was indeed the longest day. He spent thirty-six continuous hours at his battle station, sustained by navy-issued pep pills and catnaps taken in rota-tion with others on the bridge. There was considerable confusion. At one point, Gilligan was unable to determine whether the destroyer adjacent to his was firing by mistake or whether his own was, mistakenly, not firing. But he found that he experienced little fear—in part, because of the preoccupation of task; in part, from knowing that the major hazards were not being faced at sea but on the beaches. As evidence both of that exhaustion and distraction, Gilligan spent the full thirty-six hours in a group of officers that included Tom Menaugh, and "to this day I can't recollect" a single thing he and his best shipboard friend said to each other.[23]

In the hours after midnight on June 6, the *Emmons* engaged in minesweeping operations in the English Channel and then proceeded to its assigned position, 3,000 yards off the eastern end of the Omaha landing beach. Psychologically, "the period from the beginning of the minesweeping operation to daybreak of D-Day was the worst of the entire operation for the *Emmons* because of the combination of darkness and the unknown."[24] General bombardment was to commence at 5:50 A.M. A dozen minutes before that, however, an enemy shore battery began firing on the *Emmons*. Shells landed uncomfortably close. The *Emmons* returned fire (the first exchange that crew had experienced in the war) and the German guns fell silent. Minutes later, the full ear-crushing bombardment opened. By then, the *Emmons* from 2,000 yards offshore directed fire to its targets near Colleville-sur-Mer, a French fishing village with a large breakwater masking a small harbor.

Omaha Beach was heavily defended by the German 352nd Division, the stron-gest unit the Allies engaged that day, and was where most of the 4,649 U.S. fatali-ties occurred on D-Day. The *Emmons* was in a division of four destroyers offering close-in fire support to troops on the beach. Gilligan recalled how the *Emmons* was "inside the line of battleships; we fired away at the beach. The Germans had brought up some .88 millimeter guns; very high velocity, which are very hard to spot. They were chewing the beach up pretty badly. We were ordered to try to take them out— the tactic for doing that was our captain took the ship in close to shore in parallel to the coast, drawing fire from the .88s, and have the other guys shoot back at them."[25]

It was a day of unlikely events. Shortly before 4:00 P.M., a British destroyer, by design or accident, came between the *Emmons* and the beach, turned parallel to shore, and dropped anchor well within range of German guns. Since British destroyers were smaller and less shielded than their American counterparts, some on the *Emmons* trained curious eyes on the vessel. Gilligan remembered with some amazement the boson's pipe on the British ship sounding and then the galley crew carrying great steaming pots from battle post to battle post. "It was four o'clock, and the British Navy was having its tea.[26] With that done, the British resumed their bombardment of the beach.

For the gun crews on the *Emmons*, the day's high point came at 6:15 P.M., when higher command sent word that the church tower in Colleville-sur-Mer was being used as a German observation post and asked if any American destroyer was positioned to fire on it. The tower was a small target, but it was within sight and range of the *Emmons*. From the observation tower, Gilligan directed his ship's fire. Radar gunnery was then coming into use, but was not yet much trusted. Instead, Gilligan chose to use optical equipment to determine the range to the tower.[27] The order to fire was given; the *Emmons* fired sixty-six rounds and the tower fell. Thereafter and until nightfall, the destroyer was directed to seek and direct fire on targets of opportunity.

Near midnight, a lookout on the *Emmons* heard a cry for help—in English— from the waters near the ship. Crewmen lowered a small boat to find and retrieve the serviceman. But the boat returned not with the GI all had expected but with a badly wounded German pilot identified as Captain F. W. Waldemar Baetke. Flying one of the few German aircraft to challenge the landing, he had bailed out over the water. Unconscious, he was taken to the officer's wardroom, which had been converted into an operating theater. The ship's physician, C. R. Williamson, climbed up on one table end and began cutting off the pilot's flight suit. Gilligan, who had followed the wounded German to the wardroom, climbed up the other end and began to give the pilot artificial respiration. (Gilligan recalled, "I was doing my Boy Scout thing: 'Out goes the bad air; in comes the good air.'") Perhaps twenty minutes later, Dr. Williamson said to him, "Okay, Pinkie, you can quit that now. You already killed him."[28] Among his other injuries, the captured German had four cracked ribs, which, kneaded up and down, may have done considerable damage. Gilligan recalled that years later, when he was visiting a boys' school, he was asked if during the war he had ever killed a German: "I said, 'Yeah, and with my bare hands.' And the whole room was electrified."[29]

After three days of providing fire support for the later waves of troops landing on the beaches, the *Emmons* was ordered back to England to refuel and restock its ammunition bunkers. The exhausted Gilligan watched as the ship entered the Bristol harbor and turned past a grassy rise, perhaps 1,200 feet high, where the river enters open water. As the ship made that turn, Gilligan recalled, the whole bank was full of people, British civilians, perhaps several thousand, who had come to the water's edge to greet the returning ships. Once the *Emmons* docked, its captain was confronted by a delegation, telling him, "Put your lads to bed. We will restock the ship."[30] And for the next eight hours, British civilians undertook the arduous task of moving shells hand by hand along the dock, across some planking, and into the ship.

By the time resupply was completed, the fighting in Normandy had moved sufficiently inland to be out of the range of the *Emmons*'s relatively small guns. Its next assignment was thirty miles to the west, where it provided escort assistance to battleships that had trained their big guns on Cherbourg, the major port at the end on the Contentin Peninsula. And after that it returned to the Mediterranean, where it provided fire support for the much smaller Allied invasion of southern France on August 15.

That mission complete, the ship recrossed the Atlantic. For Gilligan, raised in the protected world of affluent Cincinnati and schooled in the equally insular world of Notre Dame, his service in the war was a broadening experience. Part of this, of course, was the maturing experience of combat, as well as the tens of thousands of sea miles he logged and places he saw across two hemispheres. But the war prompted a social awareness. Before his enlistment, Gilligan's world—home, school, friends—had been overwhelming middle-class Catholic. Prewar America was a world of sharp ethnic and religious divides. The Second World War brought with it a great mingling; it placed millions of young men and women in close-order contact with people of various origins, people they were unlikely ever to have met in civilian life.

Gilligan's social epiphany related to race. Growing up in Cincinnati, he later wrote, he could not recall meeting a single black child or adult who was not a servant or employed in some menial occupation. The schools he attended were all-white; the major retail stores in Cincinnati's downtown and most of the city's restaurants catered to an all-white trade. There was, he said, "virtually no social intercourse of any description between the races."[31] Nor could Gilligan recall having given this circumstance any great thought as a high school student.

What had seemed normal enough at home, however, seemed abnormal at sea. There were perhaps a score of black seamen among the *Emmons*'s 240-plus complement. It "hit me with considerable force," Gilligan said, that every black crewman had a menial assignment: "They were officers' stewards. Each was handed a white jacket and an apron and told to get in the galley."[32] He recognized that this was a restriction not only on their service but on their futures. The navy went to considerable public expense to train people to be sailors, radar operators, machinists, electricians—helping them acquire skills of potential value in a civilian economy. But a black seaman who spent the war as a steward would return home with no skill to show for the experience.

Gilligan got a view of what those on the other side of the color line were thinking when he read and censored the crew's outgoing mail, one of his tasks as an officer. He recalled in particular the letters from one black sailor who had attended Ohio State University for two years before his service. Even though he had a better education than perhaps 90 percent of his shipmates, he had been made a steward: "In every letter he wrote, he poured out his anger about the injustice of the system."[33] Gilligan could see that it was not just a matter of injustice but, potentially, one of survival. Every member of the crew had a general assignment that specified where they were to go if battle was imminent. All black crewmen, Gilligan knew, were assigned to the lowest ammunition handling room, practically on the ship's keel. If anything happened to the ship, they would be the last to get out.

The assignments were made by a Boston Irishman, Jack Griffin, who regarded the task as a thankless one since complaints about assignments were many. A year after Gilligan came aboard, Griffin secured the captain's permission to pass the task to Gilligan. By way of training, Griffin had told Gilligan how to handle complainers: "Just tell them, 'It's my job, I'm doing it. Go to hell.'" Immediately, Gilligan changed the posting of some of the black seamen, moving them from just above the keel to among the gun crews. The first one in the door to complain was Griffin. Gilligan recalled, "I told him: 'Jack, it's my job and I'm doing it. And go to hell.'"[34]

By November 9 the *Emmons* was Stateside, docked at the Charleston Navy Yard for a hurried six-week conversion into a destroyer/minesweeper. The minesweepers then in use were designed chiefly for shallow water, particularly near harbors, and had proved ill-suited for the deep, broad waters of the Pacific. The navy's response was to refashion destroyers no longer needed in Europe for minesweeping operations in the Pacific Theater. The overhaul was substantial. Heavy generators were placed on board to produce the electricity needed to detonate undersea mines, along with the huge drums that contained the cables used to detect the mines. The additional weight was considerable, so to compensate a gun mount, the torpedoes, and the torpedo tubes were eliminated, along with the equipment that tossed depth charges over the side.

The conversion was completed in the last days of 1944; at that time, military planners assumed there would be several more years of fighting in the Pacific. The *Emmons* made its way to that theater. It reached San Diego through the Panama Canal by mid-January, crossing the Pacific to Hawaii in early February. Expectations aside, the *Emmons* had only one day of serious fighting ahead of it.

6

To Okinawa and Back

On March 12, 1945, the destroyers *Emmons* and *Rodman* were resting at Ulithi, an atoll some 370 miles southwest of Guam—where, in the past year, the second-largest naval base in the Pacific had been constructed. As the destroyers were readying to sail, the *Emmons*'s captain, Lieutenant Commander Eugene N. Foss II, ordered Gilligan to transfer to the *Rodman* to take the place of a gunnery officer who had been off-boarded following an apparent epileptic seizure. The news startled Gilligan—how could an epileptic spend years on a ship without the malady becoming known? Questions aside, the switch was made without written order. Gilligan recalled, "I grabbed my shaving kit and my toothbrush, climbed over the rail, and—with no more ceremony than that—reported to my new captain."[1] The destroyers sailed an hour later. In all the many happenings of a very large war, this incidental last-minute transfer may well have saved Gilligan's life.

For security reasons, ships sailed without knowing their destination, which was revealed when sealed orders were opened once the vessels had been at sea for twenty-four hours. On board the *Rodman*, officers gathered in the wardroom before a large map of the Pacific as their orders were unsealed. The stated destination, Opikanewa Kunta, was unfamiliar, so all present crowded around while that location was tracked down on the map. The officer doing the tracking moved progressively closer and closer to Japan. Finally locating the destination, he said simply, "Oh, Christ."[2] The island string for which they were heading included Okinawa, a scant 380 miles from Kyushu, the southernmost island of Japan.

Following the liberation of the Philippines, American military planning turned to the question of the best route to take toward the Japanese archipelago. They agreed on Okinawa, the capture of which would isolate Japanese forces on Formosa and permit the building of air bases within bombing distance of Japan. Okinawa was a good-sized target, stretching eighty miles from end to end. Its conquest was to be the principal amphibious invasion of 1945, but a precondition to its assault was the capture of Iwo Jima. Located some 600 miles south of

Japan, Iwo Jima was to serve as a staging area for the assault on Okinawa and as an emergency landing site for aircraft returning from bombing runs over Japan. The capture of Iwo Jima, a mere nine square miles, entailed fighting that was among the most concentrated in the Pacific Theater. U.S. marines stormed its beaches on February 19, 1945; the Japanese contested every inch of the island, from the landings to hills planted thick with entrenchments. The four-week fight left 6,821 Americans dead; the battle was captured in the iconic photograph of the American flag being planted on top of Mt. Suribachi.

The invasion of Okinawa was a massive undertaking involving 1,300 naval vessels, including 18 battleships, 40 aircraft carriers, and 200 destroyers. The battle on land engaged nearly a quarter-million U.S. soldiers and marines. When the first wave landed on Easter Sunday, April 1, one military historian wrote, "Much to everyone's surprise, from Admiral Richmond K. Turner on down to the marines and soldiers who made the original landing, there was virtually no opposition on L-Day and for several days thereafter."[3] The Japanese had another plan, however, one without precedent in the history of warfare—as those aboard the *Rodman* and *Emmons* would soon learn.

Several days after the initial landing on Okinawa, the *Rodman* and *Emmons* were offshore providing screening and fire support for a flotilla of minesweepers. Jack Gilligan stood on the *Rodman*'s bridge: "I looked out and I thought I saw an optical illusion: an aircraft coming right at us. We rushed to man the guns. Before we got a shot off, the guy came by us—barely over us—went out a couple of hundred yards and splashed into the ocean."[4] Toward nightfall a second plane flew over. Crew on the *Rodman* manned its guns and fired a few rounds, but the enemy aircraft disappeared. No one, Gilligan recalled, knew what was happening. The answer arrived several days later.

The Japanese plan for the defense of Okinawa was, literally, suicidal. The beach landings had not been contested because the Japanese intended to draw the American ground forces further inland, where they would stall against strong defensive lines. The Japanese counterattack was to be directed by air at the offshore armada to destroy or drive off the American fleet, which would render the American forces on the island helpless through lack of supply. To this end, the Japanese built up their air forces on Kyushu and in Formosa, loaded the aircraft with high explosives and sent them, as a "divine wind" (in Japanese, *kamikaze*), to slam into the American ships off Okinawa.

Gilligan later stated that he never thought the United States might lose the war; there were moments, however, when he thought "his piece" of that war might be lost.[5] Those moments came early in afternoon of April 6, 1945, when the Japanese launched their first major kamikaze attack, an attack in which, somewhat by chance, the *Rodman* and *Emmons* were among the principal targets.

Gilligan recalled:

Around 1:30 or 2:00 P.M., I was down in the mess having a cup of coffee. I heard the general alarm go off. I started up the ladder to the gunnery officer's spot. First, I heard our 40 millimeter guns going off, which meant that something must be coming in. A few seconds later, I heard the 20s, which meant something was real close. When I got one more ladder up, the whole ship shook from the impact of a plane hitting up in the bow.[6]

The Japanese aircraft had struck square into the petty officers wardroom; half a dozen men died immediately in their bunks. And shortly thereafter a second plane crashed close enough to the ship to rupture a part of its hull. The first crash had delivered the immediate hazard. When the gasoline-loaded plane struck and exploded, it created intense fire. Flames spread down a corridor toward the *Rodman*'s bow.

Gilligan had a particular anxiety over fire at sea, a fear stoked by photographs he had seen of ships burning, their crews trapped between the uncontrolled flames and the deep blue sea. Learning of the blaze, Gilligan went below deck and hustled together several men from the gunnery crew. There was significant ammunition storage in the bow compartments down in the keel of the ship, ammunition that fed both of the forward guns. Gilligan said, "I figured if the fire got to the ammunition, we were all heaven bent."[7] Armed with a fire hose, Gilligan's impromptu detail worked its way toward the number 2 gun and then through the flame-filled passageway that led to the bow. It was, Gilligan recalled, something like fighting a fire in a tunnel. The effort took nearly an hour for the men to put out the fires.

For this action, Gilligan was awarded the Silver Star. The citation accompanying the award said that the medal was presented to Gilligan for "conspicuous bravery and intrepidity in action under enemy fire."

In complete disregard for his own safety, he entered an ammunition handling room and supervised the removal of ready service ammunition, as well as actually handling it himself, while fires were burning in the immediate vicinity and despite the fact that one projectile had already exploded. Upon completion of removing the ammunition he took station aft and directed the operation of the only gun remaining to fight in such an efficient manner as to repel repeated attacks by aircraft on the vessel. His outstanding bravery and leadership were in keeping with the highest traditions of the United States Naval Service.[8]

Early in the attack, the *Emmons* shifted course toward the *Rodman* to check on casualties and to lend fire support. From the deck of the *Emmons*, several members of the crew razzed Gilligan for letting his ship be attacked. That razzing abruptly stopped as the Japanese aerial attack intensified and the *Emmons* veered off to avoid presenting a concentrated target.

With the fire under control, Gilligan returned on deck to his battle station.

To tell you how crazy it was: I was standing out there by the 40 millimeter guns; the planes were like angry bees. One guy went by. I could see him in the cockpit. Years later—I guess I was so terrified I had nightmares about this guy still coming at me, saying, "I got you." Then I turned around to look out the ship's starboard side and one of these planes is coming in banking right down on the water and heading right for the 40 millimeter gun emplacement. He got there before we could get the gun turned around and aimed on him. His wing tip cut the sights off our 40 millimeters—incredible!—and he went out about 100 yards and blew up.[9]

Of the 300 Japanese pilots who hurled themselves and their aircraft at U.S. warships that day in April, an estimated fifty made the *Rodman* or *Emmons* their target. Perhaps the most extraordinary aspect of this was that so much fury was directed at such small targets when, only miles away, the ocean off Okinawa was jammed with larger and more valuable vessels. It appears that the *Rodman* and *Emmons* drew this disproportionate attention because they were the first American vessels operating on the direct path of the incoming aircraft, and the Japanese pilots had been instructed to strike against the first U.S. warship they encountered. American aircraft soon arrived at the scene, circling protectively above the two destroyers. American pilots shot down a number of the attackers; other kamikazes missed their targets and crashed at sea. The gunnery crew of the *Rodman* was credited with bringing down five Japanese aircraft, the *Emmons* six.

Eight attacking Japanese aircraft, however, got through to the pair of destroyers. Beginning at 5:32 P.M., five aircraft struck the *Emmons* in rapid succession. The impact of the first strike propelled Lieutenant Commander Eugene Foss from his post on the bridge out into the Pacific. A flotilla of five small minesweepers, hurrying to the scene, pulled 200 crewmen from the *Rodman* and *Emmons* from the ocean, among them Foss, who did not recover his sight for three months.

The official history reports, "After five hits within a period of two minutes, the *Emmons* was in worse condition than the *Rodman*. Although her fire rooms and engine rooms were still intact, she was unable to maneuver. All five-inch guns were disabled and on fire. There was little she could do to defend herself."[10] One crewman from below decks was "shocked and scared. I saw men swimming in the water and I thought we were going down."[11] The ship burned virtually to the water line. The order to abandon ship was given by the ship's senior surviving officer, Lieutenant John Griffin. The following day, the *Emmons* was sunk at sea.

Of the *Emmons*'s full complement of 272 officers and crew, nearly half were casualties—fifty-seven dead or missing; seventy-one others wounded. Among those killed was Ensign Ross T. Elliott, who had taken over Gilligan's post as assistant gunnery officer when Gilligan was transferred to the *Rodman*. According to the ship's history, Eliot, "spotting a strafing *kamikaze* plane, ordered the men in his command to throw themselves prone; then threw his body on top of them." He was the only one killed.[12] Thomas Menaugh, Gilligan's closest friend aboard the *Emmons,* was among the survivors. Not long after the battle, they encountered each other in port when Gilligan was visiting the wounded to see who had survived. They greeted each other with the mutually startled query, "How did you get here?"[13] (A quarter-century later, Menaugh would join Gilligan's gubernatorial staff.)

While the toll among the *Rodman's* crew was far lower, the three-and-a-half hour battle left sixteen of its crew members killed or missing and twenty more injured—one-seventh of the ship's complement. By the time the attack subsided shortly before 7:00 P.M., one of the *Rodman's* engines was out of commission and the ship was listing 10 or 15 degrees to starboard. With its radio transmitter also out of service, the *Rodman* had no way to report its location in the gathering darkness. The search signals could be heard over the radio, but no reply could be sent.

For Gilligan, one particularly ghoulish task remained. Toward twilight he learned that an unexploded Japanese bomb had lodged itself below decks, and so he went to investigate. A 500-pound bomb—apparently dropped just before impact by the final Japanese aircraft to hit the *Rodman*—had bisected the ship. It had crashed through one side of the hull, penetrated the galley, and struck the inside of the hull opposite, only to bounce off without detonating. About the size of a garbage can, the bomb lay in several inches of water in the galley passageway, sloshing back and forth with the roll of the waves.

On reaching the scene, Gilligan decided that "unless I could find some means to stabilize the bomb, its back-and-forth banging would cause it to detonate."[14] Nothing in the darkened passageway could be used to wedge the bomb in place. There was, however, the headless body of a crewman who had been decapitated by the bomb's passage through the ship. Gilligan recalled, "He was on his back with his legs drawn up. I had no room to maneuver. So I shoved his shoulder up against the bomb and forced his knees down so that he wedged the bomb. That's what kept the bomb from rolling."[15]

Through the night, the *Rodman* made slow progress to the port on Ie Shimu, a small island outlying Okinawa (and where the famed war correspondent Ernie Pyle would be killed several weeks later). Near dawn, it requested permission to enter the harbor. Permission was denied until a team of officers came to inspect the damage. They were followed by a bomb disposal expert, sent to direct removal of the bomb from the galley passageway. The expert established that the fuse on the bomb's nose had snapped off on impact. This explained its failure to explode—and apparently rendering needless Gilligan's improvisation. Crewmen teamed up to muscle the bomb over the ship's rail. As they were doing so, the disposal expert shouted, "*Stop everything!*"[16] Uncharacteristically, the bomb had been double-fused, and a possibly live fuse remained on its tail.

The April 6 kamikaze attack marked the last time the *Rodman*—and Gilligan—was sent into heavy combat, though neither was entirely out of the fray. For a month, while the fighting on and around Okinawa progressed, the *Rodman* rested in port in Ie Shima, receiving emergency repairs. Virtually every day that month, Japanese aircraft attacked, sinking several vessels, including a hospital ship. In that time, the disabled *Rodman* could not fire a single shot. Repair crews in the port patched the *Rodman*'s hull but ascertained that the damage was beyond what could be repaired locally; the *Rodman* needed to be transferred back to Guam. The ship was seaworthy but defenseless. The decision was made that the *Rodman* would sail at dusk, with the intention of clearing the battle zone by daybreak. Twice it set off, only to be recalled when its progress was not rapid enough to clear the danger zone by dawn. On the third attempt it reached Guam.

On Guam, Gilligan had business of his own to attend to. His fiancée's brother, Donald Dixon, had enlisted in the Marine Corps early in the conflict; he had done so even though he had a wife and child and was, at thirty-one, somewhat overage. Dixon was been killed in July 1944 in the successful assault on Guam. On the island, Gilligan went to the local Graves Registration Service to learn Dixon's burial site. A clerk told him that no record existed for a Donald Dixon. Gilligan, exasperated and furious, told the clerk, "He came in on the first wave. He was killed here. And you don't even have a record?"[17] The clerk suggested Gilligan check at a small graveyard on the opposite side of the island; he had no records of servicemen hurriedly buried there. There, in a makeshift cemetery near a small church near the beach, Gilligan found Donald Dixon's dog tags hanging from a simple wooden cross. Gilligan collected the tags, informed Graves Registration of the location of Dixon's grave, and, later, returned the dog tags to his fiancee's family.

By the spring of 1945, the entire Gilligan family was engaged in wartime service. Frank and Mike had both entered the navy, and Jeanne, having completed her studies at Trinity College in Washington, D.C., returned to Cincinnati, where she worked as a nurse at the Children's Hospital and spent two days a week assisting at the local USO. (Recalling her service, she said, "To my father's appalled horror, I would regale them with stories from the operating room at Children's Hospital."[18]) Harry Gilligan served as the civilian head of civil defense activities for Hamilton County.

Unbeknownst to Gilligan, the sinking of the *Emmons* had created a significant family problem. His last-minute transfer from the *Emmons* to the *Rodman* had never been officially recorded. While the *Rodman* was making its slow way to Guam, the navy announced that the *Emmons* had been lost at sea. The announcement carried with it the list of those officers and crew who survived the battle; Gilligan's name was not on it. As far as Gilligan's family and Katie Dixon knew, he was missing in action.

Gilligan's brother Michael thought so too. Michael, who had received his navy commission in February, was in Pearl Harbor in April awaiting his ship assignment. Mike was trying to catch up with the war: this he eventually did in the Philippines in August 1945, where he was assigned to service on a landing ship-tank and caught sight of only the occasional enemy aircraft. Awaiting that assignment, he spent several days in Pearl Harbor pestering people at headquarters, trying to track down news of the *Emmons* and of his brother, presumably serving aboard it. Finally, an officer took him aside: "Don't you know the *Emmons* was sunk with heavy loss of life on the picket line at Okinawa." Michael recalled, "I thought for about a month that Jack was dead; I couldn't bring myself to report that to my mother and father."[19] In fact, Harry Gilligan had already heard the news, but he refused to believe it. It may have been faith, or it may have been simple denial, but the senior Gilligan peppered navy offices in Washington with inquiries only to be told that anyone not listed as a survivor must be presumed to be dead. Harry Gilligan replied that he wasn't going to assume anything; he wanted to know where his son was.[20]

His son, entirely ignorant of his family's anguish, only inadvertently laid their worries to rest. While in Guam, Jack wrote a letter home. Its contents were inconsequential; what mattered was its postmark. Dated some weeks after the sinking of the *Emmons*, the letter was proof positive that he had not gone down with that ship.

Further confusing the situation, the *Rodman* was once again declared too damaged to be repaired locally and was sent from Guam back to Pearl Harbor. There, with time on his hands, Gilligan sought news on his brothers, both of whom were by then serving in the Pacific. Jack then bore a strong resemblance to Michael—so much so that a deeply annoyed officer told him, "Get the hell out. You've been here five times already and we told you we didn't know anything."[21] Of course, the officer who'd been there five times was Michael Gilligan. It was then that Jack learned of his supposed disappearance aboard the *Emmons*.

Moved from Ie Shima to Guam and then to Pearl Harbor, the *Rodman* had become the patient nobody wanted. Gilligan thought that the ship was beyond repair; it should be floated out past the 100-fathoms line and given a decent burial at sea. The navy, preferring to call in more specialists, forwarded the *Rodman* on to San Diego. San Diego deemed the damage beyond its powers and directed the ship on to Charleston, South Carolina. For Gilligan and the rest of the crew, this extended limping from port to port was extraordinarily boring. (As was the diet with the ship's refrigeration out of service, meals leaned heavily to ham, spam, and bologna.) Yet, Gilligan observed, "if being bored was the alternative to being attacked by kamikazes," then being bored had something to be said for it.[22]

On June 19 the *Rodman* reached Charleston. By then, the crew's boredom had given way to a macabre humor. The *Rodman*'s blackened hull sailed in just as three destroyers were exiting the harbor for their sea trials. The *Rodman* crew stood at the rail, Gilligan recalled, calling out to the rookies, "You're going to love it out there; you're just going to love it. It's a ball."[23] For an added dramatic touch, some seamen went down to sick bay and swathed themselves in bandages heavily dosed with mercurochrome to simulate bloodstains. As perhaps the ship's final indignity, the tugboat sent to steer the *Rodman* to the dock broke down.

The fighting on Okinawa continued as the *Rodman* made its way from Guam to Charleston. The Japanese surrendered the island on June 23, 1945. During that fighting, Japan launched nine more waves of suicide attacks, sinking fourteen destroyers and several dozen smaller craft and killing 5,000 American sailors at sea and 7,000 American soldiers on land. The Japanese ambition of stranding the men ashore by sinking the fleet at sea never came close to being realized; Japanese losses onshore were enormous, an estimated 110,000 dead.

In Charleston, Jack Gilligan had an ambition of his own. With thirty days of survivors' leave in hand, Gilligan telephoned Katie in Cincinnati and told her to proceed with the plans for their wedding. He was coming home. The wedding proved a somewhat impromptu affair. First, Gilligan had to drum up a best man, which was difficult since virtually every male he had known growing up in Cincinnati was off in military service. In the end, a somewhat casual acquaintance, James Farrell, home recuperating from war service, undertook the duty. Second, having arrived in Cincinnati wearing his navy dungarees, he needed something decent in which to be married. A downtown uniform shop proved up to the task, fitting and finishing a smart-looking uniform in twenty-four hours.

And so on June 28, 1945, John Gilligan, standing in Cincinnati's St. Mary's Church on Erie Avenue beside a reserve best man called into service for the occasion and wearing a suit that had been run up the day before, married Mary Kathryn Dixon.

The ceremony was something of a family reunion. The Gilligan and Dixon families, longtime friends, made up most of the wedding party. Gilligan's uncle, Father Frank Joyce, came from Cleveland to officiate. And responding to Gilligan's invitation, Frank O'Malley came down from South Bend.

O'Malley had come to Cincinnati intending to travel on to Boston to visit family. But when Gilligan took O'Malley to Cincinnati's Dixie Terminal to secure a berth to Boston, the ticket agent told them that there were no tickets to Boston for at least two weeks. Gilligan asked O'Malley where he'd like to go. Nonplussed, O'Malley said he had no idea—where were the Gilligans going? To Traverse City, Michigan, Gilligan said, for the start of their honeymoon. And so O'Malley secured a spot on a later train to Traverse City than the newlyweds were taking. Gilligan recalled, "We dined together that evening at the Edgewater Beach Hotel, batted around town a bit, and the following morning O'Malley managed a ticket to Boston."[24]

O'Malley's short-term companionship aside, Katie Gilligan had mapped out the couple's honeymoon, which began with a stay in Michigan and ended with accompanying her new husband back to Charleston, where he took his bride to see the ship that had carried him from Okinawa to Charleston. Her reaction, he said, was fairly typical: "It was a matter of wonder to her how this rusted wreck had made it that far."[25]

John and Katie Gilligan set up housekeeping in Charleston. Officers were permitted to live off-base if they could find housing. By word of mouth, Gilligan learned of a home on a street of large and graceful antebellum homes whose owners—either through patriotism, avarice, or some combination thereof—rented out rooms to navy officers. The Gilligans managed to secure a bedroom and sitting room in one particularly grand home that housed half a dozen other navy officers and their wives. It was, he later commented, an altogether cordial way to begin a marriage.

The Gilligans married in the expectation, commonly held, that the war with Japan was likely to continue for several more years. It was also part of that expectation that the war's continuation might prove fatal to Jack; the only hesitance the Dixons had about their daughter marrying was the possibility that she might end up a young widow. Jack and Katie did not rule that possibility out either; their decision to marry in part reflected the desire to claim for themselves such time as they could.

The end of the war, however, came just months, not years, later. In early August, Gilligan, serving as officer of the day, stood by the gangway of the *Rodman* checking the credentials of those wishing to come aboard. A communications officer approached and breathlessly reported that an atomic bomb had been dropped on Hiroshima. Gilligan recalled, "A lot of guys thought that ended the war right there, and they'd send us home."[26] Several days later word followed of a second atomic bomb being dropped on Nagasaki. Gilligan recalls thinking, "What are they doing—trying to exterminate the Japanese nation?"[27]

Japan's formal surrender came on September 1, 1945. Millions of men and women in arms—the newly married Gilligan not least—wanted to be out of uniform immediately. For Gilligan, getting out of the armed services proved somewhat more difficult than getting in had been. A navy directive gave ships' captains the authority to hold in service for three months those officers and crewmen minimally required for operation. Gilligan, to his chagrin, was among those so designated.

Repairs in Charleston on the *Rodman* took until October 22, after which the destroyer left port for refresher training, heading for Casco Bay, Maine. In its first day of sea trials, the ship's engines broke down and the *Rodman* had to be towed back to harbor. Learning that an additional three months' of repairs might be required, Gilligan, with some exasperation, stated his case to the captain: the war was over; the *Rodman* was going nowhere; could he please be discharged? The captain agreed. Having served just shy of three years, having seen action that included D-Day and Okinawa, the twenty-four-year-old Gilligan was again a civilian.

Xavier

In November 1945, John Gilligan, recently discharged from the navy, returned to Cincinnati and to Katie Gilligan, intending, like millions of veterans, to get on with his life. And, also like so many of them, he was uncertain as to his prospects. He had "no particular idea" of what he wanted to do.[1]

The answer all but fell out of the sky. Frank O'Malley called from Notre Dame to report that he had arranged for Gilligan to be admitted as a graduate fellow at the University of Chicago's Committee on Social Thought. Gilligan recalled, "I thought I'd died and gone to heaven."[2]

The offer represented one of academia's true plums. Founded in 1941 by historian John U. Nef and the university's influential president, Robert Maynard Hutchins, the Chicago program aimed at surmounting the separateness of the academic disciplines by bringing noted scholars from a range of subjects together to "foster awareness of the permanent questions at the origin of all learned inquiry."[3] Beyond that, the program aimed to be a model that might encourage interdisciplinary approaches at other institutions. Over time, it drew participation from such leading figures as political philosophers Hannah Arendt and Alan Bloom, economist Friedrich von Hayek, author Saul Bellow, poet T. S. Eliot, and others.

Gilligan considered the offer more a consequence of O'Malley's influence than of his own achievement. No matter. "To be at the University of Chicago in company of the individuals in that program, spending my days looking out at Lake Michigan and writing great things. It was enormously attractive."[4] It was also enormously opportune: in a single phone call, Gilligan had gone from being uncertain of his future to having a future almost any academically inclined young person might envy. And it was a possibility that Gilligan's parents and in-laws insisted he reject.

Jack and Katie were then living with her parents. The Dixon and Gilligan homes became the sites of a protracted conflict. For the older generation, the matter was a question of family. Harry Gilligan placed somewhat limited value on academia as a career, or as a future, for his son. That future, he believed, should be in the funeral business, which had provided a good livelihood to three genera-tions of Gilligans. He had long been paving the way for this: when Jack was young, his father would take him to his office on Saturdays or during school vacations to undertake various incidental tasks around the office. He "was clearly bent on my succeeding him in the business," Gilligan recalled. "He had succeeded his father, who had succeeded his father."[5]

The Dixons were equally opposed, though for different reasons. That family had been shattered by the death of their oldest son on Guam; they felt a pressing need to hold the remaining family close. The prospect of their only daughter leav-ing for Chicago threatened what remained. Edward Dixon also had a career path to offer: Jack should go to law school in Cincinnati, earn a degree, and then move into Dixon's own law office, where a spot would be available.

The twenty-four-year-old Gilligan wanted neither option. The funeral busi-ness held no attraction for him: "I thought a lot of the stuff that went on in the funeral business was just maudlin and sentimental nonsense."[6] As for the law, the life of statutes and litigation attracted Gilligan only slightly less. Circumstance presented him with a stark choice—between the parochial and the cosmopolitan, between the world he had grown up in and larger world beyond what he imag-ined. Gilligan later acknowledged that if he accepted the offer from the University of Chicago, "it was not probable we were ever coming back to Cincinnati to live." However, if he rejected the offer, "I was relatively sure it would not come again."[7]

The clinching argument was advanced by his mother: she pointed out that with all three sons serving in the military, Harry Gilligan had carried the full burden of managing the business through the war years. He needed help. Frank and Mike each had a year of navy service remaining; beyond that, they had senior years at Notre Dame to complete. So until they were able to return to Cincinnati, it was Jack's place to help his father.

Gilligan accepted the outcome, though not without resentment. "It was a very prestigious appointment. It promised to put me in association with people in the academic and literary world that I greatly admired. I thought it was the chance of a lifetime," he said, adding, "and, indeed, it was."[8] For Gilligan, this represented the second thwarted ambition. Four years earlier he had been on the verge of joining a Jesuit seminary. Either move—to the Jesuits or to Chicago—would have taken him from the city of his youth to some unknown and presumably different world. He was back where he had started, and working in a business he disliked.

But there were compensations. Cincinnati was, for Gilligan, always a favorite city; it may fairly be regarded as the most cosmopolitan in Ohio, with its museums, opera, parks, and beautiful tumbling topography. Living in a rented apartment in Cincinnati's Hyde Park neighborhood, Jack and Katie were socially active with a number of couples like themselves, younger Eastside Catholic professionals. And it wasn't long before Katie was expecting. Of this, Gilligan recalled, "Katie, with a physician brother and a dominant mother, was getting the best of care. She was so passionately dedicated to having children, she did not complain about anything associated with it."[9] With the onset of labor, the couple went to Good Samaritan Hospital, where Katie's brother, Dr. Gordon Dixon, had privileges. Gilligan commented, "He was not only a fine physician, but he was about the best-looking guy I ever knew, and he was single. Katie got the very best of care and attention from all the nurses who wanted to score well with Gordon."[10] Their first child was born on February 23, 1947, named Donald after his mother's brother, Donald Dixon, who had been killed on Guam.

Gilligan had gained one concession from the debate about his future. He would work in the funeral home, but, keeping at least a foot in academia, he would also pursue a master's degree in English literature at the University of Cincinnati. Gilligan's investment in the funeral business was something less than wholehearted. Weak at organization, he was better with people; by one account, his most valuable contribution was to counsel grieving families seeking the Gilligan Funeral Homes' services. But the work filled a good part of his day, while his graduate studies filled a good part of his evenings. And during this time his home was becoming fuller—with the birth on May 15, 1948, of his second child, Kathleen. The agreement Jack made with his family held: when his brothers returned, Jack reduced his involvement with the funeral home.

Shortly after his brothers returned home, there was another new arrival—a television set won by Harry Gilligan in a charity raffle. Mike recalled, "It was a Wednesday night; we were anxious to get it up and running so on Saturday we could watch a football game. There were only two stations you could watch. And Saturday, with everyone there trying to watch this little screen, all you could see was the back of heads and ears." Mike Gilligan acknowledged that "once television came in, book reading kind of slipped to the side."[11]

Unlike for Jack, the return to Cincinnati and to the family business was not a conflicted one for Frank and Mike. Mike recalled, "I didn't give it much thought. You went to Notre Dame; you went into the family business. That was just the way it happened. Jack had enough gumption to say 'I don't want to do this,' so he went on into teaching."[12]

Jack was working to complete his master's degree at the University of Cincinnati; his thesis, "The Vision of Margery Kempe," was a study of a sixteenth-century mystic. For American colleges and universities, the all-but-defining fact of the postwar years was the Serviceman's Readjustment Act of 1944, popularly known as the GI Bill of Rights. This entitled every ex-serviceman to a year's free tuition with an additional month of tuition for every month of military service. By 1950, 2 million veterans had entered college under the GI Bill. Their arrival not only doubled the prewar national enrollment in higher education, it energized previously somnolent wartime campuses with the worldliness and focused ambitions of the returning GIs.

A case in point was Xavier University, a small, all-male, Jesuit-run institution tucked into a compact campus in Cincinnati's Avondale neighborhood, five miles north of downtown. In the fall of 1945, Xavier enrolled 525 full-time residential students; the following year, enrollment leaped to 1,486 undergraduates, no fewer than 900 of whom were freshmen, mostly veterans. It was a squeeze. For a time, "194 students were bedded down each night on twelve rows of Army cots located in the university's field house."[13] By 1948, on-campus enrollment pushed to 1,718.

Xavier stretched to find classrooms to accommodate its students; it stretched as well to find faculty members to put in those classrooms. And in the fall of 1948, that stretch extended to the hiring of John Gilligan as an instructor in the English department. The student-run *Xavier University News* noted Gilligan's hiring in a short piece that closed, "Aiding newcomers in identifying Mr. Gilligan is his carrot-colored hair."[14]

In his first year, Gilligan taught rhetoric, drama, and poetry. With the shortage of faculty, he also taught two classes on logic through the philosophy department. In later years, he added an introductory class, Studies in Literature, an advanced class on Catholic literature, and a graduate seminar on Chaucer. As a teacher, Gilligan consciously took Frank O'Malley as his model: "I tried to teach like him. Of course, I did not have his depth. I had the idea then that the purpose of teaching was to influence thought and action; to focus on how roles within the community were to be carried out, and to find how one could build awareness of the social responsibilities that people within the society have to each other."[15] This line of thought was "the essential ingredient" that he would carry from academic to political life.

Xavier University was the second Jesuit institution at which Gilligan spent time. The university regarded its mission as clear. Its president, James F. McGuire, wrote at the time of the university's "sacred trust . . . to endow our students [not] merely with the treasures of a Liberal Education" but with "Christian education" as well. McGuire was critical of large institutions that attempted the wholesale education of students; what mattered, he said, was an education based on a core of studies that, by cultivating "intellectual excellence (combined with Ignatian spirituality)" would produce graduates capable of becoming society's leaders.[16]

"Ignatian spirituality" is a subject of some complexity, though one aspect is worth comment. St. Ignatius's "Spiritual Exercises" emphasized that if an individual could free himself from personal preferences and passions, he was more likely to be able to learn what God had willed for him. The intention was rationalist rather than emotive; the undistracted intellect would govern. And it was an intention that was both in keeping with Gilligan's nature and the furthering of it. (Two decades later, when Gilligan was criticized for the allegedly professorial nature of his campaign speeches, he replied, "My job is to help people make tough decisions to bring about constructive change and improve the quality of life for everyone. And in order for me to do this, I've simply got to give them some factual material—all those statistics—to go on. It's easy to say the things that are popular. But it's another thing to influence people."[17]

Gilligan remained at Xavier for four years. Beginning with the 1949–50 academic year, he taught a course new to the institution: creative writing. With this, he volunteered (or, more accurately, was volunteered) to serve as faculty adviser of the student literary magazine, the *Athenaeum*. Announcing that appointment, the student newspaper editorialized that previous such efforts appeared to have been "magazines put out by the editorial board for publication of their own work."[18] This Gilligan pledged to change. Submissions, he said, would come from the student body at large; the editorial board would merely advise and select. Soon thereafter the *Athenaeum* announced its standards in words and tones reminiscent of the *Scrip* at Notre Dame: "There are too many today who write in clever vein, afraid to say anything real or true. The primary objective of our efforts, however, will be to publish that which will make us think."[19] And, as ever, there was ambition: the student newspaper quoted Gilligan as saying, "There is no reason Xavier can't produce the best student literary publication of any school in the country."[20]

Xavier was a lively place—in part, it was enjoying the self-satisfaction a campus experiences due to athletic success. In Gilligan's first month at the institution, the Xavier Musketeers achieved their first football victory over cross-town rival University of Cincinnati, defeating the Bearcats 13–7. The student newspaper celebrated this news under a two-inch headline: "Famine Ends. Joy Reigns."[21] Beginning with that season, the Musketeers ran up a three-year record of twenty-seven wins, two losses, and one tie, and scored a 33–12 victory over Arizona State in the 1950 Salad Bowl.

For a time, the life of a young professor at a liberal arts college was entirely congenial to Gilligan. The family grew with the births of their third child, John Patrick, on May 10, 1949, and their last child, Ellen, on May 7, 1952. The family moved from a modest two-and-a-half-bedroom home in Hyde Park to a somewhat larger home in the same neighborhood. The academic calendar accommodated the family's lengthy summer stays in Leland, Michigan. Of these years at Xavier, Gilligan said, "I liked literature and I liked teaching literature. I wasn't going to make a million dollars, but that wasn't what I was out to do. I thought it was a perfectly attractive way to live."[22]

The attraction, however, was largely lost on the young professor's father, whose attitude was, Gilligan said, "What the hell are you doing? You're wasting your time and talent. Come on! Get out here in the real world." To the elder Gilligan, academia was not serious; business was serious. "The essential thing to him was to follow in the family tradition and keep the business going. He was kind about it, but he was obviously disappointed in my decision." The view that his son was misdirecting his own life, Gilligan said, did not completely change "until I got elected governor."[23]

Gilligan's interests beyond his family were largely literary. Along with teaching English and advising the *Athenaeum,* he contributed a column of literary criticism and comment to the *Catholic Telegraph Register* and spoke to various groups on literary subjects, including a talk analyzing the work of Gerard Manley Hopkins and T. S. Eliot to the campus French club.

But not entirely literary. In a late 1951 issue of the campus newspaper, Gilligan offered his thoughts on a question many students had: should they enlist in the military in advance of being drafted into a war in Korea in the hope of thereby gaining some control over their assignment? Gilligan was skeptical, and as a veteran his skepticism carried some weight with students. He did not have a romantic view of military life. Students, he said, should recognize that the military was "an enormous and impersonal machine . . . Anyone who has the idea of becoming a part of that machine, and then manipulating it to their best advantage, should contemplate the vision of a cotter pin determining its destiny in the machinery of a battleship, it [and he] will be used when and where the engineer decides it can be most useful."[24]

Gilligan's youth and his own military service provided common ground between him and many of his students. A school newspaper profile reported that Gilligan was "known to many students for his splendid sense of humor and wittiness." He was among those favorite faculty members who were parodied in the campus newspaper's April Fool's Day issue. The paper carried a review of a supposed play, *Passion Under the Palms,* in which the desert island survivors of some unnamed catastrophe divide their loyalties between "the island chieftain and his aspirant brother." Gilligan, perhaps significantly, was cast as the leader of the insurrectionists.[25]

Through his time at Xavier, Gilligan continued to correspond with Frank O'Malley. O'Malley remained at Notre Dame but was not entirely happy with the institution itself. He felt that its emphasis was drifting from humanism and religion to preprofessionalism. The school was becoming too large, too institutional, and too indifferent to what he saw as the finest parts of its own heritage. In his journal and in private conversations with a select few, O'Malley shared his idea of creating a new institution. Tentatively, it would be named Christ College. It would be small, with perhaps no more than 200 students. In its essence, he wrote, it "should be a community of students and teachers centered in Christ." The institution "must be characterized by inwardness, an intellectual largeness and intensity, a descent to sources from which the universe of thought and love proceeds, a meeting of the mind, and man, with the mystery of things." Its instructors would likely not be PhDs, "since the infertility and darkness of their usual pursuits cannot fail to blight the spirit," but those with "a real sense of the action of the *teacher.*"[26] (This suggests the faculty would be rather like O'Malley himself.)

O'Malley made fitful efforts to bring this college into being. In 1947, he had visited several former students in California, exploring the idea with them and viewing several possible sites for such an undertaking, but nothing substantive followed. The idea came closest to realization when he broached it to Jack Gilligan. By 1951 the pair was brainstorming by letter how such a small liberal arts Catholic institution might be created in Cincinnati.

If, like Thoreau, O'Malley was building "castles in the air," then Gilligan took it as his task to "put foundations under them." Largely from prominent lay Catholics in Cincinnati, Gilligan secured $250,000 in pledged seed money for establishing such an institution. Fortune appeared to favor the enterprise. When Joseph Bernardin was named archbishop of Cincinnati, he announced he would live in a small apartment in a church rather than in the substantial Westside mansion used by his predecessors—leaving that mansion available as a founding site for O'Malley's school.

During spring break in 1952, O'Malley made the trip to Cincinnati for a status report. Gilligan reported on steps taken and tasks remaining. Among other things, he told O'Malley that it was time for him to leave Notre Dame for the new venture. Gilligan said, "We talked and drank till three in the morning. Frank broke down and cried, saying he just couldn't do it."[27] Offering an explanation, Gilligan said, "O'Malley was to be president, dean and soul of the place, and I think being out front and center like that made him balk."

The likelier explanation is that O'Malley could not bring himself to leave Notre Dame, where he had lived since arriving there in 1928 as a student. As a young instructor, he turned down an offer to undertake a doctoral program at Princeton rather than leave South Bend. As a further note, when President George Bush gave the 2001 commencement address at Notre Dame, he quoted a comment O'Malley had made when some had urged that the brick administration building be replaced. "These bricks contain the blood of everyone who helped to build Notre Dame."[28]

O'Malley had been the project's centerpiece. Without him, Gilligan commented, "We just had nothing." Much later, he would wonder if he had been the victim of his own wishful thinking: "O'Malley endorsed the idea. But I took the next step in my own mind that he would pick it up and run with it if somebody gave him the tools."[29] Again, John Gilligan had reached for an ambition only to find that it exceeded his grasp.

Compared with the institution he and O'Malley had imagined, the appeal of Xavier University somewhat dimmed. Gilligan recalled thinking at the time, "I could continue to go back and forth to English classes, but I wasn't really going anywhere with that, so I began to think more seriously."[30] He arranged a leave of absence from Xavier for the 1952–53 school year; his plan was to complete his doctoral dissertation (on tragedy from Greek to modern times) and await whatever call might come next.

That call came by radio late in evening on Monday, July 21, 1952. Gilligan was driving home from a meeting and had his radio tuned to coverage of the Democratic National Convention in Chicago, where Illinois governor Adlai Stevenson was giving the opening speech. Stevenson was not particularly well-known nationally; most of those who heard his welcoming address, like Gilligan, were hearing him speak for the first time. Gilligan recalled: "I just heard the first few phrases and I had to pull over to the curb; I thought I was going to wreck the car. I was so enchanted by his phrasing and delivery and what he was talking about."[31] Two days after that welcoming address was delivered, Gilligan stayed up past 1:00 A.M. listening to the radio coverage as the Democratic Party made Stevenson, who had not been an active candidate, its nominee for president.

Adlai Stevenson was the first political leader, Gilligan said, who did not address his audience as though they were children. Stevenson was a presidential aspirant—somewhat like, on the Republican side, Robert Taft—who commanded the intense loyalty of many without ever commanding the votes of most. Gilligan was both a "great admirer" and "devoted disciple" of Stevenson. The appeal was not particularly programmatic; Stevenson's positions on most issues did not differ greatly from those of other liberal Democrats—indeed, on some matters he was more conservative. Rather, it rested on Stevenson's sense of the nature of politics and responsibilities of those who practice it, which he made clear in his June 23, 1952, acceptance speech:

> Let's talk sense to the American people. Let's tell them the truth, that there are no gains without pains, and that we are on the eve of great decisions, not easy decisions—like resistance when you are attacked, but a long, patient costly struggle which alone can assure triumph over the great enemies of man—war, poverty, and tyranny—and the assaults upon human dignity which are the most grievous consequence of each.[32]

The morning following Stevenson's nomination, Gilligan signed up with the local Stevenson volunteers group. Though technically on leave from Xavier, he orchestrated campus meetings on behalf of the candidate, organized letter writing to the local newspapers, and tried to "generally raise a fuss" on campus on behalf of the candidate.

Stevenson paid one visit to Cincinnati during the campaign. The Democrat's plane landed late morning, Friday, October 3, and Stevenson came into the downtown by motorcade. The candidate's own vehicle was driven by Sidney Weil, a young Cincinnati attorney who a decade later would be an important political ally of Gilligan. In his remarks at Cincinnati's Netherlands Plaza hotel, while honoring his Republican opponent, General Dwight Eisenhower, for his military leadership, Stevenson argued that Eisenhower was "selling out" his previously stated internationalist views to "Republican isolationists."[33] He said he feared that Eisenhower's election might prompt an American withdrawal from world affairs, similar to what had happened following the 1920 election of Republican Warren Harding and America's rejection of the League of Nations.

Unfortunately, scheduled activities at Xavier kept Gilligan away from his candidate's presentation. Coverage of the visit reflected the partisan nature of the local press. The pro-Democrat *Cincinnati Post* reported that Stevenson spoke to "1,200 cheering Democrats." The pro-Republican (and Taft-owned) *Times-Star* reported that the Democrat spoke to "a luncheon."[34] Local newspapers also noted that Ohio's Democratic governor, Frank Lausche, did not join his party's candidate in Cincinnati. (In fact, later that day in Columbus, Lausche all but endorsed Stevenson's Republican opponent, General Dwight David Eisenhower.)

Candidates, as people, have foibles. And those who admire them often do so not despite but because of those foibles. The 1952 campaign produced a Pulitzer Prize–winning photograph that was considered by Stevenson supporters to be evidence of his lack of pretense. It was a low-angle shot taken of the sitting candidate and revealing a hole in the sole of his right shoe.

That November, Eisenhower was elected president by a margin of 6 million votes. He carried thirty-nine states, including Ohio. Of the campaign, Gilligan said it "was a fine experience and a good campaign, and, of course, we got trounced."[35] As a memento of that losing campaign, Gilligan received and a half-century later still had a lapel ornament of a shoe sole with a hole in it.

8

Charter Politics

The Gilligan family had its brushes with politics. In the case of John Gilligan, Jack's grandfather, it was perhaps more of a brushing off. John was elected Democratic precinct committeeman for the downtown Cincinnati district where the funeral home was located—an experience that cured him of further political ambition. He ran for the post against a man named Jack Reardon, who, defeated, never spoke to Gilligan again for the rest of his life. John Gilligan concluded that if politics could be a bar to friendship, politics should be foresworn.[1]

By family telling, Harry Gilligan would have run for political office but was dissuaded by his mother and his wife. The demands of public office, they stressed, would drain time from his business, family, and civic engagements. Harry tried, not always successfully, to keep politics separate from business. In 1940, when he announced that he supported a third term for President Franklin Roosevelt, a number of Republican families threatened to have themselves buried by somebody else. That notwithstanding, Harry Gilligan was not ideologically inclined. His father's politics were, Jack Gilligan said, "Democratic, at least to the extent that he was opposed to Republican Party dominance in the city."[2]

Like many older cities, Cincinnati had a long memory. The city's substantial German population had little difficulty remembering that it had been Woodrow Wilson and the Democrats who, during the First World War, had questioned their patriotism, coerced their purchase of war bonds, and prompted the changing of good solid street names like Erckenbrecker to Mills. A good many others in the city traced their Republicanism in an unbroken line back to Abraham Lincoln and to an opposition to slavery the Democratic Party then did not share. Such Cincinnatians gave the Republicans their mass support, and the business and banking worlds help provide their leadership.

Harry Gilligan did, to an extent, confront those dominant Republicans. As a very successful businessman and, perhaps more, as a member of the board of the Kroger Company and a director of the Provident Savings Bank and Trust

Company, he was elected a member of the Queen City Club. Founded in 1874 and moved to East Fourth Street in 1927, the club was a convenient luncheon setting for the downtown business and banking world. It was the bastion of Cincinnati conservatism, where the well-born exchanged advice and invitations with the well-off, where Senator Robert A. Taft held court, and where business or civic undertakings were launched or stymied. At the time, the organization had never had a Catholic on its governing board, so Gilligan ran. Standing for election, Harry said, "Well, I've got several strikes against me right now: I'm an Irish Catholic, a Democrat, and a funeral director." He was elected.[3]

One Queen City Club story in particular captures Harry Gilligan's politics. One day in the 1950s, Harry was seated at lunch with Neil McElroy, who had served as Eisenhower's secretary of defense. McElroy commented to Harry that he must be aware that everyone in the room was an able, decent, and successful man but that Harry was the only one in the room who would be voting Democratic in the next election. How did he account for this? Harry took issue with McElroy's assumption. He bet him $100 that at least five other people in the room would be voting Democratic. McElroy declined the bet, saying that he was unwilling to take Harry's money—but, just out of curiosity, who did Gilligan have in mind? Harry then counted off the black waiters in the room—*one, two, three, four, five.* That, McElroy said, was unfair; Harry should know that McElroy wasn't counting them. To which Harry rejoined, "I know you weren't counting them. *That's* what's not fair."[4]

Harry Gilligan did play one substantial role in the world of Cincinnati politics. He was active in the Cincinnati Charter Party, an organization whose history is virtually unique in American politics. It was through the Charter Party that Jack Gilligan entered political life.

In Cincinnati, Charter was both more and less than a political party; primarily, it was an attitude toward how politics should be conducted, an attitude that had considerable influence on Gilligan's own views. The Charter movement was the city reform response to the political machine that was the turn-of-the-century creation of George Barnstable Cox.

Born in Cincinnati to English immigrants in 1853, Cox left school at age eight to help support his widowed mother. According to his most astute observer, historian Zane Miller, he was virtually a model youth: "His school principal claimed that he caused no trouble in classes, exhibited an 'undisguised love for his mother' and 'never lied.'"[5] Straying slightly, he was by age twenty proprietor of Dead Man's Corner, a saloon so-named for the frequency with which murdered bodies turned up at its intersection in the rough-and-tumble Eighteenth Ward. Cox was tall, quiet, and combative, once organizing a local baseball team with the motto "Win, Tie or Fight." His saloon fell subject to the irksome attentions of the police—which Cox thought to head off by running as a Republican for city council, to which he was elected at age twenty-four.

He served only briefly, as Cox exercised leadership from outside political office. As a young man, he discovered in himself, in his own felicitous phrase, "a peculiar fitness" for politics.[6] With the saloon as his organizing base, Cox soon dominated the politics of his ward; he then moved his office and his ambitions downtown. In the election of 1884, he was credited with carrying Hamilton County for Republican presidential candidate James G. Blaine. By 1888 Cox was the leader of the county Republicans, with 2,000 patronage jobs to dispense.

Patronage meant revenue: jobholders kicked back 2.5 percent of their earnings to Cox's organization. And patronage meant votes. As one example, a man with a patronage job as a school janitor was expected to vote as directed *and* to deliver the votes of his son and the two young men who boarded with the family. These votes added up. At the time, Cincinnati had some 500 precincts; each was home to nine or ten city employees. This meant roughly 25,000 reliable votes, enough to control the outcome in any Republican primary—which was tantamount to victory in November, as Cincinnati was essentially a one-party city; at one point its city council was made up of thirty-one Republicans and one Democrat.

Historian Zane Miller writes rather sympathetically of Cox as a figure who brought order out of the late nineteenth century chaos that then characterized urban America. By the 1880s, Cincinnati, like many American cities, had expanded beyond any capacity to govern itself. The piling of people into a confined space had created wholly new municipal requirements—transportation, sanitation, and the like—which the city generally lacked the organization or the expertise to master. The police department was corrupt, and the streets witnessed recurrent fighting between youthful Protestant and Catholic gangs. In March 1884 a local judge sentenced for manslaughter a defendant the public mind had already convicted of murder. A protest meeting drew a throng; the throng turned into a mob. At one point, barrels of kerosene seized from a nearby warehouse were rolled against the city jail and ignited (the prisoners had been evacuated). A contingent of troops was called out, Gatling guns mounted. By time the scene played out, at least fifty-six Cincinnatians were dead and 300 injured.

It was to this situation that Cox brought a measure of order. By centralizing effective power in his own person, Cox gave Cincinnati what it had previously lacked: a coherent structure by which decisions were made, directives carried out, rewards determined and distributed. As John Fairfield writes, "The machine did not represent any single class, but rather stood apart from the contending groups and accommodated one to the other." It did have its costs, however. City services were woefully inefficient, city payrolls were riotously padded, and city purchases were a bonanza for the contractor. When Cox retired in 1911, his place was taken by Rodolph Hynicka, and his dominating Republican machine remained.

The challenge to the machine started with the Cincinnatus Association, initially a discussion club formed by several dozen younger businessmen and professionals

who, given their education and affluence, felt free of any great need to defer to the
Cox machine. In 1922, the city placed a tax increase on the ballot. Cincinnati was,
in a general sort of way, broke—to meet its expenses, the city had issued $7 million
dollars worth of deficiency bonds, in effect meeting current expenses with anticipated revenues.

The Cincinnatus scheduled a forum on the issue, at which a young Harvard
graduate, Murray Seasongood, savaged the case for the increase. At city hall, he
charged, "They tell you they have no money for this, no money for that. What I
want to know is what becomes of the money?" The answer, he said, was "waste,
waste, waste—waste and incompetence in all departments."[7] Seasongood's was the
voice of the rising professional class, a class often progressive in its politics, whose
outlook was well characterized by Walter Lippmann, who wrote in 1925: "There are
more and more people in the world who hate waste, and can't rest until they end it .
. . The spectacle of people foozling and fuddling without a plan, without standards,
the whole idea of wasted labor and wasted materials is a horror to them."[8]

Such people were sufficient in number in Cincinnati to orchestrate a campaign
against the tax increase. And they were successful. The final tally—46,496 for the
levy, 60,434 opposed—was regarded as a vote of no confidence in city government. (Interestingly, voters did approve an increase in the school levy.) That was
just the opening round. Soon, Cincinnatus members upbraided city government
in public letters written in the condescending tone of presumed virtue: "The truth
is that the city has developed an inordinate appetite for granite . . . To all appearance, somebody who is very anxious to sell granite to the city has found somebody among the city officials who is very anxious to buy granite."[9] The problem,
they wrote, lay not with city council, whose members had "too little independence to steal."[10] The problem was that power rested elsewhere and out of view:
"The council of Cincinnati is not in the true sense of the word a representative
body at all. It is, on all matters of general interest, controlled from the outside
and the praise or blame for the results accomplished must belong to the outside
authority which controls it. No secret is made of the fact that the authority is the
Hamilton County Republican Committee."[11]

Reformers collected the requisite signatures to place before city voters a November 1924 referendum calling for a full reorganization of local government.
That referendum would replace the ward-based thirty-two-member city council
with a council of nine at-large members, and executive authority would be concentrated in a professional city manager hired by the council.

One opponent to the reform argued that "the adoption of the city manager
form of government for Cincinnati would take away from the people the right
to elect their own chief executive. The proposal is based on the idea that executive government is a matter of expert knowledge."[12] City manager government
appealed most strongly to businessmen progressives. In their view, citizens were

analogous to shareholders; the council was rather like a corporate board of direc-tors, and the city manager was the CEO or mayor. Still, when the referendum came up for a vote, it drew strong support across social class lines. The result was all but overwhelming: 92,510 in favor, 41,015 opposed.

A number of American cities had Charter-like reform movements. Cincinnati reformers took it even further: they would not only create a new system, they would create a standing political party, the Charter Committee, for the express purpose of fielding a slate of candidates for the reformed council. The 1925 elec-tion was a Charter triumph; six of the party's endorsed candidates were elected. Their leading vote-getter was a former judge and well-known Catholic layman, Edward T. Dixon, whose then five-year old daughter, Mary Kathryn, would, two decades later, marry Jack Gilligan.

(Another of the early Charter leaders—indeed, in time its longest-standing supporter—was Charles Phelps Taft Jr., son of President William Howard Taft and the liberal counterpart to his conservative brother, Robert Alfonso Taft, later the Republican leader of the U.S. Senate. The brothers, beyond the fact that both had graduated at the top of their Yale law school classes, were "a study in contrast": Charles, the all but indecently handsome do-gooder and the first layman to head the National Council of Churches; and Robert, the somewhat pinch-faced one pledged to block the progress of the New Deal down history's path.[13])

Instituted in 1926, Charter management professionalized Cincinnati's city gov-ernment. Colonel Clarence Sherrill, superintendent of parks and public buildings in Washington, D.C., was hired as the city's first city manager. Council members' sala-ries—raised from $1,050 to $5,000—were now sufficient to encourage them to re-gard their offices as a full-time calling. City employees were now in the civil service system, and competitive bidding brought better city services for less expenditure.

In fairly short order, Cincinnati became the most admired of city governments: "All over the land, the Cincinnati Charter movement was being hailed as the civic phenomenon of the post-war decade," wrote one observer.[14] Among other things, the city had made it through the hardest of the Great Depression years without discharging a single city employee or cutting services to the public. *Collier's Weekly* wrote that concerned citizens wishing to improve their own communities "should visit Cincinnati" to learn how best to proceed.[15] And about that time, 1935, Harry Gilligan was named to the Charter Committee's board of directors.

Cincinnati's Charter movement is all but unique among American urban poli-tics. Sidney Weil, longtime Cincinnati lawyer, commented, "Ordinarily a political insurgency rises, crests, then everybody goes home and pretty much everything goes back the way it was."[16] It lasted, in effect, by becoming a political party—complete with a central committee and dues-paying members, with memberships priced at one dollar to encourage participation from all groups. As a party, it was an anomaly. In electoral terms, it existed for the sole purpose of electing candidates to Cincinnati's city council. These it presented as a slate, with the requirement that any Charter-backed candidate support the entire ticket.

Three factors supported the party's longevity: the organizing ability of the group's early leaders, the stature it gained from identification with successful municipal reform, and the continuing weakness of the local Democratic Party. In theory, the Democrats would have been the natural opposition party, but in Cincinnati they were so weak that they often allied themselves with the independent Republicans that formed Charter's core.

With Charter reform, the city adopted a voting system known as Hare Proportional Representation, or PR. Under PR, individual voters marked up to nine candidates for city council *in their order of preference.* So if 100,000 votes were cast, then any candidate receiving 10,001 first-preference votes was designated as elected, because no more than nine candidates could receive that number. However, if some candidates received more than that minimum, fewer than nine would receive the necessary quota. In practice, if the highest first-preference total for any candidate was 18,000 votes, then that candidate's "excess" vote—that is, 7,999 ballots—would be recast for each voter's second preference. The counting would continue until this process of redistribution resulted in nine candidates with the required minimum. There was a further complication: if the dispersal of excess votes did not produce nine winners, then the candidate with the lowest vote total would be eliminated, with votes transferred to the "second choice" indicated by voters.

PR was central to Charter government. As historian Zane Miller observes, Charterites were opposed *on principle* to winner-take-all elections, which they believed tended to exclude minorities from governing. The Charterites, Miller adds, deliberately sought diverse representation within the city council to "promote inter-group understanding."[17] The various "representatives of these points of view should work together in a non-hierarchical framework to decide which policies to pursue under which particular set of circumstances unrestrained by the threat of a veto from a mayor or party boss."[18] Restated, it was the Charter view that any substantial constituency within the city should be represented on council; the proportional representation system had both the intended and actual consequence of promoting councils whose individual members were tied to some substantial group within the city. Thus, Frank A. B. Hall, a retired city detective, joined city council as its first black member in 1931, elected at a time when the city as a whole was highly unlikely to elect an African American.

The time Jack Gilligan spent with his father in the funeral business had given him a somewhat better understanding of the older man. His father was somewhat sensitive about being a funeral director; while he had pursued that calling as a matter of family responsibility, he thought that, had he felt free to extend his reach, he could have been a bank or business president. It was, therefore, of some pleasing consequence that he played an increasingly prominent role in the Charter Party.

He served as chairman of the party's speakers' bureau, vice president and chairman of its finance committee, and campaign manager during the 1947 election. In March 1948, "in a notable departure from past practice," he was the first Democrat to be elected president of the City Charter Committee, which since its founding had been led by reform Republicans.[19] He was a firm organizer unsympathetic with the desire (not unknown among political reformers) to listen to oneself talk. He believed in the four-minute speech, apparently on the grounds that anyone who could not get their point made in four minutes likely could not do so in forty.

When Harry Gilligan stepped down as Charter president in 1949, the *Cincinnati Enquirer* (which would rarely have a good word to say about Harry's son) commended his efforts, stating that Gilligan's "personal work and aggressiveness must be counted as real contributing factors to the political renaissance which the Charter movement has enjoyed."[20] Harry Gilligan remained a member of the Charter board. He had, as it happened, one further contribution to make. In 1953, he helped make his son a Charter candidate for Cincinnati City Council.

9

The First Election

Jack Gilligan's earlier career ambitions—to join a Jesuit seminary, to attend the University of Chicago, to found a college in Cincinnati—were sidetracked by circumstance, family objection, and Frank O'Malley's change of heart. But in 1953, it was an accident that set Gilligan on his career path. After the death in a boating accident of city councilman and Charterite Al Cash, it fell to the Charter Committee to nominate a candidate to stand as his successor in the 1953 municipal election.

Historian Zane Miller aptly described the nominating habits of Cincinnati political parties at the time.

> Both the Republicans and the Charterites fielded slates based on the political importance of various groups in the population. Since relatively few southern and eastern Europeans had migrated to Cincinnati at the turn of the century, each ticket usually contained German, "American," and Irish surnames (more Germans and "Americans" than Irish): Protestants, Catholics, and at least one Jew, usually of the Reform persuasion from a family of German origins; at least one black male and at least one white women; and a representative of organized labor. The ethno-racial, religious, gender and class balancing of party slates yielded similarly balanced city councils.[1]

Cash had been an Eastside Catholic Democrat; therefore, his successor would need these characteristics. Of those so qualified, two names stood out: Jack Gilligan and William Geoghegan. Both were young—Gilligan thirty-two, Geoghegan twenty-nine—and both were veterans. That August, one Cincinnati newspaper identified Geoghegan as the likely candidate. However, there were reasons for a Gilligan candidacy. Becoming active in city politics was a logical next step from his engagement with the Stevenson campaign the previous fall and his having worked on several Charter campaigns.[2] He also had some claims to civic involvement; he had been active with such charities as the St. Joseph's Orphanage and had played a role in locating new quarters for Cincinnati's Playhouse-in-the-Park theater program.

Complicating matters, perhaps, was that the Gilligan and Geoghegan families were third-generation friends: their paternal grandfathers had known each other, and their fathers were close friends. Geoghegan had been a high school classmate of Frank and Mike Gilligan and a guest at the Gilligan's Leland, Michigan, summer home. Frank and Mike had ushered at Geoghegan's wedding.

The Charterites, generally, were aware that Gilligan and Geoghegan would draw on the same voters, thereby splitting the first-preference vote cast for either. In short, if both ran, both would likely lose. Who, then, should get the nod? Gilligan, somewhat elliptically, later said that his father, long active in Charter, "denied swinging his weight around to get me the nomination."[3] In Jack Gilligan's view, the pair agreed to leave the decision to the Charter Committee, with each pledging to campaign for the other in the event he was not nominated. Bill Geoghegan suggested that a senior member of the archdiocese, someone close to the Geoghegan family, recommended to Bill's father that the nomination go to Jack. However it happened, once the Charter Committee designated Gilligan as a candidate, Geoghegan campaigned actively on his behalf.

Unlike many who enter the field, politics was never Jack Gilligan's boyhood ambition. As a teenager, he thought about entering the priesthood but never of running for public office. His motives for doing so seem mixed. He began "with the idea that politics was more than sweeping the streets and picking up the garbage; there were a lot of other issues and problems of great influence on the life of the city, issues that needed to be dealt with and weren't being dealt with."[4] It may also have been the case that he wanted something new to do with his life.

Katie Gilligan had no great liking for the role of the politician's spouse; still, she gave her slightly hedged blessing to her husband's initial candidacy. She was, he recalled, "not opposed to it. She was also not particularly enthusiastic about it, but she preferred it to the business I was in."[5] That being the funeral business, at which Gilligan was still putting in time. About this time, the Gilligan funeral home acquired the former Barrere Funeral Home in Cincinnati. One Cincinnati newspaper ran a photo of the proud new owners—Harry Gilligan and his three sons, with Jack vaguely looking like he wished to be somewhere else.[6]

In Cincinnati City Council elections, typically the Charter candidates would assert that the aspiring Republicans were lineal descendants of the corrupt elements the reformers had run out of office years before. And, typically, the Republicans would assert that the Charterites were snobs whose high-mindedness was a cloak for low-level power seeking. But there were also issues in 1953: the prospect of selling the city-owned waterworks to the county and the question of whether electric utility rates were exorbitant. More particularly, however, votes would turn to the individual standing, personality, and following of each candidate. Campaign costs were modest. Gilligan's own campaign staff was an extension of his family: Edward Dixon, his father-in-law, served as campaign chairman, and Harry Gilligan put up much of the $6,000 that the campaign spent.

The elder Gilligan also provided advice. To win, he said, Jack needed to pull good margins in his natural constituencies, Catholics and war veterans. Jack Gilligan recalled, "My father said to me: 'If you expect to get any votes out of Mt. Adams [a heavily Catholic neighborhood], you have to go talk to Pat Crowley.'"[7] Crowley was owner and proprietor of the old-style family tavern near the highest point in Mt. Adams. Gilligan duly dropped by one afternoon to introduce himself. Crowley suggested that Gilligan buy drinks for the house—adding that, as the tavern was then well shy of full, this might be an economical time to do so. Gilligan ponied up. Dues paid, Crowley shouted for the attention of the house: "I want to introduce to you *our* candidate for city council. His name is *John Gilligan.* Spread the word that he is *our* candidate."[8] (Years later, Governor Gilligan repeated the offer of "drinks on me" at Crowley's; unfortunately, the date he chose was St. Patrick's Day, and the resulting flow of beer nearly drained his checkbook.)

Gilligan's call on Pat Crowley is typical enough of local electioneering at the time, when candidates spoke to civic groups, dropped in on taverns, and contacted the friends of old friends. Gilligan characterized it as "garden party politics: everyone knew everyone; people were never really nasty."[9] But five weeks before Election Day, Cincinnati found itself swept up in a nasty, utterly non–garden party controversy over allegations of Communist subversion in local government. The reason, at least ostensibly, was Sydney Williams, who had been hired in April 1953 as the city's director of planning.

At his hiring, Williams told two members of the planning commission that before the war he had attended meetings of a California group associated with the Young Communist League and after the war had taken part in a Marxist discussion group, which he left once he decided he did not share its politics. Later, on taking a teaching post in California, he declared under oath that he had not belonged to any subversive organization during the preceding five years. But, when he signed the oath, it had actually been just four-and-a-half years since he broke with the group. When this incidental discrepancy reached official attention, Williams was advised to resign his post, which he did. So when interviewed for the Queen City position by planning commissioners Henry Bettman and Wallace Collett, Williams "voluntarily shared the circumstances of his departure from California" along with his subsequent disavowal of the views in question.[10] Bettman and Collett, aware that the Cincinnati loyalty oath "only required that the individual 'was not now' a Communist," proceeded to finalize contract terms with a man they thought highly qualified for the job.[11] Bettman and Collett, as would later become significant, were Charter appointees to the commission.

In late September 1953, the Cincinnati office of the FBI leaked the story of Williams's "radical past" to Cincinnati's city manager, Wilbur R. Kellogg. Confronted by Kellogg, Williams said he thought that the matter was a dead issue and that he had told Bettman and Collett about it when he had been hired, which came as a complete surprise to Kellogg, who had never been informed of the earlier meeting.

And with that, the fat was in the fire. The year 1953 marked a high point in the postwar public preoccupation with possible Communist encroachment into government and other aspects of American life. One response to this preoccupation was known as "McCarthyism"—which included the assertion that "disloyal" persons should be identified and driven from public life, along with any who may have aided or abetted their careers.

On October 1, 1953, the Cincinnati City Council met to demand Williams's resignation. It was a party-line vote: four Republicans versus three Charterites. Speaking to council on Williams's behalf, Wallace Collett stated, "I do not believe that a person of inquiring mind who at one time investigated a social and political doctrine and found it wrong, should be classified six years later as an untouchable who is unfit to hold public office."[12] City Manager Kellogg responded that this was precisely how he would classify such an individual.

Headlines gave the Charterites the worst of the battle. The Taft-owned *Times-Star* reported the resignation demand with a page one headline, "Planner Will Be Asked to Quit; Charterites Oppose Commission Action on Commie Charges," and the accompanying article asserted that Williams had "not denied authoritative reports that he was a member of the Communist party."[13] A few days later, a *Cincinnati Enquirer* editorial titled "Abuse of Public Trust" asserted that Bettman and Collett had been "grossly derelict in their official responsibility" in failing to make Williams's April statement known to city council.[14] It further argued that it was not a question of depriving a man of his livelihood but of "taking a chance with the security of this community and being secretive about it! Messrs. Bettman and Collett should follow Mr. Williams, in the gracious way out."[15]

Sydney Williams submitted his resignation on October 5. That the city council— again, by a 4–3 party-line vote—then demanded the resignations of Collett and Bettman for having failed to report on the April hiring discussion. The two refused. With the resulting furor, discussions of the fate of the city waterworks and other public matters were pushed aside. The election instead became about either the possible Communist influence in city government and an alleged effort to cover it up or the evils of witch hunting and the importance of intellectual freedom.

For Gilligan, it was a matter of principle that transcended the party he was campaigning to represent. He told the *Cincinnati Times-Star,* "I would rather see the Charter Party smashed than to abandon Sydney Williams."[16]

Gilligan's was a position of more than incidental courage. Throughout the country, persons accused of disloyalty or worse routinely found themselves abandoned by those they thought had been their friends, friends who, when the moment of need arrived, decided discretion was the better part of valor. Gilligan, had he wished to, had reasons enough to fudge. He had surrendered his tie to Xavier University; he was without standing in the political field he hoped to enter; he was a son in a family business that depended on the public's general approbation for its success. Ally Dick Guggenheim commented, "It certainly was a most courageous position to take and a very dangerous one to take personally and he had nothing to gain by it politically . . . I think everybody, perhaps even including his father, thought that this had been a fatal step in Jack's political career."[17]

Charter chose to stand behind Collett and Bettman. To place a nonpartisan face on the issue, they decided to form a group, the Committee of 150 for Political Morality, to argue in the press and before the public on the two men's behalf. Here, Gilligan, one of the junior members of the effort, took the lead. He proposed as the committee chair Van Meter Ames, a longtime and widely respected professor of philosophy Gilligan knew from the University of Cincinnati. Ames was not an ideologue; he was something of a moralist. He came to Cincinnati in 1925 after getting his PhD from the University of Chicago, where he served as pastor of the University Church.[18] Approached by Gilligan, he agreed to head the committee. It was "the first time in Ames' life he considered venturing into the political arena in a leadership role."[19] Ames noted in his journal, "Naturally, I'd rather be at home with my books, but with my philosophy and my teaching, I cannot always hang back with a good conscience."

The entire issue riled Gilligan—then and ever after: "I was outraged by the charges, which were based on nothing but the crassest sort of political cynicism."[20] Some of the general public, he acknowledged, may have been concerned about possible Communist encroachment into city affairs; but those who pushed the issue lacked such sincerity. Among those Gilligan held responsible for the attack was Potter Stewart, who had recently been a Republican city councilman and would later serve as a Justice of the United States Supreme Court.

As the election approached, the local press published advertisements both large and lurid. One ad run by the Republicans two weeks ahead of the vote asked, "Should Cincinnati Hire Communists for Key Jobs in City Hall?" The answers, apparently, were: "The Charter-Democrats say: YES; Republicans say: NO."[21] Three days later, the Committee for Political Morality responded with an almost identical banner headline: "Should Cincinnati Citizens Be Condemned without Fair Trial?" Its answer was, "The County Republican Machine Says: YES! The Charter Committee Says: NO!"[22] A Republican-sponsored ad that same day in the *Enquirer* informed readers that "Marxist study group" was a euphemism for Communist training school; the GOP, it stated, was for "destroying Communism wherever and whenever it is discovered . . . and that includes Cincinnati."[23]

As the November 3 election date approached, the Sydney Williams affair crowded out all other issues. The *New York Times* characterized the campaign as "unequaled, if not unsurpassed, in . . . invective" since Cincinnati's Charter movement a quarter-century earlier.[24] Privately, Charterites believed that while they were fighting the good fight, it would prove to be a losing proposition. By one account, the Charter candidates were so sure that they were going to lose that they had not even discussed who they might elect as city manager if they won.

On election night, the party's faithful gathered at the Hotel Alms to hear the expected bad news. Shortly before midnight, Harry Gilligan, reviewing precinct totals as they came in, astonished the crowd by announcing that Charter had won. By final tally, Charter candidates collected 51.5 percent of the first-preference votes and would enjoy a 5–4 majority in the new council. And one of those five was Jack Gilligan.

Gilligan was delighted—both with his own election and the general result. The vote, he believed, "marked the first time in the country that a citizens' organization had defeated at the polls a campaign premised on allegations of Communist subversion."[25] In part, he attributed this to the history of the Charter Party: since Charter's bywords were 'good government' rather than 'ideology,' it was somewhat more difficult to paint it as the abettor of subversives. Also, as some newspaper advertising pointed out, Bettman and Collett were themselves widely well-regarded for their services to the community. And it's very likely that this was a frontlash: the charges may have seemed so unfair as to prompt some to vote Charter who normally would not.

Gilligan never returned to his teaching duties at Xavier University, and his doctoral dissertation was set aside, never to be completed. On December 1, 1953, Jack Gilligan was sworn in as a Cincinnati city councilman.

Perhaps the best thing about being on the Cincinnati City Council is the chamber in which it meets. Set on the third floor of Cincinnati's City Hall, a bright 1888 Romanesque stone building with a nine-story clock tower on Plum Street, the chamber is elegant without being imposing. It appears to be an excellent place for a deliberation. The council members sit backed by a series of large stained-glass windows facing a room that, with a balcony, can accommodate 500 spectators.

That, however, is about the extent of the city's accommodation to its councilmen. When Gilligan was first elected, its nine members had no offices to use, no staff support. There was a general secretarial staff that answered the mail, but if, say, members were curious about how some other city did something, he had to do that research themselves, or else scare up a friend in some local political science department to do the chore for them. And if a council member wished to place a phone call on official business, he need only deposit two nickels in one of the pay phones in the corridor.

The job had other burdens as well. Council members were obligated to provide constituent services. Given that councilmen were elected citywide, this meant that just about any resident of the city could contact just about any councilman to complain about just about any tax assessment, pothole, or barking dog. The task for the councilman, Gilligan later related, was not made easier by the fact that in most cases the councilman in question knew nothing of the matter: "You might just as well have called the cop on the corner."[26] One older councilman advised Gilligan how to respond to complaining calls that came at 2:00 A.M. He said, "Here's what you do. Take their number. Call them back at four o'clock in the morning and ask if the garbage has been picked up. You'll never hear from them again."[27]

Jack Gilligan was reelected to six two-year terms on the Cincinnati City Council, serving on that body from 1953 until shortly before his entry to the U.S. Congress in January 1965. Defeated for reelection to Congress, he returned to council in the fall of 1967. During those years, Gilligan influenced, and was influenced by, events within the City of Cincinnati, gained experience in the craft of legislating, and refined a political philosophy. He broke with the Charter movement and lead a successful challenge that took control of the local Democratic Party. He also began, fitfully at first, to project himself as a participant in statewide politics. And, not least, he and Katie Gilligan would raise four children to adolescence.

Gilligan, by nature, aspired to success. On reaching city council, he was at some pains to prepare himself for his new task. His approach, he said, "was to learn as rapidly as possible what were the real issues and real problems in the city, and who was on which side of those problems."[28] And the first problem facing the council, Gilligan learned, was that the city was broke. The popular focus on the Sydney Williams affair had drawn attention away from a 5.41 mil property tax levy for city operations. The Queen City's generally conservative electorate may have been unexpectedly broadminded on allegations of subversion, but they were tight with a buck. The voters rejected that levy, resulting in an immediate $6 million hole in its 1954 budget of $26 million. Broadly, city council had two options: place the millage question back on the ballot in a special election or enact a temporary 1 percent income tax on individuals and businesses.

From the first, Gilligan favored the income tax. He and fellow councilman Ted Berry led the effort for adoption of a 1 percent levy on salaries, wages, and business income. The tax was intended to run only for seven months, the time needed to recoup the revenue from the failed millage. Council could take this step without a referendum, but since it was an emergency measure, six votes were required for passage. When the income tax option was put to a formal vote on January 12, however, council split 4–4, with Democrat and Charter candidate Al Jordan undecided.

Jordan had strong ties to labor organizations, including the United Steelworkers. His position was that the income tax was an effort by the "real estate lobby" to "shift the tax burden from vested interests to wage earners."[29] Charterites on city council, he added, had "sold out the interests of the poor citizens and the working poor."[30] They responded by accusing Jordan of placing the supposed interests of a segment of the population—that is, the working poor Jordan claimed to represent—ahead of the well-being of the city as a whole. With that, Jordan resigned from Charter and remained in office as an independent.

Reluctantly, the city establishment came to favor an income tax—the *Cincinnati Enquirer* declared it a "painful necessity"—despite believing that an income tax "encourages government profligacy, since it provides so easy a source of revenue."[31]

Council Republicans offered to back the tax in exchange for agreement that the city limit to 4.81 mils any tax sought later that year. Charterites favored a 5.58 mil increase. Gilligan and Berry said that this "deal" was contemplated: the offer was made in the interest of "cooperation and teamwork."

Angered, Gilligan said, "The price tag for the Republican deal is there for everyone to see." Rich snapped in response, "The compromise is now withdrawn," provoking a flurry of affirming nods from the other Republican members of council.[32]

The ante was raised with the February 2 announcement that the failure to reach a compromise could result in the laying off of 600 municipal employees and the subsequent threat from the government employees' union to "not idly stand by in the face of large-scale layoffs."[33] In the end, compromise prevailed. On February 10, the Cincinnati City Council voted 7–2 to enact the tax. Council agreed that the city could seek an increase in excess of 4.81 mils only if six of its members supported the move.

This early challenge in Gilligan's political life stands as a precursor of events to come. Gilligan was enunciating a principal he would carry into his governorship. He favored the income tax, he said, "because it is the fairest form of taxation."[34] Other forms of taxation fell basically on property, "which translated into wealth, and the people who had the taxable property got together to formally or informally protect their property from taxation."[35] Also, the strongest opposition came from Al Jordan, the councilman with the strongest ties to organized labor, who argued that an income tax represented an unfair levy on the worker's pay packet—all but exactly the position adopted by major Ohio labor leaders in their sustained opposition to the state income tax during Gilligan's governorship.

Among the peculiarities of Charter government in Cincinnati was the manner in which vacancies on the city council were filled. On taking office, each councilman executed what amounted to a political will in which they designated the individual who would choose their successor in the event of their death. In May 1954, Cincinnati mayor and councilman Edward M. Waldvogel died of a heart attack. In his political will, Waldvogel had designated Gilligan to name his successor. Some Charterites urged the selection of Harold Goldstein, an independent Democrat and twice-defeated Charter candidate. But since Waldvogel had been regarded as *the* Catholic Democrat from the Westside Price Hill neighborhood, Gilligan believed Waldvogel's successor should also be a Westside Catholic Democrat. To that end, he named Vincent Beckman, a Harvard Law School graduate who had been active in Democratic Party affairs, as Waldvogel's successor on council. With this decision, various supporters of Goldstein accused Gilligan of anti-Semitism, a charge he said was seconded by Councilwoman Dorothy Dolbey, a fellow Charter-ite who, as vice mayor, became acting mayor on Waldvogel's death.

Cincinnati council politics often got quite personal. The body was small; all were elected as individuals, and, as such, there was little pressure to suppress per-sonal differences behind a united front. Beckman filled Waldvogel's seat as a coun-cilman and restored Charter's 5–4 majority. Left hanging was the question of who would succeed Waldvogel as mayor. As it happened, the matter would turn on a falling out between Al Jordan, who had broken with Charter over the income tax, and Dorothy Dolbey and pinball. (Gilligan thought Dolbey intelligent and com-petent, but something of a pain: "I didn't say it out loud very often but she always seemed to me to be the personification of the Protestant church woman."[36])

At that time, many Cincinnati bars featured pinball games. Their glittery boards and lights were not the real attraction: if a player achieved a certain score, he could collect a small cash payoff from the bartender. This, to Dolbey, constituted gam-bling, to which she was opposed in all of its forms, and she took the lead in a campaign to have the machines banned. Jordan's perspective was that of a work-ingman's Democrat: if the average guy wanted to unwind after work by having a few beers and playing a little pinball, who was Dorothy Dolbey to interfere? The exchange soon devolved into comments on the shortcomings of each other's char-acter, resulting in Jordan announcing that he would not support Dolbey for mayor.

At a May 26, 1954, meeting, council split three ways: Carl Rich received the votes of the four Republican members, and Dolbey and Gilligan each received two Charter votes, Jordan refusing to vote. A week later, Jordan cast his vote, but since it was for Gilligan the stalemate continued. The *Cincinnati Enquirer* specu-lated that the thirty-three-year-old Gilligan would soon be chosen mayor (Gil-ligan later maintained he had no interest in the job). Over the next six months, city council on twelve occasions attempted to elect a new mayor. The results never changed: Rich, 4; Gilligan, 3; Dolbey, 2. On November 7 Gilligan announced that he was "fed up with the embarrassment of these weekly votes" and with-drew from contention.[37] Council met three days later, and Rich and Dolbey were renominated. And Councilman Jordan nominated Gilligan. Gilligan declined the nomination. Jordan then nominated Vincent Beckman. Beckman declined. Jordan then nominated Ted Berry. Berry declined. Jordan then nominated him-self. Council voted, with no majority emerging. Jordan, having nominated every

Charterite but Dolbey, finally nominated Republican Carl Rich, who, with Jordan, now had the five votes needed to reach office. The *Cincinnati Enquirer* editorialized, "The impasse ends: Cincinnati has a mayor again after more than six months of councilmanic 'deadlock.'"[38]

Though only a first-term councilman, Gilligan staked out positions on two issues that were of consequence to his own political interests and to the community he served: urban redevelopment and race.

Cincinnati had a strong tradition of planning. The city's then current 1948 comprehensive plan had placed its emphasis on creating a livable metropolis, arguing that "when a city expands beyond a certain size it reaches the point of diminishing returns in terms of the advantages which a city, as a social community, should provide for its inhabitants."[39] For improved livability, the plan urged that Cincinnati be organized around self-contained communities of 20,000–40,000 residents, each large enough to support a business district, schools, police precinct, post office, and library yet small enough to maintain a sense of intimacy and place. These communities were to be laced together by expressways, which would give all residents reasonably ready access to the business and civic institutions available in the center city. The plan, however, in an error characteristic of the time, failed to realize that while all expressways might lead to Cincinnati, they also led elsewhere. Even by the mid-1950s, the centrifugal pressures of the metropolis were tending to push people and businesses and the energies each represented away from the city center and out to the new suburbs on its periphery.

Speaking at length to city council in June 1955, Jack Gilligan called for "prompt and decisive action" to improve the city's downtown. The city's core, he argued, required "a 'sweeping' program of modernization and beautification."[40] In particular, he cited the need for better parking facilities, better public transportation, convention facilities, a modern city hall, and a general cleanup and beautification program. Such public investment would, he asserted, stimulate private investment in new office, commercial, and residential building in the downtown. He said he was "dismayed" by the general migration of merchants and professionals out of the downtown and claimed that if these problems were not dealt with in the most vigorous manner now, "we may find that the completion of the expressway system will do more harm than good, in some respects, to the downtown area."[41]

In terms of Gilligan's later actions, three points are notable. First, he asserted that the well-being of Cincinnati's downtown was properly and fundamentally the concern of city government. Second, he believed that redevelopment should be comprehensive. He noted, for example, the need for a new bridge spanning the Ohio River but argued that the bridge and its associated highway construction should be addressed not as a separate issue but in "an integrated and orderly fashion" in conjunction with other downtown efforts. And third, he assumed that the federal government would carry the major portion of the expense. Federal urban renewal funds, he suggested, should provide a two-for-one match for funds provided by the city.

Given that Cincinnati City Council then had no staff, no research budget, and no experience in securing federal funds, it is hardly surprising that Gilligan's proposal was followed by inaction.

Nor, for that matter, did action follow on a second, contemporaneous initiative. In July 1955 Gilligan cosponsored with Ted Berry the creation of a Fair Employment Practices Commission (FEPC) to investigate alleged racial discrimination in hiring by city employers and, should such allegations have merit, to levy fines of up to $500 for each instance.

Berry had been laboring for several fairly thankless decades to advance the African American community. As early as 1929, he enlisted the help of the Women's City Club to establish the status of black domestic workers in the city. As a consequence, one member urged her fellow members in need of domestic help to contact Berry, as he was in a position to "furnish trustworthy colored help."[42] With the Second World War, Berry, acting through the federal Fair Employment Practices Commission, investigated the standing of blacks in local defense industries. Nearly half of the 235 establishments surveyed replied that they did not employ blacks; others said the "lack of separate [toilet] facilities" kept them from doing so. The American Can Company, a major Cincinnati employer, reported that "the company's mechanical aptitude test barred Negro workmen," though, as Berry noted, this did not prevent the company from having blacks run its elevators.[43] At a second major employer, the union president "confirmed the union's threat to walk out if blacks were employed." After all, he added, the purpose of the war was to "preserve the American way of life."[44] Berry judged that the resistance went beyond blacks as an unwelcome presence. Evidence of an African American achieving equality as worker and wage earner, he wrote, was itself a cause for objections and animosity.

Berry, by various accounts, took in this and other information without expressing public anger. He was a tall, good-looking man, and he spoke in the measured tones of an attorney, which he was, having obtained a law degree at a time when black lawyers were not admitted to the local bar association. With his white colleagues and allies, Berry remained somewhat distant. Local attorney Sidney Weil, who had regular dealings with Berry and considered him "smarter than hell," noted that for the first fifteen years of their association, Berry referred to him as "Weil."[45] First names came later.

Because the FEPC would constitute a new city commission, its creation required the approval of seven of the nine members of city council. The motion on its behalf gained only five. One who opposed it, Al Jordan, called the proposed commission a "cheap, underhanded contrivance to confuse and deceive the Negro population of Cincinnati."[46] Berry replied with uncharacteristic sharpness, saying that he had devoted a quarter-century to advancing black Cincinnati: "You might defeat this ordinance, but you cannot defeat me or the principle behind it."[47]

Whatever issues Charterites like Gilligan and Berry right raise, the Republicans on council had one to which they returned time and again: the GOP wished to abolish the city's system of proportional representation in council elections.

Most Charter supporters saw PR as central to the city's successful governing model. Longtime Charter councilman Charles Phelps Taft wrote, "There is hardly a supporter of the City Charter Committee today who does not feel that proportional representation is the most important single element in the success of good government in the city and must be preserved at all costs."[48] The genius of PR, its supporters argued, was that it created a council whose collective membership represented all the city's major constituencies. That system might also be credited with the bringing to council a level of talent wholly uncharacteristic of municipal government. In the 1950s, for example, that council membership included Charles Phelps Taft, the son of a president; Potter Stewart, a future Justice of the U.S. Supreme Court; and Jack Gilligan, a future U.S. congressman and Ohio governor.

The system, however, was something of a hard sell. Gilligan, for one, noted that "PR wasn't easy to explain to people, especially people who were accustomed to the old comfortable system where you walked in and voted for the Donkey or the Elephant and you were done with it."[49] Indeed, a fair number found unfathomable the process whereby a winning candidate's surplus votes were transferred to others, a system which meant that often a week passed from the time votes were cast to the time winners were identified.

The city's Republicans, however, argued—with some basis, no hesitation, and little interruption—that their candidates would fare better under a more traditional electoral system. This was a point of continuing agitation for the GOP: the party placed amendments to repeal PR on the ballots in 1936, 1939, and 1947, all without success.

But in 1954, victory seemed to be theirs when, on November 3, 1954, Cincinnatians voted by referendum to abolish proportional representation by a 75,330 to 74,734 margin. However, Charter supporters, suspecting what Gilligan and others termed "clear" voter fraud, sought a recount which reversed the outcome. A year later, Republicans backed a $3 million bond issue to purchase mechanical voting machines for use in city elections. By no very great coincidence, no existing machine could accommodate the system of preference voting. An impromptu coalition of Charterites and voters wishing to avoid the expense of the machines defeated the bond measure.

The 1955 city council election offers a persuasive case of the overly complex nature of Cincinnati's proportional representation system. Not until December 10 were the

results of the city's closest-ever council contest known. This was of particular consequence to Jack Gilligan, who, following an extended and anxiety inducing recount
for the nine council seats, he retained his seat with just eighty-six more votes than
the tenth-place finisher, Albert Jordan, who ran as an independent Democrat. Gilligan characterized his margin of victory as "shocking, and to a degree humiliating."[50]
He had expected a fairly easy campaign and attributed his near defeat to his failure
to understand that, under PR, having general support was not the same as having
core supporters who would provide him with their first-preference ballot.

GOP antagonism toward PR was not lessened by the fact that, in aggregate, their
1955 candidates had outpolled the Charterites in first-preference votes—65,395 to
64,455. Republicans waited only two months to try again, when a Charter Improvement League, apparently a front for the local Republican Party, gathered
27,000 signatures seeking a referendum on PR to be held with the May primary.
The petitions, however, had their oddities—including what appeared to be multiple signatures in the same handwriting. Appointed as one of three councilmen
to examine the petitions, Gilligan secured $1,000 to retain a handwriting expert
to examine the petitions. In full righteousness, he told the press that "the whole
aura of forgery, fraud, and perjury which hangs over this petition does nothing
to inspire confidence in the sincerity, honesty or competence of those seeking to
oust PR."[51] Two weeks later that handwriting expert confirmed multiple instances
of duplicate signing. Gilligan said the Charter majority would not tolerate "even a
little perjury or a little fraud," and on March 8 the city council voted along party
lines to reject the petitions.[52]

Gilligan's narrow 1955 reelection gave Charterites a 5–4 margin on council.
With their majority, Charterites installed Charles Phelps Taft as mayor and Ted
Berry as vice mayor. Of Berry's election, the New York Times reported, "This is the
highest political office to which a member of his race has been elected in the city."
The article went on, "With tears in his eyes, Mr. Berry said at the oath taking ceremony that with his election as vice mayor, 'There are some who may have strong
reservations about the propriety of my acceptance of this office. But I accept it,
in the full conviction that in this land no one shall be denied the right to serve
because of his religion, nationality or race.'"[53]

Berry's election as vice mayor, sadly, may have precipitated the end of PR. His
election provided him some reasonable claim on a future mayoralty. But by mid-
1957, Charterites were complaining of a "whispering campaign" against Berry. The
argument, "made very quietly" and directed less to the light of day than to the ear
of prejudice, was that if Cincinnati did not abolish PR it would someday—perhaps someday soon—suffer the indignity of having a black man as its mayor.[54]
Yet another referendum on PR was placed on the September 30, 1957, ballot—the
sixth time Republicans had sought its repeal. As chance had it, that vote fell seven
days after President Eisenhower sent federal troops to escort nine black students

to a previously all-white high school in Little Rock, Arkansas. Suddenly, the topic of race was the substance of each day's national headlines. On September 30 Cincinnati voters rejected the PR system by a convincing 65,593 to 54,004 margin. The *New York Times* reported how "the Little Rock, Arkansas, racial crisis helped . . . to eliminate the Proportional Representation system of electing council members, in the opinion of political observers here. The racial campaign of some anti-P.R. spokesmen was to the effect that 'you don't want a Negro [Mr. Berry] as your mayor, do you?'"[55]

Cincinnati proceeded to add injury to insult. The 1957 council elections were barely five weeks away. While Berry's allies attempted to counter the attack on him—"We are also deeply troubled by the untrue whispering campaign against Mr. Berry and the irresponsible introduction of racial issues into the recent successful campaign against P.R voting. Such tactics have become a sinister force and can do irreparable harm to the community"—their efforts proved insufficient.[56] Under the new system, voters marked nine candidates for election. Three Charterites—Charles Taft, Vince Beckman, and Jack Gilligan—placed first, second, and third in the outcome, respectively. Their fellow incumbent, Ted Berry, finished fifteenth in a field of eighteen. With his defeat, the Cincinnati City Council became an all-white body once again.

10

The Democrats Stir

John Gilligan once described himself to a national political reporter as "a hungry fighter."[1] In the late 1950s, however, there was little a Cincinnati Democrat could feed on. Within the Charter Party, Gilligan, a Democrat, was in the minority. Within the county Democratic organization, Gilligan, an activist liberal, was again in the minority. Democrats were a decided minority in Hamilton County and a long-tenured minority in the state of Ohio. Being in the minority posed two problems for Gilligan. First, given that he viewed the Democratic Party as the natural vehicle by which the political views he favored would be advocated, advocacy was dulled. Second, given that he saw that party as the natural vehicle of his own advance, advance was stymied. The next decade would see Gilligan take the lead in the creation of a policy-oriented Democratic party in Ohio and advance in tandem with it.

What Gilligan needed was allies outside the rather genteel arena of Cincinnati Charter politics. Among the first was Bill Kircher, the AFL-CIO director for southern Ohio and West Virginia. Kircher was a native of Athens, where his father ran a successful contracting firm and where he also attended Ohio University. Kircher rejected both the business world and the Republican political views of his father to spend his life putting his solid six-foot-three-inch frame on the side of what he regarded as social justice. As an undergraduate, he attempted to end the social restrictions on Jews practiced by campus fraternities; three decades later he was the pivotal AFL-CIO contributor to Cesar Chavez's efforts to build the United Farm Workers Union in California. (At Kircher's funeral in 1989, the principal speakers were Jack Gilligan and Cesar Chavez, who termed Kircher "our greatest friend."[2])

Gilligan and Kircher met in 1956, not long after the merger of the AFL and the CIO brought Kircher to Cincinnati as an official in the newly created union. They had much in common; they were both relatively young, articulate-ranging-to-argumentative, Catholic liberals who took seriously their church's teaching on social justice. Indeed, Kircher was once so irked when a priest in his sermon blamed President Truman for communism that he tracked the cleric in question back to the sacristy to present a dissenting view. In time, Kircher would serve with Gilligan on the Catholic Interracial Council in Cincinnati; he would join Gilligan in the effort to take liberal control of the Hamilton County Democratic Party. Their first collaboration, however, had more to do with the Teamsters union.

When, in 1957, the AFL-CIO expelled the International Brotherhood of Teamsters, International Longshoremen's Association and International Bakery and Confectionary Workers International affiliates for various failures, the question in Cincinnati was whether the members of these ousted unions (save for the Longshoremen, since there was no chapter in Cincinnati) would stick with their disaffiliated organizations or join ones sanctioned by and affiliated with the AFL-CIO. Hoping to hold local members, the Teamsters sent their most able associate, Jimmy Hoffa, as featured speaker in a major pro-Teamster rally. Kircher countered by buying an hour of prime-time television; to build viewership, however, the first thirty minutes of that time was given over to the broadcast of a highly rated cowboy show, which was then followed by a panel presentation on the value of the AFL-CIO. Jack Gilligan was one of the few willing to take part in that presentation. His ringing endorsement of AFL-CIO unionism, one observer wrote, "endeared him to local labor leaders for the rest of his political life."[3]

Politics, it has been observed, "ain't bean-bag." It particularly wasn't so in 1958 when one of the disputants was the Teamsters union. Kircher also strove to attract members of the disaffiliated International Bakery and Confectionary union to the AFL-CIO-approved union. Local 213 had jurisdiction over union workers at Wonder Bread, Butternut, and other major bakeries. Kircher's son Tom (who became a Cincinnati labor lawyer) recalled it as "a very intense fight with a bit of violence."[4] One evening, Kircher was scheduled to speak to Local 213 at a local movie theater. But when he arrived, Teamsters physically prevented him from entering the hall. Finally, a group of women workers came out, surrounded Kircher, and announced that anyone trying to harm him would have to go through them.

That escape notwithstanding, Kircher, according to his son, was alarmed for his and his family's safety. The local sheriff's department offered protection. For a time, Kircher laid low at a motel room in Mt. Washington. One evening Gilligan drove to the motel to pick him up for a meeting, when, as Gilligan recalled, "a large fellow stepped out of the bushes and asked me where I was going? I said I was there to see Kircher. The fellow asked, 'Does he know you're coming?' and checked my claim. He was on the lookout for Teamsters."[5] Eventually, Kircher triumphed. Among other victories, he organized 2,200 workers in seventeen bakeries into the AFL-CIO-approved American Bakery and Confectionary Workers.

For most of political Ohio, however, a Cincinnati-area contest over union representation was akin to a squabble in a Democratic leper colony—curious to watch, perhaps, but hardly of consequence. Ohio was then a hugely Republican state—a circumstance that tightened a bottle cap on any large ambition Gilligan might have had. In the 1944 election, Ohio chose Republican Thomas Dewey over Democrat Franklin Roosevelt. In 1946 Ohio returned twenty-one Republicans and just three Democrats to Congress. In 1954 the GOP, fairly typically, captured all but one state-level office. In Columbus, Republicans enjoyed all but permanent majorities in both houses of the legislature. Republican dominance in state government was a consequence of the Hanna Amendment to the state constitution. Named for its author, Marcus Alonzo Hanna, the Ohio political boss broadly credited with having made William McKinley president, this decreed that each of Ohio's eighty-eight counties, no matter how sparsely populated, would have at least one seat in the state legislature. The rule, which remained in force until the 1960s, ensured rural dominance in Columbus by representatives known to Democrats as "the cornstalk brigade."

Ohio produced not just Republicans, but Republicans of national consequence. Robert A. Taft, "Mr. Republican," was, as minority leader in the U.S. Senate, the acknowledged spokesman of midwestern conservatism. Ohio governor John Bricker was the 1944 Republican vice presidential nominee. President Dwight Eisenhower placed two Ohio Republicans—Harold Burton and Potter Stewart—on the Supreme Court and recruited four Ohio-born figures for his cabinet: George Humphreys (Treasury), Charles Wilson (Defense), Neil McElroy (Wilson's successor in Defense), and Arthur Fleming (Health, Education, and Welfare).

There were many causes of Republican strength in Ohio. It enjoyed a secure organizing base in the city of Cincinnati; held the editorial allegiance of most every large newspaper in the state; and gathered in ample funds from its allies in business and banking. It had the solid backing, as well, of the Chamber of Commerce, which operated in virtually every place of any size. Political scientist John Fenton wrote that in small-city and small-town Ohio, "the point of view of the business community was virtually the only one that was systematically presented on a day-to-day basis."[6]

Conversely, the Ohio Democratic Party was just large enough to be at odds with itself. Its principal constituencies—longtime conservative rural voters and more recent immigrants to the state's northern-tier cities—were socially and ideologically at in conflict. In most industrial states, one large city—say, Chicago in Illinois or Detroit in Michigan—became the organizing focus for the state party. Ohio, however, had eight cities with a population of 100,000—Cleveland, Columbus, Cincinnati, Toledo, Akron, Dayton, Youngstown, Canton—but not one of them dominated. And not one of them deferred. "Each city leader preferred the role of prince of his own province to that of satrap in an effective state organization."[7] Such balkanization promoted infighting. On the Republican side, the party organization ordained candidates, and rival aspirants respected that and waited their turn, letting the party-endorsed candidate generally slide unchallenged through the primary, reserving effort—and funds—for the general election. Lacking their own clear state-level authority, Democratic primaries were rather more like food fights. The party's 1958 gubernatorial primary, for instance, drew four current or former mayors (Cleveland, Columbus, Toledo, Youngstown) plus a sprinkling of other candidates. Any candidate backed by a city base and promoted by a city newspaper was inclined to give it a shot. Such primary contests were better fitted for expending resources and inciting animosities than for fostering unity come November.

Further, Ohio lacked a politically aware labor movement. Next door in Michigan, the creative trade unionism of the Reuthers made the United Auto Workers a potent political instrument. In Ohio—in part reflecting the lack of a dominant city—unionism was local and parochial. Typically, Gilligan observed, Ohio's unions "were worlds unto themselves. They had as much control over the markets that they served as they usefully needed. Their efforts were largely directed at bringing each generation of the family into the same union, and then arguing among themselves as to who would be the top guy. They did not care a lot about the political arena."[8] Rather than provide a unified labor position in Ohio politics, local union leaders dealt piecemeal with the state's political figures, cutting such deals and forming such alliances as seemed individually expedient. Because Republicans were locally dominant in so many parts of the state, Gilligan noted, many of those union-made arrangements were with the GOP.

Ohio Republicans had a further advantage: a politically more able leadership. Preeminently, this meant state chairman Ray C. Bliss, described by political scientist Neil Peirce as "a man whose modest demeanor belied unusual intensity when it came to matters political."[9] Bliss, who later served as Republican National Chairman, brought an unrivaled level of organization to Ohio Republican politics: effective fundraising, an extensive and well-chosen staff, a research division and speakers' bureau, and a consistent message consistently delivered in weekly editions of the *Ohio Republican News*. That message had an underlying caveat: Ray Bliss did not believe any candidate should ever talk about issues; it only stirred things up.

Bliss's advice received a curious bipartisan endorsement. With a reigning Republican Party amply satisfied with the status quo and a divided Democratic Party made cautious lest it rock its own boat, statewide political campaigns tended to the superficial. Conservative Republicans like Robert Taft and John Bricker and conservative Democrats like Frank Lausche campaigned for office chiefly by invoking virtues, traditional and/or their own, and by decrying menaces, communism, and labor bosses. The general consequence of all the above was to drain the politics out of Ohio politics. A 1958 study by pollster Lou Harris found in Ohio voters "an almost complete lack of associating economic self-interest and the real problems in people's lives with their vote for statewide offices in Ohio."[10] But in 1958, Republicans other than Bliss introduced an issue into the campaign of considerable "economic self-interest," thereby roiling Ohio's political waters. When those waters settled, the policy-oriented Democratic Party envisioned by John Gilligan began to emerge.

That issue was the right-to-work (RTW) initiative, which turned on the question of the "union shop"—that is, whether employees covered by collective bargaining agreements could be required to join the union. RTW was a provision of the 1947 Taft-Hartley Act, which allowed the union shop but permitted individual states to ban it. In the 1950s, seventeen states (mostly southern and rural) took that step. In 1957, Indiana approved a right-to-work referendum; with 600,000 unionized workers, it was the first state with an appreciable industrial population to do so. Buoyed by that success, in 1958 right-to-work advocates put referenda on the ballot in six states—California, Colorado, Idaho, Kansas, Washington, and Ohio.

Ohio, the most strongly unionized of these states, was generally regarded as central to the effort. Formally, the effort was backed by the nonpartisan Ohioans for Right-to-Work, Inc., a collection of leading Ohio industrialists acting in concert with the state and local Chambers of Commerce, which gathered the signatures needed to place the issue on the Ohio ballot. The proposed Ohio amendment would ban future union shop agreements and, after two years, repeal the union shop clauses in place in 82 percent of all labor-management contracts in Ohio. Ohio, John Gilligan commented, "was regarded as the beachhead in the effort to roll back the union movement from coast to coast."[11]

Gilligan, somewhat at the persuasion of Bill Kircher, decided to take the lead in opposing the measure. His decision was rooted in part in his liberal Democratic support for collective bargaining and the union shop: "I had the fundamental belief that people had the right to organize to protect their own interests in the public arena. Efforts to prevent them were equivalent to efforts to deny people the vote."[12]

But his reasons went deeper—to the Catholic social doctrine that was never far from his thinking. Most relevant was *Rerum Novarum,* a papal encyclical on "the condition of the working classes" issued by Leo XIII in 1891. The statement takes a broad view of the effect of industrialization on the working classes. Industrialization, Pope Leo wrote, had swept away the protections once associated with trade guilds, leaving "the workers, each alone and defenseless, to the inhumanity of employers and the unbridled greed of competitors." Socialism was particularly dismissed as an alternative, as it was "destructive of individualism and therefore of the soul." Nonetheless, he argued, "if the employer class should oppress the working class with unjust burdens . . . if health should be injured by immoderate work and such as is not suited to sex or age—the power and authority of the law manifestly ought to be employed." Most pertinent, *Rerum Novarum* endorsed workers' self-protection: "Workers' associations ought to be so constituted and so governed as to furnish the most suitable and most convenient means to attain the object proposed, which consists in this, that the individual members of the association secure, so far as possible, an increase in the goods of body, of soul, and of prosperity."[13] There was a further reason Gilligan took to the field. As he acknowledged, "I was sort of spoiling for a fight."[14]

Right-to-work did not begin as the chief matter on Ohio's 1958 ballot; which, most observers held, would lead to the easy reelections of Republican Governor C. William O'Neill and Senator John Bricker. Bricker initially thought RTW would prove a disaster for Republicans. Meeting on July 6, 1958, with thirty RTW supporters at Cincinnati's Queen City Club, Bricker said the issue would galvanize a wave of union voters that would sweep away the Republican slate—himself, not incidentally, included. One account recalled how "when his assessment led to chortles of disbelief, he virtually pleaded with the group to delay the election" until the off-year election of 1959, when statewide candidates would not be on the ballot.[15] Also in attendance, Ray Bliss, advocate of "issueless" politics, seconded Bricker's assessment. The gathering was not dissuaded; their issue, they believed, was a winner. At first, Ohio union leaders shared that assessment. As the *Cincinnati Enquirer* reported, "Labor leaders are afraid that a Right-To-Work amendment will pass if Ohio voters get a chance at it at the polls next November."[16]

Initially, Gilligan anticipated the passage of Question 2, as RTW was listed on the ballot. With fellow councilman Charles Phelps Taft, Gilligan served as cochairman of the somewhat innocuously named Committee on Economic Stabilization, a loosely organized group of opponents to Question 2. It was a "civilian" group without ties to organized labor. On its behalf, Gilligan—sometimes with Charles Taft, but more frequently alone—spoke in Cincinnati, Columbus, Cleveland, and elsewhere, such appearances being his first introduction to statewide audiences. William Sheehan, business agent for the Cincinnati-area bottlers' union, recalled that "Gilligan was a good speaker—always for the underdog. He painted the picture about as emotionally as anyone could."[17] Indeed, Gilligan and Taft strove to move the issue beyond "a struggle between two power groups" by addressing the issue of "the general well-being of the community." He recalled, "If we were to have a stable and prosperous community, we needed an understanding of people's rights to organize and to bargain for their point of view." They directed their advocacy to "people who would be responsive to an appeal based on moral grounds"—church, civic, and other audiences.[18]

Reasonable sounding, perhaps, but it belies the antipathy conservative Ohio then felt for organized labor. Advocates of the measure claimed it was needed to protect the working man from union corruption and bossism, a position that Gilligan found curious since it suggested among those who made that argument a previously unexpressed concern for the well-being of the average employee. His own assessment was that RTW was a simple attack on unionism: "Who are these union guys? They aren't part of our community; they're outsiders, ne'er do wells. They strike factories and create tumult in our community. Let's get them out of

here. And that went pretty largely through the business community and the banking community and the publishing community."[19] As for "who needed" those
union guys, Gilligan commented, "Well, of course, the people who needed them
were the downtrodden and the helpless and they didn't have a voice; there was no
real way they could make themselves heard."[20] Further complicating labor's effort
was the lingering notion that unions were under some measure of Communist
influence, and it was a matter the unions felt the need to address. Writing in a
Cincinnati newspaper, Bill Kircher argued for the patriotism of unionists: "There
is no questioning organized labor's substantial contribution to the total social-
economic progress of the entire nation. Along with the church and the home it
stands as one of the three great bulwarks in this country's fight throughout the
world against the forces of totalitarian aggression and atheistic Communism."[21]

Right-to-work, Gilligan later commented, "was the bitterest fight I have ever
been part of. I was confronted in public meetings with the charge that I was a traitor to my class. We were subverting the whole system and causing terrible disabilities and suffering and get the hell out of here."[22] And the antagonism fell close to
home. Not long before the election, Jack and Katie Gilligan were attending an anniversary party at Cincinnati's Hyde Park Country Club—a club, incidentally, of
which his grandfather had been one of the five founders. Several hundred guests
were present—neighbors, friends, business associates—none of whom would
speak to the Gilligans, a circumstance Jack attributed to his pro-union advocacy.
After a certain amount of sustained avoidance, Katie said to her husband, "Take
me home. We just don't have anything in common with these people anymore."[23]

As the campaign progressed, the issue went from being nonpartisan to highly
partisan. On September 18, Republican governor C. William O'Neill endorsed
Question 2 and thereafter made the issue central to his campaign. On October
14, Senator Bricker, despite his earlier protestations, announced his support for
the measure. Right-to-work was needed, he said, "for the protection of the unions
and their rank-and-file against the abuses of the labor racketeers, the embezzlers,
the professional goons."[24] Most Democrats, including gubernatorial candidate
Michael DiSalle, ducked the issue. Indeed, Cincinnati labor leader William Sheehan said that Gilligan and Charles Phelps Taft were the only two political figures
from southern Ohio to campaign against Question 2.

To further their advocacy, the RTW campaign raised and spent over $2 million,
an extraordinary outlay for the time. The unions had nothing approaching that sum
to spend. William Sheehan recalls taking a check for $10,000—"big money at the
time"—to state headquarters in Columbus as Cincinnati labor's contribution. Without boundless coffers, voter registration became central to the opposition's effort,
and, according to Sheehan, it was "a painful proposition." The voter registration lists
supplied by the board of elections were alphabetized by county. So matching names
to precincts was a huge task for volunteers. Sheehan recalled, "We had phone banks

all over. Most of the locals provided volunteers. The clothing workers union had a downtown hall with fourteen phones going all day. The UAW had a phone bank."[25] Voter registration was key. Before the campaign began, by one estimate, only 40 percent of the state union members were registered to vote. In late-September, Ohio's secretary of state announced that registration had set a new record.

Opponents also scored a coup by bringing former president Harry Truman to Ohio to denounce the measure. Truman, who had vetoed the original Taft-Hartley Act only to have that veto overridden, warned his audience that if the measure passed, conservative Republicans would next target Social Security, unemployment compensation, and worker's compensation.

Business, however, was wholly committed to the RTW measure, which also enjoyed general editorial support from the state's press. On October 20, for example, the Taft-owned radio station in Cincinnati, WKRC, began airing an editorial message in favor of Question 2 *five times a day*. Gilligan, on behalf of his committee, filed an immediate protest with the Federal Communications Commission citing a 1949 FCC report that editorial broadcasts were "consistent with the licensee's duty to operate in the public interest" only insofar as they were part of "a reasonably balanced presentation of all responsible viewpoints" on a particular issue.[26] The matter was settled informally, with the station agreeing to run an equal number of one-minute editorials from Gilligan's group beginning on October 29.

As the election neared, *New York Times* labor correspondent A. H. Raskin wrote, the argument over RTW was so heated that "fathers and sons, husbands and wives, have been known to stop speaking to one another over the issue."[27] The vote pending, Gilligan was pessimistic: "I must confess that I thought right up to Election Day that we were not going to win."[28] But in the years before political polling became an omnipresent feature of American politics, it was possible to be entirely surprised by an outcome. Indeed, turnout was enormous—3,390,000 votes cast, better than 30 percent over the preceding off-year election. As that vote was counted, the *New York Times* reported, "a tidal wave of opposition votes from union strongholds in the big cities quickly washed away any doubt that the proposed constitutional amendment would lose. Even in farm areas and rural communities, the expected backing for the proposal failed to materialize."[29]

Question 2 was crushed: 1,160,324 for the amendment, 2,001,512 against. The vote swept from office those incumbents who had backed the measure: Governor O'Neill was replaced by Democrat Mike DiSalle, and Senator Bricker (while having the incidental satisfaction of seeing his prediction vindicated) was replaced by Democrat Stephen A. Young. And the Democrats captured both houses of the state legislature. The results "astonished and delighted" Gilligan.[30]

The vote carried national significance. With the Ohio result, the decade-long trend toward right-to-work legislation ended. That same day, RTW initiatives were defeated in California, Washington, Colorado, and Idaho, passing only in rural

Kansas. Right-to-work was dead as practical politics. Gilligan noted, "Whenever someone would, later on, agitate for the measure, the response was: 'You just can't do it. Look at Ohio; we spent all that money and we got beat.'"[31]

Gilligan's engagement with labor continued after the RTW fight. He allied himself with Jim Luken, who, as the twenty-six-year-old president of Milk and Ice Cream Drivers Local 98, tried to pull his 4,400-member organization out of the Teamsters union. As a Luken supporter, Gilligan was invited to speak to a Sunday union gathering in the 1,000-seat Emery Auditorium. When he arrived at the auditorium, he couldn't park within three blocks of the place: due to anticipated violence, hundreds of police were on hand and blocking the streets around the Emery. It took Gilligan two hours to reach the hall. Once backstage, he huddled with the other speakers before each, in turn, took the stage and denounced James Hoffa and the Teamsters. Gilligan remembered a speaker from the balcony being recognized and getting out two sentences of praise for Hoffa before a leather-throated milk driver from the back of the hall bellowed, "Your time is up, you bum!"[32] Luken then called for a vote to disaffiliate, which passed nearly unanimously with a thunderous "aye." Only two were opposed—the one who had spoken briefly and another from the front row. Luken turned to Gilligan and said, "I know the guy in the front row, but who's the SOB in the balcony?"[33]

Gilligan's association with labor was clearly a matter of principle—mixed, perhaps, with a measure of self-interest. He knew that by allying himself with Ohio's unions, he was building the rudiments of an organization that might serve his own advance.

The Democratic tidal wave in the 1958 election stirred even the somnolent waters of Cincinnati where the Hamilton County Democratic Party had been treading. For three decades, the local Democratic organization had, in city council matters, maintained an alliance with the Charter Committee, an arrangement in which they were distinctly the junior partner. Longtime Cincinnati activist lawyer Sidney Weil commented, "The Republicans in it were a rather haughty bunch, and they pretty much ran things, and since the Democrats were so very weak Charter did not have any trouble gathering them up."[34] But the bonds of partnership were fraying. The acrid dispute over the 1955 mayoral succession strained personal relations; the 1957 abolition of proportional representation deprived the Charterites of their central electoral mechanism; and now, having flexed their muscles statewide, local Democratic leaders pushed to take their party out of the Charter coalition.

Gilligan, as a Democratic Charterite member of council, opposed the move. On January 3, 1959, he went to the watering hole of local Democrats, the Metropole Hotel, to urge the Democratic ward chairmen to not withdraw from the affiliation, a move that, he insisted, would prompt the fielding of a separate Democratic council slate that November. The *Cincinnati Enquirer* reinforced this when it reported that "proponents of the coalition fear that separate Democratic and Charterite tickets will split the coalition vote and secure the Republicans a big majority in council."[35] Gilligan's protests notwithstanding, Democratic ward committeemen voted 19–6 to end the coalition. Democrats then offered their endorsement to the three sitting Charter Democrats on council: Ted Berry, Vincent Beckman, and Jack Gilligan. Berry stayed with the Charterites; Beckman and Gilligan took the endorsement.

Charter leaders responded with impressive umbrage. On January 14, the *Enquirer* quoted a Charter leader as saying, "We believe—today, as in 1924—that politics and politicians have no more place in City Hall than in our schoolhouses." Democrats, he added, "do not share this belief."[36] It was an issue of dual loyalties. "The point of disagreement apparently seems to center about the fact that the Democrats will not agree to endorse Charter-Republican coalition candidates and the Charter Committee will not have it any other way."[37]

Gilligan, caught in the middle, sought to maintain his standing with both Democrats and Charterites. On February 12, he wrote to Fred Roth, Charter president, that "this situation is analogous to one in which a knife is thrust in my hand and a demand is made that I choose which one of my two sons I would rather stab."[38] Gilligan's preference was clear, however. In that lengthy letter to the Charterites, he wrote: "I regard the new Democratic Party as the best instrument and the best hope, now and in the future, for the solutions of the problems which confront Cincinnati."[39] The Charter movement, he argued, had been a response to municipal corruption, which was no longer a major problem in Cincinnati. Council, he said, should instead be focusing now on the vigorous and imaginative use of federal and state programs to direct needed aid to the city. And here, he maintained, Charterism was at odds with broader political reality.

> It obviously makes no sense to have Republican councilmen voting urban renewal programs while at the same time Republican Congressmen from this district are voting against the Federal funds we need to continue the program. It makes no more sense to have councilmen struggling for better housing in Cincinnati while State legislators of the same party vote for unrealistically low income ceilings on families seeking to qualify for Federal low-rent housing . . . The present and future needs of Cincinnati convinces me that I can be of greater service to the community by working to build a strong and responsible Democratic party in Hamilton County than by working against it."[40]

Similarly, Vince Beckman, in his letter to Roth, cited two causes for the split: the abolition of proportional Representation and "the reorganization and resurgence of the Democratic Party."[41] Responding to this rebellion, Sidney Weil commented, "Charter simply dissolved in fury."[42]

That conflict—between Charterite cooperation in Cincinnati and party partisanship elsewhere—was felt by others, including Charterite Republican Charles

Phelps Taft. In 1960, Taft made clear in a cover letter that the monetary contribution he was making was to go to the *national* Republican Party not the state party, which had helped to finance the campaign of his opponent in the previous fall's council election. In a much later interview, Gilligan commented: "The PR system focused things on the individual candidate rather than the party platform: it was every man for himself. That is why so many younger Democrats of the era decided we were going to have to divorce ourselves from the Charter committee, or else we were never going to have a Democratic Party."[43]

The odds on Charter endorsing Gilligan's 1959 reelection to city council grew slim. In May, the Charter board of directors met to formalize its commitments. Moments before the vote, Harry Gilligan, a thirty-year veteran of Charter politics and the organization's former president—rose, announced his resignation from the board, and left. Even among Charterites, blood was thicker than politics. (Fred Roth, commenting on the senior Gilligan's dramatic departure, said, "Had I been in that position, I surely would have sided with my son rather than desert him."[44]) After the vote, the Charter board issued a statement that Gilligan and Beckman, by accepting the Democratic endorsement, had "subscribed to the principles and platform of the Democratic Party."[45] The pair had clearly opted for partisanship in municipal politics, so "on this basic division of principle, the City Charter Committee decided it could not in conscience endorse either . . . for city council."[46] The board, clearly feeling it held the moral high ground in municipal politics, cast out two of its sitting officeholders, Gilligan and Beckman, by a decisive 28–4 vote.

Jack Gilligan, somewhat in spite of himself, was now a full-fledged Democrat. And having made his bed with the Democrats, he ran as actively as any, enjoying the incumbent's freedom to campaign long hours and the name recognition that went with six years of council service. With so full a field of council candidates, the *Cincinnati Post and Times-Star* sought from all candidates answers to a series of questions presumably uppermost in the minds of voters: What downtown revitalization project should be given priority? What should be done with the riverfront, which had become a hodgepodge of disused warehouses and decaying structures? And, perhaps most important, how could the Cincinnati Reds be kept from leaving town? Pertinent to this question was that the city had committed $2 million to improving parking near Crosley Field, where the Reds played.

Gilligan's answers not only established his position at the moment but revealed the thinking that undergirded them. Regarding the Reds, most candidates were anxious to stand by their team. Republican councilman Eugene Ruehlmann stated, "It is of the upmost importance to the city to keep a major league franchise. The spending of public money for parking space was the only way to keep the ball club here." Joseph DeCourcy said, "The dollars the team brings to Cincinnati together with the prestige makes it a small price to pay." Charterite Dorothy Dolbey responded, "I certainly do think it is important enough to keep the ball club here to spend public money for parking space." While some of the Democrats offered mild objections, Gilligan objected strongly. He saw the $2 million commitment as an egregious example of public expenditure supporting private profit-making enterprise when more pressing public needs went begging. The parking scheme, he charged, was something between a smokescreen and a shakedown: "I have never believed that Mr. Crosley intended to move the franchise out of Cincinnati." He questioned whether there was "any direct relationship between the number of parking spaces and the continued prosperity of the baseball club in Cincinnati" and noted that the club had "drawn more patrons and made more money in 1956 and 1957 with fewer parking spaces than it had available in 1958 and 1959." The economics of baseball, he suggested, were straightforward: "If the ball club plays well, it will draw paying customers, whether or not there is parking. How many parking places are there within three blocks of Yankee Stadium?"[47]

Regarding downtown development, Gilligan stated, "As far as I'm concerned the downtown convention hall is a thing which could be built easily and quickly and would do a great deal to buoy the whole town." Had he the authority, he added, the project would be under way within the year. Here, his answer was fairly widely shared by other candidates, who also cited the need for funds for a new general hospital, underground parking, and improvements in the city's mass transit.

When the *Post and Times-Star* asked what was to be done with the riverfront, some candidates mentioned possibilities but pled empty civic coffers; others waxed large—a state park, high-rise apartments, a yacht basin. Gilligan's response was the most expansive. He began by referring to the "rather lengthy" 1955 report he had submitted that called for cleaning up the riverfront and addressed needs for parking, public transit, a convention hall, a new city hall, parks and recreational facilities, a new stadium, a heliport, and riverfront apartments. He noted that while the planning commission and the city council had been "wildly unenthusiastic" at the time, "I still think the job can and should be done." He went on to restate most of these needs, calling in particular for a convention hall, downtown rebuilding, and, possibly, a new baseball stadium to be developed by private and public funds.[48]

During the campaign, Gilligan was characteristically outspoken about his preferences and how they were to be achieved. He expected federal government support for Cincinnati's efforts at renewal. In July he was in the headlines with a blistering condemnation of President Eisenhower's veto of a $1.75 billion federal program to support urban renewal. The veto of the housing bill, he said, "is nothing less than disaster for the City of Cincinnati."[49] The president's action, he insisted, would cost the city the funding for 2,000 housing units needed to relocate the current residents of areas identified for rebuilding. On another matter, two weeks before the election, he condemned a much-talked-about plan to build a parking garage under Cincinnati's central downtown gathering space, Fountain Square. The proposed facility, he said, was not large enough to accommodate downtown parking needs. Further, it might involve a dangerous waiver of the fire code and would oust the public from the square during the period of construction. Gilligan promised sustained opposition—an announcement that one newspaper reported with the headline, "I'll Eat My Hat If Garage Is Built Under Square—Gilligan."[50]

The Democrats entered into the 1959 election with an optimism earned in their statewide sweep the year before. They believed they would garner much of the former Charterite vote and perhaps take control of city council. County party head John Wiethe even went as far as to say that the "need for continuation of the reform Charter movement no longer exists except in the minds of a small group of self-ordained individuals who seek to perpetuate themselves in power."[51] But, as Sidney Weil observed, "political parties are never quite as active as they claim to be."[52] The Democrats, in fact, ran third, their candidates gaining 29 percent of the vote to the Republicans' 41 percent and the Charterites' 30 percent. Only two Democrats were elected to the nine-member council, John Gilligan and Vincent Beckman. Incumbent Charterites Charles Phelps Taft and Dorothy Dolbey were reelected, along with five Republicans, who once again claimed the majority. Weil commented, "The same people got elected to city council, but the uniforms were a little different."[53]

But in politics and sports, uniforms matter. Following the Democratic-Charter split, Republicans controlled council for the next twelve years. For Gilligan, however, the 1959 election was a triumph. Demonstrating broad support, he placed among the top nine finishers in every single one of Cincinnati's twenty-six wards.

11

Urban Renewal

"My dad absolutely *loved* Cincinnati," Gilligan's daughter, Kathleen Sebelius said. To him it was "clearly one of the great American cities."[1]

Jack Gilligan was a fourth-generation Cincinnatian whose knowledge of the city was deepened by having lived at one time or another in so many of the neighborhoods that shaped its character—Clifton, Mt. Lookout, Hyde Park. Cincinnati was, Gilligan often observed, physically a very pretty place—citing the view of the effortless slow curve the Ohio River makes from a vantage from Ault Park, the hills, and the distinctive corners the roads that descend them make. In addition to the river, the hills, and the municipal parks were the city's acclaimed offerings in arts and music. Jack and Katie Gilligan regularly attended the city's symphony. He was an ardent fan of local sports. (In his mideighties he juggled his schedule to go to Cincinnati's Great American Ball Park in hopes of being on hand when Ken Griffey Jr. hit his 600th career home run.) Part of the attraction for Gilligan was that Cincinnati was large enough to offer variety and small enough to be manageable, a place where "with decent planning and a commitment to services you could keep the city useful and worthwhile."[2]

Even though Gilligan loved Cincinnati, he was hardly blind to its shortcomings—to what, with fairness, may by 1960 have been termed its decline. Gilligan's fourth term on council faced an unhappy fact: the 1960 census showed that, for the first time in its history, the population of the Queen City had declined. That decline was minimal—from 503,998 in 1950 to 502,550—but it was evidence of lessened vitality and pointed to further, steeper declines to come. As across much of the country, that vitality was moving to the suburbs. Since the completion of Cincinnati's landmark forty-nine-story Carew Tower in 1931 (at the then heady cost of $33 million), there had been little new construction in the city's center. Much existing office space was second-rate at best, and the downtown had taken on a stodgy appearance. The impulse of private capital that had built the Cincinnati of the 1920s had run its course. Lawrence Frederick Mitchell's study of the city's downtown and riverfront bleakly details the subsequent decline. Between 1937 and 1955, the city's downtown core lost 1.2 million square feet of space when 1,716 business establishments merged, went bankrupt, or went elsewhere. Between 1955 and 1962, the value of assessments in the Central Business District fell from $147 to $130 million. At the heart of the downtown—on Fifth Street north of Fountain Square—the office vacancy rate reached 17 percent, and one major storefront at a heavily trafficked corner remained empty for two years. Along the riverfront things were decidedly worse. There, the number of standing structures, by one report, had declined by better than half, from 1,010 in 1922 to 494. This reflected a shift of industrial activity away from the downtown as well as the demolition of damaged property after the 1937 flood (and later, lesser floods) and the creation of surface parking lots as a way of "banking" land against some future uncertain purpose.

Cincinnati's response to conditions common to many American cities at the time extended from the city's sense of itself. As historian Judith Spraul-Schmidt noted, however socially conservative Cincinnati might have been, city leadership self-consciously considered Cincinnati to be a leader. The city saw itself as the booming economic center of the Midwest and, as such, its task as spreading culture to the hinterlands; and with the installation of Charter government, Cincinnati came to view itself (and, for a time, be viewed) as a model of municipal government. Spraul-Schmidt, daughter of a one-time Cincinnati councilman, commented, "When you look at the city records and newspapers in the early 1960s, what you see is that they want to be modern, they want to be efficient, they want to have good, businesslike government. They want to be seen as forward-looking."[3]

They did not, however, know how to proceed. Part of the problem was the lack of resources available to the Cincinnati City Council and city government. As late as 1963, the *Enquirer* editorialized that each councilman "ought to have at his disposal at City Hall an office of his own, with the customary facilities for receiving constituents, dictating letters, maintaining files, and the like."[4]

In 1960, Jack Gilligan undertook to educate himself on the subject of urban renewal. An extended profile in the *Enquirer* reported that Gilligan—pictured smoking the pipe he then favored—was routinely paying his "own way to meetings around the country on civic renewal."[5] In doing so, he launched himself into what would be his most substantive contribution to the city's betterment during his dozen years on council. He enthusiastically told the *Enquirer* of imaginative undertakings in Pittsburgh and Detroit and described as "breathtaking" the Charles City project, which had rebuilt five blocks of downtown Baltimore. Cincinnati, he urged, needed to think larger, needed to look to public-private partnerships, needed to look past creating individual housing projects to "rebuilding a city" as a whole. As part of that thinking, the *Enquirer* added, "he also keeps having architects' plans drawn up for such projects as waterfront development and a civic center."[6] The city's approach, Gilligan said, needed to be coordinated. He condemned the fact that recent near-downtown office construction had been undertaken without referring to the city's planning commission. He argued that the $250,000 the city was annually spending on planning was woefully insufficient: "If a company allotted that figure for new product research it would be out of business in five years." Jack Gilligan loved Cincinnati, but the affection was hardly sentimentalized. He underscored his views by saying, "We'd damn well better do something about it, or we'll become just a decaying river village."[7]

Gilligan's self-education was to a purpose. Democratic councilman Phil Collins said that Gilligan was "the most informed of anybody in Cincinnati, including the city administration, on the various uses of urban development."[8] Republican Eugene Ruehlmann considered Gilligan the outstanding Democrat on city council—which, to Ruehlmann, was not entirely an advantage: "There was more collegiality then. Jack and I would frequently chat about things. Sometimes he'd say: 'Things are going fairly well, but as a minority member I have to throw a brick through the window.'"[9]

Brick tossing was something Gilligan was willing to do. In 1961, he announced that the city manager form of government was being abused by its Republican majority, stating that "unless it becomes more responsive to the public the people may demand a change"—that is, the adoption of a "strong mayor" form of government that was anathema to the Charter Party.[10] The following year he suggested that the Republican majority of the council's finance committee had made such a mess of things that Republicans should resign their seats and "turn cash control over" to the Democrats.[11] This, Councilman Ruehlmann replied, was unlikely to happen as long as the voters of Cincinnati didn't trust the Democrats with a majority on city council. At times, Gilligan gave the impression that he would rather be right than to make friends and influence people. Ruehlmann commented, "He was an excellent debater; he could get his position across, but his manner in debating was to cast the person in the other position as less than intelligent."[12]

Personality clashes, however, did not get in the way of a growing agreement on the need to redevelop Cincinnati's urban core. Earlier proposals, however—the good, the bad, and the ugly—ran afoul of the city's lack of resources needed to carry through on them. Then the federal government opened a sluice; the Housing Act of 1961 appropriated $2 billion for urban renewal.

For Cincinnati's elected government, this represented a sea change. Its conservatism was such that funds falling from Washington were not usually viewed as manna. By and large, however, local Republican leaders chose to rise above principle. One said, "I am not a Big Government fan, but this would have been much more difficult to do without government funds."[13] Principally, those monies—if secured—would be used to acquire relatively blighted blocks of the downtown and clear them of their existing structures to make way for new construction.[14]

For Cincinnati City Council, the availability of federal funding was not simply a municipal opportunity but "a whole new ballgame," according to Gilligan. "We'd been thinking about parking meter rates; now, we needed to come up with multi-million-dollar proposals to submit to the federal government for approval."[15] Educating council to the new reality was no simple task. In part, a reorientation was needed: city policy since the 1948 master plan had focused on the well-being of neighborhoods; now, that focus was to shift. The council was still without much in the way of support. As Gilligan recalled, council members focused their energy on "attempting to understand what planners and others were saying to us."[16] That process, he said, "changed the entire discussion of what city governments ought to be interested in and doing." It took a while to transform the conversation; but, he said, "by and large, the forces of enlightenment won that one."[17]

Civic discussion centered on two undertakings. The first consisted of major improvements to the central business district and the creation of a downtown convention center. The second was the development of the Riverfront that was to include a stadium to house the city's professional baseball team. Initially, everything proceeded smoothly. Following the 1961 election, council notified the requisite federal agencies that Cincinnati was initiating two urban renewal plans, one for its downtown and one for the Riverfront. Soon thereafter, council appropriated $450,000 to begin core area studies. Within several months, five potential developers submitted plans for the Riverfront. Periodically in 1961 and 1962, the front pages of Cincinnati's newspapers were adorned with architects' renderings of the great new buildings that were to come and with downtown maps showing who would drive where and what they would arrive at. Several of these called for forty-plus-story business or apartment complexes, which Gilligan saw as so out of keeping with the scale of the city that he publicly termed Planning Commission's initial approval of one such project an embarrassment.

On most matters, however, a united front prevailed. In April 1962, Gilligan joined Republican and Charterite representatives at public meetings called to preview what might be in the works, where they gave the estimated cost of the downtown rebuilding—the convention center and stadium—as $34 million and then argued that this expenditure would generate $100 million in private funds for commercial and residential construction. Gilligan's appointed role at gatherings like this was to report on what other cities were doing—which, he suggested, was more than Cincinnati was doing: the plans being presented were "a realistic proposal to head off decline of Cincinnati to village status. Other cities are on the go. If we do not act soon, some other city will grab the ball and run with it."[18]

Gilligan, urgent by nature, was doubly urgent now. "I was very interested in pushing the whole program forward. It appeared to me this kind of movement was inevitable; and we needed to do it as intelligently as possible. The alternative, of course, was that the whole thing would just bog down and we would lose the option of federal funding."[19]

In mid-1962, Cincinnati received federal approval of both its downtown and Riverfront applications. The downtown proposal focused on a dozen city blocks to establish the city center as the main concentration for business, cultural, and governmental activities and also involved the building of apartments near downtown. The Riverfront project required the demolition of 162 buildings to preserve some of the area's warehousing, make provision for the sports stadium, and leave additional space free for recreational use.

On September 23, 1962, the city council voted unanimously to proceed with what the *New York Times* termed "a sweeping improvement in Cincinnati's downtown area."[20] The $100 million development project was awarded to the Emery-Knutson Development Corporation (whose former principal, John Emery, was a Cincinnati business and civic figure who had played an important role in the 1931 construction of the Carew Tower). All concerned expected a year of planning, with construction to begin in January 1964. The city's required share passed that November in a $16.6 million bond issue for the improvement of the Ohio riverfront and for the erection of a convention center, approval that came in a 82,471 to 63,254 vote.

But then things got complicated and progress came to a halt. Emery-Knutson's detailed plan failed to win council's support. A business group next retained noted architect Victor Gruen, who was, among other things, an early developer of shopping malls. Gilligan was taken with Gruen's plan. The sticking point, however, was that the plan called for the creation of covered malls and the conversion of a number of downtown streets to pedestrian walkways, a proposal business leaders flatly rejected. It, too, failed to receive council's support. And with this, the civic chorus of newspapers and community groups that a year earlier had been crying "Onward to victory!" began deluging council with accusations of "do-nothingism."

It was only after the 1963 appointment of the Working Review Committee— described as "a small group of decision makers who could get things done"—and the imposition of an eighteen-month deadline that things began moving again.[21] Council's representatives to the committee were Gilligan, Ruehlmann, and Taft; they joined business leaders from Cincinnati Milacron, Procter and Gamble, and First National Bank. The committee retained Archibald Rogers, whose work in Baltimore Gilligan had praised.

Describing the effort, Councilman Eugene Ruehlmann said, "What Rogers did was to divide the core of the city into five or six blocks and then tackle them one block at a time."[22] Block A was Fountain Square. Here, Gilligan won a victory. He had argued for years that the construction of an underground garage on the site would not only tear up a municipal asset but would fail to solve the downtown's parking problem. Rogers accepted Gilligan's argument that a more dispersed parking was required. The plan enlarged and renovated Fountain Square and developed a string of smaller stores located nearby, with second-story walkways connecting them to additional shopping. To draw shoppers downtown, the plan established a concentrated main merchandising area anchored on the west by the city's flagship retail outlet, Shillito's Department Store, and stretching three blocks east. More generally, deteriorating office space was to be renovated or replaced—or, in one councilman's words, "the pigeon roosts were cleared out."[23] Demolition made way for new construction.

Decades later, Jack Gilligan offered a laconic assessment of urban renewal in Cincinnati: "I think it worked better than most people expected and less well than some people had hoped."[24] Ruehlmann was more enthusiastic: "The overall planning was an outstanding success. The office space near Fountain Square had been of poor quality. Development cleared that out, allowed for the enlarging of Fountain Square; additional buildings went up. It tremendously improved the downtown area."[25] He also noted that "between the University Hospital development to the west [for which voters passed a levy in 1961], the convention center and the new buildings in the downtown, we had a remarkable transition."[26]

Numbers bear this out. Urban renewal coincided with a burst of new downtown construction. In the 1960s—helped, perhaps, by the generally strong national economy—twenty-six new buildings totaling 4.4 million square feet were completed in Cincinnati's downtown business district; that figure exceeded by 200,000 square feet the highest total of any preceding decade.

David Larson, who conducted extensive contemporary interviews with Gilligan and many associated with him, offered an insightful assessment of how Jack Gilligan was changed by his decade on the Cincinnati City Council.

> The most important personal growth Gilligan experienced during his work on city council was his intellectual movement from an aristocratic view of society to a more democratic perspective. His convictions were that the people knew a lot better than the business leaders, who dominated Cincinnati, what their community needed. Gilligan thought that business leaders were usually unconcerned about the general public as long as retail trade was good, there were not too many shopliftings and that one could walk safely on the streets.[27]

Part of what drove that change in Gilligan was his engagement with the issue of race. In the years before, during, and after the attention of civic Cincinnati was focused on the remaking of the downtown, a second development—likely equal in magnitude—was taking place a few miles to the west. The West End was, in the 1950s and thereafter, rather easy to characterize as a slum. It was the site of a huge urban renewal effort, and homes were demolished by the thousands to make way for the Kenyon-Barr (later, Queensgate) industrial park to the south and the right-of-way for the Mill Creek Expressway (later, I-75) to the north. Studies of one neighborhood of 2,800 residential units determined that all but four had building code violations, all but twenty-three had multiple structural problems, 50 percent lacked adequate sanitary facilities, and 70 percent were deemed fire hazards.

West End was by far the largest substandard part of Cincinnati. Its residents were mostly African Americans and people from Appalachia, who arrived in increasing numbers as the years passed, and many of whom were "transients"—that is, husbands who found work in Cincinnati and space in a rooming house during the week and drove back to Kentucky and beyond once Friday's work whistle sounded. Gilligan said, "You could stand on the bridge on Friday afternoon and watch those Kentucky license plates and Tennessee plates going over the bridge."[28] In time, the Appalachian population of Cincinnati reached 30,000—people, Jack Gilligan noted, who were "grounded neither in Cincinnati, the city where they were employed, nor in the towns to which they returned each weekend."[29]

The city's plan, in general, was to undertake wholesale demolition of the decayed structures and resituate residents in newly constructed affordable family housing elsewhere in the city. The new construction, as it happens, never stayed remotely abreast with the demolition.

The process had its critics—among them Jack Gilligan. Speaking at an urban renewal conference in Baltimore in 1961, he termed it "economically idiotic" to demolish neighborhoods while making no effort to prevent the decay of others. As a group, he cited landlords as too unwilling to invest in the maintenance of their properties. The only justification he could see for such behavior was the view that "private property owners have a right to make money out of their property."[30] This, he said, had allowed lumber barons to devastate the nation's forests and "strip miners to mutilate the countryside." He charged that landowners did not invest because no public or private pressure forced them to—so many poor people were packed into West End that the demand for cheap, poorly maintained housing remained strong.

By one estimate, between 1950 and 1970, something between 13,000 and 22,000 low-cost housing units were demolished in the West End; more than 50,000 people—largely black and lower income—were displaced. The quantity of new construction lagged well behind the demolition because of optimism, indifference, and a certain unstated racism.

Gilligan, in retrospect, saw some good that came out of the effort. "We did clean up a lot of neighborhoods that needed to be cleaned up"—neighborhoods where, in the 1960s, 70 percent of the homes had no indoor plumbing.[31] Such neighborhoods, he said, were "worn out and there was no way to encourage the needed investment other than the urban renewal approach of sweeping it all out and starting from scratch with federal money. Otherwise, these neighborhoods would continue to deteriorate, and you had all the impact of the social tensions, racial tensions, and deteriorating public and social services."[32]

But he remained little short of appalled by the impact the federal Interstate Highway System had on Cincinnati. As constructed, I-74 (from Indianapolis), I-75 (from Detroit), and I-71 (from Columbus) all converged in Cincinnati at the Ohio River, all three crossing on the same bridge. That convergence was widely welcomed as a way of making Cincinnati "a real hub of commerce." At the time, Gilligan said, there was little questioning of "the vision of the expressway."[33] The city's own 1948 comprehensive plan had seen such through-roads as a means of tying the city together, and, in any case, the interstates, authorized by the 1956 Federal Defense Highway Act, were a major national initiative and a federal mandate.

"What we did not appreciate at the time," Gilligan acknowledged, "was that it's one thing to stand in front of a chart on a wall and say, 'Well, the expressways are going to go here, and here, and here,' without considering adequately what we were doing to those neighborhoods and what provision could or should be made for re-settling people in a way that would lessen the impact on those neighborhoods and the people who would be moved out."[34] An interstate route might be something "you saw on a chart or a graph or a map, but you didn't see it down to the flesh and blood of the importance of the neighborhood grocery store or what removing that restaurant or that youth center might do." And interstate construction "was like taking a bulldozer with a 700-foot blade and sweeping it down those hills and gullies and just demolishing everything: parishes and shopping centers and the businesses that felt local."[35] Cincinnati wasn't the only city to make this mistake; indeed, it is difficult to find an American city that in the 1960s and 1970s did not rip up neighborhoods to pave the way for passenger cars. Gilligan, in retrospect, sees no conscious malice involved in the highways' development. And to a degree, he said, it was done because those most seriously affected were black and, in the local scheme of things, "they didn't cut ice as seriously as some other people."[36] Such cynicism might suggest the displaced black population had no choice; actually, it had not a choice so much as a necessity—that of finding alternate housing in the city.

Demolition in West End breached the walls that had segregated Cincinnati. As demolition proceeded, the displaced began moving to largely contiguous areas, neighborhoods that had been mostly all-white and had little or no engagement with the black community. Across the city, large neighborhood transitions were hastened by local real estate agents telling white homeowners that the blacks were coming and that if they did not sell quickly, they would end up getting little for their property. With the West End emigration, the city's neighborhoods' characters—long a point of identity and pride—changed. Avondale, for example, a longtime largely Jewish enclave, became a low-income African American neighborhood.

Even by the sad standards of urban America, Cincinnati has had unhappy relations between the races. Even though, prior to the Civil War, the Ohio River at Cincinnati was a common crossing point of runaway slaves heading north, it was a city of slave pens, where shackled prisoners were sold back across the same river. It was the setting of Toni Morrison's *Beloved*, where a black mother drowns her children rather than see them be returned to slavery.

In 1994, Jack Gilligan tackled the topic of race in Cincinnati in an essay notable for its honesty and straightforwardness. His first conscious awareness of racial discrimination came when as a serving officer aboard the USS *Emmons*, he noticed that "when a young man reporting to duty was black, he was handed a white jacket and an apron and he became an officers' steward or cook, absolutely no exceptions."[37] He had lived several decades without really noticing the question of race. He had grown up in an all-white neighborhood, attended all-white schools and churches, and his encounters with African Americans were largely limited to those serving some menial role. He noted, without comment, that Cincinnati's major retail establishments did not serve or employ blacks and that movie theaters and parks were effectively segregated. Gilligan described his late wartime service in the South, when the *Emmons* was in port in Norfolk and Charleston. While he was in Charleston, he read of a state education commission's report that the schools reserved for black students were so run-down that both new elementary and high schools needed to be built for them and recalled how, the following day, Charleston's leading newspaper ran a page-one editorial urging officials that it would be better to abandon public education altogether than to build new schools for blacks—for the editors, maintaining black inferiority was a higher priority than free, public education for the city's white children. Cincinnati, he noted on his return, was different: in the South, segregation was enforceable law; in Cincinnati, it was "just the way things were, had always been, and always would be." At the time he thought that sentiment was wrong and troubling and that it needed to be changed but frankly admitted, "I had no notion of how that could be done."[38]

Certain steps did follow, though with limited result. As a councilman in 1954, Gilligan cosponsored with Ted Berry what proved to be an unsuccessful effort to establish a local Fair Employment Practices Commission. In 1962, Gilligan and a small group of likeminded others formed the Catholic Interracial Council with the primary intent of speaking to parish groups on segregation and racial tolerance. "The bishops had come out with this statement condemning racial segregation as a moral evil. We would go to a pastor and ask to come to his church's next meeting to discuss the bishop's encyclical."[39] The condemnation by the church hierarchy, Gilligan noted, had not been followed by any great effort to press the message home at the parish level. This is what his group intended to do.

Commonly, the presenters were Gilligan, Father Clarence Rivers (the first black priest in Cincinnati ordained by the archdiocese), and Bill Kircher, Gilligan's labor ally. As Gilligan remembered it, "the meeting would start off friendly and cordial, and as the discussion went on you could feel the temperature in the room rising. And finally some guy in the crowd would get up, just purple-faced, and say, 'What are you trying to tell us? You want our daughters to marry niggers?'"[40] At that point—and to the surprise of those assembled—one of the presenters would hand another a five dollar bill and then explain that they had a small wager going as to how long it would be before somebody stood and asked that question. Sometimes, Gilligan said, this helped break the ice.

The ice, however, was fairly thick. At one point, church officials ordered the group to take "Catholic" out of its title and remove it from its letterhead, effectively disavowing the effort. Gilligan's daughter Ellen, then still in grade school, recalled how "people would say things all the time. People would say, 'Your father is a nigger lover.' You could either stand and fight or disengage. I think I did a bit of both."[41]

Jack and Katie Gilligan themselves disengaged—not from the issue but, specifically, from Hyde Park Country Club. There were multiple precipitating factors. By one account, the break came when Katie Gilligan sought club space for a piano recital only to be refused on the grounds that some of the performers were black. By another account, it happened after a club official contacted Jack to tell him that his proposed luncheon guest, Ted Berry, the only black member of council, would not be served in the dining room.

Gilligan's ties to the club were more than incidental. His grandfather was one of the club's five founders, his father and both his brothers were members, and Jack himself had been a member since he was twenty-one and was a once- or twice-weekly golfer on its course. It was a place where Jack and Katie met up with any number of friends and family. The resignation was socially awkward but politically simple. It was "not really a sacrifice on my part," Gilligan said later, adding, "I don't think I made any new enemies."[42]

The Gilligan family in these years was living in a Victorian home on Herschel Avenue in the Mt. Lookout neighborhood. The large house sat on a double lot and had a basketball court in the driveway. The house and yard were where the Gilligan children and their friends gathered for games of pick-up football in the fall and basketball in the winter. Donald and John shared a "double room"—a bedroom and glass-enclosed sleeping porch that they often used as a playroom or study. Kathleen and Ellen each had a bedroom of their own. Donald observed, "Dinner was important. Father was home every night for dinner; Cincinnati was a small enough place that he could come home for dinner and go back out for a meeting."[43] Indeed, presence at family dinner was among the chief expectations for the four Gilligan children.

Their father had been in public life since each child's first memory. Dinner meant conversation; conversation generally meant politics. Son John commented, "At the dinner table, we'd talk about his races, about events at council and the strategy that went with them."[44] There was a bracing effect to the dinner. Not only was their father a public figure (and had been since they're very earliest memory), but he was a person who often took stands at odds with the parents of the Gilligan children's schoolmates. "From the first or second grade on, there was always pushback," John said. "It was sort of my cross to bear."[45] One purpose of the dinner table conversations was to ensure that the children were aware of why their father believed as he did and thereby be somewhat protected against the gibes of others. For Gilligan, dinner was commonly a break in the working day, rather than its end. Kathleen recalled, "My dad went back out on a lot of nights for meetings and political activities. When we would go do homework, he would go back out and do political work."[46]

According to the Gilligan children, Katie kept the very active family together. "She spent a lot of time and energy not only preparing meals but making sure that every mealtime was a social and engaged time," Kathleen said. When the children were younger, Katie was a great believer in hot cereal for breakfast and an occasional inflictor of liver for dinner.[47] As the children moved through high school, she devoted considerable time to becoming an accomplished gourmet cook, a talent she displayed at the dinner parties she and Jack hosted.

Son John offered several character notes on his mother. She came, he said, "from a family where you didn't buy a lot of stuff, but when you did you bought quality that would last."[48] Katie Gilligan's father was a common court pleas judge; he had worked his way through Xavier University, and then attended night school at Cincinnati Salmon Chase law school. In short, one should be expected to work for what one wanted.

Katie Gilligan, who held master's degrees in English and education, was an avid reader. (She and Jack both favored serious modern fiction.) A member of the Hyde Park Country Club—until politics intervened—she played tennis and golf. Daughter Ellen recalled how her mother was "terribly afraid of thunderstorms, so if it started to rain she would make her caddy drop her clubs and run for the clubhouse."[49] When not in Leland, the children spent many of their summer days at the club as well, playing "junior age" golf or caddying for the adults.

There were family expectations. Son Donald recalls, "The most important thing in my life was . . . that I excel at everything—no slacking off, no half efforts."[50] Kathleen recalled that the primary expectation was school—"we were expected to do our homework first."[51] As their parents had, the children attended Summit County Day. Kathleen played soccer, tennis, and basketball. John wrestled at St. Xavier—120 pounds as a freshman, 154 as a senior. His father, he said, "would attend our sporting events like other parents at the time, when it was his turn to drive—maybe every third or fourth contest."[52]

Church was a close second to education. Both parents wished religion to be at the center of their children's lives. The family attended Mass each week; this "was not a debatable moment."[53] (Katie Gilligan attended Mass almost every day.) But for the Gilligans, religion was not a topic solely to be discussed on Sundays but to be integrated into the family's everyday lives.

And social beliefs were to be lived. Katie Gilligan devoted her time and talent to what she regarded as good causes, about which she was quite private. One long-term political associate of her husband recalls Katie Gilligan working alone at some handwork project for the blind; it was a good work, but not one that doubled as socializing. Her son John said, "She would talk about causes of social justice as being worth your time; she instilled in us a sense of the need to be involved, to make a contribution."[54] The Gilligan children, for example, did not work at summer jobs; their mother felt that such casual employment should go to those in greater need of the income. This did not mean, however, that summers were to be spent by the pool. They were expected to volunteer—in school-based religious activities at St. Xavier or at the Children's Convalescent Hospital or at Stepping Stones, a camp for mentally and physically handicapped children.

The family had certain hangers-on, a consequence, perhaps, of the Gilligans' sense of religious responsibility. One was a man named George Moore, who suffered from "radium" in the stomach and turned up every month or so for dinner; a second was a woman who, for no certain reason, sent the family envelopes stuffed with greeting card messages, fifty or sixty at a time.

There were certain family restrictions, among them tight control over television viewing. Ellen recalled, "We had limitations on both quantity and quality; I think we got to watch about an hour a week. And no Saturday cartoons."[55] Apparently that "one hour" was each child's allotment, so if each chose a different show, total viewing time could be increased. Ellen recalled, "We got into a brouhaha once when my parents were out and John and Kathleen and I were home. We dropped the television. It rolled down the stairs. My dad wouldn't get it fixed for about ten months."[56] Donald recalled that the restrictions did have some loopholes: "At some point, sporting events became an exception to the quota."[57]

Leland, Michigan, remained the family's vacation site. In the early 1960s, Jack and Katie purchased their own vacation home two doors down his parents' and about a half-mile from his sister Jeanne's family place. Traveling to Leland from Cincinnati meant a day spent cooped up in the car; recognizing this, a certain leniency prevailed. Ellen recalled, "We were never allowed comic books, except on the drive to Michigan. Then we could go down to the local drugstore; load up on as many comic books as we could carry; and read them to stay entertained in the car."[58]

Jack's parents—Harry and Blanche Gilligan continued to make the trip to Leland. John remembered his grandfather seated in a chair, listening to the Cincinnati Reds game, and reviewing the death notices from the *Enquirer,* noting which had been handled by the Gilligan funeral home and which had gone to a competitor. (The funeral home rarely entered the children's thoughts. John commented, "I thought of the funeral home as somewhere that was elsewhere."[59] Kathleen added, "I didn't have any feelings about it; my father was never very engaged with it."[60]

Political conversation continued in Michigan. Ellen occasionally excused herself: "They would be sitting around the table debating the Vietnam War or other political events endlessly. The joke among my friends was that they would come to pick me up for a party and my family would be having the same discussion when I got home."[61]

The high point of the Gilligans' summer was the picnic held each June at the sprawling Ambleside home of Harry and Blanche Gilligan. Harry, his grandchildren agreed, was proud and protective of his political son; at times he was concerned that Jack might be tilting at windmills, but he was proud of him for making the effort. The gathering was held the Saturday closest to the shared May birthday of Jack's younger brothers, Frank and Mike. The family turnout was huge; in addition to Jack and Katie's four, Jeanne Gilligan had eight children and Frank and Mike had seventeen between them. The Gilligan grandchildren numbered twenty-nine, of which Jack's son Donald was the oldest.

Given the size of the family, Kathleen noted, the picnic was about the only time everyone saw each other. It was a fancy event—catered, with linen tablecloths and everyone dressed to the nines. For the parents, a major distraction from the festivities was making sure that none of the small ones fell into the fish pond. That parental distraction permitted opportunity for the older cousins: "Normally," Ellen revealed, "we weren't allowed to drink soft drinks. But they had a bartender on hand, and the parents weren't really minding us, so you could have as many Cokes or ginger ales as you could get your hands on."[62] In that large family, one personality stood out. Reflecting on his father, John Gilligan observed, "It's hard to believe the energy that one person could have."[63]

12

"The Miamis Are Everywhere"

John Joyce Gilligan's political career proceeded under the pressure of a fundamental restlessness. Seldom at repose, he was far likelier to be somewhat on edge—as if that edge were in fact leading to something more desirable than the present might offer. And with that restlessness came considerable frustration: as a Republican bastion, Cincinnati was simply not a suitable launching pad for a Democrat with broader aspiration.

Late in 1961, Gilligan had foresworn any interest in running for the U.S. Congress. The district, he said, was so heavily Republican "that a Democrat would have to spot the opposition 35,000 votes going in. Even if he did win one term, it would be a continuous battle to stay in office."[1] At the time, he viewed his electoral future as limited. Both county and state offices were securely in Republican hands. He commented, "There didn't seem to be any place to go. This wasn't so much a disappointment to me as much as a simple recognition that that's the way the world worked."[2]

But early in 1962, a broader possibility presented itself—the possibility to run for a statewide office. Due to the peculiarities of redistricting, Ohio would in 1962 elect a single congressman-at-large, statewide. The suggestion that Gilligan seek the post came from Governor Michael DiSalle, a Democrat. Indeed, to ease Gilligan's task, DiSalle offered to sweep the primary—that is, to arrange for Gilligan to run unopposed for the party's nomination.

Gilligan had come to know DiSalle through the latter's association with Richard Guggenheim, who, though a high-level executive with the Cincinnati-based U.S. Shoe Corporation, was a fervent Democrat. Gilligan frequently joined DiSalle and Guggenheim when the governor was in Cincinnati. Nominated for governor in 1958, DiSalle benefitted from the Right-to-Work tidal wave, which carried him to Columbus with a huge margin. Gilligan thought DiSalle was "a very decent guy, a very bright man. He and I generally shared views about state government and how it ought to function."[3]

But Gilligan, like most Ohio political observers, considered DiSalle an ineffective leader. DiSalle quarreled—and, worse, quarreled publicly—with the state legislature, which rejected his proposals on the death penalty, on "union racketeering" reform, on how claims for injured workers should be handled, and much more. Gilligan commented that DiSalle spent his mornings worrying about what the afternoon paper would say about him and his afternoons worrying about what it had said. More strangely, at least to many Ohio voters, DiSalle intervened in death penalty cases, essentially retrying the cases himself. In a case in which a divorced woman had been sentenced to death for murdering her ex-husband's presumed lover, DiSalle had the convicted woman brought to his office where he personally interrogated her after she had been dosed with sodium amatol (truth serum), the use of which had no legal standing in court (or, more to the point, in the governor's office). DiSalle subsequently commuted the woman's death sentence.

For all of that, DiSalle was the state's leading Democrat, and his endorsement of Gilligan carried weight. In the winter of 1962, Gilligan set up a small campaign headquarters at 19 East Seventh Street in Cincinnati and put together the rudiments of a campaign. The Democratic Party organizations in four of the state's eight largest counties endorsed him. He had solid Cincinnati-area labor support from Bill Kircher, regional director of the AFL-CIO, and Bill Sheehan. And he signed on a young academic, John Grupenhoff, to drum up support in university towns and other likely enclaves. And he also hit the road, pushing himself whenever time could be found to address small groups of Democrats around the state. The experience, Gilligan said, was "my introduction into state politics, traveling around the state, which I had not really done before. I found politics interesting generally and Ohio politics interesting in particular."[4] It was a low-key, underfinanced campaign that was heavily driven by the personal energy of the candidate. All seemed reasonably promising. However, the outcome of the May 1962 Democratic primary underscored the reasons why Democrats continued to play second fiddle in Ohio politics.

On the Republican side, the GOP put forward an extremely well-known candidate: Robert A. Taft, grandson of a U.S. president, son of the one-time ranking Republican in the Senate, and himself a rising member of the state legislature. Faced with only token opposition, Taft received 92 percent of the primary votes cast.

On the Democratic side, the supposed promise from DiSalle to "sweep the primary" clean for Gilligan proved empty. Eleven Democratic hopefuls were on the ballot, most only locally known. Gilligan outcampaigned them all only to lose narrowly to a candidate who had barely campaigned at all, a virtually unknown real estate agent with a very well-known name: Richard D. Kennedy. Gilligan's campaign aide, John Grupenhoff, recalled: "I remember Gilligan looking at the blackboard with the reports coming in from various precincts. He looked at the Kennedy name:

it was far outstripping everyone else but him. Gilligan was second. And Gilligan said, 'My God! I hadn't thought of that.'"[5] Kennedy received 113,523 primary votes, eclipsing Gilligan's 110,142; none of the other nine received even half as many votes as Gilligan.

After the election, Kennedy said that he doubted his last name had much to do with his victory. He described himself as liberal in economics and a moderate on civil rights, which he deemed "a difficult question to answer," adding, "I hope civil rights does not become an issue in the campaign."[6] But Kennedy's moderate take on civil rights did not prevent him from having previously unrevealed ties to a number of white supremacist organizations. After a deeply embarrassed pause, the state Democratic Party withdrew its endorsement, and Robert A. Taft cake-walked to victory and a seat in the United States Congress.

Following his primary defeat, Gilligan turned down an offer to take on the likely thankless task of DiSalle's campaign manager; he did, however, agree to direct the incumbent's speakers' bureau, a post that would allow him to further his contacts around the state. The 1962 election was a bad one for Ohio Democrats. Michael Di-Salle's reelection bid was crushed by 555,669 votes, the largest margin in state guber-natorial history. The victorious GOP candidate was the sitting state auditor, James A. Rhodes. Gilligan, who had worked for DiSalle's election, was in the Governor's Mansion the evening the results came in. Walking into a hallway, his eye caught movement on the stairway leading to a landing. Curious, he went up and pulled the drape aside, revealing DiSalle's teen-aged son, weeping.

The Cincinnati AFL-CIO's Committee on Political Education (COPE) soon thereafter minced no words in its assessment of Ohio politics and labor's role within it. Labor, it said, whose huge 1958 turnout had temporarily handed the state to the Democrats, had done little in the 1962 election. And the Democrats had done little themselves. The report stated flatly: "County Democratic organizations are almost exclusively concerned with local problems—that is, the control of jobs." It asserted more broadly, "The fact is there is no state [Democratic] party in Ohio."[7]

That assessment was one entirely shared by Jack Gilligan. By the time of his May 1962 primary defeat, Gilligan had fallen into company with a small but like-minded and energetic group—Dick Guggenheim, Vince Beckman, Bill Kircher, Jim Luken, Tom Spraul, Philip Collins, and others. To an extent, they had come to each other's attention through John F. Kennedy's 1960 presidential campaign, which lured younger Cincinnati-area liberals out of the woodwork to discover each other's exis-tence. They first met as an informal discussion group; those discussions eventually pointed to the need for action.

The group was not only Democratic but largely Catholic. This was meaningful to Gilligan, who found affirmation of his political life in the direction the church was taking under Vatican II. Religion was always central to his being: "The Church was a big thing on my mind; the intellectual way of the church—people exploring

ideas in socially conscious ways, in the fields of literature and art."[8] His own perspective was decided young. Since high school, he had been "attached to and associated with what you might call the most progressive currents within the Church."[9]
He did not see Vatican II as a wholesale departure from tradition; rather, he viewed
it as the application of much existing Catholic thought to a broadened social arena.
It was also a movement that brought to the fore the Catholic theologians and writers with whom he most identified.

Gilligan and the others in his group were in their thirties and forties—of an age
and inclination that they felt it was time they had some impact on the life of the
community. The political vehicle through which they imagined that could happen
was the Hamilton County Democratic Party, which, as it happens, was chaired by
a man who had no interest in political reform, little tolerance for political reformers, and an advanced capacity for standing his ground: the redoubtable John A.
Wiethe.

Wiethe was universally known as Socko, a nickname he acquired the old-fash-
ioned way—by slapping people upside the head. Decades before his lengthy tenure
as the intimidating chairman of the Hamilton County Democratic Committee,
Wiethe achieved local notoriety in Cincinnati as the intimidating left tackle at
Roger Bacon High School and then at Xavier University. Characteristically, when
the ball was snapped, Wiethe would head-slap the lineman facing him, earning
him the nickname that stuck long after the technique that prompted it had been
banned.[10] Football brought out Wiethe's natural strengths. He was an on-the-field
team leader, given to encouraging further exertions from his teammates by referring to them as "you coward." When he was inducted into the Xavier Hall of Fame,
the statement cited Wiethe's "dynamic drive, a keen judgment that almost never
erred, and an innate love of the game."[11]

Wiethe went on to acquire a law degree while playing semi-pro football. In 1939
he signed on with the Detroit Lions as a twenty-seven-year-old rookie. Even then,
Wiethe was small for a lineman—he was listed as six feet tall and 198 pounds. Nonetheless, he was selected to the first-team All-Pro squad in his rookie year and again
the next year, 1940 (along with fellow Detroit Lion and tailback Byron "Whizzer"
White, who, two decades, later achieved the additional honor of being named to the
U.S. Supreme Court by President Kennedy).

After his professional career, Wiethe returned to Cincinnati, established a
small law firm, and maintained ties to local sports. In 1946, he was named head
basketball coach of the University of Cincinnati Bearcats. Bearcats basketball had
been a losing proposition; Wiethe's first team posted a record of seventeen wins,
nine losses and claimed the first of five consecutive Mid-American Conference
Championships. His 1948–49 squad, finishing 23–5, was the school's first to be
nationally ranked. He left coaching following the 1951–52 season "to devote full
energies to his law practice, and budding career in politics."[12]

Wiethe played politics with the same competitiveness he did football, though initially with less success. In 1940, he failed in an attempt to become a state legislator, and in 1952, he ran unsuccessfully for county prosecutor. He then allied himself with a local politico Jimmy Sullivan, who in 1954 undertook a challenge to the sitting Democratic Party county leader, William J. Leonard. Sullivan captured the county chairmanship but died unexpectedly shortly after, and Wiethe was the unanimous choice of the Democratic executive committee to succeed him. Wiethe's first action was to appoint a committee (which included recently elected city councilman Jack Gilligan) to assess the local status of his party. That status was weak, the committee found: only 13,000 Democrats had taken part in their party's 1952 spring primary, and that fall Democrats received an average of just 39.8 percent of the vote in local two-party contests. Wiethe moved aggressively to build an organization. He expanded the number of active Democratic ward clubs in the county from twelve to sixty-eight and recruited hundreds of precinct captains. And he sent forth candidates (often, from his own law firm) to do generally unsuccessful electoral battle with the Republicans.

For Wiethe, being county chairman had certain advantages. There was a measure of prestige. There was also a certain amount of patronage to be handed out—for example, the Democrats held half the seats on the Hamilton County Board of Elections, which had a substantial number of jobs to pass out. But mostly, politics was an outlet for Wiethe's innate combativeness. For him, the work of politics was the care and feeding of the organization he had built and the dispensing of the favors, cajoling, and outright threats that kept that organization in line. It might not be fair to say that John Wiethe ruled through fear; but a lot of people were more than a little bit afraid of him.

So when Jack Gilligan and a handful of Democratic reformers decided to challenge Wiethe's control of the local Democratic Party, they chose to proceed with a measure of circumspection. The two sides had little common ground. Cincinnati historian Judith Spraul-Schmidt observed that "Socko and Jack Gilligan were just opposite sides of the world."[13] Sidney Weil commented, "John Wiethe was an organization man; his precinct executives were everything. Jack and Vince Beckman were never very interested in organization politics; they were interested in policies and political platforms—which John [Wiethe] did not give a damn about."[14]

Based on a suggestion by Dick Guggenheim, the insurgents found themselves a name. Guggenheim, who had an eye for antiques and an interest in local history, uncovered the fact that in the 1820s an insurgent group had challenged the ruling Democratic Party; they had called themselves the Miami Society. Gilligan's group of insurgents adopted this name and added a slogan: "The Miamis Are Everywhere."

Not initially. Initially, it was a clump of like-minded Democrats who met every other week for lunch at places like Lenhardt's German Restaurant on McMillan Street. Eager to keep their profile below the range of John Wiethe's well-attuned antenna, the group held each meeting in a new location. Still, there was some reason for optimism. Jack Gilligan recalled, "Our theory at the time was that there were a lot of nascent Democrats out there who had never had a chance to show their colors. If we were ever in a position to run a real campaign with real candidates, we'd win some things."[15] Fairly early, they drew in an important recruit: Sidney Weil, a key Wiethe associate, cast his lot with the insurgents.

Gilligan's public break with Wiethe took place just two weeks after his surprise defeat in the May 1962 primary at the annual meeting of Hamilton County Democrats. Wiethe was seeking a fifth two-year term as chairman. The May 22 *Post and Times-Star* headlined the event: "Gilligan, Wiethe Split in Stormy Meeting of Dems." The paper added, "Councilman John J. Gilligan has emerged as the minority opposition leader to John A. Wiethe, county Democratic chairman. The open break between the two was established for the first time before the full party organization at a stormy session last night at the Alms."[16] As a test of strength, the insurgents ran Gilligan for the post of vice chairman; their hope was that a Gilligan victory might pave the way for a broader settlement within the party. Weil commented, "We thought maybe John [Wiethe] would back off, but John did not know how to back off."[17]

During the balloting, Wiethe's own ward cast twenty-four votes for Josephine Shapiro, a Wiethe ally and incumbent, even though only ten people from that ward had been counted as present. When Gilligan ally James Luken of the local Milk Drivers union sought an explanation for this, Wiethe replied, "We use the unit rule," with no elaboration. Challenged, Wiethe shouted, "Luken, you're not in the Teamsters' Union now. If you don't stop interfering with the vote you'll be thrown out."[18] He then directed that the police be called, though the summons was countermanded before officers arrived. Shapiro won by a tally of 305–230, and John Wiethe was elected to his fifth two-year term as county party chairman.

The fight was now open and personal. In January 1963, the three Democratic members of city council—Gilligan, Spraul, and Philip Collins—demanded Wiethe's resignation, arguing that he had made "every conceivable effort . . . to vilify, to punish, or to exclude any Democrat who dares to speak his mind and conscience on matters affecting the party and the community if those ideas are not approved by John Wiethe."[19] In April, Gilligan chaired a meeting creating Democrats United, a group expressly formed to "overthrow the party's present leadership."[20]

Not surprisingly, Wiethe gave as good as he got. Those trying to topple him, he said, were motivated by nothing other than "power lust."[21] The insurgents were a self-interested clique that "had never been willing to work for the good of the party" but that would "tear the party apart and forfeit victories to the opposition in order to satisfy their lust for power."[22]

Wiethe then muddied local waters by having the Democratic organization formally propose that the current nine-member city council elected citywide be scrapped and replaced by representatives elected from each of the city's twenty-six wards. The proposal to re-create ward-style politics in Cincinnati was a complete nonstarter. Republican and Charterite leaders vowed opposition, with Charterite president Leonard Sive promising to "fight it with every resource at our disposal."[23] Conceivably, Wiethe was attempting to drive a wedge between the insurgents and Cincinnati's black community: no African American had been elected to council since the abolition of PR; under a twenty-six-member ward system, black neighborhoods might elect four to six representatives.

Wiethe had one more bone to pick with the insurgent Democrats. In July 1963, the county Democratic Executive Committee demanded that any candidate seeking its endorsement must pledge to support all positions the Executive Committee took or might take in the future. Gilligan, Spraul, and Collins declined to do so and found their endorsements withdrawn. Wiethe then lined up a slate of nine organization Democrats to challenge the insurgents in the council race.

Wiethe's next move had the subtlety of a chop block. In September 1963, he issued a press release claiming that the Gilligan funeral home had refused to bury a man because the deceased was black. The case had its curious aspects. The man, Leondres Hodge, had died September 15; the following day, the family made arrangements with the local Jamison Funeral Home to collect and dispose of the body. The bill for Jamison's services was paid by the executor of the Hodge estate, who happened to be John Wiethe. Then, on September 17, one James Alexander called the Gilligan funeral home to inquire about making arrangements for Hodge. In a later affidavit, Alexander stated that he made the call from his place of employment, the Board of Elections office, where he had been summoned by Wiethe, who was present while the call was made.

From that point, recollections differ. Jack Gilligan said that he inquired if Alexander was Hodge's nearest of kin and, learning that he was not, asked that the family get in touch with the funeral home. He claimed that this was the last he heard of the matter. In a statement issued a few days later, Gilligan said, "I further specifically denied, in answer to [Alexander's] inquiry, that our firm had ever had a policy against burying Negroes."[24] Alexander's assertion was that Gilligan had said his funeral home had "no experience in burying Negroes" and that he would have to consult his partners. He related his version of the conversation:

> I said: "Quit the double-talk, Jack; give me a simple 'yes' or 'no.' Will you bury him?"
> Gilligan: "No, I will not."
> I said: "Well, Jack, I'll be seeing you."[25]

Based on the alleged refusal to bury, Alexander filed a complaint against the Gilligan Funeral Home with the Ohio Civil Rights Commission.

In early October, the *Call and Post,* a weekly newspaper primarily circulated in the Cleveland and Cincinnati black communities, published the story headlined "Cincy Councilman Won't Bury Negro."[26] The publisher of record for the *Call and Post* was John Wiethe, who later claimed no association with the story. Gilligan filed a libel action against Wiethe and the publication, seeking $100,000 in compensatory damages and $250,000 in punitive damages. Wiethe countersued, claiming that Gilligan had been "engaged in a systematic attempt to damage [his] professional reputation as a lawyer through acts of both libel and slander."[27] He asserted that the newspaper article was "not intended maliciously but only to publish the facts as to the hypocrisy of Gilligan in his campaign among the Negro community and elsewhere in the city as the champion for fair and equal treatment for the Negro."[28] The libel case was settled after the November election in favor of Gilligan, who received a small award. The Ohio Civil Rights Commission found no basis for action on Alexander's complaint against John Gilligan or the family funeral home.

Despite this distraction, the city council elections of November 1963 vindicated the insurgents: Gilligan and Collins were reelected as Independent Democrats, and all nine Wiethe-backed organization Democrats were defeated. That same election returned Ted Berry and Charles Taft to council as Charterites, leaving the five elected Republicans with the majority.

Three weeks after Gilligan's reelection to council, he watched a newscaster deliver the report that President John Fitzgerald Kennedy had been assassinated in Dallas. He recalled how, in the days following, "the family was glued to our TV set [watching] some sort of ceremonial event. There was an image—the picture was in *Life* magazine—of an African American member of a military band standing on the sidewalk playing his instrument as the parade went by. He was standing there with tears on his cheeks."[29]

For Gilligan, "the feeling was that a real door had been slammed on what we saw as an opening to the future that was just getting under way. [Up to then,] all the stars were in line. The feeling was that we had really crossed a threshold in a new direction, with such great promise. And now a whole era, a whole chapter in the life of our nation, had been ended—idiotically."[30] The impact of the tragedy was akin to the aftereffects of a physical injury, where bruises and pains become evident over time. Gilligan described how, perhaps ten days after the assassination, he and Katie were dining at Cincinnati's Maisonette restaurant. An acquaintance stopped by the table and made some casual reference to the event, he recalled, "whereupon I burst into tears. It was uncontrollable."[31]

The president's death, however, did not deter Democrats United in Cincinnati in their active opposition to Wiethe and the county party. Sidney Weil recalled, "I remember when Kennedy was shot we asked, 'Should we cancel our next meeting?' The answer was no."[32] In December, Wiethe announced he would stand for his sixth term as Hamilton County Democratic chairman the following May. His candidacy was endorsed by the Democratic Policy Committee, which, not to miss a trick, commended him "for being the kind of leader who is not concerned with what his country can do for him, but what he can do for his country."[33] Shortly thereafter, Democrats United chose Vince Beckman to oppose him, Beckman being a less confrontational choice than Gilligan.

Wiethe's position was, in fact, well-rooted. The county chairman was elected by a vote of the county's 1,565 precinct executives—almost all of whom he had appointed. Gilligan observed, "If anybody wanted to raise a revolt against him, they would have to get a majority of those precinct executives. John Wiethe thought—and most people thought—that that would be impossible. How in hell could you line up enough precinct executives to gain a majority?"[34]

This is exactly what Democrats United set out to do. They recruited hundreds of candidates either to run against incumbent precinct executives or to stand for election in vacant precincts. Each prospective candidate had to go door-to-door in his or her precinct with a notary public. Weil recalled, "We divided up the city and went door-to-door. And these were not nice months; we were doing this in January and February."[35]

John Gilligan recalled his father bundling up and going out in his own generally Republican precinct. Beyond his full-time duties as a city councilman, he was devoting fifteen to twenty hours a week to Democrats United, including most weeknights following dinner with his family and much of his weekends. Indeed, Gilligan had added to his responsibilities as a city councilman. Following the November 1963 election, he and Charterite councilman Charles Taft joined a committee headed by Charterite Ted Berry to hold hearings on poverty in Cincinnati. The final witness the committee heard was a settlement house director who had come to Cincinnati in 1959 and was appalled by the poverty and conditions he had encountered. He worked in a neighborhood called Riverview, where families largely transplanted from Appalachia lived in dire poverty:

> I went upstairs in an abandoned house in lower Mt. Adams. No power; no water. They were heating with a kerosene stove that had a vertical pipe with an exposed flame. And all these babies—there must have been ten kids in the home. I don't know how many families they were from. And they were paying rent. And I said to them, "Why are you paying rent?" And you know what? I couldn't find them a better place to live. This was in the heart of a major city.[36]

During the hearings, the council members, in the general manner of those who spend much of their lives in meetings, were reading their correspondence, consulting documents, and the like. As the social worker waited to testify, "a guy stood up in the chamber—barrel-chested and very bellicose—and said to the councilmen, 'When my wife is talking, you listen.' He really was angry." Gilligan, who viewed politics as perhaps the community's most essential calling and believed that those who practiced it merited a certain regard, got up "very red-faced . . . He spun out of his seat and he addressed this guy, 'I'm going to tell you exactly what this witness has said, and then I'm going to ask you to apologize to this body.' Gilligan then succinctly restated the testimony just given. Partially mollified, the husband replied, 'I still don't like the fact that you don't look at her while she's talking.'"[37] The incident marked the moment Jack Gilligan came to the attention of the social worker, Jack Hansan, who would be Gilligan's future campaign manager.

The council hearings on poverty were for fact finding as well as publicity raising; while they preceded the nation's "War on Poverty," they to an extent helped make the case for it. Hansan, as it happened, had worked with Berry's successful 1959 council campaign. He claimed no particular knowledge of politics, but he did regard himself as a competent organizer—of events, of fund-raisers, of publicity drives. Hansan left the hearing carrying the view that Jack Gilligan was an articulate politician who was on the right side of the issues.

In the Democratic political war, the insurgents operated on two fronts. First, they challenged Wiethe's chairmanship through the election of reform-minded precinct captains. Second, in the May 1964 primary, they ran a full slate of candidates against Wiethe's organization Democrats. Jack Gilligan put his name forward for the Democratic nomination from Ohio's First Congressional District. As Sidney Weil recalled it, Gilligan did this principally so that the Democrats United would be able to field a full slate against Wiethe's regulars, not out of any great ambition to be a United States congressman, a recollection Gilligan shared.

The effort to overturn the pro-Wiethe precinct executives ran into a snag: apparently, no public list existed of who these individuals were. The matter was remedied by an approach not altogether in keeping with high-minded reform. One member of Democrats United learned that the weekend night watchman at the Board of Elections was open to liquid persuasion. Gilligan recounted how "one Saturday night, a group of the boys got hold of this guy and got him to a local bar and got him stiff."[38] With the guard out of the way, a truck pulled up, they proceeded to "borrow," copy, and return files with precinct executive names. All without coming to the attention of John Wiethe. (Asked to confirm this chain of events, Sidney Weil, perhaps reluctant to rule out a good story, commented only, "It doesn't ring a bell."[39])

After Gilligan joined the race, both sides amped up their rhetoric. A Democrats United release claimed: "Completely canceling the tireless efforts of hundreds of devoted Democrats in the precincts and the arduous labors of dozens of valiant Democratic candidates in Hamilton County, the high-handed and dictatorial policies of John Wiethe have torn the party to pieces and have brought about a series of crushing defeats, each worse than the last."[40] In response, Wiethe defended his tenure, claiming credit for the number of votes cast in the Democratic primary doubling in the past decade, the number of Democratic officeholders rising, and the Democratic Party share of the total countywide vote increasing from 39.8 percent to 44.5 percent. Wiethe lowered the hyperbolic boom, citing Gilligan's "glossy veneer of political gentility" and stating, "Gilligan started all the trouble that we have in the party right now. The rest of the rebels would be all right if he were done. We believe in majority rule. He believes in the cult of the individual."[41]

The May 1964 primary was a triumph for the insurgents. Twenty-four of the twenty-seven candidates endorsed by Democrats United were nominated, often by margins approaching 2–1. And Jack Gilligan found himself the Democratic nominee for Ohio's First Congressional District. That same day saw the election of 1,500 Democratic precinct executives representing each precinct in the county.

The final showdown with John Wiethe came on May 18, 1964, when the newly elected precinct executives gathered in Cincinnati's Music Hall to choose between Wiethe and Vince Beckman as county chairman. It was a spirited, to say nothing of antagonistic, occasion. Gilligan's sixteen-year-old daughter, Kathleen, and her friend Polly Guggenheim (daughter of Dick Guggenheim) passed out pamphlets for Democrats United to the arriving crowd. Kathleen recalled, "A couple of people I had known my entire life just took them, ripped them to shreds, and threw them down. They did not really confront us directly, but they made it clear they were unhappy with my dad."[42] Sidney Weil recalls the evening as "one of the most exciting elections I've ever seen—like a national convention."[43] Psychologically, Wiethe still held sway. To encourage last-minute faint hearts, Democrats United collected their supporters and, by bus, delivered them to Music Hall. Each was then issued a straw boater hat—so that on entering the hall they would see other such boaters scattered about and know that they were among friends. But Wiethe caught on; he rapped down the gavel and ordered that all "extraneous" headwear be removed. The hats were pitched.

After that show of force, John Wiethe committed what may have been the decisive error. There was a motion made for the election to be by secret ballot. According to Weil, the insurgents wanted this "because there were people who were either physically or emotionally afraid of John [Wiethe]."[44] Wiethe allowed the question to be put to the floor, something Weil says he was not required to do, and the motion passed 682 to 425. Voting booths were then brought in and ballots for county chairman were distributed, marked, gathered, and taken to a side room for counting by representatives from both sides.

Gilligan recalled that the counting seemed to take forever. Finally, a parade of officials emerged from down the hall with the ballot boxes. One of those bearers was Vince Beckman. Gilligan recalled, "As Vince went by me, he winked."[45]

Beckman had defeated Wiethe by a margin of 577 to 570.

Wiethe was "utterly surprised and devastated" by the outcome but accepted the verdict without complaint.[46]

Gilligan, Beckman, Weil, and others expected the election to usher in a whole new Democratic Party in the county. Weil said, "We hunted up and found a headquarters. We were going to have all kinds of community participation. We were going to have groups for this and groups for that."[47] But, in fact, most of those who had turned out at Music Hall "figured they had fulfilled their purpose," and before long "the organization we were left with was pretty much the same people that had been there before."[48] The regulars and the insurgents had spent nearly a year exchanging vitriol; having done so, the lions then pretty much lay down with the lambs. Once Beckman's tenure ended, Weil served as Democratic county cochair with an only somewhat chastened John Wiethe, who held a party post until 1988.

Whatever may have been his reasons for putting his name forward as a candidate for the U.S. Congress, John Gilligan was now the designated Democratic nominee—and, characteristically, running hard.

13

The 1964 Campaign for Congress

For the aspiring Democrat, Ohio's First Congressional District had the disadvantage of being one of the most famously Republican districts in the country. The most famous Republican to hold that seat was Nicholas Longworth, who held the office for all but two years between 1903 and 1931, served three terms as Speaker of the House, and had the Longworth House Office Building (one of three that today house the offices of U.S. congressmen) named for him.

Partisanship aside, there were incidental ties between the Longworths and the Gilligans. It was Longworth's grandfather whose failure at viniculture opened for development the land on which Gilligan's parents Ambleside home rested. About the time that home was being built, nine-year-old Jack Gilligan was a student at Summit Country Day School—which was on Grandin Road, one of whose branches was Rookwood Drive, which led to the Longworth mansion. Gilligan and friends were playing outside the school one April day in 1931 when a burst of motorcycles emerged, followed by a funeral cortege: the honored dead was Nicholas Longworth.

In Cincinnati, money was tied to position, and both took part in politics—Republican politics. In 1899, New York governor Theodore Roosevelt wrote to a prominent Cincinnatian, "Will[iam Howard] Taft is a very fine fellow. I wish there was someone like him here in New York, for I am very much alone."[1] Five years later, Taft joined President Teddy Roosevelt as secretary of war. By then, Nicholas Longworth had come to Washington to take up his seat in the House of Representatives. And in 1906, the trio was present at the White House when Longworth—rich, young, and ambitious—married Roosevelt's daughter, the lovely, lively, and not altogether retiring Alice.

It was a marriage that barely survived the most famous divorce in Republican history, that of Roosevelt and Taft. In 1912, Longworth's close friend and fellow Cincinnatian President William Howard Taft stood for reelection, challenged by Teddy Roosevelt, who, having broken with Taft, campaigned for the presidency as a "Bull Moose" Republican. Longworth, a party regular, faced the unhappy choice of supporting Taft, his old friend, or Teddy, his wife's father. From Alice's perspective, Longworth chose wrong, standing by the incumbent. Election year 1912 handed Longworth the only defeat of his career by a scant 105-vote margin that may have been attributed to his wife Alice, for whom blood was thicker than marriage, evident when she spoke at an election rally on behalf of her husband's opponent, John Hollister.

The district's politics may have become less interesting once the Longworths were no longer taking part, but they did not become less Republican. Longworth's successor, John Hollister, served five years before losing the seat in the 1936 Roosevelt landslide to the only Democrat to intrude on the office since Alice campaigned for her husband's opponent. The next election brought Republican Charles Elston to Congress, where he remained for fourteen years. Republican Gordon Scherer then held the seat for ten more years and was followed in 1962 by Carl D. Rich, the Republican incumbent Gilligan faced. Rich had served two terms as county prosecutor and a decade on Cincinnati's City Council, including six years as the city's mayor, and at the time of his election to Congress he was serving as a local judge.

In Cincinnati, congressional elections were not close. Often, the Democratic candidate failed to garner 40 percent of the vote in a two-way race. Even in 1958— when the proposed right-to-work amendment brought masses of Democrats out of the electoral woodwork, the incumbent Republican in the First District was reelected by more than 26,000 votes.

During this Republican ascendancy, Cincinnati Democrats were inclined to think somewhat bitterly that the U.S. House of Representatives was something of a retirement home for local Republicans who had served their party well and ably. Gilligan said, "It was a cushy job. If you didn't want to do any work, you didn't do any work. You needed a secretary or two to respond to constituent mail. You stayed out of the sight; you drew the pay and you enjoyed the perks."[2] The primary task of any Republican holding that seat, he added, was to avoid "any sort of political imbroglio that would attract attention to you or your stance on issues."[3]

Gilligan knew Rich reasonably well, having served with him on council for the better part of a decade. He regarded Rich as an amiable sort, "a friendly and gregarious fellow with tons of casual acquaintances who met him on the street and shook his hand."[4] On Cincinnati City Council, Rich had been "a popular, but not forceful, figure," Gilligan assessed, and in Congress, "he was not associated with any particular legislation or legislative battles."[5] Still, Rich was apparently agreeable to the constituents he served. In the 1962 election, Rich had claimed the congressional seat by an imposing margin of 74,392 to 44,252.

It takes a fairly sturdy optimism to believe that such an outcome could be reversed—an optimism that in politics is generally reserved for novices. Gilligan, though rather more than a novice, decided the thing could be done. He decided, in part, as a partisan Democrat who felt the good fight had to be made.

Partly I wanted to join the forces of righteousness and spread the more liberal New Deal approach to public matters and community matters. I was more than a little shaken up by Harry Truman's involvement in the Korean conflict, but it still seemed that, by and large, Truman and the rest of the party were closer to what I thought a national party ought to be saying and working for. And as I looked at the local scene, there had been some very good guys who ran for Congress in the First District of Ohio. I just decided I would take a shot at it.[6]

Two additional factors contributed to his decision to run. The first was that, after a decade of service, the Cincinnati City Council was simply getting stale for him. The second was that Lyndon Johnson, who headed up the 1964 Democrat ticket, was riding high in the polls. Overall, Gilligan said, "I felt that, locally, we would at least be competitive."[7]

Gilligan had few resources with which to compete. His campaign was all-volunteer—which meant earnest, energetic, and underfinanced. After the recent poverty hearings, Gilligan approached Jack Hansan and invited him to be his campaign manager. For Hansan, who had worked on Ted Berry's successful 1959 city council campaign, this marked his first congressional campaign.[8] He believed, however, that, despite having no particular knowledge of politics, he was a competent organizer: "As an administrator, I knew how to organize and how to delegate and how to organize a fundraising."[9] This Hansan did entirely on his own time—his agency's board of directors had approved Hansan's campaign work on the assurance that he would pursue the effort strictly after hours.

The entire campaign staff was made up of volunteers. Initially, campaign headquarters were set up in the Gilligan Funeral Home but later moved to a small storefront office opposite St. Francis de Sales's on Woodlawn. That office was managed by "Jimmy" Moyer, a past-president of the Cincinnati League of Women Voters and an energetic veteran of Charter politics. Tom Conlon Sr., a Cincinnati attorney and family friend, took charge of fund-raising; two junior faculty members at local colleges, Ed Wagner and George Wing, worked on position papers and research; and Patricia Kiefer, a student at Xavier University, organized the student volunteers who did much of the drudge work of the campaign. Gilligan's children were also among the volunteers, Hansan recalling sixteen-year-old Kathleen passing out campaign literature while wearing a straw boater. And, at every possible moment, the candidate was out, speaking to groups of thirty to fifty in neighborhood centers, churches, and ward clubs.

No one—save, perhaps, the candidate and some in the campaign—seriously believed that John Gilligan was going to win. Still, a campaign memorandum dated July 15, 1964, undertook to make the case. It stated that the First Congressional District had 584 precincts, including 235 in predominantly Democratic wards in Cincinnati. Another 250, in Cincinnati and close-in industrial suburbs, leaned fairly strongly Republican. And then there were "the Horrid Hundred"—the 100 rural Republican precincts that readily returned margins of 2–1 or 3–1 for the GOP. The memo identified three calls to action. First, the turnout in Cincinnati's predominantly Democratic wards ran 20 percent or more below that of the rest of the district; therefore, "a registration drive concentrating on those 235 Cincinnati precincts is of primary importance."[10] Second, the Democratic vote in the Horrid Hundred must be raised to 40 percent, which would require an "intensive personal campaign" by the candidate himself.[11] And third, Lyndon Johnson's "presence at the head of the ballot should add the additional five votes per precinct which would be needed to provide the margin of victory."[12]

Johnson was to prove enormously more helpful than that. Arguably, Gilligan's race for the U.S. Congress was decided by an event that took place 2,500 miles away: in San Francisco, in mid-July, when the Republicans nominated the conservative Barry Goldwater as their standard-bearer. Goldwater or not, a poll two Xavier University professors undertook in mid-September suggested that Gilligan's Republican opponent, Carl Rich, had little cause for concern. The poll was somewhat amateurish; it counted in one total the results of surveying done from July 19 to September 8. Still, the numbers were grim: Rich led Gilligan by 48 to 21 percent, with 31 percent undecided.

More usefully, the poll suggested a direction. Lyndon Johnson was running a full fifteen points ahead of Republican Barry Goldwater in the district, with voters generally endorsing the administration's stands on foreign affairs, civil rights, and poverty. Thus, the pollsters advised that Gilligan "identify himself with President Johnson and his platform" and, conversely, try to tie Carl Rich to Barry Goldwater.[13] It was hardly a novel approach; Democrat candidates nationally were measuring the likely length of Johnson's coattails, hoping they would prove sufficient to carry their own campaigns to victory. Nor was it difficult advice for Gilligan to accept, as he strongly supported the directions Johnson had taken since becoming president following Kennedy's assassination.

Rich made two missteps, which Gilligan turned to his advantage. To registered Democrats, Rich sent a suitable-for-framing version of John Kennedy's inaugural address. To registered Republicans, he sent, under congressional frank, a Department of Agriculture cookbook. Gilligan had little difficulty pointing to the hypocrisy of Rich, who had voted against most Kennedy-sponsored legislation, distributing Kennedy's best-known words and sending out cookbooks after having voted against the Food Stamp Act. Gilligan said it took considerable "gall to send cookbooks at taxpayer's expense . . . on how to cook chateaubriand and peaches flambé."[14]

Rich remained unruffled. It was, in fact, a relatively harmonious campaign. Gilligan commented: "His attitude toward me was: we'd served together on council; we knew each other; there no point in getting nasty about it. 'You go through your exercise, I'll go through mine and I'll be elected."[15] Rich, Gilligan believes, never seriously entertained the prospect of defeat. Rich may have remained confident because the Gilligan campaign had virtually no money to put behind the candidate's own energy and that of his volunteers.

In all likelihood, Gilligan's contributions were held down due to the residual bad feeling generated by his campaign against John Wiethe and the regular Democrats. Congressional campaigns in 1964 cost little by current standards, Gilligan's expenditures were minor even by the day's modest standards. They totaled only $19,000—including a $4,000 loan cosigned by Harry Gilligan and the candidate himself in the later stages of the campaign.

Gilligan remained optimistic. This, in part, was because local labor leaders—particularly, AFL-CIO's Bill Kircher and other labor leaders—United Steelworkers, United Rubber Workers, and Needle Trades—pushed their usually indifferent local membership, several times bringing in national union figures to boost Gilligan's candidacy. But even while there was optimism, there were no signs of pending victory. GOP leaders, Gilligan said, were "warning the local Republicans that this was a different year and you've got to get out there and vote because these 'mad dogs' are trying to take over—but that was pretty routine."[16]

On election night, the candidate and his campaign staff gathered at the Gibson Hotel to wait for the returns. From the first, the numbers were encouraging—enough so that Jack and Katie Gilligan, pleading exhaustion, wandered home before the final count was known. It was a clear victory: Gilligan ran up a 12,000-vote margin in the nineteen Cincinnati wards that were part of the First Congressional District and held his own in outlying areas. And while he failed to garner his 40 percent in the Horrid Hundred, his showing there was good enough to ensure his victory. (It is worth noting that in almost every ward or town, Gilligan ran ahead of the Democratic U.S. Senate candidate, Stephen A. Young.) The final count was Gilligan 74,525 and Rich 69,114.

In the end, the Johnson-Goldwater race proved to be a decisive factor in Gilligan's victory. The early campaign memo suggested that Lyndon Johnson's candidacy might mean five additional Gilligan votes per precinct; in the end it was more like two or three times that. In 1960, Ohio had given Republican Richard Nixon a quarter-million vote margin over John Kennedy; in 1964, Johnson swamped Goldwater statewide by a million votes, including Johnson's 26,209 vote margin in the First District.

However, Gilligan's congressional future was imperiled not long after his triumph. In January 1965, a Republican-controlled state apportionment board redrew the state's congressional districts. In doing so, 25,000 largely Republican suburbanites were added to Gilligan's district, and 5,000 Democratic-inclined voters in Cincinnati's inner city were removed. The district in which Gilligan would presumably seek reelection in 1966 would be, therefore, substantially more Republican. It had been a hard seat to win, and now, it would be an even harder one to keep.

14

The Great Society Congressman

The Washington, D.C., Jack Gilligan reached as a freshman congressman in January 1965 was a very different place from the federal capital city of today. The Mall, so splendidly developed since that time, did not yet include the National Air and Space Museum or the National Gallery's East Wing. Maya Lin's moving memorial to the nation's Vietnam War dead did not exist, as only a very few had then fallen in a conflict that would come to dominate the nation's political life. The Washington of 1965 was a rather provincial place—in John F. Kennedy's famous remark, "a city of southern efficiency and northern charm."[1]

Since Gilligan's congressional days, Washington has seen a double influx—first, a continuing flow of tens of thousands of educated young professionals who staff Congress, government offices, trade associations, lobbying firms, and everyone else for whom the business of America is government. Second, Washington has received a parallel though often not overlapping flow from Eritrea, Mexico, India, West Africa, El Salvador, and elsewhere. By and large, these new residents reenact the story of immigrant upward mobility: they work in tourist services and in construction; they drive cabs and wait tables; and, with startling regularity, they create for their children lives better than they themselves have had. And they have done much to make Washington an international, cosmopolitan city—a place of culture, shopping, and food. When John Gilligan reached Washington, it was all but impossible to buy either a bagel or a croissant anywhere in the city.

Kennedy's comment notwithstanding, in 1965 Washington, D.C., was a largely southern city and, despite a substantial black middle class, a largely segregated one. The prestigious Cosmos Club on Massachusetts Avenue did not admit blacks; the U.S. State Department, by report, had a running concern that African diplomats traveling by automobile between Washington and the United Nations in New York might be unable to secure overnight accommodation en route. There was a colonial aspect to life in Washington: the city lacked Home Rule and was effectively governed by a committee of Congress whose members, generally drawn from southern states, had no deep sympathy with the aspirations of its nonwhite inhabitants.

In 1965, the general and genteel quiet of the city was about to experience its most disquieting time since the early Roosevelt days three decades earlier. The 89th Congress was to be strongly associated with the Great Society, the most expansive extension of the role and responsibilities of the federal government since Franklin Roosevelt's New Deal. Part of the intellectual backdrop for this lay in three texts of peculiar consequence: *The Affluent Society* (1958), in which liberal economist John Kenneth Galbraith contrasted what he saw as the private opulence and public squalor of American life; *The Other America* (1962), in which Michael Harrington grimly detailed how short of universal that affluence was; and *Silent Spring* (1962), in which Rachel Carson started the environmental movement. What all these shared was the view that, within the general satisfaction of American success, vast problems existed, problems that could only be effectively addressed by an active and energized federal government.

Under Lyndon Johnson, the federal government moved along all these lines. The Great Society Congress of 1965–66 implemented the Voting Rights Act, Medicare, the Elementary and Secondary Education Act, the War on Poverty, Model Cities Program, national endowments for the arts and humanities, and major legislation to clean up the nation's water and air. This is, well after the fact, variously viewed as a series of needed acts, as a well-meant enterprise that became a casualty of the Vietnam War, or as an exercise in federal overreach. It was understood at the time, however, as "a liberal hour—a time in which government was in good favor with the American people, when Americans in unusually large numbers trusted the government in Washington to act responsibly on their behalf, when government seemed the proper repository for the nation's hopes, even its dreams."[2]

When Jack Gilligan reached Washington, the dominating facts of political life were the outsized figure of Lyndon Johnson and the huge majority of Democrats swept into Congress in LBJ's tidal wave victory the previous fall. The Democrats controlled the Senate by a margin of 68–32 and the House 295–140 (the latter including the extraordinary number of forty-eight new Democratic representatives). Gilligan first met with Johnson on December 9, 1964, when the freshmen class convened for a welcome and pep talk from the president. It was then when Gilligan felt that "the moment was at hand"—a Democratic president and a liberal-leaning Congress were aligned to make legislative history.[3]

President Johnson underscored the breadth of his intention in his State of the Union address on January 4, 1965. He described America's wealth—personal incomes had grown by more than 80 percent between 1945 and 1960—and then laid out the challenge: "We worked for two centuries to climb this peak of prosperity. But we are only at the beginning of the road to the Great Society. Ahead now is a summit where freedom from the wants of the body can help fulfill the needs of the spirit."[4] He urged that fundamental initiatives be framed in education, race relations, medicine, pollution, poverty, crime, and the arts. Johnson told the country, "For the first time in our history, it is possible to conquer poverty."[5]

From the first, John Joyce Gilligan adored being a Congressman. Not only was he on a much larger and more consequential stage, but the entire range of statecraft—discussing legislation, attending committee sessions, speaking on the House floor, casting his vote—greatly appealed to him. He admitted to being starry-eyed his first days in Congress: "I was just totally overwhelmed when I was first elected, wandering around the halls like a tourist."[6] But as his vision focused, Gilligan faced his initial tasks: secure a seat on a prominent committee, staff his office, and find a place to live.

Committee assignments are central to the lives of members of Congress. Gilligan's options were limited, however, as new members are rarely assigned to the most important committees. After conferring with his staff, Gilligan decided to seek a slot on the Committee on Interstate and Foreign Commerce, which held broad responsibilities for transportation, broadcasting, the stock exchanges, and public health. Gilligan put in his application and waited.

Some while later, by chance or otherwise, Gilligan ran into Speaker of the House John McCormack in a congressional corridor. Gilligan said, "Mr. Speaker, I would like to have the chance to introduce my father to you some day because you two have some things in common."[7] Speaker McCormack sought particulars. Gilligan offered that both of them were Knight Commanders in the Order of St. Gregory, both were Knights of Malta, and—perhaps the clincher—both were married to women named Blanche. With that, McCormick put an arm around Gilligan's shoulder and said, "My boy, come into my office and tell me what it is you want."[8] Gilligan got the appointment. But he may have had further assistance. Longtime family friend Bill Geoghegan was then with the Department of Justice, where, on Gilligan's behalf, he lobbied powerful Louisiana congressman Hale Boggs, who served on the body that made the committee assignments.

For the newly elected congressman, a principal task was staffing his Washington office. Gilligan first offered the key post of administrative assistant to his campaign manager, Jack Hansan. But Hansan, after seeking advice from a source experienced in Washington politics, was told that if Gilligan wanted to be reelected, he needed an assistant who knew Washington and so begged off.

In a somewhat uncharacteristic—for a congressman—move, Gilligan chose young PhDs as both his administrative assistant and chief legislative aide. As administrative assistant, he chose Dr. John Grupenhoff, the thirty-two-year-old Cincinnati native who had helped organize Gilligan's unsuccessful at-large congressional bid two years earlier. Following that defeat, Grupenhoff had been invited to join the Labor Education Research Service, a program for union officials at Ohio State University in Columbus. As chief legislative aide, Gilligan chose Dr. Edward

Wagner, a thirty-year-old history professor Gilligan knew from Xavier University and who had directed the speakers' bureau in Gilligan's congressional campaign.

The third key staff member was Margaret Moorhous, who Gilligan hired as his personal secretary and office manager. Moorhous knew Ohio well, having earlier served as executive secretary to Ohio governor Michael DiSalle; but she also had Capitol Hill experience working on the staffs of Texas congressman Homer Thornberry and California congressman Don Edwards. Gilligan also hired Lydia Hill as an assistant; she was one of the few African Americans then employed in Congress. Grupenhoff recalled, "I looked around at that time at the other congressional offices, and there sure weren't many black people working in them. Jack kind of led on that."[9] Other staffers included Susan Geoghegan, Alice Gordon, and Patricia Orth. Gilligan and his staff shared a two-room office on the fourth floor of the Cannon Building, which, as it was the oldest and least luxurious of the congressional office buildings, was the repository of many first-term members.

Even as he moved into his new offices, Gilligan knew he could hardly count on a long lease on the space. As the *Cincinnati Post and Times-Star* put it, the new congressman was "aware that his narrow win over Rep. Carl Rich last November in the Johnson landslide put him in an insecure perch."[10] From the start, Gilligan hoped to stabilize that perch by being a high-profile presence in his district. To that end, he moved quickly—on January 11, 1965—to establish in Cincinnati's main post office the first constituent services office in the district's history. The office was placed in the charge of Thomas Walker, a former assistant city solicitor of the near-in Cincinnati suburb of Norwood. Its three members pushed Gilligan's staffing allowance to within a few dollars of the $68,000 limit.

Among those who did not follow the new congressman to Washington were Gilligan's wife and children. Jack and Katie Gilligan made the decision that their then four teenage children should remain in school in Cincinnati. There was, Gilligan commented later, no really good option—there were disadvantages both to leaving his family in Cincinnati and relocating his children to new schools in Washington.

The brunt of the burden, of course, was felt by Katie Gilligan. Daughter Kathleen recalled, "All the kids were pretty busy by that point: my brother was a senior in high school; I was a junior; my younger brother was a sophomore; and Ellen was in eighth grade. As teenagers, we had active and engaged lives that did not necessarily revolve around our parents anymore."[11] John said, "My mother was a very shy person—smart, socially committed. She had three kids in high school when her husband was in Washington, with people saying mean things about him. That was difficult."[12] At the same time, Kathleen added, "she did a great job of never translating what had to be her frustration that dad was gone or busy a lot. That was not a topic of family conversation. However difficult it may have been for her, she did not put a lot of that on us."[13]

In Washington, in fact, Gilligan's was a bachelor's existence. On the recommendation of a senior congressman, he secured quarters at the University Club, five
blocks north of the White House on Sixteenth Street and just around the corner
from the *Washington Post* Offices. The club was favored as a residence for congressmen; indeed, it was also the gathering place for Supreme Court Chief Justice Earl
Warren and Justice Hugo Black during their days on the bench. Gilligan remained
there the two years he served in Congress, sharing quarters and evening meals with
a dozen or so fellow members from both sides of aisle. Most were Democrats, but,
as Gilligan noted, the resident Republicans were cordial with a bipartisanship that
has since largely been lost. Gilligan recalled that "from the outset, I decided that
whatever happened, I was going to try to make my presence count."[14] He joined
the Democratic Study Group, a caucus of the more liberal Democrats in the House,
and attended that body's briefings on a range of domestic subjects. He was, his administrative assistant, John Grupenhoff recalled, always busy—at his own or other
committee meetings, studying bills, meeting with constituents, making his presence
known to senior members.

Gilligan's first accomplishment was a minor one: the republication of an out-
of-print volume containing all the amendments and correspondence related to the
1787 Constitutional Convention. Gilligan's first official act was as the House sponsor of a resolution that led to the republication. More substantively, Gilligan sponsored a major amendment to the Johnson administration's substantial proposal in
the area of mental health and mental retardation. His amendment directed that
states receiving federal funds for mental retardation programs could not reduce
the levels of their own funding for such programs below what they had spent the
previous year. John Grupenhoff recalled Gilligan returning from a hearing to announce that his amendment had been accepted by Wilbur Cohen, the deputy secretary of the Department of Health, Education, and Welfare: "He was prancing up
and down. He was very pleased."[15]

Characteristically, Gilligan discussed pending matters with his staff before for-
mulating his own positions. Ed Wagner tracked current legislation and its related
correspondence and helped draft measures to be introduced and amendments to be
offered by Gilligan. Grupenhoff coordinated the routine work of the office. Grupenhoff also had the time-consuming chore of shepherding visiting constituents to the
House floor. Grupenhoff recalled: "I'd take the visitors over to the Congress to see
what was going on. We'd take the underground railroad [that connects the Cannon
Building to the Capitol]. Gilligan wanted to make sure that every constituent felt
welcome, regardless of party. So I'd take them over and bring them back. I bet I did
that once a day, every day. It always took an hour or two."[16] And one of the secretaries opened and read the mail—which was divided among the few personal letters,
a larger number expressing opinions on any subject before Congress, and a great

many reporting constituents' problems obtaining Social Security payments, veterans' benefits, and the like. Commonly, she marked key passages in yellow highlight, ran them past the congressman, and sent out a reply. In Gilligan's two-year term, 29,000 pieces of mail came in.

Asked what the young congressman did in Washington other than work, Grupenhoff said, "What I remember about free time was that there wasn't any—he was running all the time."[17] Gilligan, Grupenhoff said, carried a stack of three-by-five cards on all the meetings he was supposed to be attending. Evenings, Grupenhoff added, were generally spent in the office: "That was Gilligan's downtime."[18]

The new congressman did take time to pay one social call—on Alice Roosevelt Longworth. The daughter of a president and the widow of a one-time Speaker of the House, Mrs. Longworth had been an observer of virtually the whole of America's twentieth-century political life—on which she commented with a rather arched wisdom. (The adage for which she was best known was an admonition: "If you can't say anything good about someone, sit right here by me."[19]) Early in his term, Gilligan telephoned Mrs. Longworth, introduced himself as the congressman holding her late husband's seat, and asked if he might call on her. Mrs. Longworth said, "Certainly." Gilligan went to her Washington home near DuPont Circle on Massachusetts Avenue, where he was admitted to her second-floor sitting room. When Gilligan entered, Mrs. Longworth was sitting on a small couch on which rested an embroidered pillow that read, "If you can't say anything good about someone, sit right here by me." Gilligan sat instead on a small chair near the fireplace. The pair talked of the Cincinnati of her husband's years.[20]

Though a freshman, Gilligan passed on the backseat role generally assigned to and assumed by first-termers. On April 1, 1965, he introduced a measure to extend educational benefits to veterans who had served since the GI Bill had expired in 1955. As he told the House, it was "only equitable to regard those who have defended this country in the last ten years in the same way we sympathetically viewed the World War II and Korean veterans."[21] The nation, he said, had three million such "unremembered" veterans; in 1963, 210,000 of them had received unemployment compensation totaling $96 million—a "disgrace" that in part reflected the federal government's failure to provide such educational opportunities as had been made available to earlier veterans. He noted that the GI Bill had financed the educations of 625,000 engineers and 375,000 teachers and that the proposed expenditure for post–Korean War veterans was not only just but a sound investment. The measure, known as the Cold War GI Bill, was signed into law by President Johnson on March 3, 1966.

Addressing the House, Gilligan was an assured and occasionally acerbic speaker—as when on May 11, 1965, he argued against retention of Section 14(b) of the Taft-Hartley Act, which allowed states to ban the union shop. Gilligan called attention to a quarter-page ad in the *New York Times* paid for by a group calling itself the Citizens Committee to Preserve Taft-Hartley and, with mock seriousness, proclaimed himself delighted that this group wanted to "safeguard an employee's right to make a free choice regarding union membership."[22] He wondered, he said, who the fine individuals supporting this viewpoint might be. Sadly, Gilligan added, he was "shocked" by the first name of the list of cochairmen, A. D. David, president of the Winn-Dixie Stores, which, through subsidiaries, operated 600 retail supermarkets nationwide.

While he did not wish to question Mr. David's commitment to employee rights, he said, he informed the House that Winn-Dixie had, several months earlier, been found guilty by the National Labor Relations Board (NLRB) of four unfair labor practices, including illegally interrogating workers over their desire to join a union and threatening to close individual stores if employees voted to unionize. When Winn-Dixie "refused to abide by this [NLRB] finding," NLRB attorneys, he said, had taken the company to the Sixth Circuit Court of Appeals , which, on February 27, 1965, supported the federal agency's finding.[23] It was, Gilligan concluded, a "sad day . . . when a company that has broken a national law, piously preaches about preserving a law it has so flagrantly violated."[24]

Matters of particular personal political interest aside, Gilligan was an almost "straight ticket" supporter of Lyndon Johnson's Great Society. Reflecting on his votes, Gilligan said: "There were a lot of pieces [of Great Society legislation] that I was strongly for, others that I was okay with. Nothing that came up that I was opposed to."[25]

Gilligan's support for the administration's measures was particularly strong on labor, education, and civil rights issues. As a sign of this, on June 7, 1965, Gilligan placed into the congressional record the speech recently delivered by President Johnson at Washington's predominantly black Howard University. Regarded as one of Johnson's most important, it was a hallmark statement of the liberal view on racial discrimination in America, its causes and consequences, and the measures needed to ameliorate it. In his own remarks, Gilligan deemed the speech "of the greatest historic importance to the Nation and the world. I do not presume too much in saying this, or in stating it should be read as a manifesto for all men of all time who genuinely believe in democracy and the institutions of freedom."[26]

Shortly thereafter, on August 3, 1965, Gilligan voted for the landmark Voting Rights Act. This legislation, which passed the House by a 335–85 margin, extended federal protection to an estimated four million black Americans largely in southern states that had largely disenfranchised them. At about that same time he voted to extend unemployment benefits, to increase the federally required minimum wage, and to extend federal aid to education.

Even with things going largely the Democrats' way, Gilligan, Grupenhoff reported, "would get very frustrated when things went slowly."[27] He was persuaded by the urgency of the moment. He was particularly critical of himself: "He was always so upset when he had to make a decision, when he had to respond to one of Lyndon Johnson's requests when [he knew] they were not going to be popular back in Cincinnati . . . Jack commented to me that he'd never be back for another term. As a congressman, Jack said, you had to follow somebody. You have to deal with the complexity and move things along."[28]

By the time Congress broke for its summer recess, Katie Gilligan, Grupenhoff recalled, thought her husband was working too hard, was spending too much time in Washington. She was pleased that he would be taking several weeks off and spending time at the family cottage in Michigan. (Katie Gilligan, not a typical "politician's wife," according to Grupenhoff, was quite shrewd behind her quiet demeanor and more than a bit of her husband's protector.) Sons Donald and John spent part of the summer at Leland, with Donald anticipating entrance into Harvard that fall. But daughters Kathleen and Ellen came to Washington for "what was sort of an adventure."[29] They lived in a high-rise apartment building in the city's southwestern quadrant just below I-395. Among the things Ellen remembers from the summer was forming a close friendship with a girl from the apartment building: "We became great friends and would go places together."[30] The girl was of mixed race, and at the time, Ellen recalled, casual strangers tended to treat this as an oddity.

The problems of having a separated family wore on them all. Gilligan admitted, "It was very stressful. I was intoxicated with Washington; I enjoyed the House and everything about it. I was thrusting the whole burden of the family on Katie."[31] Indeed, Gilligan missed family life. He recalled declaring to Katie at one point that if he were reelected, "the family should come to Washington. I wasn't going to continue that separate arrangement for another two years."[32]

For many Democrats, the War in Vietnam began as something no larger than a cloud the size of man's hand over a rice paddy. At that time, however, most Democrats in Congress were more concerned with taking full advantage of the "liberal hour" afforded by their party's large majority than with a distant war that in the briefings then being made appeared to be winnable, or at least necessary. For many of them, the developing war in Vietnam was not a concern.

Early in Gilligan's term, John Grupenhoff sought advice from Benjamin Cohen, who had first come to Washington as one of Franklin Roosevelt's "bright young men" and had stayed on and become a Washington institution. The pair met for lunch at the fashionable Iron Gate restaurant on N Street in the city's downtown. Grupenhoff, describing himself as an outsider in Washington, asked what issues Cohen thought Gilligan should focus on. Cohen replied, "In my eye, there's only one, and that's what we're doing in Vietnam. I'm going to tell you: it will tear the country apart."[33] Grupenhoff recalled being startled by this; "people in Cincinnati were strongly in support of the war at that time."[34]

As, at the time, was Gilligan. He voiced that support both in the newsletters sent to his district and in his correspondence with constituents. In April 1965, he replied

to Margaret van Selle of Cincinnati, "I very frankly cannot see how we can pull
out of South Vietnam at this time and abandon the country to a state of anarchy
which surely would collapse. We have a moral commitment to South Vietnam to
lend whatever assistance we can when the situation calls for it to protect the territorial integrity and political independence against subversion and aggression directed
from without."[35] In August, a letter writer sought Gilligan's view of recent speeches
opposing the conflict by Senators Wayne Morse and George McGovern. Gilligan
said he had read the speeches, but "from all the information available to me it seems
as though the Senators have selected facts to confirm a conclusion they already had
reached."[36] Gilligan acknowledged experiencing some frustration on the subject. In
December 1965, he replied to Cincinnatian Edward Coyne, "While I am dissatisfied and disturbed with present conditions and policies . . . there has not been any
acceptable alternative presented. It would seem that until North Vietnam, which is
clearly an agent of Red China, decides that it will negotiate, we can do nothing else
but continue to assist South Vietnam against aggression and subversion."[37] He attempted to draw a line against broadening the conflict; when a hawkish constituent
urged that North Vietnamese ports be bombed or blockaded, he responded that
such steps would prompt serious international complications. Gilligan's position
on Vietnam was at this time is probably best summarized by his statement to Mr.
Coyne: he was dissatisfied, disturbed, and yet saw no better alternative.

For many liberal Democrats, what was most important mid-decade was the energy and skill with which Lyndon Johnson was moving major legislation through
Congress. In December 1965 and January 1966, Gilligan voted with a 237–142 majority against killing the Inter-American Development Bank; voted with the 257–
165 majority in favor of the Appalachian Regional Development Act; voted with a
263–153 majority for the Elementary and Secondary Education Act; voted with the
313–115 majority to approve Medicare; voted with the 221–203 majority to repeal
Article 14b of the Taft-Hartley Act; voted with the 249–148 majority to approve the
foreign aid bill—as well as various lesser measures.

While Gilligan regarded Lyndon Johnson as a highly skilled legislative leader,
he was not someone Gilligan ever fully took to heart—certainly not as he had
John Kennedy. He was a willing enough spear-carrier on behalf of the administration, but he questioned whether the man leading the charge was much interested
in those in the ranks. John Grupenhoff described LBJ as "so forceful he was like
a volcano; when you approached him, you thought he was about to burst."[38] A
lot of younger congressmen, Gilligan claimed, "resented the way Johnson simply
ran over them. He may have taken some of the senior members of Congress into
account and explained to them what he was doing and why, but for the freshmen
and some of the other junior members, the orders were simply issued from the
White House to line up and vote."[39]

Gilligan's view of his party's leader is suggested by an anecdote he told in an interview. Johnson, he said, strove to break people to his will. One day, the new French ambassador came to the Oval Office to present his credentials. To the diplomat's delight, Johnson invited him to stay to lunch following a brief swim in the White House pool. Johnson strode off toward the pool, stripping off his clothing on the way. By the time the president jumped into the water, he was stark naked. Addressing the ambassador, Gilligan related, Johnson said, "C'mon in! The water's fine." The newly credentialed French ambassador could not bring himself to strip down and jump in. The moral of the tale, Gilligan said, was that "from then on that ambassador was putty in his hands."[40]

Longtime congressional leader Sam Rayburn of Texas said that a politician's first job was to get elected; his second job was to get reelected. A reelection confirms the voters' original judgment; more important, with a second term the advantages of seniority start to accumulate, and the path ahead eases. Gilligan later reported that as a first-term congressman, the need to get reelected "was a very prominent part of my life."[41] And Gilligan was doubtless mindful of an additional fact: his Great Society voting record might prove something of a hard sell in a district that leaned strongly Republican.

One part of Gilligan's strategy was to paint himself as an effective advocate for his district. In addition to the constituent office, he established a constituent newsletter, in the first issue of which he asserted, "I want to create a two-way pipeline to Washington to make the national government more aware of the problems of the District, and to bring you closer to your national government."[42] He used the newsletter for constituent education—well-written essays providing an overview on the U.S. federal budget or on how personal income in America was significantly outdistancing inflation. And in it he also promoted the success of the Kennedy-Johnson economic policies with which he was associated. America, one newsletter stated, "has experienced the five greatest years of prosperity ever known by any nation in history!" The gross national product had increased 45 percent; seven million jobs had been added; after-tax personal income had risen 42 percent.[43]

In his newsletter, Gilligan showed his admiration of John Kennedy, offering this quote: "I do not believe that any of us would exchange places with any other people or any other generation. The energy, the faith, the devotion we bring to this endeavor will light our country and all who serve it; and the glow from that fire can truly light the world."[44] This was the heady view of liberalism at that time: Gilligan shared it, and to an extent hoped to inculcate his constituents with it.

Of more consequence was Gilligan's direct engagement with problem solving back home in his district. He traveled to Cincinnati several times a month. He was determined to be a presence to his constituents, sponsoring and attending meetings and conferences with various interest groups. In February and March of 1965 alone he met with representatives of the University of Cincinnati School of Medicine on the possibility of locating a federally financed research center there;

with parties concerned about the threatened closing of the regional office of the Veterans Administration; with local educators to describe benefits available under the Elementary and Secondary Education Act; with boaters and tow barge operators on safety problems on the Ohio River; and with city officials on issues related to urban renewal. Cincinnati mayor Eugene Ruehlmann credited Gilligan with providing important door-opening assistance to city officials seeking federal cooperation with Cincinnati's Riverfront Stadium project.[45]

A second part of Gilligan's reelection strategy—perhaps less intentional—was to build his stature in Washington. Though a freshman, Gilligan was, in political terms, something of a head turner. The first to notice—neither surprisingly nor perhaps persuasively—was his own staff. His administrative assistant, John Grupenhoff, said, "What was really interesting was how all the staff were already projecting in their minds that some day he could be president. I remember Margaret Moorhous saying, 'I've been around politicians for a long time—he's really big-time, he could be president if he continues with it.'"[46]

Gilligan was one of forty-eight freshman Democrats. These legislative classmen felt a strong sense of cohesion; they met frequently, and all of them typically supported Johnson's major legislative initiatives by overwhelming—at times, decisive—margins. "These freshmen had not been there before; they had no real background or standing in Washington. I think they were convinced that Johnson and the Democratic Party were onto something, that this was the wave of the future and they'd be well advised to get aboard and to support it. Some did it out of conviction; some did it out of a sense of electoral salvation."[47] Gilligan, Grupenhoff commented, "clearly was just the natural leader of this group."[48] It was in Gilligan's small office in the Cannon Building where groups of freshmen representatives would huddle up to hear Gilligan lead the strategy session or speak to the topic of the day.

Gilligan was hardly immune to ambition. It was clear to Grupenhoff and others that Gilligan had set his eye on a U.S. Senate seat; indeed, there was a standing joke in Gilligan's office that if the congressman was AWOL, he could probably be tracked down in the Senate gallery. But ambition and the high estimation of one's own staff are hardly rare in Washington, and hardly likely in themselves to lead to prominence. A legislator's knowledge on issues may well affect his standing, but such awareness frequently falls beyond the knowledge of the average voter. Public reputations are more likely to be established through the press. And it was here that Gilligan made an impression, beginning with David Broder, then with the *New York Times* and one of the nation's ranking political journalists.

On December 12, 1965, still in his first year in office, Gilligan received the kind of attention that can make a career: David Broder profiled the first-term congressman from Ohio in the *New York Times Sunday Magazine,* with Gilligan's photo adorning the issue's front cover. Broder had made it a habit, when no deadline pressed, to go over to Congress and talk informally with its members. He made a point, he said, of seeing Gilligan rather frequently: "He had a much clearer sense of what his agenda was—education and economic development—than did most of the people who entered in that big class."[49]

Ostensibly, Broder's article was about how the forty-eight Democratic freshmen elected with Johnson would fare in the 1966 congressional elections. Those districts, he wrote, "will be a testing ground of new personalities and new political techniques."[50]

> More than that, these contests will be referendums on public acceptance of the altered relationship between the Federal government and the local community that is at the root of the Great Society. Finally, they will measure the voters' willingness to return a set of Congressmen whose claim is less that they are spokesmen for their constituencies' principals and prejudices than that they are effective brokers of their interests in Washington.[51]

The fate of the Democratic freshmen in 1966, Broder contended, would go far to determine Democrats' strength in the next Congress. He described the arsenal of weapons the Democratic National Committee was putting in the hands of its most vulnerable members: a desktop system to relay news reports to radio stations in their districts, leased teletype lines to transmit statements to local newspapers, and television broadcasting capabilities for which scripts and special guests were made available.

But Gilligan, given his normally Republican district, was the article's focus. Broder described Gilligan as "a tall, florid-faced, quick moving man," "a serious fellow" whose reelection could hardly be assumed.[52] He pointed out that in 1964 Lyndon Johnson had carried the district by 26,209 votes; Gilligan was elected by just 5,411 votes. Worse for Gilligan was the Republicans' redistricting, which, Broder wrote, "added more than enough Republicans to Gilligan's district to erase his margin of victory."[53] Broder quoted a Republican charge against Gilligan that he had voted for thirty-seven of thirty-eight Johnson administration measures, a voting record considerably more liberal than his district. Broder said that "to counter the inevitable criticism [that they are rubber stamps], they need more than good arguments; they need good works."[54] He cited Gilligan's various efforts: the Small Business Administration office opened in Cincinnati, Bureau of the Budget approval for a medical research facility to be located near the University of Cincinnati, the award to a local General Electric plant of a $750 million Air Force contract to build jet engines, and others measures for which the congressman would seek credit. Perhaps reflecting these efforts, Broder wrote that he found a surprising tolerance of the liberal Democrat in Cincinnati's business community. He quoted Charles Staab, executive vice president of the *Cincinnati Enquirer* and president of the Chamber of

Commerce: "I'm not a Democrat, but I think his record is exceptional. He's always been in the forefront and he's not shy about letting people know it. He knows how to open doors and he knows the people behind the doors."[55]

The article turned to Gilligan's prospects in 1966 and a possible opponent—Robert Taft Jr., grandson of a president and son of a senator. In 1964, only one thing had stood between Taft and a seat in the U.S. Senate; unfortunately for Taft, that "thing" was Lyndon Johnson. Taft lost by a mere 17,000 to incumbent Stephen A. Young. Broder published a prediction that reflected the intimate nature of Cincinnati politics. It came from Charles Phelps Taft, Gilligan's one-time fellow Charterite on city council and Robert Taft's uncle: "I think Gilligan could beat any Republican who's held that seat in the past ten years. Against Bob, I don't know."[56]

Gilligan was "delighted" with the piece—as well he should have been.[57] It raised him from the ranks of the deeply obscure members of Congress to those on whom an eye might be kept. (Broder and Gilligan and their wives, Ann and Katie, became and remained friends.) The New York Times magazine piece had further consequences. It was read in Cambridge, Massachusetts, by a Harvard law school student named James Friedman and in Dayton by a political reporter named Bob Daley. Both, by their own statements, filed it away as of possible future interest. In 1968, Friedman was an early organizer of Gilligan's bid for the U.S. Senate; Daley signed on as that campaign's traveling press secretary.

In Congress, the Johnson legislation kept moving. The second session, though considerably less active than the first, witnessed passage of the Urban Mass Transportation Act, the Highway and Motor Vehicle Safety acts, the federal minimum wage increase, the creation of the Departments of Transportation and the Model Cities Program, and the Truth-in-Packaging and Truth-in Labeling acts.

The labeling legislation was of particular interest to Gilligan in that it was of particular interest to Procter & Gamble, a prime employer in Gilligan's district. The labeling requirement—familiar today to anyone who looks at the back of almost any item on a supermarket shelf—drew only limited opposition from the food and consumer products industries. Packaging was another matter. The bill as drafted would have empowered the Federal Trade Commission to mandate standard sizes for consumer items (in theory, everything might come in half-pound, one-pound, or five-pound packages). Consumer advocates argued that the myriad packages being vended—one inquisitive researcher identified fifty-seven separate sizes of toothpaste in a single store—made it unnecessarily difficult for consumers to judge relative value.

Here, however, the soap and detergent industry lobbyists dug in. Packaging, they claimed, was a central aspect of marketing; thereby, government-mandated sizing would restrict their legitimate business activity. They made their case, among others, to Gilligan, who recalled, "I thought they had a real point. They had so many different products—liquids, powders, whatever else. Any time the contents were changed, they'd have to go a different box. I thought it was unnecessary and ridiculous."[58] He was also sensitive to the concerns of businesses that employed so many of his constituents. Gilligan agreed to offer an amendment to sharply tone down the package size requirements. He lined up support from fellow freshmen on the committee and presented to administration officials the reasons for industry's opposition. Though a first-termer, Gilligan was credited with playing a major role in the administration's subsequent retreat on the issue.

In March 1966, Jack Gilligan was, at least publicly, a continued supporter of the administration's war aims in Vietnam. In his constituent newsletter of that month, he quoted the Truman Doctrine as committing the United States to "support free peoples who are resisting attempted subjugation by armed minorities or by outside pressures"—which, to his mind, meant continued military support to the government of South Vietnam.[59] He further argued that the nation could afford the war without jeopardizing the nation's obligations at home: Vietnam's current cost, about 1.5 percent of the country's GNP, was proportionally less than the Korean conflict had cost. But he was beginning to hedge his support. On March 15 he voted with the overwhelming 389 to 3 majority to approve supplemental funding for the war but joined with 102 members of Congress in signing a statement "making it clear that our vote was not to be interpreted as endorsing an escalation in military action, or any broadening of the scope of hostilities."[60] His press release closed, "Firmness and restraint must remain our watchwords."[61]

Vietnam was to become—if it wasn't already—an anguishing issue for the nation. For many—particularly liberal Democrats who supported the broad outlines of the Great Society legislation—views on the war moved incrementally from clear support, to private misgivings, to public doubts, to open opposition.

Gilligan's personal turning point came in mid-1966 when he and a group of younger congressman who had grown unhappy with the unfolding of events in Southeast Asia pushed for a congressional fact finding tour of the war zone. Gilligan, however, had reasons beyond curiosity or conscientiousness for going: his possible 1966 opponent, Robert Taft Jr., was being dispatched to Vietnam as a special correspondent by *Readers' Digest*. Gilligan said, "When I saw that, I figured I'm going to hear for the rest of the campaign that he knew all about Vietnam and I didn't."[62]

This delegation of fourteen junior congressmen was duly dispatched on an eight-day trip, sent as a body of the House with instructions to report back to Speaker John McCormick. The delegation left Washington, D.C., on July 2, 1966, reaching Vietnam two days later. There, after briefings from U.S. Ambassador Henry Cabot Lodge and theater commander General William Westmoreland, the group visited U.S. and Korean military forces at Cam Rahn Bay, Qui Nhon, Kahn Khe, and Dak To. At their request, Gilligan and Congressmen John Anderson of

Illinois and Robert Duncan of Oregon spent a day in the Mekong Delta region southwest of Saigon.

Evidenced by a later constituent newsletter, Gilligan was still keeping his doubts off the public record. While he routinely noted that his eight-day trip did not make him an "expert," nonetheless, "my conviction is that the people of South Vietnam without exception want the Americans to stay and help them defend their freedom."[63] He wrote that "no one who had made that delta trip could hold the opinion that the Viet Cong are a band of patriotic liberators of the people. Every few hundred feet along the roads were craters where land mines had been detonated; by each bridge and culvert we saw miserably inadequate little mud forts manned each night by local peasants in an effort to protect the roadways from marauding Viet Cong."[64] Gilligan concluded his report to his constituents: "Back in Washington, President Johnson, Vice President Humphrey and Speaker McCormack questioned us during a two-hour session in the Cabinet Room. There was no significant disagreement among the fourteen Congressmen about the U.S. role in Vietnam."[65]

Gilligan's private thoughts, however, were at odds with his stated public position. In a 2008 interview, he spoke of being startled by how poor security was in Saigon: "We were instructed by those with experience that if something came through your window at night and your room was lower than the fifth floor, then you could be reasonably certain it was a hand grenade. The recommended response was to roll out of bed and take the mattress with you, so the mattress was on top of you when the grenade went off."[66] There were firefights almost every night in Saigon—"usually a couple of guys, but it was a little unnerving."[67]

On the visit to the Mekong Delta, Gilligan and his companions stayed with an officer of the U.S. Agency for International Development. The officer was stationed in a small village; his hut, Gilligan recalled, had two kinds of screens over the windows—a fine mesh screen for mosquitoes and a heavy mesh screen for hand grenades. The official was "pretty jaundiced: we weren't making any headway and the Viet Cong were making a lot of headway."[68] He told the congressmen that the local populace did not so much support the Viet Cong as they were terrified of it; the South Vietnamese army was regarded as next to useless. More generally, Gilligan noted that pessimism was inversely proportional to rank: lead figures such as Westmoreland and Lodge were upbeat, while the lower the rank an officer had, the less likely he was to share that assessment.

Lost in the shuffle, perhaps, was that the delegation had been charged with delivering its report to Speaker McCormick. Instead, homeward bound, the delegation was instructed to go immediately to the White House to meet with President Johnson in the cabinet room. There, Johnson shook hands with the fourteen jet-lagged congressmen and asked for their report. As Gilligan much later recalled, all expressed reservations, ranging from hedged uncertainty to the flat statement that the United States could not win and should get out. "Johnson was furious. He said something to the effect that it was easy for a congressman to say whatever he wanted, but 'I'm the president of the United States and I've got this burden to bear and, goddamn it, I'm going to get it done.' And he dismissed us."[69] Gilligan recalled all those present as being sympathetic to the president: "He was a wounded tiger, and he was clearly suffering and he didn't know what the hell to do."[70]

Gilligan shared his doubts with his family. Kathleen remembers her father as "really shaken" by the trip. There was, Gilligan told his elder daughter, "a very serious disconnect between the formal presentation the president was giving people and what was actually happening."[71] It was not simply a matter of politics for the Gilligan family: Donald and John were, or were approaching, draft age. College deferments would keep them out of the military for the short-term, but the longer term was unclear. Their sister vividly recalled that "I think [my father] was really in agony about what in the world was going on."[72]

Kathleen Gilligan was herself getting ready to head for Washington, where she would start classes that fall at Trinity College, an all-female Roman Catholic institution. She had visited a number of institutions in the Boston area, where her brother was in college, but she had enjoyed her earlier time in Washington and liked the thought of attending school just across town from where her father was serving in Congress.

Gilligan went public with his private doubts on the situation in Vietnam. On October 5, 1966, he urged President Johnson to suspend the bombing of North Vietnam, a step Gilligan hoped would prompt a reciprocal move toward negotiations. The wording of his statement suggests how hesitant Gilligan and other like-minded Democrats were to break with the leader of their party. He acknowledged that two previous cessations had failed to lead to negotiations and praised the administration's "unremitting effort" to secure peace" and reminded that "not once since 1954 have the Communists taken a single conciliatory step."[73] He closed his statement: "As a nation we must show the same resolute courage in seeking peace, as is shown by our men in the fields and skies of Vietnam, and as is daily demonstrated by the citizens of that unhappy land."[74]

Those comments came a bare four weeks before what, for Gilligan's congressional career, was a make-or-break election. That election would in fair measure turn on the congruence of Gilligan's views on Vietnam—and a host of other issues—with those living in Ohio's First Congressional District.

15

Defeat

In the fall of 1966, John Gilligan was hoping—and campaigning hard—to be the first Democrat to achieve reelection to Ohio's First Congressional District since Milton Sayler in 1876. Two factors complicated Gilligan's task from the start. One was that he ran in 1964 on a ticket headed by Lyndon Johnson, whose tidal-wave victory greatly eased Gilligan's task. Gilligan would have no such help in 1966. In 1966, Lyndon Johnson and his Great Society had passed their peak of popularity; moreover, the top Ohio race was for governor, and the very popular incumbent Republican James Rhodes was expected to win in a landslide and boost his party's candidates all down the line.

Then there was the redistricting. In 1964, fully 75 percent of the First District's registered voters resided in Cincinnati; for the 1966 contest, that figure dropped to 41 percent, a share that was offset by gains made in more Republican areas. The net effect was a likely shift toward the Republicans of 8,200 votes—a total half again as large as Gilligan's 1964 margin of victory.[1] And there was a third factor. After initial uncertainty, Robert Taft Jr., chose to challenge Gilligan's for the First Congressional District seat.

It is difficult to overstate the standing of the Tafts in Cincinnati, which tended to regard the family as the city's bequest to the nation. The Tafts came fairly early to the Queen City. Ishbel Ross's family history engagingly notes, "Alphonso Taft arrived in Cincinnati from Vermont in 1838 with a box of law books, a degree from Yale, and a strong strain of ambition."[2] Indeed, law, Yale, and ambition marked the family's next three generations. From early on, the Tafts had position. In 1877, the same year in which Patrick Gilligan founded the family funeral home, Alphonso Taft was serving as attorney general in the cabinet of Ulysses S. Grant. And to position, the family added wealth, much of which came when the first Charles Phelps Taft married Annie Sinton, heiress to a considerable fortune derived from the iron business. The most famous Taft was Alphonso's son, William Howard, president and, later, Chief

Justice of the Supreme Court. Taft was prodigiously able, hard-working, and large. (He bears the peculiar distinction of being the last person who, in being elected president, weighed more in pounds, 330, than he received in electoral votes, 321.)

William Howard's children were themselves nothing if not able. Sons Robert and Charles both graduated first in their law school classes at Yale, where Helen, their sister, earned a doctorate in history. The brothers were markedly different in outlook. Charles was a reformer—an early and longtime Charterite, a booster of all good causes, and the first layman to serve as chairman of the National Council of Churches. Robert was a party regular; after service in the state legislature, he entered the U.S. Senate in 1940. And where Charles was voluble, Robert was terse. Once asked what Americans should do about the high cost of meat, Robert Taft famously replied, "Eat less."[3] On occasion, politics was thicker than blood. For instance, when Charles Taft sought the Ohio Republican nomination as governor in 1952, Robert Taft declined to endorse him.

The family had other irons in the fire, too. Hulbert Taft, son of Peter and Annie Taft, was longtime editor of the *Times-Star,* owned by his parents. The paper was deeply conservative and lent continuing editorial support to Robert Taft's ambitions. With time, family enterprises extended to include Taft Broadcasting, which operated major radio and television outlets.

In the Senate, Robert Taft rose to leader of the Senate Republicans and became the acknowledged voice of midwestern conservatism. Three times he sought his party's nomination for president. In 1952—the year before he died of cancer—Taft secured 500 first ballot delegate votes at the Republican convention, a figure falling not far short of the first ballot total of 577 secured by the eventual nominee, General Dwight Eisenhower. In 1958, when the U.S. Senate unveiled portraits of those it regarded as its greatest members, Taft was among those honored, along with Henry Clay, Daniel Webster, John Calhoun, and Robert La Follette.

By then, another Taft was on the political scene. In 1954, Robert Taft Jr., the senator's son, was elected to the Ohio state legislature. This apparently local event merited nearly a full column of flattering coverage from the *New York Times:* Young Taft, the paper noted, had "learned his lessons" politically, had a party loyalty "not unmixed with a certain independence of spirit," and was reminiscent of his grandfather, the president, "in his warmth of personality and sense of humor."[4] And young Bob was modest. The *New York Times* noted that some Ohio Republicans had wished to appoint him to his father's U.S. Senate seat after the elder Robert's death, but the younger Taft preferred to work his way up. And this he had done, becoming Republican floor leader in the Ohio House of Representatives in 1961 and the state's at-large congressman the following year. Having lost narrowly in the 1964 U.S. Senate race, Taft was now trying to reenter the political arena.

John Gilligan's life in Cincinnati variously crossed paths with the Taft legacy. His high school graduation ceremonies were held at the Taft Auditorium; he was a regular visitor to the Taft Museum; and in 1966 he and his family lived at 1875 William Howard Taft Road, a minor offshoot of William Howard Taft Boulevard. And that same year, he was challenged for his congressional seat by Robert Taft Jr.

The Gilligan-Taft standoff drew unusual attention for a congressional race, garnering lengthy coverage in *TIME*, the *New York Times,* and the *Washington Post.* Writing in the *Washington Post,* David Broder called it "one of the most fascinating off-year contests in history."[5] He added, "Their struggle is one to delight any connoisseur of political campaigns—an all-out, no-holds-barred battle between two able, articulate exponents of 1966-syle conservatism and liberalism."[6]

TIME noted Taft's advantages in family and financing but added, "Yet it is a tight race. In less than two years, red-haired, blue-eyed Jack Gilligan, who never really stopped campaigning, has earned a reputation to match the motto on his placard: 'The Congressman who gets things done.'"[7] The magazine listed the benefits that had flowed to Gilligan's district during his single term—the funds to help convert Union Station to a museum, the State Department sponsorship of a world tour by the Cincinnati Symphony Orchestra, and others—and added: "Taft does not belittle such blessings. Nor can he match Democrat Gilligan's forceful, witty platform style."[8]

Gilligan put that style to good use in a half-dozen hour-long radio debates broadcast on Cincinnati radio station WCKY. As transcripts make clear, those debates were substantive—with Gilligan and Taft each stating his views in considered answers of some length, a sharp contrast to the dueling sound bites that characterize today's presidential debates. The general impression was that Gilligan came off the victor. Indeed, one national reporter wrote that, after reviewing the radio debates, "Taft and his managers decided to refuse a longstanding offer of free time for televised debates."[9] That gave the incumbent a weapon. Gilligan asked one reporter, "If Mr. Taft is afraid to debate me—a freshman congressman—how does he expect to debate the other 434 congressmen when he gets to Washington?"[10]

Gilligan might have verve, but the Taft forces clearly had a better ground game. Taft established fifteen separate headquarters in the district and, with Gilligan tied down in Washington, got them up and running sooner. He began active campaigning in March. By one account, "Taft has plodded through bowling alleys and shopping centers, meeting the voters and doggedly trying to erase the touch of aloofness in his image that he inherited from his father along with a pleasant, bespectacled phiz."[11] The Taft campaign had significantly greater financial resources: one postelection calculation had Taft outspending Gilligan $170,000 to $90,000.

Taft's campaign stressed certain themes. First, he argued that the "rubber stamp" 89th Congress, of which Gilligan was an approving member, was responsible for a growing federal deficit that he blamed for rising prices. Second, he argued this his election was needed to help restore a strong two-party system to Congress, which had supposedly become dangerously unbalanced toward the Democrats.

Also, Taft ads stressed character. He was "a man you can trust," a phrase that played out in a series of digs at Gilligan. Taft was "Thoughtful, not glib; Warm, not slick; Sensible, not cunning."[12] For Taft, family was no minor attribute. His campaign signs simply read "Taft." As Gilligan noted at the time, the signs "don't carry his first name. Don't carry the office he seeks. Don't say vote. Don't say Republican; don't say anything else. They've just got those four gorgeous letters—T-A-F-T."[13] Gilligan's campaign literature made full use of the favorable notices his first term had brought. The *Cleveland Plain Dealer* stated, "Gilligan is a considerable star of considerable magnitude. Remember the name." The *Columbus Dispatch* called him the "hardest working first termer." The *Washington Post* editorialized, "Gilligan has done an extremely effective job."[14]

The candidates differed fundamentally on the nature of the job they were seeking. Gilligan ran unabashedly as a Great Society supporter, doing nothing to disavow a voting record that was likely more liberal than the general sentiments of his district. He termed himself "an ambassador of the Great Society to the people of southwestern Ohio."[15] This allowed Taft to counter that a congressman should represent his constituents to Washington, not the reverse.

Their differences on issues were also substantial. Serving as congressman-at-large in the 89th Congress, Taft had compiled ratings of zero and 15 from the liberal Americans for Democratic Action and 82 and 78 from the conservative Americans for Constitutional Action—outcomes roughly the reverse of Gilligan's in the 89th Congress. Gilligan favored a guaranteed annual income; Taft opposed it. Taft supported a "needs" test for Medicare; Gilligan opposed it. On Vietnam, Gilligan had somewhat backed away from the bombing pause he had earlier endorsed; both candidates could now be reckoned as supporters of the Johnson administration's war, though Gilligan's support reflected an unhappy sense that no better alternative was at hand.

The Democrats attempted to neutralize Taft's financial and organizational advantage with star power. No star was then brighter in the party's firmament than Robert Kennedy, the Democratic Senator from New York. Kennedy was featured speaker at a rally held at the Cincinnati Zoo on Labor Day weekend, something of a traditional gathering day for Cincinnati's African American population, whose support the Gilligan camp needed. The event gave ready evidence of the Kennedy appeal. John Grupenhoff, who, as Gilligan's campaign manager, organized the event, recalled that when Kennedy reached the podium, "there was a tumult of shouting and greeting. People had been sitting in the sun for a half hour, waiting to hear him speak. He gave a rousing speech. Every once in a while, he'd flick his hair; when he'd do that, the crowd would roar even more."[16] To embrace the crowd, Kennedy climbed on top of the Cadillac limousine rented for the occasion; Gilligan joined him there. Grupenhoff grabbed both men's coattails from behind to help steady them.

At one point, Kennedy, conscious of his schedule, ordered the driver to head out. In Grupenhoff's recollection, the driver replied, "I can't do that; they're all these people in front of the car. I'll run over them."[17] Kennedy, pulling rank, replied, "There's never been anyone hurt at a Kennedy rally. Drive on."[18] The car moved slowly through the crowd, exited the zoo, and headed for the airport. After stepping out of the limo at the airport, Kennedy caught sight of the Cadillac's rooftop, dented out of shape from having been stood on. He said, "I sure hope you have enough money in the campaign fund to repair that."[19] In Grupenhoff's recollection, the repair bill came to $2,000.

Taft also campaigned hard among black voters, who comprised about 15 percent of the district's electorate. He pointed to his vote for the 1964 Civil Rights bill during his sole term in Congress and argued that any hospital that practiced racial discrimination should lose federal funding. Some of his literature had a cloying, period touch: one brochure pictured a black adolescent with the text: "I pass out the literature because my Dad said it's a matter of record that Mr. Taft has shown an interest in the Negro people."[20] Perhaps that interest included gifts of air conditioning systems made by the Taft Foundation to black churches that summer.

Other speakers came to Cincinnati on Gilligan's behalf: Secretary of Labor W. William Wirtz, War on Poverty director Sargent Shriver, and Massachusetts senator Edward Kennedy. Ted Kennedy arrived at Cincinnati's Lunken Airport on Halloween night for an event set to take place in the airport hanger the following morning. Thirty minutes before speaking time, Kennedy paced around, looked at the sky, and asked Grupenhoff which way west was. Kennedy noted that when the sun came up, the audience would be looking straight into it—was that what the campaign wanted? Grupenhoff and others quickly rearranged the layout. Grupenhoff concluded that Teddy Kennedy didn't miss a thing.

Grupenhoff had some uneasiness in his role as campaign manager; he had taken part in Gilligan's 1962 statewide congressional bid but never headed up a campaign. Additionally, prior to joining Gilligan's congressional staff, he had been absent from Cincinnati for some years and was not on close terms with many who had worked on previous Gilligan efforts. In September, two months before the election, Gilligan and Grupenhoff conferred privately in the corridor outside the congressman's Capitol office. When the candidate expressed some reservations, Grupenhoff said he was perfectly willing to bow out gracefully. Gilligan declined the offer. He did so, Grupenhoff thought, because he was confident of victory; another source suggested it was Gilligan's characteristic discomfort at dismissing anyone. Gilligan, indeed, may have hedged his bets. Jack Hansan, Gilligan's 1964 campaign manager, said that late in the campaign Gilligan asked him to take on election chores he thought might be overlooked.

As expected, Gilligan drew endorsements from labor and education groups; Taft was endorsed by Cincinnati's major newspapers. The *Enquirer* rather imaginatively announced: "It is, in brief, an indisputable fact that Robert Taft, Jr., is a figure of national import. His utterances are automatically 'news' in every part of the United States."[21]

Hyperbole aside, it was a reasonably high-toned, if intense, campaign. The only sour notes came toward the end. A campaign letter signed by the chairman of Citizens for Bob Taft called attention to Gilligan's stated support for the "goals" of the American Civil Liberties Union, which, according to the letter, included efforts "to sterilize our schools, our government and our general way of life from all things god-like."[22] Further, the letter scored Gilligan for his earlier advocacy of a bombing halt in Vietnam, suggesting the incumbent believed that "a display of weakness would somehow persuade the enemy that they should surrender."[23]

Throughout his political career, Gilligan was rather nonplussed by personal attacks. The assertion of "godlessness" was notably peculiar, as Gilligan was widely known as being a devout Catholic. A further curiosity was that the letter appeared to have been mailed only to Gilligan's fellow Catholics. Gilligan wrote the letter's signer, Charles Eisenhardt Jr., to ask Eisenhardt if he actually believed what he had signed: "Is it really necessary for you to attempt to destroy your opponent's reputation and the good name that four generations of this family has worked to establish in the community?"[24] Gilligan filed a protest with the fair campaign practices committee—which, as it happened, was chaired by Charles Phelps Taft, his opponent's uncle. Gilligan rather archly closed his letter by suggesting that if the committee lacked the time in which to act, then perhaps Charles Taft might "use your position as Chairman of Independents for Taft to persuade your nephew Robert to cease and desist."[25]

A second low note came less than a week before the election when a local realty group ran newspaper ads asserting that Gilligan had supported a 1966 civil rights initiative that, if passed, "would have destroyed your basic rights" as a homeowner.[26] The ad urged a vote against Gilligan. The ad, however, failed to note that Taft had also supported the initiative in question. When the Taft campaign refused to disavow the ad publicly, the Gilligan campaign published ads in Cincinnati newspapers the Sunday before the election accusing Taft of "trying to profit from the backlash vote."[27] Gilligan used the realtors' ad in an attempt to rally support from black voters.

In the days leading up to the November election, the *New York Times* reported that the stakes for both men were high: "If Mr. Gilligan can defeat Mr. Taft, he will emerge as something of a Democratic power in the state. A victory for Mr. Taft could propel him to greater national influence, but most observers agree that a defeat would finish him in politics."[28] The race was regarded as close. Calling the contest "one of the nation's most important House races," it cited a Republican poll that gave Taft a four-point lead and an independent poll conducted by the University of Cincinnati that showed Taft ahead by "a miniscule 38.1 to 36.4 percent."[29]

Election eve, John Grupenhoff recalled, Gilligan was confident of victory. As the pair emerged from a late evening campaign event, both noted that it was a beautiful night. Gilligan told Grupenhoff, "If this weather holds, we're going to win this thing."[30] Good weather generally means high turnout, and Gilligan believed that a high turnout would mean victory.

On Election Day, Grupenhoff awoke at 3:00 A.M. to rain pouring down in sheets. And the rain didn't let up until the polls closed that evening. By late afternoon, the Gilligan campaign was out urging the few people on the sidewalks to get to the polls. The election proved to be less of a cliffhanger than anticipated: Taft defeated Gilligan by a margin of 69,586 to 61,754.

Assessing the result, *Cincinnati Enquirer* political writer Jack McDonald attributed Gilligan's defeat to the redistricting and to low turnout in city wards. Gilligan had won 56 percent of the Cincinnati vote—almost identical to the 57 percent he received in 1964—but that vote was a smaller share of the district as a whole. McDonald noted that the *Enquirer* had earlier estimated that redistricting would mean a net Republican gain of 7,000 votes—a figure about equal to Taft's margin. Taft campaign manager Carl Rubin challenged this assessment: victory, he said, came from his campaign's aggressive "grassroots" strategy and from his candidate's pulling an appreciable number of votes from black precincts.[31]

Taft clearly benefited by running on the ticket headed by James Rhodes, who was reelected governor with a crushing 62 percent of the vote. And Gilligan was clearly hindered by the long session of the 89th Congress, which limited his presence in the district across which Bob Taft was freely campaigning. This was the factor Gilligan himself considered crucial. By keeping Congress in session, he believes, Johnson sacrificed his party's "seed corn"—junior members such as himself who needed to be home campaigning.[32] Nationally in 1966, Democrats lost over forty congressional seats, including two other first-term Ohio members, Rodney Love in the Third District and Walter Moeller in the Tenth, who were both defeated in relatively close races.

But for some in Cincinnati, nothing soured them more on Gilligan's campaign than how Gilligan himself handled his defeat. Before the election, the campaign had declared on a prominently displayed billboard that Gilligan was "The Congressman who gets things done."[33] Days after, the campaign revised the board's message, redefining Gilligan as "the Congressman who got done."[34] Gilligan, it added, "would like to express to those who supported him, his appreciation to those who opposed him, his sympathy to all residents of the First District, his profound gratitude for the privilege of serving them in the Congress—Au revoir!"[35]

The rephrased billboard stands as evidence that Gilligan and many in Ohio did not have a shared sense of humor. Gilligan associate Dick Guggenheim observed, "He had a sardonic and flip wit. He got himself in trouble more often by a quick remark."[36] Regarding the billboard, Guggenheim commented, "Jack thought he was just being kind of cute."[37] The billboard prompted a tart editorial from the *Cincinnati Enquirer,* which said Gilligan appeared to believe "an adoring public should thrust office upon him."[38] The subsequent flurry of letters to the editor included one from the defeated candidate's wife. Katie Gilligan said that the *Enquirer* did not know what the word "sympathy" meant. In a rare move, she then unburdened herself of her thoughts on the *Enquirer*'s long editorial opposition to her husband, which, she said, consisted of "bitterness, distortion and ignorance."[39]

Reflecting on his single, albeit historic, term in Congress, Gilligan said he benefited greatly from the experience. He learned something about legislation, how it was formed, advanced, and passed. Most interesting, he said, "I learned that the federal bureaucracy, huge as it was, was better and more efficiently organized than what was going on at the state level in Ohio, where there was a lot of ineptitude and lethargy."[40] Further, he noted that in Washington he had formed a number of friendships that would stand him in good stead in later times.

Such reflection came later. The immediate question for Gilligan in the wake of his defeat was, "What next?" Gilligan told *Enquirer* reporter Warren Wheat that he had no intention of returning to city council. This, Wheat wrote, "dispelled Republican anxieties," as they feared their "arch-rival" Gilligan might become mayor if he regained a council seat.[41] Gilligan said he might remain in Cincinnati and work on behalf of the local Democratic Party; or, he might take a position in Washington with a federal department, either Transportation or Housing and Urban Development. But for the moment, Gilligan said, "I'm between engagements."[42]

One further possibility was raised. In December 1966, syndicated columnists Rowland Evans and Robert Novak wrote that, despite his recent defeat, "Mr. Gilligan, attractive and articulate, still looks like the hope of the future for Ohio's liberal Democrats."[43] They suggested that Gilligan might want to challenge Ohio's two-term Democratic U.S. senator, Frank Lausche, for the party's 1968 nomination.

16

Frank Lausche

Frank Lausche was not a happy warrior. Five times the voters of Ohio elected him to two-year terms as the state's governor; twice they sent him to the U.S. Senate. He won, generally, by huge margins. But he remained a worrywart, a rather suspicious and apparently friendless man who smoked and chewed his way through twenty cigars a day.

Historian George Knepper said of Lausche, "He had attractive personal qualities. Plain-living, plain-speaking, with a crown of white hair crowning what one might describe as an 'honest face,' Lausche was the sort of understated politician that Ohioans tended to trust."[1]

On the stump, Lausche was not much of an orator. He was not a joke teller. Mostly, he was mournful. But he had the common touch. He was a confiding speaker, brushing a self-deprecating hand across the side of his face as he spoke of the trials of the working poor, of his immigrant mother, of the threats of disloyalty and unchecked government spending. He would gather his audiences to him, often reducing them—and himself—to tears.

It was said that Frank Lausche could cry in four languages. Likely, those were languages spoken in the ethnic Cleveland where he'd been born in 1895, the child of Slovenian immigrants who operated the St. Clair Street restaurant and community center that served as a first home away from home for many of the 40,000 Slovenians who came to Cleveland before the First World War.

Lausche's early ambitions were entirely American. He played third base for a local semi-pro team and then, briefly in Duluth, Minnesota, in the low minors. After service in the First World War, he attended Cleveland Marshall Law School. After graduating, he established a legal practice that was no great success until he worked on the campaign of local mayoral campaign Ray. T. Miller in 1932. Miller won narrowly. Lausche's aid was appreciated, and Lausche soon found himself appointed to a vacant seat on the municipal court, to which he later won a full term.

What Ohio voters foremost knew and admired about Frank Lausche was that he was independent. He acquired that reputation early. As a Cleveland municipal judge, Lausche earned the nickname Fearless Frank after he impaneled a grand jury that moved aggressively against gambling and organized crime interests. He was supported in this by Louis B. Seltzer, the powerful editor of the *Cleveland Press*, who, in his editorials, urged Lausche to run for mayor in 1935, in 1937, in 1939, and again in 1941, when Lausche finally ran—and collected 61 percent of the vote.[2]

In office, Lausche feathered his reputation for independence. Ray Miller, now the county Democratic chairman, believed Lausche had promised to fire Cleveland public safety director, Elliot Ness, who had come to the city after his glory days in Chicago and developed a reputation as antilabor. Lausche, acknowledging no such promise, retained Ness, thereby instigating a feud with Miller that was never resolved. Writing later of the Ness affair, *TIME* magazine stated: "From that time on, Lausche walked alone. The wrath of the organization Democrats and of labor rained on his shoulders."[3] Lausche entered politics as a moderate liberal and a supporter of FDR. He began drifting rightward as mayor, however, when he discovered an affinity with a small circle of Cleveland corporate leaders. And out of office briefly in the mid-1940s, he signed on as counsel for the Association of American Railroads.

Whatever it was that Lausche sought from public office, it was not personal wealth. Lausche seemed never to push the possible financial advantages of office. When he first ran for mayor of Cleveland, he resigned his judgeship on the grounds that he should not be paid for holding one office while seeking another. When, as mayor, he ran for governor in 1944, he returned to the city his salary for each day he spent campaigning. In that election, Lausche's opponent, a well-established Republican, Cincinnati mayor James Garfield Stewart, spent $988,000 on his campaign. Lausche spent $27,132 and won, becoming Ohio's first Catholic chief executive.

As governor, Lausche was not a strong administrator. His loner style served him poorly in dealings with the Republican-controlled legislature. William Saxbe, in Lausche's years the powerful Speaker of the House, said Lausche was too mercurial to be effective. As an example, Lausche once urged Saxbe to introduce legislation that would authorize additional days of harness racing to make up for those lost to inclement weather. Saxbe introduced the bill; it passed the legislature; Lausche vetoed it.[4]

Lausche never spent money. He cast himself, unbidden and unbossed, as the protector of the public purse. When in his first term the legislature sought a retroactive wartime pay raise for the state's poorly compensated teachers, Lausche batted it down; the raise, he stated, "smacked of pork and the taxpayers deserved better."[5] That set the pattern. In 1948, political scientist John H. Fenton wrote, Ohio's state expenditures for education were close to the national par; four consecutive Lausche terms later, the state lagged the average for education by 35 percent.

Lausche did have great political instincts—in 1948, he jumped on the train carrying a barnstorming Harry Truman across Ohio. In all but unanimous assessment, Truman's campaign was bound for defeat. But Lausche, who boarded the train in Dayton intending only a brief ride, was impressed by the crowds the president was drawing, and stayed on the train for most of the day. Years later, Lausche said Truman and Reagan were his favorite presidents. If that sentiment was authentic, it was not returned. Truman's own expressed view of Lausche was, "You just can't trust the bastard."[6] When Lausche reached the U.S. Senate, one of his first acts was to vote on a bill that would authorize a pension for former presidents. At the time, there were only two living former presidents, one of whom, Truman, actually needed the money. Lausche voted against the pension.

Lausche was not without principal, however. In 1946, Lausche's first bid for reelection as governor ended in narrow defeat. Reflecting the general tenor of the Republican message that year, Lausche was tagged as soft on communism. It was a ridiculous charge. Lausche wore his Americanism on his sleeve. Back in office in 1953, he vetoed a bill that would have established jail terms for those investigated by the Ohio Un-American Activities Committee, stating, "I can see nothing but grave danger to the reputations of innocent people against whom accusations can be made on the basis of rumor and frequently rooted in malice."[7] His veto was quickly overridden, but he had nonetheless placed himself in rare opposition to the fevered suspicions of the times.

In later years, Lausche had his favorite rhetorical targets: racketeers, lobbyists, and, in particular, labor bosses. The antipathy was returned by most union leaders in the state. Elected Ohio's wartime governor in 1944, Lausche ordered the Akron draft board to induct striking Goodyear workers if they did not return to their jobs. As a U.S. senator, he was the only Democrat to vote for Republican-favored amendments aimed at toughening the Taft-Hartley Act; in 1958, he declared his support for Ohio's right-to-work amendment, which organized labor viewed as a death knell. Lausche's record moved opponents to hyperbole. Mike Kerwin, a Democratic congressman with strong ties to labor, described Lausche as "a menace to mankind."[8]

But in the back-scratching world of politics, Lausche felt no itch to be a team player. By one evaluation of seventy-five major Senate votes, he voted with the majority of his own party only 27 percent of the time. He was, however, on congenial terms with the state's leading Republicans. They had no real hope of beating him, he knew, and, given his largely Republican voting record, no great wish to do so. He drew tons of Republican votes: in the 1962 election, Republicans captured eighteen of the state's twenty-four congressional seats; Lausche, surfing against the tide, was reelected to the U.S. Senate by an astounding 692,521 votes.

As his party's unchallenged leading figure, Lausche was, for aspiring Democrats, the only game in town. And Lausche played that game for keeps. He paid unusual attention to patronage appointments: those who challenged or crossed him did not advance. One Ohio Democrat stated, "He had this air of being a foxy grandfather, but he was tough and mean as hell."[9] Political appointees who spoke favorably of labor unions or who urged reform soon discovered they no longer had appointments.

Once, a campaigning Lausche announced he would speak in Cincinnati. For local Democratic leaders, this amounted to a test: their effectiveness would be judged by the size and the enthusiasm of crowd they assembled. However, they learned that no candidate but Lausche was to speak from the platform; and at the reception that would follow, no one but Lausche was to be introduced. So however much Democrats standing for lesser offices might benefit from Lausche's public blessing at the event, that blessing was, characteristically, not going to be given.

One local Democrat concocted a scheme to aid two candidates running for state representative. Moving through the receiving line, one of the candidates took Lausche's right hand and, without releasing his grip, moved to the senator's left side. The second candidate then grabbed Lausche's free left hand and moved in close. By arrangement, a photographer emerged from the crowd to snap their picture before taking off down the hall and evading the state troopers an infuriated Lausche sent in pursuit. The following day, the picture appeared in a political ad in Cincinnati newspaper, with the headline, "Lausche's Winning Team." The evening of the prank, Lausche confronted Jack Gilligan: "I know who's responsible for this, and I'm never going to forget it."[10]

17

The Unbeatable Foe

In June 1967, a young Cleveland-area law clerk named Jim Friedman invited himself to lunch with John Gilligan. Friedman is an individual of considerable energy, much of it directed toward politics, which he practically exhales. During his days at Harvard Law School, Friedman had read and been impressed by David Broder's 1965 *New York Times* profile of Congressman Gilligan, filing it away for future reference. Back in Cleveland following graduation, Friedman mingled with various reform Democrat groups; then, he managed to get an invitation to a seminar at the Kennedy School of Government at Harvard, where he was shown about by future Congressman Barney Frank and where he learned how the Kennedy campaigns organized their citizen support groups. As his day job, Friedman clerked for the chief judge of the Sixth Circuit U.S. Court of Appeals; when that court convened in Cincinnati to hear cases, Friedman traveled to the city. His lunch invitation to Gilligan came during one such visit.[1]

The two met at Cincinnati's Vernon Manor Hotel, a grand building then somewhat past its prime and where Gilligan had an insurance office. Following his unsuccessful bid to retain his congressional seat the previous November, Gilligan was, for all practical purposes, unemployed, a circumstance complicated by his having three children in college—Donald at Harvard, Kathleen in Trinity College in Washington, D.C., and John Patrick soon to leave for Dartmouth. Soon after the election, he accepted an offer from longtime friend William Sauter to join the latter's insurance agency.

The insurance business notwithstanding, Gilligan was keeping himself in political circulation. That spring, Governor James Rhodes had endorsed what he unabashedly called "the most important piece of legislation I've ever known of since I've been in public life."[2] The proposal was to create a body known as the Ohio Bond Commission, on which Rhodes-appointed members would have the untrammeled authority to commit up to 6 percent of the state's general revenue for capital improvement projects as designated by the commission. In the words of one political journalist, it "was essentially asking voters to give up their historic right to approve or disapprove individual bond issues."[3] Still, Rhodes was riding high; he had been overwhelmingly reelected the previous fall, and voter approval of the bond commission was widely anticipated.

Gilligan thought it a flat-out terrible idea, in both theory and practice. In theory, it took the power of the purse strings from those who should be controlling them: voters and their elected representatives. In practice, Gilligan thought, it would give free rein to what he regarded as one of Rhodes's more objectionable habits: a fondness for building buildings that was not matched by an interest in funding the operations housed in them.

Much of organized labor and many Democrats opposed the proposal, Gilligan quite publicly. He spoke around the state to business and civic groups, "Frequently," he said, "these groups knew very little about the real issues on the ballot. My effort was to educate them."[4] To almost general surprise, the bond commission proposal was voted down by nearly a 2–1 margin in the May 1967 election. With that outcome, wrote political columnist Abe Zaidan, "Gilligan stood tall at state Democratic headquarters for putting his personal reputation on the line against what had appeared to be a popular state development."[5]

Friedman's lunch with Gilligan took place that June and lasted three hours. The young lawyer arrived with sheaves of voting statistics and ideas of how a modern, progressive Democratic party—one that made use of computers, polling, and television—could be created in Ohio. More to the point, in Gilligan's recollection, was that Friedman "had carefully worked out that I could beat Frank Lausche."[6] Gilligan's initial response, he recalled, was that the idea was "goofy."[7] Liberal Democrats in Ohio had for years talked about the need to get rid of Frank Lausche, but that "need" never led to the name of the candidate who would undertake the task. Gilligan had himself been party to numerous such discussions but claimed that, prior to his lunch with Friedman, he had never given serious thought to running for the U.S. Senate. He did so now: "The long and short of it was that Jimmy Friedman convinced me I could do it."[8]

Gilligan put Friedman in touch with his former congressional staffer, Ed Wagner, then at Cleveland State University. They recruited a few like-minded souls, and that summer they all gathered at a hotel in Mansfield—strategically located between Columbus and Cleveland—to form a loose organization that evolved into Citizens for Gilligan. Soon thereafter, Wagner and Friedman began seeding pro-Gilligan groups around the state.

Elsewhere in Ohio, Democrats were stirring. Much of this owed to Morton Neipp, a Toledo attorney who became state Democratic chairman in 1966, and to Eugene "Pete" O'Grady, an energetic reformer from Cleveland whom Neipp recruited as the party's executive director. Pete O'Grady was a second-generation politico; his father had been a political journalist in County Mayo and was smuggled out of Ireland after the 1916 Easter Rising, ending up in Cleveland and, not surprisingly, a Democrat. O'Grady was an experienced political organizer for Democrats and labor leaders. He had run I. W. Abel's campaign for presidency of the United Steelworkers, and he had been active in the campaign to defeat Rhodes's bond commission. O'Grady had a quality relatively rare in activist Democrats: he was ecumenical. He stood apart from and was dissuasive of the internecine battles that often erupt between Democratic factions eager to determine which one is slightly more correct. A longtime associate said, "Pete was a guy who could relate to anybody in society—millionaire or panhandler. He had a vision of the Ohio Democratic Party as a place where everybody had a home."[9]

At this time, the state Democratic Party was pretty much broke. Neipp pushed the fund-raising agenda. He secured Senator Robert F. Kennedy to headline a fund-raising dinner and raised $70,000—which was then real money for Ohio Democrats. He and O'Grady also worked with Ohio labor unions to build the sort of Democratic-labor alliances that existed in other big states. Labor's own activity increased as a result: in 1967, the state AFL-CIO launched a voter registration drive, supporting that effort with a monthly publication of political information, *Focus,* sent to 800,000 union members.

Looking down the path to the future for Democrats in Ohio, Niepp, O'Grady, and the Ohio AFL-CIO agreed that the bump in the road was Frank Lausche—who, based on his Senate voting record, they agreed was a Republican in all but name. Gilligan had a further objection to what he saw as Lausche's self-centered dominance of the state party: "We would never have a Democratic Party in Ohio worth the name until we got rid of Frank Lausche, who spent his time and energy decapitating any Democrat in this state who stuck his head up, so he would never have a rival."[10] With his antilabor voting record and attacks on "labor bosses," Lausche had enemies elsewhere—including in Washington, D.C., where the national AFL-CIO was moving to target him in the 1968 election. Those who wanted him out acknowledged that, in a general election, Lausche had tremendous crossover appeal to Republicans and independents. So if Lausche was to be beaten, someone would have to challenge him in the party primary. Gilligan, with his active opposition to right-to-work and pro-labor record in Congress, was on labor's short list of possible contenders.

In September, Gilligan and Friedman went to AFL-CIO national headquarters in Washington to meet with Al Barkan, longtime director of the Committee on Political Education (COPE). The meeting was brokered by Gilligan ally Bill Kircher, who by 1967 was a national AFL-CIO officer. At a private lunch at the Hay Adams, a labor organization pollster ran down the results of an Ohio survey matching Gilligan against Lausche among Democratic voters: Lausche 55 percent, Gilligan 7 percent, with 38 percent undecided.

Gilligan piped up: "Okay. We've got them right where we want them."[11] He was, in fact, entirely serious. Gilligan's judgment was that if Lausche—who had been the state's leading Democrat for over two decades—could pull only a 55 percent preference in his own party's primary, then he was ripe for the taking. This comment launched the campaign.

Gilligan was willing to make the fight—but, as he stressed to those around him, he was "not willing to do it alone."[12] He feared that many who encouraged him to take on Lausche would discreetly exit to the sidelines once the battle began. He wanted two things. First, he wanted assurances of major financial support from the national AFL-CIO. Second, he wanted the state Democratic Party executive committee to endorse his primary election challenge of Lausche. As a practical matter, the latter was a prerequisite to the former. These requests were not casually made; national labor had never committed funds to a primary candidate, and the state Democratic Party had never withheld its endorsement from a sitting officeholder— much less from one who was the greatest vote getter in the party's history.

Gilligan at this point sought to create a minor political base, and perhaps some income. In November he stood for election to the Cincinnati City Council. Feeling confident, the Democrats put together a blue ribbon ticket, which they referred to as Nine Fine Men. Gilligan, however, was the only one to gain a seat.

State party leaders moved to address Gilligan's conditions. The executive committee met on January 11, 1968, in the Ulysses S. Grant Room of the Hotel Sheraton–Columbus. According to press accounts, state chairman Neipp opened with a fifteen-minute talk urging a Gilligan endorsement. They reminded the committee that Gilligan drew support from more populous counties and Lausche from rural areas. One Lausche supporter, Belmont County chairman Frank Vanelli, asked, "We are finally at a point where we can win an election. Why are we going to have a primary fight and tear our party apart?"[13] The endorsement vote, however, was decisive: for Lausche, 8; for no endorsement, 6; for Gilligan, 45. The national AFL-CIO bestowed its own endorsement four weeks later. Both of Gilligan's conditions were met.[14]

The man left without honor in his own party, Frank Lausche, shrugged off the rebuff. Those who had rejected his candidacy, he said, "would have been glad to support me if I had allowed my thinking and voting to be dictated by them. Those forces have unsuccessfully opposed me in every political contest in which I have been since 1943"—from virtually every one of which he had emerged victorious.[15] The state's political press largely shared Lausche's view of the matter. The *Cincinnati Enquirer,* never an admirer of Gilligan, said the endorsement had been made "in the expectation . . . of getting someone who will adapt himself more readily to the party powers, so to speak."[16] Needling Gilligan further, the editorial observed that as Gilligan had finished second in the 1961 city council race, fifth in the 1963 race, and eighth in the 1967 race, it was "understandable that he should feel the need to seek a broader base."[17] A blunt January 14, 1968, editorial cartoon in the *Columbus Dispatch* depicted "labor bosses" and a Democratic donkey telling Gilligan, "We're endorsing you because Lausche wouldn't jump through the hoop when we told him to!"[18]

Most predicted that Lausche would stave off the challenge. The *Youngstown Vindicator* reported that unnamed senior Democrats believed the Gilligan endorsement was "an obvious takeover of the party by labor groups," which would leave Democrats a permanent minority in the state.[19] Lausche, it said, would be renominated "by a large majority."[20] Ohio congressman Wayne Hays weighed in with a similar judgment: "Lausche will win two-to-one over Gilligan in the primary and he'll win in the fall, too."[21] Even one friendly reporter, O. F. Knippenburg of the *Dayton Daily News,* expected Gilligan's challenge to do more harm than good. Lausche would prevail, Knippenburg predicted, and Gilligan, "one of the most attractive Democrats to come along in years, [will] emerge so damaged from the primary battle as to nip a promising political career."[22]

The Democrats' disavowal of Frank Lausche occurred near the start of what was easily a most extraordinary year in American political history. Central now was the continuing conflict in Vietnam. By mid-1967, the war in Vietnam had become an aching frustration for Americans—one felt by both those who did not understand why America could not push through to victory and those who believed the war was a catastrophic misuse of American power. The power engaged was immense—more than 500,000 U.S. military personnel were serving in the theater—and the toll was stark: 200 American soldiers were dying each week.

Opposition, generally the province of the young, was expressed at campus teach-ins and in demonstrations of considerable size: 200,000 marched against the war in Manhattan in April 1967; 50,000 gathered in protest that October at the Pentagon, the symbol of U.S. power. That opposition and outrage was increasingly expressed and felt in homes across the country—such as within the Gilligan household. John Gilligan was a student at his father's alma mater, St. Xavier High School, in April 1967 when Dr. Martin Luther King joined the issues of race and war in a speech delivered at Riverside Church in New York City. When the *Cincinnati Enquirer* blasted King editorially, John wrote a response, got 250 St. Xavier students to cosign it, and delivered it to the newspaper. The *Enquirer* was not amused and ran a second editorial suggesting that the son of a local politician had hoodwinked a number of students into signing something they did not understand. That second editorial prompted a rare public response from Katie Gilligan, who wrote the *Enquirer* taking issue with the newspaper. That action, John said of his mother, "reflected who she was. She was standing up for her son, standing up for her husband, making a political point, and standing up for Dr. King."[23]

Still in 1967, such expressions of protest mostly occurred outside the bounds of electoral politics. This began to change when, in November 1967, U.S. Senator

Eugene McCarthy, a Democrat, announced he would challenge President Johnson in the coming year's presidential primaries; his intention was to give war opponents a way to express their opposition within the electoral framework.

Events in America were driven by unexpected news from Vietnam. On January 31, 1968, the North Vietnamese and Viet Cong launched a coordinated assault across the breadth of the country. The Tet Offensive was the largest military operation undertaken by either side thus far in the conflict; an estimated 80,000 attackers struck at cities and towns, including thirty-six of the country's forty-four provincial capitals. Militarily, the attack failed; the attackers suffered enormous losses and failed to hold their territorial gains. But the political and psychological effect it had on Americans was startling. The attacks appeared to belie months of optimistic reports on the progress of the conflict. With Tet, not even the compound of the American embassy in Saigon was secure from assault. The assertion that the enemy had been defeated was undercut by reports that General William Westmoreland had requested an additional 206,000 U.S. troops be placed in the region.

Jim Friedman recalls spending much of the spring primary campaign waiting for the "adults" to turn up and take charge. They never did. John Gilligan's challenge to Frank Lausche was largely the work of the young, energetic, and inexperienced. Thirty-seven-year-old social worker Jack Hansan was again named campaign manager. Campaign aide Ed Wagner was Gilligan's administrative assistant during his term in Congress. Not one of the key staffers had any experience running a statewide campaign. In fact, many just wandered in. One of the first to do so was twenty-two-year-old Ohio State University law student Alan Melamed, who in early January presented himself at the small Gilligan headquarters in the Lincoln-Leveque Tower in downtown Columbus. Melamed, troubled by the war in Vietnam, wanted to do something more meaningful than study torts. He dropped out of law school and spent the spring as Gilligan's driver. Peter Hart arrived the following month. Hart—today one of the nation's most highly regarded pollsters—was then a twenty-six-year-old assistant to pollster Lou Harris. Similarly concerned over Vietnam, he had written letters to various antiwar candidates offering his services. After a brief interview with Jack Hansan, Hart signed on for what he recalls as "a minimalist salary."[24] Hart had no difficulty securing a leave of absence from Harris. (Told that Hart would be campaigning against Lausche, Harris "didn't think I would be gone long.")[25]

Volunteers streamed in, too. Chris Buchanan, a sixteen-year-old Ohio high school student, got bored stuffing envelopes for Eugene McCarthy and went to the Gilligan campaign office in Columbus, where Peter Hart assigned him the task of doing a voter breakdown by county and media market to be used as background for media buys. Buchanan worked through his spring break; at the end of the week, he recalled, Jack Hansan handed him an envelope with $5 in it—the first "real money" he had ever earned. Buchanan, comparing the work he had been doing with the typical summer jobs his classmates had, felt rather pleased with himself.[26]

Other campaign workers were recruited. Bob Daley, a thirty-four-year-old political reporter for the *Dayton Journal-Herald*, emerged from a dinner with Gilligan at Dayton's Pine Club restaurant as Gilligan's traveling press aide and general assistant. Daley, who had been tracking Gilligan's career since his unsuccessful congressional bid in 1962, met Gilligan for the first time in 1967 when Daley took part in a seminar series entitled "Piety and Politics," for which Gilligan was a lead presenter. Of the early campaign staff, Daley may have been the only one who anticipated victory: "Here I was with a wife and two young kids. If I hadn't felt so strongly, I probably would not have taken the chance to give up a job and take a flyer on something like a campaign that would only last three or four months."[27]

The primary campaign's formal launch came on February 10 in Columbus. Gilligan then outlined the "three legs" of intended support: the state Democratic Party, whose endorsement had been gained; labor unions; and the Citizens for Gilligan organizations (by then in Akron, Athens, Cincinnati, Cleveland, Columbus, Dayton, Elyria-Lorain, Springfield, Toledo, and Youngstown). But Gilligan had already taken to the road. In the first week of February, he completed a five-day swing through Toledo, Elyria, Cleveland, and Akron. In these early stops he made a point of taking a nominating "oath," pledging, unlike Lausche, to "support and abide by the principles enunciated by the Democratic Party in its national and state platforms."[28] He also managed to work repeated references to his opponent's age into campaign press releases, one of which read: "Mr. Gilligan, who is forty-seven years old—twenty-five years younger than Lausche—recently stated that . . ."[29]

Generally, the traveling campaign was made up of Gilligan, Daley, and Melamed—candidate, aide, and driver. A typical day began with a breakfast planning session at the hotel followed by a small fund-raiser and three or more meetings with voters, and then the drive on to the next city after the evening's final event. Early on, twenty-five to fifty was a decent-size audience at a union or Kiwanis hall; crowds were larger on some campuses (more than 100 people turned out at Bowling Green State University, Melamed recalled). Gilligan made a point of getting on local radio stations, which often had time to fill and were rarely visited by a statewide candidate. The candidate generally returned to Cincinnati, and home, very late on Saturday, heading back out Monday morning.

The traveling campaign originally hit the road in a bulky Clark camper bus, which, Daley recalled, had been "borrowed from somebody's brother-in-law."[30] The vehicle's flat front had no particular tolerance for headwinds; once, on the road from Mansfield to Youngstown, the power steering went out, rendering it all but uncontrollable. Melamed got the whimpering vehicle to Youngstown, dropped Gilligan at the candidate's next event, and threw himself and his vehicle on the mercy of local Democrats.

Youngstown Democrats at the time were led by one of Ohio's few remaining local bosses, Jack Sulligan. (Sulligan had bestowed that odd surname on himself when he was informed that success in local politics required an Irish last name, and had concluded that "Sulligan" qualified.) The Democratic headquarters were located near the Mahoning County Courthouse, where petitioners queued on the ground floor and friends of the party played cards on the second. A local supporter heard of the bus's plight and ushered Melamed into the upstairs club where a game of pinochle appeared to have been in progress for some weeks. The supporter told Sulligan, "The Gilligan bus has broken down and we need to get it fixed." Without removing his eyes from his cards, Sulligan told an associate, "Call the city garage; we've got a bus coming over and we want them to fix it."[31] Given his emergency, Melamed decided it would be tactless to suggest that there might be something wrong with having the city garage fix a campaign vehicle at taxpayers' expense.

Gilligan, Daley, and Melamed traveled all over the state. Melamed recalled a swing though southwestern Ohio:

> We'd go out on these windy roads as far as we could go. I remember one place. This house was on cinder blocks. Just one room. Fourteen children. One of them had cerebral palsy, and they would mash the food to feed the child. They had a little cornfield. The guy worked at a gas station all week and then on the weekend he would tend this field. Their entire diet was starches. This was 1968. No running water. An outhouse. I remember it having a pretty profound impact on Jack, seeing all this.[32]

The campaign traveled, but hardly in style. Early on, to save on airfare, Gilligan and Daley hitched rides on private aircraft whenever they could. Daley recalled hopping a ride from Athens to Lima aboard a four-seater flown by a local dentist. The co-pilot and navigator, seated next to the pilot, was the dentist's mother. Daley recalled, "His mother was reading the maps on her lap. Jack and I were in the back, scared to death."[33]

While Gilligan was the endorsed Democratic candidate, support for him within the party was not universal. The state's largest county organization, Cuyahoga, with its usual standoffishness, sat out the primary. The reason, said Friedman, was simple: "They, like 98 percent of the civilized world at the time, thought we had no chance."[34] Such skepticism complicated fund-raising. Friedman once sought a contribution from the father of a friend, someone who had known him all his life: "He said to me, 'Jim, look—this guy has no chance.' He didn't say it in a nasty way, just as a fact."[35]

Arguably, there were two Gilligan campaigns under way that spring. The first, which might be termed the "new politics" effort, was broadly motivated by the desire to stop the war, reform the process, and, perhaps, feel some youthful oats. This effort was characterized by Hart and Melamed, by low-budget scrambling, and by the 10,000 volunteers the campaign hoped to have roped in by Election Day. By way of example, Friedman recalled: "On Sundays, I'd get up and drive down to Notre Dame College, which was a Catholic girls' school near where I was living, pick up four college girls, take two big cartons of literature in the back of my truck, and drive the students to every Catholic church in the eastern suburbs of Cleveland to leaflet with Gilligan stuff."[36] The second campaign was the union effort, which, with no particular sentimentality, had fixed its target on Frank Lausche and was committed to removing him from the U.S. Senate. A difference between the two was that the new politics crowd did not know how to raise money.

Part of the fund-raising problem was Howard Metzenbaum, a wealthy and politically active young Cleveland attorney (and later a U.S. senator). Following Gilligan's state party endorsement, Metzenbaum told the *Toledo Blade*, "I am very much for Gilligan and I will support him all the way."[37] With this, Metzenbaum was put in charge of fund-raising. But he failed to raise much in the way of contributions, forcing campaign manager Jack Hansan to go to Cleveland with an ultimatum: raise $100,000 or resign. Metzenbaum, Hansan says, replied that "he didn't think the Gilligan campaign was worth ten cents."[38] Hansan requested his resignation. By the time Hansan got back to headquarters in Columbus, Metzenbaum had informed Cleveland media that he had quit due to the amateurish nature of the Gilligan effort, thereby adding insult to penury. The money crunch was severe. One staffer remembered that everyone looked forward to the occasional visits from Walt Davis, a Washington-based labor leader who backed Gilligan, because Davis and his credit card characteristically sprung for dinner for whatever staff members were present.

Indeed, labor had deep pockets to draw from. Following the February 16 endorsement of Gilligan by the AFL-CIO, labor funds started to flow in. In Washington, lawyer and longtime Gilligan friend and associate Bill Geoghegan acted as intermediary, collecting $150,000 from national unions and forwarding those funds to Ohio. Statewide unions, particularly the United Auto Workers, provided additional funds. Originally, the Gilligan campaign hoped to raise $500,000. They only raised $319,000, of which $280,000 came from organized labor. Labor's financial role prompted charges from Lausche that "big labor" was pouring a million dollars into the state to defeat him. As much as Gilligan might have liked this to be the case, the charge was untrue. Challenged by the Gilligan campaign, Lausche withdrew that figure. It was the case, however, that donations from labor organizations kept the campaign afloat.

Labor money aside, the Gilligan campaign ran primarily on the candidate's energy and that of his youthful staff. Jack Hansan, Peter Hart, Ed Wagner, and Bob Daley spent the spring living in two inelegant apartments just off Broad Street, which someone described as bachelor pads—absent the women. The apartments were places to crash; the campaign—as campaigns do—became for them a 24/7 activity.

With this came strong personal bonds. Friedman and Daley became lifelong associates of Gilligan. Peter Hart, who came to Ohio in hopes of gaining some political "combat experience," characterized his work for Gilligan as the political equivalent of first love: "To me, Jack was a huge hero and a magnificent candidate and magnificent politician. It was exceptionally special. Maybe anybody feels that way for a first campaign, but I don't think so."[39]

By March, Gilligan was campaigning hard. His schedule for Thursday, March 7, began with the candidate shaking hands with workers arriving at the Ford plant in Toledo, followed by a visit to the dock on Lake Erie, a meeting with local building trades officials, and a second plant visit—all before a press conference held at a UAW-sponsored health and retiree center. The afternoon included meetings with a student group at the University of Toledo, the taping of a ninety-minute interview with local radio stations, and, closing the day, an off-the-record meeting with local Democratic officials.

Gilligan was a somewhat uneven campaigner. His strongest appeal was to younger, better educated voters, those more interested in program and policy than in the well-worn stories from the old neighborhood that Frank Lausche told often, even if graciously and well. Writing for the *New York Times,* James Naughton noted that before liberal groups, "Gilligan is a master of incisive and witty commentary."[40] He was less effective in other settings, in part, perhaps, because the somewhat professorial Gilligan simply did not look like an Ohio politician. (Naughton reported being seated in a restaurant with a group that included Gilligan when someone asked the waitress if she might guess who at the table was running for office. The waitress pointed to a union official. When told that Gilligan was the candidate, she replied, "Oh my. Good luck.")[41]

Frank Lausche was slow to respond to his challenger's campaign. Lausche's biographer James Odenkirk wrote, "By the time Lausche had begun to campaign seriously day-to-day, Gilligan had visited twenty-nine of the eighty-eight counties, given 180 speeches, held six major news conferences and visited the editors of every major newspaper in the state."[42] And when Lausche responded, he did so with the kind of retail politics that had worked for him in the past: meeting with small groups of likely supporters. Journalist Abe Zaidan observed that "Lausche patterned his campaign to reinforce past loyalties rather than to encourage new ones."[43] The typical Lausche gathering was "much like a religious ceremony: they come to give and to receive blessings, joined in spiritual communion, exalted by a generation of true feeling. They offer up faded postcards and brown newspaper clippings and old political buttons. They ask only in turn that each gift revive the memory of a happily shared moment in history."[44]

His own campaigns aside (and he never campaigned for others), Frank Lausche maintained an extraordinarily low profile in his home state. He operated no standing office in the state for constituent services or self-promotion. His single campaign office was in Cleveland's Carter Hotel and was managed by a one-member staff. At one point in the primary campaign, Gilligan and press aide Daley stopped at the Cleveland address at which Lausche was registered to vote. "It was an apart-ment building, and his name wasn't on the mailbox," Daley said. "Here's a U.S. sen-ator, and he isn't even a resident. Gilligan made a point of that in the campaign."[45]

The Gilligan campaign was sensing progress but had no hard evidence that showed it. With his background with the Lou Harris organization, Peter Hart put together a poll, with campaign volunteers telephoning respondents. The poll showed Frank Lausche with 37 percent support, a significant drop from the per-cent he had before the challenge began. And while Gilligan still trailed at 22 per-cent, 41 percent of voters, a huge share, remained undecided. Most importantly, Hart said, the poll showed the Democratic Party organization and the labor unions that were backing Gilligan that their candidate was in the game.

Besides, it was proving to be a year for the unlikely in politics. On March 12, the little heralded McCarthy campaign obtained a surprising 42 percent of the vote in the New Hampshire primary, the nation's first. (Those boosting McCarthy's candi-dacy included Gilligan's son John, who had headed to the Granite State to canvas on behalf of the senator's campaign.) That surprising news was trumped on March 31 with Lyndon Johnson's announcement that he was stepping down: he would neither seek nor accept renomination for president in 1968. (Gilligan, listening to the presi-dent's speech in a Cleveland hotel room, had had a sudden intuition. He noted that Johnson, whose speeches never ran longer than their announced time, was running long now. He alerted others in the room to this, adding, "He's going to quit."[46])

Surprise turned to shock days just later when James Earl Ray fired his rifle through an open window of a Memphis flophouse, fatally wounding the leader of the American civil rights movement, Dr. Martin Luther King Jr., who was standing on an opposite balcony. Alan Melamed remembers that as the campaign's worst day. He recalled eating dinner in a Toledo motel with Bill Mallory, an African American political activist from Cincinnati, when the television broadcast news of the assassination. Mallory tried repeatedly to reach his family in Cincinnati by telephone, but the lines were jammed. It was, Melamed recalled, "just a horrible, horrible night."[47] The next day's campaigning was through a western tier of conser-vative Ohio counties, ones not greatly sensitive to the cause of civil rights. In Lima, the local host had run for Congress as an anti–civil rights Democrat. Gilligan of-fered the crowd no words of comfort; in Melamed's recollection, Gilligan told the crowd, "Any of us who has contributed to the atmosphere of racial hatred and intolerance in this country has the blood of Martin Luther King on their hands."[48]

In the hours and days following King's assassination, rioting broke out in scores of American cities. Kathleen Gilligan, then a junior at Trinity College, recalled standing on a college dormitory roof watching sections of Washington, D.C., be engulfed in flames. Gilligan returned to Cincinnati, where, on April 8, rioting broke out in the city's Avondale neighborhood. A curfew was invoked, though this may not have been generally known, and police arrested 260 people, mostly as curfew violators or for disorderly conduct. These violators were run through municipal court, where, following proceedings that commonly lasted barely a minute, most were sentenced to six to twelve months in the workhouse. Notified of this by a local minister, Gilligan went to the court and watched as justice was meted out wholesale. He was appalled, a reaction not softened by the fact that all court personnel were white.

A volunteer observer later wrote that the judges took the position that as long as the "riot act" had been read, it did not matter if particular defendants had actually heard it. Among those defendants fined $500 and sent to the workhouse for a year were an honorably discharged veteran who worked for the IRS, a long-term employee of a local restaurant, and "a steady worker and the father of two children." The observer wrote, "The lawyers protested feebly, stunned, as was almost everybody else." When bail was sought, it was set at the prohibitively high figure of $10,000.[49]

On April 10, Gilligan wrote his fellow members of city council. While he provided full praise for the police and firefighters, he attacked the court: "Everyone, without regard to individual circumstances, the person's past behavior or mitigating conditions, was automatically found guilty as charged, and promptly given the maximum penalty." It would, he added, "be extremely difficult" to encourage the community to have "a proper veneration for justice, if our courts continue to be conducted in such a manner."[50]

And, with that, a fair portion of the sky over Cincinnati fell on Jack Gilligan. The response included a letter signed by five of Gilligan's fellow city councilmen, who said his criticisms violated the constitutional separation of the legislative and the judiciary, the independence of which, they rather archly informed Gilligan, "was formally recognized by King John on the 15th day of June, 1215, in Section 29 of the Magna Carta."[51] They also affirmed the view that "the efficient and effective apprehension of criminals under a riot condition . . . and the swift and certain administration of justice" was the best method of maintaining law and order for the city's citizens.[52]

One councilman who did not sign the response to Gilligan, Republican Eugene Ruehlmann, thought Gilligan's criticism of the courts was "courageous but wrong."[53] Some of the judges might have been excessive, he conceded, but "the curfew arrests stopped the rioting cold."[54] Recalling the reaction, he added: "There is no question about it. Gilligan caught unholy hell."[55] Gilligan's statement, one longtime associate said ruefully, "was Jack Gilligan at his best and his most politically uncalculating."[56] There may be a good time to stand up for the civil rights of alleged curfew violators, but, in conservative Cincinnati, the immediate aftermath of rioting was not it. The episode likely had little influence on the primary vote, but the assertion that Gilligan was soft on crime would dog him through the fall campaign.

As much as anything, the Senate primary turned on age, style, and energy. The Gilligan campaign discovered time and again that Lausche's core supporters were extraordinarily loyal. Odenkirk noted that Gilligan "found it nearly impossible to change the opinions of longtime Lausche supporters. Even with his Silver Star from World War II, he encountered difficulty getting across to veterans groups that the Senator voted against the Cold War GI Bill, against the 1959 Veterans Readjustment Act and against the 1960 Veteran Life Insurance Act."[57] But while Lausche supporters were loyal, they were dwindling in number with age. Many, indeed, were not even Democrats. (At one Lausche gathering, a local radio reporter drew the senator's ire by asking, "Would all the registered Democrats here today raise their hands?"[58])

Largely, the candidates' positions on issues reflected their opposite sides on the age and cultural divide. On Vietnam, for example, Lausche slammed those who "denounce our country as a liar, an exploiter, a cheater."[59] Gilligan represented a different worldview: America, he said, must end "our holy war on Communism. The question this nation must ask itself is whether it intends to be a police force for the world. [If so], it will mean bringing our boys home in boxes for a long time."[60] Gilligan was almost righteously outspoken. In mid-May, for example, Gilligan told a union group in Columbus that organized labor must set aside its "fears and prejudices" and take a stand for civil rights.[61]

From the first, Jim Friedman had talked of having the Gilligan campaign take advantage of such "new" technology as televisions and computers. Indeed, they had major success with TV. The campaign commissioned a thirty-minute biographic production on Gilligan made by the noted documentary filmmaker Charles Guggenheim. Titled *Against All Odds,* it tracked Gilligan's life through Cincinnati, Notre Dame, the navy, city council, and Congress and into the present. By current standards, the film was slow—the candidate strolls purposefully down a sidewalk with his jacket tossed over his shoulder, the candidate sits at home while daughter Ellen plays the piano in the background. But for the time it was well and cleverly done. One shot showed Gilligan in his high school football uniform. Next, the viewer hears the Notre Dame "Fight Song," which blended smoothly into a shot of a Notre Dame halfback breaking free. Peter Hart commented, "People watching that documentary could easily have thought Jack was a player for the Notre Dame team."[62]

The campaign's general financial troubles, however, made it difficult to book much air time. The documentary was shown somewhere in Ohio thirty to forty times, often during off-peak hours. Still, the program caught considerable attention. For most viewers, it was the first professional campaign film they had seen, and it ranked high among the reasons for the primary's outcome.

Curiously perhaps, while it had been Jim Friedman who talked about the need to employ computers, it was labor that actually did it. The national AFL-CIO made the Ohio primary its first statewide use of the technology. It assembled lists of its Ohio members and then paid teams of high school girls $1.75 an hour to track down the ward, address, phone number, and party identification for 800,000 union members. This information was then returned to Washington for processing on rented computer time, with the results given to thousands of door-to-door and telephone solicitors. Ohio labor threw its ground troops into the contest in earnest, distributing 1 million pieces of literature the day before the election. The *New York Times* credited labor's effort "with bringing up Mr. Gilligan from an upstart challenger a few months ago to a serious contender in the last ten days. Labor's effective use of the computer has implications for every state with a large union membership."[63]

Labor was central in other ways, too. For the four months preceding the primary, the state labor publication, *Focus,* highlighted the race, with the April issue providing side-by-side comparisons of the voting records of Lausche and Gilligan on labor and other matters. The state AFL-CIO treasurer commented: "Four issues—the last one a real blast at Lausche—showing his voting record in Congress, right into the living room of every union member in the state."[64]

In 1968, no news agency in the state did professional polling during a primary. Predictions were made, however. The handicapper who then carried the most prestige was Richard L. Maher of the *Cleveland Press,* whose predictions were published the Saturday before the vote. Maher saw it as a wipeout: Lausche would beat Gilligan by "two-to-one."[65] Such was Maher's standing that his prediction left some Gilligan supporters downcast. Other prognosticators offered some hope. James Naughton predicted that "Gilligan is within range of a stunning upset."[66]

Gilligan's campaign staff and supporters gathered at the Alms Hotel in Cincinnati to hear the returns. Their chit-chat was that it was going to be a "long night." This was, in fact, a sign of their optimism: if victory came, they believed, it would be narrow and not secured until the early hours of the morning.

They were wrong. From the first, the tide ran entirely Gilligan's way. He posted solid margins in most of the populous counties—57 percent, for example, in Lausche's home, Cuyahoga County—and ran close to even in many of the smaller, conservative counties that Lausche did carry. The final total was Gilligan 544,814, Lausche 438,588. A one-term congressman had taken the nomination away from a twelve-year incumbent senator.

Despite considerable head scratching—both in Ohio and in Washington, D.C.—no one could recall that having been done before. Indeed, when Gilligan and Hansan met after the election with the chairman of the Democratic Senate campaign committee, they were told that Gilligan's victory had "scared just about everybody in the building."[67] Incumbents were not to be defeated within their own primary, not even incumbents nobody much liked.

Curiously, Lausche in defeat polled almost the exact same total as his winning primary margin six years earlier: he received 438,588 in 1968 compared to 437,902 in 1962. The difference was the huge upsurge in non-Lausche voters, a tide that justified Gilligan's belief that there were a great many "real" Democrats out there—if they could only be rallied to the polls. It was a victory that Gilligan shared with organized labor. The week after the primary, the *Washington Post* reported that Ohio labor "made its most impressive showing in a decade" in Gilligan's victory.[68] The article went on to call attention to the impact of labor's computerized efforts and its likely success in elections to come. For the moment, at least, the tie between Gilligan and the unions was strong.

The Gilligan-Lausche contest caught the headlines, but somewhat less noticed that day was the nomination of William Bart Saxbe, Ohio's third-term attorney general, as Gilligan's Republican opponent come November.

Saxbe was a career politician, having won election to the Ohio House of Representatives in 1946 at age twenty-three and risen to the post of Speaker. During his first term, he wrote later, he never rented an apartment in Columbus as he could not afford one. At the time, he was still a full-time law student and supplemented his low legislative salary by performing various odd jobs, including that of proofreading proposed changes to the Ohio Revised Code. By the time that code actually became law, Saxbe was Speaker of the House of Representatives. He was a fairly powerful Speaker in part because Governor Frank Lausche took little interest in legislative matters and also because he enforced a measure of decorum in the House. (He banished lobbyists from the floor and forbade one representative, Patrick J. Dunn, from clipping his toenails during session.)

Saxbe styled himself—and was styled by others—as the Squire of Mechanicsburg, named for the tiny Champaign County crossroads where he and his wife, Ardath, known as Dolly, acquired a farmhouse. He liked Mechanicsburg, he said, for its versatility; there he could practice law, sell real estate, repair cars, and go hunting and fishing, all as mood and moment suggested. Saxbe claimed to have done all the remodeling of the farmhouse himself, a statement that prompted one visitor to say it explained why nothing in the dwelling worked quite properly. He was agreeably profane and chewed tobacco, both for pleasure and for show; he could with some regularity shoot a stream of a tobacco juice into an unresisting tin can, a skill quite likely Jack Gilligan never spent much time attempting to master.

William Saxbe, unlike Jack Gilligan, had no surpassing wish to be a United State senator. He was, at heart and by nature, a statehouse politician. Along with everyone else, Republicans believed that the victor of the 1968 Senate election would be incumbent Frank Lausche. By multiple accounts, party leaders approached Saxbe with an offer: if he would "fight the good fight" against Lausche in 1968, they would clear his path to the 1970 gubernatorial nomination—the post Saxbe most wanted. With Gilligan nominated, however, Saxbe and those in his campaign realized they were in a race they might win.

18

The Summer of Discontent

Through his career, Jack Gilligan took part in fourteen campaigns, be they primary or general election. Of those, his victory over Frank Lausche was likely the most satisfying. With that victory, Gilligan was suddenly big political news—"the hottest political property in America," state Democratic leader Pete O'Grady said, with perhaps a touch of parochial pride.[1] But within three weeks of victory, a cold rain fell on Gilligan's parade. This happened within the Democratic Party's larger political story: the race for the presidential nomination between Vice President Hubert Humphrey, who represented the party establishment, and the dueling insurgent candidacies of Eugene McCarthy and Robert Kennedy.

Gilligan had early been drawn to the Kennedys. For Gilligan, John Kennedy's 1960 election victory represented an opening to the future: "We had had a win with Kennedy, which for the first time in a long while generated around the country the idea that there might be a political future."[2] Even before the Democrats United challenge in Hamilton County, Gilligan sought contact with the Kennedy circle. In this he succeeded, coming to know Kennedy aide Kenneth O'Donnell, speechwriter Ted Sorenson, and, to an extent, Robert Kennedy, then attorney general.

In Gilligan's view, Robert Kennedy was his brother's "enforcer": "He was a really tough guy and he didn't mind carrying that reputation; he had the confidence of the President, and that's all he needed."[3] Robert Kennedy, Gilligan said, was a political omnivore who would remain after the meeting, retire to a local saloon, and pick the brains of all present. Where does this guy stand? What does that group want?—information used to clothe and feed the network Robert maintained for his brother.

The Kennedys' circle extended to include historians, litterateurs, athletes, and the occasional astronaut. After John Kennedy's assassination, the gathering place had moved from Hyannisport to Robert and Ethel Kennedy's Hickory Hill farm in McLean, Virginia, near the nation's capital. Gilligan had been a guest at the farm, though in relation to the extended clan he considered himself to be no more than a distant neighbor. But he was close enough to observe the transformation Robert Kennedy underwent following his brother's death. Gilligan recalled, "Jack's death shattered him."[4] Though elected to the Senate from New York in 1964, Robert Kennedy largely withdrew from the routines of politics.

> I always said he grew more as a person in a few years than anybody else I had known. Jack's death did it. He was almost catatonic; he could have walked off a bridge. His personal suffering and loss made him aware that there were good people who had suffered troubles over which they had no control, people born in unforgiving circumstances. That drew him back into politics. And as a candidate he managed to communicate this empathy to others.[5]

The empathy communicated nowhere more strongly than in impoverished urban black neighborhoods, where Kennedy's hand, his touch, his acknowledgment were urgently sought. Campaign chronicler Theodore White wrote: "Touring a deep ghetto with Robert Kennedy was like being in the eye of a hurricane, and as dangerous . . . He would clamber up on the slippery red leather back-rest of his open car and there, balancing, would talk through a bullhorn. The hands would reach for him, grabbing for a thread, a shoelace, a shoe; in the near hysteria, anyone in the car with Bobby would become a bodyguard, protecting him."[6]

Through the spring primary campaign, Gilligan, with his own race to run, had adopted a carefully neutral stance on the presidential nomination. Peter Hart commented, "Through the primaries Jack had been very close to Bobby; there were a lot of phone conversations between them. Clearly, Jack's heart was with the Kennedys."[7] This was evident when, on May 14, 1968, Robert Kennedy stopped in Columbus to confer with Ohio delegates to the upcoming Democratic National Convention. Gilligan met him and his contingent at the airport. They headed downtown in an open convertible. Bill Berry, Kennedy's bodyguard, rode up front; Gilligan and Kennedy rode in back, with Ethel Kennedy seated between. Several carloads of reporters followed. About a mile from the Statehouse, the lead car for some reason turned off the main road and into a black neighborhood. There the motorcade stopped. In minutes, a throng of 500 had gathered around Kennedy's car. Kennedy climbed onto the trunk of the car shaking hands, with his bodyguard's arms wrapped around his legs. (At that point Gilligan's chief concern was for the safety of Ethel Kennedy, who was six months pregnant.) Gilligan recalled: "Then a big guy took Bob's hand, took his arm in his other hand, and just pulled him out of the vehicle. He was riding on top of people's arms, like you see at a football game."[8] The bodyguard and Gilligan pushed their way through the crowd to drag Kennedy back. The convertible eased its way out of the neighborhood, through the crowd, and continued on to the Neil House for the scheduled meeting with state delegates.

The encounter may not have been unusual for the Kennedy campaign, but for Gilligan it had unwelcome consequences. His challenge to Lausche had been largely financed by labor, and in the 1968 race the AFL-CIO was hardly neutral. The labor organization was solidly behind Hubert Humphrey, the inheritor of the Johnson mantle and a longtime, strong, and forthright supporter of labor issues. Mark Shields, who joined the Gilligan campaign later that year, commented, "Labor was 100 percent for Humphrey. Anything that in their judgment would hurt the vice president's chances was not just an aberration, it was disloyalty."[9]

AFL-CIO president George Meany was not slow in making his displeasure known. Gilligan had been invited to a mid-May lunch with Meany in Washington, D.C. However, on arriving in Washington on the morning of the meeting, Gilligan was unceremoniously told that the session was cancelled. According to *Washington Post* columnists Rowland Evans and Robert Novak, Meany was "furious" over Gilligan's decision to ride with Kennedy from the Columbus airport. While there were reports that Meany had been informed that Gilligan went to the airport as a courtesy, not an endorsement, this apparently cut no ice with the labor chief. Meany wanted Gilligan to endorse Humphrey. "But Gilligan is staying neutral," Evans and Novak reported, "and Meany is fuming."[10]

The division within the Democratic Party was widening into a chasm. It was divided between those who supported American policy in Vietnam and those who were appalled by it; between party regulars who felt they had paid their dues and citizen insurgents who felt their own moment had come; between those who viewed the day's much-ballyhooed "counterculture" of "sex, drugs, and rock and roll" as a threat to traditional values and those inclined to see it as a warranted response to those values. As much as anything, though, it divided the old from the young.

Meany's snub had hurt. But for Gilligan, the cruelest cut came a few weeks later. He spent Tuesday, June 5, campaigning in northwestern Ohio, returning exhausted from Toledo to his home at 10:00 P.M., arriving in Cincinnati just as polls were closing for the California presidential primary. Several hours later, he was awakened by a phone call from an Associated Press reporter asking for his thoughts on Kennedy being shot.[11] "I said, 'That was years ago. Why are you asking me about it now?'" The reporter clarified: "No, *Robert* Kennedy; he was shot in California tonight." Gilligan recalled blurting out "Jesus Christ Almighty!" and hanging up. "It just couldn't happen."[12]

Kennedy died shortly after he had claimed victory in the California primary, where he bested Eugene McCarthy 46 to 42 percent. Gilligan's view was that this victory would have propelled Kennedy to his party's nomination and his country's presidency: "I thought he would be nominated and elected. I thought the victory in California would lead to that."[13]

A week later on June 12, 1968, Jack Gilligan paid tribute to the slain senator at a memorial service held at the Xavier University chapel.

He was the third son of his family to die an untimely and violent death in the service of his country and it must be noted that in each instance these young men who possessed from birth all that the world is supposed to hold dear—wealth, position and security—each voluntarily risked everything, including life itself, not to enrich themselves or their families but to make this a better nation and a better world for all men. Their lives and their deaths present all of us with a challenge and standard of performance against which to measure our efforts and our concerns.[14]

At the time, Gilligan said, "we were devastated, everyone in the [Democratic] party was."[15]

Gilligan traveled to New York City for Kennedy's funeral mass, held at St. Patrick's Cathedral. He obtained the required tickets through longtime friend Bill Geoghegan, who had worked on the Kennedy campaign in California and had last seen Robert Kennedy the night before his assassination. Gilligan then boarded the train that carried Kennedy's body to Washington, D.C., for burial in Arlington National Cemetery. It was a grueling trip, he recalled, with the gloom compounded by delays that extended the normal travel time of three-plus hours to more than six. Gilligan sat with Geoghegan, somewhat fitfully discussing politics. Gilligan wondered whether any Kennedy campaign staffers—now without a candidate—might be interested in coming to Ohio to assist his own campaign. As it happened, they were sitting opposite Pat Lucey, a rising Democrat with a reputation for political savvy. Lucey crossed the aisle, chatted with Gilligan, and recommended Mark Shields be asked to join the Gilligan campaign.

Raised in the Democratic, blue-collar town of Weymouth, Massachusetts, Shields was political almost from birth. As a teenager he knew the names of the ninety-six U.S. senators as well as he knew the line-up of the Boston Red Sox, and Adlai Stevenson's defeat in the 1952 election, he said, was the first time he saw his mother cry. In 1964, Shields went to Washington looking for political employment. In 1968, he worked with Pat Lucey on Kennedy's behalf in the Nebraska primary; thereafter, Shields and his wife, Ann, moved on to the Kennedy effort on the West Coast. Following the assassination, the couple headed for a cottage on Cape Cod, intending to find a piece of quiet. Three weeks later, Shields received a telegram from Gilligan, inviting him to Ohio. Shields went. Gilligan found him to be "bright, knowledgeable, funny as hell—and very shrewd politically"—a judgment he never altered. In mid-July, Shields joined the campaign; he was Gilligan's first experienced campaigner.[16] Jim Friedman recalled how he arrived wearing a PT-109 tie clasp, a nod to the navy patrol boat on which John Kennedy had served in World War Two and a defining Kennedy insignia, and something that enormously impressed Jim Friedman.

Other former Kennedy hands signed on to the Gilligan campaign that summer. Phil Peloquin, age twenty-three, had been teaching in the Chicago public schools when he left his classroom to lick envelopes for Kennedy. He stayed with the campaign through the Nebraska and California primaries, by which time he was working as a campaign advance man, organizing and overseeing each campaign stop. The day before the Golden State voted, Peloquin was among a half-dozen campaign staffers sent to New York to work on that state's pending primary. Television brought the news of Kennedy's death their first night in town. Peloquin's next task was to help organize Robert Kennedy's funeral train. Shortly after the funeral, Peloquin met with Gilligan, Jack Hansan, and Bob Daley. He recalled, "I was very impressed with Gilligan. He struck me as incredibly bright; a wonderful sense of humor; and a sense of what is and what is not possible. I was kind of bowled over."[17] When a post was offered, Peloquin (an admitted "Ohio virgin—I'd never been there") signed on.

A second newcomer was Jim Dunn, who had been a soundman for Kennedy. This was in the days when tape recording was all reel-to-reel and editing was done by slicing and splicing the tape. Dunn spent the campaign at Gilligan's elbow, recording his remarks and then editing them—on occasion, in public bathrooms—into bits that he could transmit by telephone to Ohio's radio stations. Such transmissions generally began, "This is Jim Dunn . . . reporting live from the campaign trail with Jack Gilligan."[18]

In speaking about his political ambitions, Jack Gilligan said, not altogether in jest, "I would have given my soul for a seat in the United State Senate."[19] In the summer of 1968, Jack Gilligan was on the doorstep of that ambition: he had gained the Democratic Party nomination for the Senate from Ohio. Yet, over that summer, he focused much of his time on an issue outside the immediate demands of his own campaign, an action that, in retrospect, may have cost him the election.

That issue was Vietnam. In March 1968, Gilligan had publicly called for the United States to halt its bombing of North Vietnam. At the time, the question of continuing or stopping the bombing was the common demarcation line between those supporting a continuation of the Johnson administration's policy and those seeking alternatives to it. "In the course of the war," Gilligan said much later, "I had become more and more convinced that our position—and that of the Democratic Party—was a total disaster that we would be pay a terrible price for our country in the world if it continued."[20] Gilligan believed that a pro-war policy would be a disaster for the Democratic Party in the 1968 national election, and conversations with other Democrats in the course of the year persuaded him that his views were fairly widely shared: "There was deep opposition, and it wasn't from just a bunch of long-haired kids camping in the park. It was from serious people who approached government in a serious way and played serious roles within the national party."[21]

It was out of this feeling that Gilligan initiated an effort to draft a peace plank for inclusion in the Democratic National Convention platform. He believed that no possible Democratic candidate could win in November unless the platform adopted by the convention distanced the party from the status quo of the present Vietnam policy. The story of this episode is well told in what is perhaps the best account of America's 1968 presidential season, *An American Melodrama,* by three British journalists. The account largely parallels those of Gilligan and Bill Geoghegan, who served as deputy counsel to the platform committee. (Geoghegan, interestingly, was a close friend of Hale Boggs, the Louisiana congressman who served as convention chairman. The latter friendship dated to Geoghagen's days as an official in the Justice Department under Robert Kennedy. It was Boggs, Geoghegan said, who appointed him deputy counsel.)

Beginning with former Kennedy aide Kenneth O'Donnell, Gilligan enlisted various Democratic leaders he felt might be sympathetic to the effort. On August 1, the group—Senators Claiborne Pell and Wayne Morse; Kennedy supporters Fred Dutton, Frank Mankiewicz, and Ted Sorenson; McCarthy supporters Blair Clark and Joe Rauh; O'Donnell and Gilligan—met at the Carroll Arms Hotel in Washington to map strategy. Gilligan was, if nothing else, traveling in fairly heady company. To be in a better position to support the effort, Gilligan soon secured a position as an Ohio representative on the Platform Committee.

Gilligan's involvement with the peace plank, however, put him at risk of stepping on the toes of organized labor, since AFL-CIO support for Johnson and the war was nearly total. Anecdotal evidence of this, William Sheehan, a Cincinnati labor leader friendly to Gilligan, recalled the AFL-CIO 1967 convention in Bal Harbor, Florida. A series of Johnson administration speakers—and the president himself—assured the convention that there would be no retreat on Vietnam. After the talks, Sheehan recalled saying to Bill Kircher, the longtime Gilligan associate who had brokered Gilligan's first meeting with the AFL-CIO, "What happens when you start to have doubts on the war?" According to Sheehan, Kircher replied, "You keep them to yourself or you get out of the [labor] movement."[22]

Two weeks after the gathering at the Carroll Arms, the *New York Times* reported that the AFL-CIO had cut off its funding to Gilligan's fall campaign—specifically, the *Times* said the unions had stopped payment on a $10,000 check sent to the campaign "following a complaint from Vice President Humphrey that Mr. Gilligan was not supporting his bid for the Presidential nomination."[23] As reported, the incident began when the Humphrey campaign sought a formal endorsement from the Ohio delegation and Gilligan responded that he intended to remain uncommitted. Humphrey then wrote Al Barkan, AFL-CIO political director, and, describing Gilligan as "ungrateful," sought his help in "persuading this fellow Gilligan" to support his candidacy.[24] For his part, Barkan insisted no funds had been cut off; none had been committed. The *New York Times* quoted Gilligan aides as saying that the national labor organization had "tentatively promised as much as $200,000" to the effort. Humphrey dismissed the *Times* story as "plain unadulterated bunk."[25] Gilligan, too, perhaps attempting to mend fences, said he did not know "the foundation" for the news report.[26]

As a matter of practical politics, drafting the peace plank required finding wording that urged a change in policy without directly condemning the Johnson administration. On August 21, the *New York Times* identified the tentatively arrived at key points: a halt to the bombing of North Vietnam; a cease-fire; and a call for direct negotiations between the South Vietnamese government and the National Liberation Front, the political arm of the insurgents. That draft, the *Times* reported, had been written by Kennedy aide Fred Dutton, assisted by Gilligan. Two days later, the newspaper identified Gilligan as among the five-member "ex officio subcommittee" that was pursuing negotiations on the peace plank.[27]

At the time, Gilligan's assessment of the peace plank's prospects ebbed and flowed: "It was like any campaign," he said later. "You have your ups and downs. You get some information from one part of the battlefield that things are going well; and then you get bad news from other areas."[28] He added, "I became more and more convinced that whatever position Johnson took and whatever else happened, we had to get out of that war."[29] At one point, success appeared within reach. Late on Friday, August 23, Gilligan met with David Ginsberg and Bill Welsh, two high-ranking associates of Vice President Humphrey. For more than an hour, the men refined phrasings of the plank language, narrowing the distance between the Vice President's and the peace advocates' positions. The meeting occurred in the Statler Hilton hotel room of Bill Geoghegan, playing the dual role of host and lookout. At one point, Geoghegan recalls, Hale Boggs knocked on the door, and, entering briefly, asked: "Do you mind if I come in and find out what you fellows are doing?"[30] Actually, Geoghegan did. He knew Boggs' chief loyalty was to Lyndon Johnson—if Boggs learned what was up, Johnson would likely have word of it soon thereafter. In leaving, Boggs cast what Geoghegan termed an "et tu, Brute" look in his direction.

After studying the draft, Ginsberg said, "There is not ten cents of difference between this and the Vice-President's policy."[31] This meeting has been characterized as "one of those poignant moments in politics when a tiny group of men, just below the top rank, feel capable of staving off disaster."[32]

This did not prove to be the case, for "the real power, that of Lyndon Johnson, had not been represented" at the session.[33] Johnson was not budging on the war. And Humphrey, not yet the nominee, was unwilling to break with him on the issue. Gilligan concluded that Humphrey was trapped: if he sent out word that he wanted the peace plank included on the platform, then that word would quickly reach Johnson, and then, Gilligan suggested, "Johnson would have gotten on the phone and said, 'What's this I hear, Hubert?'"[34] Geoghegan—though as deputy counsel officially neutral—sided with Gilligan. The administration was offering nothing, or, as he pithily put it, "Johnson was giving us the sleeves out of his vest."[35]

On Monday, August 26, rival Vietnam planks presented their statements to the platform committee. The peace plank, written in part by Gilligan, called for an immediate bombing halt and for deescalating America's involvement; the administration version said a bombing halt could come only when it would clearly not endanger U.S. troops and that further, de-escalation depended on the ability of the South Vietnamese army to take on a greater share of the fighting. Within the platform committee, the administration view prevailed by a 65–35 vote; the issue was next to go to the convention floor.

The Democratic National Convention, held in the last week of August 1968 in Chicago, was not only a gathering of Democrats but the target of thousands of people, largely young, who came to protest the war, the probable nomination of Hubert Humphrey, and, perhaps, American society in general. Some who showed up were student radicals, of whom at least a few actively sought to sow disruption. More, however, were supporters of the various peace candidates. And a fair number were merely curious. Anticipating the protests—perhaps, indeed, anticipating much larger crowds than occurred—Chicago had girded itself, taking on appearance of a city under siege, with National Guard units reinforcing the city's police forces.

Kathleen Gilligan, now twenty, and Ellen Gilligan, sixteen, arrived in the city with their mother in a station wagon driven by Jack Hansan. Kathleen recalled, "As we headed to the convention center, there were armed soldiers on the street. And as you got closer, they were closer and closer together. And when you got to the convention center itself, they were arm to arm. There was real tension. This was something [none of us] had ever seen before."[36] Gilligan, concerned for their safety, told his daughters not to leave the Sherman House hotel where the Ohio delegation was lodged; he told his sons to cancel their plans for coming to Chicago, paying their way to the family cottage in Leland to ensure they would be beyond temptation's reach.

At the convention itself, Gilligan split his time between the peace plank effort and his own Ohio delegation—"so they would not think I was just freelancing and ignoring them."[37] That delegation was split, Gilligan said, as it was both "pro-Humphrey and pro-me." A national convention, Gilligan observed, is not a straightforward thing—the crosscurrents of competing ambitions swirl around the floor. One example of this was when Gilligan shared a cab ride with Senator William Benton of Connecticut, who was working hard for Humphrey. He was doing so, the senator told Gilligan, because he believed he had Humphrey's commitment that if Humphrey was elected, Benton would be appointed ambassador to Great Britain.

The full convention debate on the respective Vietnam planks occurred on Wednesday, August 28. The two-hour session was curiously muted: by design, speakers for each side alternated in five-minute presentations, an arrangement that made it difficult to build momentum for an argument. Gilligan traced this to the control of the hall by the Johnson forces; it was they who decided "who got admitted to the building; who sat on the committees; who got to do the speaking, and on what terms and conditions were they able to speak."[38]

U.S. senators Gale McGee and Ed Muskie, Congressman Hale Boggs, and Missouri governor Warren Hearnes were among those speaking for the administration's majority plank. Those arguing for the minority plank included Kenneth O'Donnell, Senator Al Gore Sr., Ted Sorenson, and John Gilligan. In his remarks, Gilligan urged delegates to consider the impact the war had had not only on the "tortured nation" of Vietnam but on America itself:

> We have lost 25,000 young American lives in Vietnam, lives and talents which this nation desperately needs for the solution of problems at home. We have spent $100 billion, money and resources that are again needed for the repair of the ravages of our own society. Scripture says: "What fathers, if asked by their sons for bread, would give them a stone?" Our young men have asked for a chance to build and develop, and we have sent them over the seas to destroy and kill.[39]

When delegate votes were cast, the majority plank prevailed by a 1,567 to 1,041 margin.

But the debates in the hall were being overshadowed by the events in the streets. David Broder, among the most moderate of men, said of 1968 that "it was the first time I ever thought the country might actually be coming off the rails."[40] The year's first six months included the assassination of Martin Luther King, which saw widespread rioting in its aftermath, soon to be followed by the assassination of Robert Kennedy. And the angry campaign of Alabama's George Wallace attracted millions of belligerent adherents who were either opposed to the tide of racial progress or to the presumptions of Great Society social planners. But no moment so typified the year's unraveling as what happened on the streets of Chicago shortly before 8:00 P.M. on Wednesday, August 28.

For several hours, demonstrators, with the general agenda of marching on the convention site, had been stopped by lines of policemen near the corner of Michigan Avenue and Balbo Drive. Then, police permitted a mule train organized by the Poor People's Campaign to come through its lines. Many demonstrators, apparently believing they were free to follow, moved forward. As described by Theodore White:

> Slam! Like a fist jolting, like a piston exploding from its chamber, comes a hurtling column of police from off Balbo into the intersection, and all things happen too fast: first the charge as the police wedge cleaves through the mob; then

screams, whistles, confusion, people running off into Grant Park, across the bridges, into hotel lobbies. And as the scene clears, there are little knots in the open clearing—police clubbing youngsters, police dragging youngsters, police rushing them by the elbows, their heels dragging, to patrol wagons, prodding recalcitrants who refuse to enter quietly.[41]

A local Chicago reporter wrote:

Scores of people under the Palmer House canopy watched in horror as a policeman went animal when a crippled man couldn't get away fast enough. The man hopped with his stick as fast as he could, but the policeman shoved him in the back, then hit him with a night stick, hit him again, and finally crashed him into a lamppost. Clergymen, medics and this crippled were the special pigeons that night.[42]

In the course of the week, more than 1,000 demonstrators were treated for injuries; most occurred on that Wednesday evening. (A subsequent report, "Rights in Conflict," compiled by Chicago attorney Dan Walker, cited "unrestrained and indiscriminate police violence." The mass police movement into the demonstrators at the intersection of Michigan and Balboa, the report said, "can only be called a police riot."[43])

Kathleen and Ellen Gilligan had obeyed their parents' injunction to remain in their hotel; mostly, they watched television, played cards, and ordered room service. Still, Kathleen recalled, "If you'd go down to the hotel lobby, there would be kids who had been in Grant Park. You could tell they'd been pushed around, coming into the lobby saying, 'We're being beaten.'"[44]

Jack Gilligan commented, "All the tumult in the streets began to filter into the hall, including delegates being roughed up on their way to the arena. The emotional level of the campaign in the convention hall just rose dramatically; delegates were screaming at each other and getting up and marching around the hall in the midst of someone else's speech."[45] But in the end all this sound and fury signified nothing. In Gilligan's judgment, "The outcome was pretty well determined by the control Johnson had of the hall."[46]

The following night that control was sufficient to ensure the nomination of Johnson's preferred candidate, Hubert Humphrey, who received 1,760.5 delegate votes. Eugene McCarthy got 601, and the others, together, received 261. Jack Gilligan—possibly with mixed feelings, possibly as a fence-mending gesture—cast his vote for Hubert Humphrey.

Mark Shields saw Gilligan's role in Chicago as evidence of both political commitment and political skill: "Jack very much took the lead on the peace plank. His argument was that the party needs this. To win Ohio, we need a peace platform. He wasn't just scratching his ideological mosquito bites or proving his purity; he saw it was an absolute practical matter."[47] At the same time, Shields said, both knew that with labor support now in doubt, a new source of financial support would be needed. The affluent liberals who had backed McCarthy were one possibility. Mixing his metaphors, Shields said McCarthy "had brought in a dairy herd of fat cats, and it would be a disservice not to continue to milk them."[48]

To build support among such donors during the convention, Shields undertook to get Gilligan on television as often as possible. The task proved relatively easy. Shields said, "There were three networks covering the convention gavel to gavel. And they loved conflict. There wasn't going to be a threat to the nomination—McCarthy and McGovern didn't have the votes—but there was going to be a fight on the peace plank. So they wanted to cover that."[49] By one count, Gilligan received twenty-two minutes of national television time at the convention.

Gilligan's strategy, however, had the defects of its virtues. In working-class Youngstown, the phone started ringing at the home of Bob Shipka, the high school social studies teacher who was heading the Gilligan volunteer effort in Mahoning County. The county was steelworkers' territory; indeed, it had been the United Steelworkers' local that had ponied up $2,500 so that Shipka could open a storefront office during the primary. And the phone callers were not happy. Shipka observed, "Your average blue-collar steelworker was not in love with the peaceniks."[50] Shipka's father, a former union leader, called to say, "Get him [Gilligan] the hell out of Chicago."[51] Jim Griffin, the director of Steelworkers District 26, called to deliver the same message. County Democratic chairman John Sulligan thought Gilligan was "being outrageous."[52] And soon after the convention a poll in the *Youngstown Vindicator* showed a marked tightening of the race with Saxbe in Mahoning County, what should have been secure Democratic territory.

Gilligan believed at the time, and later restated that belief, "that if Johnson had backed off an inch, the peace platform would have been adopted."[53] Gilligan added that what he and other peace plank promoters "failed to recognize was not only Johnson's persuasive powers and his general powers, but the degree to which he ultimately identified himself with the war. For anything to be adopted that to a degree discredited him would be a serious blow to his legacy."[54]

Gilligan's postmortem of his own efforts was not entirely happy. For the better part of six weeks—time he might have spent visiting courthouses and shaking hands in Ohio—he had devoted his time to the platform effort. "In many respects," he said, "I had no damn business getting involved. My main objective should have been the campaign for the Senate. All it wound up doing was alienating a good part of the labor support, which I believe cost me the election."[55]

Indeed, as the Democrats began picking up the pieces after their convention, Gilligan's Senate prospects looked shaky. Ohio political journalist Abe Zaiden wrote, "When Gilligan mounted the platform at the Democratic National Convention to support the minority peace plank, there was strong feeling within the hawkish Ohio delegation that he had all but written the epitaph for his own political funeral."[56]

19

"My Purpose Holds"

In his pursuit of a peace agenda, John Joyce Gilligan was not exactly AWOL from his Senate campaign: that campaign had almost ceased to operate. Following the spring victory over Lausche, the Gilligan effort went into hibernation. The major campaign headquarters were shuttered. This had occurred, perhaps, less because the nominee was in Chicago than because the campaign was broke.

On the Saxbe side, the tenor was entirely different. When Lausche was the expected opponent, the Saxbe campaign was not an entirely serious undertaking. One staff member recalled, "We were running around eating watermelon and not keeping expense accounts."[1] But with Gilligan's removal of Lausche from the Ohio political scene, it became at least an even-money bet that the GOP could pick up the contested Senate seat. At this point the Republicans sent in Robert Teeter.

Teeter, already a ranking Republican strategist at age twenty-nine, became the principal architect of the Saxbe effort, among other things coining the slogan "It Should Be Saxbe." Teeter believed in television advertising every bit as much as anyone in the Gilligan campaign, but unlike them, Teeter had money to spend. During July, Teeter dumped serious money into statewide television commercials. Campaign advance man Vince Rakestraw recalled, "I don't remember how much money was spent on TV, but it was a hell of a lot."[2] One estimate had spending at $250,000. Some commercials boosted Saxbe; some blasted Gilligan. A particularly effective one showed an American eagle under assault by the naysayers who presumably rallied to Gilligan's banner. All were aired without response from the Gilligan camp. Jack Gilligan's uphill defeat of Frank Lausche had given him a certain cache, momentum, and a more than modest lead. The Saxbe campaign's early television blitz challenged that.

This well-orchestrated thrust by the Saxbe camp contrasted painfully with the problems facing the Democrats. Their national convention had degenerated into a street brawl. While that gathering may have nominated Hubert Humphrey, for the moment Humphrey seemed diminished rather than enlarged by his victory. Millions of antiwar Democrats shied from supporting him; many traditional donors, believing Humphrey's campaign hopeless, kept their checkbooks firmly in their pockets.

Gilligan, meanwhile, was also faced with a divided party. In his primary victory, 40 percent of the ballots had been cast for Frank Lausche, largely by conservative Democrats who cast a doubting eye on the peace movement, the protesters, and those who associated with them. Portage County conservative party chairman Roger DiPaolo never forgave Gilligan for his support of the peace plank. The Franklin County party organization was lukewarm toward him. Hamilton County cochair Socko Wiethe still carried a grudge against the man who had tried to unseat him. And, in a move that was hardly surprising, Senator Frank Lausche eventually endorsed Republican Saxbe.

The political tone of the Gilligan campaign was to be largely shaped by Mark Shields, who on arriving in Columbus in July, like many political newcomers to Ohio, was struck by Ohio's complexity. He discovered that the state's northeast was industrial liberal; the middle band was pure Midwest conservative; the southeast was transplanted southern; and the southwest was congenitally conservative. There was no Chicago, no Milwaukee, and no Boston to dominate the media markets. Shields observed, "Toledo is so much different from Akron, which is so much different from Columbus. Each is almost autonomous."[3] This meant that one could not run a one-size-fits-all campaign; rather, the campaign must be tailored to the state's peculiarities. He also noted that Ohio had something of a one-and-a-half-party system: "The Republicans had a presence, a statewide organization, structure, and discipline. The Democrats did not."[4] And then there was the opponent, whom Shields had a fair regard for: "Bill Saxbe was an interesting and thoughtful man; we were not running against some cardboard cutout."[5]

State headquarters for the Gilligan campaign was on one of the upper floors of a building at 88 East Broad Street in Columbus, near one of the city's major intersections. Campaign manager Jack Hansan provided overall management of the effort, and Ann Shields (Mark's wife) managed the office and the volunteers who wandered in. Peter Hart was in charge of building the field organization, an effort he coordinated through five regional directors: "We concentrated in maybe as many as twenty counties. I can remember places like Tuscarawas, where we had a person and a little bit of an organization. But it was not as though all eighty-eight counties were organized."[6]

The Gilligan campaign was long on talent and short on resources. Jim Friedman, who coordinated Gilligan efforts in northeastern Ohio, later said, "It was a very traumatic experience of constantly being broke and being forced to forego certain campaign techniques for lack of money."[7] And the campaign was not without internal stresses either. Steve Kovacik, originally one of three assigned to manage Cuyahoga County, emerged largely by force of personality as the effort's sole director. In the view of many, he directed to headquarters in Columbus a stream of demands for resources the campaign simply did not have.

The strategy for the Gilligan effort rested on three premises, Shields recalled:

> We have a good television candidate; we have to get him television. We had separated from the Johnson administration on the war. Nixon is probably going to carry Ohio; we have to push the issues that divide us from Saxbe and Nixon. We have to get Jack and Jack's persona—message and messenger—out there. Television—both paid and free—was to be the vehicle for doing that.[8]

The campaign didn't expect much help from the Fourth Estate: other than the *Akron Beacon Journal* and the *Dayton Daily News,* which were friendly to Gilligan, most of the state's newspapers, particularly in Columbus and Cincinnati, were hostile.

But television meant money. Gilligan recalled how Peter Hart and others in Washington put together a campaign television budget: "We were to have so much money by this month and so much money by that month . . . Of course, we missed every deadline. The money wasn't there, so the programs were cancelled."[9] Jack Hansan pressed for another, fresh campaign film for the fall election. In the end, however, funds were insufficient to complete it, and an edited-over version of the primary film was aired instead, with Senator Ted Kennedy providing a fresh lead-in. Even scaled back, that effort cost $90,000; nearly as much was spent on the revised film as on the air time purchased to show it.

As early as September 15, the *New York Times* reported that the Gilligan campaign "is withering for want of the financial nourishment that union labor supplied last spring."[10] The *Times* noted that Gilligan had pared his budget to $700,000, "which is petty in a state with six TV markets, and he may have to cut it again."[11] Indeed, he would.

So what did the Gilligan campaign have? First and foremost, Gilligan said, the campaign had first-rate people—Mark Shields, Phil Peloquin, Jim Dunn, Peter Hart, Jim Friedman, and others. And, Gilligan said, "we had an enthusiastic base of volunteers"—thousands of them, in fact.[12] In Columbus, Ann Shields helped recruit an all-women citizens' group for the county and had hundreds of block workers doing door-to-door leafleting. Elsewhere, Gilligan for Senate committees were organized on thirty-five Ohio campuses, this coming at a time when most students still did not have the vote. Many of those who volunteered were moved by the peace issue. Vivian Witkind was one. An Ohio native attending college out of state, Vivian had returned home for summer break: "My family brought Gilligan to my attention. They said, 'There's this terrific guy from Cincinnati.' I was looking for an antiwar candidate, a McCarthy candidate."[13] Gilligan was her choice. She came to work at the state office in Columbus, doing "press release stuff."

And, perhaps surprisingly, Gilligan was able to make peace with much of the state-level labor movement. Journalist Abe Zaiden, who had written that Gilligan's pro–peace plank speech in Chicago appeared to be his death knell with labor, amended that view when he wrote that "a post-convention assessment of Gilligan's health indicates that reports of his suicidal death may have been premature."[14] It was a split decision, however. National labor organizations kept their distance, while the Ohio AFL-CIO—perhaps mindful that Gilligan had gone out on the limb for organized labor ever since the 1958 right-to-work controversy—bestowed its unanimous endorsement at a September 27 meeting in Columbus's Fort Hayes Hotel. The national AFL-CIO, Gilligan said "showed its support of Humphrey by cutting off my support and showing what happened to people who faltered."[15] Financially, he added, that was the main impact on the campaign. Ohio unions made up a portion of that loss: led by the United Auto Workers, about $100,000 in largely Ohio union money came to Gilligan's fall campaign—barely a third of what the campaign had received from labor in the spring primary race.

Of course, the campaign's chief asset was the candidate himself. Syndicated columnists Rowland Evans and Robert Novak summed up the obstacles facing the Gilligan candidacy and added, "Against this Gilligan has only his own style, wit, and charisma."[16] The issues Gilligan stressed on the stump—the war, the environment, the unmet needs of American's cities—were fairly standard fare for anti-war Democrats that season. But Gilligan often went beyond that to pose the more fundamental question: What kind of country did America wish to be? As a campaigner, he was still at times a bit stiff, but more generally he found his comfort and his voice and presented the aspect of being that relatively rare thing in politics—a serious man. Campaign worker Vivian Witkind said, "He was thrilling to listen to; he was exciting. He cared about what he said; no one can speak that well unless it is grounded in his character."[17]

Somewhat uncharacteristically in a campaigner, Gilligan never suggested that his audience was indebted to him. One report compared his rhetorical style against that of the Democratic nominee: "Unlike Humphrey, Mr. Gilligan never mentions accomplishments of the past in his appeals to the young, Negroes, low income whites and others who might feel alienated."[18] Asked about this decades later, Gilligan said: "I was always very uncomfortable with that line of thinking and talking. Any real accomplishment in the world reflects the efforts of a lot of people. I knew—and thought any thinking individual would know—that for an individual to claim personal responsibility was the height of arrogance."[19] If there was a weakness in Gilligan's style, it was that the professor in him was inclined to stray from his text. He would speak, invite questions, and often turn the question into a new disquisition, thus competing with his own original message. Campaign manager Jack Hansan noted that the speeches Robert Kennedy delivered in 1968 "were pretty much the same. Jack didn't have the discipline to stick to three or four points and repeat them. He was the professor, and a great story-teller."[20]

And Gilligan was seemingly indefatigable. From September to Election Day, he appeared at six to eight events a day—speeches at union halls, gatherings with supporters, radio interviews, and the like. Actually, as he recalled, "I was in a perpetual state of exhaustion."[21] What buoyed him at each stop "was the response that comes from the crowd if it is going well. I remember going into meetings not anticipating much turnout or enthusiasm; and found a lot of both. And this affected others: people in the field would get a response greater than they had anticipated, and that encouraged them to try harder."[22]

Virtually all public events were advanced by Phil Peloquin: "Jack would be giving a speech in town X at the Rotary. First question: Where's the Rotary Club? How do you get there? What's the lighting situation? Does the sound system actually work?"[23] (When he'd worked with Bobby Kennedy, each event had half a dozen advance men. Gilligan had Peloquin, and a few volunteers.) All matters must be considered. Where does every door lead? "You don't want to lead your candidate out a door and onto a loading dock when the television cameras are running?"[24] Some problems had no solutions, however. How do you keep local dignitaries from speaking beyond their supposedly agreed on five minutes? When the day's final event ended, the candidate headed for a motel room and Peloquin headed for the next day's site.

Bob Daley traveled with the candidate, often by car but more commonly by chartered executive aircraft as the campaign progressed. Daley's tasks involved everything from dealing with the local press to keeping the candidate on schedule. Gilligan, strapped for cash to buy radio time, made a point of seeking out what was local and free. Daley recalled, "He told me one time how important it was to spend an hour at a rural radio station, because instead of talking to a dozen people you'd talk to 500 or 1,000. Any opportunity for media took priority."[25] And time was not to be wasted. Daley recalls waiting for a rally to begin in a southeastern Ohio county seat, and Gilligan saying, "C'mon, let's shake some hands."[26]

Interestingly, and perhaps surprisingly, those at the core of the Gilligan campaign gave little thought to how the race was faring. Asked if he had been optimistic about the election, Peter Hart replied, "I can't really remember. I was just totally involved and totally committed. It was 24/7, and I loved every minute of it."[27] He added, "To give you a sense of how naive I was, Mark [Shields] came to me ten days before the election and asked whether I wanted to go on staff in Washington in the event Gilligan won. I had never thought about it."[28] As seasoned campaigner Mark Shields put it, "When you're in a campaign, you don't think, 'Gee, we're going to lose.' You think, 'What do we have to do today?'"[29] Still, Shields added, "we always figured we were competitive."[30]

While Gilligan was reaching out to young or disaffected, the "new politics" vote, Saxbe was poaching on what should have been Gilligan's home turf: the union vote. The Ohio AFL-CIO had endorsed Gilligan, but it did not represent all the unionized workers in the state. Among others, the Teamsters stood apart—and gave Saxbe their blessing. Gilligan recalled how Teamster leader "Big Bill" Presser explained the facts of politics to him: "He said, 'I got nothing against you, Jack, but Bill Saxbe and I have been friends for a very long time. He's done more favors for me than I can count, and I've done favors for him. He's a friend of mine.'"[31] Saxbe foraged for union votes in a used Greyhound bus (purchased for $13,000 and refurbished with $3,000 more). The Republican candidate later wrote, "We stopped the bus at a lot of plants and talked to a lot of workers."[32] And at each stops—Ohio Brass in Barberton, Timken Roller Bearing in Massillon, American Shipbuilding in Lorain, Ohio Screw Products in Elyria, and elsewhere—Saxbe would pop a plug of Mail Pouch tobacco into his cheek (brand chosen, Saxbe campaign staffer Vince Rakestraw said "for political reasons," since the candidate's real chew was Red Man).[33] Then, while speaking to an assembly of workers, Saxbe would shoot a stream of tobacco juice into some undefended receptacle, a feat that always proved popular.

When Saxbe toured Youngstown Sheet and Tube, Bob Shipka, who was coordinating the Gilligan campaign in the area, drew an anxious breath. Shipka recalled, "I heard from a lot of people in the mills: 'Here's Saxbe at the plant opening at 6 A.M. with coffee and donuts. The guy is really making an impression.'"[34] Shipka was sufficiently concerned to contact campaign manager Jack Hansan, but nothing came of it: Gilligan, perhaps taking these industrial workers for granted, rarely toured steel mills. Nor did he have what might be judged the approved wardrobe. Shipka remembers a big 1968 Labor Day picnic in Lake County: Howard Metzenbaum, one of Ohio's least likely cowboys, turned up in shirtsleeves and boots; Gilligan was attired in a white shirt and tie. Shipka managed to talk Gilligan out of the tie, which he judged "a historic achievement."[35]

Saxbe had many of the strengths of a retail politician—he was comfortable, casual, and given to telling those whose hands he shook that he knew they still had the same wife, but did they have the same .12 gauge? While touring plants, a Saxbe aide would snap a Polaroid picture of the candidate and whoever he was talking to and then give it to that person at the conversation's end. The Republican candidate's rhetorical range was limited, however. As Rakestraw recalls, "He did 'law and order,' because he'd been attorney general."[36] And, he added, "in Ohio, all politicians can do the 'jobs and progress' speech as easily as breathing. Those were the prologue and the postlogue of just about everything he said."[37] Demonstrating this, in his autobiography Saxbe summarized matters laconically: "The two major issues were Vietnam and crime. The voters wanted an end to both, and I promised I would do what I could to get that accomplished in Washington."[38] Saxbe drew further points with labor when, late in the campaign, he declined to cross a picket line set up by cafeteria workers at the University of Dayton, where he was scheduled to speak.

Saxbe had another notable advantage. For most of the race, Republican nominee Richard Nixon was running way ahead of Democrat Hubert Humphrey, a lead likely to mean extra votes for Republicans, who, like Saxbe, were down ticket of Nixon. Indeed, just weeks before the election, there was evidence that Humphrey was not heading for defeat but for disaster. On October 6, the *New York Times* reported that Nixon was leading in thirty-four states, George Wallace in seven, and Humphrey in just four, with five states undecided. That same day, in Ohio, the *Mansfield News Journal* published conflicting polls: one in "bellwether" Montgomery County gave Saxbe a seventeen-point lead, while a statewide poll showed the Republican a scant two points ahead of Gilligan.

Significantly, there was no one down ticket from Wallace; his American Independent Party was not running a Senate candidate in opposition to Gilligan and Saxbe. Early October predictions gave Wallace upward of 20 percent of the Ohio vote. How these voters split between Saxbe and Gilligan might well decide the outcome. Peter Hart recalled, "The key to understanding that election was the Wallace vote; we had to get Wallace votes to want to vote for Gilligan. That was the major challenge."[39]

The challenge was not lessened by the fact that the somewhat patrician Mr. Gilligan and rather rough-edged Mr. Wallace were not natural allies. Yet there was some evidence that Gilligan was drawing Wallace voters. The *New Republic* stated that "reports from southeastern Ohio, a rural Democratic stronghold where Wallace is running strong, say that comment on the county-fair circuit this fall disclosed strong voter support for a Wallace-Gilligan combination. The reason: both are speaking out."[40] The *New York Times* printed a similar assessment: "Mr. Gilligan is expected to get a good share of the [Wallace] vote . . . as both come through as fighters independent of established authority."[41]

But if Gilligan was seeking the Wallace voter, he was not doing so by cutting any slack for the Alabama governor. While Bill Saxbe made little mention of Wallace, Gilligan was more pointed. One newspaper reported, "Before labor groups, Gilligan has been known to look his audience in the eye and tell them if they want to 'vote for hate' then go ahead and support Wallace, and then to suggest that it would be easier just to move to Alabama where they 'know how to take care of their blacks and of labor at the same time.'"[42]

The campaign drew in the Gilligan family. After working for Allard Lowenstein, an insurgent Democrat on Long Island, John returned to Ohio to help out with his father's campaign. On October 10, he showed the campaign film at nearby Wilmington College and spoke to the Clinton County Democratic Committee; the following week he addressed the Auglaize County Democratic Dinner in Wapakoneta.

On October 15, Harry Gilligan, the candidate's father, spoke to the local Democrats in Grove City, just west of Columbus. Kathleen Gilligan joined the campaign following the end of her college term. None was more active than eldest son Donald, who maintained an almost full-time schedule speaking to small county Democratic dinners and student groups.

The Gilligan campaign was starving for funds. National labor's refusal to fund Gilligan's candidacy was drawing criticism. On October 10, Evans and Novak wrote that "with characteristic irrationality, labor is concentrating on the near hopeless Humphrey campaign in Ohio while ignoring Gilligan's more realistic prospects."[43] But that criticism wasn't generating any funds for the campaign. Jim Friedman organized a major fund-raising dinner in Cleveland in early October. The effort brought in over $30,000, the largest return on any in-state event, but it was a one-time occurrence and, realistically, the campaign needed ten times that sum. Part of the problem, campaign manager Jack Hansan noted, was that, unlike California or the Northeast, Ohio lacked "well-heeled" liberals who might provide substantial underwriting to a candidate who caught their fancy.[44]

So Gilligan went to the mountain. Gilligan was an onstage participant at two major fund-raisers for Senators for Peace, gala events held at the Boston Garden and Madison Square Garden in New York to raise funds for a group of Senate candidates opposed to the war in Vietnam. For the campaign as a whole, perhaps 40 percent of all funds came from out of state, much of it raised during these events.

On October 21, Senator Eugene McCarthy came to Cincinnati to headline a fund-raising rally at the University of Cincinnati field house, with the popular folk trio Peter, Paul, and Mary warming up the crowd. McCarthy spoke with a characteristic asperity about the American political process in general and the U.S. Senate in particular—which was, he told the crowd, why the election of men like Gilligan was so important. The *New York Times* reported, "As Mr. McCarthy departed under a resounding ovation, Gilligan workers took names of volunteers to work the neighborhoods of southern Ohio."[45]

McCarthy had spent that day traveling Ohio on the Gilligan campaign plane. Gilligan's younger daughter, Ellen, was excused from high school to go along with them. When her father asked what she had made of McCarthy, Ellen said: "Well, Dad, for somebody who is campaigning for you, he spent a lot of time talking about himself"—a comment, she recalled, that appeared to please the campaign advisers within earshot.[46]

McCarthy fared no better in the estimation of Gilligan's elder daughter, Kathleen, who attended the Madison Square Garden fund-raiser. By that time, the race between Nixon and Humphrey had narrowed sharply. Despite her antiwar sentiments, Kathleen Gilligan said, "I had been convinced by my father that there was a huge difference between having Hubert Humphrey as president and having Richard Nixon as president."[47] She expected McCarthy to give a rousing call of support for Humphrey; instead, the Minnesota Senator urged those present to wait until 1972 to readdress the issues insurgent Democrats had raised. Kathleen Gilligan recalled being "stunned" that, in her judgment, anyone could be so preoccupied with his own defeat as to be unable to "make a distinction between somebody who had been fighting for social justice issues his entire life and Richard Nixon."[48]

What goes often unreported is that as Election Day nears, most of those involved are drop-dead exhausted. The Friday before the election, Donald Gilligan, who was down to two or three hours of sleep a night, spoke as his father's stand-in at a Cleveland rally for Hubert Humphrey. The Democratic presidential candidate, Donald said, was so exhausted that he did not know where he was. For some reason, Donald's remarks followed Humphrey's. Someone handed Donald a stuffed animal that he for some undisclosed reason was to give to Humphrey. Donald spoke to the younger people in the crowd and, perhaps forgetting that Humphrey was standing behind him, observed that many of them were likely disappointed in the election's nominees. Still, he said, they had a responsibility to make a choice. (Afterward, Don recalled, Louis Stokes, the brother of Cleveland mayor Carl Stokes and himself a candidate for Congress, patted him on the back and said, "Good job."[49])

Exhaustion may have also played a role in the campaign's final major event. Throughout the campaign, Gilligan had repeatedly challenged Saxbe to meet in a debate. Given his combative articulateness, his grasp of detail and quick wit, the debate platform generally showed Gilligan at his best. At one point, Gilligan observed that twenty-two different television stations, forty-seven radio stations, and "the League of Women Voters in seven cities" had urged Saxbe to take up the challenge.[50] Saxbe declined. The Republican, Mark Shields observed, was following a frontrunner's logic: "if you are ahead in the polls and ahead in funds, you don't risk your standing in a debate."[51]

In Ohio politics, however, one venue is unavoidable: the debate hosted just days before the election by Cleveland's City Club. Saxbe bowed to protocol. One of his campaign staff member recalled, "I don't think he necessarily wanted to debate Gilligan. He respected Gilligan as an intelligent man and a good debater—and a debate in [heavily Democratic] Cleveland was not the best setting for us."[52]

As is the City Club's practice, the debate was held in conjunction with a luncheon. Roughly 700 people packed the ballroom at the Sheraton Hotel; many more followed the exchange through a live statewide radio feed financed by a Gilligan campaign that was confident of the outcome.

Saxbe spoke first. He was casual and composed. He began with a few general comments—change was needed "to pull this country together; to wind up this war; to get to the serious problems of poverty and pollution"—and then went on the offensive.[53] He called Gilligan a "rubber stamp" congressman for Lyndon Johnson who "voted ninety-four percent for the Johnson program." The Great Society had failed, Saxbe said, because Washington did not trust local expertise. Money needed to be spent on pollution and housing, but it had to be spent intelligently. Gilligan, he said, spoke of the need to do "new" things, but his model for the new was the 89th Congress. This, as campaign comment, was straightforward enough: Gilligan had been a strong Great Society supporter, and the liberal Democratic approach that stressed the federal government's role in problem solving was a fair subject for criticism.

Then Saxbe moved into rougher terrain. He quoted from a student newspaper account of a Gilligan visit to Cincinnati's Xavier University in 1964, which claimed Gilligan had said that "the university crowd should start riots and political revolutions in the area of what this country so obviously needs." Further, Saxbe said, the editor of the student paper was in the audience ready to vouch for the comments. This quotation had been dogging Gilligan for years. It had, in fact, been written by someone not present at the event; in fact, the moderator at the Xavier event had written that the student paper owed Gilligan an apology.

But Gilligan was often taken aback by character attacks. Several in the Gilligan camp believe their candidate was being set up but was too exhausted to realize it. At that point in the debate, Gilligan set aside the positive case he intended to make for his candidacy and instead took issue with the "attack" approach to politics. He repeated the various denials of the Xavier remarks. He then asserted that "$10,000 or $12,000" had been spent on a statewide newspaper ad alleging that he opposed law and order, "was an evil person, a subversive." Did the people who placed that ad, he asked, actually think it was an achievement to "sow dissension; seeds of suspicion; to pander to the worst elements in our society?"

Gilligan continued, consciously or not, restating the major influences on his political career. Sounding rather like Adlai Stevenson in 1952, he stated that "the prime responsibility of the candidate and the officeholder is to talk directly to the people and to point out to them the problems we have and to suggest the effort and sweat that is going to be required to solve them." Then, sounding rather like Robert Kennedy in 1968, he ticked off ways in which Americans could do better. Americans, he said, spent twice as much on alcohol as on higher education and twice as much on chewing gum as on the Model Cities Program. "I don't think the American people are content to live in a society—whether our income is $15,000 a year or $50,000 a year—if our children are half-educated; our cities are filled with violence; our air so polluted we can hardly dare breathe and our water so dirty we can barely bathe in it." The question, he asked, and which was met with considerable applause, was not "which team" would win this election "but what kind of nation do we wish to be?"

Saxbe responded to Gilligan's challenge. He agreed that pollution and poverty must be addressed. Gilligan, Saxbe charged, believed that "a more aggressive use the federal treasury is necessary to build the kind of country that we want." Saxbe said he believed the "spending power" of the country was limited, that "the

American taxpayer has about had it." Saxbe, quite simply, did not share Gilligan's faith in the efficacy of the federal government. Moving again to the attack, he said that Gilligan "summarily" dismissed public concern with law and order. During the April riot in Cincinnati, Saxbe said, Gilligan had "resisted the curfew" and had subsequently opposed both an antiriot ordinance and a tax issue to raise the pay of Cincinnati policeman. He cited his own efforts as attorney general to work with police; "sound, firm, but fair law enforcement is the answer to peace in our cities," he said. Saxbe added that the people Gilligan believed would benefit from the spending programs he proposed would do so only if they "are going to be safe going out of their houses at night"—a comment that drew strong applause.

Gilligan rose to the defense. Many people, he said, had worked to stave off the employment of "police state tactics" as a response to civil disturbance. Yes, he *had* violated the riot curfew in Cincinnati—and so had every Cincinnati city council-man, including the mayor, who had been on the streets as a hoped-for calming influence. His protest had been simple, he reminded: eighty-six people, none of whom was charged with riot, arson, or any serious crime, had been charged as curfew violators. No matter what their previous arrest record, family situation, employment history, reason for being out on the street, or demonstrated knowl-edge that a curfew had been issued, "each and every one of them was given a year in the workhouse and a $500 fine. Each and every one—including a recently returned Vietnam veteran—was slapped with a $10,000 bond."

Gilligan's tone gained urgency, reaching a crescendo when he said that "every American has the right to be judged on the basis of the circumstances of their case." Amid the applause, Gilligan, all put pounding the lectern, asserted, "If we abandon those principles, we may win an election; we may frighten a few votes into our pockets. But we will destroy our nation and I will have no hand in it." His comments concluded to loud applause.

The question-and-answer period that followed produced little beyond one agreement: Saxbe asserted that the federal budget could be balanced if the $30 billion annual expenditure on Vietnam was returned to the economy, and Gilli-gan agreed, claiming that the federal deficit was largely due to the war in Vietnam. Gilligan noted he had been one of the five men who had written the peace plank, which had drawn 40 percent support at the convention, and added, "We can look forward to the day when the war will stop."

In his autobiography, Bill Saxbe stated that by the time of the City Club debate his lead in the polls had narrowed to fewer than ten points, an acknowledgment that Gilligan was gaining ground. (Actually, most polls had the two closer.) Saxbe claimed to have won the debate or, at least, "it had been no worse than a draw."[54] A recording of that debate suggests that Gilligan's principled defense of his actions found strong support among the immediate audience in the Sheraton Hotel. How-ever, his recurrently being placed on the defensive—in protection of "rioters" and high taxes—likely made a less favorable impression on those listening by radio. Indeed, the Saxbe campaign used snippets of Gilligan's remarks in its radio advertising during the final weekend of the campaign.

The following Tuesday, both sides were guardedly optimistic. Saxbe campaigner Vince Rakestraw recalled, "Given Gilligan's ability, I was never overconfident."[55] From Columbus, he made repeated calls to Cleveland to seek a projection of Gilligan's margin in that Democratic stronghold. The Republican campaign believed that Gilligan needed a 175,000-vote edge in Cuyahoga County to offset Republican strength in central and southwestern Ohio.

Gilligan's Columbus-based campaign staff—not without bias—took an office pool of predictions: all saw victory with 51–53 percent of the vote. Jim Friedman flew to Cincinnati to join Mark Shields to focus on the vote in Hamilton County. Gilligan suggested that his deficit in the strongly Republican county might be held to 20,000 votes. Results reached Friedman and Shields with painful slowness, however; the computer that tabulated the county vote had broken down. Amid this flurry of activity, Bill Saxbe was asleep: "Dolly and I went to bed, thinking I had lost."[56]

He thought wrong. Needing a 175,000-vote margin out of Cuyahoga County, Gilligan was held to 130,438. And when the numbers from Hamilton County did finally come in, they were dreadful. In his home county, Gilligan was swamped 219,219 to 131,046. The statewide totals were Saxbe 1,928,964, Gilligan 1,815,152.

Jack Gilligan was in Columbus when he learned that his political ambition—a seat in the U.S. Senate—would, at minimum, be postponed. The two dozen people crowded into Gilligan's hotel room included advance man Phil Peloquin, who recalled: "First, he made a rally speech. Then, he made a concession speech. He looked very much the same each time. He was very well in control of himself. Intelligent, elegant, spoke well."[57]

At the presidential level, Ohio's electoral votes went to Republican Richard Nixon: Nixon 1,791,014 votes, Humphrey 1,700,586, and George Wallace 467,495. Gilligan's margin of defeat was about 20,000 votes greater than Humphrey's. What is striking, however, is that outside of his home Hamilton County, Gilligan ran closer to Saxbe than Humphrey did to Nixon. While Gilligan lost Hamilton County by 88,173 votes, Humphrey did so by 48,524. It is difficult to attribute that difference to anything other than voter reaction to Gilligan's actions in the disturbances following the assassination of Martin Luther King Jr. In general, Gilligan fared better than Humphrey among the better educated voters and in the more affluent suburbs. Bill Saxbe may have been correct when he attributed his victory to the site visits he made to places like Youngstown Sheet and Tube and Tyler Roller Bearing. While Humphrey carried blue-collar Mahoning County by 25,485 votes, Gilligan did so by only 19,209.

Narrow defeats hurt worse. Ann Shields, the Columbus office manager, recalled, "It always felt like a winning campaign. We were very disappointed; we expected to win. It was really the first campaign I'd been in, which may have been why I expected to win."[58] Peter Hart remembered being "sad, disappointed, but I don't think I felt crushed. I thought we had given it a very good run. I thought Gilligan would be around again. I may not have been smart enough at twenty-six to know that this is how life is going to play out, that you don't get all the chances you expect."[59] Indeed, the Gilligan staffers may have been protected by their very youth, by the thought that time was on their side, that there would be another election to win. In acknowledgment of this, Gilligan, ever the professor, gave a number of his campaign workers plaques, each bearing an inscription from Tennyson's "Ulysses":

For my purpose holds
To sail beyond the sunset, and the baths
Of all the western stars, until I die.
It may be that the gulfs will wash us down;
It may be that we shall touch the Happy Isles,
And see the great Achilles, whom we knew.

Narrow defeats also prompt postmortems. In the Gilligan camp, the common refrain was the lack of money. Jim Friedman said, "If we had had anywhere near the money Bill Saxbe had for television, we'd have beaten him easily. I'm sure of that."[60] Campaign manager Jack Hansan said that the expenditure on the fall campaign was $504,000—a figure considerably under the earlier $700,000 projected budget the New York Times had termed "petty" for a state the size of Ohio. Some, both inside and outside the campaign, placed the blame at labor's doorstep. The Dayton Daily News editorialized that organized labor, having pushed Frank Lausche, its "aging nemesis," from office, had "abandoned its champion in the general election."[61]

Reflecting years later on the campaign, the person most directly involved in the outcome—John Joyce Gilligan—questioned these common theories regarding his defeat. "I don't think money was the issue. More dollars would have helped, [but] I don't know how much difference it would have made."[62] Instead, he focused on what had been achieved: "For years in Ohio, we Democrats had been going through the motions of running campaigns, but without hope of winning. We finally saw things moving our way. We identified volunteers and sources of money; there was some union militancy we had not anticipated. We had something to build on for future campaigns."[63] From Gilligan's perspective, something of substance had been accomplished: the 1968 election had made Gilligan the leading Democrat in the state. Stephen Young, the state's senior U.S. senator, was increasingly inactive in the party; the popular John Glenn had yet to run for statewide office; Howard Metzenbaum was still best known as the man behind Young's Senate campaigns; Carl Stokes had a limited base outside his home city of Cleveland; and Frank Lausche had been ousted.

Not all Gilligan supporters took defeat easily. In Youngstown, coordinator Bob Shipka "was devastated by the loss."[64] This was, no doubt, on his mind when, three days after the election, Shipka called Gilligan out of the blue and said, "Jack, you've got to run for governor."[65]

20

Setting Sail for Columbus

In the immediate aftermath of the Senate campaign, Jack Gilligan was weary beyond words. The defeated candidate, Jim Friedman recalled, "was in poor health for about six months following the election. The election had taken quite a bit out of him. He later told me he had suffered some fainting spells."[1] In defeat, he faced the immediate tasks of restoring his physical vigor and securing the means to support his family.

Gilligan returned to the insurance business in Cincinnati with Bill Sauter, who was engaged in marketing a then new type of group plan that combined mutual funds and insurance coverage. Such work paid the bills, but it hardly held Gilligan's full attention. He continued to ruminate on American politics and the career he might chart therein. With the election of Richard Nixon and the continuation of the Vietnam War, American liberals were in a dismaying mood. Their expectation that little good would come of the Nixon administration tended to feed pessimism about the nation generally. As others, Gilligan focused his concern on what he saw as the dangerous deterioration of America's cities.

Two months after his loss to Saxbe, Gilligan wrote an essay arguing that virtually every American city of more than 500,000 people was "rapidly becoming ungovernable if it is not already so."[2] He traced this to the disempowerment of inner-city communities. He contrasted the life of Norwood, a close-in suburb, with Cincinnati's impoverished Basin. Norwood had it own mayor, police, fire department, school system, and sundry other institutions, all in fair measure answerable to the needs and wishes of the community. The Basin had none of these; it could not even determine on which day trash would be collected. What the Basin did have, however, was a per-capita income that was less than one-third of Norwood's, 30 percent adult illiteracy, and 31 percent unemployment.

The most interesting aspect of Gilligan's essay is its sharp departure from the top-down assumptions of the Great Society that he had supported so strongly when he was in Congress. Many federal programs, he wrote, took "the Community Chest approach in which the beneficiaries of the program are supposed to be respectfully silent in the presence of the administrators . . . who are [presumed] brighter, better, and wealthier than they."[3] The authorities, he added, suggested to the poor that the system was "dispensing to them . . . more than their due."[4] He questioned whether the expertise to rebuild America's cities actually existed: the "nation-building" efforts aimed at America's inner cities, he thought, were little different from, and no more successful than, those being taken in South Vietnam. For him, the issue was one of social cultures. How did a sophisticated nation like the United States deal with a "backward" people—be they in Southeast Asia or southwest Cincinnati— who lacked the high-end job skills, the financial capital, and the traditions of self-government that the majority culture assumed necessary to success?

Gilligan distributed his essay to some like-minded sorts, though not to any particular outcome. In its writing, he was perhaps not so much moving to the Left as moving toward the pessimistic. Nixon in the White House, the continuation of the war in Vietnam War, the Democrats' distance from power, and, perhaps, Gilligan's uncertainty about how Democrats might use the power they did not have—all combined to move Gilligan and others into a stance that verged on despair.

Nor, closer to home, was there much to prompt hope. Writing in the *Christian Science Monitor* on October 29, 1969, David Hess stated: "In Ohio politics, war and misfortunes seem to run in cycles for the state Democratic Party. Every two years, party luminaries batter each other in the primary election, then lie hopelessly stunned while Republicans flee with the general election prizes. Next year promises little if any change in the Democrats' lot."[5]

One underlying reason for the Democrats' disadvantage was money, and in 1969 there was little cause for optimism. Longtime Ohio reporter Brian Usher wrote that in the 1960s, the Ohio Republican Party raised $500,000–$1.5 million annually, an amount determined by the significance of the elections to be fought in a given year. Meanwhile, "Democratic state chairman Eugene [Pete] O'Grady ran the party from an aging hotel room with worn rugs, bare light bulbs, and a mimeograph machine on a budget of about $50,000 a year."[6]

Jack and Katie still lived at 1875 William Howard Taft Road, but their nest was all but empty, with Ellen, a high school student at Summit Country Day School, the only Gilligan child still living at home. Each of the three older children had adopted some variation of their parents' politics and social consciousness and, in some cases, some of their father's combative nature. Donald, who graduated from Harvard in 1969, taught at a Cleveland public high school, a "difficult" assignment that qualified as an alternative to the draft. After assigning his students James Baldwin's *Another Country,* which was not on the school's approved reading list, he was "more or less" asked to leave (after several parents objected to what they regarded as sexually explicit passages, something Donald found odd given that three students in the class were pregnant at the time). He then moved to a parochial school in Columbus and, with the Catholic school system in the city verged on bankruptcy, helped organize a union and publically advocated the sale of diocese-owned property, with the pro-ceeds to be applied to the schools. He was, he said, "fired the next day."[7] John, who had drawn a low draft lottery number, enlisted in the Ohio National Guard in 1971, completing his basic training at Ft. Ord, California. Kathleen was a senior at Trinity College in Washington, D.C., and was increasingly active in the antiwar movement: "I was in Washington, so we were at the front edge of a lot of the mobilization marches that were taking place there"—notably the November 15, 1969, march that brought a half-million protesters to the capital.[8] She recalled, "We had kids who were coming and staying at the college, sleeping on sleeping bags. I was involved in a number of antiwar activities. Being in Washington during that time was feeling like you were sort of at the edge of the earth."[9]

It was a welcome respite from the insurance business when, in the spring of 1969, Gilligan received a six-week appointment to the Kennedy Institute of Politics at Harvard. It was not only a congenial, collegial setting in which to discuss American politics; it was a vantage from which to consider his next political move. The U.S. Senate remained the primary object of Gilligan's political affections: "My interest—intellectual interest—was the Senate, national legislation and politics."[10] In mid-1969, Gilligan gave sustained thought to a 1970 run for the Ohio Senate seat held by Democrat Stephen A. Young, who, at age eighty, was expected to retire. Gilligan explained, "I always had my eye on the Senate; I thought it was a great position."[11]

His was not, however, the only glance being cast in that direction. While Gilligan was considering entering the race, he recalled, "Howard Metzenbaum came to see me and said he wanted that Senate race and would run against me." Metzenbaum, Gilligan noted, "was a single-minded guy."[12] As, indeed, was John Glenn, who it was generally assumed would also be a candidate. Gilligan concluded, "I didn't want to end up in a primary with Metzenbaum and/or Glenn."[13] Even if successful, Gilligan believed a two- or three-way primary fight would so absorb resources and divide the party as to make success unlikely in the fall campaign against the expected Re-publican nominee, Robert Taft Jr.

As one door closed, another was opening. The governorship was also due to be filled in 1970. Gilligan said that the Ohio governorship was "a much bigger position than any I had previously encountered in my political career."[14] This was particularly so given that he was, essentially, without administrative experience, still, he recalled, "the more I looked at it, the more interested I got in the potential of the position."[15]

At home, Gilligan found slim support for the idea among his family: "They didn't want to see me get banged up."[16] Several of his children expressed doubts. "They argued that, first, I could not be elected as a liberal Democrat to the office of governor; and second, if elected, I would never be able to change anything."[17]

In Gilligan's recollection, only his sister, Jeanne Derrick, was unabashedly for the undertaking.

He sought other opinions. Jim Friedman, the first to urge Gilligan to take on Frank Lausche, was among those arguing that he set his cap on Columbus. An underlying logic applied. Since the days when Democrats United challenged John Wiethe for the Hamilton County party chairmanship, Gilligan had worked to create a modern Democratic Party in Ohio. That task would not be complete, Friedman argued, until a Democrat sat in the governor's mansion. It was an argument that helped push Gilligan's thinking: "I became convinced, first, that for the party and the political movement, the governorship was the great teaching prize and, second, that I could win it."[18] Further, seeking the governorship would let him finesse the expected Metzenbaum-Glenn battle for the Senate nomination. Remaining outside that contest, Gilligan noted, "would make it easier for them to support me in return."[19]

By fall 1969, Gilligan had decided to make the run. He had further decided that he wanted his campaign to be directed by Mark Shields, who was then director of campaigns for the Democratic National Committee (DNC). (Shields attributes being hired at the DNC in part to the warm letter of recommendation Gilligan sent to DNC chairman Fred Harris after the 1968 election: "Jack, having lost a heartbreaker of a race, then devoted his time and energy to helping those who had worked for him."[20])

Gilligan formally announced his candidacy for governor on December 18, 1969, in words that called on the nation's capacity for change: "The feeling is everywhere. We need a change. We need a fresh start. We need to sweep away all of the slogans and double dealings of the old time politics and politicians, and we need more than anything else to deal honestly and straightforwardly with the problems that beset us."[21]

Gilligan, by his own acknowledgment, had no extensive background in state politics. So after announcing his intention for the state's top job, he began cramming for it. Jim Friedman directed the three-month effort: "We felt our primary task was to educate Jack Gilligan, very deeply and very quickly about the issues in state government—its operations, the numbers, the people, the problems, the whole thing."[22] The prep team created task forces on education, taxation, and other areas and recruited experts, including a number of people from New York City consulting firms who volunteered time for the opportunity to influence a potential governor. Gilligan was, as ever, a quick study with a retentive memory and analytical mind. Friedman said, "It was very obvious during the campaign that, because we had bathed Jack in all these facts, he knew much more about the state government and the issues confronting it than [his opponent] Roger Cloud."[23]

To this detailed course of study Gilligan added several broader perspectives of his own. The first was that Ohio's state government, lacking clear direction, was suffering from a general malaise that undercut whatever efforts individual state employees might wish to make. The second was that the state's public schools were in dreadful condition. "I visited communities around the state. They had a constant theme: their schools hadn't been very good to begin with and now they were going broke."[24] Gilligan believed that the Republicans who had been governing Ohio paid lip service to education, but, "aside from periodically kicking the teachers unions around," were unwilling to take needed action.[25] This circumstance continued, Gilligan believed, "because no one was prepared to bite the bullet."[26] And that bullet was taxes: Ohio had neither a state personal income nor a corporate income tax, thereby restricting the funds available to public schools.

The campaign staff came together fairly smoothly. Mark and Ann Shields arrived in late January. Key campaign slots included a number of familiar faces. Steve Kovacik as field coordinator. (His tenure was brief, however. There was considerable static between him and other top campaign figures; further, he may well have wanted the campaign slot that went to Shields. His unhappiness was no secret, and he was replaced by Dennis Shaul.) Jim Friedman, working as a volunteer, was deputy campaign manager and chief fund-raiser. Bob Daley, as before, traveled with the candidate, nationally prominent documentarian David Garth handled media, and Pat Cadell directed polling in the spring, with Peter Hart taking over thereafter.

Completing the inner circle, Gilligan hired Bob Tenenbaum as press secretary. In 1968, Tenenbaum's Army Reserve unit had been visited by Peter Hart, who urged that Tenenbaum take an interest in the Gilligan Senate campaign. Then, in 1970, when Tenenbaum, a journalist, was working for the Columbus United Press International office, he received a call from Friedman (a junior high school classmate from Cleveland Heights) that led to the offer to be Gilligan's press secretary. Tenenbaum said, "I did not have a clue what press secretaries did, but I knew the Statehouse press corps. So I said yes."[27]

While Gilligan's defeat of Lausche and close run against Saxbe had made him Ohio's ranking Democrat, the gubernatorial nomination was not quite his for the asking.[28] In the May 1970 Democratic primary, he faced challenges from Mark McElroy, a former Ohio attorney general, and Robert Sweeney, a former Ohio congressman-at-large. Confident of victory in May, Mark Shields chose a strategy that looked past the primary to focus the candidate's rhetoric on the alleged failings of eight years of Republican administration. In line with this, he limited primary expenditures to $100,000, a figure that precluded a media campaign. (By contrast, the victor of the GOP primary spent $400,000.)

Gilligan's low-key campaign appeared to work. During his race against Lausche, Gilligan could barely get a phone call returned by an editor; now, with the exception of the *Youngstown Vindicator,* every major state newspaper that made a primary endorsement endorsed Gilligan. In early April, a Pat Cadell poll showed Gilligan comfortably in the lead.

The three Democrats shared the stage at the Cleveland City Club on April 3. Speaking first, Gilligan gave a fair summary of the major points on which he would campaign. Ohio, he asserted, had a "long tradition of stumbling into the future" without considered plan or agreed purpose.[29] As a consequence, "We are finally coming to the realization that the great and wealthy state of Ohio is in a condition of collapse and chaos. Every school district in Ohio is on the brink of bankruptcy." Gilligan also ticked off Ohio's low ranking in almost every aspect of state government. Relative to wealth, Ohio ranked forty-seventh in public health; forty-ninth in police and law enforcement; fortieth in public welfare; forty-sixth in support of hospitals; forty-fourth in efforts to develop and protect natural resources. But he would not agree that Ohioans were the victims of bad government; rather, they were its author. The responsibility, he said, lay with the citizens and the voters. "Everyone has a contribution to make; whoever does not becomes a part of the problem . . . Government is we, the people, working in concert to accomplish together what we cannot do as individuals. We can make of our state whatever we want it to be."

In his own remarks, Mark McElroy seconded much of what Gilligan had said, but with less urgency and no clear call for action. Robert Sweeney took a different tack, contending that Ohio was paralyzed by fear, "the all-encompassing fear that nothing can be done to bring our Ohio society back to a state of unity." He said, "Fear has paralyzed us—on the extreme Left, the ultraliberal thrashing around with wild revolutionary schemes to solve deeply rooted problems overnight; on the extreme Right, we have the present administration—immobile, reactionary, in the hands of a plutocracy that will not move or experiment." To succeed, Sweeney added, any governor must engage the support of those in the middle.

The question-and-answer that followed offered one piece of clarity. When an audience member inquired, "Is there a candidate with the candor to tell us that state taxes are too low?" Gilligan responded: "I'll be happy to make that statement."

One opponent, Robert Sweeney, who had spoken of the fear abroad in the land, identified Gilligan as the cause of some of that fear. Traveling the state, Sweeney met with Democratic county chairmen, for whom he played what was alleged to be a recording of a meeting between Gilligan and a group of Black Panthers. Jim Friedman commented, "The one instance in the whole campaign where Jack lost his temper was when Sweeney challenged his patriotism. Jack gave an awfully curt response and Mark [Shields] and I were very disturbed at the way he replied."[30]

On the Republican side, Gilligan's likely opponent was State Auditor Roger Cloud. In the primary Cloud faced opposition from Attorney General Paul Brown, a former Ohio Supreme Court justice, and the bearer of a greatly popular Ohio political name, and Donald Lukens, a conservative two-term congressman from Middletown. On April 10, these three gathered on the same City Club stage, where Roger Cloud took to task Gilligan's criticism of their state: "Gilligan said last Friday: 'We are finally realizing that the great state of Ohio is in a condition of chaos and collapse." Now, nothing could be more ridiculous. One cannot govern Ohio's people by degrading and belittling their achievements. Such negative political rhetoric well underscores the difference between a candidate who ridicules the past and one who proposes solutions for the future." Cloud cited five areas of significant achievement under Republican governor James Rhodes: higher education, elementary and high school education, highway development, industrial expansion, and job development. He outlined those matters most pressing to him—crime, prison reform, education, and the environment—and then questioned whether Gilligan had the experience to succeed in state government.

> The urgency of these problems allows no time for on-the-job training. Problems can be solved only by drawing upon the wealth of legislative and executive experience. Ohio's toughest job requires someone who has the executive competence to recognize the state's needs and the innovativeness to spell out their solution. The governor must be able to work successfully with the legislature—the '70s require a governor who consistently demonstrates stability and mature judgment, someone the people can trust with Ohio's future.

Cloud targeted Gilligan's vulnerable spot: his lack of experience with state politics. Still, Cloud was the opponent the Gilligan camp most hoped to face in November. As a ranking member of the state's Republican Party, Cloud was doubly hobbled: first, he could not dodge responsibility for whatever might have been the failings of Republican rule; and second, he could not propose anything new without explaining why it had not already been undertaken.

During the 1970 primary season, however, most of the interest was not focused on the governor's race but on who would fill the seat of retiring U.S. senator Stephen Young. On the Democratic side, former astronaut John Glenn faced a challenge from wealthy Cleveland businessman and lawyer Howard Metzenbaum. In the GOP primary, the two biggest names in Republican Ohio, James A. Rhodes (forced from the governorship by term limits) was facing off against Robert A. Taft Jr. As it happened, the outcome of each primary race complicated Gilligan's political life.

John Glenn's early political career cannot be separated from that magic moment in February 1962, when Glenn, a much-decorated former Marine Corps pilot and original Mercury astronaut, became the first American to orbit the Earth. Since the Soviet Union's launching of *Sputnik* in 1957, the United States had seen itself as trailing in the "space race." This was more than a matter of national prestige, as millions of Americans feared a possible Soviet weaponizing of space, with nuclear devices orbiting above America's cities. Glenn's flight showed the world that America was still in the game. Tom Wolfe, who wrote of Mercury astronauts in *The Right Stuff,* described in a *New York Times* article the extraordinary public response to Glenn's feat:

"During his ticker-tape parade up Broadway, you have never heard such cheers or seen so many thousands of people crying. Big Irish cops, the classic New York breed, were out in the intersections in front of the world, sobbing, blubbering, boo-hoo-ing, with tears streaming down their faces . . . John Glenn, in 1962, was the last true national hero America has ever had."[31]

All across America, "roads, bridges, streets, schools and hundreds of babies" were named for him.[32] Biographer Richard Fenno noted two of Glenn's traits: his "civics book" view of politics as activist, high-minded, and optimistic and his "soaring ambition."[33] So it wasn't too surprising when, less than two years after his trip into space, John Glenn announced that he would challenge incumbent Stephen A. Young for the Democratic nomination to the U.S. Senate. Perhaps only a fluke prevented his election. Glenn slipped in a bathroom, cracking his head in the fall and leaving him with a persistent dizziness that forced him from the race.

Glenn, though widely seen as having all the virtues of an Eagle Scout, proved in 1964 to be a dreadful campaigner on behalf of his fellow Democrats. One observer wrote, "His campaign was badly organized, lackluster, and underfinanced. His unsophisticated polls told him what he wanted to hear, that hero status was transferable into votes."[34] As a "citizen politician" he had no deep ties to any major Democratic constituency—labor unions, blacks—nor did he make any great effort to create them. One political reporter wrote, "Glenn didn't do much but say, 'I'm John Glenn. Here I am. Vote for me.'"[35]

Though initially little known outside his native Cleveland, Howard Metzenbaum had been in Ohio Democratic politics for a quarter-century. And hustling. A biographer wrote that Metzenbaum's determination was rooted in "a strong work ethic molded by hard times, resentment of anti-Semitism and class consciousness, and an expectation that nothing in life would come easily."[36] He had grown up poor. At one point during his adolescence, he made extra cash by delivering groceries, a business that ended when his father sold the car to meet a mortgage payment. He ran a scattershot of enterprises while attending Ohio State University; graduated, and then graduated from its law school.

A member of a political family, Metzenbaum ran for the state legislature in 1942, just barely squeaking in: of the eighteen representatives Cuyahoga County sent to Columbus, Howard finished eighteenth. In Columbus, Metzenbaum was smart, liberal, and assiduous; he was named an "outstanding member" by the Ohio Legislative Correspondents Association during each of his four terms. In 1948 he was elected to the Ohio Senate, where the Democrats had a 19–14 majority. Metzenbaum wanted the post of majority leader but dropped out of the race when he learned that five Democrats planned to vote for a Republican rather than for him. According to family sources, Metzenbaum believed ever after that the defection had been prompted by anti-Semitism. He retired from the legislature following that term.

He did not, however, retire from politics or business. His largest enterprise was a string of airport parking lots. By 1965, he had 98,000 spaces in sixty cities. He was also a practicing and successful attorney, widely regarded as the brains (and the wallet) behind Stephen Young's successful 1958 and 1964 U.S. Senate campaigns. He maintained ties with state politics, serving as the chief lobbyist for the AFL-CIO. And he was drawn into the civil rights movement, joining Dr. Martin Luther King's famous march from Selma to Montgomery, Alabama, and helping arrange legal representation for arrested civil rights workers.

By 1970, Metzenbaum may not have been everyone's friend, but he was nobody's fool. He was backed by a great deal of money—much of it his own—and fronted by the most sophisticated use of television advertising Ohio had yet seen. Produced by cinematographer Charles Guggenheim, the cinema verité spots showed Metzenbaum in conversation with grocers, housewives, and painted-spattered workmen, among others. An admiring article in the New York Times said that "every commercial projected truth, reality, believability, both about the candidate and the voters with whom he was swapping ideas."[37] Ohio political journalist Richard Zimmerman wrote, "In one ad Metzenbaum was shown sympathetically chatting with a burly construction worker who suddenly began sobbing because he could not afford to buy a home for his wife and children. These spots finally convinced me that Metzenbaum was a serious, formidable candidate."[38]

On the Republican side, the most unusual thing about the standoff between James Rhodes and Robert Taft was that it was allowed to occur. In the Republican political process, candidates for particular offices were not so much nominated as ordained. Contested primaries were avoided, allowing money and venom to be reserved for the fall contest with the Democrats. (As, perhaps, an extreme example of this, in 1956 Ohio Republican senator John Bricker proposed that William Saxbe and Chalmers Wylie settle who would get the nomination for Ohio attorney general by flipping a coin.) Taft and Rhodes represented, however, distinctly different strains of Ohio Republicanism. Taft was a Yale-educated scion of the state's leading conservative family; Rhodes was the hard-scrabble product of Jackson County who dropped out of Ohio State University during his first semester. James A. Rhodes was also the most successful state politician in Ohio history.

Traveling once with a campaigning Ohio governor James Rhodes, journalists pooled their predictions of how often Rhodes would use the word "jobs" in his next talk. Hearing of this, the governor dropped a quiet bit of advice to newspaperman Richard Zimmerman: "Bet high."[39] Zimmerman did so. Rhodes then delivered the goods; he closed his speech affirming that "the goal of my administration will be to create jobs, jobs, jobs, jobs and more jobs."[40]

For James Rhodes, jobs were life's universal solvent. If a person had a secure, decently paying job, he argued, they would be less likely to turn to drink, to crime, or to divorce—the very things that raised the demand for the sorts of state services that Rhodes, in his many years as Ohio's governor, had no great inclination to fund. Any number of Republican candidates talked in favor of the needs of business, the virtues of the free enterprise system, or the perspective of the Chamber of Commerce, but Rhodes talked about what, to most people, was the most important consequence of such enterprise: a good job. It may have been a Republican's argument, but it was dressed in the democratic desire for self-sufficiency and well being that crossed class, ethnic, and racial lines.

Unlike Ohio's previous governors, who were reliably dour, Rhodes was ebullient. He was a booster, a salesman, and he never saw anything Ohio that he wouldn't endorse, praise, or eat. (Sometimes he could parlay two of those actions into a single statement, as when he told Ohioans that if they each drank only one additional sixteen-ounce can of Ohio tomato juice a year, the state would be blessed with another 2,000 jobs.) His appearance matched his persona. Carl Stokes provided a good physical description of Rhodes: "[He] stands over six feet tall and looks like a football player turned mortician. His gray hair is combed up in a small pompadour and then swept back. In the 1960s, he wore almost a uniform—blue suit, blue shirt, blue tie. He must have had a dozen suits, all the same cut and color. Yet somehow, on him it didn't look as plain as it sounds. He managed to look natty."[41] He also looked fit, the result of innumerable rounds of golf, a game to which he was devoted.

James Rhodes was born in 1909 in Jackson County, a landlocked bit of southern Ohio's coal country. Rhodes's father, who had worked his way up from shaft mining to a post as a mine superintendent, died when James was nine; in his high school years, he moved with his mother to Springfield, near Dayton. He retained his Appalachian accent, however, and his earthy country humor. (He once asked a visiting Nelson Rockefeller, the New York governor Rhodes greatly admired, if Rockefeller knew how to keep flies out of the dining room. Easy, Rhodes told his patrician guest, put a bucket of manure in the living room.)

In 1930, Rhodes headed to Columbus ostensibly to study at Ohio State University. He was only briefly, and irregularly at that, a student, withdrawing after a single quarter (during which he was placed on academic probation). Rhodes bore no grudge against the institution; in fact, he remained fabulously loyal to OSU, which was later the site of one of his most famous malaprops. Addressing a campus gathering as governor, he thanked his hosts for giving him the opportunity to speak at "this venereal institution."[42]

Rhodes was not in the classroom because he was busy with more urgent things. He was the proprietor of Jim's Place, a popular university hangout. During that time he also helped organize the first Ohio State Young Republicans Club and boosted the Knothole Gang, a sports club for children. In all of this he was making himself known, ingratiating himself, as preparation for the political career he intended. In 1934, "with a few dollars' worth of campaign cards and a door-to-door, flesh-pressing style that would characterize his campaigns through his political life," Rhodes beat the incumbent Republican ward committeeman.[43]

From there, he stair-stepped his way upward—in 1938, he won a five-way race for the Columbus school board; in 1939, he was elected city auditor; in 1943 (at age thirty-four), he became the city's mayor. Wartime Columbus was nearly broke; surprising given his later and long-term opposition to taxes, Rhodes worked to defeat a referendum that would have overturned the .5 percent payroll tax enacted by the Columbus City Council. In Columbus, Rhodes formed a valuable alliance with the powerful Wolfe family, which owned WBNS (the call letters standing for banks, newspapers, and shoes, which the family also owned, or sold).

With his eye on the Governor's Mansion, Rhodes in 1952 sought and secured the office of state auditor. In 1954, he gained the Republican nomination to run against incumbent governor Frank Lausche, who was seeking an unprecedented fifth term. Rhodes criticized this, saying, "No man has squatter's rights to the governorship of the great state of Ohio"—a remarkable statement given that Rhodes would eventually hold that position for sixteen years.[44] Lausche beat him handily. The governorship finally came Rhodes's way in 1962, when he swamped an ineffectual Democratic incumbent Michael DiSalle, gaining 59 percent of the vote.

Rhodes, like most of his predecessors, was deeply averse to asking Ohio voters to pay higher taxes. Unlike them, however, he loved spending money. Particularly, he loved the ground-breakings and ribbon-cuttings that went with new state projects. He hit on a scheme that allowed expenditure without apparent taxation: the bond issue. Normally, when a taxing district floats a bond, taxation to cover the interest payments and pay off the principal is part of the package. Rhodes presented Ohio voters with a series of bond issues that included no such payoffs; the costs of financing and retiring the bonds were to be borne out of the existing general revenues of the state. True, over time this was a detriment to the state budget, but in the short term it created money to spend.

In Rhodes's first eight years in office, 1963–71, Ohio voters approved four bond issues totaling $1.8 billion (easily $10 billion in 2010 dollars). This money Rhodes directed to highways, colleges, industrial development, and parks. That Rhodes spent on highways was hardly surprising; constituents loved highways, as did the construction firms that built them and were reliable contributors to Rhodes's campaigns. He also poured money into building colleges. His 1962 campaign for governor had featured a "Blue Print for Brain Power," which argued that the state needed to invest mightily in higher education. In office, he created a Board of Regents to coordinate higher education within the state. Virtually every sitting public university president opposed the move; none felt any great wish to be coordinated. Rhodes called the university presidents together and told them he was thinking of seeking $175 million for college construction—or maybe not if his regents bill failed. The gathered presidents decided the Board of Regents was a fine idea. In all, Rhodes's first two terms as governor saw $770 million spent to expand the state system, with new four-year campuses opened in Akron, Toledo, Cleveland, Youngstown, and Dayton and two-year institutions scattered around the state. In this, Rhodes more or less made good on his campaign pledge to put a state institution of higher learning within thirty miles of every young person in Ohio.

Like the bond issues passed without a dedicated means to pay them off, Rhodes's approach to college construction pushed costs into the future. Most of the buildings were not finished until after he left office. And while Rhodes had financed the bricks and mortar, he made no provision for funds to put books on the libraries' shelves, professors in the classrooms, or financial aid in the pockets of students. These were matters that Rhodes devolved on his successor.

His approach to his job was similarly casual. He was most comfortable with Chamber of Commerce types, boosters such as himself. He kept a first-class billiard table in the basement of the Statehouse, where he hosted regular games and gabfests with those he found congenial. He arrived to his office early, took care of whatever was on his desk, and then lunched at the Columbus Club at a big table reserved for him. After lunch, Rhodes sometimes napped on a chaise lounge in a small room off his executive office and, refreshed, went out for a round of golf.

But with Rhodes, it always came back to jobs. He opened state offices in New York and Washington, D.C., to promote development in Ohio and dispatched teams of state officials and businessmen—known as "Rhodes's Raiders"—to drum up business from other states. He ran full-page ads in the *Wall Street Journal* proclaiming that "Profit Is Not a Dirty Word in Ohio." He rounded up sixty Ohio businessmen and took them off to Europe looking for customers (even the Pope) and, covering all bases, also paid visits to Israel.

Among Rhodes's successes was the sparkling new Lordstown plant that General Motors opened in Mahoning County in 1966, which helped make Ohio the clear companion state of Michigan in the auto industry. But, according to historian Neal Peirce, "with automation making its impact ever more obvious and the aging facilities in such heavy industries as steel, actual manufacturing jobs in Ohio registered only modest [employment] gains in the 1960s."[45]

Events were catching up with James Rhodes, as two considerable embarrassments demonstrated. The state had long skimped on financial support of public education. In 1968, 19,000 schoolchildren in Youngstown and elsewhere in the state were sent home when their underfinanced districts simply ran out of cash. Rhodes's pro-business policy paired with weak regulatory standards burdened the state's environment and made acid rain one of Ohio's leading exports. In 1969, the environmental cost was underscored when a portion of the Cuyahoga River, flowing its polluted way through Cleveland, actually caught fire. Rhodes was a booster, a sincere lover of his native state, and something of a joke teller. But by the end of the 1960s, late-night talk show hosts were telling jokes about Ohio.

While Rhodes was a consummate Statehouse politician, he was not statesmanlike, a quality some associate with being a U.S. senator. At least that was the argument advanced by his opponent in the 1970 Republican senate primary, Robert

A. Taft Jr. Rhodes, Taft suggested, was not senatorial, or even particularly honest. The Taft campaign was aided in this by an April 1969 story in *Life* magazine, "The Governor and the Mobster."[46] The governor in question was Rhodes. And while the text that followed that headline did not entirely justify the inferences that might be drawn from it, the story hardly did Rhodes any good. The "mobster" was one Thomas "Yonnie" Licavoli, imprisoned in 1934 for involvement in a series of gangland murders. By lore, the mob had made a standing offer of $250,000 to anyone who got Yonnie out of the joint. This Rhodes did by pardoning the aged felon. The magazine offered no evidence that any money had changed hands but maintained that Rhodes should in any case have known better.

Quite possibly, all Rhodes knew of the matter was what he had been told by John McElroy, his chief administrative assistant, who took full responsibility for recommending the pardon. One Statehouse reporter who investigated the matter spoke with McElroy and "firmly believed he had acted in good faith."[47] Still, the issue was tailor made for Taft, who, referencing one of Rhodes's favorite statements, commented, "Integrity should not be a dirty word in Ohio."[48]

There was another matter that had been dogging Rhodes since it was first posed by Democrat Michael DiSalle in their 1962 race. At issue were campaign funds Rhodes had converted for personal use. This was legal enough under Ohio law, provided one paid taxes on the amount—which it appeared Rhodes did not do until the tax authorities raised the matter a good while later.

Still, Rhodes was hanging in the race. When the pair debated at the Cleveland City Club, "Rhodes, quoting extensively from Taft's earlier praise of the Rhodes administration, seemed to get the best of it. Before the confrontation, Rhodes had been slowly cutting into Taft's lead, according to the polls. His Saturday performance—telecast extensively in the state—may have given him still another boost."[49]

The day before the City Club debate, President Richard Nixon had sent large numbers of American troops into Cambodia in an attempt to maintain tacit neutrality in the war in Southeast Asia. This move sparked protests at many of the nation's campuses, including Kent State University in northeastern Ohio. On May 2, the campus ROTC building was torched, apparently the work of an arsonist. Historian Andrew Cayton wrote: "A Kent resident, fifty-nine year-old Luther Lyman, Jr., who was a car dealer active with the campus ministry center, later recalled the palpable sense of fear among the townspeople." On the evening of May 2, when they saw the flames rising from the ROTC building, "many people in this town thought their houses and their property was going to be next."[50]

Governor Rhodes ordered units of the Ohio National Guard to the campus. The Monday following, "hundreds of people formed a volatile crowd on the Commons. Some were cursing, jeering, and throwing rocks at the 113 young, inexperienced National Guardsmen clustered off to one side on an elevated area called Blanket Hill."[51] The guardsmen began falling back; then, at 12:25 P.M., some opened fire on the crowd. Sixty-one rounds of ammunition were fired off in thirteen seconds. The fusillade killed four students; wounded nine others.

The event produced a national outcry. For students and those who sympathized with them, it was the militarism of Vietnam being directed at civilians, with perhaps more to follow. For others, it was a fate the students brought on themselves through the self-indulgence that marked their generation. Gilligan's response was inequivocable: "I was outraged and said so from the highest hill."[52]

And, with the tragic event still undigested, Ohio was asked to vote the following day. Jack Gilligan posted a decisive victory, receiving 59 percent of the vote in a three-way race—and posting the largest plurality in state Democratic primary history. Roger Cloud did somewhat less well, receiving a shade over 50 percent in his three-way race. Both Senate primaries were extraordinarily close. To the surprise of most, Howard Metzenbaum claimed the Democratic Senate nomination over John Glenn by a final margin of 430,469 to 417,027. The Republican race was even closer: Robert Taft edged James Rhodes by 472,202 to 466,932. Journalist Richard Zimmerman noted that a week prior to the vote, three polls had Rhodes trailing by 7 percent or more: "There is no question that Rhodes' give-no-quarter stance [at Kent State] generally enjoyed wide support at the time."[53]

Both primaries had consequences for Jack Gilligan. John Glenn regarded the Senate seat as something of an earned reward; his defeat left him convinced Metzenbaum must have run a dirty campaign. Several decades of animus followed. In early 1974, it was Gilligan's unwelcome task to decide whether to fill a vacated seat in the U.S. Senate with Howard Metzenbaum or John Glenn.

Jim Rhodes's defeat in the Senate primary left him free to consider other options; after all, he was still the best-known Republican in the state.

In his victory speech, John Gilligan looked beyond the moment's triumph to the tragedy at Kent State: "Beyond any sense of hope for victory in November is a source and frustration. There is bloodshed on one of our college campuses . . . What has happened is that somehow, we have all lost our way."[54]

21

The 1970 Campaign

John Joyce Gilligan's 1968 campaign for the U.S. Senate carried with it elements of romance—it was a campaign of hope and, at times, of hope against hope. John Gilligan's 1970 campaign for the governorship of Ohio was an exercise in professionalism; it was about a politics whose time had come. As Gilligan recalled, "I think we were pretty confident that we could win."[1] State government was clearly deteriorating: "After years of inertia, there were a number of problems at the state level that had just sort of festered with no organized efforts to deal with them. As I got around the state, it became evident that there were lots of people who were ready for change."[2]

In general, campaigns have rhythms. As Gilligan press secretary Bob Tenenbaum noted, they resemble sporting events: there's a back and forth as first one side, then another, seizes the initiative or fumbles an opportunity. The 1970 race for the Ohio governorship between Jack Gilligan and Roger Cloud was not like this. Gilligan held a solid lead when the race began, and that lead only widened as that race progressed. One extensive series of polls reported by John H. Beavers in his 1971 study *Reconstructing a Republican Majority* showed Gilligan with a 6.8 percent lead at the outset of the campaign, a lead that stretched to 13.2 percent by Election Day.

The Gilligan forces mapped out the campaign at a Memorial Day weekend retreat at the Imperial House off I-75 in Cincinnati. In addition to Gilligan and Mark Shields, among those in attendance included Jim Friedman, scheduler Kathy Daveney, field coordinator Dennis Shaul, Columbus office manager Ann Shields, researcher Anne Bingle, and Bob Daley. By general assent, Shields was the most sophisticated political operative Jack Gilligan had worked with. One campaign staffer said "Mark was able to read people and separate out the real people from the phony. Mark knew who he could count on and who he couldn't count on."[3] He also had a gift for bracing the troops: "He's Boston Irish; he has a wit and a sense of people that manages to keep a campaign staff loose, which is, I think, terribly important."[4]

Financially, the 1970 campaign was a world apart from Gilligan's bid for the Senate, which had left Jim Friedman painfully aware of the restrictions that a financial squeeze placed on a campaign. Following that defeat, Friedman had vowed to Gilligan that no future campaign would ever go hungry again. And Friedman proved as good as his word. In the two months following the primaries, the campaign focused on fund-raising. Friedman orchestrated dinners in Cleveland, Columbus, Cincinnati, Toledo, Akron, and Canton, raising $50,000 or more at each. It was, Friedman noted, the first time state Democrats had charged $100 a ticket for a fund-raiser, an entry fee previously considerable impossible. "My job was to motivate them and show them it could be done."[5] These big donation events were supplemented by a series of smaller cocktail party–style meetings with the candidate, each meeting intended to raise $3,000. The funds, Friedman reported, were squirreled away in bank accounts to cover future media costs.

All consequences were favorable. It meant that campaign decisions could be made without reference to financial constraints or the need to raise money. It also meant that from July on the candidate's time could be devoted to campaigning. An additional benefit was that the general sense that things were going well and people were donating was itself an inducement to further contributions. In October, former Democratic governor Michael DiSalle forwarded a check for $500; a Sandusky attorney sent along $505 in checks collected at a cocktail party; and Harry Gilligan reported to his son that the general president of the Hotel and Restaurant Employees and Bartenders International Union had "money which he wants to put into your two little hands."[6]

And by 1970, money meant television. The 1970 campaign spent more on television, about $600,000, than the 1968 campaign spent on everything; indeed, according to Friedman, only the campaign of New York's Nelson Rockefeller spent more on media. The Gilligan team produced fourteen different commercials, all by David Garth. Gilligan's tagline—"He's honest, he's tough, and he'll fight for Ohio"—had a bit more edge than the Cloud's "He's the one man ready to govern Ohio." Cleverly, the campaign made heavy buys during the premieres of new television shows.

Gilligan commercials were characteristically keyed to some issue his campaign was raising. In one thirty-second shot, Gilligan stood by an archway that Rhodes had had erected on I-70 as it crosses into Indiana west of Dayton. He talked about the cost of the arch and about how a nearby school had closed down for lack of funds. These, he said, were Republican priorities. (Chris Buchanan, at eighteen a veteran of the 1968 campaign, assisted with this shoot, which had to be repeated a number of times because the sounds of semitrailers going past kept drowning out Gilligan's voice. Buchanan also assisted with a spot in which an older gentleman, having sung Gilligan's praises, ended saying, "I should know. I'm his father."[7]) Set in Greeneville, a slice of Americana northwest of Dayton, another commercial showed Gilligan strolling down a shaded street ruminating on the beauty of Ohio and urging that efforts be made to preserve it. Some of the spots had more edge. One featured Slim Hinzelman, with whom Gilligan had served on the USS *Rodman*. "Hell," said Hinzelman, "I knew this guy. He was on the ship with me, and he was the only guy with the guts to do down into that ship and pull out the ammunition before it blew up."[8]

Gilligan's field campaign was run out of the eleventh floor of the Lincoln-Leveque Tower in downtown Columbus, under the office management of Ann Shields, who thought Columbus more than marginally less interesting than Washington, D.C. She recalled, "We worked all the time. Then, one rainy day, we decided to go see a movie, *They Shoot Horses, Don't They?* It was a seriously depressing movie. Then we came out of the theater to discover we were still in Columbus."[9] Still, she added, "when you're part of a winning campaign, your view of things is improved."[10]

Phil Peloquin, chief advance man from the 1968 campaign, returned from a tour of duty in Vietnam in May 1970 to enroll in the University of Illinois law school. "Jack called. He said, basically, I need your help on the advance staff." Peloquin told his former boss that he was in law school, to which Gilligan replied, "I'm running for governor *now;* you can go to law school anytime." Two days later, Gilligan called again. Peloquin recalled, "He talked me into it."[11]

John McDonald joined the campaign shortly after the May primary. McDonald, the Democratic minority leader in the Ohio House, had made an unsuccessful bid for his party's nomination for attorney general. As McDonald tells it, following that defeat, "I went back to Newark and sulked for a week. Then Mark Shields called."[12] McDonald brought to the campaign inside knowledge on the state legislature—issues, history, and personalities—and he spoke on Gilligan's behalf in counties he knew well, often appearing with the candidate's father, Harry Gilligan, who, McDonald said, "was better with crowds than Jack or I."[13]

Jack Davis, a former McCarthy campaigner in the Columbus suburb of Bexley, served as campaign scheduler. His task, he said, was to "move Jack around the state—all eighty-eight counties, county fairs in small communities." Gilligan, Davis said, often wished to skip the smaller venues: "He did not want to go to some of the smaller places; I was blunt about it."[14] The schedule was largely determined by Mark Shields and Jim Friedman, with the events for each day marked out on a yellow tablet, generally with each day built around some "must do" event. Davis recalled, "One of them would say, 'There's a Jefferson-Jackson Day dinner in Mahoning County. What are other invites for the day?'"[15] Maybe six invitations arrived each day, Davis said; maybe half were accepted. The candidate was bounced around:—"Dayton in the morning, Youngstown in the afternoon, Marietta in the evening—just zipping him around the state."[16]

A triumvirate of Democrats—James Kaval, Jim Schiller, and Bob Moss—directed the campaign in Cuyahoga County. All signed on, Kaval said, "before we comprehended in any detail everything that would be involved."[17] By Election

Day, the trio had fifteen field offices scattered around the county—most of them housed in rented trailers—and were coordinating the efforts of 3,000–5,000 volunteers. The volunteers, Kaval said, "came from all over the ballpark. We tapped into union groups like steelworkers, oldsters, party members, youngsters. Cleveland had a very active chapter of the Americans for Democratic Action, and we tapped into that."[18]

The campaign had five field coordinators, including Alan Farkas, who had organized students for Gilligan at Cleveland State University in 1968. He became coordinator of thirty-three counties in southeastern Ohio, where he organized citizens groups and helped advance the candidate. (Farkas, memorably, tagged along with Mark Shields for a lunch meeting with a dozen labor representatives in Mansfield. When the waitress came to take drink orders, Farkas asked for a particular French cocktail. The waitress looked clueless. Later, Shields took Farkas aside, threw an arm around his shoulder, and informed him that, in Ohio, "Democrats drink beer."[19])

On the campaign trail, Gilligan pushed a short list of issues. Education was a natural; with schools closing throughout the state, it took little argument to persuade audiences that the Ohio schoolhouse was in trouble. Gilligan drew the support of the Ohio Education Association, the state's major teachers union, which gave his campaign its first ever endorsement. Gilligan also talked about the need for state action on crime; pointed out the absurdity of Governor Rhodes proposing to spend $750 million for a bridge across Lake Erie when many of the bridges in the state were in disrepair; and about workplace safety, the 70,000 Ohioans who had been injured on the job in the past year, and the inadequate workers compensation they had received.

Staff researcher Anne Bingle kept an updated map of school and plant closings in the state, material that might be fed into a speech to give it local relevance. If the campaign wanted to focus on pollution in Toledo, Bingle could supply not only facts on the subject but suggestions as to where best to make the announcement—"a great big smokestack here, a dirty river there, or something that had happened two days previously that was topical and would gain media impact."[20]

Donald Gilligan said that the 1970 campaign "was a much more organized campaign. The 1968 campaign had an ad hoc feel that was both its strength and its weakness; 1968 was about the war, and there was an emotional edge to everything."[21] In 1970, he said, that emotional element was gone; even the shootings as Kent State were played down. The theme of the 1970 campaign, he said, was that his father's opponent, Roger Cloud, "was a 'crook.' We didn't have to take it very much further than that."[22] Actually, Roger Cloud was not a crook, though a lot of the people around him could fairly be so accused.

"Everyone," said Mark Shields, "should be so lucky as to run against a Roger Cloud once in their careers."[23] Gilligan's Republican opponent in 1970 was not a

nonentity. Indeed, prior to his race against Gilligan, Cloud had never lost an election in thirty years of public life. He had served nine terms in the state legislature,
five of them as Speaker, before becoming state auditor in 1966. Statehouse reporter
Lee Leonard stated, "Guys would say that when Roger was Speaker he knew more
about the bills than anybody else because he actually read them all."[24] Future Democratic Speaker Vern Riffe said, "Roger Cloud wasn't a lawyer, but he knew the
Ohio code like some people know the Bible. When I first came to Columbus, Roger
Cloud knew more about state government than anybody around."[25]

Cloud had something of an all-Ohio upbringing. His father was a tenant farmer
and his mother was a schoolteacher. At age sixteen he graduated from high school in
DeGraff, having been both quarterback and class valedictorian. He once won $100
as a tenor in a singing contest. Later, he played semi-pro baseball in Des Moines.
In 1936, at age twenty-six, he was elected to the DeGraff School Board. A dozen
years later, he won a seat in the Ohio House. Cloud was not a mossback. During
his campaign, he put forth fairly well-considered positions on crime and vocational
education. Nor was he a committed antitax Republican, favoring a county income
tax whose proceeds would be largely directed to public education.

The fates, however, were multiply unkind to Roger Cloud. First, he was, by general consent, entirely without charisma. Lee Leonard termed Cloud "meticulous,
colorless, bland."[26] Perhaps the unkindest cut came from Cloud's own press secretary, who told one national reporter, "To know Roger Cloud is to forget Roger
Cloud."[27] Jack Gilligan commented: "Cloud wasn't a salesman like Jim Rhodes, who
went around the state enjoying the hell out of saying the same thing, preaching the
same nonsense wherever he went. Cloud was not a very vigorous opponent; just
one in a long line of people who went through the various chairs and offices on the
organizational chart of the Republican Party, and had won his spurs."[28]

Second, Cloud was a creature of the Ohio Republican organization at a time
when it was in decline. According to John H. Beaver's polling, the percentage of
Ohioans who rated Rhodes's performance as "good" dropped from 52.6 percent in
February 1970 to 36.4 percent in October 1970.

Third, Cloud was ill-served in his campaign, though possibly at his own behest.
He appointed his son, Clifford, as campaign manager. At one point, Kip, as Cloud's
son was known, was rumored to be having an affair with an out-of-town media consultant the campaign had hired. *Plain Dealer* political reporter Richard Zimmerman wrote, "To quash the rumors, Kip, his wife, and the media consultant jointly
appeared before a meeting of a rather nonplussed campaign staff to insist that domestic tensions among the three had been candidly discussed and resolved."[29]

But most of all, Cloud fell victim to a slowly unfolding financial scandal that,
where Ohio Republicans were concerned, hurt the just and unjust alike. On April
14, future campaign scheduler Jack Davis was sitting in a Manhattan hotel reading
the *Wall Street Journal* when he saw a note on Crofters, an investment scheme, and

thought, "Oh, my god. The whole Ohio GOP is tied into this frigging mess."[30] The immediate tipoff was that the American Stock Exchange announced it would be investigating Four Seasons, a company that operated retirement homes in Oklahoma and elsewhere. Four Seasons had received $4 million in loans from a fund controlled by Ohio's Republican treasurer, John Herbert. Herbert was authorized to invest up to $50 million of currently idle funds from the School Employees Retirement System (SERS) with the stipulation that such investments be securely made in federally guaranteed housing projects that carry a prime credit rating. Herbert, however, had invested $62 million, rather than $50 million. Moreover, these funds had been invested not solely in secure federal undertakings but in speculative private ones. This included $8 million lent to King Resources of Denver; $4 million lent to Four Seasons Nursing Centers of America in Oklahoma City; and $5 million lent to the Jim Walter Corporation in Tampa. These transfers had been brokered by an organization named Crofters, Inc., which had been paid $604,978 in finders' fees. The principal executives at Crofters were Gerald Donahue, a former Ohio tax commissioner and one-time assistant state attorney general under William Saxbe; Sidney Griffith, a Columbus attorney; and Harry Groban, described in the press as a "full-time money finder."

The scandal's payoff—figuratively and literally—was that Crofters had in turn donated over $30,000 to Republican candidates for statewide office: $15,000 to Treasurer John D. Herbert, running for attorney general; $7,500 to Senator Robin Turner, running to replace Herbert as treasurer; $5,500 to Attorney General Paul Brown, for his failed bid for the gubernatorial nomination; and $1,000 to Roger Cloud. (Both Herbert and Cloud returned the donations once they became known.) Additionally, it was revealed that Governor James Rhodes had accepted a $3,000 donation from Crofters during his primary campaign against Robert A. Taft that spring.

Reporter Richard Zimmerman's conclusion was that "three Republican candidates for state office in 1970 had been involved in approving millions of dollars in questionable, perhaps illegally speculative investments of state retirement funds" and of receiving campaign contributions in consequence.[31] Given that campaigns were in 1970 much less expensive than they are today, the Crofters' donations represented a significantly higher share of a campaign's total costs.

The story, in the parlance of journalism, had legs. For example, the *Plain Dealer*'s David Hopcraft did his first piece on the scandal just before Memorial Day; he was still reporting new revelations (some of them leaked by the Gilligan campaign to keep the pot simmering) on Labor Day. The story dragged, Zimmerman noted, "primarily because those involved desperately tried to cover up their shenanigans. Each new nugget of incriminating information had to be dug up step by tedious step, and each new revelation merited page one display."[32]

Consider a single week:

On May 24, five days after he had returned the $1,000 donation from Crofters, Cloud wrote House Democratic minority leader John McDonald that he had never accepted a dime of such money and was caught in the misrepresentation.

On May 26, Republican candidate Paul Brown announced that, whatever actions others might take, he was keeping the $5,200 contribution from Crofters.

On May 27, Cloud, as head of the Republican ticket, demanded that Herbert and Turner withdraw from the election. He also asserted that as the investments had been the province of the state treasurer, they were no responsibility of his as state auditor.

Beginning with the *Plain Dealer* on May 27, newspapers across the state began pressing the Ohio GOP executive committee to "act decisively . . . digging deeper into the mess, making findings completely public and expressing clear votes of confidence or no confidence in their present candidates."[33] When the executive committee met in Toledo to address the matter, it decided that unless "mitigating" circumstances were identified, Herbert and Turner were to be ousted. The *Dayton Daily News* editorialized, "If Mr. Herbert is telling the truth, he is guilty of not knowing what was going on in his own office. If he is not telling the truth, his integrity is as shaky as a high-rise soufflé. Either way, he should bail out of the attorney general race."[34] On May 31, the *Akron Beacon Journal* reported itself as "baffled by the casualness with which all involved have treated the disclosures about Republican campaign donations from a company apparently doing illegal business with the state. None of the individuals have publicly indicated that they feel they have done anything wrong or that their integrity has been challenged at all."[35] The GOP candidates were not resigning.

On June 16, the *Wall Street Journal* announced that Roger Cloud, acting under his investigatory powers as state auditor, reported that "a series of loans made by the state of Ohio to various companies appear to have been made illegally." His 400-page report fixed primary blame on state treasurer John Herbert, who "served in a unique fiduciary capacity and therefore was directly responsible for improper acts of his employees."[36]

As state auditor, Cloud had argued that while the loans were probably illegal, the state was making good money on the investment. This argument collapsed, however, when one of the firms in question, Four Seasons, filed for reorganization, a step that commonly precedes default. When that bankruptcy followed, Ohio found itself on a lengthy list of creditors and with no great hope of ever seeing that $4 million the state had lent Four Seasons.

By this point, Cloud was widely implicated in voters' minds. As one observer noted, while Cloud had name recognition, he was without "character recognition." And because of his relative blandness, few Ohioans had any definite fix on what sort of person he was. And because few Ohio voters had any definite idea of Cloud, it made it simpler for them to imagine him guilty. By July 1970, Beavers's polls reported that 21.4 percent of voters identified Cloud as the single individual most worthy of blame; another 18.8 percent named him as somehow at fault. Cloud also caught grief from the GOP establishment, which thought its gubernatorial candidate could have conducted some nice, discrete investigation whose revelations would not have been made known until after the election. Nor was Gilligan letting Cloud off the hook. On September 24, the Democrat released a statement charging that "Roger Cloud, auditor of state, under the statutory responsibilities of his office, was the first elected official in Ohio to know about these loans . . . He kept silent about this mess through the Republican primaries. He kept silent about this mess until after it was revealed by an Eastern newspaper."[37]

Crofters practically brought the Cloud campaign to a halt. By one account, Cloud was simply aghast at the effect the scandal was having on his personal reputation. He regarded himself as an honest public servant. He had returned the improper donation. He had led the investigation that pointed the finger of wrong at his fellow Republican candidates yet was still being tarred with the same brush. "To Cloud and his family, the blemish on his honesty and integrity had to be removed."[38] And that became Cloud's focus—"No thank you notes written, no follow up to May victory; no strategy for general election, virtually no personnel hired for the upcoming campaign; practically no direction or leadership, no morale inspiration."[39] The Gilligan campaign issued a press release which stated that a planned $100-a-plate dinner for Cloud had been cancelled because only twenty-five tickets were sold. To add insult, Turner and Herbert announced they would remain on the ticket, and the state GOP, claiming it had no practical way to launch a write-in campaign to replace them, decided to let them do so, a move which suggested that Cloud, who had demanded their departure from the ticket, had limited standing within his own party. This brought the matter to the attention of syndicated columnists Rowland Evans and Robert Novak, who declared Ohio "A Republican Disaster Area" and noted that the approval rating for the once well regarded Mr. Cloud had dropped from 67 to 51 percent.[40]

Singly and collectively, Ohio Republicans remained indecisive. On July 20, U.S. Senator William Saxbe endorsed the entire Republican ticket, Turner and Herbert included. Two months later, the state committee and Roger Cloud reendorsed Herbert and Turner, a step that Warren Wheat, the generally conservative *Cincinnati Enquirer* columnist, called "disgusting."[41]

Through all of this, the campaign for governor continued, though fitfully. The *Wall Street Journal* commented, "While there were plenty of other issues in Ohio (taxes and campus unrest) the whole style and content of the campaign became shaped largely by one thing, the scandal."[42] And with all this in the background, Gilligan returned repeatedly to the state's need to spend more on education, on the mentally ill, and on others who were the its most vulnerable citizens. He attacked Cloud's proposals on education as being inadequate, saying that Cloud's plan was "so wholly irresponsible that he abandoned it in a Celina speech the other day but his speechwriters haven't caught up so he repeated it here again."[43] More particularly, Gilligan said, "what is needed is a massive increase in state spending on education."[44]

And Gilligan talked about taxes—specifically, on the need for Ohio to adopt a corporate income tax, a statement beyond which he was careful not to go. Any talk of taxes made certain Ohioans—some of them Democrats—uncomfortable. Democratic chairmen from smaller counties advised, "Don't let them talk about taxes; don't let them do this. He's going to throw it away."[45] Drawing a rather careful line, press secretary Bob Tenenbaum said, "Gilligan never said the word 'income tax.' He talked about the environment, education, mental health, prison reform." Tenenbaum, however, acknowledges that "people knew they were voting for higher taxes."[46] (Interestingly, to the extent that Ohio voters had a tolerance for new taxes, it was not for the tax Gilligan favored. By one poll, 51.2 percent said that if a new tax was required, they would prefer that it be a sales tax increase; only 26.5 percent said an income tax and 4.0 percent an increase in property taxes.)

And if voters did not know that Gilligan favored a tax increase of some sort, Roger Cloud told them. In late-August, columnist Hugh McDiarmid wrote that Cloud "uses words like 'exorbitant' and 'unthinkable' and 'irresponsible' to describe Gilligan's proposals, which is strong language from Roger Cloud."[47] At an event in Cleveland, McDiarmid reported, Cloud referred to Gilligan's "infinite capacity to propose spending plans" and accused Gilligan of advocating "massive new spending—a billion dollars' worth."[48] Cloud continued to stress that as an experienced Statehouse politician and a Republican, he had the necessary skills to work with the state legislature.

In the background of the Crofters scandal, the Democrats were stealing a march on the Republicans, a move that would turn their pending election victory into a long-term advantage. With 1970 came the U.S. Census, after which all 132 seats of the Ohio General Assembly would be redistricted, and whoever controlled that redistricting would shape Ohio politics for the next decade. If Gilligan was elected, the five-member redistricting commission would include two Democrats—Gilligan, as governor, and one Democrat from the General Assembly—one Republican from the legislature and in all likelihood Republican secretary of state Ted Brown, regarded as certain of reelection; and the newly elected state auditor.

The Democratic candidate for this position was Joseph Ferguson Sr., a diminutive individual popularly known as "Jumping Joe" because of his habitual bouncing up and down. Ferguson was a longtime fixture in Ohio Democratic politics but was not considered one of the party's major assets. In 1950, syndicated columnist Joseph Alsop wrote that Ferguson was "something of a caricature of the genus American politician . . . a small turkey-cock of a man . . . [who] is virtually illiterate.'" Whatever might have been Ferguson's limitations, his election as auditor would give the Democrats the deciding vote on reapportionment.

As Gilligan's own election appeared probable, his campaign turned to ways to support the election of "Jumping Joe" Ferguson. By one account, the campaign transferred $26,000 from its own fund to that of Ferguson. Another story is that Gilligan campaign manager Mark Shields called Ferguson and recited for him the text of pro-Ferguson radio ads. Did Ferguson approve? Why, yes he did. Good, Shields purportedly said, because we started running them yesterday.

Taking the broad view, Jack Gilligan noted that Republicans "had simply overlooked the importance of the auditor's race"—further evidence, he thought, that the GOP's vaunted discipline was breaking down. During the Ray Bliss era, he suggested, candidates as compromised as Robin Turner and John Herbert would have awoken to learn they had been maneuvered from the ticket in a manner that almost seemed like a promotion.[50]

As his own victory seemed likelier, Gilligan added a third piece of his strategy: campaigning for a few younger, more liberal candidates for state representative. He attended a fund-raiser for Richard Celeste in Cleveland and campaigned for Henry Lehman in a suburban Cleveland district.

In mid-September, the Cloud campaign underwent a sharp shift. Apparently, national Republicans had concluded that Cloud's son, Kip, was the obstacle to whatever slim chance the Republicans had in Ohio. GOP national chairman Rogers Morton arranged to have the younger Cloud replaced by an experienced South Carolina political operative, Harry "Buck" Limehouse. Jim Fain, publisher of the pro-Gilligan *Dayton Daily News,* referred to Limehouse as "the hired gun the Nixon administration sent out to show Roger Cloud how to campaign dirty."[51]

Immediately, the Gilligan quote from the Xavier University student paper was front and center in the Republican campaign, presented, among other places, in each week's edition of the *Ohio Republican News.* Cloud backed that message with semi-tough talk of his own, announcing that where crime and civil unrest were concerned, blame needed also to be attached to politicians like Gilligan who had endorsed rioting as a suitable means for advancing an agenda.

By late September, the Cloud campaign had taken to the airwaves, painting Gilligan as a fomenter of civil unrest. The Gilligan campaign was ready. Mark Shields and Jim Friedman called a number of the stations to suggest, in their mildest tones, that the message being broadcast might be libelous. At least five Ohio stations discontinued the ad, though not WLW, a leading Cincinnati radio station, whose station manager said, "Documents submitted by [Gilligan] do not refute the quote attributed to him, in our opinion."[52]

In a mild way, the Cloud campaign managed to rally. Limehouse's influence, the *Dayton Journal Herald* wrote, brought "more professionalism, or at least the appearance of more professionalism, to the Cloud campaign than it had seen in the previous four months."[53] And there was also the effect of the "recent hard-hitting radio ads that infuriated Gilligan and loosened the purses of a number of Republicans who had been complaining about the campaign's inaction."[54]

In August, prior to Limehouse's arrival, Cloud gave a speech in which he laid out what he saw as the accomplishments of the Rhodes years: six new state universities had been opened; the number of vocational courses offered had risen from 1,100 to 5,000; 95 percent of the Interstate system in Ohio had been approved for completion, the highest in any state; seven years of balanced budgets. Looking to the future, Cloud then called for controlling social and campus violence, shifting the burden of school financing away from property taxes, and (modestly) taking steps aimed at reducing pollution. He closed, as he generally did, by emphasizing his experience in state government: "It is not possible for a governor to be extremely successful in dealing with the problems unless he is able to secure the compliance and the good will of the legislature."[55]

The following month, with Limehouse now involved in the campaign, Cloud spoke to Republicans gathered at the Ohio Fairgrounds. By this time his campaign had gone negative, painting Gilligan as a dangerous radical. Following predictable statements that Gilligan would tax the state to death, Cloud (who wasn't much of a hatchet man) quoted what Gilligan allegedly said at Xavier University. But he got it wrong. Gilligan, he said, had recently told a crowd at Oberlin College, "You can talk and march, pray and sing, shout and demonstrate—but, nothing is going to happen until you take into your hands the processes of government and shake it up and make it what you want it to be."[56] This statement might be translated: stop protesting, get involved—hardly a radical sentiment. And the Cloud campaign had no better luck with its repeated assertion that a Gilligan governorship would see Ohioans paying an additional $1 billion in taxes. The Gilligan campaign scoffed at the figure (though when the time came to submit a budget, the increase sought was greater than that).

The negative campaign failed. Bob Tenenbaum, the Gilligan campaign's press secretary, stated that "the Xavier thing was mishandled by the Republicans."[57] In part, this was a simple matter of resources: the negative Cloud radio ads were nearly lost amid the far larger number of Gilligan announcements. The Cloud campaign had been urged by national advisers to attack Gilligan across a broad range, yet make no attack until solid evidence was in hand, and to wait until a positive image had been created for Cloud. None of these things happened.

A more significant failure of the campaign was that the attacks did not get under Gilligan's skin and prompt him to say anything that might be used against him. Gilligan maintained a certain archness in his reply: attack him, he suggested, and you attack all who stood with him. He told one audience, "When anyone—politician or otherwise—questions my patriotism in seeking office, he insults the nearly two million Ohioans who in 1968 voted for me and what I stand for."[58]

By October, the Gilligan campaign was receiving favorable coverage not only in Ohio but nationally. This, John McDonald said, happened because the Washington press had been "carefully and assiduously cultivated" by Mark Shields, who told them that Ohio had a candidate that any national reporter should meet the next time he passed through the Midwest.[59] In an unusual pairing, Max Frankel of the *New York Times* commented that of all the candidates clamoring to be at the center of the public clamor, "only those who have come across as vigorous individuals, such as Governor Ronald Reagan in California and John J. Gilligan, seeking the governorship in Ohio, have managed to evoke what could be termed real enthusiasm."[60] Joseph Kraft of the *Washington Post* called Gilligan "a shoo-in for governor," noting that Ohio's commitment to "issueless politics" had been replaced by the Gilligan-pressed issues of education, pollution, and race relations.[61] And Kraft made explicit something the Gilligan campaign had been only hinting at: namely, that if a new corporate income tax did not produce the revenue the state needed, Gilligan would ask for a personal income tax. David Broder, likewise, in the *Washington Post,* reported Gilligan as well ahead of Cloud, adding that "most observers would be surprised if the standing were reversed."[62]

Indeed, Election Day brought no such surprise. Gilligan's margin of 378,954 was huge by Ohio standards, and Cloud's 43.5 percent was the second lowest a major party candidate had received since the Second World War. From Gilligan's perspective, the next most important result was the narrow victory Joseph Ferguson achieved in the auditor's race over Republican Roger Tracy. Ferguson's 1,477,000 to 1,427,000 win was likely attributable to the resources Gilligan had shifted his way. In the U.S. Senate race, Robert Taft defeated Howard Metzenbaum by 73,000 votes. And the two Republicans most directly implicated in the Crofters scandal, were defeated.

Gilligan's victory resonated beyond Ohio. John Herbers of the *New York Times* wrote in his national election recap, "Probably the most important gain is in Ohio."[63] Some Republicans, however, were reluctant to concede that it had been a victory of party or policy, insisting, like Representative William Batchelder, that "Crofters was the biggest factor in his victory."[64] Representative George Voinovich offered, "I think a lot of people believe that had it not been for the Crofters scandal, [Gilligan] would not have been elected. So there was a feeling that he was occupying that job by accident."[65]

However it may have been achieved, the victory was one the Gilligan camp acted on quickly. By noon on the day after the election, Gilligan aide Thomas Menaugh headed for Columbus to establish a transition office. Meanwhile, the Gilligan campaign staff was packing up the campaign. Among them, campaign worker Chris Buchanan paid pollster Peter Hart $125 for the Honda 50 Hart had used for getting around Columbus. The motorcycle, Buchanan noted, came with two helmets—one of which smelled rather strongly of the pipe tobacco Hart favored.

22

Ohio on the Verge

In the interregnum between his election and inauguration, both John Gilligan and Katie Gilligan paid courtesy calls on Governor James Rhodes and his wife, Helen.

Gilligan was looking for help. He told Rhodes that he regarded the job of governor of a major state as among the most difficult that existed and that he would welcome any advice the outgoing governor might have to offer. As Gilligan recalled the encounter, "Rhodes said, 'Don't kid yourself. This is about the easiest job I have ever had. Get yourself about twenty-one people [to head the various departments]. And if one of them comes in with a problem, just tell them you know five or six guys who'd love to have their job.'"[1]

Gilligan regarded the administrators Rhodes had thus assembled as a mixed lot. Some, he felt, were only slightly to the right of felonious. But a few were quite able. John McElroy, Rhodes's chief of staff, was regarded throughout political Columbus as extremely hardworking, competent, and reliable, and he lent considerable assistance to the incoming administration. Dr. Howard Collier, the director of finance, was widely credited with keeping the ship of state's finances somewhat above the waterline. On November 25, 1970, Collier sent Gilligan a detailed twenty-five-page report on the state's financial status. Collier's report stressed three points. First, the state should reach the end of the fiscal year (June 30, 1971) with a $15 million surplus, enough to meet about two days' expenditures. (Collier told the *Dayton Daily News* a couple weeks later that if all unpaid bills were met, the year-end surplus would be $800,000—sufficient cash flow for "about an hour."[2]) Second, current revenue sources (existing taxes and fees) would likely carry the state for two more years, provided no programs were added or enlarged. Funds would allow for scheduled raises for state employees, but no general pay increases. And, finally, there would be "little if any money available for capital improvements."[3]

In short, the state under its existing tax policies could remain solvent for two years, provided nothing additional was undertaken. Gilligan, however, had campaigned on the notion that the state needed to expand its level of services to its citizens. He had, however, been rather cautious in saying how this was to be financed. While he endorsed a corporate income tax, the specific words "personal income tax" never crossed his lips. What he did say, however, was that he would appoint a blue-ribbon citizens task force to address the matter. That approach not only provided Gilligan some cover during the campaign, it also provided a means of creating some consensus on the issue once he was in office.

On December 17, 1970, Gilligan met with the task force and pointed them to the future: "I urge you to keep in mind that the reforms you recommend for Ohio's tax structure must be designed not just to meet the current financial crisis, but to serve the needs of our state for at least the decade that lies ahead."[4] Gilligan had selected as the group's chair Jacob Davis, chairman of the Kroger Corporation. The two had long ties: not only had Gilligan's father and grandfather served on the Kroger board of directors, but their respective grandfathers had been best men at each other's weddings. Along with corporate prominence, Davis had served on various Cincinnati school tax levy committees and education commissions.

The balance of the thirty-four-member task force, however, was selected by aide John McDonald and others. McDonald said, "It was not explicitly a committee that would support a state income tax but which understood that substantial sums were needed."[5] The group included representatives from industry, education, local government, public utilities, labor, and banking. John Mahaney, the longtime head of the Ohio Retail Merchants Association, said, "That was probably the best citizens committee appointed by any governor. It was wall-to-wall, powerful, successful, and untouchable people who were not beholden."[6]

Gilligan pledged not to interfere, telling the task force that its conclusions would be its own. In his study of Ohio tax reform, Ohio State University professor Frederick D. Stocker wrote that Gilligan's hands-off approach "suggests the great confidence he apparently took in the task force."[7] The group's report was due February 15, 1971, so that its findings could be incorporated into the 1971–72 state budget—itself due for submission to the General Assembly on March 15.

About the time the task force was created, Gilligan named his transition staff: James Friedman as executive counsel; John McDonald as assistant for legislative affairs; Robert Daley as appointments secretary; and Robert Tenenbaum as press secretary. Tom Menaugh oversaw the transition operation, with help from campaign researcher Anne Bingle and Gilligan's longtime secretary Susan Geoghegan. The transition office was inundated with mail; as many as 15,000 letters arrived in the two months prior to the inauguration, many from Democrats who had decided the time had come for their state government to give them a job.

In December 1970, Katie Gilligan, accompanied by her son John, paid a courtesy call on Helen Rhodes at the Governor's Mansion, where they chatted of various matters while drinking ice tea in the living room. The Ohio governor's official residence is located at 358 North Parkview, a decidedly upscale street in Bexley, an affluent enclave within the city of Columbus. Commissioned by a local industrialist, the Jacobean Revival home was completed in 1925; three decades later, it was turned over to the state as a residence for the Ohio's governors.

By one account, when the Gilligans arrived, the household staff consisted of seven trusties, five of whom, Gilligan recalled, were murderers. These included Joe, who had been convicted of first-degree murder, and Lee, a wife killer sufficiently well-educated to help with the household clerical tasks. Usually an Ohio state trooper was in evidence to keep an eye on things. But this did not reassure Katie Gilligan. Early on the First Lady asked one trusty what crime he had committed. Raped and murdered his seventeen-year-old girlfriend, was the reply. This proved too much for Mrs. Gilligan, whose own seventeen-year-old daughter had a bedroom one floor below the trusties'.

One former trusty, Jordan, did remain. Gilligan recalled him as a placid man who, having killed his wife in a "crime of passion," had completed his sentence and remained on at the Mansion as butler, doorkeeper, and general man-of-all-work: "He knew everything about the Mansion and he knew about the groceries and the tradesmen and the ordering."[8]

The Gilligans lived in an apartment on the Mansion's second floor. There they had a sitting room and a bedroom, which they filled with their own furniture. The apartment was situated in the corner of the house, and it caught the morning sun. Katie commonly cooked breakfast in the small kitchen. Katie was meticulous about not making personal use of state property. For example, purchases for state events and purchases for family use were accounted for separately—a level of honesty, her husband remarked, that, in Ohio, was "a considerable novelty."[9] She also preferred driving her own car to riding in the governor's chauffeured Lincoln Continental.

At the time the Gilligans moved in, it was probably the case that not one Ohioan in a thousand had ever been inside the Governor's Mansion. This, Katie Gilligan addressed in part by turning a portion of the first floor into an art gallery, using the displays as occasions to invite women's groups and art groups for tea. Working with the director of agriculture, Gene Abercrombie, she also coordinated a series of plantings on the rather threadbare grounds and saw to the partial redecoration of the Mansion, with new upholstery, window treatments, and fresh paint.

While the four Gilligan children each had an assigned bedroom on the Mansion's third floor, these were seldom occupied for long. Ellen, the youngest, was midway through her senior year at Summit County Day School and the only one still in Cincinnati. Gilligan wanted his daughter to transfer to the Columbus School for Girls, but there were limits to how far Ellen was prepared to let her father's political career interfere with her adolescence. (At one point, she recalled, having been teased for the being "the governor's daughter," she pointedly informed her father, "You've ruined my life."[10]) She persuaded her parents to let her stay in Cincinnati with the family of a classmate so she could complete her education at the only school she had ever attended.

At the time of the inauguration, John was a senior at Dartmouth. After graduation, since he carried a low draft number, he would enter basic training and become a member of the Ohio National Guard, during which time he would live in the Mansion for several months. Kathleen, who graduated from Trinity University in June 1970, had returned to Ohio to work on her father's campaign and remained "at home" through the inauguration and several months thereafter. The Mansion, she recalled, was "not a very welcoming place. It felt like somebody else's property. It was fine if you had 100 people in the living room for a reception, but it wasn't a very great place to plop down and read a book."[11] Donald had graduated from Harvard in 1968. Also the holder of a low draft number, he had as noted arranged to teach in a series of "troubled" high schools as his alternative service.

When the newly elected legislators assembled in the Ohio Statehouse in the first week of January 1971, they convened in one of the world's great rabbit warrens. The building, which dominates the major Columbus crossroads of Broad and High streets, represented a kind of legislative enactment of Virginia Woolf's urging of the importance of having a room of one's own. Originally, the building contained fifty-three rooms, most of them high-ceilinged and amply proportioned. Reacting to the desire of state officials to have individual accommodations, those fifty-three rooms eventually became 317. Floors with high ceilings became two floors with adequate ceilings, or three floors with low ones; closets received battlefield promotions to the rank of office. James Thurber, a native son of Columbus, wrote in the mid–twentieth century that it was "almost impossible to find the governor's office, or any other, unless you have been accustomed for years to the monumental maze of corridors and rooms. Even the largest rooms seem to have been tucked away in great, cool, unexpected corners by an architect with an elephantine sense of humor."[12]

Despite this, individual legislators had no offices at all. The seats in both the Senate and House chambers sat in semicircles, with small gaps between each table, and these gaps were the closest thing legislators had to desk space. As such, they were stuffed with copies of bills under consideration, the legislator's mail, and other sundry items. Henry Lehman, a freshman representative from suburban Cleveland, discovered that the forty-four sitting Democrats shared a large room in the basement, two Democrats to each of twenty-two desks; each pair of desks had a single telephone, which was also shared. The shortage of space had policy implications. David Johnston, an early director of the Legislative Service Commission, could not fill positions since there was no place to put new hires. Johnston managed to wangle some spots in the basement, where the staffers had to endure musky odors, cracked walls, and, when the air conditioning broke down, intolerable heat even in winter. And cockroaches flourished.[13]

The legislature that convened in the Statehouse in 1971 was a body doubly in transition. Following the 1962 U.S. Supreme Court "one man, one vote" decision, which reapportioned representation across the state, for various reasons, the transition from legislators who represented counties to legislators who represented people took a few years to take effect. The consequence for the Gilligan administration and those who shared its liberal outlook was that the roadblock to progressive legislation the Cornstalk Brigade represented was losing power.

A second change was generational—those serving as state legislators were getting younger. For generations, a seat in the state legislature had been the capstone of years as a county commissioner, a township trustee, or some other local official. These citizen-legislators had other employment, and, though perhaps one-third were attorneys, the range of occupations they pursued was a reasonable cross-section of those they represented. One state representative, an accountant, announced he would not attend legislative meetings until after March 15, then the deadline for income tax filings. Another, a farmer, said he would leave as soon as it was time to bring in the hay. None thought this unreasonable behavior. (The citizen-legislator practice died slowly: as late as 1973, only thirteen members reported their service in Columbus as their primary livelihood.)

With the 1960s, however, the legislature became a place where people *began* their political careers. Among them were Republican Stanley Aronoff, elected at age twenty-eight to the legislature in 1961, served with increasing influence until 1996; Republican William Batchelder, who entered the House as its youngest member in 1966 and in 2011 was elected Speaker; and George Voinovich, who was elected to the legislature in 1967 and whose subsequent service to the state included two terms as mayor of Cleveland, two terms as Ohio's governor, and twelve years as a U.S. senator.

At the same time, the work was not particularly arduous. The legislature made budgets by the biennium. Until the 1950s, the legislature's first term, the budget-making session, was held in the odd-numbered year and generally adjourned in May; the even-numbered-year session might last six or eight weeks. Effectively, the legislature operated on a three-day week: out-of-town members arrived in Columbus on Monday night, and the calendar for the following week would be set on Thursday. The state legislature that convened with Gilligan in January 1971 ended up working the entire year.

Legislatures that met up until the 1970s were greatly more collegial than those that followed. One reason for this collegiality was the tunnel that led from the capitol basement under South High Street to the bar at the Neil House Hotel, where good men and, occasionally, women of all political faiths converged. Warren Harding, who served four years in the state Senate before moving on to the U.S. Senate, said the Neil House "might fairly have been called the real Capitol of Ohio. On its floor, I first saw and felt the pulsing movement of the political throng."[14]

Patrons dropped by the Neil House less to fill stomachs then to rub elbows. John Mahaney, longtime head of the Ohio Council of Retail Merchants, recalled the camaraderie which once ruled. "A leading Democrat and I would go to the Neil House after night hearings. We'd go to the dining room, sit down at a table. Before long, ten or twelve people would join us—Republicans, Democrats, press. Nobody ever reported anything that was said at the table. It was an unwritten rule, but it was a rule."[15] John Johnson, a freshman Democrat elected in 1970, said that the Neil House "was also a place where leading members of the legislature hung out, and you had the chance to talk to them; where you could meet with the Speaker and make sure the leadership knew who you were. You could learn a lot from those conversations."[16]

Legislators not only gathered at the Neil House; a goodly number of those from out of town lived there, perhaps fifty at a time. Senator Harry Meshel prized its "bipartisan fraternizing," but added, "It became a place where it was easy to abuse your privileges. You'd come out of a meeting late; go under the tunnel to the bar. You would eat and drink too much too late."[17] (It was inconveniently convenient: "If you lived at the hotel; you could get to an 8:00 A.M. meeting. But you didn't see any sunlight."[18] After a time, Meshel moved into a condominium on the city's west side.)

As told by historian David Gold, in those ethically more tolerant times, lobbyists routinely dispensed food and drink.

> Each January, they had the hotels stock up on steaks and liquor; at session's end they had farewell parties, and in between, they invited particularly important legislators to private dinners. The Ohio Trucking Association [OTA] maintained an open bar for members at the Neil House. "If you had no one else to buy you a drink," recalled one lawmaker, "you were always welcome at OTA." At least one lobbyist was always ready to play poker with and lose to any legislator, although an unwritten code of ethics prohibited a legislator from winning more than he needed.[19]

The lobbyists carried considerable influence. According to Bill Chavanne, who began the Gilligan years as assistant legislative liaison, that was because most lobbyists then had long-term ties to a particular industry whose ways and needs they knew and could articulately represent. They had not yet been replaced by the independent lobbyist who, somewhat less expertly, represents a range of clients, rather like an advertising agency. In the 1970s, it was the trade association lobbyists—the utilities, the bankers, the manufacturers, the insurance interests—who dominated the scene, remaining for decades in Columbus and cultivating their understanding of their industry and the legislators who were, or might be, sitting on committees of interest. Chavanne added, "You had to work not to have some lobbyist pay for your dinner."[20] Legislators were not particularly shy about claiming what they regarded as their due. Stories abound about how Senate minority leader Anthony Calabrese would walk into the Neil House and ask who was going to buy him dinner. When Calabrese learned that the lobbyist he was expecting to pick up that evening's tab was home sick in bed, he called his missing host to say, "Send your credit card over in a cab."[21]

The general public learned about its representatives in Columbus through the press and radio and television broadcasts. At that time, the newspaper was still the most influential medium for news. The legislative press corps during the Gilligan years was large, consequential, and competitive—all of which made it rather more likely to be critical of the doings of politics and politicians. (It may also have been somewhat less committed to sobriety, as Statehouse reporters were among those who joined the legislators and lobbyists after hours at the Neil House and elsewhere.) The competitiveness stemmed from the fact that many Ohio cities still had multiple newspapers that vied for readers and stories. An editor in Cleveland might be annoyed by being beaten on a story by a Cincinnati paper but would be livid if beaten by the paper's cross-town rival. The complement of reporters included those working for the wire services, United Press International and the Associated Press, and for the three state papers owned by the Scripps-Howard chain. Within the general hierarchy, the *Cleveland Plain Dealer* and the *Columbus Dispatch* were considered the lead dogs in the pack. In addition, much of political Columbus read the *Ohio Report,* published by the Gongwer News Service, an independent agency that reported in considerable depth on the activities of the state government and legislature.

The governor-elect, the new and returning legislators, and the press that wrote about both would, whether they as yet suspected it, spend most of 1971 writing about Ohio's taxes.

During the primary campaign, the moderator of the Democrats' debate at the Cleveland City Club wondered, rhetorically, why anyone would wish to be governor—particularly if they had read a recently released study on Ohio taxation. The study in question, "A Profile of State Government Taxation and Revenue for Ohio," written by two junior economics professors at Cleveland State University, John F. Burke Jr. and Edric A. Weld Jr., documented the financial limits on what state government could—or was willing—to do and suggested the large measures required to alter the situation.

Burke and Weld asserted that "no other state in the nation has fewer resources per person with which to finance public services" than Ohio.[22] In 1968, the average state government received $297 per capita with which to address public needs;

Ohio's per capita revenue of $213 was 28 percent lower than the average. Further, that gap was widening. In percentage terms, the shortfall between what Ohio received and the national average had more than doubled since 1950. Breaking expenditures down by category, the report showed that Ohio spent less per capita in virtually every area, including about one-third less on education, public welfare, and hospitals. The state did slightly exceed national averages in two of the eleven categories: highways and prisons. Burke and Weld stated, "In public services as in other areas of human activity, people generally get what they pay for. Being forty-ninth in state expenditure probably indicates that Ohioans have been receiving substantially lower levels of public service than the inhabitants of most other states."[23]

But Ohio was not a poor state. Indeed, when its relative affluence was factored in, that gap between Ohio's per-capita revenue and other states' increased. Nationally in 1968, for every $1,000 in personal income, Americans paid an average of $58.55 to state government through local sales, real estate, gasoline, business, and "sin" taxes. Ohioans paid, on average, $40.77.

The figures were somewhat muddled by the circumstance that perhaps 300 Ohio municipalities collected local income taxes. As a consequence, Burke and Weld noted, "Ohio relies to an unusual extent on local government units to provide the public good and services needed by its citizens."[24] Still, even when state and local taxation were aggregated, "Ohio ranked fiftieth in revenues relative to income."[25] The state's residents enjoyed "the lowest total tax burden relative to income and capacity to pay of any state in the nation."[26]

Ohio took a long time getting to this place. The Second World War had had the unintended effect of filling the state's coffers as never before. As economist Frederick Stocker pointed out, wartime demand for armaments meant boom years for Ohio's industry, and wartime rationing limited state expenditures. So by 1948, the state had a $218 million surplus, a tremendous sum at the time (about $2.4 billion in 2013 dollars). Governors like John Bricker and Frank Lausche kept taxes low by drawing on that surplus. A curious consequence is that for some years, while the people of Ohio might not be getting much from state government, they had the satisfaction of knowing they were underpaying for what little they did get.

That Ohioans were, proportionate to income, the lowest-taxed people in the country was not universally viewed within the state as any great outrage. For while "taxation without representation" was a major battle cry behind the American Revolution, taxation *with* representation has been a major grievance since. In few states did the citizenry feel as aggrieved by taxation as in Ohio. As one Republican legislator acknowledged, "Actually, real estate taxes in Ohio are not very high when compared to other states. But they are high psychologically, in the minds of the people, and so it cannot be ignored."[27]

James Rhodes endlessly argued through his first two terms as governor that Ohio's low tax rate would make the state attractive to industry. This would not only create a good many jobs, he said, it would also allow state government to finance needed services out of the incremental revenue brought in by economic growth. Rhodes pledged no new taxes—a pledge he kept provided that one accepted his definition of what was a tax—a sales tax—and what wasn't a tax: motel room tax, auto license tax, tax on utility bills, and any tax a county or municipality enacted in part to compensate for low levels of support from Columbus. Stocker rather pithily characterizes Rhodes's approach as "a unique blend of chutzpah, luck, skill, and bombast."[28] The luck was that the 1960s were boom years for Ohio, in part due to the demands the Vietnam War placed on Ohio industry; the skill was Howard Collier, Rhodes's director of finance; and the bravado was Rhodes himself.

The Governor himself projected a personal image of tremendous energy and enthusiasm. His repeated assertions that Ohio was far outstripping the rest of the nation in economic growth engendered wide acceptance of the notion that growth would somehow solve the state's fiscal problems. His profound conviction, against all evidence, that whatever economic growth Ohio enjoyed was attributable to "favorable tax climate" solidified support for his hold-the-line tax policy; his pride in Ohio's low tax position, coupled with noisy claims to Ohio's national leadership in this or that public service area, drowned out the evidence of gradual deterioration.[29]

According to Stocker, Ohio's tax system leading into 1971 was not only questionable in its ability to finance public purposes but was structurally flawed. First, it was inelastic. It relied largely on taxes—sale, excise, real estate—that changed little with the fluctuations of the economy. Second, it had an uneven impact—"Some people, some businesses, some communities were hit very hard, while others were almost completely missed." The consequence was that, even in a low-tax state, some people were being overtaxed. Third, it was regressive. As Jack Gilligan had quite accurately stressed in his campaign, in general, the lower a household's income, the greater the share of its income went to state and local taxes. And fourth, it resulted in great disparities. Public education, for example, was largely funded by taxes on local real estate, which meant that while one Ohio school district had $205,000 of appraised real estate tax for each student, another had just $3,090.[30]

In 1968, Ohio, Texas, Florida, Nevada, and Wyoming were the only states with neither a corporate income nor personal income tax. Burke and Weld's report showed that nationally such taxes accounted for 24 percent of total state revenue—a figure that roughly equaled the difference in per-capita expenditures between Ohio and the rest of the country. The report concluded that bringing Ohio's expenditures up to the national average would require from $1.2 to $1.6 billion in additional revenues.

This is what John Gilligan faced when he arrived in Columbus in January 1971.

23

Setting Up Shop

On January 11, 1971, John Joyce Gilligan was inaugurated as the sixty-second governor of the state of Ohio. Four decades later, he said that his strongest recollection of the day was "astonishment that it was actually occurring."[1] A certain amount of astonishment was in order. Gilligan had spent most of his life in the political minority on the city council of Cincinnati, a city that only somewhat grudgingly regards itself as part of the state. He had never previously sought state office; indeed, friend and foe alike often commented that he was better suited for national than state politics.

For Gilligan and his family, that cold, brisk day began with Mass celebrated at St. Joseph's Cathedral on Broad Street. At 11:00, they were transported by limousine to the Statehouse. At noon, John Joyce Gilligan stood on a platform on the High Street side of the capitol and took the oath of office as administered by C. William O'Neill, Chief Justice of the Ohio Supreme Court and a former Ohio governor. Gilligan took his oath of office on the family Bible. A crowd of 4,000, largely Democrats, was present and in an ebullient frame of mind. Press accounts noted the governor's relative youth, age forty-nine, and that his hair was still red.

In his characteristically crisp, slightly rising voice, Gilligan's inaugural address outlined three themes. First, he affirmed the power of popular sovereignty, calling on Ohioans to direct their elected officials "to undertake the fearful struggle to build a society based upon justice, order and mutual respect, enriched by compassion and hope."[2] Next, he spoke to the social needs of the state: "Are we in the midst of wealth and power never before seen in the long history of mankind, content to live in dirty and decaying cities whose streets are haunted by violence and crime?"[3] Americans, he said, enjoyed the wealthiest of societies; could they be "content to see thousands of our children left hungry and ragged in the midst of plenty? I do not and I will not believe we are so content."[4] Finally, he made a call for personal responsibility: "The first thing we have to do is to stop making excuses for ourselves, for each other, for our society, for our economy and for our government."[5] Individuals, he said, did not live "in the grip of blind and irresistible forces; greed, violence, waste and brutality are not the necessary characteristics of our way of life"; rather, "We are what we want to be."[6]

The ceremony was followed by an afternoon gala held in the Ohio Theatre, adjacent to the Statehouse. After that event, Gilligan and his press secretary, Bob Tenenbaum, stopped at the Maramor Restaurant to exchange introductory banter with the Statehouse press corps. Finally, Gilligan and family headed to the state fairgrounds' Frank Lausche Building (ironically) for an early dinner and ensuing entertainment. The $100-a-ticket affair drew 3,000 people, with the proceeds going to retire the accumulated debt of the state Democratic Party. The evening featured a dance band led by well-known band leader and pianist Peter Duchin and Columbus-born jazz singer Nancy Wilson. (But when Wilson couldn't gain the boisterous, jubilant crowd's attention, she commented pithily on its manners and left the stage.)

By this time, Gilligan had selected his inner circle of advisers and aides. Gilligan first offered the chief of staff post to Mark Shields, who declined, just as he later declined the chairmanship of the state party. As Shields explained, "I really felt I owed it to my wife. We had always thought that our home was in Washington, D.C. That was where we met; that was where we owned a house."[7] Gilligan next offered the post to Jim Friedman, who had misgivings of his own. He was not certain he wished to make politics his livelihood, he said, and, further, as a longtime Cleveland resident, "I had doubts about relocating my wife and young daughter to Columbus."[8] After some reflection, though, Friedman accepted Gilligan's offer.

Gilligan made Robert Daley his appointments secretary. Daley was a gut-level Democrat ("You see the results from the poor people that have to live in horrible homes and have underfed and undernourished kids, and kids who don't go to school with the right clothes and don't go to school with food in their stomach") and as unabashed a believer in the efficacy of activist government as Gilligan, to whom Daley was deeply loyal.[9]

Tom Menaugh took on the role of managing the governor's office. Of the staff, he had known Gilligan the longest, their association going back to the navy, to Okinawa and the day in April 1945 that they both survived. Menaugh's father was a Chicago newspaperman and political liberal. Prewar, Menaugh attended and graduated from Wisconsin's Beloit College. Postwar, he worked in advertising before transferring to the Fred Harvey restaurant chain, where he was eventually in charge of personnel, purchasing, and construction. He maintained some ties with liberal politics, with, among others, the Illinois chapter of the American Civil Liberties Union. Gilligan thought Menaugh "a very bright and dedicated guy."[10] Beyond their personal relationship, it was Menaugh's experience in business that prompted Gilligan to recruit him to head the elected candidate's transition effort and then to manage his office.

John McDonald was to serve as the administration's liaison with the state legislature, a job McDonald was well-suited for given that he was the only member of Gilligan's inner circle to have served in the General Assembly. Starting out as a state representative from Newark in 1964, he later served as Democratic minority leader in the House. As minority leader, McDonald merited an assistant—in 1968, he chose Bill Chavanne, who at the time was a reporter for *Gongwer*, the independent newsletter that reports on Ohio state government. The Democratic caucus McDonald led was very much in the minority, holding barely a third of the ninety-nine seats in the House chamber. As noted, McDonald joined the Gilligan campaign following his unsuccessful 1970 bid for his party's nomination as Ohio attorney general.

The press secretary job once again went to Bob Tenenbaum. As a subject of news, Jack Gilligan proved himself rather different from his predecessor. When Jim Rhodes had been in a selling mood, he might hold five press conferences a week; on other occasions—such as after the shootings at Kent State—he could, in the words of reporter Lee Leonard, "get very lost."[11] Rhodes was also noted for his uncertain syntax, which often left it to the discretion of the reporter to decide what the governor had said. (Leonard recalled once backing the governor into a corner and insisting that Rhodes clarify an apparent discrepancy. In Leonard's telling phrase, Rhodes responded nonchalantly, "I lied."[12])

In contrast, for Gilligan the press was a simple fact of political life. As Tenenbaum put it, "Gilligan came in with the notion that the press was your conduit, so you should work with them as best you can."[13] Part of this was simple organization, and then letting that organization be known. The governor's office issued daily schedules of Gilligan's whereabouts. He also held routine press conferences, which were generally scheduled for the morning so that the Cleveland television crews could get their film back to their studios for broadcast on that evening's news. Gilligan met two important criteria for success with the press: he was always coherent and generally quotable; and, under his direction, state government did a great deal that was actually newsworthy.

Tenenbaum as press secretary, McDonald as legislative liaison, Daley as appointments secretary, and Menaugh as office manager—all had tasks that, in politics, were fairly standard and straightforward. James Friedman's chief-of-staff job was somewhat more difficult to characterize. In theory, a chief of staff's position is whatever the chief executive wishes it to be. Friedman's job was framed by the actions of Gilligan's predecessor. Jim Rhodes was impatient with the details of the job and so delegated much of those to his own chief of staff, John McElroy. McElroy applied himself with considerable diligence to the job and was regarded by members of both parties as highly competent. (All of which was fine with Rhodes, who went so far as to direct passage of a state law creating the post of authenticating officer, which empowered McElroy to sign various documents in Rhodes's absence.) It was to McElroy that many came to get things done, a circumstance that in time became not only standard procedure but an expectation.

Friedman began with this broad definition of his office and expanded it from there. He handled patronage and personnel and was heavily involved in hiring. (The new administration made appointments to innumerable bodies.) He also played a major role in state Democratic Party politics. Once a week he and John Jones, executive director of the Ohio Democratic Party, piled into a motor home and headed off for dinner with half a dozen Democratic county chairmen in some corner of the state. And he handled seemingly trivial matters. For example, the state retained title to land that had once been the right-of-way for the Miami & Erie and the Ohio canals. The land was leased, often to farmers, and these leases came into the governor's office by the dozens, and Friedman attended to these.

Friedman, whose office was next to Gilligan's, had an hour or two of direct contact with the governor each day, separate from working lunches and early-morning breakfasts at the Mansion. Also, Friedman's office had a direct line from the governor, a phone that rang until it was answered, something Friedman found annoying. He worked most weeknights until 2:00 A.M. before returning to his sub-urban Columbus home, where he had erected a basketball hoop in the driveway. Keyed up from the day's efforts, Friedman would unwind by shooting baskets. (He perfected what he called "the azalea shot," which was made from behind an azalea bush. He considered the shot unmakeable by any opponent—until Mark Shields came to town and aced it.[14]) Eventually, complaints from the neighbors brought the early-morning basketball to a halt.

Friedman related an anecdote rather telling of his approach to the chief-of-staff job. In 1971, the Democratic National Committee scheduled a large dinner in Washington for September. Gilligan and Friedman wanted Ohio, with its newly elected Democratic governor, to make something of a splash at the event. Fried-man, determined that Ohio would sell more tickets and fill more tables than any other state, began pushing tickets. Indeed, the banquet boasted a dozen tables from Ohio, the most of any state, and each featured a small Ohio flag. Fried-man said, "We had the biggest delegation. But as chief-of-staff to a governor, that should not have been a focus of my time."[15]

When Gilligan came to Columbus as governor-elect, he was an outsider in the city. Cincinnati, Gilligan noted, was "just sort of on a sidetrack in state politics, particularly Democratic Party politics, which had their core in Cleveland, Columbus and Toledo."[16] So as far as state politics was concerned, he said, "he knew who the players were, but not much more."[17] But because he was little known in Columbus, he was not beholden to particular individuals and local groups. Gilligan had a decidedly low opinion of many who had served in Rhodes's cabinet—"I think there were a number of people in the Rhodes administration and even in the Lausche administration who in my book were evil people. They weren't just neutral; they weren't just time servers, but people who were doing bad things."[18] For his part, Gilligan wanted to fill his cabinet with people whose credentials went beyond just working on someone's campaign; he wanted individuals with a working knowledge of some significant aspect of state government: "I wanted people who wanted to be part of state government not because they were looking for a job but because that's where their capabilities and interests were."[19]

With a proposed 1971–72 budget due to the General Assembly on March 15, 1971, filling the finance director post was a priority. Gilligan's choice was Hal Hovey, a Toledo native. Although only thirty-two, Hovey held a law degree and a doctorate from George Washington University, having previously attended graduate school at Harvard University on a Woodrow Wilson Fellowship. In D.C., he worked in the office of the secretary of defense and at the U.S. Bureau of the Budget. At the time of his cabinet selection, Hovey was head of the Public Policy Economics Division at Columbus's Battelle Memorial Institute, a premier private research center where he had worked on issues of taxation and spending and school construction financing. Hovey came to be regarded as one of the stars of the Gilligan cabinet. John McDonald commented, "Anyway you look at it, I think Hal was far and away the best and brightest of the cabinet."[20] (Hovey's tendency to affix seemingly abstract names to things did not always sit well with legislators, however. Hovey once made reference to "multiple prime double-A," prompting Senate minority leader Anthony Calabrese to respond, "I'm not going to vote for multiple sclerosis."[21])

A second key appointment Gilligan made was naming Jack Hansan to the welfare post. With a graduate degree in social work from the University of Pennsylvania, Hansan was a long-term associate of Gilligan, having managed the latter's 1964 and 1968 campaigns. Hansan, offered a range of cabinet posts, chose welfare. Prior to the 1970 election, Hansan had been working on his doctorate at Brandeis University's Florence Heller School of Social Welfare. Much of Hansan's professional work had occurred in Gilligan's home city of Cincinnati, where he directed the Seven Hills Neighborhood Houses, Inc., settlement house.

Development director David Sweet, thirty-one, joined the administration from Battelle, where he had worked since 1963 and where, at the time of his appointment, he was program director of its social systems science section. Sweet had completed his dissertation on regional development at Ohio State University in previous August 1970. (He was interviewed for the post by Tom Menaugh, Jim Friedman, Mark Shields, and Gilligan. Gilligan listened, but said little. Out of the blue, Shields asked, "There's a manufacturer of D-cup bras in New Jersey—how would you attract him to Ohio?" Sweet doesn't remember his answer, but apparently it sufficed.[22]) In announcing Sweet's appointment, Gilligan said, "Dr. Sweet will bring to the department the kind of expertise and imagination we will need if Ohio is to carry out an aggressive, intelligent development plan for the next decade."[23]

These three appointments were generally regarded as nonpartisan. Others on Gilligan's cabinet, however, were less so. Pete O'Grady stepped down as executive chairman of the Ohio Democratic Party to become director of the Department of Highway Safety, which held jurisdiction over the state highway patrol and the bureaus of motor vehicles. O'Grady was a popular figure with Democrats and enjoyed wide contacts throughout political Ohio. According to a close associate, O'Grady felt he should leave the state chairmanship for the cabinet so that it was clear he was "on the team" and not an outsider or possible rival.

J. Phillip Richley, forty-four, accepted the position of director of highways, a post often associated with political patronage and expected to "turn out the troops" during campaigns. Richley held an engineering degree from Youngstown State University and was midway through his first term as Mahoning County engineer when he took the job with Gilligan's administration. *Gongwer* reported, "Mr. Richley's appointment had been widely rumored—as being in part a patronage result of Mahoning County's strong campaign support of the new governor."[24]

Paul A. Corey, forty-four, joined the cabinet as the director of state personnel. At the Cuyahoga County Commissioners' office, Corey he had been responsible for contract negotiations, personnel, purchasing, and other administrative functions. John McDonald said that—given the question of public employees' right to organize and to strike that was pending and that state employees would expect to pay a significant share of the anticipated tax increase—the appointment of someone with Corey's professional skills was important.

Gilligan's only specific suggestion was that of Gene Abercrombie as director of agriculture. Abercrombie held a degree in agricultural economics from Purdue University and headed a company that managed sixty Ohio, Indiana, and Kentucky farms. Gilligan said, "He was not a political type, but he believed quite passionately that Ohio was missing the boat, was squandering a lot of opportunities for export in the field of agriculture."[25] It angered Abercrombie that talk of economic development focused on industry, when so little was being done to support the state's farmers. Gilligan, despite many summers at Leland, was a city boy; his interest in agriculture was limited. That being the case, he said, he was "more than grateful" to have Abercrombie come aboard.[26]

Others in Gilligan's original cabinet included:

- Ronald Coffey, 34, Commerce. At the time of his appointment, Coffey was on the law school faculty at Case Western Reserve University, where he specialized in corporations, securities regulations, and business planning.
- Benjamin J. Cooper, 49, Corrections. The lone carryover from the Rhodes administration, Cooper had been a department employee since 1957, when he was named chief psychologist at the Mansfield Reformatory.
- William E. Garnes, 47, Employment Services. Garnes was an international representative for Region 2-A of the United Auto Workers Union in Cincinnati and a full-time UAW staff member since 1957.

- Martin J. Hughes, 49, Industrial Relations. At his appointment, Hughes was serving as assistant to the international vice president of the Communications Workers of America (CWA), having previously served nine years as a CWA legislative representative in Washington, D.C.
- Kenneth DeShetler, 42, Insurance. DeShetler worked in private and public practice in Toledo prior to his election as a Toledo Municipal Court judge.
- Richard E. Guggenheim, 57, Liquor Control. Former vice president and secretary of the U.S. Shoe Corporation in Cincinnati, and one of Gilligan's earliest allies in the Miami Society, Guggenheim, had served as chairman of the Ohio Civil Rights Commission and as chairman of the state Democratic platform committee in 1966 and 1970.
- William B. Nye, 37, Natural Resources. Reelected to a second term in the state Senate, Nye resigned the office to join Gilligan's cabinet. In the Senate, Nye had been a leading exponent of environmental legislation and had chaired the subcommittee on the environment for the state's 1970 Democratic convention.
- Robert J. Kosydar, 39, Taxation. Kosydar was an assistant state attorney general before entering private practice.
- Bruce L. Newman, 34, Urban Affairs. Newman, assistant director of the Cleveland Foundation, was a short-term appointment; Gilligan planned to merge Urban Affairs with Development headed by David Sweet.
- William J. Ensign, 46, Youth Commission. Ensign had just been elected to his second term as mayor of Toledo when he accepted Gilligan's appointment. He had worked as a welfare case worker, probation officer, parole officer, and welfare director for Lucas County before being elected mayor in 1967.

Several things stand out about Gilligan's staff and cabinet. The first is youth; six were in their thirties when Gilligan appointed them. The second is education; seven held law degrees and three had PhDs. And third, while the appointments included two African Americans, no women were appointed to the cabinet.

Two cabinet positions proved difficult to fill: adjutant general of the Ohio National Guard and director of the Department of Mental Health and Retardation, a new post Gilligan planned to create by separating its activities from those of the Department of Corrections.

The National Guard directorship was sensitive because of the tragedy at Kent State. A month after his election, Gilligan spoke at Kent State, a spot many in state politics avoided even years after the shootings. In his prepared remarks, he pledged that no such tragedy would happen during his own tenure and placed blame on the Nixon administration's having "split the nation, black from white, rich from poor, young from old, with their bitter rhetoric of fear."[27] At the same time, he pointed out that the public, which financed Kent State and other public institutions, believed that students, by accepting that aid, were responsible to act "for the betterment of the whole community."[28] Such citizens, he noted, reacted "with shock when they saw the violence and vituperation not only here but on many of our campuses earlier this year."[29] And he proposed an agenda that he wished his audience would adopt: "We will not permit youngsters to grow up ignorant. We will not tolerate subhuman hospitals, or a prison system which warps and deforms people we should be trying to reform . . . We will not ignore the many Ohioans who live in misery, lacking nourishing food, decent housing, purposeful employment and adequate medical care."[30]

Calling Ohio's youth an untapped resource, he said that he planned to create the Volunteer Corps for Young Ohioans, to be headed up by a young lawyer and recent Cincinnati congressional candidate named Gerald Springer. (Springer, better known as Jerry, went on to serve as Cincinnati's mayor and become a daytime television host.)

That, however, did not answer the question of what to do about the National Guard. Gilligan's recalled: "What was clear, at least to me, was that the top leadership had to go—the top two or three people. It wasn't exclusively their fault. There had been a breakdown in communications, but you could never square it with the general public and go on as though nothing had happened."[31] Gilligan sought and secured the resignation of the National Guard's commander, General Sylvester Del Corso, and several others. Finding a successor proved somewhat more difficult.

By law, the adjutant general of the Ohio National Guard had to be a West Point graduate with the rank of colonel or higher. Barely ten individuals met this criterion; of these, only two were Democrats. The first Democratic candidate interviewed for the post startled John McDonald by saying he thought the mistake at Kent State had been the failure to use tanks. Other prospective appointees were similarly bellicose. At one point, Mark Shields asked if it was permitted to find someone reasonable lower in the ranks and then promote them to colonel. Tom Menaugh recalled the phone call he made to the final candidate, Colonel Dana Stewart: "I called General Stewart, who is a lifelong Republican, and then I said, 'Would you be interested in talking with the governor?' He said, 'It never entered my mind. You know I'm a Republican.' I said, 'Yes, the governor knows that. We'd like to talk to you.'"[32] When Gilligan, Menaugh, John McDonald, and Jim Friedman met with Stewart, Menaugh said, "we knew right away he was our guy."[33]

The directorship of Mental Health and Retardation was also difficult to fill because of the governor's keen interest in how Ohio treated those who were utterly dependent on the state for their well-being. As governor-elect, he paid several visits to state facilities:

There was a facility for the mentally retarded; probably 200 patients. I wondered what these people did all day: what was being done for them or to them? They sat in big rows around the walls of this room in chairs, side by side, not really talking to each other. I became aware that most of these people were heavily sedated; and that was their life. They were sedated and they sat there, all day long. They slept in large dormitory rooms with double-decker cots placed eight inches apart. I thought: My god, what's going to happen if there's ever a fire in this place? How are they going to get these people out?[34]

Gilligan conducted a nationwide search, which was complicated both by the discouraging nature of the task and the low salary the administration was prepared to pay whoever undertook it. The existing position of director of Mental Hygiene and Correction paid $27,539—this at a time when Alabama, Georgia, Illinois, Indiana, and many other states paid $35,000 or more. Holding to his pledge to find the individual he wanted, Gilligan allowed the post to remain vacant through the first months of his administration. During that time, John McDonald approached legislative leaders and negotiated a higher salary for the post.

Under Jake Davis's leadership, the Citizens Task Force on Tax Reform was a hard-working group. Former Gilligan campaign staffer Alan Melamed, who provided logistical support to the undertaking, reported that 67.5 hours of meetings had been concluded. It was also a well-informed group, receiving eighteen white papers covering everything from county-by-county figures for school expenditures, a critique of the state's tax structure, issues related to property tax relief, and the relative merits of state- versus county-based income tax collection. Additionally, as *Gongwer* reported, "a seemingly endless line of witnesses, representing virtually every interest group in the state, came before the task force."[35]

The task force considered a wide variety of alternatives. On January 14, 1971, the *Columbus Citizen Journal* reported eleven possibilities under consideration by the group: eliminate the business "direct use" exemption in sales tax; apply sales taxes to services like beauty shops and TV repair; tax groceries; raise the sales tax; enact a state lottery; enact a severance tax on minerals extracted in the state; equalize the tax on domestic and non-Ohio insurance companies; replace the corporate franchise tax with an income tax; and/or enact a personal income tax. On February 15, the task force presented its report. Key recommendations included enactment of a steeply graduated personal income tax, rising from 1 percent on incomes of $3,000 to 8 percent on incomes of $50,000; the enactment of a 4–8 percent corporate profits tax, coupled with repeal of the existing .5 percent corporate franchise tax on net worth; and a 10 percent rollback in real estate taxes.

However, four of the thirty-four members of the task force declined to sign the report. One was a conservative businessman who simply could not accept the size of tax increase the report projected, and the other three were representatives of organized labor. At the time, the fact that labor would oppose a strongly progressive income tax struck Gilligan's inner circle as a curious anomaly. As the year unfolded, that opposition became curiouser and curiouser.

The task force findings fed into the flow of data being managed by finance director Hal Hovey, who was devising the 1971–72 tax program, with some assistance from Friedman, McDonald, and Menaugh. While the administration's specific plans remained under wraps until the March 16, 1971, budget presentation,

Governor Gilligan made it clear that he was thinking large when, on March 1, he delivered to the legislature his first State of the State address.

The twenty-five-minute address was a forthright statement of how and why Gilligan intended to greatly expand the role of state government in Ohio. His administration, he said, "would recommend a substantial increase in state support for education" while at the same time act to reduce the property tax burden placed on homeowners.[36] He said he also intended to push for educational equality at the postsecondary level, reporting that while families earning under $7,500 a year paid 56 percent of all state taxes, only 23 percent of the students enrolled in Ohio's universities came from such families.

For many legislators, the speech marked the first time they had heard their new governor speak at any length. Those who had been raised on a diet of bromides from James Rhodes were perhaps startled to learn that Gilligan had not come before the joint session to praise the state he now governed. There was, Gilligan had said soberly, much that was inadequate in the state of Ohio. In the mental health field, he said, nine hospitals had been cut off from federal funds for failure to meet minimum federal standards. One such institution, Cambridge State Hospital, had 2,500 patients, no staff psychiatrists, and only two physicians. Bluntly, he added that in a visit paid to Columbus State Hospital, "two mothers who have mentally retarded children told me they would rather see their children dead than placed in an Ohio institution."[37] He said Ohio's support for Aid to Dependent Children was woefully inadequate. He recalled the embarrassment the state had suffered when thirteen school districts had closed for lack of funds. Ohio's working men and women, he said, needed safer workplaces, more generous unemployment compensation, and improved employment services and training. Further, he pledged to strengthen the Ohio Civil Rights Commission so that it could "eradicate from our society every last vestige of racial and religious discrimination."[38]

In the nub of the address, Governor Gilligan attacked head-on the logic by which James Rhodes and the Republicans had been governing the state.

> In recent years we have heard over and over the boast that Ohio has the lowest taxes in the nation. We heard, too, the boast that spending by Ohio's state government was the lowest in the nation. Both these boasts are true. But the results of the low taxes and the consequent low spending are all too evident: a nearly bankrupt educational system; decaying cities; polluted air and filthy water; totally *unnecessary* suffering for thousands of people who need our help—the aged; the blind; the disabled; the mentally retarded child; the injured or unemployed workman. We are not helpless to change these things. We have the resources—as many societies do not—to build a better life. We can do better, if we choose to.[39]

Republicans made much of the fact that the maiden address by Ohio's new governor was not once interrupted by applause.

24

Round 1: The House

Tax increases are places angels and governors rightfully fear to tread. On March 17, 1971, *New York Times* political reporter R. W. Apple Jr. wrote that "the necessity of raising taxes cost at least a half-dozen Governors their jobs last November, and governorships are coming to be regarded among politicians as dead ends."[1] He then quoted Ohio's governor John Gilligan: "I think I can get away with higher taxes. But when I get the money, I'll have to produce or they'll throw me out. But what the hell—if I can't improve the quality of life in this state in four years, I don't deserve to be here."[2] Apple commented that the proposed taxes, "if enacted, would amount to a revolution in Ohio, which is the foremost example of the low-tax, low-service state in the country."[3]

By almost any standard, the tax increase Gilligan was seeking was very large. The budget he submitted for the 1971–72 biennium was $9.1 billion—nearly half again as large as the last budget submitted by his predecessor. Opposition was immediate and heated. Conservative state representative Robert Netzley (R-Laura) announced that the House Finance Committee, of which he was vice chairman, "would cut that program up so badly that even the Gilligan funeral homes won't be able to handle it."[4] And while, as Gilligan noted, thirteen Ohio school districts had closed for lack of money, some argued that added school funding was not needed. Republican Representative Alan Norris, vice chair of the Judiciary Committee, told reporters that "better management and planning by school boards would go a long toward solving education problems" and that he doubted that his own district "would ever support a state income tax."[5]

The battle over what to tax and how much to tax it waged on to the end of the year. It bitterly divided the House Republicans and fueled animosity between the House and the Senate.

By Ohio statute, the state budget is due to the General Assembly for completion by June 30. Instead of completion, however, impasse ruled—an impasse during which the legislature voted eight consecutive interim budgets so that the state could continue to pay its bills. Gilligan, who had a considerable agenda he wished to enact, staked his governorship on the outcome of the income tax contest: "Everything we wanted to do was dependent on passing that tax."[6]

From the first, Gilligan believed the income tax would pass if the voters of Ohio were sold on it as a necessity. Early in the legislative session, Gilligan undertook a statewide tour arguing on behalf of his tax proposals, beginning April 1 in Columbus, April 7 in Cleveland, April 13 in Dayton, April 14 in Cincinnati, April 27 in Toledo, April 29 in Akron and Canton, and April 30 in Youngstown. Each stop was a full-scale press: the governor or his budget director met with the local mayor and city council; individual cabinet members paired off with local officials who held parallel responsibilities; Gilligan's education adviser, Robert Cecile, met with superintendents and school board members. (At his Cincinnati stop, Gilligan passed up on the opportunity to toss out the first pitch of the Reds home opener, giving that honor to Gordon Roberts of Lebanon, a former army sergeant who had recently received the Congressional Medal of Honor.) Gilligan addressed other audiences along the way. On April 23, he spoke in Conneaut to the Ohio Mayor's Association, telling them bluntly that he would not siphon money from education and mental health to increase the funds available to cities. If the cities needed more money, he urged the mayors to demand publicly that Gilligan raise further the tax increases he was seeking. It was not reported whether Gilligan had any takers on this suggestion.

The income tax question received an intelligent airing when Democratic state representative James Flannery (D-Cleveland) and Republican state senator Stanley Aronoff (R-Cincinnati) shared not entirely opposing perspectives before the Cleveland City Club on April 23. Representative Flannery advanced the Gilligan administration's basic arguments: Ohio bore the responsibility to educate the young, sustain the poor, and care for the mentally ill and others in need; however, the state lacked the revenue to provide such "good and desired services" to its citizens. For the first time in a long time, Flannery said, "We plan to meet our full responsibilities, and to provide the services you want and need. And for the first time, we are going to make an honest effort to reform the tax structure here in Ohio."[7] He said that the additional education spending would cut class size from thirty to twenty-five and bring Ohio's payment for Medicaid and public assistance up to the national average. He also cited the need to raise the pay of state workers—"We pay our lawyers $12,000 a year to defend the state against corporate attorneys"—and to act against water and air pollution.[8] Coupled with rollbacks in property taxes and the repeal of the corporate franchise tax and the intangibles tax, Flannery said, the results would be a tax system that was "more fair, equitable and elastic."[9]

Senator Aronoff observed an anomaly. In the past election, he said, "We had a man running for governor, putting it openly and without shame, that if elected he was going to put to the state of Ohio a state income tax—and he won, and he won big."[10] Aronoff noted that in that same election, "representatives and senators campaigning throughout the state were opposed to raising taxes. They won also. What does this mean?"[11] What it meant to Aronoff, he told the audience, was that while the public might support new approaches to taxes, they wanted the effort "moderated by experienced legislators who will bring their experience to bear and not spend us into bankruptcy."[12]

He believed there would be new taxes; further, he believed there would be an income tax—though whether at the county or state level he did not know. He agreed with Gilligan that education was the top priority; but he questioned whether the bill actually reformed education taxes. He said that simply rolling back real estate taxes by some set percent allowed the often substantial differentials between school districts to remain. He further questioned whether "this legislature is going to buy $1 billion in new spending in the welfare field."[13] Welfare, he said, was a tremendous problem. Costs in Ohio were rising 20 percent annually; soon, the state would be spending more on welfare than on education.

Speaking "off the top of my head," Aronoff said, "I think someplace along the line we will have an increase in revenue of approximately 50 percent of what the governor is proposing."[14] As for his own position, he felt torn between enacting a state versus county tax. He closed by quoting former Governor James Rhodes's longtime finance director, Howard Collier: "It's all going to end, as it always does, with some kind of vast compromise."[15]

The individual who proved to be crucial to the outcome of the tax battle in the Ohio House of Representatives was Charles Kurfess, then serving his third term as Speaker. In 1948, eighteen-year-old Kurfess, son of a farmer from Perrysburg Township in Wood County, listened to the radio broadcast of Minneapolis mayor Hubert Humphrey presenting his eloquent advocacy of civil rights at the Democratic National Convention. That fixed Kurfess on a career in politics—but as a Republican. In 1955, Kurfess served as a page in the Ohio Senate; the following year, he graduated from Ohio State's law school, got married, and ran for the state legislature. That race involved taking on incumbent Republican Roy Longnecker in the primary. Kurfess felt honor-bound to tell Longnecker of his intentions, though he was advised against doing this since the incumbent, he was told, might likely plead for one more term. Kurfess told Longnecker anyway, though not without taking the precaution of dropping off press releases announcing his own candidacy at most of the district's small newspapers. Kurfess won the three-way primary, he said, simply by out-campaigning his opponents.[16] During his legislative tenure, Kurfess was a believer in the citizen-legislator and for years split his time between the Statehouse in Columbus and his own law practice in Wood County. He found it a happy balance: "As a legislator, on Thursdays I couldn't wait to get back to law practice; as a lawyer, on Mondays I couldn't wait to get back to legislature. I might have gone further if I'd focused on either, but that was a life choice."[17]

He remembers in particular speaking in favor of an open housing measure when that controversial measure came before the assembly in 1965. Kurfess told the House: "If you put this on the Ohio ballot, it would be defeated; it would be defeated in my district."[18] He said voting for the bill was simply the right thing to do and gave his reasons. It pleased him that two members stood up to say that Kurfess's remarks had persuaded them to support the measure.

When House Speaker Roger Cloud became state auditor in 1966, Kurfess was not next in line for the Speakership but campaigned for it anyway. The election had brought in a sizeable number of new members, and Kurfess traveled the state to meet them, greet them, and gain the support that elected him Speaker. As Speaker, Kurfess had a broad charge: he represented his own party caucus; he represented the House to the Senate; he represented the legislature to the governor, and he represented the legislature to the press. Kurfess pushed to expand the resources available to legislators. He created the Legislative Fiscal Office, which gave each party a staff person independent of the governor's office. He also pushed for broader member involvement in policy making. And he hired the first female page ("though eventually she married a Democrat."[19]) In his history of the state legislature, David Gold wrote that Kurfess "called for improvement of the General Assembly's stature in the eyes of the public through the formation of citizens' committees to recommend reforms, and the adoption of ethical standards."[20]

Kurfess was well-regarded. State Representative William Batchelder (R-Medina), who would rather pointedly cross swords with Kurfess over the income tax, nonetheless said that Kurfess "was held in very high personal regard. He was ethical, moral. I remember the way he opened the process up to the members. I recall, he would say to the visiting children of legislators, 'This is where your father is working; this is his workshop. You are welcome to come here any time.'"[21] And George Voinovich, a junior state representative when Kurfess became Speaker, said that he had "the highest regard for him and his integrity. He was a straight shooter."[22] Kurfess had some reservations about the de facto leader of the opposition party, Jack Gilligan: "He was an intelligent guy; he had what he thought were some good ideas about government which he favored philosophically and practically."[23] He was uncertain as to what extent Gilligan was "owned" by labor: "Obviously, he was heavily indebted to labor—and I don't like it when someone is heavily indebted to anyone."[24]

For his part, Gilligan described Kurfess as "a fairly big-sized guy, pleasant, outgoing—who very clearly knew his own mind. He clearly enjoyed the confidence of those people on his side of the fence, and a lot of Democrats, who might never have voted for him, had respect for him. I had the feeling very early on from some conversations with Kurfess that if he could be persuaded that an income tax was necessary he would stand up for it, even if it would cost him among his Republican brethren."[25]

With Republicans holding a 54–45 edge in the House, the GOP could pass any tax package its members could agree on. They could not, however, agree. A strong handful supported Gilligan's call for a graduated state income tax; another group inclined to support a 1 percent income tax collected at the county level and directed to public education and local government; still others supported an increased state sales tax; and a good many opposed new taxes of any kind. Fifty votes were required for passage. But as Speaker Kurfess stated on multiple occasions, "I do not have fifty votes for anything."[26]

The long tradition of "Republican dominance and adamant opposition to taxes of any kind" was still present in the House, Gilligan said, and adamant.[27] State representative Keith McNamara (R-Columbus) said that "the clash between the Governor and me began *on* the day the budget was on the House floor."[28]

Representative Batchelder said of his own reaction to the governor's budget proposal: "I was flabbergasted. There were those of us who were believers in 'supply side economics' before the term was invented. Gilligan's budget was, in my perspective, too much government in both cost and breadth."[29] Conservative opposition was determined. Batchelder said that "some of the new Republicans elected in 1966 were Goldwater's children; they did not come here to negotiate."[30] One repeated Republican assertion was that the proposed tax increase was more aimed at increasing welfare payments than at funding education. Interviewed by the *Troy Daily News,* State Representative Robert Netzley (R-Laura) charged that 62 percent of the tax increase would go to welfare. Kurfess, among others, shared this concern—if not Netzley's arithmetic. Responding to a citizen's letter, Kurfess asked rhetorically: "Is it necessary to double welfare payment programs of this biennium? [Governor Gilligan] has made no commitment at all in attempting to support a basic revision of the welfare programs."[31]

The Gilligan administration orchestrated a broad-based campaign in favor of the income tax. At the direction of legislative liaison John McDonald, aided by his assistant Bill Chavanne, representatives of twelve to twenty pro-tax groups met on Monday mornings in the Statehouse press room. The purpose of these regular meetings was to keep the groups informed and energized. Chavanne recalled, "We'd help them think about names of people they could talk to—say, a hospital administrator in Xenia who could call on his representative."[32] The volunteers, Chavanne recalled, were often somewhat too ready to believe that a politician who listened politely was a politician who was agreeing with them and their position. In one instance, he watched as Representative Ethel Swanbeck agreed with everything said by a pro-tax advocate. Chavanne later approached Swanbeck and asked if she was going to vote for the bill. The representative replied, "Oh, no. oh, no."[33]

Three major players signed on to the reform effort early: the Ohio Education Association (OEA), the Ohio Farm Bureau, and the Ohio Council of Retail Merchants. The first, the politically active union of the state's public schoolteachers, had the most to gain from Gilligan's proposals. Finance director Hal Hovey ran the numbers and then informed each school district in the state what its new appropriation would be if the tax was enacted. When Republicans presented a counterproposal, Gilligan responded, saying that their plan would "virtually assure wholesale school closings later this year."[34] The governor added that under the GOP plan, 565 of the state's 639 school districts would receive less aid than from the administration's plan. The differences were not trivial: in Franklin County (Columbus), for example, the Republican plan called for $49.8 million and Gilligan's for $70.4 million. In time, other education groups joined in support of the tax measure, including the Ohio School Boards Association and the Ohio Superintendents Association.

Self-interest was readily apparent among adherents of the proposed income tax. The farm association backed the plan in part out of concern that the alternative to an income tax would be higher taxes on land. Similarly, the retail council hoped to head off an increase in the state sales tax. John Mahaney, the longtime head of the retail association, and someone highly experienced in state politics, argued that "the income tax was absolutely necessary for the state."[35] It was, he said, one tough fight—"really the most difficult thing I was ever through. I was the traitor to the party and the bastard at the family picnic for supporting it."[36]

Among those groups *not* backing the income tax were, notably, organized labor—specifically, the Ohio AFL-CIO and, in particular, that body's leader, Frank King. Gilligan found King's position unfathomable. What, he wondered, could be fairer to the working men and women of Ohio than a graduated income tax? Somewhat speculatively, Gilligan said, "Someone early on in [King's] presence referred to the tax as a payroll tax. He got it into his head that it was going to fall only on payrolls. And you could not talk him out of it."[37] Legislative liaison John McDonald offered a different explanation: "King was an old-school Democrat. He had seen Rhodes be very successful [by opposing taxes], and he thought if we could duplicate what Rhodes had done, we'd be successful without sticking our neck out on something as risky as new taxes."[38] This was not a minor obstacle: in addition to his state labor post, King was a former Democratic minority leader of the Ohio Senate, where he continued to wield considerable influence.

Gilligan met individually with legislators whenever McDonald or Chavanne thought such a session might advance the cause. Occasionally, they got it wrong. Chavanne believed State Representative David Weisert (R-Muskingum) would vote yes if he received a little private attention from the governor. A meeting was duly set up, with Gilligan providing a big-picture view to the apparently receptive legislator. When the governor finished, Weisert said, "Is there any way we could do all this with a bond issue?"—repeating the financing approach Gilligan had found reprehensible in James Rhodes—Gilligan, Chavanne reported, was "definitely not amused."[39]

While McDonald and Chavanne organized pressure from outside the legislature, "aggressive Gilligan aides, led by chief of staff James Friedman, began stalking the legislative halls day and night."[40] Meanwhile, Republican lieutenant governor John Brown launched broadsides against Gilligan, charging that the governor "opposes a public vote because he is afraid Ohio voters would reject it" and arguing that Gilligan would "set Ohio on a course to fiscal ruin."[41] The importuning of Gilligan staff members was not always welcome. State Representative Gertrude Polcar (R-Parma) denounced the "Democratic orangutans and their gorilla tactics."[42] On May 28, Speaker Kurfess complained to Gilligan: "Throughout the afternoon members of your staff have threateningly approached a number of our House members, not just cajoling or pleading . . . but with bleak political threats and innuendos concerning elections in which those members might in the future be involved."[43] The Speaker observed that the power to eject nonmembers from the House floor was his, and he would exercise it if presented with "similar behavior in the future."[44]

Kurfess, by this time, was presiding over a very unhappy Republican caucus. George Voinovich noted that the 1966 election had produced a substantial number of new Republican members: "We came down in 1967 as a band of brothers; there was quite a good esprit d'corps, camaraderie."[45] That feeling was lost by 1971. "It was not a happy time. Roommates stopped rooming together. A lot of Republicans never forgave Kurfess."[46] At one point, Kurfess and others in the Republican House leadership acquired tiny gavels, which they wore on their lapels as inconspicuous emblems of leadership. One House conservative went to a hardware store and came back with some wood screws. Reporter Lee Leonard recalled that "they stuck them in their lapels, and of course it meant 'screw Kurfess.' They paraded around with these little wood screws. Everyone knew what it meant."[47] Feeling was such, Leonard added, that some Republican representatives did not speak to each other for years thereafter.

John Mahaney, who talked strategy with Kurfess and Democrat Vern Riffe, recalled that "it got so bitter that the Republicans were talking about ousting Kurfess. When things came to a head, Vern was shaking with rage. He said to me—I was the go-between—'Go across the hall and find out if Kurfess has four friends.' If he did, Riffe added, House Democrats would join that quartet to reelect Kurfess as Speaker."[48] Mahaney said that it never came to that, "but Vern could have done it."[49] By report, Kurfess was rattled by the opposition within his own ranks. Keith McNamara, who, despite being a tax opponent, considered himself close to Kurfess, said of his party's leader, "He may hold a grudge; but if so, it's hard to find."[50]

On May 28, Gilligan announced that if his original tax proposal was put to a vote, he was confident the House would enact it. Representative Keith McNamara, certain no such thing would happen, immediately moved that Gilligan's original budget proposal be voted on. The Democrats caucused. It was clear that the votes were not there, so they directed their members to vote no. The upshot was that the governor's budget was rejected by a 99–0 vote. Almost as odd was the GOP's decision to approve and send to the Senate the appropriations half of the budget without sending any tax plan to pay for it. The $7.8 billion budget approved by the GOP was more than $1 billion less than what Gilligan had proposed.

As both sides maneuvered, speculation spread. In early June, the *Columbus Dispatch* carried a report that the House would likely approve a 1.50–1.75 percent income tax, collected and spent at the county level. Democrats opposed the measure. Representative James Flannery said a graduated income tax was needed "to provide the revenue elasticity that is needed to grow with the state."[51] Concurring, Representative John Johnson (D-Orrville) said a flat rate tax would only be a stopgap: "We should not have to come back each session to nickel and dime the public on taxes."[52]

On June 15, *Gongwer* reported that "Majority Republicans in the Ohio House, hopelessly deadlocked over the past several weeks over the hot taxation issue, indicated willingness Tuesday to work toward a compromise with Administration Democrats."[53] Not all Republicans were ready for compromise, however. The following day, Representative Richard Reichel (R-Massillon) proposed a flat 0.8 percent county income tax, not to be increased except by popular referendum.

With the June 30 budget deadline approaching, the first of what would become numerous interim budgets was introduced in the House. Finance director Hal Hovey stated that, as things stood, "Ohio was capable of paying bills through February."[54] For a time, agreement seemed near. On June 23, *Gongwer* reported that Kurfess and Democratic minority leader Lancione had reached agreement that the tax bill should include a 1–4 percent personal income tax, a 4–7 percent corporate income tax, and a 10 percent rollback in real estate taxes. After meeting with the Democratic caucus, however, Lancione revised his position, saying that the "compromise is only possible if there is a new omnibus appropriations-education funding bill on which Democrats and Republicans would compromise on both levels and means of raising revenues."[55] In short, the Democrats wanted more spending. To Kurfess, this shut down efforts to find common ground.[56]

On Saturday, June 26, Gilligan and his fellow Democrats enjoyed a brief respite from the tension and turmoil at the annual Democrats' State Dinner—which, for the first time in nine years, was chaired by a sitting Democratic governor. The 3,000 Democrats in attendance heard featured speakers Birch Bayh and George McGovern, two U.S. Senators widely believed to be harboring presidential ambitions. The event raised an estimated $300,000, a fair down payment on the $2 million the state party hoped to raise during the year.

Such interruptions aside, the tax question became all but all-consuming. On June 30, the General Assembly ratified the Twenty-sixth Amendment to the U.S. Constitution, thereby giving eighteen-year-olds the vote. As Ohio was the thirty-

The parents—Harry and Blanche Gilligan. (Courtesy of the Gilligan family)

Jack Gilligan graduated from Notre Dame in November 1942 as part of an accelerated program that hastened his enlistment in the U.S. Navy. (University of Notre Dame Archives)

On June 28, 1945, John Gilligan married Mary Kathryn Dixon, a Cincinnati native he had known most of his life and who he had courted largely by letter. (Courtesy of the Gilligan family)

The Gilligans some decades later. (Ohio Historical Society)

Jack Gilligan, then a young Cincinnati City Councilman, and Katie Gilligan in their early-model Volkswagen, well-stocked with the couple's four children. (Ohio Historical Society)

At a 1956 presidential rally in Cincinnati's Music Hall. Gilligan stands to the left of his first political hero, Democratic nominee Adlai E. Stevenson. To Stevenson's left is Michael DiSalle, future Ohio governor, and John A. Wiethe, Hamilton County Democratic chairman and future Gilligan nemesis. (Ohio Historical Society)

Fellow Cincinnati councilman Theodore Berry and Gilligan were often aligned on issues of race and poverty, not generally high priorities in this conservative city. (Ohio Historical Society)

Newly elected congressman Jack Gilligan with Speaker of the House John McCormack of Massachusetts. That McCormack's wife and Gilligan's mother were both named Blanche was of some small assistance to Gilligan gaining the committee assignment he sought. (Ohio Historical Society)

Even as a young congressman, Jack Gilligan caught the eyes of many in the Democratic Party establishment, which kept his campaigns well-supplied with well-known speakers. Gilligan felt particularly close to the Kennedys; both Edward (shown here) and Robert campaigned for him. (Ohio Historical Society)

Gilligan, Georgia congressman James A. McKay and California representative Lionel Van Deerlin flank Lyndon Johnson as the president signs a $280 million, three-year extension of the Research Facilities Construction Program, a measure Gilligan had championed. (Ohio Historical Society)

In Congress, Jack Gilligan was a Great Society liberal and yet was still aggressive in pursuing his district's interest. In 1966, seeking reelection as the "Congressman Who Gets Things Done," he lost narrowly to the "crown prince" of Cincinnati conservatives, Robert Taft. (Ohio Historical Society)

James Friedman, probably Gilligan's most important political adviser, was a young federal appeals court clerk when he descended on Gilligan to announce that the one-term congressman could defeat Ohio's reigning Democratic officeholder, Frank Lausche, in the 1968 party Senate primary. (Courtesy of James Friedman)

Frank Lausche was Ohio's champion vote-getter: the five-time governor and two-term U.S. senator anticipated little difficulty in dispensing with Gilligan's challenge in 1968. (U.S. Senate Historical Office)

By 11:17 on election night, Gilligan had opened up a 25,000 vote lead on the incumbent. As totals swelled, Gilligan's margin topped 100,000 votes. (Ohio Historical Society)

An editorial cartoon contrasts the relative penury of Gilligan's general election campaign with that of his better-financed opponent, Republican William Saxbe. (Ohio Historical Society)

Republican William Saxbe, seated, listens to Gilligan speaking at the Cleveland City Club debate which, coming just days before 1968 November election, marked one of the traditional high points of the campaign. (Ohio Historical Society)

Jack Gilligan ran for office—primaries and general elections combined—well over a dozen times. Here, he goes one-on-one with a voter. (Ohio Historical Society)

Gilligan takes on the electorate two at a time. (Ohio Historical Society)

A voter decides it's time for Gilligan to do a little listening. (Ohio Historical Society)

On January 11, 1971, John Joyce Gilligan was inaugurated as Ohio's 62nd governor. Sitting at left is outgoing Republican governor James A. Rhodes, Harry Gilligan, Katie Gilligan, and the new chief executive. The Gilligan children—Ellen, John, Kathleen, and Donald—stand behind. (Ohio Historical Society)

An editorial cartoon suggests that the size of the legislative program of the newly installed governor was pitching to the generally conservative Ohio General Assembly. (Ohio Historical Society)

Gilligan (left) with Senator Edmund Muskie (D-Maine), to whom Gilligan gave an early endorsement for the 1972 Democratic presidential nomination. Muskie may have been the most plausible nominee, but he generated little excitement, disappointing many. (Ohio Historical Society)

Gilligan's inner circle, 1973. Left to right: Robert Tenenbaum, press secretary; Phil Moots, legislative liaison; Governor Gilligan; Robert Daley, assistant to the governor; Jack Hansan, chief of staff; Max Brown (back to camera), director of communications; and Jay Tepper, executive assistant for administration. (Courtesy of Robert Daley)

Built for an Ohio industrialist and donated to the state, the Ohio Governor's Mansion was not entirely a place that "a lot of living" could make a home. (Ohio Historical Society)

Katie Gilligan's own efforts as First Lady focused on the well-being of children. (Ohio Historical Society)

Jack Gilligan, a lifelong and devout Catholic, pauses outside a downtown Columbus church where he had been a special guest at a Lenten service. (Ohio Historical Society)

Following his term at the U.S. Agency for International Development, Gilligan was re-cruited to return to his alma mater by Notre Dame's legendary head, Father Theodore Hesburgh (third from left). Gilligan taught in the law school and then directed the uni-versity's vibrant Peace Studies program. Notre Dame would prove Gilligan's longest pro-fessional association. (University of Notre Dame Archives)

Retiring from Notre Dame, Gilligan returned to his native Cincinnati, where he found work on the faculty of the University of Cincinnati as well as an elective office on the city's school board—and Dr. Susan Fremont, who, on September 30, 2000, married the former governor at St. Anthony's Church in Madisonville. (Courtesy of Robert Daley)

eighth state to endorse the measure, its action secured adoption of the amendment. Pleased with that distinction, Governor Gilligan flew to Washington that same day to hand-deliver Ohio's approval to the president pro tempore of the U.S. Senate. Years later, when journalist Lee Leonard undertook to write an article on the topic, he could not recall the date of passage. Hoping to have his memory refreshed, Leonard called James Friedman, who, according to Leonard, responded, "I don't remember a thing about that. We were up to our asses in the income tax."[57] For the moment, it appeared everyone was talking past one another. Before getting on the plane to Washington, Gilligan threatened to attempt to break the impasse in the House by beginning budget discussions with the Senate. House Republicans, he said, "need help from the Democrats but are unwilling to let the Democrats have any say in what is in it."[58] On July 6, Speaker Kurfess said there was more support in the GOP caucus for a 1.5 percent flat-rate personal tax than for any other measure. That same day, Minority Leader Lancione said Democrats wished to restore $187 million previously cut from the budget by Republicans—an amount the 1.5 flat tax would not cover. And on July 9, the Ohio AFL-CIO announced it was "opposed to this bill in its entirety and will notify members of the House by letter of our opposition."[59] No end appeared to be in view. Representative Robert Netzley said, "It wouldn't surprise me if we wound up putting the income tax question on the November ballot."[60]

As it happened, all of the above was the storm before the calm, an effort by virtually all parties to make their complaints known before arriving at an agreement. On July 14, following what the *Columbus Dispatch* termed "four months of backroom bickering and three hours of floor debate," the Ohio House approved a comprehensive tax package that included Ohio's first income taxes: 4–8 percent on corporations and 1–4 percent on individuals.[61] The bill, largely drafted by Speaker Kurfess, sent money principally to local schools and libraries and the local government fund, while providing a 10 percent rollback in property taxes and an income-based homestead property tax reduction for those over age sixty-five.

Passage came with a 54–42 margin, with thirty-eight Democrats and sixteen Republicans supporting the measure and six Democrats and thirty-six Republicans opposing it. The budget called for a $1.5 billion increase in expenditures. Amendments on the floor restored $167 million in Gilligan administration programs cut during the spring—notably for aid to dependent children and the environment—and added $23 million for state employee pay increases.

The package also:
- Reduced the assessment rate on tangible personal property from 50–70 percent to 40 percent
- Retained the current direct use of exemption on equipment used in industrial processes (tightening this exemption, which would have produced $60 million per biennium, was eliminated from the bill by floor amendment)

- Eliminated the 5 percent state intangible personal property tax on investment earnings
- Provided homestead property tax exemptions of $2,500 for persons over age sixty-five with an income of $6,000 or less and $1,000 with higher incomes
- Enacted a 10 percent across-the-board reduction in real estate taxes
- Instituted a 1 mill increase in the intangible tax paid by financial institutions and dealers and the excise tax paid by Ohio insurance companies and established a 2 percent increase in the estate tax for estates between $40,000 and $100,000.

The overall increase in taxes drove some Republicans to despair. House Judiciary Committee chairman Joseph Tulley (R-Mentor) characterized the passed measure as "a tax upon initiative, a tax upon hard work and a tax upon success."[62] He and other conservatives argued that the tax provided benefits to the rich and poor at the expense of the middle-income earner. The bill now went to the Senate, where, the *Dispatch* reported, leaders hoped to "wrap up" the measure by August 15.

Gilligan fully expected to have the income matter resolved by July 30, and at that point his administration could begin pressing the legislature on other matters. The issue of strip mining in eastern and southeastern Ohio, however, did not wait for the resolution of the tax question. This was not only a substantive matter in its own right but one that tied to more general environmental concerns. The House proceeded on the question immediately after sending the tax and budget question on to the Senate.

Within Ohio's general pattern of environmental degradation, strip mining stood out in its egregiousness. The rise of the practice in Ohio followed simple economic incentive. After the Second World War, as the deep shaft mines in eastern Ohio began to play out, and the cost of bringing coal to the surface rose sharply. Where coal seams lay close to the surface, it was far less expensive simply to strip clean the overburden of soil, sand, and clay, exposing the seam for easy harvest. Strip mining became increasingly common: in 1941, 10.7 percent of the nation's coal supply came from such mines, a figure that by 1961 reached 32.3 percent. Ohio's share was far higher: 37 million of the 55 million tons of coal harvested in the state in 1970 came from strip mines.[63]

Strip mining in Ohio was localized in about 13,000 square miles in twenty-seven eastern and southeastern counties. Accessible seams of coal were generally four feet thick; an acre could yield about 6,000 tons of coal, which, at mid-1960s prices, was worth about $22,000, a one-time return far in excess of the long-term commercial value of the land for agriculture. Harrison and Jefferson counties were the two most ravaged by the strip mining. Researcher Jack Hill reported that 59,549 of the 521,000 acres in these two counties had been strip-mined.

Strip mining did not add much to the local economies. One study concluded that there was "no evidence to indicate" that the coal and strip mining industries "are supporting the county with strong complementary industries, such as retail trade."[64] Rather, wealth traveled a one-way route out of the region—for example, to the Ohio Power Station in Washington County, which in the mid-1960s converted 1.2 million tons of coal annually into electricity. Describing the industry as it operated in the early days of his governorship, Gilligan said: "There were power plants operating along the banks of the Ohio, from Youngstown virtually all the way to Cincinnati. There were trains, and the trains ran on a circular track that never stopped."[65] When the trains reached the mines, "they would slow, and a huge shovel would dump a load of coal into each car as it passed. The train would then head for the steel mills or the power plants and dump their load. They changed crews, of course, but the trains themselves never stopped."[66]

Much of the land being stripped was agriculturally marginal. These "were desperately poor communities," Gilligan said. "The farmers were eager to sell."[67] Commonly, farmers sold the coal rights to their land believing the coal companies planned simply to dig a shaft, not that they would strip the entire surface—"And the devastation!" Gilligan recalled. "They were making large areas of Ohio look like the dark side of the moon."[68] Worse, the coal seams of Appalachia contain pyrite, an iron sulfide that, when exposed to air and water, produces sulfuric acid, which drained from the heaps of slag deposited by the strip mining operations to poison soil and streams.

Strip mining was a matter previous state governments had done little about. The insufficiency of state action was underscored in mid-1971 by the testimony of two Ohio representatives during congressional hearings on a proposed nationwide ban on strip mining. Wayne Hayes (D-Flushing) stated, "A disaster of enormous magnitude is occurring in my home [Belmont] county and in many like it throughout the land."[69] And John Seiberling (D-Akron) said that "ninety-nine percent of state regulation to date has been an abysmal failure. My own state of Ohio is no exception."[70]

Ohio decided to act. Gilligan said, "We just happened to hit the crest of the wave. It was a period in American generally where environmental matters were first being given some serious attention."[71] Commonly legislative proposals to crack down on polluters are watered down in committee, often under industry or lobbyist pressure. Ohio's proposed strip mining bill, however, became tougher as it moved through the House. The original bill "permitted" the Ohio Division of Forestry and Reclamation to write regulations for reclaiming land; the amended version "required" such action. Legislation decided that local coal companies could appeal rulings only in the Franklin County Common Pleas Courts, not a local court that might be susceptible to the blandishments of a local enterprise. The licensing fee charged for strip mining increased from $15 to $150 an acre; state inspectors had the "absolute right" to enter a mining operation and the power to make arrests.

Gilligan believed the mine owners were taken by surprise by the strength of public sentiment—and found themselves largely without allies or arguments. "They did not have any natural constituency. In the areas in which they were operating, they were regarded as evil. They were ruining communities and ruining farms."[72] Further, as surface mining was far less labor intensive than shaft mining, no strong argument about "protecting jobs" could be advanced. "They had dislocated the [shaft] miners; there wasn't any work left in the mines," Gilligan said. "You could run one of those strip mining operations with just a handful of people, plus the railways. So it was very tough for the mine operators and strip miners to build any public opposition to these measures."[73]

On September 30, 1971, the state's House Committee on Environment and Natural Resources voted 16–0 to forward the bill to the House floor. The *Dayton Daily News* reported, "The bill will impose the strictest control on strip coal miners in Ohio history. Its land reclamation and anti-pollution sections are at least as strong as provisions in the laws of all other nearby strip mining states."[74] As evidence of the measure's popularity, the bill had at this point gathered thirty-two cosponsors—twenty Republicans and a dozen Democrats.

Speaking to the press on October 21, Gilligan said that while the bill was not perfect, it represented "a long step towards the complete elimination of the ravages—past and present—of strip-mining in Ohio."[75] In terms of his own administration, Gilligan noted that in April, the Ohio Department of Natural Resources had for the first time refused to issue a license to a coal mining company that wished to expand its operation in Richland County. A week later, the House voted on the measure. Four hours of speeches preceded the vote. John P. Wargo (D-Lisbon) stated, "This bill is too late for my [Columbiana] county—thirty years too late. I implore you to support this bill so that your county can be saved from ruin."[76]

George Nicolozakes, vice president of the Marietta Coal Company, told a reporter that passage of the bill would force smaller operators out of business and force larger operators to pass their increased costs along to the consumer. The argument carried no weight within the House chamber: the *Dayton Daily News* reported, "Attempts to amend the floor were resoundingly defeated, causing legislators who hoped to weaken the bill to give up in frustration."[77] The measure passed and carried to the Senate with considerable momentum. That momentum was checked, however, when Republican senator Robert E. Stockdale, chair of the committee handling the bill, suffered a heart attack. He was absent better than a month, and Senate action on the bill was deferred until the spring of 1972—ample time for its opponents to rally.

With the tax issue stalled, the Gilligan administration moved on a second front, one that looked past the current legislative entanglement to the long-term goal of making the Democrats the legislature's majority party. As a consequence of the 1970 U.S. Census, in 1971 Ohio was to redraw the boundaries of its legislative districts. It was a task the state Democratic Party welcomed with combative glee, since, for a change, they would be in control of redistricting. Gilligan had been sensitive to the importance of redistricting to Ohio since his 1965–67 term in Congress. The U.S.

Supreme Court's "one man, one vote" decision required states to create legislative districts of approximately equal population, and Ohio's Hanna Amendment was struck down. In December 1964, a lame duck Republican-controlled legislature approved a scheme highly likely to favor Republicans and placed it on the May 1965 state ballot for voter approval.

With that matter before the voters, Congressman Gilligan rose on April 8, 1965, to attack the GOP-proposed measure. Ohio, he noted, had a considerable history of the Democratic Party receiving a majority of the aggregated popular vote only to wind up with minority representation in the State House of Representatives. In 1960, he noted, Democratic candidates drew 53 percent of the statewide ballots but gained only 39 percent of Ohio's legislative seats. This experience was repeated in the elections of 1962 and 1964. Gilligan called attention to the language of the GOP-backed proposal, which required districts be "as similar in economic and community interests as possible," a deeply ambiguous phrase that "could mean anything the [Republican-controlled reapportionment] board wishes it to mean."[78] Faced with strong Democratic opposition, Issue 3 was trounced at the polls. At that point, the legislature adopted the plan devised by Attorney General William Saxbe, which created a thirty-three-seat Senate, with each Senate district divided into three House districts. Though generally considered an improvement over what it replaced, the effort resulted in districts ranging from 61,479 to 187,208 in population. Speaking in 1971 as governor, Gilligan said there "is no doubt whatever that the current system is not in accordance with the requirements of the United States, because it fails to provide equal representatives for every Ohio citizen."[79]

With Gilligan's election, the Democrats gained nine seats in the House, cutting the GOP margin from 63–36 to 54–45. Now in control of the state Reapportionment Board, the party hoped that redistricting would produce a Democratic majority in the legislature in 1972.

That goal, John McDonald noted, pitted the wishes of individual legislators against the best interests of the party. Reapportionment, he said, "is a very emotional issue. You are dealing with legislators' districts, their political livelihoods. Everybody wants to be elected by 75 percent of the vote."[80] Such comfort for the individual, however, has the effect of concentrating the party's vote into fewer districts. Rearranging those voters could produce more Democratic legislators, but at the expense of making any given member's election less than certain. Incumbents, McDonald said, wanted 75 percent, "and once we'd explained to them that that wasn't going to happen, the conversation got a little bit chilly."[81] The argument that McDonald and others spent months repeating to incumbent Democrats was: "Do you like being in the minority? If so, you will never get your name on a significant piece of legislation. We have to get more people here."[82]

The Gilligan administration's task was simplified by the fact that the other two Democratic members of the Reapportionment Board—Auditor Joseph Ferguson and Senate minority leader Anthony Calabrese—had specific and limited agendas.

Ferguson had a particular concern with Representative Keith McNamara, who had introduced legislation that would bar anyone serving in statewide office if they were seventy years of age or older. Since the public had approved a constitutional amendment that had set an age limit for anyone becoming a judge, McNamara, who did not necessarily agree with that stricture, felt that the same standard should apply to statewide officeholders. Asked decades later if he knew at the time that the sole individual to which his proposal would apply was Joe Ferguson, McNamara responded, "Yes, I probably knew that."[83] Asked if he considered Ferguson's prospective departure from public life as no great loss to the citizens of Ohio, he said, "Yes, I probably did."[84] So Ferguson returned the favor, deciding that McNamara's departure from office would be no great loss to the public. Ferguson's sole request, where redistricting was concerned, was that Keith McNamara lose his seat. McNamara took the loss philosophically. He had been in office a dozen years, he said, and likely that was enough.

Calabrese's demand was equally straightforward. Bill Chavanne said, "All Tony wanted was to have every Italian in Cuyahoga County in his district."[85] This was somewhat more difficult to accommodate, as a Senate district defined the outline of three House districts and imposed its shape on all adjacent districts. The mapmakers spent some time on what came to be called "the Calabrese Corridor." Commenting on the result, John McDonald said, "There's a very strange-looking district that managed to pick up all the Italians in Cuyahoga County and put them into one district, and that district can elect and reelect Tony until he meets his maker."[86]

So, with the relatively minor sacrifice of one Republican legislator and some fancy line-drawing in Cuyahoga County, the Gilligan administration had the votes it needed to redraw the rest of the state to its party's advantage.

McDonald and James Friedman wanted a computer-driven mapping operation. Ira Gaffin, director of research for the state party, directed that effort. To maintain some secrecy, Gaffin and several assistants worked in a low-profile, rented office over the Arthur Murray Dance Studio on Broad Street several blocks east of the capitol, where U.S. census data was delivered on huge reels of tape.

Much of the statistical work was an even more secluded setting. That spring, Chris Buchanan got a phone call from Mark Shields. Buchanan, who had undertaken demographic research used to plan media campaigns for Gilligan in 1968, agreed to spend his summer crunching numbers for the reapportionment effort. Buchanan, who "loved election statistics," was a student at Boston University.[87] He recalled working for $67.20 a week in a windowless room in the Forrest Industries Building on Massachusetts Avenue in Washington, D.C. Buchanan started the complicated process (which today, with computers, has become a sophisticated art) with 8½-by-11-inch sheets of paper on which county outlines had been drawn; his first step was to hand-shade the political percentages. Buchanan spent May and June loading data—some of it from an upstart Columbus firm named CompuServ—from five different statewide races. From this data, he was able to determine the likely Democratic vote of any district that could be devised. (Buchanan had only limited contact with Gilligan; at one point, the governor, in Washington for an event hosted by Mark Shields, told the college freshman to "keep up the good work."[88]) In mid-August, Buchanan delivered his statistical goods to Columbus, driving through the night in his prized yellow Opel Cadet to the office above the dance studio.

On receiving the data, John McDonald said, "we looked at individual districts. You can't have incumbent Democrats sitting on an 80 percent district; that's just wasting Democrats. You could carve that down to 55 percent."[89] In some cases, if there was a particularly well-established incumbent, they might carve as low as 51 percent. For McDonald, there was irony at play in this process. During his term as minority leader of the House, he had worked with Republican Charles Fry on standards for redistricting. Among other things, they determined that districts had to be compact and contiguous. In the work he was doing under Gilligan, he noted, "I had to work against my own ground rules."[90]

In addition to voting behavior, the data provided information on median income, race, and age for each of the ninety-nine proposed new legislative districts. By modern standards, the approach was preprimitive: all calculations were done on adding machines. Errors were made. McDonald recalled, "We came up with a district in Toledo. Along with black/white, age, economic—one of the indices was people per household. We kept running this district that looked perfect, except it had fourteen people per household."[91]

Buchanan's work on the data continued. When his classes at Boston University resumed in September, he'd take the first flight to Columbus after his last Friday class and then take the last flight back to Boston on Sunday. By this time, McDonald and Chavanne had started to test reactions to their work by showing the proposed new map for each county to the incumbent. Negotiations ensued. Then, according to Buchanan, "McDonald would say, 'He's fine with it' or 'You got to make a change.'"[92]

McDonald and Chavanne did their best to keep their work secret from the individuals most concerned with its outcome, the Democratic incumbents. Chavanne said, "I don't remember talking to any incumbents. They may have told me, 'I got to have this' or 'I got to have that,' but [if so] I didn't pay much attention to it."[93] He added, "You can't make deals at the beginning, because everything affects everything else. I was trying to make sure no one got hurt. I had information from being legislative liaison and from campaigns. I got to know these guys and when they needed help."[94]

One incumbent who got such help was John Johnson (D-Orrville). Johnson had been narrowly elected in 1970 as the first Democrat to hold the district since 1936. At that time, the district included Wayne County—a dairy and grain region, and home to Smuckers—and four fairly Republican townships from Ashland County. Bill Chavanne, Johnson said, "was interested in my staying in office."[95] The Republican townships in Ashland County were moved out of his district and more balanced districts from Summit and Holmes counties moved in. Johnson was comfortably reelected four more times before deciding to leave the legislature in 1980.

Factors beyond demographics came into play. McDonald and Chavanne didn't want to draw a line that separated an incumbent from their campaign manager or most important supporters. But one number was central: 107,596, Ohio's population divided among ninety-nine House districts. McDonald and Chavanne tried to stick within a 1 percent variance—a stricter standard than state courts might require but the standard the U.S. Supreme Court preferred.

McDonald said, "We tried desperately, and I think fairly successfully, to keep our apportionment activities a big secret."[96] Another reason for keeping the redistricting activities a secret was the administration's desire to avoid doing anything that might cost votes on the tax package that was pending. The secrecy was not much appreciated, however. On September 15, in the *Dayton Daily News,* several Democratic legislators complained that their input had not been sought; at the same time, two Republican senators from Montgomery County, Clara Weisenborn and David Holcomb, expressed confidence that their seats would be protected: "Both have let the governor's office know they support his personal income tax and an official in the administration said they will be remembered for their support."[97]

When, on September 15, the proposed remapping became public, it brought howls from Democrats, largely from Cuyahoga County, the party stronghold. Bill Chavanne commented, "We got a lot of heat. Everybody thought they knew their counties better than we did. We got everything from 'You've left out my main fundraiser' to 'You put my mother on the wrong side of the street.'"[98] James Celebrezze demanded of Jim Friedman, "What are you doing to me? I can't possibly win in this district."[99] Actually, Friedman said to Celebrezze, he thought he would have an easy time, noting that Celebrezze's brother had recently been a candidate and urging him to "check the overlay of your brother's result against this new district, and then come back."[100] Friedman wrote down his own expectation for Celebrezze's November vote—58 percent—and sealed it in an envelope. Celebrezze's vote that November was 61 percent.

Until 1970, Cleveland had four districts with black majorities. With demographic changes, however, only three could be justified. The odd incumbent out was Troy James, who found himself in a district that was 65 percent white, mostly Polish. James unhappiness with this was furthered by the likelihood that his 1972 opponent would be Ralph Perk Jr., son of Cleveland's mayor and, unlike James, someone strongly connected to white ethnic voters. The county Democratic chairman suggested to James that Gilligan might be trying to dump him. Further, the district James inherited was not itself overjoyed with the arrangement. When Bill Chavanne met with leading Democrats in the Polish community, they said that, as a matter of party loyalty, they would support James—once, and once only. Jim Friedman told James that he had "the governor's word" that he would be re-elected: if funds were needed, funds would be forthcoming; if gubernatorial visits were needed, those visits would happen.[101]

Feelings ran high. On September 30, 1971, the final day of Yom Kipper, Jim Friedman was at the Columbus home of press secretary Bob Tenenbaum for the holiday's traditional breaking of the fast when he received an emergency call. Cuyahoga County Democrats were meeting at the Statehouse where they were receiving their first look at their proposed new district lines. The delegates were not happy campers. Friedman headed over to join the meeting. One point of contention was how strongly Jewish and heavily Democratic Shaker Heights would be divided between incumbents Harry Lehman and Leonard Ostrovsky. Emphasizing his feelings on the matter, Ostrovsky grabbed Lehman by the throat. Calm was eventually restored (and the two were both eventually reelected).[102]

But if some Democrats were concerned about the plan, the Republicans were consternated. On October 1, the *Cleveland Plain Dealer* headlined the news: "State Remap Perils GOP Hold."[103] The reapportionment, the report said, "creates at least twelve new Democratic districts in the House . . . Most importantly, eight of those new Democratic districts will have incumbent GOP lawmakers thrown into races against each other in the same district."[104] This, the *Plain Dealer* continued, "could bring Democratic control of the House in 1972."[105] Overwhelmingly, those at risk of losing their seats were Republicans. For example, tax opponent Robert Netzley and Jack Oliver (R-Arcanum) were moved into the same district. The *Plain Dealer* reported that Netzley, anticipating the reapportionment plan, had purchased a home in Piqua, but Piqua wasn't in his new district either.

Republican Speaker Charles Kurfess, whose support on the income tax measure was vital, was less than pleased: "Without regard to the fate of any particular legislator, this is a sad day for responsible government in Ohio," he said to a reporter from the *Dayton Daily News*. "Never before has the will of the people, the concept of effective community representation, common sense and decency been so patently abused."[106] There was a further grief for the Republicans. Under Ohio election law, a candidate must live in a district at least a year before they are eligible to represent it in Columbus. This meant that those who had been displaced had nowhere to go, since it was already less than a year until the May 1972 primary. One noncombatant, reporter Lee Leonard, offered: "Twenty House Republicans either quit or got put in against incumbents in their home districts. The Democrats did a masterful job."[107]

Numbers-cruncher Chris Buchanan attended the Reapportionment Board's September 29 meeting when the plan was formally presented. He was expecting some knock-down and some drag-out. Neither occurred. The five board members sat at the front of a room packed with press and legislators. It took the Democrats less than ten minutes to present their plan and approve it by a 3–2 party-line vote.

Redistricting is both potent and partisan and, as such, often ends where such matter may be further adjudicated—in the courts. Knowing a challenge was inevitable, the Gilligan administration much preferred that the matter be settled in federal court, since its plan met the narrower federal standard for population discrepancy and because a federal court was likely to be less intrusive into what was, fundamentally, a matter of state prerogative.

Therefore, the administration was not altogether disappointed when a suit challenging the redistricting was filed on November 15, 1971, in federal court by a Youngstown tavern owner who claimed it contained population discrepancies. The fact that the tavern owner in question had twice been an unsuccessful Democratic candidate for the state assembly lent some credence to the belief that it was a friendly suit—that is, one filed to be convenient to the defendants and their redistricting.

On November 27, State Senator Alan Norris (R-Westerville) filed a suit with the Republican-leaning Ohio Supreme Court claiming that the Democratic plan was full of errors, including the fact that his own residence had been omitted. This suit urged the court to enjoin Ohio from using the proposed plan, claiming that "ample time" remained for a new one to be drawn up. The suit was argued by John McElroy, one-time chief of staff to Governor James Rhodes.[108]

The three-judge federal panel in Youngstown gave the Reapportionment Board until December 21 to present a plan that addressed the concerns raised; the federal judges held: "It is clear that the apportionment plan is unconstitutional on its face and no conceivable ruling by the Ohio Supreme Court could alter this situation."[109] Further, on behalf of the panel, District Judge Frank Battisti directed that no other lawsuit be filed in any court so long as the federal panel had the matter under consideration. Jim Friedman said that the "reactivation of the apportionment board would give it another chance to correct mistakes made in its first effort."[110]

None of this, however, was accomplished without hard feelings. State Representative William Batchelder regarded Battisti's action as "a federal usurpation of a state's right. Our supreme court interprets Ohio law."[111] Indeed, the Republicans were getting somewhat squeezed. On December 7, Gilligan vetoed an item from the interim state budget that would have permitted the secretary of state—a Republican—from hiring private attorneys in litigation related to legislative reapportionment. Then, as good as his threat, on December 13 Judge Battisti fined State Senator Norris $100 and John McElroy $5,000 for contempt for bringing the matter to the Ohio Supreme Court and then threatened to jail Rhodes's former chief of staff. Someone in court said to McElroy, "He's kidding, right?" McElroy opened his jacket to show that, in case of incarceration, he had brought his toothbrush.[112]

On December 20, 1971, the Reapportionment Board—again in a party-line vote—voted 3–2 for a redistricting plan little changed from the original.

25

Round 2: The Senate

Ohio's Senate hearings on the tax proposals opened before the Ways and Means Committee, chaired by Michael Maloney (R-Cincinnati) on Wednesday, July 20, 1971. No shortage of opinions was brought forward. On July 28, the committee heard the testimony of twenty-four witnesses—representatives of the Ohio Manufacturers Association, Goodyear Tire and Rubber, Chamber of Commerce, Ohio Municipal League, Ohio Library Association, as well as the mayor of Cincinnati and others. Somewhat unusually, the Senate body also heard from a clutch of state representatives—including Joseph Tulley (R-Mentor), John Bechtold (R-Cincinnati), and Robert Netzley (R-Laura), who spoke on behalf of the more limited tax proposals unsuccessfully advanced by House conservatives.

With the close of hearings, one House Republican, Speaker Pro Tempore Charles Fry, issued a statement attacking the "basic rationale" for the income tax: the needs of education. Gilligan's proposals, he argued, did not point to any real reform in public education. By his math, fully three-quarters of the added funds to be spent would go to increased salaries for those in the field. The Ohio Education Association, he asserted, was more interested in higher salaries, more restrictive bargaining practices, and the defense of existing tenure law than in such matters as merit pay, teacher evaluation, year-round schools, and other measures he characterized as actual reforms.

The question for the Gilligan administration, however, was not school reform but tax reform. And the question for the Senate was what the price tag might be. After two weeks of hearings, tax subcommittee chairman Michael Maloney concluded that funding the amended appropriations bill would require $1.246 billion in new revenue. At the same time, certain reductions would have to take place: chiefly, $184 million in property tax relief and a $90 million reduction to follow from elimination of the intangible taxes.

As at the national level, the Senate was a rather different body from the House. With just thirty-three members, it was smaller, more intimate. Because senators served longer terms than representatives—four years instead of two—the tenor of the body changed more slowly. Given this, the GOP was more firmly in control than in the House, holding a 20–13 majority.

The Senate's presiding officer was Ted Gray (R-Piqua). First elected from the 3rd District in 1950, Gray served for more than four decades, the Ohio Senate's longest tenure. In his service as president pro tempore, said one longtime political observer, "Gray was not doctrinaire. He was a fair-minded legislator who would make buddies on both sides of the aisle."[1] Statehouse reporters describe Gray as a consent leader, an opinion shared by William Batchelder, the one legislator whose tenure in the House nearly matched Gray's in the Senate: "Ted Gray was very pragmatic. He was not primed to lead a grand charge to change the basic tax structure of Ohio."[2] Though not greatly given to compliments of Republicans, Gilligan thought Gray was "a pretty reasonable guy."[3]

Gray was not the major obstacle to Gilligan's tax reform, however. Rather, that opposing force was Anthony Calabrese, the Democrat's own Senate minority leader. Calabrese was a character, even if only half the stories told about him were true. Richard Zimmerman wrote, "We never knew for sure whether Tony had or ever had ties to the mob, but he seemed to go out of his way to make one think so. A former night club bouncer, Calabrese spoke wise-guy English with a noticeable Italian accent, wore expensive, light-colored silk suits with dark blue or black silk shirts and white ties, and at times escorted flashy young women to the Senate chamber, where he would introduce them as 'my niece.'"[4]

Calabrese also had nerve. One story goes that he sought worker's compensation for injuries he received in a fall in the Senate parking lot. Another account described in his Senate office a wall densely covered with inscribed photographs of various notables, all signed in the same handwriting. He was, however, in the words of Senator Stanley Aronoff, "not a man without substance."[5] And reporter Lee Leonard described Calabrese as "an old-school Italian politician who liked to live the good life. If an issue got to him, he could get active, but it was mostly about having a good time."[6] He was, at least outside the Senate chambers, popular with most members, who enjoyed his bonhomie and dinner table companionship. But in Columbus, there was no love lost between Calabrese and his fellow Democrat and ostensible leader, Jack Gilligan. Calabrese apparently regarded Gilligan as just a little too blue-blooded to be a real Democrat. Of Calabrese, Gilligan, said, "I don't think Tony was putting people on; I think he was genuinely a buffoon."[7] (In the May 1970 primary, Calabrese gained the Democratic nomination for lieutenant governor; had he been elected, he would have stood next in succession as Governor. Gilligan's discomfort with this possibility amused Calabrese. At one point, he came up behind Gilligan, gave the gubernatorial nominee a nudge with his elbow, and said, "Hey, Jack. I'm only a heartbeat away."[8] Calabrese lost that November to Republican John Brown by 150,000 votes, a matter of no small relief to Gilligan.)

Stanley Aronoff said that Calabrese "was shrewd enough to know he needed people to guide him."[9] In the summer of 1971, with the tax fight under way, the individual offering that guidance was Frank King, president of the Ohio AFL-CIO and former Democratic Senate leader. King was not easy to pigeonhole. Some reporters said King tended to play to whoever was in the room. Gilligan's own people disagreed: John McDonald said that while King sometimes sought to please his immediate audience, "he was perfectly willing to stand up and take on people if he thought they were wrong."[10] Possibly, King considered Gilligan a rival. Journalist Hugh McDiarmid said, "He was a very ambitious guy. He didn't like Gilligan being more of the leader."[11] Or possibly King was simply a traditionalist: his background was in the trade unions, which are generally more conservative than the industrial unions. But what was clear was that King—and, by extension, the Ohio AFL-CIO—opposed any tax package that did not put the primary burden on business.

King may not have controlled Calabrese, but his influence on the Cleveland senator was strong. As, in turn, was Calabrese's influence over a handful of Democratic Senators with strong union ties. In the House, Democrats had supported Gilligan's income tax by a 38–6 margin; without the backing of King and Calabrese, however, there would be no such margin in the Senate. McDiarmid described how "through the summer Calabrese lobbied successfully not only against a House-passed plan that was more or less acceptable to Gilligan but also against anything that did not please King (which, in turn, was anything acceptable to Gilligan or to cautiously pro-compromise legislators)."[12]

The antipathy between Gilligan and King was something less than a Statehouse secret. On August 4, Bill Chavanne wrote the governor to press concern that Senate Republicans might rush a Senate vote forward. Their reason, he said, was that "they sense a lack of unity in the Democratic ranks in the Senate."[13] He said that if the income tax bill did not receive the support of at least eleven of the thirteen Democratic senators, it would fail. The Republicans knew the Democrats were divided: "Most specifically they are sensing this lack of unity because the Senate Leader, Tony Calabrese, has made some open statements that he is not in favor of the bill."[14] Chavanne added that an aide to Calabrese told lobbyists that "Frank King has told them it's an unfair bill and Frank King has never lied to them."[15]

August was a shaky month for the tax reform agenda. Republican Senator Robert Shaw, chair of the Financial Committee, and Michael Maloney, chair of Ways and Means, were working on alternative budget plans. Maloney said, "If it's going to be in the neighborhood of $850 to $900 million in new spending, I can't see anything other than an income tax."[16] He said that if the increase was in "the range of $650 million, then increases in the sales tax; franchise tax; etc., should suffice."[17] In late August, the Senate Ways and Means Committee accepted a "high" bill of $1.064 billion and a "low" bill of $703 million. Senator Gray said the caucus would decide which bill would go to the Senate floor. But for Gilligan, there was only one acceptable outcome: "There is no chance whatsoever of a sales tax increase. A sales tax is just brutally unfair."[18] At the same time, AFL-CIO leader King said that his well-staffed labor organization would start circulating petitions to put an alternative to Gilligan's tax plan on the state ballot by August 29.

And at this point, Gilligan raised the ante. With the tax question in limbo, state expenditures were outrunning current income. At the end of August, Governor Gilligan announced his intention to impose a program aimed at shedding $6.7 million in monthly expenses. Its principal elements were layoffs of state employees, cuts in welfare payments, and state park closings.

The layoffs of 2,840 state employees, including 750 from the state highway department and 500 or more seasonal employees in the Department of Natural Resources, were set to begin September 1. (When layoffs were first rumored, Gilligan received a note from GOP Senate leaders Ted Gray and Michael Maloney asking him to ensure that no "over-zealous personnel directors" use austerity as a shield for dismissing public servants hired by Republicans.[19]) Included in Welfare reductions were cuts of $1 a day for those recipients living in nursing homes, 1.5 percent in payments to recipients of Aid to Dependent Children, and 5 percent in general relief payments, as well as layoffs for thirty-seven department employees. (The planned reduction in welfare payments—intended to save $700,000 a month—was deferred when a Columbus welfare recipient gained a court order ruling that the state had failed to abide by the federally required notification procedure for such a step.)

To share this pain, Gilligan took, and ordered his top aides to take, 10 percent pay cuts, and an August 23 memo from Hal Hovey instructed cabinet members on how they could refund to the state the appropriate share of their salaries.

Gilligan also ordered the closing of forty-six of the fifty-seven state parks, those that were not self-sustaining through fees charged. The closing was to go into effect the Tuesday after Labor Day. Forty-four state memorials and other facilities operated by the Ohio Historical Society closed the following week.

Of the cutbacks, legislative liaison John McDonald said, "I think Jack wanted to demonstrate to the public that 'you can't have something for nothing.' His feeling was, everyone would become enraged with the legislature."[20] Gilligan said that he hoped the step would prompt "Ohio to break out of its self-imposed paralysis."[21] He claimed at the time that "the Republicans have the votes to pass any budget and any tax they want to pass. There is no excuse for their not acting."[22]

The public, however, saw it otherwise. Hugh McDiarmid wrote, "Gilligan, whose style was confrontational, decided to turn the screws further by ordering up an austerity program that, among other things, closed state parks. It was a move which, even though it dramatized the legislative gridlock . . . infuriated the public and provided fodder for the Republican campaign ads two years later."[23] People let Gilligan know of their unhappiness directly. Gilligan recalled how "Bob Hargenow, a golfer I knew from Cincinnati, had some sort of relationship with the parks.

I found out from him, among others, about the damage I was doing to the whole human race."[24] Indeed, the park closings brought only rare defenders, among them the state *Democratic Newsletter* of September 20, which announced that "GOP Cowardice" had closed the parks, saying all fault rested with the legislative Republicans who were compiling "an unenviable record of ineptness" in budgetary matters. The move engendered immediate opposition even from administration supporters.[25] State Representative Don Pease (D-Oberlin), a strong Gilligan supporter, wrote the governor urging that the park closings be delayed in hopes that progress on budget talks might ensue. The Republican opposition was rather less tactful. On the day the austerity program went into effect, House Speaker Charles Kurfess described the move as "cheap politics," adding, "The governor is using his so-called austerity program as a façade to hide his own apparent ineffectiveness in getting the support of even his own party members in the legislature behind his excessive tax and spending plans."[26]

And Gilligan came in for some mockery, too. With the groundskeeping crew at the Governor's Mansion laid off, the gubernatorial grass grew long. One Saturday, a group of Republican state legislators led by Robert Netzley turned up in Bexley dressed in coveralls and pushing lawnmowers. They had, not surprisingly, alerted the press to what they claimed was their own contribution to saving the state money. Gilligan was not amused. At a September 10 press conference, he characterized their incursion, coming as it did at a time when thousands had been laid off, as in "the poorest taste."[27]

Members of the public took similar steps. Within a week, 150 campers picketed at the main entrance to Mohican State Forest; going at least a step further, campers at Stonelick State Park burned Gilligan in effigy. The park closings, said Donald Lukens (R-Middletown), showed "a lack of concern for the Ohio taxpayer. The majority of Ohio taxpayers cannot afford to travel out of state every weekend."[28] John McDonald said, "Public opinion was unanimously against him: 'He's going to Michigan and Lake Leelanau for God's sake, and we can't go to Burr Oak State Park.'"[29]

News from elsewhere, however, reinforced the extent of the state's financial plight. On September 13, *Gongwer* reported that Ohio's superintendent of public instruction, Martin W. Essex, announced that twenty-two school districts enrolling 139,000 students might be forced to close due to lack of funds.

Yet Republicans continued to declare Gilligan's austerity measures a sham. In a September 28 press release, Speaker Kurfess argued that funds existed to maintain all state functions: "The decision not to expend these funds and instead close Ohio's state parks, reduce state aid to local schools, cut back on assistance to the blind, aged disabled and disadvantaged children, and take other actions under the guise of austerity clearly was a decision of the Governor alone."[30] All such services, he said, could be immediately restored.

Within Gilligan's immediate circle, no one remembered urging that the parks be closed. Press secretary Robert Tenenbaum said, "Apparently, it was one of those miraculous ideas that was implemented without it ever having occurred to anyone."[31] A vacationing Tom Menaugh was "horrified" by the decision.[32] John McDonald commented, "I did not recommend closing the state parks. I was out of the country, on a camping trip in Canada."[33] The suggestion had come from John Jones, head of the state Democratic Party. Jones, during previous service as director of personnel for Columbus mayor Jack Sensenbrenner, had urged closing city parks as a way to highlight the city's financial plight following the defeat of a May tax levy. The parks were duly closed and the tactic apparently worked: in November, the resubmitted levy passed. (Later, Gilligan sent Jones a photograph with the inscription, "I wish you hadn't talked me into closing the parks."[34])

Senate Republicans, Jim Friedman said, were stonewalling, hoping to isolate and exhaust the Gilligan administration and thereby prompt some mistake. And the park closing was just such a mistake. Gilligan acknowledged that he was initially mystified by the outcry:

I frankly did not consider the state parks as a primary interest to the general well-being of the population. Other things were more important, especially to the poor and less well protected, who were not big users of the parks. I knew we would get a scream whatever we did. I was not ready for the violence of the reaction we got over the parks; it took place in what was a beautiful September and many people had made their plans to vacation in the parks and use the lodges there. For that part of the population, it was really a very heavy blow.[35]

Perhaps surprising, Gilligan's position got a sympathetic hearing from Keith Mc-Namara, one of the firmest of tax increase opponents: "It was part of [Gilligan's] idealism: 'I'd rather close the parks than close a mental institution.' In the abstract, that may make sense, but not to the guy in the public who wants to take his kids to the parks."[36]

The parks remained closed for sixty days, into early November. The closings would stand in the public mind as one of the cardinal errors of the Gilligan administration. Gilligan came to understand this too late. Speaking in December 1972 to the Cleveland City Club, he announced that he had some advice for his fellow governors: "If the legislature won't give you enough money and you're forced to cut back—close the schools, shut down the hospitals, fire all the state employees—but *don't close the state parks.*"[37]

Austerity, rather than putting pressure on the state legislature, became the occasion for the Senate to dig in its heels. On September 8, the *Dayton Daily News* reported that Senate leaders had agreed to abandon the proposed income tax in favor of a sales tax increase. One Democratic leader was quoted as saying, "We

told him [Gilligan] that two weeks ago he had eleven of the twelve Senate Democrats in favor of the personal income tax. Since that austerity program of his, he
doesn't have them. He took his own poll a few days ago and it showed he had only
six in favor."[38]

Closer to home, Gilligan said, two things happened during the austerity period. First, department heads "were really horrified, they were outraged, they were
screaming bloody murder that we were tearing their departments to pieces. They
were literally pounding on the door of the governor's office to get in there: 'Do it
someplace else; cut someplace else; don't cut us . . . I'll have to give up; I'll resign."[39]
Second, Gilligan said, a number of department heads assumed that "someone" had
it out for them and demanded to know whom.[40]

At this point, Gilligan took a step in labor's direction. On September 14, reports
circulated of a discussion between a Gilligan administration official and the Senate
Ways and Means Committee in which the official urged adoption of a 4 percent
severance tax on minerals extracted within the state; a 1 mill franchise tax on federally chartered banks (state-chartered banks were already paying this assessment),
and a 2.5 percent tax on the gross premiums written by insurance companies operating in Ohio. Combined, these would yield an added $71.6 million in the next bi-
ennium from business sources. Four days later, the Gilligan administration yanked
it from consideration. The administration was in an exquisite bind: any effort to
lure support from pro-labor senators was likely to cost it support from business-
minded Republicans. The *Columbus Dispatch* reported: "Labor sources indicated
. . . that any administration retreat on its earlier proposals to equalize the tax load
between business and individuals will result in continued union opposition to the
plan."[41] The article continued, contending that "without labor support, no personal
income tax bill is likely to pass the Senate." It reported that in a meeting with the
Ways and Means Committee, budget director Hal Hovey "acknowledged at least
temporary defeat." Hovey according to the article, said, "To levy four to eight percent corporate and personal income taxes while repealing the business direct use
tax, was 'unobtainable.'"[42]

Gilligan was not yet ready to call retreat. If the legislature rejected his income
tax this year, he said, he would simply resubmit it—and continue to do so every
year until the taxes were passed. Gilligan said, "Sooner or later Ohio has to join the
twentieth century. The longer we delay, the longer other things—pollution, mental
health, and other services—will continue to be at the bottom of the barrel."[43] He asserted, hardly for the first time, that Ohio's present tax structure was "unproductive,
regressive, inequitable and uneconomic."[44] He described his own proposal as "the
greatest single tax reform package ever offered a state legislature . . . [It] would give
the state the fairest and the most productive tax structure in the fifty states."[45]

Gilligan's clarity regarding his own proposals was not matched in Columbus.
The *Columbus Dispatch* reported that the five Republican Senators counted as

likely supporters of an income tax were "remaining watchful." Concerned about Gilligan's support for greater taxes on business, Senator William Taft (R-Cleveland) predicted that Gilligan would abandon the income tax proposal: "Certainly, once that plan is dead there's no question that an increase in the state sales tax remains a viable alternative."[46]

Tempers were fraying; patience was thin. The September 16 *Dispatch* headline read, "Aura of Compassion Missing from Budget Bill Sessions." (This corresponded with the approaching deadline for redistricting.) The governor's own patience ended. In late September, he announced that he would sign no more interim budgets: "I will no longer be a party to this exercise in bad government."[47]

Gilligan tried again to reach out to organized labor. On September 22, he met at the Bavaria Haus in Columbus's brick-lined German Village neighborhood south of the capitol with state AFL-CIO chief Frank King, United Autoworkers president Ray Ross, and eleven of the thirteen Democratic senators. Senate deputy leader Oliver Ocasek offered this assessment: "There were no hard words, but then there was no compromise either."[48] Several days later, the *Dayton Daily News* reported that "about half the thirteen Senate Democrats would not vote for the income tax plan, because organized labor has opposed it."[49]

Long after the fact, Gilligan acknowledged there were "one or two" times when he felt the tax might fail. The first may have been after that meeting. *Gongwer* reported, "Although he stopped short of throwing in the towel on an income tax, the governor conceded that he has been unable to put together a united Democratic front or a coalition in the Senate."[50] On September 23, The *Toledo Blade* reported Gilligan as citing two causes for the Senate "paralysis" on taxes: first, Republicans were listening to the voices of business and industry, which argued that someone else should pay for needed state services; second, some Democrats were listening to "certain segments of organized labor" who maintained their opposition to the taxes.[51]

Gilligan's protestations aside, the current in the Senate was running in favor of a sales tax. State Republican chairman John Andrews weighed in on the issue, saying sales taxes gave the individual more control over her money; further, they were easier to collect. On September 22, the *Toledo Blade* reported, "Informed Statehouse sources said an Ohio vote on increasing the four percent Ohio sales tax could come as early as Friday."[52] Gilligan dismissed the pending Senate vote as pointless. Whatever the Senate passed would go to a Senate-House conference committee. A pro–sales tax Senate version, Gilligan thought, would prove impossible to reconcile with the pro–income tax version passed by the House. Speaking in Dayton to the Ohio Municipal League, Gilligan noted, "Half the House members who voted for an income tax in July would have to change their votes and vote for a sales tax three months later. I don't know that they will do that. I think there will be an impasse."[53] Or, possibly, he hoped there would be. The one possibility that lurked behind the scene for the administration was that both bodies would approve a sales tax increase and then override a Gilligan veto.

On September 26, in a rare Saturday session, the Ohio Senate voted 18–15 to enact a corporate income tax and to increase the state's sales tax from 4.0 to 5.5 cents on the dollar. The Senate was, on that occasion, acting under a constraint: the OSU Buckeyes were hosting the University of Colorado, and most senators had tickets to the game. When the vote was announced at 2:40 P.M., senators scampered from the chamber and headed to the stadium. (Reporter Lee Leonard recalled, "I wrote my story and ran to the stadium for the second half of the OSU-Colorado game. OSU lost.")[54]

The September 26 budget passed by the Senate provided for a $7.6 billion biennial budget, funded in part with $790 million in new tax revenues. The earlier House version called for $9 billion in expenditures, and $1.6 billion in new revenue. The House had chopped $385 million from Gilligan's education request; the Senate reduced this by an additional $114 million, passing $1.47 billion. Similarly, the House had reduced Gilligan's $1.8 billion welfare request by $300 million; the Senate cut an additional $210 million. Republican Michael Maloney acknowledged that "everyone" was dissatisfied with some aspect of the result. However, he added, "We have to realize that this package is the one with seventeen votes, and in tax legislation that's the name of the game."[55] Gilligan financial adviser Jay Tepper said that the Senate-passed version "does not provide enough funds to meet the needs of the state. It also has virtually no property tax relief and expands and perpetuates the regressive tax structure of the state."[56] Gilligan was blunter. He called the Senate version "a tax increase, not a tax reform" and "a typical Republican attempt to put the burden on low-income and middle-income Ohioans."[57] It would now fall on a Senate-House conference committee to reconcile what Gilligan termed "the unreconcilable versions."

About the time the Ohio Senate passed its sales tax–based budget, the youngest member of the House, James Mueller (D-Chesterfield) proposed an amendment to withhold all paychecks to state legislators until the budget was completed. Advancing a somewhat modified proposal, a Republican member from Cincinnati rose to propose that all legislators be paid except Mueller.

The House was not in a terribly good mood. Following four months of often acrid debate, the House had, on July 14, settled on a budget that would enact the first personal and corporate income taxes in state history. Now, ten weeks later, the Senate had bounced that idea in favor of a 1.5 cent increase in the state sales tax, a move many in the House regarded as simply irreconcilable with its own action. Nor did any clear path present itself. Not for the first time, House Speaker Charles Kurfess stated, "I don't have fifty votes for anything today."[58] Also, legislators of both parties were unhappy with the recently unveiled state redistricting. Senator Anthony Calabrese, despite being granted "the Calabrese Corridor," declared that redistricting had cost Gilligan "several" Democratic votes in the Senate. The *Dayton Daily News* reported that "Gilligan's reapportionment plan, which has upset legislators of both parties, has engendered a lot of feeling against the governor and his programs."[59]

It also appeared probable that Gilligan would make good on his promise to sign no further interim budgets. The legislature passed the year's sixth such budget on September 29 to pay expenses through October 31. With Gilligan withholding his signature, however, the budget did not become effective for ten days, during which time the state had no authority to spend money. So Representative Mueller ended up getting part of his wish: the state's legislators received their paychecks ten days late.

And it was *October*—a month by which virtually every previous legislature had completed its work and gone home. For most in the assembly, their service there was part-time employment; most had a business or law practice or other responsibility to attend to. The *Columbus Citizen Journal* reported that many of these citizen-legislators had "virtually abandoned their back-home jobs," a step that could mean a substantial loss of income.[60] One reporter recalled how "some of the lawyers were threatened with being put out of their own firms because they weren't doing any of the business they were supposed to—they didn't have any time, being constantly in Columbus."[61] This was a problem even for those lawyer-legislators whose practices were *in* Columbus, like Keith McNamara: "People will stop me on the street: 'I bought a house last week. I would have had you represent me except I knew how busy you were.'"[62] Perhaps of more personally pressing concern, the extended session and its consequent common loss of personal income created for legislators an unwelcome measure of family strife, occasionally relieved with weak humor. When one legislator's wife had a baby, a second legislator asked him, "How is that possible? You have not been home in eleven months."[63]

By October's end, the bickering and backbiting had exhausted even the considerable equanimity of House Speaker Kurfess. Jay Tepper issued a press release urging the GOP to provide enough votes for a permanent two-year budget and thus end the prolonged deadlock. To Kurfess's thinking, Tepper had gone public with a matter still under negotiation, a betrayal of the process. Soon thereafter, Kurfess recalled, "I walked out in the hall and this budget guy [Tepper] is at the other end of the hall, and I don't know exactly what I said, but it might have been, 'Get your ass out of here.'"[64]

Nor was the pressure any less on the Gilligan administration itself. As the deadlock was prolonged, a sprinkling—and then more of a sprinkling—of Ohio Democrats expressed the view that perhaps the personal income levy went too far. Jim Friedman recalled how at this time the Democratic chairman for Cuyahoga County, Joseph Bartunek, was working quietly to undercut the income tax; chairmen from smaller, conservative counties were expressing worry. Friedman said,

"They'd go to barbershops and hear stuff; they'd walk down the street and hear stuff; they'd start worrying about their local candidates being reelected."[65] And, not least, Gilligan was worried. If the income tax failed, it would have amounted to a repudiation of his leadership while he was still in his rookie year. Gilligan added, "I was convinced the income tax had to happen, or the state machinery would collapse."[66]

The tax battle had a claustrophobic effect on Ohio politics. While broader perspective may have been obscured in the moment, it was clear that states across the nation were scrambling for funds. This was particularly so in states with divided government—one party in control of the legislature and another party seated in the governor's office.

In California, the *New York Times* reported that October, the Republican governor Ronald Reagan and the Democratic-controlled legislature fought on how to bridge a $350 million deficit in a $6.8 billion state budget. There, the state finance director argued that the gap could be closed by "increasing levies on cigarettes, liquor and horse racing."[67] Minnesota, too, like Ohio, saw its legislature "enmeshed in the longest session in its history."[68] The governor, Democrat farmer-laborite Wendell Anderson, had sought $762 million in new taxes—again, most of it earmarked for education. The Republican opposition had countered with a $471 million package to come from the same combination of corporate income tax and sales tax increase advocated by the GOP in Ohio.

In Wisconsin, Governor Pat Lucey was seeking to alter the state's "revenue sharing" system in ways more favorable to Milwaukee and other urban areas. He had the support of the Democratic-controlled assembly, but the Republican-controlled Senate was opposed. Stalemate had ensued. Governor Lucey, in words that many in Ohio could easily have shared, declared, "The situation has reached critical proportions and is fast approaching intolerable limits."[69]

Similarly, the school budget crisis that was the single biggest driver of tax reform in Ohio was being felt across the country. The *New York Times* reported, "The money crisis in the nation's public schools, compounded of sharply rising costs and shrinking local revenues, has entered a new, more acute, and more threatening phase."[70] Chicago would end its school year eleven days early unless $22.8 million could be rapidly found in the budget. Independence, Missouri, started its school year two weeks late and announced it was likely to end that year early. Kalamazoo, Michigan, planned to shut its schools for twenty-three days. Portland, Oregon, announced the school year would end seventeen days early. Philadelphia had discharged 800 teachers and was planning to cut five weeks from its school year.

The National Education Association reported that forty-one of sixty-three large school districts in the country were operating under "crisis conditions."[71] It was a crisis of multiple causes. One reason was that local real estate taxes, historically the major source of school finances, were becoming insufficient, in part due to decreased voter willingness to approve tax increases. A second complication was that lawsuits were in progress in thirty states challenging the constitutionality of the funding formulas used, generally, because they led to greatly varying levels of per student expenditures around the state.

The key complicating matter for Gilligan was Frank King's continued opposition to a personal income tax. This conflict made its way to the *New York Times,* which ran a lengthy article on the "embarrassment" that a liberal governor was suffering at the hands of labor unions that were the traditional ally of Democrats.[72] King was adamant, and he—in part through Senate minority leader Anthony Calabrese—controlled or influenced enough Democrat votes in the Senate to put the income tax initiative out of reach. The *Times* went on to report one piece of possible good news for Gilligan: "Reports that the UAW [the Ohio AFL-CIO's single largest member union] is discussing a break with Mr. King on the income tax issue and an announcement of support for Governor Gilligan's position."[73] Indeed, meeting in Cincinnati, the UAW announced it could support an income tax provided it was linked to "meaningful tax reform"—a phrase the labor organization did not define.[74]

From Gilligan's perspective, "Labor leaders at the national level began to understand that King was holding this whole thing up—and that if he succeeded in defeating it, labor was going to be blamed for the failure of the effort to aid the schools. So he grudgingly backed down; in effect, he released his Democratic compatriots to vote for it."[75] Incongruously, on October 14, the *Columbus Dispatch* reported that King, standing at the elbow of Anthony Calabrese, said, "I've always preferred an income tax to a sales tax."[76] The newspaper could not resist adding a previous King comment—"We're against an income tax and we're opposed to a sales tax"—and commenting, "The inability of the Senate to agree on an income tax earlier was blamed largely on King whose labor organization controlled six or seven Senate Democrats. At those discussions more than a month ago, Senate Republican leaders said that only five GOP senators would vote for an income tax. This meant that twelve of the thirteen Democrats would have to support it if it were to pass."[77]

From the standpoint of the Gilligan administration, that was progress on only one front. The six-member House-Senate conference committee appointed to resolve the differences between an income tax–and a sales tax–based budget increase was deadlocked. The *Dayton Daily News* reported, "The prospect grew stronger last week that a six-member House-Senate conference committee appointed three weeks ago will never reach agreement on a new two-year budget and tax package."[78] Some Democrats were blaming Gilligan for the imbroglio. Bishop Kilpatrick (D-Warren), the only Democratic Senator to have voted in support of the 1936 adoption of the state sales tax, said, "This guy is harder to support than any governor I've ever known."[79]

Also, though the shift by unions may have lessened opposition from Gilligan's Left flank, opposition from the Right continued. On October 21, Bob Netzley wrote the conference committee to state that what Ohio most needed was "a revenue source, other than real estate taxes, for the operation of local schools."[80] He noted that for a decade a tug-of-war had taken place between welfare and education, with welfare winning in recent years. "To enact tremendous tax increases without this tax reform can only be interpreted as a sell out by the majority party to the Gilligan administration, the labor bosses and the welfare spenders in this state."[81] And in an October 22 statement, Speaker Kurfess reminded all that his support for an income tax was not unconditional: "Any attempt to use a personal income tax solely as a means of raising more revenue on top of existing taxes should be doomed to failure. The conference committee should consider a personal income tax only with substantial property tax relief, including a meaningful homestead exemption for our elderly."[82]

For Gilligan, the shift by organized labor did appear to be a light at the end of the tunnel. On October 22, the *Columbus Dispatch* announced, "Assembly OK Expected on Income Tax."[83] The pending measure included an across-the-board rollback of real estate taxes and a string of measures sought by organized labor, including the corporate profits tax, the severance tax, the domestic insurance company tax, and the tax increase on financial institutions. Six days later, the paper offered, "Senate Leaders Hope for Vote on Budget."[84] The tunnel, however, proved longer than expected. One Republican Senator said the addition of the labor-backed amendments would cost the measure the votes it needed from his party for passage. Essentially conceding this point, the Gilligan administration delayed the Senate vote.

On November 1, following Gilligan's refusal to sign the seventh interim budget, the state of Ohio's lost its authority to spend money, something it normally did at the rate of $800,000 an hour. With this, workers in the auditor's office stopped issuing checks of any kind.

That same day, a bipartisan coalition led by Senator Bill Taft and Representative James Flannery began meeting in a Columbus hotel in hopes of coming up with an acceptable compromise. Theirs was not the only gathering. On November 2, Governor Gilligan and aides met with representatives of the United Auto Workers, the Retail Merchants Association, and others to assess the political ground ahead and plan their next move. November 3, as a reminder of the pressure all were under, marked the third day Ohio could not legally pay its bills. Optimism was in short supply. One newspaper reported, "'It's like trying to fight your way out of a bowl of whip cream,' one legislator remarked. 'Others openly cursed the day they decided to seek office.'"[85]

Reviewing the landscape, Gilligan decided to put his chips on Taft and Flannery. On November 4, he wrote House minority leader A. G. Lancione, "You will soon be called to vote upon a compromise budget and tax package. That package, while far from perfect, and substantially less than the administration's original tax reform and budget recommendations, is obviously preferable to any other bill that is likely to be approved by this General Assembly."[86]

Before any such action might occur, the first conference report—the Senate-based one advocating a 1.5 percent increase in the state's sales tax—was released to the House. This was politic on Kurfess's part. "When I appointed my conferees, I told them just one thing: the first conference report has to include a sales tax and no personal income tax. I decided I owed it to my caucus to give them a chance to vote."[87] That vote came Friday, November 9, in a House chamber packed with lobbyists—corporate interests urging its passage and retail merchants and labor organizations urging its defeat. Speaker Kurfess stated his lack of support for the sales tax. The House went into session at 11:00 A.M.; twelve hours later it emerged, having rejected the sales tax by a decisive 66–28 margin.

Complications pended. Unless the legislature acted by Tuesday, November 13, 50,000 state employees would not be paid the following Friday. This prompted Herschel Sigall, representing 5,500 state workers through the American Federation of State, County, and Municipal Employees, to offer the telling phrase: "No contract, no work." And AFL-CIO chief Frank King introduced a new wrinkle. He had opposed a sales tax, as unfair to his members; he had opposed an income tax, as unfair to his members. Now, he announced opposition to increased corporate income taxes, which, he said, by reducing corporate profits, left his members with much less to bargain for.

Senate and House leaders moved to appoint a third conference committee. Governor Gilligan announced that, at least from his perspective, the House defeat of the sales tax made passage of an income tax a near certainty. At least one problem was averted. On Saturday, November 10, the legislature finished action on yet another interim budget, one that would allow state employees to be paid provided it gained the governor's signature. Gilligan signed the bill an hour later.

That same day, Gilligan reiterated his support for the Taft-Flannery bill. Speaking to a university group, press secretary Bob Tenenbaum said the Taft-Flannery bill enjoyed majority support in both Houses. In response, John Hall, principal lobbyist for the Ohio Education Association, said the bill had been drawn to benefit "high income individuals and high profit, low net worth corporations."[88] Taft-Flannery, he added, was intended to shift the tax burden from "some big industries represented by the Ohio Manufacturers association and the state chairman of the Republican Party."[89] Nonetheless, passage was expected—indeed, the House of Representatives was notified to schedule a special Saturday-morning session the next week, at which it was expected to add its approval to the measure.

Then Gilligan pulled the plug. Somewhat late that Saturday, he decided that the proposal would reduce the share of state taxes paid by business from 35 percent to 23 percent. Gilligan met the following Thursday with lobbyists from the "big four" supporters of the income tax—the United Auto Workers, Ohio Education Association, Ohio Retail Merchants Association, and Ohio Farm Bureau Federation—urging them to weigh in their opposition to the bill. In a statement delivered shortly before midnight Friday, November 16, just hours from the scheduled vote, Gilligan called the Taft-Flannery measure "a poorly written bill that will let big business off the hook, hurt low and middle income taxpayers and provide inadequate level of support for state programs." Warming to his text, Gilligan accused Senate GOP leaders of spending "forty-eight hours closeted with representatives of big corporate manufacturers" drafting a bill "even they are embarrassed to vote for."[90] With that statement, Democratic support for the measure evaporated: the final vote was 23–10.

Republicans, who'd thought they had a deal, were apoplectic. Senator Mike Maloney, claiming that legislative liaison John McDonald had told him just hours before the scheduled vote that the bill was acceptable, called Gilligan's statement "a sham and the epitome of deceit."[91] He added that if the governor did not butt out of the legislature's business, nothing would be achieved. Representative Norman Murdock (R-Cincinnati) decried Gilligan's "unbelievable hoax [as] simply unforgiveable."[92] Democratic Senate minority leader Anthony Calabrese told reporters (and others within earshot) that the governor was a "son of a bitch."[93] About the only upbeat statement came from Republican lieutenant governor John Brown, who found a silver lining in the imbroglio: "After all, we are not paying any new taxes during this impasse."[94]

On November 17, a third conference committee was appointed. According to Gongwer, the committee decided to test immediately Gilligan's contention that the Taft-Flannery bill could pass both Houses. That bill called for a personal income tax ranging from .5–4 percent and a corporate income tax of 4–8 percent. When the Senate convened on the evening of Monday, November 22, passage was expected. Both McDonald's assistant, Bill Chavanne, and the bill's cosponsor, William Taft, considered passage imminent. Taft said: "I thought we had it right up until the time of the vote."[95]

But there were two surprises that day. Senator Robert Stockdale (R-Kent), considered a probable vote for passage, had been hospitalized earlier in the day with an apparent heart attack. And then, when the roll was called, a second presumed supporter, David Holcomb (R-Dayton) brought "audible gasps to the Senate chamber" by voting no.[96] This, in turn, brought a no vote from Ron Mottl (D-Parma), who, according to a press report, "had been expected to support the plan if Holcomb did." The Senate rejected the measure by a vote of 17–15.

Some Republicans celebrated its defeat. Robert Netzley told the *Troy Daily News* that the tax reform feature of the bill was "an outright fraud" and, sounding his favorite theme, claimed the proposal was "obviously a tax bill for welfare and not for education or tax reform."[97] Concerned with the state's burgeoning school funding crisis, Netzley urged quick action on a short-term 0.5 cent or 1 cent sales tax increase to stave off school closings.

While Gilligan's rejection of Taft-Flannery had prompted what one newspaper called "near hysterical rantings and ravings" among legislators that November, the governor (at least outwardly) maintained an air of bemused indifference.[98] Speaking on November 15 to a group of elected African American public officials in Dayton, Gilligan said his staff had become sufficiently concerned for his popularity that they'd commissioned a poll rating him against two historical figures with image problems: Typhoid Mary and Jack the Ripper. The governor told the Dayton throng that he was encouraged by the results: he had rated only six points behind Typhoid Mary. Querying an aide how he had polled against Jack the Ripper, Gilligan said, an aide told him, "Seventy-six percent of the people think that you are Jack the Ripper."[99]

The banter obscured two points of some consequence. First, to get a tax package he regarded as suitable, Gilligan was prepared to hold out until Lake Erie froze over. As he told the Dayton audience, "It may take six months or it may take six years, but the state will have to do it."[100] Second, Gilligan was, consciously or not, following a dictate of Henry David Thoreau, who asserted that one man in the right constituted a majority. The Ohio governor was quite comfortable in his belief that he was right and confident that the majority would eventually agree. Given both this patience and certitude, he felt largely immune to the slings and arrows of legislators and journalists. According to John Mahaney, "They couldn't say enough bad things about Gilligan. I don't think Jack much cared."[101] (Gilligan had other, happier matters on his mind that November. Several days before Thanksgiving, his son Donald married Betsy Tarlin in a ceremony at the Governor's Mansion—not, as Donald Gilligan recalled, the warmest venue for a wedding.)

The session ground on. The first conference committee had tried unsuccessfully to push a sales tax on the House. The second and third committees had tried unsuccessfully to push an income tax on the Senate. Representative John Johnson recalled "considerable frustration. We thought at times the income tax would not pass."[102] Gilligan's press secretary Bob Tenenbaum recalled: "If you look back, there were always points at which you thought it might not get done."[103] As the impasse continued, William Batchelder said, "There was antagonism between the Senate and the House: we [the House] thought they wanted to pass an income tax but were afraid to do so."[104]

The determining decision was made by Senate president Ted Gray. When Gray appointed a fourth conference committee, he replaced Senators Mike Maloney and Max Dennis with Howard Cook (R-Toledo) and Stanley Aronoff (R-Cincinnati), presumed income tax supporters. John Mahaney said, "Gray put Stan Aronoff and Howard Cook on the conference committee, and twenty minutes later they had the income tax."[105] Statehouse reporter Lee Leonard agreed: "Aronoff was the key.

When he was put on the Senate conference committee, we knew the income tax would pass. I gave Aronoff the credit for turning the tide."[106]

Aronoff was a first-term senator; rarely were freshman legislators appointed to conference committees. He recalled being "frustrated. The state was going to hell unless something was done. I gave a signal to Ted Gray: If he put me on the conference committee, I'd be willing to find a compromise."[107] Aronoff said his position wasn't ideological—"We can't let the state sink while we wallow around in philosophy"—but the pragmatic need to find something moderates from both parties could support.[108]

From the first, the new committee demonstrated a "more open and conciliatory" mood.[109] Legislative liaison John McDonald and budget director Jay Tepper joined in the committee's discussions. Throughout the very long session, Republicans had repeatedly argued that the proposed increase in welfare spending was too high; the Republican conferees maintained that position now. Negotiation followed. By rough numbers, Republicans wanted $100 million in welfare cuts. To make such a cut, McDonald stated, would be an absolute nonstarter with newly elected members of the legislative black caucus.

Then, a longtime state budget department employee named Helen Samuels brought an interesting piece of information to McDonald's attention: the state welfare office was currently running ninety days in arrears on payments to suppliers. Welfare director Jack Hansan's proposed budget aimed at making the state current in its obligations—in effect, paying twenty-seven months of bills in twenty-four months. The state could "cut" about $100 million simply by letting the float continue. McDonald told the committee that it could take credit for the cut, but it needed to know that it meant the doctors and people who were mostly their constituents would be paid late.[110] At the same time, McDonald said, the black caucus could protest the cutback, knowing that welfare rolls and payment levels would not be affected. House conference member Keith McNamara announced that he believed further cuts were possible, but his Republican cohorts declared themselves satisfied.

On December 9, 1971, the Ohio Senate convened to vote on the fourth conference report. As that meeting came to older, the Reverend Alvin Duane Smith invoked a prayer not found in scripture: "Dear Lord: Now that nine months have passed since we started expecting, may we be pregnant enough now to be delivered. Amen."[111] The measure before the body called for a graduated income tax ranging of .5–3.5 percent and was expected to generate $790.6 million in new taxes. The bill proposed a $388 million (30 percent) increase for K–12 education and a $122.6 million increase for higher education. Proposed expenditures on welfare rose from $854.9 million to $1.2 billion; and $86 million was added to the mental health and correction budget, raising it to $424 million. From the standpoint of Governor Gilligan's March 16 budget requests, the measure represented nearly half a loaf.

In the final debate, the principal speakers for the bill were Republican Stanley Aronoff and Democrats Anthony Calabrese, Oliver Ocasek, and Harry Meshel (D-Youngstown). In response, Robert Coles (R-Elyria) argued that the bill was a gift to the public utilities: "If this is a tax reform bill, I don't want any part of it. This is a big business bill. The property rollback is a gimmick."[112]

The bill passed 17–15. It was not a party-line vote. Democrats favored the bill by 11–2, and Republicans opposed it 13–6.

Passage by the House the following day was pro forma. Debate still ran for four hours, with Speaker Kurfess, confident in his support, allowing opponents to have most of the air time—perhaps in the hope that giving them their say now might mollify them in the future. Representative Lloyd George Kerns (R-Richwood) said the tax "can only result in driving out industry."[113] Robert Netzley said the legislature was losing "all chance of true tax reform and [was setting] the pattern for spending and waste."[114] Patrick Sweeney of Cleveland, one of the few Democrats to oppose the measure, called the bill "another broken down effort" that entailed "lying to the people."[115]

Keith McNamara was the only member of the fourth conference committee to decline to endorse its handiwork. He said that conference committees were permitted only to address differences between House and Senate versions, but this committee had gone far beyond that. Acting at the behest of the Cleveland law firm of Squires, Saunders, and Dempsey, he claimed, it had altered language related to state bonding requirements. He also contended that this bill violated the state constitution's mandate that a single piece of legislation could deal only with a single subject. To these points McNamara added his general lack of enthusiasm for the income tax. He later commented, "Ohio had not had an income tax before. People were fearful that once it was adopted, sooner or later it was going to go up."[116]

At the time of the vote, Gilligan was in San Francisco, traveling on a trade mission with development director David Sweet and special projects coordinator Richard Neustadt. When the phone rang in Gilligan's suite bringing word that the battle was over, the income tax had passed, a modest celebration ensued. On December 20, Governor John Gilligan formally signed the $7.686 billion two-year budget into law in noon ceremonies held in his executive office.

The tax didn't have to pass. Press secretary Bob Tenenbaum said, "The tax thing overwhelmed everything else: not because it was a huge fight, but because it actually got done."[117] No one, including Gilligan, went through the year without doubts on this point. The income tax fight was a benchmark; it drew lines. Stanley Aronoff said, "The income tax defined you politically. For years thereafter, the income tax was the relevant past. It influenced politics well beyond the next term, until media politics took over. Memories of this vote were indelible, as much as any single vote."[118] Chuck Kurfess's support for the legislation split the Republican caucus. Lacking a majority for anything, Kurfess decided the caucus would take no collective stance on the issue; this opened the door to the support from Republicans the income tax required for passage. In his history of the state legislature, according to David Gold, "the anger of conservative Republicans with the defectors caused a split in the House caucus and suspicion of the party's legislative leadership that lasted into the 1990s."[119] George Voinovich, a great admirer of Charles Kurfess, said simply, "A lot of Republicans never forgave Kurfess."[120]

There is one rarely cited yet possibly pivotal reason why the income tax was enacted. An analogy is suitable. In one Sherlock Holmes story, the great detective tells his companion, Dr. Watson, that the secret to the case's solution was the unusual behavior of the dog at night. But the dog, Watson replied, did nothing at night. That, responded Holmes, was the unusual behavior. The "dog" who, in the case of the Ohio income tax, did nothing during the income tax fight was former Republican governor James Rhodes. Though out of office, Rhodes likely remained the most influential Republican in state politics—and there is no evidence he ever placed a single phone call urging that the tax be defeated. John Mahaney stated, "Rhodes was contemplating a comeback even then. He knew the state was broke. Why not let the other guy get hold of the money for him, then run against him for getting it, then spend it yourself?"[121] It is worth noting that for all of Rhodes's pronouncements of "no new taxes," what that phrase meant in practice was "no new taxes" for which he, James Rhodes, might have to take the blame. (At the time, Mahaney and Rhodes maintained offices in the same downtown building; the pair had social ties and almost daily contact. Mahaney recalled, "I'd go over and visit him on the eleventh floor. He knew I was for the income tax, so he could have said, 'Johnno, you are making a mistake.' But he never said it.")[122]

Conservatives, though defeated, were neither contrite nor without recourse. State Representative William Batchelder denounced the new tax in an interview with the *Ashland Times* three days after the House approved the measure. Robert Netzley made of his opposition more than rhetorical. He and a few liked-minded legislators initiated an effort to gather the 350,000 signatures it would take to place repeal of the income tax on the 1972 statewide ballot.

26

The High Point

On December 16, 1971, just days after the income tax was signed into law, Jack Gilligan and Jim Friedman boarded a flight to New York's LaGuardia Airport, where a private plane collected them and delivered the pair to the Manchester, New Hampshire, home of Maria Carrier. Carrier was the state coordinator for the Muskie presidential campaign; she was hosting the dinner at which Gilligan would commit to Edmund Muskie as his 1972 Democratic presidential preference. The deal was sealed over sirloin steaks. For Muskie, Gilligan's endorsement was the most significant he'd received thus far; for Gilligan, the endorsement's announcement ended speculation that he would stand as the "favorite son" candidate for Ohio's 153 delegates.

The arrangement had been encouraged by Mark Shields. Though Shields had declined to work for Gilligan in Columbus, he headed up Ohio's Washington, D.C., office—acting as the state's eyes and ears in the nation's capital—when he was named political director of the Muskie campaign. During the month before the announcement, Gilligan had met with Muskie, Shields, and Muskie's administrative assistant, George Mitchell. For their part, Gilligan and Friedman wanted assurances that Muskie would commit personal time and campaign resources to Ohio. Due diligence appeared to have been practiced. Peter Hart was commissioned to do a poll, which in late 1971 showed Muskie leading easily among Ohio Democrats.

For Gilligan, Muskie was the most plausible pick: "I did not know him well, but knew him well enough to think he would make a good President. We could campaign for and build around him without any fear of being embarrassed down the line. He was a good guy."[1] The announcement had some immediate political payoff for Gilligan when the *New York Times* reported the news "above the fold." Gilligan fairly consistently drew favorable coverage in the national press. In part, this was because he was, to eastern sensibilities, a welcome and literate alternative to whatever stereotypes they might carry about Buckeye politicians. It also reflected Mark Shields's skill in working the press on Gilligan's behalf. The Gilligan endorsement ran so prominently because Shields promised *Times* political writer R. W. Apple an exclusive on the story if Apple would secure the front-page placement.[2]

Gilligan's formal endorsement of Muskie came on December 22, 1971, at a Columbus joint press conference. Gilligan cited "his intelligence, his understanding, his compassion and his courage."[3] Muskie, for his part, responded, "It's good to have a friend like John Gilligan at this early stage. I can't think of a better happening during Christmas week."[4] All concerned deny that the senator and the governor discussed a possible place for Gilligan on a Muskie ticket. Still, as Shields observed, if you are a major state governor and an early endorser of the eventual nominee, you are likely to land on any short list of individuals under consideration for the vice presidency.

If the early endorsement was intended to stop rival aspirants Hubert Humphrey and George McGovern from entering the Ohio primary, it failed. Humphrey paid a call on Columbus two weeks later. Speaking at the Neil House, Humphrey accused Gilligan of "using a good deal of pressure" to line up leading Democrats for Muskie.[5] The *Columbus Dispatch* broadened that indictment: "There have been numerous reports that county chairmen are being called into the governor's cabinet room in small groups where the facts of political life, as seen by James Friedman, the governor's top aide, are explained to them."[6] In any case, both Humphrey and McGovern promised to make full-bore efforts in Ohio.

In Columbus, politics proceeded at the state level. On January 5, 1972, the House approved a redistricting of Ohio's congressional seats, now reduced to twenty-three under the 1970 census. On January 6, the Senate voted to grant state employees a pay increase—either thirty-eight cents an hour or 10 percent, whichever was greater. Other actions came early in the new year. Governor Gilligan issued a pair of executive orders. The first combined the Department of Development and the Department of Urban Affairs into a single Department of Economic and Community Development, directed by David Sweet. The second directed that all hiring on projects undertaken with state funds be done on a nondiscriminatory basis. And on January 7, an ad hoc committee of five House Republicans announced its intention to seek a ballot referendum to repeal the recently enacted state income tax, saying: "The overwhelming adverse public response to the recently enacted Ohio state income tax makes it essential that the people of Ohio be given an opportunity to vote on this issue."[7]

Since his earliest days with Democrats United in Cincinnati, John Gilligan had argued two things. First, that government was "we, the people" acting in concert to do that which could not be achieved individually. And, second, that the Democratic Party was the natural vehicle through which this progress could be made— or, would be made, provided it achieved some semblance of unity and order. The year 1972 brought Gilligan to both the low and high points of his governorship. The spring witnessed a setback to his own national ambitions and serious dissension

within his own administration. Midyear saw passage of a long-overdue bill restricting strip mining and, separately, the creation of the Ohio Environmental Protection
Agency. And the fall brought vindication of the income tax he had championed and
victory in the state's legislative elections—both by thumping-good margins that easily exceeded the governor's hopes.

Politics has deadlines. In 1972, the first of real deadline of consequence was
February 15, the date by which those seeking nomination to the state legislature
were required to file their paperwork. In 1972, Gilligan and the Democrats were
seizing on the opportunity redistricting presented to create as many winnable
seats as possible in the Statehouse. Unintentionally, perhaps, the Democrats had
put themselves out on a limb: in creating numerous districts that in normal years
would be 52, 53, or 54 percent Democratic, they were wagering that 1972 would
be a normal year—not a year in which Republican Richard Nixon would trounce
Democrat George McGovern by nearly a million votes statewide, with likely consequences all down the ballot.

Candidates for state representative were traditionally "the orphans of politics."[8]
Nobody at the county level paid much attention to their success because, unlike, say,
a county engineer, a representative had no patronage to dispense. Many were more
or less self-nominated, collecting some requisite number of signatures on a petition
and scurrying among friends to secure the needed funds. (The money involved in a
state representative race was at that time tiny: $5,000–10,000, about what Jack Gil-
ligan had spent on his first campaign for Cincinnati City Council.)

Jack Gilligan observed that at the time, the state legislators' lot was not an altogether happy one. Salaries were modest—$12,750 annually—and the legislators
were not particularly appreciated by their constituents. Jack Gilligan commented:

> My general impression was that they were better than their constituents deserved—
> Republican or Democrat. In many cases, they had been in or had been seeking the
> office for some time; in consequence, they were more acquainted with the realities
> of the political situation than their constituents. And one of the problems—a prob-
> lem to this day—was that of educating their own constituents as to what really was
> an issue and why going in this direction made sense, and going in that direction
> did not.[9]

In 1968, John McDonald, then minority leader of the House Democrats, had
made an initial effort to recruit candidates for state representative. And early in
1970, Bill Chavanne, as McDonald's assistant, made a similar effort. In November
1970, propelled in good measure by Jack Gilligan's decisive victory, the Democrats
had picked up ten seats in the House, cutting their deficit from 64–35 to 54–45. And
so in 1972, the Democrats set their eyes on acquiring majority control of the House

of Representatives. (They targeted the House over the Senate because the mix of senators actually up for reelection in 1970 was unfavorable to Democratic gains.)

The Gilligan administration approached the task with a three-stage strategy: first, control redistricting; second, find good candidates; third, "clear the primaries"—that is, attempt to ensure that the candidate designated by the party would not waste time, resources, and goodwill facing opposition in the primary. This was a central part of a party-building effort.

For 1972, Bill Chavanne identified eighteen districts as possible gains for the Democrats. Each needed a candidate. McDonald and Chavanne solicited prospects from county chairmen, interest groups (like the Ohio Education Association), and others, including Vern Riffe, a rapidly rising legislator who noted that "for the first time the governor's office was involved in a significant way in recruitment."[10] Since reapportionment had created new districts, the task was to find candidates who suited those districts. And the less people know about the names on the ballot, Chavanne argued, the likelier they are to vote for someone they see as being like themselves—so in a Catholic district you run a Catholic; in a strongly union district a union member; in an upscale district a college-educated professional. Chavanne added, "The best candidates are about thirty-five years old; they're mature enough, but they still have the energy to win."[11]

Many have an itch for public office, but not all want that itch scratched. Pressing for commitments, Chavanne said he learned the difference between "I'll run" and "I'll run." The former meant that the prospective candidate needed first to talk to his wife, his family, his boss, and the guy he'd like to have as campaign manager—"It meant he wants to get elected, but doesn't really want to do the work." The latter "I'll run" meant the candidate was ready to work.[12]

The next step was to assess the district—Was it winnable? Was it winnable by this candidate? This involved calling the county chairman and other folks and saying, "This guy wants to run: Did you ever talk to him?" And then someone had to decide which candidates to back. Chavanne said he never flat-out told a candidate they could not run; the message was softer: "We might say, 'We don't think this is your year.'"[13]

Not all candidates ran to win, Chavanne noted. It was important to seek the strongest possible candidates for districts in which defeat was probable. The reason, he said, was that "not everybody in public life is as confident as they seem." Usually, the most nervous person in any campaign is the incumbent. If challenged by a strong candidate—"someone who works hard, who goes door-to-door"— Chavanne said, that incumbent might expend resources his party could have more effectively used elsewhere.[14]

The administration was very much on the lookout for opportunities. In mid-November 1971, George Voinovich resigned his House seat to become the auditor of Cuyahoga County. (Bill Chavanne maintained that Voinovich timed his resignation to avoid having to vote on the final income tax compromise, which he had pledged to support but something his strongest supporters opposed.) Learning of this resignation, Jim Friedman urged the local Gilligan organization to suggest a candidate. The following week, Friedman flew into Cleveland for an evening audition with the hopeful. Tim McCormack, a law student, lived in Euclid and served on the city council; he had almost been elected Euclid's mayor at age twenty-three. When broached about running for a seat in the Ohio House, McCormack hesitated: he had no money. Friedman assured him that money would be found. Further, McCormack said he had unpaid debts from his mayoral campaign. Friedman said that those debts would be paid. Finally, McCormack added that he needed a job. Friedman said, "We'll get you a job. Any other questions?" There were none, and the Democrats had a candidate.[15]

The party was looking for candidates at least as aggressively as prospective candidates were putting themselves forward. In January 1972, Larry Christman was grading papers for the senior government course he taught at Northmont High School, a dozen miles northwest of Dayton, when he was summoned to the principal's office to take a phone call. The call was from John Hall, the chief lobbyist of the Ohio Education Association. Christman, who was locally active in the OEA, knew Hall from work he had done on a teacher union legislative liaison group. Casually enough, Hall began by asking Christman if he lived in "that new district" (the 67th, which combined parts of Montgomery and Miami counties). Christman said he did. The pair then chatted about potential candidates, with Christman believing he was serving as a sounding board.[16] Shifting tone slightly, Hall then said, "Well, Larry, would *you* want to run?"

Christman declined. Pressed for reasons, Christman said he was busy completing the college coursework he needed to be certified as a curriculum specialist; further, he was just six weeks into a four-year term on the Englewood City Council, having been elected the previous November.

Hall's tone brightened: "So, you mean your name has been on a ballot and you won?"[17] Christman acknowledged this and, under slight prodding, added that he had placed first in a field of five. This "got Hall real excited," Christman recalled: "We went around and around for fifteen minutes." Attempting to extricate himself from the conversation, Christman agreed at least to speak with "someone named Chavanne" at a phone number Hall supplied.[18]

When Christman called, a secretary answered: "Good afternoon. Governor Gilligan's office." Christman awkwardly said he'd dialed the wrong number. The secretary then asked who was calling. When Christman identified himself, she said, "Mr. Chavanne is awaiting your call. He's in with governor; he'll call you back as soon as he's free."[19]

When Chavanne called back, Christman detailed the reasons why he could not run. He had no time; he had no savings; he had a mortgage; he wasn't known. He had attended exactly one Young Democrats meeting in Montgomery County, but that was just to see a friend be sworn in. He didn't know anyone in Miami County, but he thought there might be another Democrat running, which would mean a primary battle, something he didn't want. In his characteristic unruffled manner, Bill Chavanne told Christman, "We will get you the money." And according to Chavanne, being unknown in Montgomery County was "not a problem. We will tell [county chairman] Paul Tipps that you are his candidate." The potential primary challenger was also not a problem, because, Chavanne said, "he will not run."[20] After taking a weekend to think it over (a weekend he spent advising his school's debate team at a tournament in Marysville), Christman returned home with his decision made: "I thought it might be fun. In any case, it would really enhance my teaching of government. So I did it."[21]

And so that February the Democrats were gathering in their hopefuls and ensuring that their nominating petitions, appropriately signed, were filed in Columbus by the 15th.

Two weeks after the deadline passed, the State Senate settled into its first good fight of the year—a fight not so much within the Senate as between the Senate and a special interest group. The issue was strip mining. When a tough bill had sailed through the House the previous fall, Gilligan in part attributed its smooth passage to the mining companies having been caught unaware. Now, they were ready. On March 1, Governor Gilligan sought to dramatize the issue by inviting senators to join him aboard the state's aging DC-3 for an aerial tour of the strip-mined regions. The previous evening, however, Ralph Hatch, president of Hanna Mines, had stolen a march on Gilligan. Hatch announced before 1,000 of his company's workers gathered in Cadiz High School that he would shut down all operations if the bill passed as currently written. It was not a trivial threat: Hanna mined 11 million tons of coal annually, 20 percent of the state's total coal production.

The confrontation drew national attention. The governor's response was "vintage Gilligan."[22] As quoted in the *New York Times* on March 5, Gilligan said, "I hope the members of the Senate will resist and reject the brazen and brutal attempt of the president of a giant coal company to blackmail this government by threatening the livelihood of hundreds of miners and their families."[23] In the following days, miners and their wives—perhaps 400 in all—came to Columbus to sit in on hearings and to confront Frank King, president of the Ohio AFL-CIO, which had endorsed tough strip mining legislation. It was not altogether clear—not least, perhaps, to the miners themselves—whom they felt most aggrieved by. The *Columbus Dispatch* reported that "a shouting match between King and strip mine workers erupted at the Statehouse moments after a subcommittee reviewing strip mining legislation recessed Thursday."[24] The miners claimed King was selling them out; King suggested that the miners were being "snowed by the company" they worked for.[25] At the same time, senators came under contrary pressure from environmental groups opposed to any concessions to the mine owners.

One possible concession at the heart of debate had to do with the high wall, the vertical landform that remains once the side of a hill has been strip mined, the bottom removed. As proposed, the bill called for high walls to be reduced by grading, a measure the mine owners said, with marginal credibility, would bankrupt them.[26]

That view, however, was shared by Harry Meshel, generally a strong Gilligan supporter. Meshel, a former steelworker, thought coal vital to east central Ohio: "There were thousands of jobs at stake over the strictures Gilligan was pushing. I was supporting all the controls—restoring the land, containing the drain-offs, doing whatever was needed to keep runoff out of the aquifer. I was supporting everything except for the high wall."[27] He thought the industry was right that the expense was excessive relative to the environmental good achieved. "I thought it was just far too early to give up on coal mining as an industry."[28]

Meshel served on the Senate subcommittee assigned the bill. He recalled being instructed by Senate president Ted Gray to come to Gray's office, sit down, and write a bill he thought would pass. Under Meshel's amendment, the high wall could be left in place provided the mine operators could persuade the state reclamation chief that it would not detract from the land's future value. That amendment was part of the Senate bill adopted when the Senate passed its version of the bill on April 4, 1972. More generally, the Senate bill permitted water impoundments, water-oriented real estate developments, recreation area developments, industrial site development, sanitary landfill, and agricultural in the reclamation.

While tracking progress on the strip mining legislation, Gilligan was attending to that variety of chores that fall on a chief executive. On Wednesday, April 5, he cut the ribbon on the Muskie for President headquarters on Dayton's South Wilkinson Street and, that evening, attended the Cincinnati Reds home opener in Riverfront Stadium (the same stadium whose bond issue he, as a city councilman, had voted against). The following day, he hosted an hour-long breakfast session for a dozen state legislators at the Mansion, had his picture taken with the mayor of Ashtabula, and, that evening, spoke at a Muskie fund-raiser in Dayton.

On April 7, the House concurred unanimously with the Senate-passed bill. Representative Sam Speck (R-New Concord), the original sponsor of the 1971 House bill, said the measure would put Ohio "at or near the top of the fifty states to strip mine reclamation law."[29] In his April 10 signing, Governor Gilligan noted two purposes of the bill: first, to protect the environment; second, to allow an important industry to operate profitably. He paid tribute to the members of the General Assembly, "who stood up against the strongest pressure ever exerted in these halls."[30] He added, "We will enforce this bill; we will use it as a tool to put an end to the senseless and greedy destruction of huge portions of our state."[31]

But this wasn't the end of Gilligan's fight with the coal mining industry. The exchange was with Hanna Coal over the GEM (giant earthmover) of Egypt, which, standing ten stories high and weighing 7 million pounds, was the largest strip mining machine in the state. Hanna wanted to move the machine across I-70. As Hanna outlined in an April 12 letter, the company planned to protect the highway from the machine's weight by covering the road with a six-foot layer of dirt covered with a wooden mat. And, it informed, given the machine's slow speed, the Interstate would need to be closed for twenty-four hours to permit passage. Hanna outlined its intentions in this regard in an April 12 letter to John McDonald of the governor's staff.

The thought of a 7,000-ton strip mining machine bringing eastern Ohio to a halt was appalling to Gilligan. Press secretary Bob Tenenbaum commented, "Gilligan did not like to do things he thought were demagogic; he was not going to stand in the schoolhouse door. But he thought about calling out the National Guard."[32] A collection of twenty-seven church groups sent telegrams Gilligan opposing the move. Hanna, they noted, had promised to reclaim all lands stripped south of I-70 if the move was allowed. The company could show good faith more rapidly, the telegram read, by restoring the lands they had stripped north of the Interstate.

On April 14, highway director Phillip Richley urged that the required permit not be issued. However, Hanna had the law at least vaguely on its side. During the first Rhodes administration, general terms for such an undertaking had been agreed on. (Gilligan characterized it as "one of a number of goofy enterprises to which Rhodes gave his blessing."[33]) By one account, Gilligan suggested that Hatch disassemble the 7,000 ton machine and carry it piece-by-piece. Hanna head Ralph Hatch said the arrangement with Rhodes was something of a "gentlemen's agreement"—perhaps leaving Gilligan to wonder whether it was Hatch or Rhodes who was the gentleman.[34]) In the end, matters proceeded rather as Hanna wished. The roadway was buried beneath six feet of protective earth; an operation center was built out of plywood; traffic was rerouted for twenty-four hours along a county road to US 40; and the GEM of Egypt made its clanking way from the north to south side of I-70, where it remained in operation for several years.[35]

Strip mining was an activity carried out near the surface, and consequently highly visible. Below the surface in Columbus, however, something was turning rotten in the Statehouse of Ohio. An opposition faction was developing within the Gilligan administration—not in opposition to the governor but to several of his closest staff members. According to Dave Larson, who conducted numerous interviews at the time, a rump group of Gilligan cabinet members began meeting shortly after the first of year. They were worried about how the income tax fight had diminished the administration's popularity and worried that the administration itself was being poorly run and was unresponsive—unresponsive, in particular, as demonstrated by their insufficient direct contact with the governor.

In late April—then just days before the Ohio primary—nine members of Gilligan's cabinet confronted the governor with a bill of particulars and, going well beyond that, demanded the ouster of legislative liaison John McDonald and office manager Tom Menaugh and the transfer of Jim Friedman to a post that lacked direct access to Gilligan. (Subsequently, the group also sought the dismissal of John Jones, executive director of the state Democratic Party, a demand Gilligan was able to sidestep on the grounds that Jones was not a state employee.) One newspaper account reported, "The consensus seems to be that cabinet members dealt frankly, even harshly, with the governor."[36] Frankly enough to state that unless those named were moved over or out, all nine would submit their resignations. Gilligan recalled, "They did not come to discuss the matter: it was them or us. Flat out."[37] The two-hour session ended with Gilligan's agreement to read and respond to the group's demands.

The nine disgruntled cabinet members were Gene Abercrombie, agriculture; Paul Corey, personnel; Henry Eckhart, public utilities; Jack Hansan, welfare; Pete O'Grady, highway safety; Phil Richley, highways; Dennis Shaul, commerce; Joe Shump, industrial relations; and Joseph Sommer, workmen's compensation. William Garnes, employment services, was traveling but extended his proxy to the group, which then became known as "the Gang of Ten." Jack Hansan served as the group's spokesman. Hansan said he had been sought out for this role based on his long association with the governor, back to his management of Gilligan's 1964 congressional campaign.

Gilligan said that he was startled by the personal animosity expressed. He had been aware of conflicts but had believed the issue was the conflict that fairly often exists between department heads and the executive staff that stands between them and the governor's appointment book: "Most of the [departmental] guys, especially the more talented ones, run not for the salary but the psychic income of feeling that they're on the inside, that they are movers and shakers. And when they feel they're being shut out of it they want a chance." Further commenting on the complaint, Gilligan said that during the austerity crisis, "the department heads were really horrified; they were outraged. They were screaming bloody murder that we were tearing their departments to pieces."[38] At least some department heads believed passage of the income taxes would bring a bonanza of new money. Instead, what it brought was the insistence of budget director Hal Hovey that departments receive no additional funding until they demonstrate how the public would benefit by their expenditure. (There may have been pettier issues: McDonald and Menaugh were among those who regularly played doubles tennis with the governor, Gilligan's standard and frequent exercise, which some of the "ten" thought gave them a "pillow talk" advantage with the governor.)

Meeting a second time with the group, Gilligan announced that McDonald and Friedman would be removed from their present posts, though he hoped to accommodate them elsewhere in the administration. Gilligan invited Jack Hansan to join him on a trip to Toledo for an appearance with Senator Muskie. During that trip, he offered Hansan the chief of staff post. Hansan first wanted clarity— Did he have the power to hire and fire, and was that power inclusive? Gilligan said it was. That condition met, Hansan accepted the post.

There were several sound reasons behind the selection of Hansan. First, Gilligan had settled confidence in the latter's character and judgment. Second, Hansan had demonstrated considerable administrative skill as director of the state welfare office. One Ohio newspaper quoted Gilligan with crediting Hansan with having taken "the overwhelming welfare bureaucracy we inherited" and turning it into "an efficient, flexible and capable department."[39] Bob Daley, the governor's astute appointments secretary, saw Hansan as the fairly obvious pick: "He had the organizational talent to run the office and run the administration. He also had the governor's confidence because they had been through some hard times together; and thirdly, he was tough enough to do the things that had to be done and the governor knew had to be done."[40]

Hansan's own assessment was that Gilligan was a poor administrator and that he "could do for Gilligan what the governor could not do for himself—master the daily nuts and bolts and build and nurture an organization." Hansan rated his own abilities as considerable: "I know that everything I have touched was better off in consequence: I knew how to select people; delegate to them; support them."[41] He planned to announce the shakeup at a May 3 press conference. A statement Hansan made in an interview in 1974 suggests that he was not shy about wanting a clean break and clear control.

> That afternoon I made another move, which was to cut [budget director Hal] Hovey off at the pass. Hovey and McDonald and Menaugh [had] arranged to meet with the Governor on the afternoon prior to when I was going to have this hypothetical press conference . . . I called Hovey and said: "I'd like to see you." I called him over here and I said, "Hal, there's going to be a change made and you're very important part of this administration and I'm telling you we need your help. I need you, Hal; your role is not going to change. But if you side with McDonald and Menaugh, you're through."[42]

With little of the palace dispute having leaked to the press, Hansan's news conference occasioned considerable surprise. In reporting the news, the *Plain Dealer* noted that "several top Gilligan lieutenants said they were not informed of the change until 11 a.m. yesterday at an administration staff meeting."[43] Principally, the Gang of Ten consisted of individuals with some stake and standing within Ohio Democratic politics. The "professionals" in the cabinet—like economic development director David Sweet and mental health director Ken Gaver—were pretty much in the dark over the pending shakeup. Curiously, perhaps, the shakeup appeared to cause no great reaction among legislators.

John McDonald attributed his ouster to the often apt phrase, "No good deed goes unpunished."[44] His tenure as legislative liaison had witnessed passage of the income tax and a federally approved redistricting of the state, the administration's most important legislative achievements. These steps, McDonald freely admitted, had not been accomplished entirely by charm: "Let's face it: Jim [Friedman] and I stepped on a lot of toes and twisted a lot of arms."[45] Further, according to press accounts, McDonald enjoyed poor relations with Democratic legislative leaders. In the Senate, he—like everyone in Gilligan's inner circle—had wanted someone other than Anthony Calabrese as leader; in the House, he favored Donald Pease for the leadership post eventually gained by A. G. Lancione. His role in redistricting had further bruised feelings. His removal, he speculated, might have been a way for Gilligan to distance himself from the bloodletting.

McDonald declined the offer of some other position within the administration; he did not wish, he said, to work with people who had wanted him fired. Nor was he happy that it was Hansan who delivered the news of his discharge. By McDonald's account, the new chief of staff said, "The governor wants you to resign." To which McDonald replied, "Then let the governor ask me."[46] "I at least deserved the courtesy of [Gilligan] looking me in the eye and saying, 'Hey, I appreciate the work you did, but now it's a problem and you've got to leave.'"[47] McDonald's May 16 letter of resignation to Gilligan made the case for his own tenure: "During the past eighteen months we have witnessed the enactments of better than three-fourths of our legislative program, including adoption of a state income tax and federal court approval of our reapportionment plan."[48]

The case of Jim Friedman was, for Gilligan, a good deal more complicated. Friedman did not lack for detractors, who saw him as brusque and unwilling to delegate. State Democratic chairman John Jones said, "Jimmy Friedman was smarter than hell. But he micromanaged; he had to have his finger in everything. It became impossible to get decisions out of the governor's office."[49] Similarly, Tom Menaugh commented, "We had an absolute fiasco because Friedman tried to have everything funneled through his office before it got to the governor, and nobody could ever get to Friedman, and there were long periods of time when nothing happened."[50] Cabinet member Richard Guggenheim added, "Friedman got most of the cabinet irritated. That was really the basis."[51] Similar comments surfaced in the press. The *Cleveland Plain Dealer* added, "Access to Friedman was frequently difficult and many officials complained of his tough personality. Democratic county chairmen around the state were angry when they were often unable to get through to Friedman by phone."[52]

Press secretary Robert Tenenbaum raised a point in Friedman's defense: part of the job of a chief of staff is to protect the chief executive from all the things that have no business reaching his desk. Some who complained Friedman was keeping them from seeing Gilligan, Tenenbaum said, were people Gilligan had no need to see. Tenenbaum said Friedman was "very sure of himself, very direct, politically very astute. He was the governor's SOB; and every governor needs an SOB."[53]

Whatever the complaints, Jim Friedman had been Jack Gilligan's closest political ally—at least since the day in 1967 when he had surfaced in Cincinnati to urge Gilligan to take on the unlikely task of challenging Frank Lausche, the most popular Democrat in state history. Friedman since that time had made a virtual career of Gilligan's advancement. "Jim had been with me from the beginning, through the campaign and all the vicissitudes," Gilligan said. "He got to the point—not unreasonably—that he thought he not only knew where we were going but how we were going to get there, that our views coincided. Therefore, he felt a certain freedom in speaking out. We shared views on virtually everything, so whatever he decided probably had to be okay with me. He got out in front a little bit."[54]

Gilligan later said that he had had several brief chats with Friedman on the matter but speculated that perhaps it would have been wiser to rein in Friedman more forcefully. In the end, Gilligan called Friedman in: "I said that despite my appreciation for everything he had done during the campaign and the administration, I just couldn't let the whole shooting match go down the drain."[55] According to Gilligan, the dismissal of Friedman was the toughest single decision he made in politics. He urged Friedman to meet with Hansan to define some other task for him within the administration. That exchange with the new chief of staff foundered, however, on Friedman's insistence on having direct access to Gilligan and Hansan's refusal to permit it.

Friedman did not fault Hansan for this. "My view is pretty simple," he said. "Were I Jack Hansan, I would have done the same thing. He was a good bureaucratic infighter, and he did not want anyone with direct ties to the governor."[56] And, from the distance of years, Friedman acknowledged some merit to the complaints against him. First, he noted that having inherited from Governor James Rhodes's aide John McElroy a very broad definition of what a chief of staff did, he had broadened that definition further. He acknowledged difficulties with delegating and added that it had never really occurred to him that department heads might resent taking directions from a twenty-nine-year-old.

At the time, Friedman went somewhat less than gently into that good night. According to Hansan, Friedman said to him, "This is the worst thing you've ever done or will ever do; it's the biggest mistake of your life."[57] Part of Friedman's pain reflected the unexpected nature of the dismissal: "I had not spent a lot of time covering myself. I always viewed myself as the cutting edge, the point of the spear. I never looked behind me to see if someone was gaining on me."[58] (That comment was seconded by Pat Leahy, who then assisted state auditor Joe Ferguson: "Friedman was looking forward, not paying attention to who was slapping him on the side."[59]) "It was embarrassing," Friedman said. "Not too many people get fired on the front page of the newspapers."[60]

Gilligan clearly hoped the break with Friedman would not be final. On May 25, he appointed the Cleveland attorney to a five-year term as chair of the Ohio Civil Rights Commission, a part-time post carrying a salary of $11,794. In making the appointment, Gilligan said, "Jim Friedman is young, able, energetic and totally devoted to the cause of equal rights for all."[61] Beyond that task, Friedman devoted himself to the practice of law and, at Gilligan's request, worked outside the governor's office on strengthening the Democratic Party for the 1972 election.

Those ousted tended to blame Hansan—and in fairly hyperbolic terms. Tom Menaugh, who departed the administration quietly several months later, accused Hansan of having executed something akin to a coup (he termed the new chief of staff either "Haldeman" or "Ehrlichman," the disgraced Nixon aides with particular reputations for playing hardball).[62] John McDonald said, "My perception was that it was all done on Jack Hansan's advice."[63] But Hansan maintained that he was "not the arranger of any cabal."[64] Things were in danger of floundering, he said, and he was called on to stabilize things. Gilligan backed that judgment: "I think it's a bum rap to say that [Hansan] in any way plotted, or inspired, or instigated that revolution."[65]

In his new role, Hansan rather quickly brought his administrative skill to bear on the governor's office and operations became notably smoother. First, as chief of staff, he met almost daily with a core group that included four department heads: Phil Moots, legislation; Jay Tepper, finance; Max Brown, communications; and Bob Daley, administration. Second, as secretary of the cabinet, he served as liaison between its members and the governor. Monthly cabinet meetings with set agendas were held, though Hansan admitted their most useful outcome may have been to prevent cabinet members from claiming they had not had the opportunity to have their say. He took other steps, as well, scheduling face-to-face meetings between Gilligan and younger staff members. Hansan gained favorable press. Four months into his tenure, the *Akron Beacon Journal* reported that "in more than a dozen interviews in the past ten days, Hansan often was described in glowing terms. Associates, both inside and outside the administration, said he has proved himself 'extremely capable,' willing to delegate responsibility, people-oriented, an outstanding organizer, always ready to listen to someone's problem and help solve it."[66] The idea of some merit was that Friedman and McDonald had been needed to do the bruising work of the income tax fight; now, a more organized touch was required.

However, one matter remained unresolved, a matter that grew in consequence as time passed. By common consent, Jim Friedman was the sharpest political mind within Gilligan's easy reach. Friedman was also Gilligan's connection to Mark Shields and pollster Peter Hart, rising stars in the national Democratic Party. Gilligan's hope—in mid-1972 and for some while thereafter—was that the breach between Friedman and Hansan would heal or blow over or somehow resolve itself in a way that would allow the trio of Friedman, Shields, and Hart to play key roles when reelection became the pressing matter in Gilligan's life.

In addition to, and simultaneous with, the intramural conflict within the administration, another setback Jack Gilligan suffered that spring was the slowly deflating campaign launched by Senator Edmund Muskie and endorsed (early and quite publicly) by Governor John Gilligan. Gilligan had placed Jim Friedman in charge of the effort, and now Muskie was not only finishing out of the money, but he wasn't even finishing.

As a candidate, Muskie was favorably regarded by many but passionately supported by few. Mark Shields noted the irony that befell Muskie: in the Florida primary, Muskie trailed Hubert Humphrey, Henry Jackson, and George Wallace to finish a disappointing fourth; that same day, a *New York Times* poll showed Muskie as the only Democrat who could beat Nixon. As Gilligan himself acknowledged of his own pledged choice, Muskie "didn't generate a lot of passion, or exhibit much."[67]

Gilligan expressed his chagrin in an April 12 interview with R. W. Apple of the *New York Times*, saying he found it "impossible to hide his dismay" at the campaign Muskie was waging.[68] He said he had hoped that a Muskie candidacy would avoid the sort of the Left-Right split the Democrats had experienced in 1968, but Muskie's failure to focus on a few key issues was preventing this. Several weeks later, Gilligan transmitted his assessment directly to Muskie: "I told him that I was confident early of his ability to win in Ohio but that his chances now were less than fifty-fifty."[69]

Gilligan, after Florida, hoped for a strong showing in Pennsylvania, whose primary fell just before Ohio's. In Ohio, however, the Muskie campaign achieved little traction. As a campaign coordinator for Muskie, Jack Davis tried to sell the Maine senator's candidacy in southern Ohio, but "in Ironton and the Ohio River towns, they just weren't buying."[70] The Gilligan endorsement had not been entirely popular within the governor's own administration. Following the primary, health director John Cashman wrote Pete O'Grady that the younger members of his staff "particularly resented" the big push that Gilligan appeared to be making for Muskie, adding that he did not "know of a single young person in my department who was for Senator Muskie even though all of them have been firm Gilligan supporters."[71]

Voters in Pennsylvania didn't buy Muskie either. Following a poor showing there, Muskie withdrew as a candidate. Jim Friedman was with Gilligan and California senator John Tunney, another early Muskie supporter, when word of their candidate's withdrawal came over the television news. Friedman recalled, "We were in a hotel suite. When the news came in, I literally thought Tunney was going to jump out the window."[72] Gilligan's own reaction was less dramatic. With the Ohio primary itself less than a week away, he resisted pressure to declare for some other candidate. Ohio's governor, having arrived early for the 1972 presidential sweepstakes, was now dressed up with nowhere to go.

Arguably, this was Gilligan's low point. His chief aid banished. The cabinet distracted. The man he had early on backed for president—backed, possibly, with visions of vice presidential–shaped sugar plums dancing in his imagination— had given up the fight. Gilligan at this point took a revealing step—revealing in that it was a straightforward attempt to address a deficiency he saw in himself. He urgently requested a meeting with John Olsen, an official with the Cleveland Foundation—the nation's oldest and, at the time, largest community foundation. The governor sent the state DC-3 to bring Olsen to the Mansion, where Gilligan detailed the rift in his cabinet. Gilligan, Olsen said, "was remarkable and engaging. He said he had never managed anything in his life. Could I undertake a study on how to improve the effectiveness of his cabinet?"[73] Olsen completed a report and sent it to the cabinet as "Gilligan's basis for mollifying things."[74]

What followed was a series of monthly two- and three-hour sessions between the pair, held for privacy's sake at the Governor Mansion, in which they addressed individual topics, such as workmen's compensation and the search to find a new welfare director to replace Hansan. Olsen found Gilligan "witty and engaging, and with that wonderful Irish charm."[75]

Olsen made a distinction between the managerial and the administrative. Gilligan was strong as the former, according to Olsen, at setting administration objectives, but weak at the latter. "He assumed that he did not have to see personally that follow-through was occurring."[76] Olsen commented: "The detailed questions— How to allocate and implement priorities? How to implement budget over time?— these things might be said to be cabinet responsibilities, but there still needed to be a mechanism by which they get done. Gilligan did not have the mechanics of how a CEO actually organizes his office to be able to achieve those kinds of objectives."[77]

Olsen stressed to Gilligan that a governor's power derives less from his formal standing than from the quality of the people appointed and the use to which they are put. As it happened, Olsen did not have a terribly high view of public administrators. It was his view that government generally did a far poorer job of training managers than was done in business and that the stronger the ideological bent of an administrator, the less effective they were likely to be at their job. (Olsen's tutorials continued into early 1973. Gilligan found in Olsen a useful sounding board for whatever matter lay at immediate hand. In mid-1973, he formalized the relationship when he named Olsen to head the newly created Office of Budget and Management.)

Whatever effects John Olsen's tutorials with the governor had on the public perception of the latter, they were hardly surprisingly slow to register. What did register in mid-1972 was that Gilligan's personal popularity with the electorate was low, perhaps dangerously so. Officially, the Gilligan camp had likely all but given up on the idea that Ohio would conclude that Jack Gilligan was a "hail, fellow, well met" and the "life of the party." It is not certain that a chief executive's program can be more popular than the chief executive himself, but that was Gilligan's hope—that Ohio would recognize good government even if it tended not to perceive a warm and genial governor. This was in contrast to Gilligan's predecessor.

An aphorism attributed to Jim Rhodes is that it is easier to like someone you do not trust than it is to trust someone you do not like. People did not particularly trust Jim Rhodes; as reporter Hugh McDiarmid wrote during the 1974 campaign, Rhodes "figures that about ninety-five percent of the press corps thinks he's a liar and he's probably right."[78] Still, for all his malapropos, evasions, and self-misquotations, Rhodes was fairly popular with reporters, who considered him a good sport and who were informally welcome in the governor's office. Gilligan, by contrast, was not particularly chummy with the press; those journalists who sought to wander back to the governor's office did not find the welcome sign posted. Gilligan's recollection was that he tended to like those reporters who represented newspapers he thought fair or favorable. Among his favorites were Abe Zaiden of the *Akron Beacon Journal* and Hugh McDiarmid of the *Dayton Journal Herald*. (A few members of the press corps thought McDiarmid mimicked Gilligan's distinctive speaking style, something that may have been less attributable to any tendency to curry favor than to the simple fact that both had grown up in Cincinnati.) Gilligan was on first-name basis with most reporters, except for Haskell Short, who, as bureau chief for Scripps-Howard, had been a big fan of James Rhodes. Gilligan referred to him as Mr. Small.

Gilligan read much of what was written about him and his administration, occasionally calling his opinion of a reporter's work to the latter's attention. Once, reporter David Hopcraft, believing that one Gilligan statement contradicted a previous one, wrote a Sunday column calling attention to the apparent discrepancy. Walking near the governor's office the following Monday, he had his arm taken by a cheerful governor, who, in Hopcraft's telling, pointed to his gubernatorial visage and said, "Clear eyes. Straight teeth. Honest John Gilligan," and walked off smiling.[79] Lee Leonard also recalled writing columns with which Gilligan did not agree: "One day, I was going past his office and he came out and in that haughty way he had, he said, 'I've been reading what you've been writing about me.' And he didn't smile."[80]

It was hardly to Gilligan's advantage that the newspaper that may have been most unreservedly hostile to him was the lead paper in the capital of the state he governed. That paper, the *Columbus Dispatch,* routinely gave the governor and his

administration a hard time—often over matters of lesser importance, and sometimes over matters of no importance. In June 1971, just five months after Gilligan
was inaugurated and during the heat of the tax battle, the *Dispatch* carried an editorial cartoon of a dreamy-eyed Gilligan with his preoccupied face in the clouds
of national ambition and his feet in the mud of "Ohio problems."[81] Two months
later, the paper printed a three-column, page one photo of a Ford LTD County
Squire. This state-owned station wagon, the newspaper said, was being used by
Bill Nye, director of the Ohio Department of Natural Resources, on a family vacation on Kelley's Island. Two weeks later, a *Dispatch* editorial criticized Gilligan for
attending the National Governor's Conference rather than minding the shop in
Columbus. When Gilligan replied that Ohio governors had been attending such
conferences for fifty-two years, the *Dispatch* usefully dug up the obscure fact that
Governor Mike DiSalle had skipped out on the 1959 conference. Gilligan deemed
the *Dispatch* "a total pain in the neck."[82] Gilligan regarded it and the *Cincinnati
Enquirer* not so much newspapers as "organs of political warfare."[83]

For all the grumping, Gilligan's press secretary generally thought the press
played fair with the governor—the notable exception, Tenenbaum said, being a
considerable flap kicked up over Gilligan's use of the state DC-3 aircraft to travel
to the family summer home in Leland, Michigan. The DC-3 was hardly luxurious
travel; Katie Gilligan, the governor's wife, never boarded the aircraft without first
having a martini. Tenenbaum thought the key offending word in the proposition
was "Michigan"—Ohio State University's great rival. Had the Gilligan vacation
home been in Wisconsin, Tenenbaum suggested, no one would have cared. The
flap bothered Tenenbaum because the Gilligan's had been vacationing as a family
at Leland for four decades, and he thought the press was trying to make a big deal
out of a family matter.[84]

The Gilligan administration ran a more organized public relations function
than Ohio politics had previously seen. One aspect of this, coined the TV Beeper,
allowed the governor to talk to ten local television news reporters during one-
hour sessions held in the basement of the Statehouse. It was an economical arrangement for the local television stations—the state provided the technicians, the
camera, the studio, and the governor, and news directors from WSPD in Toledo,
WSMJ in Youngstown, and elsewhere provided the questions. The project was the
brainchild of James Dunn, Gilligan's sound man in the 1968 Senate campaign. At
the end of these sessions, once the questions were answered, the finished film was
distributed by couriers from the Ohio Department of Highways. The *New York
Times* commented, "The arrangement comes close to giving the Governor access
to his own free statewide TV network once each week."[85]

A second element of the operation allowed news editors at the small radio stations scattered about the state to call in and get live comments from the governor
on "current news" for broadcast use on their station. The calls came into a dun-

geonlike room in the basement of the Statehouse, Between these morning calls, Gilligan, by report, would sip his morning coffee and read his *New York Times.* Gilligan was diligent about the matter, though it was hardly his favorite enterprise. He was at times dismayed by how many of the news editors who queried him gave no evidence of having read that morning's headlines. Still, the project was generally regarded as a success, as it gave smaller radio stations at least the opportunity to give their listeners up-to-the-moment comment on local matters.

The antipathy of several major newspapers aside, Gilligan's troubles with the press were often self-inflicted. Rhodes, when governor, refused to be drawn into discussion of any topic that was not Ohio; he told one reporter, "I'm not going to be talking about things like North Dakota," which all present interpreted to mean that the governor would not be discussing North Vietnam.[86] Gilligan, however, at press conferences could be goaded into discussion of issues ranging from U.S. foreign policy to the current boycott of nonunion lettuce (which, on August 19, 1972, he urged state agencies to support). This carried some suggestion that Ohio's governor would rather be in Washington, D.C., a suggestion not without plausibility. Lee Leonard recalled, "I asked Tenenbaum why Gilligan talked about all these things." The governor's press secretary responded, "Because he believes in them."[87]

Gilligan's biggest problems with the press came from comments he volunteered. On September 1, 1972, he was strolling with development director David Sweet along the midway at the Ohio State Fair. Admittedly, the state fair was never Gilligan's favorite event—his interest in pig racing was slight, and the close collection of barns aggravated his hay fever. An announcer asked the governor where he was heading. To the sheep shearing, Gilligan replied. "Are you going to shear a sheep?" asked the reporter. No, said the governor, "I shear taxpayers, not sheep."[88] Unfortunately for Gilligan, this may have become the best remembered sentence of his administration. Press secretary Robert Tenenbaum recalled, "I knew it was a problem the second I heard 'sheep.' The fact that he said it and the way he said it—I could just imagine people saying, 'I don't need my governor to be a comedian.'"[89] David Sweet, who was standing with Gilligan at the time, later commented, "I figured we'd be hearing more about that."[90]

Despite that moment, however, events in Ohio in the fall of 1972 had all begun to move Gilligan's way. Passage of the corporate and personal income taxes had been the great success of 1971. But for the measure's opponents—particularly a clump of conservative state representatives—the tax battle continued. They had vowed to place the income tax question on the November 1972 ballot and let the people of Ohio decide directly if they wished their taxes increased. The effort faced both legal and practical hurdles. The first was overcome when the Ohio Supreme Court ruled 5–2 to permit the initiative's placement on the ballot. That ruling directed Secretary of State Ted Brown to certify a summary of the proposed amendment, with that summary being printed on the petitions tax opponents began to circulate. The proposal would do more than reverse the enactment of the income and corporate taxes. As worded, the amendment would not only repeal the 1971 income tax, but it would ban any future graduated income tax whatsoever and require that any flat-rate income tax could be enacted only by state referendum. The practical obstacle was the simple difficulty of gathering the signatures needed to place the measure on the November ballot.

But even as the task of signature gathering began, some significant Republicans were peeling away from the effort. The *Dayton Journal Herald* reported that Republican state chairman John Andrews "has been lobbying cautiously and privately against the movement to repeal the new state income tax."[91] Representative E. W. Lampson, chair of the Ways and Means Committee, urged Republicans not to circulate pro-repeal petitions. If the issue reached the ballot, he said, Republican candidates risked being inundated by a flood of tax-supporting Democrats. Further, Lampson argued, "The corporate-personal income tax is better than any possible alternate source of tax income."[92]

Bob Netzley was the key figure and spokesman for the repeal effort, with help from his fellow representatives Joseph Tulley (R-Mentor) and Gordon Scherer (R-Cincinnati). Netzley was something of a gadfly, with a flair for publicity. He was well regarded among House conservatives. William Batchelder said, "Netzley was a hero to the conservatives because he didn't change his vote" on the income tax.[93] He was, perhaps, part conservative and part libertarian, which might account for the variety of arguments he put forward in opposition to the tax legislation. Netzley told one radio interviewer that state expenditures had increased 175 percent in the preceding fourteen years, and that the income tax would simply feed the beast. At times, he invoked popular sovereignty: the public had had no direct say in the tax that had been passed or in the "tremendous increases that are going to occur probably next year and in two more years or three more years and so on."[94] And at times, he raised the issue of local control, insisting he was not opposed to income taxes per se but that he favored a county-level tax aimed at supporting public schools and local government. One problem with a statewide tax, he argued, was that whatever money went to Columbus tended to stay in Columbus.

But consistency was not the issue. Many in Ohio did not need, or want, an intellectual rationale for opposing a tax. In August, tax repeal petitioners filed 366,000 signatures with Secretary of State Ted Brown; when some were ruled invalid, they gathered an additional 71,000—a significant grass-roots achievement and one that required Brown to place the issue on the November ballot.

Characteristically, Jack Gilligan took the long view: "A lot of our people thought 'We're down the tubes on this one.'"[95] What Ohio-born voter would pass on the opportunity to abolish a tax? The attitude reminded Gilligan of 1958, when opponents of the right-to-work amendment had initially expected to be trounced at the polls.

Gilligan was pinpoint clear that the tax referendum was not a challenge but an op-portunity.

> It was an opportunity to get people to think in these terms—about the relation-
> ship of services and taxes, about what was needed in the future, and how any
> idea they had to improve anything in the state was at risk without this source of
> financial support. We were arguing—through this campaign and through this
> administration—about the need for improvements in many fields. We were not
> going to get any of those things until we got more resources.[96]

He thought that "if we did it right, not only would we protect the tax, but we could al-ter the political balance in the state of Ohio."[97] Part of the task, he said, was to ensure that Democrats campaigning for the General Assembly faced the issue square on.

> I said to all our people: Don't treat this as a defensive issue; treat this as an of-
> fensive issue. Go after your opponent for the legislature and say, "You're opposed
> to the income tax. Fine. Now, you tell me how we're going to pay for everything.
> How are we going to pay for education?" If you're opposed, then you have some
> responsibility to come up with an alternative. And if you don't, then you are sim-
> ply being obstructionist.[98]

Gilligan campaigned in every one of the eighteen state representative districts Chavanne regarded as winnable. Generally, Gilligan visited local fund-raisers where politics was a retail undertaking—not too many hands to shake, not too much money to raise, hardly any babies to kiss. Chavanne commented, "It was not difficult to get Gilligan to do it. He didn't want failure; he wanted those candidates to win."[99] And he honored individual requests whenever possible. Don Pease wrote seeking a Gilligan appearance at the local Lorain County Jefferson-Jackson Day dinner, as such an appearance, Pease stated, "will have a very definite bearing on my re-election campaign."[100] McDonald passed the memo to the governor's executive assistant, Bob Daley, with the penciled memo, "Accommodate if at all possible."[101]

John Jones, executive director of the state party, supplied the manpower for these campaigns. He insisted that the several dozen people he could count on must not be scattered about the state supporting the McGovern campaign; rather, they should be concentrated on the winnable House races. Jones recalled, "I was sending those young people around the state to set up organizations, from the precinct level up," along with $200 to $500, depending on the candidate's prospects.[102]

Campaigns are often a sort of organized scramble. Two weeks before a sched-uled fund-raiser in Shelby County, Chavanne telephoned the candidate to see how plans were advancing. They weren't; in fact, the event had been cancelled. Chavanne blistered: "What the hell do you mean? It's on the governor's schedule. Get your butt on the phone and make it happen."[103] On the day of the event, Chavanne cautioned Gilligan not to expect too much. In fact, they were met by 400 people and the high school band, and, as an added amenity, the candidate's brother had rented a trailer for the governor's convenience. A hat-passing produced a pleasing $800. After the event, the candidate's brother begged a private moment with Gilligan, assuring Chavanne that he wasn't going to ask for anything. Instead, when both stepped into the trailer, he gave Governor Gilligan a watch. Gilligan, completely taken back, told Chavanne, "I can't accept this; I've got to send it back." Chavanne cut him off, saying, "you can throw it away, you can give it away. But if you give it back, this guy is going to be embarrassed."[104] (Four decades after the event, Gilligan did not recollect the watch.)

On another occasion, Gilligan campaigned in Ashtabula County on behalf of a young man named Robert Boggs. Chavanne had been impressed with Boggs but had doubts as to whether his was the right last name to run against a fairly well-qualified Italian Republican in an Italian district. Gilligan's visit began with the "high roller" event—the nine people who had come up with $25 to attend. Gilligan, Chavanne recalled, was considerably less than pleased. Then, all headed downtown, where a crowd of 500 was waiting. To Chavanne's eye, every single person in the audience was over age sixty-five; how, he wondered, was a candidate one-third that age going to come across? Boggs stood up, went to the podium, and started talking about Franklin Roosevelt, the Democrats, and the Great Depression. He won the crowd and, subsequently, the election.

Gilligan spent much of October campaigning, dividing his time between the campaigns of would-be state legislators and the unlikely-to-be national ticket of George McGovern and Sargent Shriver. He met with groups of Democratic legislative candidates in Columbus on October 3 and 4, in Toledo on October 5, and in Cleveland on October 6—in all cases, restating his instruction that they make a positive case for the income tax. He gave a pep talk on the income tax to administration public information officers gathered in the Statehouse press conference room; discussed the tax issue with a group of African American ministers in Toledo and black media executives in Cleveland; and spoke at fund-raisers in Dayton and Toledo. He also spoke twice at fund-raisers for George McGovern, spoke once to a school group about the dangers of drugs, and, on Saturday, October 7, attended a play-off game between his hometown Cincinnati Reds and the Pittsburgh Pirates. On the daily schedule, this last item carried the uncertain note "Collect bet."[105]

As Gilligan campaigned, much of establishment Ohio was coming around to support the income tax—including establishment Republicans. The *Christian Science Monitor* reported that former Governor James Rhodes had declined to help the tax repeal effort. The Republican majority whip in the State Senate, Mike Maloney, came out against repeal.[106] Howard Collier, former state finance director under James Rhodes, said that, after having reviewed the pending state budget drawn up by Gilligan finance director Hal Hovey, "the only way the state could continue spending levels set by the General Assembly would be for that body to impose new taxes. Which could mean some people eventually would pay more— not less—on taxes."[107] In late October, that most Republican of organizations, the Ohio Chamber of Commerce, came within an ace of opposing repeal: a survey of its 109-member board showed that "forty-two percent opposed repeal," while only 5 percent favored it (the rest being either undecided or unavailable).[108] And, with the exception of the *Columbus Dispatch,* virtually every major newspaper in the state—from the *Akron Beacon Journal* and the *Cleveland Plain Dealer* to the *Youngstown Vindicator* to the *Cincinnati Enquirer*—urged a no vote on the repeal.

In October, Democratic state party official David Meeker sent a memo to Gilligan chief of staff Jack Hansan detailing the scale of the effort: 1.2 million pieces of literature distributed; press kit and speaker's kit developed and in use; mailings to all Democratic precinct captains; distribution of newspaper ads; surveys of radio stations; and more. The work with radio included scripts tailored to parents, senior citizens, small businessmen, and others.

State representative Netzley kept up the counter–battery fire. The bulk of the tax increase, he argued, would go not to education but to welfare; indeed, the current state budget had $1.2 billion for education and $1.1 billion for welfare, and to Netzley's eye it was the latter figure whose growth bore checking. While Netzley was entirely correct—welfare expenditures were the most volatile item in the budget—Gilligan was quick to point to figures from the U.S. Department of Public Welfare and noted that Ohio's proportion of residents on welfare—41.44 out of every 1,000— ranked thirtieth among the states. Ohio's welfare rate was lower than California's, New York's, and Illinois'—all of which had Republican governors. Gilligan said that states had little leverage over welfare costs, which were influenced by such "uncontrollable factors" as unemployment, federal regulations, court decisions, and, in Ohio, the lack of state control of caseworkers on the local level.

Not giving up, Netzley accused Gilligan appointees of engaging in scare tactics: he charged Martin Essex, superintendent of public instruction, with misstating the decline in school levies being sought since the income tax had passed; he accused Phil Richley "the $30,000 a year Director of Highways," of threatening to fire one-quarter of his department's employees if the tax was repealed"; and he asserted that "high-salaried Bill Nye" of the Department of Natural Resources had stated that "there would be fewer fish or rabbits if repeal passed."[109]

The anti-repeal force wheeled out its largest guns in the final days before the vote. On Friday, the bishops of the seven Catholic dioceses in Ohio endorsed retaining the tax. And, topping that, Saturday brought the endorsement of Ohio State University football coach Woody Hayes, who said, "I received a good public education at Newcomerstown and at Ohio State University. I hope young people of today will receive the same opportunity, so please join me in voting 'No' on Issue 2."[110]

Hayes's statement was distributed to the 86,000 Buckeye fans in the stands for that afternoon's game against Minnesota (which the Buckeyes won, 27–19).

But a few doubts remained. The campaign employed targeted marketing—a message for seniors, a message for parents, a message for union members. One radio spot aimed at union workers began,—"I'm Frank King, president of the Ohio AFL-CIO. Here is one reason working people oppose State issue 2."[111] *Columbus Dispatch* writer David Lore pointed out the irony: barely twenty months ago, King and Ray Ross of the United Autoworkers had declined to sign the task force report calling for a personal income tax, and both, for some while thereafter, had led the fight against the tax. Lore wondered if union members would believe what the pair said in 1971 or what they were saying now. He wrote that the *Dispatch* had polled 124 employees at a local industrial plant and found that seventy-four were planning to vote for repeal.[112]

Press coverage focused on the income tax issue. This was fine with Bill Chavanne, who was attempting to remain tight-lipped on the likely outcome of the House races. Still, he recalled, "As the election neared, people were asking, 'How many seats will we get?'"[113] Most people, Chavanne said, were predicting fifty or fifty-one, which would give the Democrats the thinnest of margins in the ninety-nine-seat chamber. Chief of staff Jack Hansan called a full staff meeting, at which Governor Gilligan asked, "How many seats will we win."[114] Chavanne said he thought the Democrats would do pretty well. To which Gilligan asked, "*How many seats?*" Chavanne recalled that when he replied, "Fifty-eight," there was an audible gasp. Jack Hansan told him, "If we win fifty-eight seats, you get an autographed picture of the governor thanking you."[115]

On election eve, Robert Netzley predicted a close outcome on tax repeal. He told the *Plain Dealer* that "the real issue is the people's right to vote," that the structure of the tax system was something upon which the people were entitled to pass direct judgment.[116] For his part, Governor Gilligan predicted that the income tax repeal would be "resoundingly defeated."[117] (Somewhat less convincingly, Gilligan said the presidential contest between Republican Richard Nixon and Democrat George McGovern had become "a real horse race.")[118] The *Cleveland Press* hedged its bets, reporting that "soundings around Ohio indicate the income tax battle is a rough one with the outcome likely to be close."[119]

Not remotely. In tiny Crawford County, the income tax was upheld by a vote of 10,794–8,878—a spread of about 9 percent. And that was the closest county in the state. Repeal of the income tax was defeated in all eighty-eight Ohio counties; in sixty-four of those counties, it was defeated by a margin of better than 2–1. The total vote was 1,164,857 to repeal the tax and 2,582,109 to retain it.

For Jack Gilligan, there had not been an electoral result so surprising, so pleasing, and so overwhelming since the Right-to-Work vote in 1958. There was a lot at stake: "If we had lost that one, then all the other plans we might have had—mental health, etc.—would have been just so much wreckage." Though he had believed all along the issue was winnable, "still, I was surprised by the numbers—something like 70 to 30 percent, which seemed like an absolute miracle."[120]

The result was something of an anomaly. In an Ohio election in which Republican Richard Nixon trounced Democrat George McGovern by almost 900,000 votes—a 22 percent margin—Ohio voters by an even larger margin chose to maintain the heaviest tax ever levied on them.

For the Gilligan administration, success was double. The Democrats gained thirteen seats in the state legislature, which, when it convened, would have fifty-eight Democrats—the exact number Bill Chavanne had predicted—and forty-one Republicans. (Apparently, Chavanne and Jim Friedman were the only Democrats in Columbus confident that their party would make such gains. In the days prior to the election, Friedman said, "we made a number of bets with people here in town. And we collected on those bets."[121]) Additionally, the Democrats gained three seats in the Senate, reducing the Republican margin in the upper chamber 17–16.

Some results were particularly pleasing. In Cuyahoga County, Representative Troy James had feared his career had ended when reapportionment turned his district from largely black to mostly Polish. Richard Nixon carried the district with 60 percent of the vote, but James was returned to office. The Polish community, which had expressed doubt about James's candidacy, warmed to their legislator once he was in office, where he remained until 2000.

And in Cincinnati, Republican Stanley Aronoff, whose addition to the fourth and final House-Senate conference committee helped prompt the income tax's passage, faced what he considered the most difficult election of his life. He made no pretense that he had voted his district's wishes on the issue. Rather, "I went to every church event, to every block party, to every public forum and did my best to explain."[122] He was reelected with an increased margin. For him, the lesson of the election was "to have faith in people," that "people would respect you if you said you had acted from [your] conscience."[123]

Gilligan drew a similar lesson: "Not for the first time or the last time, my faith in humanity was restored."[124]

27

The Progressive Moment

John Joyce Gilligan marked the beginning of his third year as governor of Ohio on January 1, 1973, in Pasadena, California. Gilligan had never yielded an inch in his loyalty to Notre Dame and its Fighting Irish; still, as governor, he was present to watch the Ohio State Buckeyes take on the Trojans of the University of Southern California in that year's Rose Bowl. It was not a good year for Buckeye pride; the Trojans trounced Ohio State 42–17. Postgame, Gilligan headed down to pay a call on the Ohio State locker room, only to encounter Buckeye's coach Woody Hayes, who was in a somewhat less affable mood than he had been when he spoke against the income tax repeal two months earlier. Actually, as Gilligan recalled, Hayes was in the act of throwing chairs. The football coach asked Gilligan what he was doing there. The governor responded, "I thought I'd congratulate the team on their hard play." "What the hell," said Hayes, who had locked half the team out of the locker room. "We lost."[1]

As events were to prove, there is, in politics as in football, no substitute for victory. Jack Gilligan had every reason to feel that the new year would prove a good one for him personally.

The General Assembly that had been elected the previous November convened in the early days of January. Ever since 1958, when Ohio established four-year terms for the governorship, a governor's time in office was divided into two biennia—each with its own budget, each with the General Assembly elected the fall of the even-numbered year, and often with their own agendas.

In Gilligan's 1971–72 biennium, the governor and his staff had by force of fact and perseverance secured from a reluctant legislature Ohio's first personal and corporate income taxes and then seen this measure resoundingly sustained by public referendum. Further, the Gilligan administration had enacted a redistricting of the state's legislative boundaries that was generally conducive to the election of Democrats; they had seen this strategy pay off when the November 1972 election turned a House of Representatives that had been 54–45 Republican to one that was 58–41 Democratic and cut the GOP's margin in the Senate to a single seat, 17–16. The tax increase provided Gilligan with the wherewithal to expand the role of state government within Ohio, and the legislative gains provided the political base for securing approval for such actions. In short, the years 1971–72 had left Gilligan and the Democrats financially and politically positioned to carry into being the progressive government they had long argued Ohio needed.

Delivering his State of the State address to the General Assembly on January 17, 1973, Gilligan outlined the policy moves he had a mind: the restoration of public confidence in popular government through adoption of ethics legislation; progress on environmental protection; improvement in the lives of Ohio's mentally and physically disabled; action to curb the explosive growth in welfare costs; creation of a Business and Employment Council to determine how best to bolster the state's somewhat faltering economy; stronger support for education. All these, he emphasized, would be achieved with no new general taxes being imposed or increased. Near the close of his long address, Governor Gilligan stated: "Our job now is to demonstrate that we can make government work; that we can make government truly responsible to the real needs of the people; that we can force government to measure up to the highest standards of economy, efficiency and basic honesty. And that is *exactly* what we are going to do."[2]

In the General Assembly, the leadership positions had been decided. In the Senate, Republican Theodore Gray remained as president pro tempore, with Anthony Calabrese returning as minority leader for the Democrats. In the House of Representatives, now controlled by the Democrats, former minority leader A. G. Lancione was elevated to Speaker, with Vern Riffe as Speaker pro tempore, Barney Quilter as majority floor leader, William Mallory (the first African American to hold a Democratic leadership position) as assistant majority floor leader, and Richard Celeste as majority whip. On the Republican side, former Speaker Charles Kurfess was named minority leader, with Norman Murdock as assistant minority leader and Alan Norris as minority whip.

The core of Gilligan's own administration consisted of Jack Hansan as chief of staff, Bill Chavanne as legislative liaison, Phil Moots as counsel to the governor, Jay Tepper as finance director, Max Brown as communications director, and Bob Daley as assistant to the governor. People—governors included—are influenced by those with whom they surround themselves. But Gilligan's term in office was more broadly influenced by two general factors.

In the early 1970s, the Democratic Party nationally was in neither a particularly imaginative or unified place. The party carried deep fissures from the war in Vietnam, a matter around which there were long and not entirely forgiving memories. These fissures were not closed by the 1972 nomination of South Dakota senator George McGovern, an early and outspoken opponent of the war, whose landslide defeat was not universally mourned by party regulars. The general party infighting was an obstacle to outward-looking and creative governance. Paralleling this, Gilligan later pointed out that the "ball was pretty much in Nixon's court." And the game Nixon and those around him played was "hardball." Gilligan commented, "Nixon's modus operandi was a very personal kind of politics. It was venomous stuff."[3] Most Democratic office holders were not anxious to present the high profile that might call presidential wrath down on them. As a consequence, Gilligan recalled, "there wasn't any [Democratic] governor around that was out there leading the pack and organizing the armies. It was, in a sense, every state for itself."[4]

Gilligan's biennial administration was also heavily influenced by his experience with the Charter movement in Cincinnati. Charter, he felt, raised a central question not often seriously answered: What is politics for? In Gilligan's view, many, if not most, in politics regarded the undertaking as rather "like baseball," a contest in which everybody cheers for his or her team with no test other than victory and no measure other than the rewards which flow from that victory. What Gilligan had internalized from Charter was that politics was the self-conscious act of changing society for the betterment of those individuals who comprised it. In Cincinnati politics, Gilligan had broken with the Charterites to pursue a career as an independent Democrat. In office as Ohio governor as an independent Democrat, he found himself still influenced by the Charter approach. "I don't think there's any question that it had a direct influence on what our administration did. Our administration was not that which could have been expected from the conventional Democratic Party proposals of that time."[5]

Speaking the previous December to the Cleveland City Club, Gilligan noted that on taking office he had been given charge of twenty-three departments, eighty-seven agencies and bureaus, and 183 boards of commission. "No one, the governor of Ohio included," he commented, "knew how they all fit together. As a matter of fact, they didn't."[6] For Gilligan, one aspect of addressing the state's problems was a rationalizing of its administrative structure. That Ohio had a combined Department of Mental Hygiene and Corrections was, Gilligan often commented, why the prisons were run like asylums and the asylums were run like prisons. One action was to create separate departments to oversee the state's prisoners and to tend to its mentally and physically disabled.

Gilligan had four other reorganizations in mind: merge the Department of Development and the Department of Urban Affairs into a single agency; establish an Environmental Protection Agency; divide the Department of Finance between the Department of Administrative Services and the Office of Management and Budget; and create the Department of Transportation by combining previously scattered transportation functions.

In all, the State of Ohio had approximately two dozen governmental departments, each of whose directors and staffs were generally engaged in tasks of utility and consequence. The Gilligan administration can be best illuminated not with a laundry list of what was attempted by each of these departments but, rather, by its treatment in some depth of four areas—areas in which the Gilligan administration's actions represented abrupt departures from the practices of past state administrations, both Republican and Democratic: mental health and prison reform, the *humane environment;* environmental protection, the *physical environment;* economic development, the *economic environment;* and ethics and campaign financing, the *political environment.*

28

The Humane Environment

In October 1969, *Columbus Dispatch* reporter David Lore undertook a five-part look at Ohio's mental health and intellectual and developmental disability programs. Lore may have felt under some pressure not to paint too bleak a scene, to be even-handed in the journalistic sense. So among other things, he wrote of programs in operation for the educable disabled and of the marginally increased receptivity some Ohio towns had shown in easing younger patients back into the community for short-term employment. But his more typical articles offered readers information like this:

> In one typical Hawthornden ward, one hundred or so elderly patients share five sinks, three toilets, and two bathtubs in a crumbling fifty-year old building. The chief activity on the ward is television, but the set is broken.
>
> At Orient State Institution, one woman attendant struggles to keep up with thirty-seven severely retarded young boys in a ward dayroom. The odor of the room indicates few of the youngsters are toilet trained.[1]

The day of his visit, Lore noted in the piece, was sunny and pleasant: still, none of the patients was allowed out to enjoy it since there were not enough attendants to keep control of them.

Part of the problem, of course, was money—the state spent about $7 a day on each inpatient in its institutional care, which compared to what one public administrator reported was the $82 dollars a day typically spent per patient in private clinics. Money tied to chronic understaffing. On "bad days and usually during the night shift," Lore reported, one attendant might be singly responsible for several hundred patients.[2] Chronic understaffing fed low morale and high turnover. And, given the age of the state's institutions—the lack of sprinklers, the crowding of beds packed just inches apart, the shortage of attendants, the drugged state of many individuals, and the locked doors—there was the ever-present hazard of fire. Also,

most of the patients under the state's care were in large institutional settings—
Cleveland State had 1,125 patients, Columbus State 1,800, Hawthornden 1,500. And
then there was the anomaly that the department responsible for Ohio's institutions
for the mentally and physically disabled also operated the state's prisons—in effect,
the Department of Mental Hygiene and Corrections was, in reality, the Department of Incarceration. During the late 1950s, Governor Michael DiSalle had toured
such facilities, sometimes with reporters in tow, and on at least one occasion was
said to have vomited on his exit. Coming a decade later, the Lore series showed
how little had changed.

John Joyce Gilligan was a man of opinions, many of them strongly held. But
no issue during his four-year governorship was as close to his heart as the desire to improve the lot of those citizens of Ohio most dependent on the state for
their survival and well-being. At the time he took office, Gilligan said, "the mental
health facilities in the state of Ohio were just a stinking disgrace."[3] Nine of the ten
mental hospitals had been declared ineligible to receive Medicare funds because
they failed to meet the pertinent accrediting standards. "All of these facilities were
badly understaffed," Gilligan said. "Maintenance was absolutely deplorable. The
provisioning of these places—food and medical supplies, especially the food—
was a source of income for the managers of the facility . . . Usually the administrators had a comfortable working relationship with their major supplier."[4]

Things looked no better at closer range. Early on, Gilligan paid a visit to Orient
State Hospital, about thirty miles outside Columbus.

I was the first governor, so far as anybody knew, to set foot on the grounds. There
was a large building that had been a home for the aged, with some smaller buildings around it. I asked what was going on in these smaller buildings and I was
escorted to have a look. Incredibly enough, on the first floor there was no furniture; there was what amounted to a cage taking up about a quarter of the room.
In the cage was a very large fellow of indeterminate age. He could have been in
his twenties or his forties. He was clearly beyond being able to communicate with
anybody. He was kept in there, and he was fed three times a day by sliding a tray
under the door and into his cage. He ate what he ate and left the rest. And I asked,
"How do you keep him clean?" He had no clothes on beyond shorts. What it
amounted to was that they hosed him down a couple of days a week.[5]

And the most appalling part, Gilligan said, was that the individual in question
was not intellectually disabled; he was a deaf mute. Born profoundly deaf to parents who soon thereafter died or disappeared, he never had his disability diag-
nosed, and no effort was made to teach him the rudiments of communication.
During his visit, Gilligan ordered that some better provision be made for the man
and then made some point of tracking his progress. (By the time the governor left

office, the man in question was employed in a sheltered workshop.) At a second facility he visited, Gilligan said he encountered "people sitting in a circle around a large room. I realized, these people were just doped. They spent their lives just sitting in chairs staring at other people. It was just weird and ugly."[6]

Staffing was a particular problem. Gilligan later stated, "As a general observation, which may be unfair, the level of personal competence of the state employees was modest. They were timeservers; not particularly interested in rocking the boat." This, he added, was "especially true in areas like mental health and the prisons."[7] Gilligan's efforts in the areas of mental health and mental retardation began with two steps. First, he moved to sever the operation of the state's mental institutions from those of its prisons, establishing a separate Department of Mental Health and Retardation. The House of Representatives approved this step on November 4, 1971, and the Senate did so unanimously on March 24, 1972. With that vote, the *Dayton Daily News* editorialized, "Ohio can make strong, solid progress in an area which state government neglected too long, at a great cost in human misery."[8]

His second move was to create a citizens' task force to review the state's programs in mental health and developmental disabilities and to make recommendations. Headed by Cleveland psychiatrist Dr. Victor M. Victoroff, the task force included an expected range of medical and lay personnel. Its report, submitted in mid-October 1971, "accent[ed] the failure of leadership and the absence of professionally trained persons in crucial levels where decisions are made in the department . . . [and] documented the low quality and quantity of manpower; the decrepit equipment; poor morale; lack of coordination; and impoverished funding as faults of the system."[9] This being said, the task force nonetheless stressed that the system's "most grievous fault" was the lack of competent leadership.[10]

Here, Gilligan focused his efforts. He later recalled that through contacts with various national mental health organizations, "we came up with the names of some experienced people in this area. We wanted to bring them in to redesign and reinvigorate the program."[11] The obstacle to this happening, he said, was that Ohio "couldn't touch the salaries that most of these people commanded."[12] Ohio's long-standing commitment to tightened purse strings extended to the salaries of those who headed state departments. Two highly regarded candidates for the state position turned down the directorship of Mental Hygiene and Corrections; each was already making $7,500–10,000 more to run a city-level program. In this circumstance, legislative liaison John McDonald persuaded Republican legislative leaders to make an exception to the state's salary schedule and raise remuneration for the director post to $37,500, thereby making this position the highest-paid in the state, after the governor.

For this post, Gilligan sought someone with "academic knowledge and a working knowledge of systems of government."[13] Gilligan found his candidate in Dr. Kenneth Gaver, a psychiatrist who had served for five years as deputy director of the Oregon mental health system. Gaver had entered public service after having found "private practice not to my liking—sitting in the same chair day after day, listening to the same patients talk about the same problems. It was pretty boring."[14] As deputy director in Oregon, Gaver had worked with a mix of mental hospitals, facilities for the intellectually disabled, and substance abuse programs. He had found the work intellectually appealing: "I had to analyze, create, advocate, and learn to write legislation."[15] Gaver, a Republican who had largely worked with Republican officials in Oregon, felt he had a sure hand in dealing with state legislatures. He accepted the position in Ohio even before passage of the December 1971 tax increase that would bring considerable additional money to the program he would direct. Ohio's historic low budgets did not concern him; he had considerable confidence in his ability to get money out of a legislature, though whether the confidence he'd gained in relatively liberal Oregon would have proved effective in Ohio was never put to the test.

Gilligan was committed to the issue. He received monthly county-by-county reports of how often his name had appeared in the local press on matters related to mental health and development. And he paid routine visits to the state facilities, where, accompanied by superintendents and staff, he would ask, among other questions, "What do you need to improve this?" On those visits he learned that it was often "the first time that most of these people had been asked that question by anyone in a position to do anything about it. Many had just abandoned hope of ever improving things."[16] As Gilligan recalled:

> The pleasant surprise was to find people, often in intermediate positions, who were dedicated people—to caring for the sick or building highways. They were not only decent people; they were often heroic people in many respects. When word began to get out and around that I was visiting such places—and I always had Bob Daley with me taking notes, to ensure there'd be some follow up. As the word got out in those institutions, people began surfacing and speaking their minds and stating their experiences. We were inundated with lament and complaint. I confess I hadn't known a damn thing about it. I had lived in Ohio all my life and had no reason to believe that there was anything untoward going on [in state-run institutions], and I'm sure the vast majority of people in Ohio had no reason to think so either.[17]

The need of the mentally and physically disabled was the public issue that most engaged the attention of First Lady Katie Gilligan. She visited—perhaps with some distress—a number of state institutions, including an October 3, 1973, stop at the Warner School for the Mentally Retarded in Cleveland, and attended the National Mental Health Association gathering in Atlanta, one of the few times she traveled out of Ohio on state business.

Gilligan had no training or particular expertise in the field of mental health. Kenneth Gaver, however, found him to be an informed ally: "Governor Gilligan had about as good a knowledge of mental health issues as anyone whose primary business was state politics."[18] That understanding, and the governor's strong support for the measures that Gaver wished to undertake, was, according to the doctor, "crucial."[19]

That was something of a later judgment, however. Kenneth Gaver reached his new position only to be dropped into a controversy. The Ohio system included nineteen mental health institutions, six institutions for the intellectually and developmentally disabled, and three institutions through the division of forensic psychiatry, which included the Lima State Hospital for the criminally insane. At the time of Gaver's appointment, the *Cleveland Plain Dealer* was undertaking an investigation into charges that staff at the Lima State Hospital had severely beaten a number of inmates. Reviewing the situation, Gaver concluded that the newspaper's accusations were accurate. Eventually, indictments were handed up against thirty-two employees. The first two trials ended in acquittals—possibly, Gaver believed, because Allen County juries lacked sympathy with the alleged victims of the assaults. Attorney General William Brown then secured a new venue for the remaining trials. (The judge receiving the cases was apparently less than happy with the arrangement, as it would make his jurisdiction responsible for the costs of prosecution.) In the end, the thirty remaining suspects each pled guilty to misdemeanor assault; they retained their positions of employment at Lima State but were ordered to undergo job retraining. Gaver said that the feeling against those thirty among the general employee population at Lima State was sufficiently strong that virtually all left the state's employ within a month.

Despite that unpleasant start, things proceeded fairly smoothly. Gaver had the great advantage of being the first Ohio mental health director who was both a board-certified psychiatrist and an experienced public administrator. The existing staff, Gaver said, "knew that I was a professional. It was an entirely new light at the top."[20]

The staff Gaver inherited, a department report said, was "poorly trained."[21] An executive order issued April 10, 1972, mandated improvements. First, staff improvements were, Gaver believed, key to the whole reform. In 1970, each of the 100 employees had been responsible for 199 patients; by 1974, the patient load *per hundred staff* dropped to 124.3; the number of trained psychiatric aides increased from 3,348 to 4,830; the number of attendants (those with no formal patient care training) dropped from 2,488 to 854.

Second, Gaver established priorities for improving the physical condition of the state facilities. The conditions in the schools for the physically disabled were very bad—"people slumping in old broken benches and wooden chairs."[22] Such defective furnishings and other unsafe conditions were more of a cost than a savings, since the failure to meet applicable safety codes was a major reasons state institutions had been declared ineligible for Medicare reimbursement. Adoption of the 1973–74 state budget proved a watershed. That budget carried a 31 percent increase in spending on mental health, the largest of any department. It was a figure that drew some expression of doubt from House minority leader Charles Kurfess, who noted that the increase was three times that being received by public education and asked on the floor on the General Assembly whether such a disparity indeed reflected the priorities of the state. In 1973, only two members of the state legislature took part in a bus trip to the Orient State institution, with "some members complaining that the tour was just a poorly planned exercise in lobbying."[23] But if state legislators did not greatly wish to see the condition of state institutions, they were nonetheless prepared to vote substantial sums to improving them. New furnishings arrived at most institutions. Gaver recalled being present when several tractor trailers arrived at Orient State delivering new furniture for virtually the whole institution.

Beyond additional staffing, training, and equipment, the increased funds went to a "humanization" program, a series of incremental improvements in facilities and programming—everything from $80,000 to remodel the gym at Cambridge State, $15,000 for a "time out" room at the Athens Mental Health Center, and $7,260 for a barbershop at Lima State to $80 for two ping-pong tables at Longview State Hospital. Laboratory facilities were reequipped and darkrooms added. Kenneth Gaver commented, "You have no idea how happy the dentists were that they no longer had to develop a child's x-rays inside of old battery boxes."[24]

Not all improvements were financially intensive. The department, for example, initiated a program in which ordinary citizens "adopted" individual children in facilities for the developmentally challenged, acting as a sort of foster parent to visit the child and provide the greater level of attention that was an important part of the care. The effort, Gilligan said, "drew an enormous turnout."[25] Governor Gilligan shared with Gaver an appreciation of the ceremonial. Ohio, at the time, presented a certificate to any institutional resident who lived to age 100. On one such centennial, Gilligan turned up at Orient State to bestow such a certificate on a patient. Gilligan was also on hand when an acetylene torch was used to cut the iron doors off of one of the buildings, a matter of both practical and symbolic significance.

The Gilligan-Gaver era in state mental health programs fell within a major transition in professional thinking within the field, one characterized by the word "deinstitutionalization." The general reckoning was that mentally ill and developmentally disabled individuals would fare far better if they were removed from large, impersonal institutions and placed into smaller, community-based programs that could facilitate their reentry into society. Describing the approach at the time, Gaver said in a March 1974 interview that large institutions never have the staffing or funding necessary to be of significant help to their inmates.

For some years, deinstitutionalization was generally viewed as the welcome wave of the future—better for the suffering and more cost-effective for the states. (In most states, mental health services ranked with education and welfare as the three largest expenditures.) Ohio had started to move with this trend prior to Gilligan's inauguration. Since 1971, one departmental report stated, "the department has been developing a computer-assisted diagnosis and periodic review system to maximize the match of patient needs to institutional resources."[26] As a consequence, the average daily resident population fell from 16,264 in 1970 to 14,377 by the end of 1971, 12,848 in 1972, 11,980 in 1973, and 10,220 by 1974.

Despite the apparent advantages of deinstitutionalization, it was also the subject of unintended consequences. While, from the patient's standpoint, it made great sense to be moved out of large, impersonal institutions, the fact was that the outside world was not particularly anxious to see the mentally ill move into locally established community-based facilities. In part, Gaver said, the problem was simply one of "not in my backyard": individual neighborhoods fought becoming the setting for a half-way house for people they regarded as different and potentially dangerous.[27] Another issue was money: on a per-patient basis, community mental health proved to be more expensive than state care and placed a burden on counties and cities. Quite simply, large institutions enjoyed economies of scale; supervision was simpler when patients were aggregated, meals were less expensive when prepared in bulk.

The most serious failing of deinstitutionalization, in Gaver's view, was the failure to appreciate the necessity of providing low-cost, supervised housing for those released from large institutions. Deinstitutionalization received widespread support from lay groups nationally; unfortunately, Gaver said, many public advocates of deinstitutionalization lacked an adequate understanding of the needs of those they advocated for: "We had a bunch of people who didn't understand that you had to prepare a place for the people to live."[28] The discharged patient would "need support and supervised living in the community. There was a deficiency of understanding on the part of people who were pushing so hard."[29] And, he acknowledged, "We in the field didn't understand that either." Four decades later, the subject still rankles. In a 2010 interview, Gaver stated, "I wish I had understood the key factor of housing."[30]

Gaver's thinking paralleled Gilligan's own. In reflecting on his public life, Gilligan called attention to two mistakes he made. The first was that, as a city councilman, he had not been more sensitive to how the Interstate highways converging on Cincinnati would tear up that city's neighborhoods and had not sought means to lessen the impact. The second was deinstitutionalization.

It was a big mistake that we made—and which I have since regretted through the years. The idea was that these people needed a different environment in which to live; they needed training. We thought if we closed these warehouses, the burden would be taken up by facilities in the various communities, closer to the patients' homes. What I failed to appreciate was that there was not a terrible amount of enthusiasm on the local level to pick up the funding burden. It was in many respects a disaster. These people began showing up at police courts and drunk tanks and in many cases simply being abandoned to the streets. We helped some people in some ways, but we also caused a lot of trouble.[31]

The debate over deinstitutionalization, and the lessons that might be learned from it, continued within the mental health field well after Jack Gilligan and Ken Gaver passed from the Ohio government scene. The fact remained that the level of care and attention paid to Ohio's mentally disturbed and physically and developmentally challenged was raised enormously during the administration of Jack Gilligan. Money is not the measure of all things, but measures of money are suggestive: under Gilligan, Ohio's expenditures per patient rose from $3,914 in 1970 to an average of $8,468 in 1974.

Gilligan had in Dr. Gaver a considerable admirer. The psychiatrist labeled Gilligan as simply "a great governor."[32] Among other things, he said that Gilligan kept political concerns out of the department's administration. And Gaver saw the prospect of continued improvement. In a comprehensive 1974 document entitled "Promise," he outlined in detail an ensuing decade for Ohio that would be characterized by services delivered closer to a patient's home, care that would be more comprehensive with the rights of patients better protected. He was optimistic that this and perhaps more could be achieved. He said he drew up that plan at a time when he felt "a general sense of progress within the department" and that his own standing was secure. Nonetheless, shortly after submitting his "Promise" for the future, Gaver submitted his resignation.[33]

Gaver's record in Ohio had brought him some attention. He was interviewed for the post of director of the American Psychiatric Association, and the State of Texas attempted to recruit him, among other possibilities. Still, it was not visions of sugarplums that prompted his resignation. He had concluded that Gilligan was not going to be reelected. It was, he recalled, "a gut feeling, and one I felt fairly strongly."[34] He recalled attending a Gilligan campaign appearance in Cleveland at which the governor talked at some length about the progress Ohio was making in mental health and disabilities reform. "I was thinking, 'Oh, my gosh! This is no way to get votes.'"[35] Gaver believed that if Republican James Rhodes was returned to the Governor's Mansion, the days of generous funding of and executive concern for mental and developmental health programs in Ohio would be over. And so he resigned.

Later, following the defeat that Gaver predicted, Gilligan reflected on his administration's work with the mentally and developmentally disabled. He told a campaign volunteer disappointed by the election's outcome: "Because all of us worked together, thousands of Ohioans—especially the weak and the helpless, the poor, the ill, the elderly and the handicapped—will have had a little better life. No one can call that a defeat."[36]

As in mental health, in prison reform the Gilligan administration's energy was largely directed at reversing the legacy of earlier thinking. Again, Gilligan created a citizens' task force, which he assigned to Bernard Friedman, a judge in Cuyahoga County's Common Pleas Court. The task force's final report, issued in December 1971, advocated creation of smaller prisons more closely located to the urban areas that were the homes of many inmates; the immediate closing of the Mansfield Reformatory; community-based alternatives to incarceration; and higher salaries for all prison personnel to attract a better workforce, particularly more young people and more blacks. The report stated that Ohio's prison system "must share at least part of the blame" for the general increase in crime.[37]

   One phrase used in both the mental health and prison reform efforts was "humanization"—what was thought of as the simple better treatment of those who were in the custody of the state. On August 4, 1971, Gilligan ordered an end to censorship of prisoner mail so that inmates "may retain some sense of dignity."[38] While both incoming and outgoing mail was examined for contraband, letters themselves no longer were read by a censor. Within a week, the number of letters mailed from the Ohio Penitentiary in Columbus increased from 1,800 to 4,000 daily. Planning also began on a system that would eventually establish a secondary school system that would operate in seven state prisons. Also instituted was a prisoner furlough program, a measure Gilligan described as "a significant step toward turning our correctional system into a true rehabilitation system."[39] Under the program, inmates who had served one-third or more of their sentences would be eligible for furlough provided a suitable employment or training setting could be identified.

   There were, however, limits to the reform efforts. Gilligan and Commissioner of Corrections Benjamin Cooper rejected a petition from the all-male inmates at the Ohio Penitentiary seeking permission to place phone calls to inmates at the Marysville Reformatory for Women. On Friday, March 24, 1972, 50 of the 135 guards scheduled to work the 6:00 P.M. shift at the Ohio Penitentiary in Columbus called in sick; the following day, 83 of the 185-man scheduled crew did likewise; and on Sunday night, only 11 guards showed up for duty. Behind the action, said a union spokesperson, was the guards' demand for hazard pay and other benefits, a demand they pressed even though a 38-cent hourly increase over the normal hazard pay was pending. In the meantime, supervisory personnel and "healthy" guards working extra shifts were called into action. Prisoners were for several days kept in their cells. That Monday, Gilligan directed the state personnel director to initiate efforts to hire replacements for guards who refused to work. His position was backed by the Ohio Civil Service Employees Association, which called on all employees to return to work immediately. With those steps, the sick-in ended.

More generally, Gilligan faced prison reform problems similar to those in the mental health field: oversized, outmoded, and physically decrepit facilities and understaffing and underfunding. In January 1972, Gilligan announced that the state was spending $32 million a year to maintain prisons that were "not much more than human powder kegs."[40] Elaborating on his theme, Gilligan said the state prison system served neither the inmate nor society, "for instead of preventing crime, the prisons have in fact been encouraging it."[41]

The worst of the state system was the 140-year-old Ohio Penitentiary at 245 West Spring Street near the Columbus downtown. The prison had various claims to notoriety. At the turn of the century it had housed prisoner number 30664, William Sydney Porter, better known for his pen name, O. Henry. Gruesomely, the prison had also been the site of a horrific 1930 fire, in which 322 inmates died, most of them trapped in their cells. On January 18, 1973, Gilligan announced his intention to "abandon and demolish" the facility, which he termed "a symbol of all that is wrong with the existing penal system in Ohio."[42] Events moved more slowly than that statement would suggest, however. On June 29, a number of the prison buildings closed, and the prisoners were transferred elsewhere. A portion of the remaining facility was remodeled as the Ohio Correction Medical Center. A later court order directed that the remainder of the facility be closed by 1979.

The closing of the state pen had been made possible by the opening of the long-planned $30 million prison at Lucasville. The new prison was just the sort of large, impersonal facility that both Gilligan and the task force under Judge Friedman had opposed; further, it was located a considerable distance from the homes of most of its inmates. The prison was located in Scioto County, in which barely 2 percent of the population was African American, while the prison population was about 50 percent black.

On July 24, 1973, two guards at the facility were slain by inmates. Gilligan stood by his Department of Corrections director Bennett Cooper. On August 10, the *Columbus Dispatch* reported that former members of Gilligan's prison task force, having toured the Lucasville facility and talking with both prisoners and "a few" guards, were "broadly critical of prison management" and that individual guards had "sought revenge" on prisoners following the murders of their coworkers.[43] In turn, Gilligan blamed "irresponsible journalists and scandal mongers" for reports that the facility was riddled with narcotics and homosexuality and virtually controlled by prisoner gangs. He further noted, "On the one hand, we hear Lucasville is a country club; on the other hand, that it is a hell hole."

Gilligan stood by the facility he had not welcomed, telling a town meeting in Lancaster that the new Lucasville prison was "a heckuva a lot better than the Ohio

Pen as far as physical facilities are concerned."[44] Two days later, Lucasville superintendent W. J. Whealon submitted his resignation. And several days later agreement was reached between the administration and the unions representing the employees that guards would be permitted to carry nightsticks and mace inside the prison.

Despite the troubles at Lucasville, Gilligan was inclined to believe that the efforts in the prison field had been more successful than those in mental health: "We did a much better job over the span of time with the prisons, because there were a smaller number of institutions involved and there were some professional people already in there who when given some support and some resources were able to do a better job."[45]

29

The Physical Environment

Characterizing the physical environment he inherited, Gilligan said: "When I became governor, every public beach on Lake Erie was closed as a health hazard. And as I drove along the highway, you just saw sign after sign: No swimming, No fishing, etc. It was an outrage that a natural resource like Lake Erie was being shut off to the public."[1]

It was a judgment shared by many others. A month following Gilligan's inauguration, the February 12, 1971, issue of *Science* carried a report of how an established biologist "startled and amused" an audience of ecologists by proposing that the western third of Lake Erie be given up as lost. The speaker proposed that a dam be built from Cedar Point on the lake's Ohio shore to Point Pelee on the opposite Canadian side. This separate section of the lake would be used as a "sewage lagoon" for the waters of the Detroit, Maumee, Raisin, and Portage rivers. There, aerobic degradation would reduce the level of the water's pollution before it was released into the eastern two-thirds of the lake, thereby affording that portion of Lake Erie a measure of protection. As the article indicated, the speaker was finding a new way to emphasize a widely entertained possibility: Lake Erie might be passing the point of no return.[2]

Pollution not only prevented recreational use of Lake Erie; it had largely killed off the lake's once-thriving fishing industry. Early in his administration, on May 8, 1971, Gilligan invoked a sixty-day ban on commercial fishing for white bass in Lake Erie due to high concentrations of mercury. The causes of the lake's woes were simple enough to identify. As Gilligan noted, "Industries and municipalities were the main sources of the pollution; municipal sewage and industrial dumping went right out into the lake" in vast and unending quantities.[3] Gilligan noted that, though "a pretty broad statement, . . . when I took office, for all practical purposes there was no environmental law in Ohio."[4] Journalist Richard Zimmerman attributed this in part to "Rhodes' preoccupation with industrial development ('Jobs!

Jobs! Jobs!') [which] resulted in his abysmal record for controlling pollution in general and acid rain in particular."[5]

Again, Gilligan sought to clarify direction and to build consensus through the creation of a task force—in this case, the Citizens Task Force on Environmental Protection. The body's chairmanship went to John Glenn, to give the state's most popular Democrat a public role. The fifty-one-member body drew broad representation from industry, academia, and environmental and civic groups, with its efforts supported by a team of experts, among them Ira L. Whitman, then director of urban and regional programs at the Battelle Memorial Institute.

In its introduction, the task forces' report, which was submitted on June 22, 1971, acknowledged that the nation was pointing its finger at the Buckeye State: "A 'dying' Lake Erie, the burning Cuyahoga River, the air-polluted city of Steubenville . . . [have become] nationally recognized symbols of environmental degradation."[6] The chief recommendation made of the task force was that a cabinet-level Department of Environmental Protection be created to coordinate all existing and new environmental efforts. Beyond that, the report urged Ohio to limit discharge of pollutants into rivers and streams and, by the mid-1970s, charge polluters for doing so. Additionally, the state should move to protect its natural resources; encourage use of recycled materials; undertake soil conservation and erosion control; and keep environmental considerations in mind when deciding where new power plants should be located.

On August 11, the Gilligan administration introduced its environmental protection bill to the General Assembly. The proposal, *Gongwer* noted, was "based almost exclusively on the recommendations of Colonel Glenn's task force."[7] Gilligan's message accompanying the bill said that it represented "the first response to what I believe is one of the most urgent and complex challenges facing our society."[8] Notably, the bill carried bipartisan sponsorship—at this stage of things, environmental protection had considerable appeal to both political parties. In the Senate, the bill gathered nineteen cosponsors, led by Oliver Ocasek (D-Summit); in the House, the thirty cosponsors were led by Chester Cruze (R-Cincinnati).

In politics, timing may not be all, but it is a great deal. Gilligan's decision to move on environmental protection came barely fifteen months after the first celebration of Earth Day, April 22, 1970, which drew a level of participation that impressed even its organizers. That event was shortly followed by passage of the Clean Air Act of 1970, the first in a series of major federal actions that included the 1972 Water Pollution Control Act Amendments and the 1974 Safe Drinking Water Act—landmark legislation that established a framework of federal law and set minimum performance standards. Federal regulation allowed states the option of establishing their own environmental protection agencies or of locating the function within an existing state agency or agencies. Failing this, the federal government would administer the laws directly—an option most states were anxious to avoid.

Gilligan decided that Ohio would have a single-focus Environmental Protection Agency (EPA), the model that in practice was adopted by most states. Bill
Nye, director of the Ohio Department of Natural Resources (ODNR), however,
was widely believed to want the environmental function placed within his agency.
This was made clear when, by chance, Alan Farkas, who had served as executive
director of the environmental task force, was in a legislative corridor one evening
when he heard Bill Blair, ODNR's legislative assistant, talking in a darkened committee room with an unnamed state senator. Farkas, in eloquent recollection, "assumed nefarious intent."[9] He confronted the pair, who acknowledged planning an
amendment that would put EPA within ODNR. Farkas said: "I took Bill Blair to a
pay phone and I called Jimmy Friedman at home, and I told Jimmy Friedman that
Blair was standing outside the phone booth and I wanted him to tell Blair that in
no way, shape, or form did the governor support this."[10]

Indeed, Ohio's EPA was evidence that the state's government was not immune
to infighting. In August 1972, shortly before the agency's actual establishment, Bill
Nye urged that the Ohio EPA and ODNR be housed in the same building due
to the "inherently interrelated" functions they served. One Gilligan staffer wrote
Jack Hansan, chief of staff, saying, "I think we all understand that his motive on
paper is to stay close to the EPA thing in hope of some future development."[11]
This prompted Hansan to write to Nye that "the need for EPA to be separate at the
beginning of its existence outweighs all other considerations."[12] Further, once in
operation, Ohio EPA at times crossed swords with the attorney general's office. Not
formally part of the Gilligan administration, the attorney general at times undertook legal actions against polluters with which EPA was simultaneously attempting to reach voluntary compliance. A certain amount of bad blood ensued. When
EPA director Ira Whitman, likely intending a compliment, said that the attorney
general's office had "some good lawyers over there," it drew an offended response:
"Why just 'some'? Why just 'good?'"[13]

Within the General Assembly, the notion of a strong EPA had more support
in the House than in the Senate. Not until May 9, 1972, nine months after the
original legislation had been introduced, did a "far less ambitious" version emerge
from the Senate Environmental Affairs Committee.[14] The Senate version dropped
the requirement that the EPA director's approval was needed in determining new
utility sites; it eliminated a planned trust fund to finance antipollution measures;
and it removed the option that private citizens could file environmental lawsuits
(which drew sharp criticism from Ohio Chapter of the Sierra Club as a serious
weakening of the proposed legislation).

Gilligan's own thinking remained expansive. Speaking that same day in Columbus to the local chapter of the Sierra Club, Gilligan said he still favored folding
the existing pollution control boards, the existing ODNR, and the newly mandated functions into a single agency, as advocated by the citizens' task force the

previous year. Such an agency, Gilligan told the audience, would allow the state "to work on the causes of environmental pollution and not just its effects, and by doing so begin to prevent pollution rather than simply react to it."[15]

On June 20, *Gongwer* reported that the House would defer until July 6 any effort to pass the EPA bill. At the time, only twenty-five Democrats and seventeen Republicans were pledged to support the weaker Senate measure, eight fewer than required for passage. With the House and Senate divided, Speaker Charles Kurfess took the lead: "I got a call—'things have blown up in the [conference] committee; everything is falling apart.'"[16] Kurfess directed that a dozen key people from the legislature and administration be in his office the following morning. His recalled, "We spent the day creating that bill—'this is in, this is not in.' Even my own legislators criticized me for putting it together behind closed doors."[17] The press, however, generally gave Kurfess credit (which, Kurfess said, "told me that when the media passes judgment on the legislative process, their judgment of the process depends on how well they like the product").[18]

The question, then, was whether Gilligan would settle for the result. Farkas recalled, "I remember very distinctly having a meeting in the governor's office talking about what to do next. And he said, 'Alan, I learned as a young man that sometimes the devil is described as the perfectionist. The bill that gets past the Senate may not be what you and I might want it to be, but we need to get a bill passed, and you have to work with the Senate to get that done.'"[19] At a subsequent press conference, the governor said, "We will take what we can get and go from there. I will sign the bill and wish that it were stronger. I can't control the Assembly, the bill is considerably weaker than we intended."[20]

On July 24, Gilligan signed the legislation in a ceremony staged near the smokestack of the electric power station at the Columbus Municipal Lighting Plant, an example of the pollution the law was intended to attack. Gilligan vowed that the new agency would clean up the environment and make Ohio a better place for us to live."[21] Gilligan appointed Ira Whitman as director of the new agency. The agency, Whitman said, would be ready to go when the law became effective on October 23.

Two deputies were named prior to that date. Farkas was selected as deputy director for policy development, and Samuel Bleicher, on leave from the University of Toledo law school, was named deputy director of regulation. Farkas and Bleicher had had a curious meeting. Farkas, in his association with the task force, was speaking at the University of Toledo. He recalled being distracted by someone sitting in the front row, who he thought was kibitzing more than listening. After the talk, Farkas approached the individual, who proved to be Bleicher and who identified himself as a professor of environmental law. Farkas recalled saying, "This is no time to be teaching law. This is time to be making law."[22] (Additionally, in the 1968 Senate race, Bleicher had cochaired the Gilligan campaign in Lucas County.)

At about this time, the EPA, under a consultant's advice, decided to organize along functional lines—permitting, surveillance, etc.—rather than along "domain" lines, water, air, etc. The decision was to avoid any likelihood that a water problem might be declared solved simply by declaring it to be an air pollution problem. Environmental protection was then a hot topic with the media. Whitman, Bleicher, Farkas, and others were routinely invited to speak—to the press, to the Rotary, to local environmental groups. But with the agency's top officials preoccupied with hiring staff (eventually, agency employment reached 500, compared to ninety in its predecessor agencies), assigning responsibilities, and writing regulations, they had as yet very little to say. Bleicher recalled, "The press, almost on a daily basis, was asking, 'What are you going to do about pollution?'" What the agency wanted to say, Bleicher recalled, was "come back in six or eight months when we have something definite to report."[23]

Some early actions did occur. In late October 1972, Avon was selected to receive the EPA's first air permit, having "presented an admirable example of air pollution, water, and solid waste control."[24] On November 20, the agency issued permits to the Columbus & Southern Ohio Electric (C&SOE) generating facility, which the EPA praised for "taking the initiative when equipment is still under technological development while others are adopting a 'wait and see' attitude."[25] At the same time, the EPA ordered construction halts on three projects in Cambridge until approval of plans had been received, and it also was considering the possibility of taking legal action against Irondale, which had for eight months declined to respond to notification that it was violating a clean water order. In January 1973, the agency ordered Chemline Corporation of Lisbon to "cease and desist" the disposal of industrial waste into an abandoned strip mine in Columbiana County, as the waste was leeching into nearby waters.[26]

Within the charge given the Ohio EPA, three matters stood out: air pollution from coal-fired generation of electricity, water and air pollution from Ohio's heavy industry, and the waste dumping that was polluting Lake Erie.

In the early 1970s, the combustion of coal to produce electricity was the single largest source of air pollution in the state. Indeed, Ohio was the state most dependent on coal-generated electricity; it drew the highest percentage of its electricity from coal. EPA director Whitman recalled, "We put more time—Sam Bleicher, I, and others—into dealing with the electrical utility industries than into any other program."[27]

Two broad alternatives existed for reducing the resultant air pollution. One was to switch from relatively high-sulfur coal mined in Ohio to low-sulfur coal carried in by rail from Wyoming. The second was the installation of "scrubbers" to reduce the sulfur content of Ohio coal. Clearly, the Gilligan administration favored the latter course, which would protect the state's substantial mining industry. Whitman's position was that "since Ohio's utilities were the biggest coal burners in the country,

they should take the lead in advancing scrubbing technology."[28] The utilities de-
murred. Such technology, they argued, was unproven; its use might well make the
generating plants less efficient. (The EPA's case was less than airtight. Sam Bleicher
commented that "the cost of cleaning coal with 'scrubbers' seemed high enough
that it might not be warranted."[29] Indeed, later environmental thinking questioned
the efficacy of scrubbers and suggested that "clean" coal was simply a misnomer.)

The utilities did propose a solution: tall stacks. These 1,000-foot-high chim-
neys, the utilities argued, would expel pollution high enough into the atmosphere
that it would naturally disperse and cease to be a major problem to anyone. (In
time, tall stacks were associated with the acid rain that fell many miles to the east,
reinforcing the principle of what goes up must come down.)

On March 15, 1973, the Ohio EPA held a press conference in Cleveland at which
it announced that the fourteen major electrical generating stations in Ohio were
to bring their operations into compliance with the Ohio sulfur emissions regulations by July 1, 1975. The agency held public hearings on the feasibility of the mandate; the EPA issued a statement that "evidence presented . . . has not convinced
us that sulfur dioxide removal equipment is not available or proven."[30]

The electrical utilities ranked among Ohio's more sophisticated industries.
Whitman commented that they were "the hardest group with which to work. They
were respectful. They went through the motions, and they hired their lawyers."[31]
Their sophistication was not lessened when American Electric Power (AEP), a
New York–based utility holding company, acquired Columbus & Southern Ohio
Electric, adding it to its previously owned Ohio Power. As part of the acquisition,
AEP, in response to charges of being an absentee landlord, agreed to relocate its
corporate offices to Columbus. This caused something of a spilt in the Gilligan administration. According to Whitman, development director David Sweet favored
the move for the jobs it would bring. Whitman, however, thought otherwise: "I was
definitely opposed to them bringing their political clout to our backyard."[32] It was
clout, Whitman recalled, that AEP was soon exercising. In 1973, the corporation
began running large-scale advertisements in the Wall Street Journal and New York
Times "celebrating themselves on what good power providers they were and making the case for not having to submit to EPA's regulation."[33]

In drawing up Ohio's regulations, the state agency in some instances had adopted standards more stringent than those of the federal government. Thirteen
major utilities sued, arguing on narrow grounds that the regulations had been
improperly drafted. Hearings were held. On September 10, 1973, the hearing ex-
aminer ruled on behalf of the utilities. The examiners' report directed the Ohio
EPA to reduce its quality and stack pollution standards, adopt the more lenient
federal standards, and postpone its July 1, 1975, cleanup deadline for two years.

An editorial in the Akron Beacon Journal stated that "the report has rocked
the EPA, which sees it as undermining its efforts to make Ohio's air breathable."[34]

Nonetheless, the *Beacon Journal* headline editorialized, "A Little Easing Is Wise" and suggested that the EPA's "zeal to clean Ohio's air out-ran common sense." The generally liberal newspaper endorsed the two-year postponement, arguing that "the technology simply doesn't exist to provide proven [antipollution] systems. The investment required—estimated at $2 billion—would have to be paid for by the customers even if the systems don't work properly."[35]

Ohio had its heavily polluted districts. In Ironton, 100 miles south of Columbus, the *Dayton Daily News* reported, "the fog which reduces visibility here to one hundred feet or so on many mornings is not strictly nature's curse on the people. It is smog thickly laden with foul-smelling emissions from two large Allied Chemical Co. plants, a Dow Chemical Co. facility, the Armco Steel Works across the river in Ashland, Kentucky, and other industries."[36]

Nowhere in the state, however, were the residents more likely to gasp for air than in Steubenville, a community of 31,000 on the Ohio River's west bank. The pollution traced to the area's heavy industry: 11,000 jobs in steel, 1,150 in titanium, and 3,000 more in rail, coal, slag, and other industries. On January 26, 1973, Governor Gilligan issued a pollution warning for the Steubenville area, ordering all industries in Jefferson, Monroe, Belmont, and Columbiana counties "to curtail production to the greatest extent possible without actually shutting down."[37] State EPA officials had tagged a reading of sulfur dioxide of 292 micrograms per cubic meter of air—appreciably above the warning level of 263. The high reading, the National Weather Service reported, followed from a pollution-trapping inversion of warm air and little wind, conditions the forecasters expected to continue for at least another twenty-four hours. The following day, Gilligan took a similar action in Cleveland, ordering "all industry in the region to curtail all pollution emissions."[38] Air samples there had shown a particulate concentration of 499 micrograms per cubic meter of air for a twenty-four-hour period, nearly one-third higher than the alert level of 375.

Subsequently, the Ohio EPA issued pollution alerts for Steubenville again in early June 1973; on October 17, 1974, during which the highest readings ever recorded were reached; and on November 6, 1974. Industrial operations were curtailed each time. But some locals thought the bad air was a fairly minor price to pay for Steubenville's 15,000 good-paying jobs. One local official asked a representative of the state attorney's office: given that it took thirty years to get black lung disease, did a few days of bad air really matter?

(Steubenville was infamous for its low air quality. Harvard University's "Six Cities" study, conducted from 1974 to 1988, reported that Steubenville had the highest mortality rate, attributable in fair measure to inhalable particles and sulfates. A December 15, 2010, article in the *Pittsburgh Post-Gazette* noted that air quality had improved measurably since power plants in the region had installed scrubbers, but that the city was "still polluted."[39])

The largest concentration of heavy industry, however, was in the state's northeast quadrant. In early 1973, the U.S. and Ohio EPAs announced they would hold joint hearings in Youngstown on the issuance of pollution permits for major steelworks, including Republic Steel, U.S. Steel, and Youngstown Sheet & Tube. At that hearing, the various EPA officials were met with a united front: corporations and their workers stood together in opposition. Ira Whitman recalls, "The steel mills gave their union workers a half day off so they could picket the hearings."[40] Many carried signs—"Steel, Not Eels" and "Brass, Not Bass"—suggesting that jobs in heavy industry were of greater consequence than the well-being of Lake Erie's aquatic life. A vice president of U.S. Steel, Whitman reported, said that if his corporation was forced to spend 10 cents on water control, "we're shutting down this plant."[41] (Whitman said the plant was one of the less efficient in U.S. Steel's operation; it was possible, he speculated, that the corporation wanted to close it but welcomed the chance to lay the onus on the EPA.) The session in Youngstown, Whitman recalled, "was the one place in the state that there were unfriendly voices; the one place I felt uncomfortable."[42]

Youngstown Sheet & Tube was something of an exception—it was a home-grown industry and a source of considerable local pride and it was an aging facility. Several of its main competitors sat near the docking facilities of Cleveland. Those companies didn't have to haul their ore from the lake by rail to Youngstown; and they also had access to the water, the Cuyahoga River and Lake Erie, to use in cooling. Youngstown's Mahoning River was little more than a stream; and often the cooling process raised its temperature above 100 degrees Fahrenheit. One official commented, "We can remove all the pollutants, and once we've done that, it will be just fine for taking a bath."[43]

Of the steelworks involved, Whitman believes Youngstown Sheet & Tube was the most sincere in arguing that compliance would mean insolvency. It did make what appeared to be a good faith effort. On June 26, 1973, the *Youngstown Vindicator* announced that the Sheet & Tube would spend $20 million in the first year and eventually as much a $50 million in a pollution abatement program. Gilligan was present to award the company the Governor's Award for Community Action for undertaking the effort. Gilligan called it "gratifying" that such a large company began such "an ambitious program."[44] The residents of Youngstown, he said, would benefit from the cleaner air that would result. EPA director Whitman praised the Sheet & Tube for its cooperative and straightforward approach. The following September, the company announced that it would finance a fair measure of the improvements through the sale of tax-free revenue bonds.

In January 1974, the U.S. EPA endorsed water-quality standards for the Mahoning Valley. Labor union leaders expressed alarm that enforcement of such standards would render the Sheet & Tube untenable. Whitman wrote to Gilligan, "Friday, I issued a statement aimed at combating rumors that Youngstown

Sheet & Tube and other major manufacturers would be forced to close if the new standards were adopted, noting that the Ohio EPA has made a policy to work with industry and to take into consideration economic problems."[45] Sam Bleicher commented, "The Sheet & Tube was in the process of trying to issue bonds for pollution control—what should our enforcement position be with those industries that were trying?"[46]

Ohio was a relatively expensive place in which to achieve environmental cleanup. For electricity, the state relied heavily on high-sulfur Ohio coal and had to choose between the expense of scrubbers and the job losses that went with using a less polluting fuel. Heavy industry, so important to Ohio's economy, was a major polluter in its own right. Given that it was becoming relatively inefficient and less profitable, heavy industry had less financial margin to draw on for pollution control.

The steelmakers were a prime example. The domestic steel industry was in decline nationally; that decline was sharper among Ohio steelmakers, with lower production efficiency and higher labor costs. Before Ohio started losing jobs to Mexico and Asia, it was losing jobs to Texas and the Carolinas. Youngstown Sheet & Tube was among the first to announce the bad news. In the first nine months of 1975, its raw steel production dropped 38 percent. On "Black Monday," September 19, 1977, 5,000 workers were laid off, with the mill's remaining business transferred to Illinois. Whitman acknowledged that the negative effect of the mill's closing on Youngstown was considerably greater than the positive effect that its closing had on the Mahoning River.

Ohio's steelmaking belt was hardly the only place in the nation where there was negative reaction to the demands of environmental improvement. Writing in 1974 in *Science and Public Affairs,* Sally Jacobsen called attention to Illinois, where, in 1970, Republican governor Richard Ogilvie oversaw passage of strong environmental legislation and "appointed aggressive people to run the environment agencies and set the program on a course of strong environmental advocacy."[47] This was during the issue's early hey-day: the key measure passed the Illinois Senate by a 40–0 vote, with nine abstentions. For the moment, one legislator commented, opposing environmental action was akin to being "against Motherhood."[48]

Ogilvie's successor, Democrat Dan Walker, characterized the state EPA as arrogant and arbitrary. Major industry groups started totaling up the costs, actual or putative. The Illinois Chamber of Commerce said its review showed that five Illinois industries—industrial chemicals, blast furnaces and basic steel, petroleum refining, nonferrous secondary metals, and automotive and farm machinery—would be forced to lay out $720 million in capital expenditures to meet the costs of pollution control equipment. The Illinois Manufacturers Association asserted that the costs of complying with environmental standards had forced the closing of fourteen plants. Coal industry officials argued that enforcement of the original standards would cost the state 8,500 mining jobs and $110 million in lost revenues. In consequence, the

Illinois legislature voted in June 1973 to pass legislation preventing the state EPA from enforcing the existing sulfur standards "until the technical feasibility of sulfur removal devices is proven by continuous operation for one year."[49]

The reaction against environmentalism was heightened by the 1973 Middle East oil embargo, with its consequent concern about the adequacy of gasoline supplies. On December 13, 1973, Ira Whitman wrote to Gilligan about his appearance before a crowd of 400 at a Columbus energy seminar hosted by the lieutenant governor.

> I spoke out strongly against the energy producers who have caused so many of our current environmental problems and who now seem equally incapable of dealing with fuel shortages. I emphasized that no long-term relaxation of environmental requirements should be made at the present time, especially in the absence of "straight talk" about fuel supplies from the energy industry and the federal government. Since the audience was heavily industrial, my speech was not received with enthusiasm.[50]

In an August 1, 1974, memo to agency staff, Whitman noted the current economic uncertainty that had prompted some to argue that environmental improvements and pollution control standards "should be softened, delayed or suspended" to ease the burden on business.[51] The key point of rejoinder, Whitman said, was that this "burden" was largely imaginary. He distributed a *Wall Street Journal* analysis from that morning reporting that second-quarter 1974 corporate profits, far from being swallowed up by unreasonable environmental demands, had in fact increased 25 percent over the previous year. He called this to the agency's attention so that staffers would be versed in how to put the question of environmental costs into proper perspective. His memo reminded them that "legitimate hardship situations will continue to be given close scrutiny and appropriate consideration where legal, but legitimate hardships among big industry are presently the exception, not the rule."[52]

Lake Erie had been treated as a dump for almost as long as people lived in any great numbers along its shore. John D. Rockefeller, founder of then-Cleveland-based Standard Oil, said of early industry behavior: "We used to burn it [crude oil] in distilling the oil, and thousands and hundreds of thousands of barrels of it floated down the creeks and rivers, and the ground was saturated with it."[53] Eventually, the creeks and rivers reached the lake, carrying the pollution of hundreds of enterprises, including that of America's first billionaire.

Three factors combined to kill the fish, close the beaches, and sour the smell of Lake Erie. First, Ohio municipalities and Detroit dumped raw sewage into the lake. Second, rivers—particularly the Maumee, which drained rich agricultural land—added the runoff of chemical fertilizers. The third was the nature of the lake itself. Generally no more than thirty feet deep in its western basin, Erie was far shallower than the other Great Lakes (the *average* depth of Lake Michigan is 279 feet). For the other Great Lakes, in the summer months lake water nearer the surface becomes warmer than the water deeper down; in winter, the reverse occurs. When winter cools the surface water, it makes it denser, heavier than the water beneath. At some point, the higher and lower water essentially change places, flushing the deeper, dirtier water to the surface and exposing it to the cleansing power of sunlight. Lake Erie, however, is not deep enough to allow for this inversion to occur. In consequence, whatever contamination accumulated at the bottom of the lake continues to accumulate.

On October 26, 1972, still in its first week of operation, the Ohio EPA appointed Earl Richards to head its Lake Erie Task Force. Richards, Sam Bleicher said, "was a throwback. A solid engineer, well known around the state, who sucked it up, did what was needed."[54] Where water pollution was concerned, Lake Erie was clearly the priority. It was the state's most important body of water. And politics applied. The northern third of Ohio contained half the state's population at that time and more than half of its Democrats. (Interestingly, under Governor Rhodes, what limited funds for water pollution abatement existed went largely to the southern, and Republican, two-thirds of the state.)

There are some problems that can be solved by throwing money at them. In the case of Lake Erie, this money was largely federal, allocated under the 1972 federal Clean Water Act, which created a revolving loan fund to finance the upgrading of municipal waste disposal. President Richard Nixon had vetoed the original bill, arguing that its $1.8 billion price tag was excessive; Congress overrode the veto.

On March 20, 1973, the Ohio EPA received tentative federal EPA approval for a priority list of grants for municipal pollution control; with that announcement came the news that only about half of the $115 million originally appropriated would be available. By federal law, the Ohio EPA had been obliged to establish criteria for how it ranked possible projects. Here, some politics entered in. EPA staff member Vivian Witkind recalled, "We were determined to come up with a formula that made Cleveland the number-one priority."[55] In June 1973, the Ohio EPA was informed that about seventy-five of the projects it had proposed would be funded, with most of the money targeted to the Lake Erie basin.

Governor Gilligan was "about as engaged in environmental matters as we needed him to be," according to Ira Whitman.[56] One instance came in the Cleveland area—the largest single source of municipal pollution—where a newly formed Cleveland Regional Sewer District (CRSD) was created under court order. In time, EPA director Whitman said, it became "a very effective body."[57] But not immediately. Early on, Whitman said, there was a protracted dispute between Cleveland and its suburbs over the larger city's unwillingness to surrender control of the operation. At Whitman's urging, Gilligan agreed to tour one of the large treatment plants CRSD operated (it is not often, Whitman commented, that "you see a governor taking a walking tour of a sewerage plant").[58] Whitman believed the city utilities official hosting the event had put together a staged tour, for at each step, the Cleveland official's comments were contradicted by those of the Ohio EPA engineer that Whitman had invited. This all occurred in the presence of the press; the resulting publicity helped prompt Cleveland to cooperate. CRSD operated three major treatment plants. On June 1973, Whitman spoke at ground-breaking ceremonies for the Cleveland Westerly Wastewater Treatment Plant: "I stressed the favorable impact the new plant would have on the quality of Lake Erie."[59] In a later interview, Whitman added, "We worked closely with CRSD. It took ten or twenty years, but they progressively upgraded their operation."[60]

Between the founding of the Ohio EPA and the end of the Gilligan administration, Ira Whitman estimates that $150 million was spent to improve wastewater treatment in Ohio, most of it in Cleveland and other municipalities that sat along Lake Erie. About three-quarters of this money was federal; most of the rest was raised through the sale of bonds, with the municipalities in question putting up relatively little of their own funds. The work was done in increments and, as such, produced incremental improvements. Whitman noted, "The reopening of the individual beaches happened over time; in any given summer, there were more days when a beach was open than it had been the previous year and fewer when it was closed."[61] Speaking in Cincinnati in September 1973, Governor Gilligan said that two-thirds of the Lake Erie beaches had been reopened for public use.

Whitman and others were well aware that theirs was an agency that could enmesh itself in partisan politics quite easily—indeed, without even knowing that it was doing so. Bleicher recalled that wholly without intending to, the Ohio EPA "was driving the state's farmers crazy."[62] The agency had created standards for allowable air pollution based on studies of steel making, coal-generated electrical production, and related matters. Bleicher said, "We never thought about grain dryers. They would use natural gas and spew out chaff, most of which landed within ten feet of the dryer. Still, it's air pollution; and by weight, it's a lot of air pollution. We were told we were making it difficult for farmers to dry their own grain; they would be forced to have the work done by large operators."[63]

This left the agency in a bind. It did not wish to aggravate every voting farmer in the state of Ohio; at the same time, Bleicher said, the agency's "position was that we could not touch the regulations." If you weakened regulations for one group, "then the utilities and everyone else would come in and seek a waiver."[64] So the agency decided to take an off-the-record stand: it would simply forego enforcement where grain dryers were concerned. Bleicher felt justified in this, because the chaff blown about by the dryers did not add to the sort of pollution the agency was most concerned about. Bleicher commented, "This was a perfect example that no matter how smart you think you are when you are writing the regulations, the world is always more complicated than you thought."[65]

On July 2, 1974, Ira Whitman sent Gilligan a memo outlining those steps he believed would be necessary in the first two years following Gilligan's expected reelection. There was, he wrote, "no question that Ohio's environmental protection efforts are succeeding—to a degree."[66] He rated that state's efforts as about on par with those of Wisconsin, Indiana, Michigan, Illinois, and Minnesota. He stated, as a general thought, that "it takes more effort to enforce than to establish."[67] He said that the agency was dealing with some 5,000 serious polluters, so resources should be commensurate. Whitman added, "I believe we had within our grasp the ability to provide a meaningful, permanent improvement in the quality of Ohio's air, land, and water. The present program effort is not adequate to do this . . . and will allow the state to do little more than put out fires." Breaking into a sports metaphor, he asked, "Do we drop the ball at midfield and punt, or do we follow through and carry the ball into the end zone?"[68] Whitman was being rhetorical; his statement assumed that come January 1975, the team quarterbacked by Gilligan would still have control of the ball.

Reflecting years later on the early experience of the Ohio EPA, Sam Bleicher cited two major points of progress. First, the infrastructure needed to do environmental regulation was created with general public agreement that such regulation was worthwhile. Second, "industry and others installed a lot of pollution control equipment."[69] This was not always done at the behest of the Ohio EPA, he noted, but by companies that "saw the way things were headed. Often, such equipment provided energy and material savings to the company in question."[70]

For Ira Whitman, in physical terms, the "most significant reduction was in sulfur oxide; many Ohio electrical generating plans moved to low sulfur coal."[71] A chief frustration for him, however, was that the agency had no authority to address automotive emissions; it could not even act against the innumerable garages in the state that advertised their willingness to disconnect the catalytic converter installed to diminish emissions. What pleased Whitman most, though, was his association with John Gilligan: "He was a joy to work for."[72] Whitman was aware that his was a politically sensitive post, that he was, in the broader sense, expendable. But in working for Gilligan, he said, he was "never afraid of that—Gilligan was honest and aggressive."[73] After the defeat in 1974, Whitman recalls, Gilligan took him aside and said, "At least we gave them hell."[74]

30

The Economic Environment

In his first two terms as governor, James Rhodes spent eight years selling Ohio on itself. It was the "low tax state" where "profit was not a dirty word." It was because of these policies, Rhodes argued, that the state maintained an economic prominence and security that undergirded the good life for all Ohioans. And it was a message Rhodes exported nationally through promotional campaigns and the efforts of Rhodes's Raiders—select Ohio businessmen who called on business leaders in other states to assure them that the Valhalla of their profit-making dreams lay invitingly between Lake Erie and the Ohio River.

David Sweet, director of the Department of Development (which merged with the Development of Urban Affairs to create the Department of Economic and Community Development) believed Rhodes had been half right.[1] Sweet credited the Republican with being among the first governors to realize and perhaps the most assiduous to pursue the idea that state government could play an active role in promoting a state's economy. Rhodes, who thrived on attention, believed that attention focused on Ohio would help make the state thrive. However, the problem with Rhodes's approach, Sweet said, was twofold: the Republican governor's ideas on how prosperity could be achieved were entirely wrongheaded; and the fact that Rhodes had brought a good many Ohioans around to his way of thinking was an "enormous obstacle" to initiating more effective approaches.[2]

Just thirty when appointed, Sweet was the youngest member of the Gilligan cabinet. He was one of three high-level appointees, along with Ira Whitman and Hal Hovey, to come to state government from the regional economic development office at the Columbus-based Battelle Memorial Institute. Sweet had been spotted by Jim Friedman, who had engaged the young PhD in preparing background papers for the Gilligan educational effort that preceded his candidacy. Sweet's appointment came rather swiftly after Gilligan's election. His familiarity with Ohio Democratic politics was, however, a touch uncertain. (He recalled being perhaps the only person to show up at Gilligan's postinauguration Ohio fair-grounds celebratory blowout wearing a tux.)

The Gilligan administration took power just as some comfortable assumptions about the Ohio economy were meeting up with some uncomfortable truths. True, the 1960s had been generally good years for Ohio: the state's heavy industry had been bolstered by the Vietnam-induced demand for munitions. But that strength was deceptive, as Sweet pointed out in a lengthy August 3, 1971, memo to Chief of Staff James Friedman.[3]

Since 1955, Ohio's share of the nation's GNP had dropped from 6.1 percent to 5.5 percent.[4] The state's median personal income had in the same period dropped from 12.6 percent to 2.2 percent above the national average.[5] Also, Ohio employment was badly skewed toward the slow-growing manufacturing sector and away from the technology and service sectors from which most of the next decade's jobs were likely to come. Sweet told a *New York Times* reporter, "In the decade of the 1960s, manufacturing employment increased six percent while the service sector increased sixty percent."[6] Moreover, Ohio's bounty was rather badly distributed: statewide, per-capita income was $3,775, but in the core of its larger cities and the state's southeastern Appalachian fringe, that figure was $2,173—a full 40 percent lower.

Sweet also believed that Rhodes's high-profile out-of-state recruitment efforts were simply posturing. New jobs, he said, did not surface in Canton or Celina because they had been lured there by a pipe-playing governor; principally, new jobs were created by existing employers, by a company that employed 500 adding a second shift in one department to reach 520 or a business with 20 employees gaining a new contract sufficient to raising its work force to 22. In rough, Sweet said, there were three steps to be taken to build employment opportunities in the state: first, retain the employers Ohio had; second, help those employers expand their operations; and third, create through entrepreneurship and venture capital new employers. He agreed that there was a role to be played in attracting employers from other states, but it was less likely to come about through boosterism than because some out-of-state firm wanted better proximity to a major Ohio-based supplier or customer.[7]

Sweet was not persuaded that Rhodes, with his emphasis on low taxes and a profit-friendly administration, really had the answer to that fundamental question: What does business want? In his memo to Friedman, Sweet wrote, "No longer is economic growth, with any imbalance, hailed as the route to well-being. Quality of life for all the citizens is the overall goal and economic expansion is only an element of, and partial means to, improved quality of life for all."[8]

The different approach Sweet saw for Ohio was evident in his department's earliest promotional efforts. One of these was a full-page magazine ad, broadly placed, that simply showed three young boys walking across an open and welcoming field.

The advertisement's message consisted of the statement: "Ohio: A nice place to raise a business."[9] Another early message reflected the view that 80 percent of new jobs in Ohio came from enterprises already located in the Buckeye State: "Ohio: Minding our own businesses."[10]

Sweet spelled out his approach in a special advertising segment published in *Fortune* magazine in November 1972:

> Traditionally, state governments—including Ohio—have mounted vigorous sales campaigns aimed at drawing new businesses within their borders. What happened to those firms after the plant cornerstone was laid was often "outside" state government responsibility. In Ohio in the 1970s, we believe state government must rethink its responsibilities and reshape its role in the industrial development process.
>
> We believe in Ohio that economic development depends on quality education as well as quality sites, decent health care, efficient law enforcement and a livable environment as well as available transportation and utilities.[11]

In addressing the obstacles to the growth of new jobs in the state, Sweet emphasized that 95 percent of the state's incorporated businesses employed fewer than fifty people. Small business commonly lacked the in-house expertise—in marketing, in employee recruitment, in securing financing—that major enterprises enjoy. To help address this, the department created what it termed its Ombudsman Program, which it launched in August 1971 with advertisements announcing: "Starting today: Every business in Ohio has a man in Ohio."[12] The program, Gilligan stated, "will unravel red tape, provide answers, guidance and invaluable aid. [The ombudsman's] services are discreet and confidential, without charge, and available to all Ohio business—big or small, in Ohio now or expanding operations from another state."[13] More prosaically, the program pledged to:

- Provide a central clearing-house for receiving and answering complaints, criticism, and suggestions concerning state activities related to business
- Refer inquiries to appropriate state departments agencies and then follow through on referrals to determine if further action was required
- Assist in arranging meetings and conferences with appropriate officials in state department and agencies, when necessary
- Suggest changes for redress of business complaints, referring these suggestions to the proper departments or agency for disposition or further action
- Provide advice on site selection, financing, technology transfer, international trade, and economic research.[14]

In the program's first thirty-three months, the program handled 7,800 cases: "An Ohio minibus manufacturer called for help in finding a location to expand facilities; a businessman inventor from Greenview asked aid in marketing a new cleaning agent; an Ohio sink and bathtub products manufacturer asked information on where to obtain special wood pallets; an Ohio worker asked how to get his Workmen's Compensation check and had it in two days. Bellaire, Ohio got help in obtaining soda ash for its water purification plant."[15]

Sweet regarded development work as a professional undertaking, offering yet another contrast with Rhodes. During Rhodes's second term, the governor was dining with a small group interested in spurring transportation activities within the state. Rhodes asked where the largest automotive test track in the country was located. Michigan, he learned. Then Rhodes asked how big it was. Told it was 1,000 acres, the governor stood up and committed Ohio to creating a center ten times that size. Rhodes made good on his word, building the Transportation Research Center in East Liberty. On taking his post, Sweet became an ex-officio member of the board that managed the East Liberty facility. He was startled to learn it was being run from within the state bureaucracy by persons with no particular expertise in automotive science. This, Sweet said, was characteristic of Rhodes: "He put money into infrastructure and not into staffing."[16] Sweet was able to switch management to the OSU's College of Engineering, which had the talent to run it. Sometime after Gilligan left office, the state sold the facility to Honda, for whom it was an important consideration in locating a manufacturing plant in Marysville.

Such efforts were numerous; and many were piecemeal. Sweet urged creation of a Governor's Task Force on Employment and Economic Expansion to address the longer-term questions of Ohio's economic future. As its mission, he said, the task force should

> appraise Ohio's present conditions, problems and opportunities; make recommendations to the governor with respect to maximizing state employment and income "within the broader goal of quality of life for all the citizens." The task force will consider current employment-reduction and plant closing problems, imbalance in economic development by region; the reasons for Ohio's long-term decline; the range of the state's strengths and weaknesses; and the whole range of actions that state may take.[17]

Following up on this recommendation, Gilligan on May 23, 1972, announced establishment of the Governor's Business and Employment Council, under the chairmanship of George S. Dively, head of the Harris-Intertype Corporation of Cleveland and author of a book on business management. Additional members were drawn from manufacturing, labor, finance, education, research, and small business. The council's purpose was to "tangibly improve business and employment opportunities in Ohio."[18] Gilligan identified six issues that needed to be addressed:

- Improve the business climate for new and small business
- Pay special attention to improving opportunities for minority enterprise

- Accelerate innovation in Ohio
- Improve labor-management relations for improved efficiency
- Raise employment of the undeveloped manpower in inner cities and Appalachia
- Improve state policy for employment and economic health.[19]

The council had a budget of $80,000 drawn from the Ohio Bureau of Employment Services, with W. R. Purcell Jr., president, Planning Systems Corporation, as executive director.

In announcing the council, Gilligan gave a list of reasons why it was needed. Ohio industry had become outdated; inner cities and the Appalachian regions of the state were depressed; Ohio had lagged in research and development and in creating service industries. He noted that, unlike Massachusetts, which had seen a spurt of high technology development in the "Route 128 Corridor" surrounding Boston, Ohio had no geographic center in which growth could feed on itself. These problems, Gilligan said, "may sound new. But they aren't new—what is new is a state government in Ohio.[20]

(On July 6, 1972, the General Assembly formally approved the merger of the existing Urban Affairs and Development departments into a combined Department of Economic and Community Development under David Sweet. The measure passed the House, 58–28, with the Senate voting 26–5 to concur with the House amendments to the original bill.)

Assaying the situation, the council's executive director W. R. Purcell wrote David Sweet on September 5, 1972, that Ohio in the forthcoming decade would require 1.5 million new jobs to be created at a required investment of $20 billion. Purcell was well aware of the politics of the circumstance: "While the Council regards itself as nonpartisan—and must be permitted to continue its nonpartisan approach and image to perform effectively—its results will not only help provide the jobs and money base for achievement of other Gilligan programs but, also provide sufficient specific new results and information to pull the business-and-jobs rug from any other would-be 1974 governor."[21]

On September 9, 1972, Governor Gilligan spoke at the kick-off event for the Governor's Business and Employment Council, an Entrepreneurial Seminar held at Ohio State University. He stressed the importance of small business to the state's economic future: 80 percent of job growth would come from Ohio companies, most of them small and which in aggregate employed half the state's labor force. He noted with pleasure that while organizers of the event had hoped that as many as 400 small businessmen might attend, 500 had in fact applied to do so. The weekend event offered seminars on entrepreneurship, developing a business plan, developing a financial plan, financing a new business.[22]

In March 1973, the council announced its first set of five recommendations. On May 16, Sweet wrote task force chair Dively that the Gilligan administration had requested funding to implement three of those recommendations—increased service industry recruitment, an Ohio foreign office, and an information program on vocational and technical education opportunities—and that the two other recommendations, intended to ease the flow of venture capital, required legislative action. He noted that the Securities Act (SB 338) had been introduced to the Senate, with hearings pending.[23]

For his part, Sweet considered entrepreneurship to be key to Ohio's economy, but lacking. The business environment did not in general support innovation, and those innovations created often did not take productive root in the state. Sweet's favorite example was Xerography, a breakthrough technology developed in Columbus through the collaboration of inventor Chester Carlson and the Battelle Research Institute yet never manufactured in Ohio.

A major obstacle was the absence of venture capital available to Ohio's entrepreneurs. In January 1973, Business and Employment Council director Purcell released to the press figures that were hardly reassuring. He cited the *Guide to Venture Capital Sources,* which gave the number of such sources by state. Clearly, Sweet noted, Ohio trailed badly: for every 1 million Massachusetts residents, there were 10.5 venture capital sources available; 9 in New York; 6 in California; 3 in Illinois; 2 in Pennsylvania; and .7 in Ohio.[24]

The need for venture capital, Sweet acknowledged, was a problem the state proved unable to address, though he noted that a number of individual Ohio cities did take action. However, according to historian George Knepper, the slow or stagnant growth of Ohio's banks after 1970 "did little . . . to ameliorate a pressing need for new industrial seed money and venture capital. Local entrepreneurs found it difficult to find financial backing . . . Few venture capital firms operated in Ohio, and those that did frequently invested in out-of-state enterprises."[25]

Meanwhile, in memos to Chief of Staff Jack Hansan, Sweet kept the administration apprised of his department's actions. In May 1973, the Department of Economic and Community Development sponsored international trade seminars in Springfield, Middletown, and Mansfield to instruct small business owners on how to find and tap international business. In June, the Ohio Development Team called on 203 firms during a week-long trip to Canada, and the Office of International Trade contacted 510 Ohio manufacturers, advising them of foreign trade leads for purchase of Ohio-made products. In October, more than $1 million in sales agreements for Ohio products were finalized during an Ohio public-/private- sector trade mission to Japan and Taiwan, a series of six-week seminars for Ohio minority business owners began in Columbus, and, later in the month, 185 members of Ohio's private-sector travel industry attended the 1973 Governor's Conference on Tourism at King's Island amusement park.

Sweet's Development office was responsible for promoting tourism as well. In Sweet's first year, Ohio had the advantage of being the state chosen to present arts, crafts, and other activities on the National Mall in Washington, D.C. Also, following her selection as Miss America on September 12, 1971, Laurie Lea Schaefer of Bexley was a regular participant in events boosting Ohio.

And, perhaps partly in response to Gilligan's tendency to call attention to Ohio's shortcomings, Sweet, in January 1973, urged the creation of a "Let's Hear It for Ohio" campaign, which was straight-up boosterism for the Buckeye State. Ohio, Sweet noted in his memo to Gilligan suggesting the campaign, was "not simply the birthplace of aviation, it led the nation in the production of balloons, baseballs, batteries, Bibles, business machines, cash registers, cutlery, detergents, dishwashers, earth moving equipment, electric refrigerators, fertilizer, footballs, glassware, gold balls, lawn care products, pottery and much more."[26]

More substantively, from the standpoint of state government, the campaign was to focus on the state's efforts in environmental protection, mental health and development, honesty and openness in government, occupational health and safety, and public education. The campaign launch date was March 1, 1973 (Ohio Statehood Day), and included everything from speech contests for students, free bumper stickers, and public forums at which Gilligan took questions from whoever chose to show up. In Cincinnati, Riverfront Stadium agreed to carry the "Let's Hear It for Ohio" logo on the electronic sign outside the stadium. Actual administration of the campaign was the province of Ron Castell, hired that spring as the administration's communications director.

Sweet was careful to report what good news there was to report. On September 6, 1973, he sent a memo to Gilligan citing "several of the economic indicators we are bragging about."[27] Among them, state employment had hit 4,594,000—a full 350,000 more jobs than when Gilligan took office. Also, the jobless rate remained a low 4.3 percent, and Ohio's GNP for the year 1972—$59.9 billion—was almost a 16 percent increase over the two previous years (in fairness, perhaps half that increase was attributable to inflation). And finally, the number of new firms opening for business had increased from 768 in 1971 to 1,134 in 1972. These numbers were distributed to the press as well, and a number of journalists gave the figures substantial play.

Not everything went smoothly, however. For administrative purposes of their own, each of the state's departments and agencies divided the state into a dozen or so districts. This meant that Ohio had more than three multijurisdictional planning districts, each somehow engaged in delivery of some or another service to Ohio residents, often without reference to the actions of other state agencies.

Early in his tenure, David Sweet began arguing for the creation of uniform planning districts, perhaps a dozen of them statewide. On April 26, 1971, he told the Ohio Planning Conference, meeting in Warren, that "if we are to deliver the services which state government is chartered to provide to the people of Ohio—at minimum cost, with maximum efficiency and for optimum benefits—the first major step which must be taken is to functionalize our present structure and firmly link ourselves up with the planners and implementers at the local level throughout the state."[28] The following June, he delivered a similar message to the County Commissioners' Association of Ohio, meeting in Toledo: "State government got bigger to help communities solve problems more effectively. But, you all know what happens when an organization gets big, centralized and bureaucratic—it gets out of touch with the individuals and communities surrounding it. So, when local government sought help, they encountered red tape and buck passing. Face-to-face contact between state government people and local officials began to diminish and a communications gap set it."[29]

His department produced brochures to support the regionalization effort; among other things, these reported that Ohio was the only major state that had failed to adopt planning/service regionalism, even though such regionalism would

- Make state government more responsive to local needs
- Meet federal requirements and facilitate flow of funds
- Serve as centers for data gathering
- Be a means of pooling limited resources
- Serve as a framework for planning, coordination, and delivery of state and federal services.[30]

He then invited people to express their preference for how the borders should be drawn. In September 1973, Sweet told the Ohio Municipal League convention in Cincinnati, "We feel that the State of Ohio is moving to take a leadership position among the forty-three states which have initiated statewide system for regional planning and development. We are committed to a state-local partnership in accomplishing this goal."[31] Indeed, Governor Gilligan had by executive order divided the state into eleven multicounty service districts as of April 30.

The administration's move triggered a reaction by those who saw the enterprise as an assault on local control and long-standing prerogatives. The Ohio Campaign to Restore the Constitution, Inc., objected to actions that flowed from executive direction rather than from the ballot box. Those objections became part of a campaign which argued that Gilligan's order was part of a "great conspiracy" toward statism that had begun in 1913 "when Paul Warburg of the German banking family and a relative of the Rothschilds came to the United States to establish a Central Bank" and been followed by the amendment legalizing the income tax (a move "borrowed from the Communist Manifesto") and was somehow tied to the creation of tax-free status for the Rockefeller, Ford, Carnegie, and other foundations that, among other things, was "aimed at destroying local government."[32]

Rather more effective than charges that the Red Menace was on the loose was simple foot-dragging by a number of the state agencies involved that believed current arrangements operated for their convenience. Jim Rhodes, by that point Gilligan's likely 1974 opponent, attacked the plan, telling the *Zanesville Times Recorder* that while it "might be a good idea as far as business is concerned, but after all, government should not be run as a profit system, but should be there to rule and serve the people. Perhaps, most important, government should be run for the benefit of the people, and any plan that does not further that concept should not and must not be implemented."[33] In the end, the plan was only partially implemented. The whole annoying matter left Sweet with the belief that "you can't institutionalize change in four years."[34]

More important, perhaps, Sweet realized that you cannot in four years "transform an aging industrial economy to one oriented to high-technology and service industries."[35] A range of interrelated tasks was involved in creating the "newer" economy that Sweet, Gilligan, and a too-small number of Ohio business leaders spoke about. One central requirement was a better-educated workforce. In February 1974, the Gilligan-appointed Citizens Task Force on Higher Education reported the doleful news that while Ohio ranked fifteenth in per-capita income, it ranked forty-eighth in per-capita expenditure on higher education. Worse, Ohio trailed the national average in the proportion of its high school graduates going on to college by a full 10 percent. Part of the reason, doubtless, was cost, evidenced in the fact that at the time Ohio State University charged the highest in-state tuition of the Big Ten schools.[36]

The task force made various recommendations for improving this situation, but none that was an overnight fix. Gilligan recalled: "We thought the only way to the future for Ohio or any other industrial state was to elevate the level of education and job skills. There was a new economy developing. And what we were unable to say at the time with any confidence [was] that we knew how to do it. We needed people at the machinist, design, and entrepreneurial levels—we needed them all—and we needed them trained to a certain standard. But it was not something that was going to happen in four or five years."[37]

Indeed, Ohio was not to be afforded the luxury of time. The late-1973 oil embargo sent the price of crude oil soaring from $9 to $30 a barrel—a price rise that particularly affected Ohio's aging, relatively inefficient, and energy-intensive industrial plants. The results were startling: "Between 1972 and 1982, Ohio lost 246,553 manufacturing jobs, an 18.3 percent decline."[38] Moreover, job losses in high-paying steel, rubber, and automotive industries were not matched by gains of equally well-paying jobs in computer technology and other fields, even if those who lost the one somehow qualified for the other. It was a decline that Gilligan believed was beyond the scope of the state to reverse: "The decline would have come anyway, whether or not we had done the things we did. Given the development of Japan, China, and other offshore economies and, prior to that, the movement by American industry to Mexico—we had only the resources of a state to address a problem that was simply international in scope."[39]

It was an increasingly acute problem for Ohio's near-neighbor states as well—Michigan, Indiana, Illinois, and beyond, an area that would soon become known as the Rust Belt.

31

The Political Environment

On becoming governor of Ohio, what surprised John Gilligan most was that "on their way out, the Rhodes people burned most of the financial records."[1] Gilligan spoke of his predecessor in tones ranging from awestruck bemusement to a deep-seated contempt. On discovering the missing records, Gilligan was simply "outraged."[2] He did not know—nor was he ever to learn—what potential embarrassments had been put to the flame. He did, however, have his suspicions. The appointments process, he said, "looked a bit like they had gone out in the back alley and shot craps for it." Still, while there appeared to have been considerable wheeling and dealing in the political arena, "there was no documentary evidence that we became aware of."[3]

The incoming governor did learn, however, how the state contracted out its business. So far as Gilligan could tell, Ohio employed a single printer to produce everything from the marriage license forms used in Noble County and the speeding ticket forms used in Lucas County to the reimbursement forms various state agencies in Columbus used in triplicate. The printer in question, Gilligan said, had been receiving all of the state's business for years on a no-bid basis. Similarly, a single company did all the purchasing for Ohio's state parks—from the railway ties that demarcated parking spots to the toilet paper that stocked the outhouses. So far as Gilligan could determine, while records existed on what the state had paid to the firm in question, there were no records of what the state had received in return. Commonly, newly elected chief executives say their biggest surprise on reaching office is the discovery that things are as bad as they had said they were while campaigning. Gilligan said, "While I was running, I criticized the inefficiencies, but I had no idea what were the realities."[4]

Gilligan's view of public administration was likely best summarized in that variously attributed phrase, "A public office is a public trust." In his third "State of the State" message, delivered to the General Assembly on January 17, 1973, Governor Gilligan stated: "Our American system of self-government . . . depends for its vitality upon the faith of the people in their political structures and processes, and in the personal integrity of our public officials. But in recent years, repeated revelations of corruption in government and the failure of public officials to protect the interests of the public have contributed to dangerous erosion in public confidence in the basic integrity of government here in Ohio and throughout this nation."[5] It was time, he said, for Ohio to demonstrate that nothing less than "absolute honesty" was acceptable from its public officials. And that being the case, he was making ethics legislation—laws defining and prohibiting conflicts of interest and requiring officials to disclose their sources of income—his administration's highest priority for the 1973 legislative term.

In Ohio and elsewhere at the time, "ethics," however construed, was not entirely a bar to partisanship. While it was not an Ohioan who said, "to the victor belong the spoils" (the words were actually uttered by New York senator William Learned Marcy during an 1832 senate debate), it may as well have been.[6] If one headed a state government department, then it was fairly well acknowledged that any job that lay within your power to bestow was likely to be better performed by a member of your own party, all things being equal (as they rarely were). Little shame was attached to arranging matters accordingly. In 1971, when one well-schooled Democrat went to work for Joseph Ferguson, the new state auditor identified as a priority task the ridding of the department of Republicans, "particularly blacks and Catholics," who, Ferguson is said to have determined, had no excuse for not voting Democratic.[7]

A staff member working with state personnel director Paul Corey reported how aspiring Democrats made their needs for employment known. A typical conversation began: "My cousin needs a job."[8] Queried as to where in the human enterprise the cousin's talents resided, the relative asked to see the salary list. As the story goes, the cousin's advocate scanned down the list of available jobs until they saw a particular salary level, and said: "He's good for this one."[9] Nor was it considered shameful that the employees hired this way should experience a certain financial loyalty to the political party that had been the source of their good fortune. During one 1973 legislative session, Representative Charles Fry, a ranking Republican from Springfield, rose on the floor of the General Assembly to decry the alleged efforts of Democrats to seek donations from state employees. Possibly Fry undercut his argument by acknowledging, "The only defense I've heard is that when Republicans were in power the same thing happened."[10]

There were blandishments of various sorts directed at the lowliest bureaucrat up the line to governor. Gilligan delighted in the machinations of those members of his party who were, perhaps, either less fastidious or simply more direct. He relished telling of an exchange with Jack Sulligan, the longtime Democratic chief of Mahoning County. Sulligan was, among other things, one of the few Buckeye Democrats who routinely referred to Gilligan as "kid."

In Gilligan's telling, Sulligan opened the conversation by saying, "I got a guy who wants to be some help to you."

Gilligan responded that he could always use some help—"What kind of help is this going to be?"

"Well, kid, he wants to give you some money."

"That's very nice. How much?"

Sulligan said, "Well, I don't know—I think it depends on how you play your cards. But I think it might be $15,000 or $20,000."

This, Gilligan allowed, was a lot of money. "What does he want for this?"

Sulligan replied, "Aw, kid. You don't want to know. I told him you wouldn't do anything, kid, but you got to listen. You got to listen. You got to be practical."

Gilligan asked what "practicality" his prospective benefactor had in mind.

Sulligan replied, "You're going to name some people to the liquor control board, kid. And he'd like to name a few in our area."

Gilligan told the disappointed Sulligan that his own practicality would not stretch to meet the request.[11]

The ethics of politicians is a subject of which one hears rather more than one sees. It is not a topic those in political life are particularly fond of, as it offers them a lose-lose proposition: they can lose with the public by opposing it, and they can lose for themselves by abiding by it.

Patrick Sweeney, a Democrat from Cleveland, entered the Ohio House of Representatives in 1967 as, in his own words, "the youngest and dumbest member."[12] But what bothered him was seeing the business card of a fellow representative: one side listed him as vice president of a savings and loan on Cleveland's Euclid Avenue, and the other side gave his position in the state legislature. The juxtaposition bothered Sweeney: "I thought, 'That's not right.'"[13]

So Sweeney dropped a legislative ethics bill into the House hopper. That same year, 1967 the national Council on State Governments drafted its first model ethics legislation, which no state rushed to adopt. Sweeney reintroduced his bill each year thereafter, but neither he nor the cause of legislative ethics—in Ohio or the nation—made much progress. In the early 1970s, only eight states had ethics legislation of any sort in force. One of Sweeney's attempts did garner supporting testimony from finance director Hal Hovey, who told the House Select Committee on Legislative Practices, "I will call the public's attention to this bill again and again. If the bill dies in committee this session, at least the public will know . . . who killed it."[14] The bill did die, and hardly anyone inquired as to the cause of its demise.

In 1973, three factors came together to make possible what the *Cleveland Plain Dealer* called "the near-impossible feat" of passing ethics legislation in Ohio.[15] First, Democrats gained control of the House of Representatives; second, Governor Gilligan made ethics legislation his priority for the year; and third, the slow, inexorable unfolding of Watergate offered a very public lesson in the harm unethical government could do. Senator Harry Meshel (D-Youngstown) commented, "Watergate was a great influence; it really exposed the nerves of inner government to the public: the president's enemies list, the misuse of the IRS."[16]

The introduction of an ethics bill followed considered background work, much of it done by Phil Moots as legislative liaison. An early question, he said, was whether Gilligan could, on his own authority, establish ethics standards for state employees. The answer, in rough, was no: the governor could set standards for those working directly within the executive branch but lacked the authority to establish standards for the state departments or the legislature. That would require legislation. Then, a more political question was, If reform occurred, who would get the credit? Clearly, Gilligan, whose image as a reformer would be further burnished. And who would get the benefit? That is, would a given ethics bill work to the advantage of one party over the other? Also being considered at that time, Moots recalled, was the possibility that ethics legislation might discourage qualified persons from entering public life if they had "things" they did not want to reveal. Was this a loss, and one to be regretted? And finally, if Gilligan took the public lead as chief advocate of ethics reforms, would that not end in his being held to the highest standard? Moots commented, "Some people raised the concern, 'It's the guy on the white horse who gets muddy.'"[17] Presented with all this, Moots recalled, Gilligan said, "I want to do it."[18]

With Sweeney as its chief sponsor, the ethics bill was introduced into the Ohio House of Representatives on January 11, 1973. (Interestingly, Sweeney was one of the few House Democrats to vote against the income tax.) That day the *Cleveland Plain Dealer* reported that "a sweeping administration ethics bill requiring full financial disclosure and including tough prohibitions against conflicts of interest for elected and appointed officials was introduced into the Ohio House today."[19] The report quoted Gilligan as saying the bill was "absolutely essential if we hope to be able to restore public confidence in government" and noted that the proposal "faces a tough fight in both houses of the legislature, where lawyers—traditionally hostile to conflict of interest legislation—are the dominant occupational group."[20] The *Plain Dealer* praised Gilligan for introducing the legislation and stated that "this could be the year when a bill banning conflicts of interest finally makes it through the Ohio General Assembly."[21]

But this wouldn't happen easily. Two issues arose immediately. First, as proposed, legislators would be banned from receiving income from any state body other than the legislature itself. This, as was quickly pointed out, would require resignations from the nineteen members of the General Assembly who were public school teachers. Second, House minority leader Charles Kurfess objected that the proposal would require legislators who were attorneys to reveal the names of their clients, which Kurfess, a practicing attorney in Bowling Green, regarded as a breach of confidentiality. (But as Senator Harry Meshel said, "If a corporation wanted to influence you, they could pay money to your law firm and claim it was for legal work you had done."[22]) This sparked considerable controversy. The *Dayton Journal Herald*, which termed the proposal both "badly flawed" and "overly ambitious," added tersely: "The bill does not speak to a gut conflict of interest issue—the all too common practice of lawmakers who are lawyers representing clients in cases before state agencies."[23] Similarly, a *Plain Dealer* editorial said of the House majority leader, A. G .Lancione, a lawyer who practiced before state agencies, "We think we know enough of [Lancione's] character to doubt he would ever use his influence consciously for private gain, yet there may be officials on state boards who, in awe of his power, would go out of their way to favor his clients."[24]

Simultaneous with the introduction of the administration measure, House Bill 55, the Republicans presented an alternative that had one principal difference: the Gilligan administration required reporting of all sources of income above $500 *and* the actual amount received; the GOP version required *only* that sources, not amounts, be listed. The weaker Republican version prevailed. On April 17, 1973, when the measure received the unanimous approval of the House State Government Committee, the requirement that legislators must report amounts received by source had been eliminated. The *Columbus Dispatch* said the stricter requirement was "a large stumbling block, with large blocs of Democrats and Republicans opposed to it."[25] Further, in this version, attorneys and physicians were excused, on confidentiality grounds, from revealing the names of clients and patients.

The House bill established a six-member ethics committee, three members from each party to be appointed by the governor and confirmed by the Senate. That commission would be authorized to issue subpoenas and take statements under oath, statements subject to perjury laws. The commission was given the discretionary power to require any group of officeholders or officials who had "substantial administrative authority" to file a financial disclosure statement. The committee-approved version required all state employees to file by April 15 a statement listing sources of income; investments of $1,000 or more in any enterprise that did business with the state; property owned, other than one's personal residence; all gifts above $500; and several lesser matters. Further, state employees were forbidden from practicing before any state body that had employed them and were subject to restrictions on disclosing "confidential" information. Failure to file the form could lead to a $250 fine and a thirty-day jail term.

Though his initial proposal had been weakened, Gilligan's backing of the bill remained strong. Days before the committee measure moved to the full House, he wrote to each member of that body urging passage of the legislation: "There is no infallible means of ensuring the honesty of all employees of government, but HB 55, I believe, makes a substantial contribution to ensuring the integrity and honesty of public officials."[26] That measure easily passed the House on May 2 by a vote of 91–6.

The debate over this ethics legislation included two commonsense observations. The first, from the bill's chief sponsor, Patrick Sweeney, was that serious ethics violations were far more likely to be committed by "the bureaucrats and administrators who move dollars" than by members of the legislature.[27] He urged, "We want to watch all public officials."[28] Expressing a conservative view of human perfectibility, Representative William Batchelder said, "Government needs ethical officials more than it needs an ethics law. We can only pass it and pray."[29] A few Republicans went further, such as John Galbraith of Toledo, who said that the bill "would drive people out of government. We can't legislate honesty. We can always throw the rascals out."[30]

The bill then moved to the Senate, which gave the measure a fairly thorough chewing over. The *Cleveland Press* reported that the Senate "knocked one serious hole" in Gilligan's bill by exempting school board members, local officials, and local board members paid less than $1,000 a year.[31] Harry Meshel pointed out that the important criteria was not how much public figures earned, but the level of expenditure they oversaw and determined. One amendment proposed to include under the law the owners and chief executives of newspapers and television and radio stations. A second amendment, offered by Gene Slagle (D-Galion), required lobbyists to comply with the bill, though, as one Statehouse reporter put it, "Judiciary members who supported the attempt could scarcely keep straight faces as they voted for it."[32]

On July 27, the Senate deleted the media and lobbyist requirements by votes of 21–10 and 24–7, respectively. This left an exasperated Senate minority leader Anthony Calabrese to ask rhetorically, "Are you going to take everybody else [out] and let us [public officials] be the fall-guys for everything?"[33] The final bill passed the Senate by a 26–5 margin. It was left to one of the few female members, Marigene Valiquette (R-Toledo), to suggest the limits of the legislation: "Ethics is either something you have or you don't . . . I don't think this bill is going to change one thing."[34]

On August 28, the conference committee measure easily passed both houses: 88–1 in the House and 27–4 in the Senate. By general consent, the committee version more closely resembled the weaker Senate version. The revised bill replaced the single six-member commission with separate ethics commissions established for the executive branch, the judicial branch, and each house of the state legislature. Application of the law was withdrawn from school board members, local officials, and members of boards and commissions who were paid less than $1,000 a year. This latter had been a sticking point between Senate and House conferees, who favored the most inclusive definitions. One newspaper reported that Representative Sweeney "said the logjam broke when word came from Governor Gilligan's office to 'get a bill' regardless of the exclusions."[35]

Passage did bring a few dissenting voices. The *Dayton Journal Herald* noted acerbically that the law as passed would have meant that Treasurer John T. Her-

bert's 1970 acceptance of the $15,000 Crofters payoff would have brought no pun-
ishment and that an Ohio University trustee who had sold insurance to the university while serving on its board would have escaped punishment. The biggest flaw,
according to the Dayton newspaper, was the abolition of the proposed six-member
ethics board and its replacement by individual bodies to oversee each branch of
state government.[36] This was echoed by Representative Richard Celeste, who had
taken a lead role in pushing the ethics measure; he thought the replacement of the
six-member board by separate boards for each branch of government was the bill's
"biggest failure."[37] Ethics, he argued, could not be effectively enforced by bodies
that sat "as judge and jury on themselves."[38] Here, Celeste parted company with
the bill's chief sponsor, Patrick Sweeney, who thought legislators had a better understanding of the issue than "those good-government guys who think everybody
in politics is a crook."[39]

Generally, press coverage was favorable. Writing in the *Cincinnati Enquirer,*
Warren Wheat stated, "Finally, running out of excuses to delay the moment of
truth, Ohio lawmakers last week reluctantly put an ethics law on the books governing themselves, elected state officials, city and county officeholders and other
public servants in key decision-making positions."[40] The *Akron Beacon Journal*
editorial declared the "ethics law a solid gain, even with its weaknesses."[41]

As passed, the legislation required disclosure of the names of family members
and family-owned businesses; sources of income over $500; investment of over
$1,000 in Ohio corporations; real estate owned beyond one's personal residence;
debts and creditors of over $1,000; and nonfamily gifts of over $500. Additionally,
on leaving office, legislators were forbidden for a year from representing private
interests before state bodies. To these were added a general prohibition against the
use of official position to secure any personal benefit beyond legal compensation.

The case for the legislation was made best, perhaps, by an internal administration memo that rather deliberately called attention to the anemic state of ethics
legislation nationally. Only fourteen states then required financial disclosures of
any kind from public officials—of these, "California and Texas had been declared
unenforceable; Pennsylvania, New York and Missouri cover a far more limited
range of officials."[42] Unlike the handful of states that had ethics legislation, Ohio's
applied to all branches of government. Only two states covered local officials,
and only two more—Ohio among them—covered judicial officials. A key disagreement in Ohio had been whether to cover the amounts of income or just
the sources. In 1973, no state required its public officials to report the amounts of
income received from any particular source.

On September 14, 1973, Bill Chavanne wrote Gilligan: "I think it is more than
fair to say that this legislation represents ninety-five percent of the Administration's proposals to the General Assembly. I recommend that you sign the bill."[43]
This Gilligan did on September 19, calling the bill "the most significant action that

the General Assembly has taken in a number of decades in terms of elevating the standards of conduct of public officials." *Gongwer* commented, "A code of ethics law was an important legislative priority pursued dutifully by the Gilligan administration throughout the year."[44]

As numerous parties noted, the bill as passed was considerably weaker than the one Gilligan had originally proposed. Still, the governor had three good reasons for supporting the legislation as amended. First, getting any ethics legislation enacted was a considerable feat. Second, as chief sponsor, Gilligan was willing to "accept anything" because he wanted credit for the bill when he ran for reelection. And third, Gilligan had a faith in what might be termed the not-better-angels of legislators. An ethics bill might be weakened when being discussed; however, human nature was such that subsequent misdeeds were likely, with such misdeeds leading to pressure for stricter enforcement. The important thing, to Gilligan, was that the law was on the books and a firm start had been made.

Considering the bill nearly four decades after its passage, two who most firmly advocated it, Patrick Sweeney and Harry Meshel, give it positive marks. Meshel equated the law to legislation aimed at reducing any form of crime: "If you cut crime by 20 percent, then you've made a contribution."[45] Further, he noted, the bill made it easier for legislators to resist the blandishments of lobbyists. Sweeney, who began sponsoring ethics legislation in 1967, described himself as "almost satisfied; it was not the best, but the best we could get. It's like laws on seat belt use or no smoking in public places. They're not universally obeyed, but they have an influence."[46]

Even before the ethics bill was signed into law, Gilligan was angling for larger fish. On September 11, he informed legislative leaders of his intention to call a special late-October session of the legislature to address the related, and highly contentious, issue of campaign finance. The case for reform was sharpened when, on October 10, Vice President Spiro Agnew resigned office as part of a plea bargain tied to his nonpayment of income taxes. With Gilligan's call for a special session, a bipartisan study commission was established to begin drafting legislation.

The special session convened on October 23. Perhaps surprisingly, Gilligan brought a fairly weak hand to the table. As Vern Riffe, increasingly the de facto leader of House Democrats, complained to Dick Celeste, Gilligan "did not have a position going in; he had not hammered out what he wanted."[47] This, Riffe said, was a problem for many rank-and-file Democratic members who had no great wish to get far out on a limb in favor a measure they did not much like to begin with. Celeste quoted Riffe as saying that many House Democrats "didn't want to limit what they could accept in cash. They didn't want to limit who they got money from."[48]

Republicans were even less enthusiastic. Longtime Statehouse reporter Lee Leonard described campaign finance reform as "an issue that was pushed by the media, not by the general public."[49] While the measure had the support of "the usual people on the left-hand side of the spectrum," Leonard estimated that only five of the seventeen Senate Republicans favored it.[50] And for Gilligan, there was a further problem: the Republicans had no interest in passing a campaign finance reform law that would add luster to the credit the governor had just received for passage of the ethics bill.

As Brian Usher wrote in *Campaign Money,* agreement was reached on certain points: individual candidates were required to have a single body to collect their funds, and amounts raised were to be reported prior to the election in question. Beyond that, however, agreement was thwarted by the fact that the Democratic-controlled House and the Republican-controlled Senate had different interests to protect. Each was unassailably positioned to pass amendments whose principal purpose was to interfere with the traditional fund-raising methods of the opposition.

Republicans, for example, with their 40,000 dues-paying members and strong party organization, were traditionally most successful financing campaigns through party and individual donations. Democrats sought to restrict what political parties could do financially. For their part, Democrats raised far greater sums from labor unions, a portion of each member's dues aggregated for bulk political donations. Democrats, Usher noted, claimed that this was the only way the "little guy" could make his preferences felt against the privileged. Republicans claimed this made individual candidates beholden to the preferences of the handful of union officials who decided where contributions would be channeled. They preferred "freedom of choice," whereby individual union members would have the option of deciding to which candidate their own contribution would go.

The special session adjourned on November 16, 1973, in time for Thanksgiving but without anything to show for its efforts.

The new year broke not with campaign finance reform but with two other problems with ethics legislation. On January 4, 1974, one-time Gilligan chief of staff Jim Friedman resigned his post as chair of the Ohio Civil Rights Commission because the new ethics legislation appeared to state that his service on the rights commission meant he could not, as a private attorney, represent clients before other state agencies. Gilligan, stating that Friedman had "turned the Civil Rights Commission into an active, positive force working for equal rights for all Ohioans," hoped the soon-to-be-appointed Ethics Commission would clarify the situation.[51]

Three days later, Gilligan appointed to the Ethics Commission Republicans Bruce Petrie of Cincinnati, E. W. Lampson of Jefferson, and James Slater Gibson of Toledo and Democrats James C. Kirby Jr. of Columbus, Reverend Robert A. Raines of Columbus, and Barbara Rawson of Shaker Heights and inaugurated their activities at a luncheon at the Governor's Mansion. (The Senate Judiciary Committee urged easing ethics laws restrictions on lawyers to allow people who served part-time on hundreds of state and local boards and commissions to do other work for the government.)

In his fourth "State of the State" address, delivered January 15, 1974, Gilligan said that Ohio had made unparalleled strides in building the society that citizens wanted for themselves and their children. He called the ethics bill passed the previous fall "the clearest, toughest and, I believe, the most effective law on the books of any state in the Union."[52] More, however, was needed. Finishing the job, he said, required enactment of "a tough, enforceable campaign spending law that will eliminate the sleazy practices that have outraged the people for so long."[53]

Here, Gilligan's wishes suffered at the hands of the slender Republican majority in the Senate, which in mid-January introduced its own proposal. The GOP measure largely restated the position the party had taken in the previous fall's special session, maintaining the requirements that all candidates have but a single committee for soliciting funds, with amounts reported both before and after the election. And the GOP set limits of $3,000 in contributions per candidate and $25,000 from any given individual. But the Republicans held to their controversial "freedom of choice" clause, which, rather than permit labor unions to make block donations to political candidates, generally Democrats, would require union members to individually designate their contributions. Among other things, this would give unions the considerable clerical task of summarizing those donations.

Four weeks later, the Senate, by a 17–15 party-line vote, passed and sent to the House a bill still containing the freedom of choice provision. Further, the Senate adopted an amendment offered by Michael Maloney abolishing the elections commission intended to oversee enforcement. The bill did set spending limits—10 cents per capita for candidates for governor and senator, a figure that Senator Tony Hall (D-Dayton) said would "make politics the sport of rich men and women and well-financed lobbies."[54] A month thereafter, the Democratic-controlled House approved by an 82–11 margin a bill starkly different from the Senate version. Freedom of choice was eliminated; limits on campaign expenditures were set for all offices; pressuring state employees to make donations was declared a crime; and the state elections committee to enforce the provisions of the act was reinstated. In one aspect, the Democratic bill was weaker: it set no limits on personal and organizational contributions.

What has been termed "a quite modest reform bill" was passed by the General Assembly on April 4.[55] The bill had four main features. The first, on campaign organization, required candidates to have a single fund-raising body with preelection reporting of amounts raised. The second, on conflict of interest, forbade contractors from receiving nonbid contracts from any officeholder to whom they had donated $1,000 or more. The third, enforcement, created a bipartisan Ohio Elections Committee to be appointed by the secretary of state. The fourth feature, and likely the most important, set campaign spending limits for each level of office, including $16,139 for state representative, $38,734 for state senator, $1,065,201 for governor. Prominent members of each party were unimpressed with the legislation as passed. Tony Hall asserted that "the bill is only a shell designed to fool the public into thinking the legislature has enacted" something tough.[56] Republican state chairman Kent McGough described it as "a very weak law" that would have "almost no effect on our operations."[57]

Given the enormous sums of money that find their way into political campaigns today, and given the multiplicity of committees and means (not always revealed) by which those funds reach individual candidates, any law that established unitary fund-raising committees, required preelection reporting of sums raised, and limited campaign expenditures was a reform that is unmatched at present. Ethics and campaign funding are subjects that those who hold or aspire to gain elective office characteristically shy away from. Given this, Ohio in 1973–74 made notable progress—as much, perhaps, as any state in the nation. This drew some deserved recognition. On April 21, 1974, Christopher Lydon of the *New York Times* wrote, "Ohio, not heretofore noted for Puritanism, is quickly becoming a state where it is the rule that candidates must walk financially naked into the political arena."[58]

When ethics legislation was first under discussion within the administration, Gilligan aide Phil Moots suggested that it was the man on the white horse who was likeliest to get himself muddied. The man he had in mind was Gilligan. And the irony of campaign finance reform in Ohio is that in the 1974 gubernatorial election, the candidate to be hemmed in by the newly established expenditure limit was Jack Gilligan.

32

The Sure Thing

John Joyce Gilligan, a man with a taste for the classics, may have seen in his 1974 election effort something akin to Shakespeare's War of the Roses cycle, in which rival factions seek the kingship of England with no quarter sought or given. In his own case, the rivalry was not between the Houses of York and Lancaster but between Jim Friedman and Jack Hansan and all those who sided with one or the other.

Gilligan greatly valued Hansan both as a person and as an administrator: "It was just perfectly evident that here was a guy who was true-blue all the way. He wasn't out to feather his own nest; he was out to improve the society."[1] Hansan generally received high marks as chief of staff, for seeing that the paper flowed, the decisions were made, the proper person was appointed, and the deadlines kept. Further, Gilligan placed value on what might be termed Hansan's dispassion—his disinclination to allow his judgment to be influenced by personal likes or dislikes. This, Gilligan believed, allowed Hansan to put people where they would be of most use, or to dispense with them if usefulness proved not to be their strong point. Of himself, Hansan said that, unlike most people, he knew what power was and how it was meant to be deployed.

Jim Friedman was politically a powerhouse, perhaps more of a workhorse than a show horse, but one with the shrewdness to identify the issue most in need of tackling and the energy to then tackle it. Appalled at how the lack of funds had constricted Gilligan's 1968 Senate battle with William Saxbe, Friedman had vowed that, financially speaking, Jack Gilligan would never go hungry again. He had made good on that commitment. Friedman headed up fund-raising for the 1970 gubernatorial bid with such success that virtually the entire sum required was raised and banked by Labor Day, allowing the candidate two months of campaigning unencumbered by any need to meet with or solicit donors. And, perhaps curiously, while Friedman was something of a freelancer, he did not ride alone; he was personally and politically close to both Mark Shields and Peter Hart, two individuals whose political skills were highly and rightly esteemed by the governor.

The difficulty was that Hansan and Friedman could barely stand to be in the same room. For his own part, Gilligan had hoped the ill will would fade with time, a hope that itself faded. Gilligan later commented, "They weren't going out in the alley to fight it out, but they weren't going to play on the same terms, either."[2] Gilligan was well aware of Friedman's association with Shields: "Did I regard [Friedman and Shields] as a "two-fer"? Yes. And Peter Hart was much the same. They were personally loyal to Friedman. They felt he had not been dealt with fairly [in being dismissed]. They were disinclined to get involved in the campaign."[3] Gilligan said that "the break had been made." Hart and Shields were incomparable in their fields, but when it came down to a decision, they didn't want to play on the new team. "I was grievously wounded, but there wasn't much I could do about it."[4]

That things were bad became evident on November 22, 1972, when various administration insiders met at the Madison Hotel in downtown Washington, D.C., to begin planning the 1974 campaign. Bob Daley recalled, "It very quickly broke down into a simmering disagreement between, on one side, Jack Hansan and the other side Jim Friedman, and to some degree Mark Shields. The result of that session was a bust! It took us a year to get the thing put back together."[5] There was considerable backbiting. Communications director Max Brown recalled, "Friedman and Shields would make overtures; the Hansan group always rebuffed these. They did not want Gilligan to revert back to his true nature."[6] At meetings of Hansan and staffers, Brown added, "someone would say, 'We've got a problem; the governor is on the phone with Shields again.' The innocent and unknowing one was Jack Gilligan."[7]

The stakes were high. It is likely that at this time Jack Gilligan was casting an acquisitive eye in the direction of the White House and the 1976 election that would determine its next occupant. This was hardly mere daydreaming. Any two-term governor from a major swing state was likely to have at least sugar plum thoughts of Pennsylvania Avenue. Gilligan acknowledged at the time that it would be difficult to campaign nationally if one had the responsibilities of a sitting governor and that the nomination, if it was to come, would have to be from a "brokered" convention in which he emerged as the most acceptable to the broadest constituency.[8] In terms of possible rivals, given Watergate, Gilligan thought it probable the Democrats would go outside Washington for a candidate, choosing a governor or ex-governor. Those he saw as likely included Reuben Askew of Florida, Jimmy Carter of Georgia, and Pat Lucey of Wisconsin—all from states with fewer electoral votes than Ohio. As late as August 1974, Gilligan discussed the prospect of establishing a commission somehow tied to the nation's bicentennial in 1976 that could somehow serve as a possible launching pad for a presidential campaign.[9]

And, a straw in the wind, Gilligan began accepting more out-of-state speaking engagements, a common enough way for a prospective candidate to test his appeal. A fine public speaker, Gilligan enjoyed the podium and the play of language on an audience. On June 1, 1973, Gilligan spoke in Washington, D.C., to the National Urban Coalition; on August 25, he addressed the convention of the Indiana Democratic Editorial Association in French Lick; on October 25, he addressed the National Association of Democratic State Chairmen in Louisville, Kentucky. While his remarks tended to be straight-on assaults on President Nixon, he did not spare his own party. He told the Louisville audience, "Obviously, the most important thing that we [Democrats] did was to permit the re-election of Richard M. Nixon as President of the United States"—a feat accomplished, he argued, through the party's division.[10] He was scathing of Nixon: "This is the man who called the students who marched, cried out and wept for peace *bums,* while he lied to Congress and the American People about what he was really doing in Southeast Asia."[11] Gilligan spoke of unmet responsibility, as when he told the National Urban Coalition that the "federal government is responsible for assuring a minimum level of income, education and health care below which no American must be allowed to fall."[12] He asserted that political leaders shied from this due to a "basic inability to believe that the people are capable of understanding and choosing what is good."[13] To the Democratic editors in Indiana, he quoted the remarks of Walter Lippmann, made on the verge of the Second World War: "Upon the standard which the wise and honest will now repair, it is written: You took the good things for granted. Now you must earn them again."[14]

Some national observers saw a Gilligan candidacy in 1976 as well within the realm of possibility. National political reporter David Broder thought a Gilligan candidacy "very plausible. If he'd been re-elected, he would clearly have been one of the six or a dozen plausible Democrats in 1976, which turned out to be a good year for the Democrats."[15] And Clayton Fritchey in the *Washington Post,* while noting that Senators Edward Kennedy, Walter Mondale, and "Scoop" Jackson were the frontrunners, called attention to three dark horses: Senator Adlai Stevenson II of Illinois, Birch Bayh of Indiana, and Jack Gilligan. Of Gilligan, Fritchey wrote, "a landslide reelection would transform him into a national figure."[16] *New York Times* analyst Christopher Lydon included Gilligan among a dozen prospective candidates.[17]

Such speculation was not universally pleasing, however. In May 1973, Jody Powell, a key strategist for Jimmy Carter, surfaced in Columbus, where he bent various ears, including that of Statehouse reporter Brian Usher. Usher, perhaps mildly touched by state pride, told Powell that Ohio had a governor of its own who might be making the run. Powell, Usher recalled, managed to restrain his pleasure at the news.

At the same time, there were skeptics. When *Plain Dealer* reporter David Hopcraft met in Cleveland with a visiting Robert Strauss, then the Democrat's principal fund-raiser, Strauss indicated no interest in Gilligan whatsoever. As a possible indication of Gilligan's own interest, when Hopcraft wrote an article describing Strauss's indifference, the reporter got a very cool reception at the Governor's Mansion. Further, one longtime Washington insider said that Gilligan's thoughts of a brokered convention were the wishful thinking common to candidates who could not be nominated in any other way; the Democrats had not had a brokered convention since Adlai Stevenson's nomination in 1952 and were unlikely to do so in the future.

Through 1973, however, the main obstacle to Jack Gilligan's political advancement was the continuing uncertainty over who would head his 1974 campaign. Bob Daley recalled: "The governor said, 'I'll have a campaign manager by the end of June.' Well, June came and went. So it just drifted. We missed deadline after deadline."[18] Things drifted, likely, because Gilligan still hoped to involve Friedman and Shields and sought a draft campaign plan from Shields. Shields was ambivalent, acknowledging, "We had a little bit of a falling out, me and Gilligan."[19] Shields remained close to Jim Friedman, occasionally calling on him for assistance with campaigns he was working. "I did not have confidence in Jack Hansan. I said I would do the campaign if Jimmy [Friedman] was involved."[20] The view from the other side was that Hansan would work with Shields but not Friedman. Shields thought that this was a way of getting rid of them both. Gilligan considered separating the campaign from the administration: let Hansan run the government and let Friedman run the campaign. Hansan was hardly the only one to argue that this was not a sustainable distinction; governing and campaigning interacted in so many ways that no line between them could be drawn and held.

Gilligan's interest in the matter became another cause for delay. In July 1973, while Jack Hansan was vacationing in Europe, Gilligan invited Shields and Friedman to the Governor's Mansion. Friedman recalled, "We talked about the two of us running the reelection campaign for 1974 and how that might segue into a presidential effort."[21] Friedman left the meeting believing it was a done deed. Bob Daley recalled that "a day or two later, Jim called me and said, 'Well, we're all set to go.'"[22] When Daley professed ignorance, Friedman, he recalled, said, "Well, if [Gilligan] didn't tell you, he will, so let's do this and that."[23] But Gilligan never spoke to Daley about it; indeed, when Daley raised the matter with Gilligan, the governor stated, "Hell, we never decided that."[24] Nor did Gilligan override the objections raised by Hansan when the latter returned from vacation. Eventually, Gilligan met with Friedman to spell it out directly: given the heritage of animosity, there would be no place for Friedman in the forthcoming campaign. And Friedman felt quite sincerely burned. He wrote a four-page, single-spaced letter to Gilligan expressing "disappointment and some anger."[25] It was a letter he never sent.

Throughout all this backbiting and intrigue, time was passing. The administration did not seem to view this as a great problem. It was all but universally assumed throughout the Ohio political world that Gilligan would be reelected and reelected easily. One leading Republican media consultant recalled, "Not only did every Democrat in the state of Ohio think Jack Gilligan was going to be reelected, just about every Republican thought so, too."[26] Gilligan may not have been someone with whom the average voter would delight in sharing a beer, but he had a solid record of accomplishment and a reputation for honesty that would stand well in an election cycle heavily influenced by the misdeeds known as Watergate. This expectation of Gilligan's invulnerability was widely rooted: as late as April 28, 1974, a survey of the Statehouse press corps conducted by the *Cleveland Plain Dealer* returned the unanimous verdict that Gilligan would gain another term.

The second reason for Democratic confidence was the growing expectation that Republicans would nominate James A. Rhodes for a third term in office. Rhodes filed his nominating petitions in January 1973—early, because he expected a court challenge. Ohio had a two-term limit to the governorship, and Rhodes had already served two terms. But did the restriction mean two terms "in a lifetime" or two terms "consecutively"? Gilligan and other Democrats clearly hoped the Ohio Supreme Court would take the latter view, clearing the path for a Rhodes candidacy. On May 10, the state's high court declared Rhodes eligible to run. Asked if this decision left the state's Democrats "off-the-record" happy, Gilligan press secretary Robert Tenenbaum said, "The Democrats were not 'off-the-record' happy; we were flat-out happy."[27] A good many Republicans quietly shared doubts about Rhodes's attempted comeback.

> There's a distinct uneasiness within Republican ranks over former Governor James A. Rhodes' bid to return to the governor's office next year. Although many party veterans recall Rhodes . . . built a political dynasty as Ohio's Number One salesman, they will also confide that past allegations about Rhodes' income tax problems are certain to surface again in the campaign—and could be even more damaging in the context of the Nixon Administration's trouble the past year.[28]

Rhodes's strongest primary opponent was Representative Charles Fry (R-Springfield), a Kurfess lieutenant who had nonetheless voted against the tax increase. The *Plain Dealer* reported: "Fry and his lively family are touring Ohio in a chartered bus preaching that Rhodes is a scandal-smudged politician who cannot defeat Gov. John J. Gilligan in November. With the political atmosphere dominated by Watergate, Fry's chief campaign theme is integrity in government. It is a theme that the moderately conservative Fry hammers at every campaign stop."[29] Fry's statement that Rhodes's political morals were suspect was a statement that everyone associated with Jack Gilligan welcomed and seconded. Many Democrats regarded Rhodes as a throwback to some earlier quasi-Paleolithic age of Ohio politics, when the governor fiddled the books while the Cuyahoga River burned. Republican representative William Batchelder was likely correct when he said, "They thought Jim Rhodes was a buffoon."[30]

There was, however, a specter haunting the Gilligan campaign—the possibility that Gilligan might be a candidate for president in 1976. If, indeed, Gilligan did leave Ohio for Washington, then he would be succeeded by the sitting lieutenant governor. State senator Anthony Calabrese had won the 1970 Democratic nomination for that post, only to lose in the general election that November. Clearly, he intended to try again. Gilligan was not indifferent to Calabrese's ambitions; the governor bluntly declared the state senator as "the last Democrat on Earth" fit to be governor of Ohio.[31]

And here, another matter intervened, one that requires something of a flashback.

On June 17, 1972, five men were apprehended breaking into the Democratic National Committee headquarters in the Watergate complex in Washington, D.C. This, which Republicans initially dismissed as a "third-rate burglary," was the point of departure for one of the great American political scandals—one that would eventually drive Richard Nixon from the White House and, less noted at the time, considerably complicate the political life of Ohio governor John Joyce Gilligan.

The Watergate scandal is here only summarized—How a $25,000 cashier's check, supposedly a donation to the Nixon campaign, wound up in the bank account of one of the burglars. How the *Washington Post* provided evidence that Nixon's attorney general, John Mitchell, controlled a fund for intelligence-gathering on the Democrats then reported that the Watergate break-in was part of this effort. From there, matters snowballed. Former Nixon aides G. Gordon Liddy and James W. McCord were convicted on burglary and wiretapping charges in connection with the Watergate break-in; principal White House staffers John Ehrlichman and H. R. Haldeman resigned, as did attorney general Richard Kleindienst. The U.S. Senate held nationally televised hearings on the matter, chaired by North Carolina's Sam Ervin. A former presidential appointments secretary, Alexander Butterfield, revealed that President Nixon customarily tape-recorded all conversations in his Oval Office. Nixon declined to turn the tapes over to Congress. The president then ordered the acting attorney general, Elliot Richardson, to dismiss Archibald Cox, the special prosecutor appointed in the affair. Rather than do so, Richardson resigned on October 20, 1973.

At this point, the story takes an Ohio turn. On November 1, Richard Nixon nominated Senator William Saxbe of Ohio as Richardson's successor. Saxbe was a doubly odd choice. First, though a Republican, he had not been a notable supporter of the Nixon administration. In the Senate, Saxbe opposed deployment of the administration-backed anti-ballistic missile program and voted against Nixon's controversial Supreme Court nominee Clement Haynsworth. Indeed, *The Congressional Quarterly* reported that Saxbe had opposed the Nixon administration on five of nine major issues. Also, Saxbe had rather earthily dismissed Nixon's claims to ignorance of alleged Watergate misdeeds, which he likened to the piano player in a brothel claiming "he didn't know what was going on upstairs."[32] He did, however, have two characteristics to recommend him. First, as a former Ohio attorney general, he had some actual qualification for the post. More important, Saxbe was a U.S. senator. Any prospective attorney general nominated by Nixon was likely to face sustained and hostile confirmation—unless, that is, the nominee was a sitting U.S. senator, in which case senatorial courtesy might hold sway. Indeed, when William Saxbe was approved as attorney general on December 13, the entire undertaking lasted twelve minutes.

By Ohio law, the Senate vacancy created by Saxbe's appointment had to be filled by Ohio's governor, and on nobody's say-so but his own. For Gilligan, this was very much a Hobson's choice between his top candidates, Howard Metzenbaum and John Glenn. However, the 1970 U.S. Senate primary in which Howard Metzenbaum had narrowly eclipsed John Glenn had left both men with considerable dislike for each other and mutually antipathetic supporters. Gilligan knew that the appointment of either would make him about as many enemies as friends.

The vacancy could hardly have occurred at a worse time in relations between two of the principals, Governor Gilligan and would-be senator John Glenn. Looking to his 1974 reelection bid, Gilligan had urged Glenn to stand for lieutenant governor, as his running mate. The common thinking in the governor's camp was that the halo of Glenn's achievements in space would warm Gilligan's somewhat austere image. The sweetener was that service as lieutenant governor would position Glenn, who had never held public office, for a future statewide campaign for U.S. senator or governor, for which he could expect enthusiastic party support. Gilligan recalled, "I told Glenn that he could be lieutenant governor if he wanted that. He did not take it with any great grace."[33] Communications director Max Brown reported Glenn's response to the offer: "Let *Howard* be lieutenant governor."[34] According to Richard Fenno, Glenn's biographer,

> Gilligan invited the reluctant Glenn to a closed-door meeting at the drafty governor's mansion on a tree-lined street in suburban Bexley. With Gilligan were union leaders, warning that they would back Metzenbaum if Glenn rejected the governor's offer and ran against the Clevelander. To seal the deal, Gilligan told Glenn he had also lined up Democratic chairmen from about a dozen large Ohio counties—all in favor of a compromise that would keep Glenn out of the Senate race.[35]

On August 31, Glenn sought what became a rather lengthy meeting with Gilligan's chief of staff, Jack Hansan. Hanson's detailed notes of the occasion begin: "[Glenn] introduced the subject with a long list of points, which required a half hour."[36] According to Hansan, Glenn was startled to have Gilligan press the lieutenant governorship on him, as he had already rejected the offer. He believed he was being told that if he declined that offer, he faced "political extinction." He affirmed his

intention to "fight back" and said that he would stand in the May 1974 primary
for the Democratic Senate nomination. Glenn, Hansan said, repeated criticisms of
Gilligan and others present at the Governor's Mansion, "frequently using the terms
hoax and sham; worst type of hypocrisy." Further, Hansan said, Glenn accused
Gilligan of trying to "rig" the ticket and of unaccountably preferring Metzenbaum,
who Glenn said was a "bad guy" who tended to "buy" elections.[37]

Hansan, in response, told Glenn that the offer of the lieutenant governorship was
entirely sincere; that Gilligan and party leaders believed it in the best interest of all
concerned; that the Bexley meeting had not been stacked but represented a "good
and reliable cross-section" of the party leadership. Their consensus was that if the
primary were held that day, Metzenbaum would win; the party had an interest in
avoiding a bloodletting primary. He believed Glenn should see the wisdom of helping the party now in exchange for being helped in 1976 and suggested that any public attack by Glenn was likely to "bruise" Gilligan more than anyone, which would
hardly benefit the Ohio Democratic Party, whose good graces Glenn sought.[38]

Hansan later said, "Glenn thinks everybody is wrong except him."[39] Prior to that
meeting, he and Glenn had been on good terms; following that session, Hansan
said, "he never subsequently spoke to me."[40] In his political life, John Glenn was
widely credited with fine character, but he was also known to have the competitive
instincts of a Marine fighter pilot. Ohio political reporter Tom Suddes said, "Glenn
was a gentleman. But he had a sense of entitlement that would stop a train."[41]

Glenn's final rejection came at an Ohio Democratic Party meeting on September 18 when the executive committee formally endorsed Metzenbaum as the party's candidate in the 1974 Senate race. Glenn was outraged, and very publicly so. He
issued an eleven-page letter characterizing Gilligan's offer of the lieutenant governorship as backstabbing and announcing that the state Democratic leadership had
made him "a target marked for political extinction . . . because I will not go along
in a deception of our Democratic voters."[42] He further commented, "I didn't think
what they were doing was right. I felt I had earned my opportunity by my life in
public service to run for the Senate . . . I did not want to be told what to do. I see
myself as fulfilling a better role than lieutenant-governor . . . Besides, I don't like
deals . . . I am a target now marked for political extinction . . . because I will not go
along in a deception of our Democratic voters."[43] Fenno wrote that Glenn's crossing of swords with Gilligan did much to shape his political persona: "It affirmed
his public service view of politics and created a degree of political independence."[44]
His standing as a "citizen-politician" would prove appealing in an election year
dominated by the word "Watergate."

So, with Saxbe's confirmation pending, the issue of Metzenbaum versus Glenn
was the principal question in the state's political press. Gilligan recalled, "Every
time I stuck my head out the door, a reporter would ask me which I was going to

appoint."[45] The matter also became a principal point of discussion within the Gilligan administration. Press secretary Bob Tenenbaum recalled, "There was a real donnybrook of an argument; it went for days."[46] Tenenbaum was one of the few without a favored horse in the race: "I had an enormous admiration for Howard [Metzenbaum] as a politician and admiration for John Glenn as a person. He is an incredibly decent human being."[47] Jim Friedman recalled, "I told the governor I thought Howard could be elected."[48] Among the party hierarchy, there was little straight-out advocacy for appointing John Glenn—not terribly surprising, given the unsparing and righteous tones in which Glenn had shortly before denounced the state Democratic Party.

Mark Shields, however, proposed an alternative: "My view was that Gilligan should support anyone but either."[49] Nothing Gilligan might do in January, Shields believed, was going to head off a brawl of a primary between Metzenbaum and Glenn in May. Since Gilligan could do nothing to prevent a brawl, Shields urged him not to step into the middle of it. Shields, with support from Pete O'Grady and Bob Daley, argued for a "caretaker" appointment. The choice might be former House leader John McDonald or possibly Denny Shaul, a Rhodes Scholar who had run unsuccessfully for mayor of Akron. Such an appointment, Shields told Gilligan, would burnish the credentials of the Democrat chosen and help their future in state politics. Alternately, Gilligan could select a well-known and respected college president. In any case, Shields said, it should be a "quality" choice made with the understanding that the individual selected would step aside once the primary result was known.

John McDonald said, "I was told at one point that I was the governor's choice."[50] McDonald drafted a statement on how his appointment could take Gilligan off the hook. To his chagrin, he learned that Gilligan had made a similar statement to House Speaker A. G. Lancione. Ultimately, Gilligan rejected the caretaker approach. In Bob Tenenbaum's words, "Jack felt he had an obligation not to fiddle around with the U.S. Senate."[51]

Personal sentiment was not a significant factor in Gilligan's appointment. Gilligan was not fond of either man. Tom Diemer, Metzenbaum's biographer, quoted Gilligan as saying, "Howard Metzenbaum is the most offensive politician I have ever met, and John Glenn is always on the defensive."[52] Likely, Gilligan recalled that Metzenbaum had disappeared as Gilligan's chief fund-raiser during the 1968 challenge to Lausche; by the same token, Glenn had only months previously publicly accused Gilligan of shafting him in the worst sort of backroom deal.

But Gilligan did credit Metzenbaum's lengthy service to the party: "He was an outspoken Democrat who had been through the wars; Glenn was a celebrity who had not been in the forefront of any issue."[53] Again, the important perspective was Gilligan's: "I don't want to be nasty about it," he said, "but at the time I don't think

John Glenn ever did anything for anybody. All he had to do to win was go out in the street and shake hands, so he didn't undertake political chores like campaigning for others."[54] Further, when the pair had faced off in the 1970 primary, Metzenbaum had emerged the winner. This Gilligan regarded as a further argument in his favor.

And there is fair likelihood that Gilligan simply considered Glenn naive. He relates how, at the 1973 Ohio State Fair, Gilligan was in a trailer reserved for his use, showering and getting ready to change for a more formal event that evening. An aide informed him that John Glenn was at the door; the matter was urgent. Glenn entered to say that if Gilligan would appoint him to the Senate, he would declare his support for Gilligan for vice president. Gilligan recalled: "I said, 'John, do us both a favor and don't ever say that out loud. It's not going to do either of us any good.'"[55] Not only was Gilligan not a candidate for vice president, but, by all tradition, the presidential running mate would in due time be selected by the party's eventual nominee, who would likely make that decision without squaring it with John Glenn.

Gilligan believed Glenn should be patient: "I felt John could have virtually any position he wanted in the state if he just cooled off a little bit. He could well afford to step back and support Howard and do a little work in the party and then get the nomination he wanted."[56] In this, Gilligan misread the man: patience was not among the many virtues of John Glenn. An anecdote that underscores this recounts how Ohio Democratic executive director David Meeker posed Glenn a hypothetical: He could fly in a rocket ready to launch today but that, because of unsolved problems, might well not make it back to Earth, or he could wait two years and fly in a vehicle whose return was certain—which would he choose? "Why, the one this year, of course," Glenn said. "I might never get another chance."[57]

On December 19, 1973, Governor Gilligan announced the appointment of Howard Metzenbaum to the seat vacated by William Saxbe. Anticipating that move, Glenn had the previous week announced he would challenge Metzenbaum in the forthcoming May primary. However, the controversy did not entirely end there. Glenn and Metzenbaum had of course been vetted, with closets scoured for any skeletons that Gilligan should know about. Metzenbaum affirmed there were none. Then, two days before his Senate appointment was made public, Metzenbaum quietly paid $118,102 in federal back taxes. Because of this and some other possibly unresolved tax questions, the U.S. Senate delayed seating Metzenbaum until January 21, 1974, and then by the not entirely complimentary vote of 53–22.

That the case for Metzenbaum had been made by ranking Ohio labor leaders was of no small consequence. Such backing mattered: if you were a Democrat in the 1970s without fairly strong union support, you were a Democrat unlikely to gain public office. For Jack Gilligan, such support was an unambiguous combination of personal belief and political advantage. Indeed, in mid-1973, Gilligan had overseen passage of measures sought by labor. On June 28, the State House had passed Ohio's first minimum wage and sex discrimination bills. The bill fixed minimum compensation at $1.60 an hour for most workers and $1.30 an hour for agricultural workers with time-and-a-half for every hour above forty worked in a given week. The bill's chief sponsor, Barney Quilter (D-Toledo), was quoted in *Gongwer* as terming the measure "a step forward for more than 500,000 workers not presently covered by the federal minimum wage."[58] Not long thereafter, Gilligan signed into law a revised worker's compensation bill raising maximum benefits from $56 to $110 a week. The legislation, Gilligan said, "will enable Ohio's benefits to be more closely equal to those of our sister states in providing a livable income for those injured or disabled at a time when they need the income most."[59]

Speaking in Cincinnati to the state carpenters union, Gilligan highlighted his administration's record with labor. Not only had the weekly worker's compensation level been raised, but, to forestall Republican efforts to weaken the measure, the law established automatic increases based on two-thirds of the average weekly wage. Since taking office, Gilligan added, "we have nearly doubled unemployment benefits," raising them from a maximum of $66 to $114 a week, with built-in cost-of-living increases.[60] Additionally, the state extended unemployment protection to the 3,200 Great Lakes seamen whose ports of call included Lake Erie. Further, the state had greatly strengthened compliance with occupational safety laws, creating a Division of Occupational Safety and Health to broaden workplace inspection. Gilligan noted that when "the Industrial Commission came under our control, I removed the darling of the auto industry from its helm and appointed a steelworker."[61]

The Ohio General Assembly had moving on other reforms as well in 1973. On July 10, the House passed by a decisive 79–14 vote a bill giving consumers the means to identify outdated food products; the bill defined any food item with a safe shelf life of less than sixty days as "perishable." On July 18, following an "emotional, pointed, grueling and long" debate, the Ohio House voted 76–20 to authorize the state's Public Health Council to establish rules governing abortion procedures.[62] The measure, while it did not contravene *Roe v. Wade,* was strongly opposed by many abortion-rights legislators. Representative Henry Lehman (D-Shaker Heights) argued that the council was "totally unqualified" for the task it was being assigned and termed the bill "the greatest giveaway of legislative power."[63] If standards were to be set, the argument was advanced, it should be done by a physician body, the State Medical Board. The issue remained in limbo, however, as the Senate deferred action at the time. And on August 21, Gilligan signed into law a ban on the use of the cognovit note in consumer transactions, a statement signed by a debtor that, in the event the debtor fails to make repayment, waives any defense the debtor might have offered for that default. The bill, *Gongwer* reported, "was one of Governor John Gilligan's legislative priorities this session."[64] Judiciary Committee chairman Arthur Wilkowski called cognovit notes "a gimmick sought by those seeking an indentured servant."[65] The bill ensured that a judgment could be granted only after the consumer had been notified that a complaint had been filed, told the amount being sought, and ensured the right to retain counsel and to a court hearing. At the bill signing, Gilligan said, "I believe that allowing a consumer's money or property to be taken in payment of debt without giving him a chance to explain his reason for defaulting is an unconscionable act."[66] This list of actions showed both Gilligan's support for labor and his concern that fair treatment not be dependent on wealth or legal sophistication.

The conflict between Metzenbaum and Glenn over the Senatorial nomination ran almost to Christmas 1973 and into what, for Gilligan, was a troubled holiday season. On Christmas Eve, his mother, Blanche, died at the Cincinnati nursing home where she had been resident the better part of the previous five years. Her last years had been difficult, and she had withdrawn, barely noticing the visits regularly paid her by Harry Gilligan, the man who had determinedly wooed her more than half a century before.

The Glenn-Metzenbaum imbroglio had left hanging a further matter—who would Gilligan endorse as his running mate? One possibility was Representative Richard Celeste. Though only thirty-six, Celeste was a rising figure in Democratic state politics. He was on good terms with Gilligan, who had made Celeste one of the few local candidates with whom he had campaigned in 1970. In his fourth year in the legislature, Celeste had been elected majority whip, a post Celeste actively sought, spending four days visiting seventeen Democratic Party county leaders. Celeste recalled how various county chairmen told him, "Well, we think John Glenn ought to be on the ticket with Jack."[67] When Celeste said that this simply was not going to happen, one county chairman replied, "Yes, we know; isn't it a shame." In early January, Gilligan, persuaded that Celeste could hold off Anthony Calabrese in the Democratic primary, endorsed Celeste's candidacy for lieutenant governor.

By this time, the Gilligan campaign team was finally taking shape. Several possible campaign managers from out-of-state were interviewed, without result. Pete O'Grady's name surfaced. O'Grady, the former leader of the state Democratic Party, was the current director of the highway department. Bob Daley recalled:

> I don't know who it was that suggested Pete to Jack Hansan, but it was Jack's suggestion to the Governor that Pete O'Grady be the chairman. There were a number of reasons: Pete had experience; one, he was the former director of the party; he knows the powers around the state; secondly, he's been a good cabinet member. Thirdly, one of the things that was appealing to me was that he had a proven ability of working with us and with the Governor.[68]

Along with personnel, the campaign themes were being clarified. One reflected the continuing Watergate scandal. Richard Nixon was likely the American political figure that Jack Gilligan held in lowest regard: "I had such a consuming distaste for the guy that if he'd driven off a bridge I wouldn't have turned my head to watch him fall. He was a poisonous human being."[69] Further, he felt Nixon and his associates exercised a generally intimidating influence that prompted Democrats in general and reformers in particular to lay low when they should have been raising cane. So Watergate's role in the Gilligan strategy was central. Continued polling showed that voters regarded Gilligan as honest. For example, in May 1973, a poll conducted by Peter Hart showed 70 percent of respondents agreeing with the statement, "I admire Jack Gilligan for his honesty"—an eleven-point jump over the previous year.[70] Hart added, "Governor Gilligan continues to be held in a fairly high personal regard by the electorate. He is definitely regarded as an intelligent and active governor, and considered by most to be honest, responsible and courageous."[71] In a year of great cynicism about politics, the fact that 45 percent of respondents *disagreed* that Gilligan resembled "all politicians" who promised much but delivered little was seen as good news.[72] The character card, the Gilligan camp calculated, would be played, with James Rhodes's rather mixed financial history in the foreground and the Watergate scandal and possible impeachment trial of Richard Nixon in the background.

Gilligan would also run on his record—in school finance, fiscal responsibility, environmental protection, mental health, and other areas. Again, in the Hart poll, 71 percent of respondents agreed with the statement, "The Gilligan administration is working hard to solve the problems facing Ohio," a full fourteen-point jump over the previous year.[73] All this was, for an American political figure in the 1970s, very good news. The Gilligan camp believed that emphasizing character and achievement would offset what was seen as the governor's acknowledged weakness—that he was a figure to whom many in Ohio did not warm. As Hart reported:

> In the areas of friendliness and humility, voters are highly skeptical. Jack Gilligan is not a folksy, down-home type, and there is no reason to try to make him into something he is not. But in a contest against Rhodes, there will be a sharp difference in style, and Gilligan will lose ground in this area. This is acceptable as long as the governor can counteract this by demonstrating his intelligence, honesty, competence and candor. In essence, it is a question of whether the voters seek a governor who is well-liked or well-respected.[74]

The personal perception was important. Gilligan was much admired by most of the young and articulate members of his own cabinet. Executive assistant Jay Tepper said Gilligan was "far and away the best public servant I have ever worked for. As good as he was as governor, he was that good a person."[75] Similarly, Ohio EPA official Alan Farkas said of Gilligan, "He may not have been charismatic, but he was inspirational. I was not in his office that often, but any time I was, he didn't really care about the politics. He wanted to do the right thing."[76] But Gilligan's affinity for the quick foxes did not extend to those he regarded as lazy dogs. Representative William Batchelder said that Gilligan "did not suffer fools gladly," which, in Batchelder's mind, is "a big fault in a politician."[77] There is in politics, as in life, a fair sprinkling of fools, including those whose votes you may need. Gilligan did little to cultivate relationships with those in Ohio's General Assembly, leaving most dealings with the legislature first to John McDonald and then to Bill Chavanne.

Republican representative Keith McNamara told of how he was first elected to the House in 1960 by attacking "Tax Hike, Mike," the incumbent Democratic governor Michael DiSalle. Two weeks into the new office, McNamara and a number of other freshman Republicans were invited to dinner at the Governor's Mansion. DiSalle, a notable chef, cooked and served what McNamara called "the best Italian food of my life."[78] The guests left, McNamara added, still persuaded that DiSalle was wrong but thinking that "at least he was a pretty nice guy." The point of his story, McNamara added, was that McNamara could not recall Gilligan ever speaking to him.

Dick Celeste observed: "This was the political failure of Jack Gilligan and he could never distinguish between old timers who were honest-to-goodness liberals in the sense that they wanted a purposeful, active, progressive party in the state, but their manner was old time. They did worry about patronage. They wanted to have a drink and sit around and curse and be a little gruff and that wasn't Jack Gilligan's style."[79] About that style, Representative John Johnson (D-Orrville) recalled a 1971 dinner Gilligan hosted at the Governor's Mansion for new members: "There were hors d'oeuvres, cocktails, wine, and no beer. A representative from Lorain said, 'What kind of an organization is this?' Somebody went out and got some beer."[80]

Two lines of thought present themselves. First, Gilligan was an extraordinarily self-directed individual. Perhaps this was in fair measure the Jesuit influence— that while he might at times be uncertain as to what to do on personnel matters, he was not greatly afflicted with doubt on either the value of his person or the rightness of his values and was inclined to assume that others were similarly confident. Gilligan said in a 1974 interview:

> The other thing about politics that fascinates and baffles me—it is extraordinary to me how much hand holding people need out there; how badly they need to be reassured over and over and over again that they're doing a good job and they are just where they belong and that you really depend on them. I just think I don't require as much of it as other people do, and I am unable sometimes to understand other people's insatiable need for that. What happens—people begin to feel they are elbowed away from the crown. They're not talking about the merits of the decision anymore; they're talking about who won.[81]

The second, more prosaic possibility is that for a man who found his vocation in politics, he was not a glad-hander or a back-slapper or even terribly at ease with those who were. Gilligan said that he was aware of being considered aloof; the likelier, simpler truth of the matter was that he was socially shy, a shyness compounded by a lifelong inability to remember names.

> I've always had a problem remembering names. I remember in high school tak-
> ing a girl out dancing to the Pavilion Caprice. I saw a couple across the floor. I
> should have known her name, but I couldn't think of it. Racking my brain, waltz-
> ing around the floor. We bumped into them on the dance floor, and I couldn't
> remember *my* date's name, and I was finally reduced to saying, 'And what is your
> name, little girl.' And, boy, she was blistered.[82]

The meet-and-greet that is the meat-and-treat for many in politics, Gilligan said, was "the bane of my life."

> The inability to remember names often got encounters off on the wrong foot. I
> think a lot of people interpreted that as my being aloof. I found, by and large, I
> made a hell of a lot of friends, of high and low degree and of various circumstances.
> Some shared my political beliefs; some for other reasons. I never had trouble meet-
> ing people in that general way. I think that in groups I wasn't as comfortable; I'd try
> to come up with people's names and there would be nothing there.[83]

Gilligan was not, in the view of those around him, an easy man to get to know. One-time legislative liaison John McDonald commented, "I used to play tennis with the governor three mornings a week, and yet I don't think I know him that well."[84] Gilligan adviser Phil Moots picked Gilligan up at the Governor's Mansion at 6:45 A.M. twice a week, on the way to golf at an indoor facility in Columbus: "I did a lot of that. You might have thought that with that we would have developed a kind of personal relationship, but we did not."[85] Communications head Max Brown did advance work for Gilligan on mental health issues: "He was always a bit intimidating. You'd better be ready with the information. He was the smartest guy in the room. He was not your buddy."[86]

Another key decision—made personally by Gilligan—was to turn the media campaign over to Charles Guggenheim, one of the country's premier documentarians and among its most expensive. Explaining the decision, Gilligan said that the media campaign had "to be very quiet; it can't be blatant; it can't be brassy; it can't be overwhelming. It's got to be subtle. The David Garth approach [Garth was thought to have the instincts of a refined street fighter], which was good in [1970], but in my view doesn't fit the mood of the country this year."[87]

Robert Alan Cohen, who wrote a dissertation on the 1974 campaign, identified five main themes to the Gilligan effort: identification of Gilligan with Ohio, emphasis on accomplishments, use of surrogates to make strong attacks on Rhodes, comparisons of the Gilligan and Rhodes administrations, and an emphasis on open and financial disclosure. Finally, to carry news of this record to voters, the Gilligan campaign outlined plans for a massive volunteer effort, tens of thousands of mostly young Democrats organized by former Gilligan aide Michael Ford to bring the reelection campaign to Ohioans' doorsteps. Jack Hansan said, "The plan, in my head and on paper, clearly called for much of 1974 to be devoted entirely to the development of a citizen's organization for John Gilligan."[88]

The Gilligan campaign entered 1974 sufficiently confident of victory that it shrugged off the Metzenbaum-Glenn rift. It reacted somewhat similarly when, on February 16, the Government Accounting Office (GAO) issued a sixteen-page report detailing alleged transgressions committed by Ohio's Democratic and Republican parties in 1972, with the greater blame falling on the Democrats. These charges included, among many, preferential hiring of Democrats in positions partly paid for by the federal government and the soliciting of campaign contributions from state employees. Specifically, the report noted that approximately half of the $414,644 in ticket sales to the party's largest fund-raising dinner had been made by state employees. The GAO submitted the report to Attorney General William Saxbe and urged that it be reviewed by the state attorney general and the director of personnel.

In Ohio, the report drew mixed reactions. True, the deliberate hiring of identified Democrats to federally funded positions was a serious offense. But the hiring of "one's own" was also the long-standing tradition of both political parties. It was uncertain how forcefully, if at all, Attorney General Saxbe would act on the report; Saxbe, after all, as a longtime Ohio Statehouse politician, knew more than a little about how campaign funds were raised in his home state. Jack Hansan was not particularly concerned with legal repercussions: "There has never been an indictment [under the relevant statutes], there have never been arrests, there has never been a trial, there has never been anybody ever cited from one of those statutes. But nobody wants to be the first."[89] Still, he acknowledged that from a public relations standpoint, the report was not good. In part, it led to befuddlement, giving the Democrats pause on how to proceed, particularly on whether they could continue to draw on the employees of the state highway department to supply the "troops" needed to keep a campaign on the march. In the end, while no indictments were forthcoming, there was considerable confusion.

As Gilligan noted, a prospective presidential campaign of a sitting governor is subject to all manner of unanticipated interruptions. On the late afternoon of April 3, a massive, slow-moving tornado struck Xenia, the county seat of Greene County in southwestern Ohio. The tornado gouged a half-mile wide gash across the town of 25,000, toppling the local high school barely an hour after students had left for the day. To those who reached the scene soon after, the twister had left a range of curiosities—a full-sized mattress sucked halfway through a bathroom window; an apparently undamaged home that had been separated from its foundation; block after unrecognizable block of streets denuded of their trees; and thirty-six people dead.

By 6:30 P.M., barely two hours after the twister's touchdown, Governor Gilligan and press secretary Bob Tenenbaum were driving to the scene. Tenenbaum said, "We just got in the damn car and drove to Xenia."[90] Approaching the city, Tenenbaum recalled, "at some point, all of a sudden you could see the devastation. All the trees down, all the emergency vehicles."[91] They headed for the home of a relative of Tenenbaum, who, unaccountably unaware of the damage, answered the door saying, "What's wrong?" The National Guard, hundreds of rescue workers, and volunteers were on the scene. Assured that the situation was in good hands, Gilligan and Tenenbaum returned to Columbus.

While planning for the Gilligan campaign went forward, most public attention in spring 1974 focused on the no-holds-barred Democratic Senate contest between John Glenn and Howard Metzenbaum. The *New York Times* early on applied the word "bitter" to the race.[92] An early-March poll in Ohio showed a near tie: Glenn, 41 percent, Metzenbaum 40 percent.

One point of contention was that the self-made Metzenbaum chafed at the belief that while he had worked hard for what he had gained financially, Glenn's own affluence had come from cashing in on his status as astronaut. He suggested that Glenn lacked the background to be a U.S. senator because he had never held a job. Likely, what Metzenbaum meant was that Glenn had never worked in the private economy, but that distinction was entirely lost on the audience of the May 3 debate between the pair at Cleveland's City Club. Glenn said in part:

> I ask you to go with me . . . as I went the other day to Veterans hospitals and look at those men with their mangled bodies in the eye and tell them they didn't hold a job. Go with me and tell a Gold Star mother her son didn't hold a job . . . You go with me on Memorial Day, coming up, and you stand in Arlington National Cemetery—where I have more friends than I like to remember—and watch those waving flags and you stand there, and you think about this nation, and you tell me those people didn't have a job . . . I tell you, Howard Metzenbaum, you should be on your knees every day of your life thanking God that there were some men, some men who held a job.[93]

Coming from Glenn, generally a man of little eloquence, the remarks brought down the house and prompted a sustained standing ovation. Years later, Mark Shields said that having heard Glenn's speech, "I was all but certain that someday he would become president."[94] That was speculative; what was all but obvious was that John Glenn had taken Howard Metzenbaum down for the count. When primary votes were tabulated that May, Glenn emerged a relative easy victor—571,871 to 480,123.

For Gilligan, this was bad news. It meant that Ohio's Democratic Senate nomination had gone to a candidate who felt he owed Gilligan little, or nothing. That sense of grievance was exacerbated by Glenn's principal adviser, Steve Kovacik, who had been unceremoniously fired from the post of managing Cleveland's 1970 Gilligan campaign—a campaign for which Kovacik, stories vary, may have harbored expectations of serving as campaign manager.

Glenn aside, the Democratic primary was a victory for Gilligan. He had long believed that Ohio Democrats should act as a unified party, not simply as a vaguely associated group of somewhat like-minded people. It was therefore to Gilligan's pleasure that Richard Celeste defeated Anthony Calabrese, by 30 percent to 19 percent in an eight-candidate lieutenant governor race. According to Gilligan interviewer David Larson, Gilligan had hoped to run a black candidate for secretary of state. His candidate, Dayton state senator Tony Hall, was a former Peace Corps member and an articulate liberal. Hall competed in a six-candidate field that included the better-known William K. Brown (in Ohio, anyone named Brown is better known), defeating him by a 233,779–213,084 margin. And Gertrude Donahey and William J. Brown won essentially uncontested races for state treasurer and attorney general. The upshot was that Gilligan would lead a fairly united ticket of committed liberals. Jack Hansan commented at the time, "The Celeste-Hall thing were [sic] just sweet, sweet victories, because that really is the test of two things: one, the governor's political strategy continues to be the best of anybody's in the state. And two, it was particularly sweet because it means we have a ticket we can run on and be proud of, and that gives us momentum."[95]

From Gilligan's perspective, there was also good news from the Republican side. James Rhodes, who Gilligan considered his weakest potential opponent, was renominated with 59 percent of the vote. On his own side of the ledger, Gilligan collected 71 percent of the vote against a virtual unknown, James D. Nolan, whose campaign consisted of mimeographing and mailing out press releases about him and his views. In his victory statement, Gilligan said:

> I believe the Democratic Party stands for something in Ohio. It stands for programs that direct the services of government toward the needs of the people. That is what our administration has tried to do in these past three-and-a-half years with, I believe, a great deal of success. Now—in the next six months—we will put that record on the line. We will be presenting the work, discussing the achievements of the first Gilligan administration, and our ideas for the next four years.[96]

James Rhodes launched his own campaign on May 10 with a statement previewing his major campaign thrust—that Gilligan was a wasteful and disorganized administrator.

> My campaign will be a fight to eliminate waste, overlapping duplication, and wanton extravagance in the reckless spending of the taxpayers' money . . . It's a shabby operation, and a messy approach to management. Gilligan follows the Parkinson's

concept: when you can't solve a problem add 200 people to the payroll. While Ohio's income tax has been hailed as a panacea for schools, they are actually facing acute financial problems. There is widespread dissatisfaction in our schools.[97]

Rhodes particularized his viewpoint with a claim he repeated throughout the campaign that Gilligan was taxing everything that walked, crawled, or flew.

Rhodes's rhetoric notwithstanding, campaign manager Jack Hansan considered the May primary a significant victory for Gilligan. A second triumph followed just weeks later. Ohio AFL-CIO President Frank King, a thorn in Gilligan's side at least since his 1971 refusal to back the income tax proposal, was voted out of office when the state labor body met in Cleveland on May 27. King, head of the 900,000 member state AFL-CIO for a decade, was Gilligan's major rival within the Democratic Party—the New York Times termed him the "head of a vocal, anti-Gilligan faction within the state Democratic party."[98] King was defeated by Milan Marsh, a state building trades official from Youngstown, by a 3,014 to 1,801 tally. (The Gilligan administration had been behind the ouster. Gilligan commented: "A number of people from my administration worked on a day-to-day basis with labor. It was widely known that King and I didn't get along; no one felt that King's continued presence was essential to the administration or to the state or to anything else."[99])

Marsh's campaign drew key support from Warren Smith, secretary-treasurer of the organization, who openly broke with King, accusing him of mishandling both political and legislative matters. Smith was a Gilligan favorite: "He was quiet, anything but bombastic, soft-spoken. He had a vast knowledge of the labor movement and people out there. He was not interested in taking over the organization and running it. He wanted to have a good labor movement; wanted it to work well for the working people in the state."[100] Unsurprisingly, Marsh promised full support for Gilligan's reelection campaign.

In his own campaign, Rhodes was like a boxer who kept jabbing at the same spot—the spot being the wallet of the average Ohio voter and John Gilligan's presumed evil intentions for it. Rhodes gained a measure of credence when two pieces of news surfaced. First, news leaked that Gilligan was considering seeking a significant tax increase in his second term. The consequential public outcry pushed Gilligan to issue a "no new taxes" pledge. This, in turn, implied postponement of major highway projects, which suggested that highway contractors and their donations would gravitate in Rhodes's direction. Then, in June, the Legislative Budget Office, the financial arm of the state legislature, reported that the state was likely to reach December 31 with a $40 million to $60 million surplus. Gilligan, speaking perhaps too quickly, dismissed the matter, saying that anyone who thought the state was in surplus was "chasing moonbeams."[101]

But even moonbeams can aggregate—and, indeed, in the end, the state surplus edged above $80 million.[102] Today, that might be considered wonderful news. At the time, however, it was variously interpreted by Gilligan's doubters as evidence of financial incompetence or proof that the income taxes enacted had been larger than necessary. The man on the spot, finance director Jay Tepper said his task was to estimate income and expenditures as accurately as possible, with certain important caveats: if you projected a surplus, the state legislature might proceed to spend it; if that surplus did not materialize, then the state of Ohio would be bouncing checks. Therefore, he believed, a conservative course was best. The actual sum—the $80 million—was no bonanza, he pointed out; it was equal to approximately three days of state expenditure.

Accounting, however, is not generally as lively as politics. The surplus hurt Gilligan's campaign, said press secretary Bob Tenenbaum: "Suddenly, there was this '$80 million' surplus in the budget. That was raw meat for the Republicans."[103] The problem was made worse, Tenenbaum added, by the administration's apparent inability to explain how the extra money had come to be. In rough, the problem seemed to be that smaller errors made by each of three state departments had aggregated rather than offset each other. Gilligan saw one thing clearly: so far as his administration's credibility was concerned, this "was just about the worst thing that has happened to this administration and to me personally since I closed the parks in 1971."[104] And Jim Rhodes was quick to jump on the matter. Quoted in *Gongwer* on July 8, he said, "Because of the faulty planning and management, too much money has been earmarked by the present governor for welfare and the bureaucracy, while education has been left to suffer."[105]

By the standards of campaigns in the 1970s, the Ohio governor's race was still in its early days. On July 22, Pete O'Grady officially opened Gilligan's statewide headquarters with a balloon-busting press conference in a funky old bank building at 22 West Gay Street in Columbus. James Rhodes opened his own campaign with a press conference at the Neil House, where he claimed that 40 percent of those on welfare were there illegally. (He also said that Jack Gilligan should be worried because George Steinbrenner was being investigated by the Senate Watergate Committee. Why this should have caused Gilligan angst was left unexplained by the Republican candidate.)

Much later, Gilligan said that by the summer of 1974, he "began to have misgivings that things weren't going as well as they ought to be or seemed to be. We were running without a couple of cylinders, or something."[106] Quite possibly, he missed the professional and consequent comfort that might have come from Mark Shields and Peter Hart, had that pair been on the campaign. Possibly, his misgivings simply reflected a truism offered by Jack Hansan: the candidate is the individual who worries the most. And, maybe, quite simply, the candidate was exhausted. Son Donald Gilligan seriously questioned whether his father "had taken four consecutive days off in the entire time he was governor."[107]

Max Brown, Gilligan's communications director, recalled that on August 10, the day after President Richard Nixon resigned, Gilligan uncharacteristically called a full staff meeting. "He was almost angry at our incomprehension that a huge event had happened—'Don't you understand? *Huge*. This has huge ramifications for the state.' I thought, Nixon's resignation was huge, but what changes does that dictate? I didn't make that connection."[108] The connection Brown and the others hadn't made was that Gilligan had anticipated campaigning against the backdrop of the impeachment of President Nixon; a campaign premised on holding the moral high ground was weakened when it no longer had Dick Nixon to kick around.

There were also questions as to who was in charge. As time proceeded, it became clear that Pete O'Grady was head of the Gilligan campaign largely by proxy and that the real decision maker was chief of staff Jack Hansan. R. Dean Jauchius, a close Rhodes aide, later wrote, "Officials high in the Ohioans for Gilligan organization noted that Hansan's marching orders to O'Grady made clear that the [campaign] committee existed solely to handle the mechanical details of the campaign. Policy decisions and directives would come from Hansan and Gilligan."[109] Jauchius added that communication within the Gilligan campaign appeared to travel only one way—from headquarters to the field; there was little listening being done in Columbus: "Dissenting voices were ignored, dismissed as alarmist or simply screened out."[110]

This extended to the candidate's own family. All four Gilligan children were active in their father's campaign, and each had some level of doubt about the generally optimistic assumptions. Ellen, who took time out from college to campaign chiefly in Ohio's smaller counties, encountered considerable criticism that the governor had spent too little time in the rural parts of the state. John, coordinating the campaign in more-populous Mahoning, Trumble, and Portage counties, was restless that the statewide effort did not become more aggressive. All four Gilligan children passed their misgivings on to their father. Around Labor Day, Hansan summoned the foursome to his office and instructed them to stop bearing bad tidings to the governor. The election, they were told, was in the bag; negative reports risked upsetting the apple cart. Similarly, Michael Ford, who headed up the get-out-the-vote effort, felt that negative news was simply unwelcome at headquarters. As a twenty-something, Ford said he didn't believe he had the standing to take issue with the higher-ups. These actions and attitudes had the effect of isolating Gilligan from the fray, isolating a candidate who Republican Jauchius and others felt had the best political intelligence of any Democrat in the state, including his own campaign staff.

For the first four months following his nomination, James Rhodes ran a low-budget campaign, wandering the state and irritating Jack Gilligan with patently false statements. He accused Gilligan of hiring "plumbers" to dig up dirt on him, of presiding over more school closings than any governor *ever*, and of using state funds to "get" former AFL-CIO president Frank King. On August 24, the *Columbus Dispatch* quoted Rhodes as saying that budget mishandling by Gilligan was responsible for "the financial crisis in Ohio's school districts."[111] Further, Rhodes said Gilligan had falsely claimed the income tax would forestall the need for schools to seek more funds. Rhodes declined to prove or withdraw these statements. To many, Rhodes was the "old dog" of Ohio politics, undertaking a somewhat mangy campaign and one to whom no new tricks could be taught.

But they were wrong. In his successful 1962 and 1966 campaigns for governor, Rhodes did not spend a single dime on television advertising. Nor did he spend on television in his 1970 Senate primary battle with Bob Taft. That defeat made Rhodes a convert. Against Gilligan, Rhodes faced likely defeat, said Republican media operative Doug Bailey, one of two Ohio natives who formed a then-rising Republican political media agency, Bailey-Deardourff. The 1974 campaign, Bailey said, had two hallmarks. First, Jim Rhodes being Jim Rhodes, there was an emphasis on "jobs, jobs, jobs" coupled with the assertion that he could attract the jobs he alleged Jack Gilligan was driving off. The second was that Rhodes, uncharacteristically, took personal leadership of fund-raising and that all that money went for television. Bailey commented, "Part and parcel of the thinking was that because the national picture was so awful [for Republicans], the race had only one possibility of success, and that possibility was television." Bailey stated, "When I say Rhodes put *all* that money into television, I mean he put ALL into television. If it was a question of paying for an additional poll or putting the money into television, it went into television."[112]

Rhodes's media blitz struck on September 9, with a five-minute biographical spot that made the former governor sound like the true son of Ohio—hard working, responsible, a doer. The spot repeated the phrase, "When *he* was governor, taxes were low; jobs were plentiful. Ohio *prospered*."[113] John Deardourff claimed that the five-minute ad "showed Rhodes to be a lot warmer person, a more friendly person; that he related more to the common man than did Gilligan. We knew there was a lot of uptightness about Gilligan. On the other hand, Rhodes was easy-going, one of the most unassuming guys you could imagine."[114]

Far more effective, though, were ads that took direct digs at Gilligan. This was before negative advertising was so pervasive as to be entirely tolerable. In one ad, a pair of hands played a shell game, looking for the $80 million that Gilligan had at first denied existed. A series called "Days to Remember" reminded voters of Gilligan's closing of the state parks and the governor's comment that he "sheared taxpayers."

Meanwhile, Gilligan campaigned hard. Thursday, October 3, he was in Dayton for a media event at Wright State University and for meetings with state legislators and newspaper officials. Friday, October 4, he was in Cincinnati, meeting with high school newspaper editors and briefing the local press and attending a legislative fund-raiser and a reception for county Democrats. Saturday, October 5, he hosted a major luncheon with Ohioans for Gilligan at the state fairgrounds in Columbus, attended a fund-raiser, made an appearance at a labor reception in St. Clairsville, dined with the Belmont County Democratic committee, and arrived in Cleveland at 10:00 P.M. In Cleveland on Sunday, Gilligan attended morning Mass at Our Lady of Peace and a series of fund-raisers; he then headed to Kent for a "minority conference" and back to Cleveland for a visit to a Slovenian home, followed by three more fund-raisers before his 10:30 P.M. return to Port Columbus airport. At most of these stops, he talked about the successes of his administration—tax equity, school funding, mental health, and environmental reform—a great deal more than about any real or alleged shortcomings of James Rhodes.

Still, his actions suggested a certain divided attention. With the election just weeks away, Gilligan went to Washington, D.C., to meet with what were termed "a group of wealthy, Democratic liberal reformers."[115] Others present—all of whom were thought to nurture presidential ambitions—were Senators Lloyd Bentsen of Texas, Walter Mondale of Minnesota, and Henry "Scoop" Jackson of Washington as well as Congressman Morris "Mo" Udall of Arizona. Rhodes was quick to respond: speaking to a large Republican crowd in Columbus on October 17, the Republican said that his election would free Gilligan "to run for President on his own time."[116]

Back in Ohio, Gilligan, as in all his races, pressed his opponent to debate. It was, he argued, the best way to let voters know the stands each candidate took; it was also a forum that showed his articulate, informed, and combative personality to best advantage. Rhodes, rarely described as articulate, declined all such offers. Assessing the stump styles of gubernatorial candidates John Gilligan and James Rhodes, Abe Zaidan wrote: "Gilligan, a former English literature instructor, jauntily prods his opponent with a mock heroic humor that is sometimes imperious. Of his own goals and achievements in office, he is deadly serious. His speeches come amply adorned with statistics that, by the look of some of his after-dinner listeners, are at best, only half-digested . . . Still . . . Gilligan—despite pedantic tendencies—offers the best-balanced command of subject and style."[117] He also showed flashes of a self-mocking humor. (One story told of the time a reporter suggested that Gilligan's stage manner was "didactic and professorial," the candidate interrupted to add, "and arrogant."[118]) By contrast, Rhodes was "a torrential downpour, half-evangelist, half-prosecutor, slaying thousands of dragons with two flailing arms and a blur of rhetoric that bestirs the viscera, albeit numbing the intellect."[119]

But in the end, it was not Rhodes he faced across the podium. Having told an Ohio State University crowd that debate was "essential," Gilligan was taken aback when a young woman, Nancy Brown Lazar, came to her feet, identified herself as a candidate for governor, and accepted Gilligan's offer to debate. Although Lazar had been a member of the Socialist Workers Party and chair of the Cleveland Young Socialist Alliance, she was listed rather innocuously on the ballot as an "Independent." Good to his offer, Gilligan did indeed debate Lazar before an audience at the Cleveland City Club—an event that can only have added to her visibility and credibility.

In the final weeks of the campaign, Rhodes's media effort expanded to include twenty-six television stations and 226 radio outlets. It was a campaign that frequently closed with a message that undercut Gilligan's advantage of incumbency: "Let's Make Governor Rhodes Governor Again."[120] Rhodes spent heavily; in the dozen days between October 16 and 28, the Republican contender spent $328,000 on media alone, a third of his campaign's entire expenditure. Much of the money came from those who, having benefited from the first Rhodes administrations, could reasonably expect to benefit from his return to Columbus: highway construction firms, large business, and nursing home interests that faced substantial regulatory costs under Gilligan. In late October, Rhodes borrowed $110,000 from a small group of longtime supporters to drive his final push.

Rhodes's campaign expenditure was geographically targeted. *Plain Dealer* reporter Brian Usher calculated that in 1970, Gilligan received 46 percent of his total vote from eleven counties in northeastern Ohio. Counterintuitively, Rhodes spent most heavily there. His campaign's apparent thinking was that much of the Gilligan vote in the region was soft. Voters there backed the governor on economic and labor issues but were likely to be put off by his concern for social causes and perceived upscale manner.

In mid-October, the *Cleveland Plain Dealer* assayed the impact of Rhodes's media campaign:

Uneasy supporters of [Gilligan] believe Rhodes is on an uptrend and Gilligan on a downtrend with the election just about three weeks away . . . Gilligan's TV commercials, some believe, have been poorly done, with little impact on the public. The governor has taken an above-the-battle approach in his TV spots, which are packaged like public service material.

[Gilligan media director Charles] Guggenheim may be the best, but several media experts interviewed here last week agreed that Rhodes material is far superior. In his own commercials Gilligan is not the warm, issue-oriented governor who can win an audience with his off-the-cuff humor and well-grounded facts about the state's needs. Gilligan's new five-minute commercial features a mentally retarded youth being helped by a state "humanization" program. A media friend of Gilligan said, "That commercial is awfully heavy."[121]

Hugh McDiarmid noted that Rhodes "unleashed a barrage of slick ads, saturating the volatile Cleveland market and portraying Gilligan as an arrogant, uncaring, dangerously anti-business liberal . . . Yet for the most part the Gilligan team stood pat, convinced that its well-financed juggernaut of a campaign would prove a winner against Rhodes."[122] Communications director Max Brown admitted that Gilligan's media campaign "was not compelling," saying, "We hired Guggenheim to do the paid TV. In hindsight, and maybe earlier, I thought it was too esoteric, not an attack on Rhodes. Gilligan was impressed with Guggenheim . . . Guggenheim was aloof, aristocratic—a little like Jack himself."[123] Three weeks

before the election, Guggenheim urged the campaign to produce a series of negative ads but was waved off by Hansan and others.

The Gilligan effort had heavily committed instead to a ground campaign. Gilligan had forty full-time and eighty part-time staff, compared to Rhodes's six full-
time staff. Much of Gilligan's staff's time went into organizing tens of thousands of
volunteers to hit the telephones in the evenings before the election and the streets
the day of the election. The operation was run by twenty-six-year-old Michael
Ford, a former administrative assistant to Gilligan, who coordinated efforts with
Pete O'Grady. The ground campaign was budgeted about $280,000. While most
volunteers were young, Ford stated, "It was not a children's crusade. We had a
large number of housewives, faculty, labor leaders, and others."[124] The effort began, he said, with "building a campaign in as many of the eighty-eight counties as
we could, and deciding who would be the public faces of that campaign—would it
be established party figures or new folks?"[125] The next step was to coordinate volunteer activities with Gilligan's campaign schedule. Ford built in a "check-back"
protocol: doubtful of the optimistic results a good many volunteers were reporting from their door-to-door canvassing, he had volunteers write follow-up notes
to those they had talked to (with the notes read by coordinators before being
mailed). He also undertook "blind" telephone polling—that is, by callers who said
they had no association with the Gilligan campaign—to check the results.

It was a considerable undertaking. Perhaps 30,000–50,000 volunteers were involved. Ford says he never really knew the count; his efforts were focused on the total
number of volunteer hours needed and worked rather than the number of people
working them. The same day the *Plain Dealer* warned of Rhodes's cresting media
wave, the *Columbus Evening Dispatch* ran a laudatory piece on the ground operation.

> The scope of the operation is almost unbelievable. Since September 16, more than
> 200,000 telephone calls have been made and about 250,000 households have re-
> ceived literature. By Election Day, half a million. On Election Day, 500,000 calls
> will be made to people who haven't voted yet . . . Last week, Ford accompanied
> by a reporter, inspected field operations in Springfield, Troy, Hamilton, Cincin-
> nati and Columbus. The inspection trip is not unusual. From Ford on down, the
> field coordinators have to spend time three or four days a week personally mak-
> ing phone calls or literature drops—[this] serves to emphasize to the volunteers
> the importance of their work . . . In Cincinnati, sixteen girls dressed in jeans and
> plaid shirts were out on the streets dropping literature at doorways. Four girls
> can cover a precinct in an hour. There is a contest among Cincinnati parochial
> schools to see which can supply the most volunteers.[126]

State Republican Party chairman Kent B. McGough acknowledged that his own
party's operation couldn't touch the sophistication of the Gilligan effort, likely the

largest volunteer effort in Ohio political history. Still, the volunteers worked at a disadvantage: every time a Gilligan volunteer spoke to a voter out on the front porch, that same voter was seeing a dozen Rhodes advertisements in the living room. Ford observed that there was only so much the field organization could do about the advertising blitz. His operation, he said, was intended to "find and pull" Gilligan voters and get them to the polls. He added, "You can't control message on the ground."[127]

Broadly, the Gilligan campaign decided it could not shift gears to negative television ads in part because it was nearing the $1,065,000 limit on campaign expenditures established by the campaign finance reform bill the Gilligan administration had championed. One Democratic source said, "We had to make the choice of whether to put more into radio and television by cutting the hell out of our field organization." The choice was to go with the field organization.[128]

The campaign continued to receive good news. In mid-October, Gilligan received a series of strong newspaper endorsements, including those of the *Cleveland Press, Akron Beacon Journal, Dayton Journal Herald,* and *Lorain Journal.* He even received some kind words from one Ohio news outlet, the *Cincinnati Enquirer,* which had rarely in two decades said even a tolerant word of him: "Mr. Gilligan has faced and made a number of genuinely tough and highly consequential decisions." That paper, nonetheless, endorsed Rhodes.[129] Some still saw a Gilligan victory as inevitable. On October 20, Ronald Clark wrote in the *Akron Beacon Journal* that "not since 1958 has the Ohio Republican Party been so near a wipeout. That's not to say that one will occur, but the signs are obvious."[130]

They were not, however, universally obvious. In mid-October, Brian Usher reported in the *Cleveland Plain Dealer* that a poll by "a nationally recognized firm" gave Gilligan "a shaky six-point lead over Rhodes."[131] The poll had been leaked by the Glenn campaign. The Gilligan camp rightly suspected this move and discounted it. Usher recalled being told, "You are being used by the Glenn people. We're ten to twelve points up."[132] Usher was doubly offended—first, by the notion he was being used and second, by the fact that he wasn't believed. He added, "I was one of the few people who thought they could lose." Other polls gave the nod to Gilligan, but by widely varying margins. An Ohio poll reported in the *Cincinnati Enquirer* on October 11 gave the incumbent a secure-looking 44 to 33 percent lead, though with a perhaps concerning aggregate of 23 percent who were undecided or would vote independent or not at all. A more partisan poll commissioned by the Ohio Republican Party and taken by Market Opinion Research gave Gilligan only a three-point margin.

Vern Riffe, perhaps the sharpest member of the House Democratic caucus, was having doubts. Campaign manager Jack Hansan told Riffe he expected a quarter-million-vote victory and that Gilligan would be "the strongest, most powerful elected official at the Democratic National Convention in 1976."[133] To which Riffe responded to Gilligan, who was present, "This election isn't wrapped up." In his travels around state, Riffe had sensed considerable anger over the income tax and the park closings and just plain cussedness. He said, "If the Governor is reelected by 50,000 votes, I'll be satisfied. I'll be the happiest man in the room tonight."[134]

For much of the campaign, Gilligan spoke most often of his accomplishments in office. Speaking October 10 to 3,000 union members in Columbus's Memorial Hall, he rattled off his achievements—state aid to schools greatly increased, workmen's compensation and unemployment payment virtually doubled, Ohio's first minimum wage law enacted. He also attacked Rhodes's best-known phrase—that "profit is not a dirty word in Ohio." But, Gilligan added, the air and water *were* dirty because of Rhodes's unwillingness to crack down on polluters.[135]

Rhodes, even by the standards of stump speakers, felt no particular commitment to fact, in the factual sense. At one point, Gilligan communications director Max Brown sent telegrams to every television station in the state trying to head off a series of assertions that would be made in pending Rhodes advertisements. Rhodes claimed that thousands of jobs for Ohio's working men and women had been lost. Actually, Brown said, employment in the state had risen from 4,143,000 to 4,569,000 since Gilligan took office. Rhodes claimed that when he was governor, "almost half" the state budget went to education; the actual figure, Brown reminded the media, was 37.6 percent. Brown closed his telegram, "We respectfully request that these erroneous statements not be aired."[136] (Since the media air erroneous advertisements all the time, Brown's request may have been ignored.)

Faced with the media barrage, Gilligan decided it was time for sterner stuff. Speaking to an assembly of Democratic women at the Neil House, he declared Rhodes to be a "political swindler" who made promises he had no intention of keeping. Rhodes's world, he said, was the "politics of ribbon cutting and blow-off huckstering."[137] His campaign told the *Plain Dealer* on October 19 that it would reorient its media message from a soft sell praising the governor's accomplishments to "attacks on the integrity of his Republican opponent."[138] The new ads would emphasize the 1970 Crofters scandal, in which Rhodes had been at least a peripheral participant, and Rhodes's refusal to disclose the sources of his campaign funds or his own personal finances. The campaign would reportedly spend $65,000 on radio and $85,000 on television in the final three weeks.

On October 21, Gilligan blasted Rhodes over a deposition the former governor had recently given in connection with the trial of the National Guardsmen who had fired on unarmed students at Kent State University. Rhodes testified that he did not know that the guardsmen had been armed, or with what weapons, and "that the then Adjutant General, Sylvester Del Corso, would not take orders from him."[139] Gilligan said Rhodes had been "derelict in his duties" and noted that Rhodes's unsuccessful effort to keep the deposition secret until after the election was "understandable" given his performance at the time.

Indeed, the deposition can hardly be regarded as Rhodes's finest hour. The *Akron Beacon Journal* reported that "frequently in the testimony, Rhodes evades direct answers to questions from [Steven] Sindell, [attorney for parents of the four slain students], either by offering lengthy circular statements that miss the point or by responding rhetorically:

> [Sindell] "What is your recollection?"
> [Rhodes] "Just what the law says."
> [Sindell] "What do you think it means?"
> ["Rhodes] "Well just exactly what the article says."[140]

Candidate Gilligan issued a press release saying he felt the need "to express shock and outrage" at Rhodes's statements, including his apparent ignorance that the state's governor was commander-in-chief of the Ohio National Guard, and at Rhodes's assertion that he had not known the guardsmen were carrying live ammunition.[141] Gilligan was hardly alone in his reaction. The *Akron Beacon Journal* carried an editorial headlined, "Jim Rhodes' Mental Lapse At Kent Defies Belief."[142]

On October 22, Gilligan was in Youngstown speaking to a group of African American leaders. According to the *Cleveland Press,* Gilligan "mounted the stage and listened to them gripe at him for awhile. On the way into the hall he stopped to embrace his son, John Patrick, who is organizing in Youngstown."[143] The black leadership meeting ended with the assembly vowing loyalty to him in the election. In the car later on, the governor chuckled about the affair. "You have to walk in and let the leader slap you around a little bit to prove he has machismo," he said. "Then, after he's proved he has some clout, he'll let you know he's with you."

Republican media specialist Doug Bailey observed that the Rhodes campaign was little concerned with ethics charges brought against Jim Rhodes. Rhodes had been in statewide politics a quarter-century and had been the subject of continuing accusation—not all serious, not all baseless. In Bailey's mind, Ohio voters had long ago individually decided whether Jim Rhodes was a good old boy who occasionally bent the rules or whether Jim Rhodes was a crook. Bailey believed that as long as no new and serious allegation against Rhodes was made, rehashing what was long known would have little effect. Also, even with the Gilligan campaign spending $150,000 on media buys during the final three weeks up to Election Day, they would be overspent by Rhodes, who as noted was spending $328,000 just between October 16 and 28.

Still, Gilligan continued to consider the election a choice between government conducted by principle and government conducted by any means convenient. In his final television ad filmed the week before the election, he played what he regarded as his strongest card.

. . .

In this election year the people are entitled to some straight talk, but they are not getting it in the race for governor because my opponent refuses to discuss the issues. In the four years I've been in government we've accomplished many things and we've also made mistakes; I know I've made my share. But one thing I have never done is lie to the people. I've tried to say where I stand on the issues, and I've made my personal and campaign finances a matter of public record. My opponent refuses to disclose his own personal finances despite the fact that there have been questions for years about where he gets his money. Jim Rhodes refused to disclose his campaign finance despite the fact that thousands of dollars have been reported missing in the thirty years he'd been running for public office. I know you want honesty in your state government. I need your vote on November fifth.[144]

33

A Long Night, and the Morning After

The day before the election, Governor Gilligan took a moment and called Peter Hart, national pollster and longtime associate to thank him for the effort he had contributed that election year. He also spoke with Mark Shields, suggesting that the two of them might meet soon to discuss possible futures. In his own call from Gilligan, Hart recalled not a trace of anxiety in the governor's voice or any suggestion that victory might not be his when the ballots were counted twenty-four hours later. Hart, who would be advising CBS News on its election night prognosticating, said that he was "much less confident than I think Gilligan was."[1] By no small irony, it is possible that Peter Hart would be the first person in America to know that Jack Gilligan would go down to defeat.

Later, a number of Gilligan officeholders and campaign staffers talked about having had doubts, which, likely enough they did, if for no other reason than such is human nature. But whatever doubts might be retrospectively identified, they were not articulated sharply or soon enough to prompt any redirection in the campaign.

Jack and Katie Gilligan and James and Helen Rhodes voted early, with airs of outward cheerfulness and with hopes that the pictures of their balloting might make the front pages of some of the day's Ohio newspapers. Throughout the state, Gilligan's army of volunteers—perhaps 30,000 or more strong—descended on the electorate, phoning, urging, and coaxing them to the voting booths.

By the time polls closed, more than 3 million Ohioans had cast their ballots. The 1974 election was before the era of exit polling, but by early evening a strong Democratic tide was running. With the exception of the race for secretary of state—where Democratic state senator Tony Hall trailed incumbent Republican Ted W. Brown, en route to his ninth consecutive victory—the Democrats held healthy leads in every statewide race down-ticket from the governorship. It was clear that the Democrats, having gained the Ohio House of Representatives in 1972, would add control of the Senate by a healthy margin—thus, apparently ushering in a period of strong party dominance.

That, of course, depended on the outcome of the race between Gilligan and Rhodes. By 8:00 P.M., analysts at NBC and ABC had called the election for Gilligan. Over at CBS, Peter Hart was not following suit. Hart spoke the simple truth when he said, "At that point, I knew Ohio better than anybody else [at the competing networks]. I didn't like the numbers I was seeing from particular counties. It didn't look good."[2] Hart was not the only one unnerved by the data. Chris Buchanan, who had crunched numbers for the 1971 redistricting effort, was in Columbus poring over the data as it came in, then comparing it to county voting totals from 1968 and 1970. Looking at the numbers, Buchanan was "devastated."[3] Representative Richard Celeste, the Democrats' candidate for lieutenant governor, spent much of the day ferrying coffee to party volunteers. By 8:15 P.M., his victory seemed secure, and he headed for Columbus and the Democrat's traditional gathering place, the Neil House.

Among those present were Bob Tenenbaum and his wife, Judy, who had been active in a closely fought congressional campaign. Tenenbaum recalled, "At some point early in the evening—8:30 or 9:00—we got the notion that the turnout wasn't what we needed it to be. Maybe ten or fifteen people knew that."[4] With perhaps two-fifths of the vote counted, Gilligan led by 644,239 to 622,314, but as the earlier votes counted were more likely to be Democratic, this did not bode well. Celeste arrived, took the temperature of the room, and found it chilly. Someone reported seeing one of Gilligan's inner circle stride by "with tears streaming down his face."[5] Celeste's feelings were understandably mixed: he had regarded a Gilligan win as the likely precondition of his own. Now, by campaign convention, it was his supposedly happy chore to stride down to where Democrats were mingling in the ballroom and claim victory—even though the man he intended to serve under appeared to be losing. Sometime before 10:00 P.M., Celeste went to see Jack and Katie Gilligan in their suite. Pete O'Grady and Bob Daley were there, too, tabulating results. Celeste recalled, "Jack Gilligan was a defeated man. I mean to look at him, he was defeated."[6]

Indeed, the only politician in the state willing to go on record as stating that Jack Gilligan had won was Gilligan's opponent, James Rhodes. At 12:50 A.M., Wednesday, November 6, Rhodes walked out before the press and graciously conceded defeat: "The election is over. Governor Gilligan has won it, and we're not going to discuss the past at all. I want to wish him well, he and his wife."[7] Shortly thereafter, Jim and Helen Rhodes stood alone at an elevator, where they were spotted by several Gilligan workers. One noted that he looked defeated and that "she appeared frankly relieved at not having to reenter public life."[8] Almost simultaneously, Katie Gilligan urged her husband to go make his acceptance statement. Jack Gilligan begged off; he wanted to wait until some more numbers came in. Actually, watching Rhodes's concession speech on television, Gilligan was astonished. He said, "Rhodes was wrong. I knew we were down the drain."[9] The Republican's concession, however, prompted some Gilligan staff to consider that perhaps they were mistaken, perhaps they had won after all; and in a flurried way they began to work through the numbers looking for some basis to affirm this.

Republican media consultant Doug Bailey did not regard Rhodes's concession as odd in the least. Rhodes, he said, could inhale and exhale Ohio election statistics. Based on the reported vote splits in the counties Rhodes knew, it was clear to him that he had suffered a close but definite defeat. For Rhodes, Bailey added, the reasonable thing to do was to call it a night and head home to bed.[10] What Rhodes failed to consider, Bailey added, was that while Gilligan was pulling the predicted high percentage of the vote in Cuyahoga County, the total vote being cast was a great deal below expectation. And it plummeted on the Democratic side of the ledger. Compared to the previous gubernatorial race, Rhodes picked up only a few thousand more votes than Roger Cloud had received in 1970; Gilligan's county total, however, dropped by 100,000.

At the time, Rhodes's concession and Gilligan's refusal to claim victory complicated matters for reporters, who wished to put both their newspapers and themselves to bed. Reporters sought out press secretary Bob Tenenbaum, pressing him for a formal Gilligan victory announcement so they could bring the long day to a close. Hugh McDiarmid of the *Dayton Journal Herald* told Tenenbaum, "I'm going with 'Gilligan wins.'" Tenenbaum recalled, "I literally took him by the arm and led him into a hallway and said, 'You cannot attribute that quote to anyone associated with this campaign. Don't go with that story, just don't.' And he went with it, anyway."[11] Perhaps by way of explanation, Tenenbaum added, "Of all the reporters in the press corps, McDiarmid had this sort of affinity for Gilligan. He could not allow himself to believe that this defeat could happen."[12] Nonetheless, a Gilligan victory was announced in the earliest editions of the *Journal Herald*—before they were pulled back off the street. The *Journal Herald's* was not the only headline complicated by the shifting stories. The lead headline in the *Cincinnati Enquirer's* first Wednesday postelection edition announced, "Gilligan Beating Rhodes in Race for Statehouse." The second edition gave the incumbent a second term in Columbus: "Gilligan Defeats Rhodes in Contest for Governor." The next edition took that victory away: "Rhodes Beating Gilligan in Contest for Governor."[13]

Rhodes's concession had, among other things, thrown the Democrats who had assembled in the ballroom into high celebration. Those in the Gilligan suite knew that there was nothing to cheer about. The best thinking was to keep Gilligan away from the throng. Max Brown said, "We decided to take Gilligan home through the corridor; a lot of reporters wanted to talk to Gilligan, the victor. It was a tremendously odd experience—to know that we were losers and have everyone think we were winners."[14]

By 2:00 A.M., the continued low turnout from northeastern Ohio confirmed that Gilligan was defeated. At that hour, Gilligan still led by 10,000 votes, but the reduced number of Democratic votes flowing in from the Cleveland area was being slowly overtaken by Republican votes from the more rural and conservative parts of the state. Gilligan spoke now of defeat, which he acknowledged with a quiet dignity and calm.

At 3:30 A.M., one of Rhodes's daughters awoke her sleeping father to inform him that, despite anything he might have said the night before, he had been elected to a third term as Ohio's governor. At a 9:00 A.M. Wednesday news conference, Rhodes accepted victory, calling the outcome the greatest victory in his life. But because the closeness of the vote suggested a recount would occur, he said he would make no further statement. (Since the result was by fewer than .5 percent, a recount was mandatory.)

Gilligan spoke to the press an hour later. He was subdued. He said he thought the likelihood that a recount would reverse the result was "negligible." Given, he added, that it had been a day of generally Democratic victories, he ascribed his defeat as "purely and simply a repudiation of me, personally."[15] Asked if the perception that he was arrogant had been a factor, Gilligan replied, "Quite possibly, but I would say here stands before you now one of the least arrogant men in the human race."[16]

By the full though unofficial vote, Rhodes had defeated Gilligan 1,493,679 to 1,482,191—less than one vote per Ohio precinct.

The day produced from each man a rather uncharacteristic statement. Asked why he had conceded defeat the previous evening, James Rhodes almost poetically replied, "Concession is good for the soul."[17] Watching his own defeat being tallied, Jack Gilligan turned to Bob Daley, a close associate, and with atypical bluntness said, "We blew it. We really blew it."[18]

Ellen Gilligan had taken a break from college to campaign for her father. She noted that her father had often gone into an Election Day facing the possibility of defeat: challenging Carl Rich for Congress in 1964; defending that seat against Bob Taft two years later; challenging Frank Lausche for the U.S. Senate nomination in 1968; taking on Bill Saxbe in the general election that followed. In each of these, she noted, there was cause to imagine defeat as being possible. But against Jim Rhodes in 1974, "there had been no doubts whatsoever"[19] It was a view her siblings shared. The three-county area John Gilligan had worked had come in solidly for his father, but overall he was dismayed by what he considered the timidity of the campaign. Kathleen Gilligan recalled, "My reaction was more one of shock, and that went on for twenty-four hours. I kept thinking, 'This can't possibly be; something is going to change this.'"[20]

The notion that Gilligan was unbeatable spread to his larger campaign family. Press secretary Bob Tenenbaum said, "I don't think anybody had it in their heads that there was a strong chance we could lose. That impacted the way the campaign was run and the eventual outcome. The pervasive feeling was we did not need to be that well organized."[21] That assumption spread beyond the campaign. Family friend Bill Geoghegan, attending a conference in Hawaii on Election Day, woke up, turned on the radio, heard Gilligan had been defeated, and decided "I was dreaming."[22] Soon after the votes were counted, the *New York Times* editorialized on the election nationally and in Ohio:

> The brutal realities of inflation and recession, the fear of depression, and the memory of Watergate worked together to wreak heavy damage on the GOP from New York to California . . . It is hard to believe, for example, that Ohio voters had much concern for post-Watergate morality when they defeated Governor John Gilligan, one of the abler Democratic state executives, and replaced him with ex-Governor James Rhodes, a routine partisan with a questionable record.[23]

Much of the Ohio press—or at least the press sympathetic to Gilligan—commented along similar lines.

With defeat confirmed, John and Katie Gilligan went to Florida for a week—if not away from the fact of defeat, at least away from its immediate surroundings. While there, Gilligan wrote a pained, somewhat rambling 2,500-word statement—a mea culpa—that began with the simple statement, "First of all, it was MY FAULT."[24] Fleshing out that statement, writing, "[I had] persuaded myself that I could run this campaign in a defensive crouch and that, in fact, it would be safer to do so than to run the risk of 'losing my temper' or making some rash statement. So, in fact, I said nothing."[25] More specifically, Gilligan said he had broken faith with the Ohio voter by disclaiming that his second administration might have any need to seek a tax increase. In Gilligan's sense of consequence, a politician unwilling to stand behind his own beliefs was unworthy of office. Further, Gilligan said, he had erred in not attacking Rhodes earlier and harder. Given, he said, that "all of us deeply believed that Jim Rhodes' moral character, his maladministration of public affairs, [and] his almost incredible insensitivity to human concerns" were a matter of great importance to voters, the campaign—and the candidate—should have been forthright in making this clear.[26] Instead, Gilligan said, the campaign had waited for the press to nail Rhodes to the wall.

Intended for private circulation within his campaign, Gilligan's statement soon jumped the fence into the hands of the press. Some newspapers condemned Gilligan's confessed disingenuousness on taxes. The *Dayton Journal Herald* editorialized, "We daresay the confession merely confirmed public suspicions."[27] But what is interesting about Gilligan's statement is the gap between the personal and the political. At least in his own mind, Gilligan had failed—and, in effect, been punished—because he had fallen short of the standards he had set for himself; he had broken his central commitment, the one he made with his own nature.

In purely political terms, however, this statement is perhaps not the best explanation for his defeat. In assessing the causes for Jack Gilligan's 1974 defeat, three things need to be kept in mind. First, Gilligan's defeat was so narrow that any of a long list of factors could have accounted for the 11,000 votes by which he was defeated. Second, while reversing any one of those factors would likely have returned Gilligan to the Governor's Mansion, Rhodes's victory required that *all* of them occur. And finally, these factors were not mutually exclusive.

One factor was the specific actions of the Gilligan administration—in particular, the 1971 closing of the state parks during the income tax fight; specific statements by Gilligan, most notably his offhand comment that he "sheared taxpayers"; and the election year embarrassment of a budget surplus that was denied rather than celebrated. Any of the above could readily have made a difference of 10,000 votes.

Another factor was Nancy Brown Lazar. The independent candidate for governor received 95,625 votes—the highest total achieved by a third-party gubernatorial candidate in Ohio since the Progressive Era. Additionally, a strikingly high number of voters, 79,396, cast no vote at all for governor. Both totals may reflect some desire to "chastise" Gilligan for faults real or imagined. In a postelection review, Jim Fain of the *Dayton Daily News* quoted an unnamed voter as saying, "I voted for Rhodes because I wanted to teach Gilligan a lesson in humility, but, my god, if I had had any idea that Rhodes would get elected, I never would have voted for him."[28]

Then there was the tendency to look past the battle being fought in the present and focus on a possible run for the presidency in 1976. Whatever Gilligan's own thinking on this may then have been, the lure of the White House distracted some staffers and persuaded at least a few voters that their state was not Gilligan's top priority. As Kathleen Sebelius later commented, her father's belief was that "the election was well in hand and he was going to win, so he was almost leaping over 1974 and looking down the road."[29]

Another factor was the mishandling of John Glenn, who the same day Jack Gilligan squeaked to defeat was elected to the U.S. Senate by 1 million votes, the largest margin in state history. Following Gilligan's appointment of Howard Metzenbaum in early 1974, there was not only no love lost between Glenn and Gilligan, there was active antipathy on Glenn's part. An admiring *Washington Post* profile of John Glenn noted that in 1973 Gilligan "entertained grandiose national aspirations" but made one fatal mistake: "He kissed John Glenn off as a political rube."[30] Citing a particular grievance, one Glenn aide reported that Gilligan kept Glenn waiting in the Governor's Mansion kitchen one morning while he and others discussed Glenn's political future. That, the *Post* added, "was no way to treat a hero."[31] In the general election, Glenn came within distance of Gilligan only to engage in occasional sniping. In consequence, the state's strongest Democrat, Gilligan, and the state's most popular Democrat, Glenn, added up to a net minus.

Also, Gilligan had adopted an incumbent's strategy. Robert Cohen insightfully wrote in his dissertation: "When political considerations indicate re-election, the incumbent, confident of victory, is unwilling to alter what is perceived as a winning campaign. For these reasons a campaign of incumbency is inflexible and difficult to adapt to changing situations."³² One aspect of an incumbent strategy is to hold the votes of previous adherents. At least in one instance, Gilligan failed to do this. In the largely African American wards on Cleveland's East Side, Gilligan's 1970 vote total of 74,594 dropped to 46,279 four years later. One wonders why. Gilligan had a solid liberal record on civil rights, and beyond that, he had embraced the issue personally. He had resigned from the country club his grandfather helped found because of its segregationist policies, and he had publicly challenged the Cincinnati courts over their handling of curfew violators arrested during the city's 1967 civil disturbance, a stand that brought down considerable wrath upon him and which contributed appreciably to his 1968 defeat at the hands of William Saxbe. Yet, for all of this, no deep resonance existed between Gilligan and the black community. Perhaps this was a matter of style; perhaps it was a consequence of there being no blacks in high-visibility posts within his administration. Further, "None of the Ohioans for Gilligan advertisements dealt with problems of greatest concern to the black community": civil rights commissions, affirmative action programs, open housing legislation, welfare programs, urban housing, and inner-city development.³³

Yet another factor was how, during the campaign, Gilligan embraced the cause of Cesar Chavez and the deeply impressive effort he and the United Farm Workers Union were undertaking to organize agricultural laborers. Gilligan did this, apparently, despite having given a pledge of neutrality to Teamster leader Jackie Presser, whose own union was conducting a rival organization effort. The action prompted Presser to switch his endorsement to Rhodes.

And finally, some in the Gilligan campaign felt that, in the expectation of victory, their candidate did not campaign with sufficient diligence. Senator Harry Meshel reported, "We had a big rally in Columbiana County—a pig roast. Fifteen hundred people. Everybody running statewide came but Gilligan. I don't know why he didn't show. I won the county; Gilligan lost the county. I always thought he lost the election in Columbiana County."³⁴

Arguably, the single greatest cause in Gilligan's defeat was the sustained underestimation of James Rhodes as a candidate. Postelection, the *New York Times* commented on how the Gilligan campaign's chief mistake "was miscalculating the roguish charm and strategic brilliance of Mr. Rhodes, the Republican 'boy wonder' of Ohio politics, now sixty-five years old," qualities that overshadowed "many old stories of financial manipulation and . . . the Kent State killings in 1970."³⁵ Rhodes was for many voters (particularly Republicans, particularly rural) in his mode and manner, the definitive Ohio politician. George Voinovich, a later Ohio governor, commented, "I always felt Gilligan wasn't comfortable as governor, in comparison with Jim Rhodes, who fit the office like a glove. John had a little bit of aloofness about him. I had conversations with him and it was not true in those conversations. But he brings to mind a Serbo-Croatian saying: 'Is he one of us?'"[36]

Further, the Gilligan camp seemed to ignore the fact that Rhodes himself ran as a semi-incumbent. As a former two-term chief executive, he had universal name recognition and a history of association with groups that prospered during Rhodes's first incarnation and donated accordingly. And, of course, his campaign tagline muddled the issue of incumbency: "Let's Make Governor Rhodes Governor Again."

And the Rhodes media effort beat the Gilligan effort all hollow. Gerald Austin, campaign coordinator for Gilligan in Cuyahoga County, was unsparing in his assessment. The person who cost Gilligan the election, he told an interviewer, was an autoworker earning $17,000–$20,000 a year living in a Cleveland suburb with a wife who worked part-time and several children. First, this voter sees a Rhodes ad: "You are being asked to approve a school tax levy; why do you have to do that if Jack Gilligan did so much for education in this state?" The guy, Austin says, "starts scratching his head: 'That's a good question.'" Then, Austin adds, his putative voter sees a Gilligan ad showing "John and Katie sitting on the couch discussing the finer points of arrogance" and why Gilligan is perceived as such by many. Austin concluded, "Here is one guy talking my language, talking to me about an issue that concerns me, and here is another guy talking about arrogance. Arrogance is not something you can put your hands on, not something you can stick in your pocket and see if you can come out with any change."[37]

The election's most notable numbers emerged from Cuyahoga County. Compared to 1970, the drop-off in votes for Gilligan there was fully nine times his margin of defeat. One argument is that the negative advertising that the Rhodes campaign targeted to northeastern Ohio drove down the vote, though Doug Bailey of Bailey-Deardourff told the author he felt this argument received more credence than it deserved. Turnout, likely, was also affected by the end-of-the-campaign strike that brought publication of the pro-Gilligan *Plain Dealer* to a halt. Jack Hansan, Gilligan's campaign manager, suggested that the Cuyahoga County effort fell short because it was largely under the direction of lieutenant governor candidate Dick Celeste, who, certain of Gilligan's election, focused too much attention on his own campaign.

Later, Pete O'Grady, perhaps only nominally the head of the Gilligan campaign, offered this judgment: "We lost the governorship; Jim Rhodes didn't win it."[38] On this point, agreement was bipartisan. Rhodes said of Gilligan, "He gave the election away."[39]

The individuals notably absent from the 1974 effort—Jim Friedman, Mark Shields, and more than a few others—laid the blame for the defeat at the feet of Jack Hansan, the man who had supplanted them. The argument, in rough, was that Hansan may have been a skilled administrator, but campaigns are not administered, they are fought. His mea culpa released, Jack Gilligan also redirected responsibility. He later told Dayton newsman Brad Tillson that while the defeat had been a "wrenching, harrowing shock," he regarded Rhodes's campaign as "a super saturation lie" intended not so much to elect Rhodes as "to defeat me." In consequence, he said, "I was destroyed by a media campaign on television, radio and in the newspapers as if a rifle shot me."[40]

Whatever national ambitions Gilligan may have had for 1976 ended with this defeat. Of great consequence in Ohio was that Gilligan's defeat came just as his two decade effort to build a progressive Democratic Party in Ohio was bearing fruit. Beyond the governorship, Democrats held every statewide office but one and strong majorities in both houses of the legislature. But for Gilligan, the man and the moment did not meet.

Many saw Gilligan's defeat as rather more than routine, as the *Lorain Journal* editorialized:

> Nevertheless, Gilligan's defeat is a more tragic loss for the state than for himself. Gilligan had the courage to challenge the state to meet its responsibilities. He did things for the people that most politicians only talk about. He is a classy guy, a decent man with good instincts. You might say that Gilligan had the election won if the people he had helped the most—the poor, the sick, the elderly, the students, the minorities, the mental patients—could have turned out to vote for him.[41]

John Joyce Gilligan—at fifty-three, in his political and intellectual prime—would never again hold major elective office.

34

Departure and the Next Step

For press secretary Bob Tenenbaum, the morning after the votes had been counted felt like he'd awoken with a dreadful hangover from a party at which no one had had a good time. But as press secretary, he could not take the day off, and so he headed to the office. There was, he said, "a lot of 'What happened?' and a lot of shrugs."[1]

Given the closeness of the vote—less than .5 percent—state law mandated a recount. Campaign worker Christopher Buchanan was among those who threw themselves into the recount effort—less, perhaps, in hopes of reversing the result than from simply being unable to accept it. He was "in a state of disbelief that in the year of Watergate, James Rhodes of all people would win against the White Knight. It was completely implausible."[2] The Columbus campaign office at 22 Gay Street, Buchanan said, was "like a funeral home." Buchanan stayed at his task for two weeks, finding, he said, "lots of little mistakes in the numbers, but nothing substantive."[3]

By November 21, Rhodes's lead over Gilligan had dropped—but only marginally, to 12,980. Secretary of State Ted Brown said the formal canvassing of voters would be completed by the end of the month, at which time, Gilligan could request a formal recount.

Tenenbaum said the prospect of a recount brought campaign workers "some hope, perhaps misplaced."[4] He had not been a major policy maker in the administration, he said, but he did take sole responsibility for stopping the recount, which was agonizing and going nowhere. It was bad for the state, Tenenbaum said. "I argued and argued and argued that we should stop it."[5] On Friday afternoon, December 13, Tenenbaum read to the press a short statement from Gilligan asking that the recount be halted. By that time, 11,145 of the state's 12,831 precincts had been recounted, producing a net gain for James Rhodes of 106 votes.

Elections notwithstanding, life continued. Four days before Gilligan formally conceded defeat, the family formally announced the engagement of Kathleen Gilligan to Gary Sebelius, a recent graduate of the Georgetown University School of Law and son of three-term Kansas congressman Keith Sebelius. The couple had met in the nation's capital while Kathleen was working for the Center for Correctional Justice and Gary was in school. Considerable mention was made at the time that, unlike the bride, the groom was a Republican. The couple was married at the Governor's Mansion the day before Christmas, December 24, 1974.

John Joyce Gilligan addressed the Ohio General Assembly for the last time on Tuesday evening, January 7, 1975, when he presented his final "State of the State" address. He congratulated the newly elected Democrats who brought the party control of the State Senate and an expanded majority in the State House, but he said nothing of his own defeat. Gilligan wasn't yielding much. He recounted the progress that had been made during his tenure in tax equity, support for education, reform of mental health, protection of the environment, and other matters, stating, "We have real reason for pride in recent accomplishments."[6] He reminded those present that popular government worked no better than those who were its leaders worked at it. He called for expansions in education funding, both primary and postsecondary; for further property tax relief; for efforts to increase the number of physicians in the state; for collective bargaining protections for the state employees; and more. Gilligan closed on a slightly more personal note, expressing his "heartfelt gratitude to the people of Ohio and to the members of the legislature for the privilege that I have had of working with them and for them."[7]

But that was not Gilligan's legislative farewell. Under a quirk of Ohio law, the newly elected and heavily Democratic General Assembly took office on Monday, January 6, 1975; James Rhodes, however, would not officially succeed Gilligan as governor until seven days later, January 13. So for that intervening week, the Democrats controlled both the executive and legislative branches, creating a loophole through which the outgoing governor and the incoming legislature hoped to pass and have signed into law legislation that, not surprisingly, would favor the Democrats.

Doing so, however, required some rule changes. Since action must come swiftly, the existing House rule that required a two-thirds vote to expedite legislation had to be changed. The House of Representatives, by a partisan 54–37 vote, adopted a rule allowing a simple majority to suffice. By existing rules, legislation was not deemed to have passed the Senate until it was signed by the state's lieutenant governor, John Brown, who, like Gilligan, was a lame duck. But a Republican. The Senate voted 18–11 to extend the power of signature to the Senate's president pro tempore, Oliver Ocasek. Senate minority leader Michael Maloney noted that "there was not a shred of fairness or impartiality" to the Democratic rule changes.[8] But these rules, at least for the time being, were rules.

About this time, Jack Hansan contacted Chris Buchanan and asked him to redraw the state's congressional districts, just as he'd done in 1971. Buchanan, working on a large board laid across twin beds in his parent's Columbus-area home, produced a map that offered some likelihood of producing three additional Democrats in the state's Washington delegation.

In all, the outgoing Gilligan administration introduced six bills. Beyond redistricting, the measures sought to transfer the Ohio Consumer Protection Division from the Commerce Department, which Rhodes would control, to the office of the attorney general, William J. Brown, a Democrat. A similar transfer of power moved the patronage-rich Ohio Income Tax Collection Division to the state treasurer, Gertrude Donahey, also a Democrat. Other measures strengthened unemployment insurance protections; limited the authority of the secretary of state, the newly elected Ted W. Brown, a Republican, to appoint or dismiss members of county election boards; and established various changes in voter registration laws considered favorable to Democrats.

Republicans were apoplectic. Legislative historian David Gold wrote, "Republicans expressed their feelings about the legislative railroad by playing the sound of a train over the House sound system and calling out 'all aboard' during the roll call."[9] The six bills passed nonetheless.

On January 11, the Franklin County Court of Appeals struck down the provision allowing Senator Ocasek to sign any bills as long as Lieutenant Governor Brown was available to do so. The following day in Cleveland, Ohio Supreme Court Chief Justice Frank Celebrezze, a Democrat, ordered a stay on the Franklin County decision. Meanwhile, Democratic leaders, fearful that Brown would simply sit on the bills until after Rhodes had been inaugurated, supplied the Republican lieutenant governor Brown with copies of the bills, not the originals to which Brown was entitled. The Democrats calling on Brown promised to deliver the originals if he promised to sign them.

According to the *Columbus Dispatch,* word of Celebrezze's decision reached Columbus at about 5:30 P.M. Forty-five minutes later the Republican lieutenant governor announced that he was not going to be rushed into signing bills he had barely had the chance to read.[10] Gold wrote, "To deprive the Democrats of an opportunity to claim that he was absent and that they could therefore present the bills to the Democratic president pro tempore [Ocasek], Brown hunkered down in his office for the weekend."[11] That Friday evening, Governor John Gilligan signed the bills at the home of a Columbus friend with whom he was staying—perhaps to avoid the Republicans, perhaps to avoid the press.

On Monday morning, January 13, two Gilligan aides presented the bills to Brown for filing. They were acting, they said, on Governor Gilligan's authority. Brown informed them that Gilligan was no longer governor. The explanation is murky. Possibly, the aides assumed that Gilligan remained governor until Rhodes formal inauguration, scheduled for later that day. Apparently unbeknownst to all but a few, Rhodes had taken the oath of office the previous Friday, so that his powers as Governor would date from the official ending Gilligan's term, which had occurred at 12:01 a.m. the morning of January 13. Cutting to the chase, Senate minority leader Michael Maloney filed a taxpayer's suit to have the six laws voided. This, the Ohio State Supreme Court, which then had a 5–2 Republican majority, did some months later.

The question for Jack Gilligan, of course, was, What next? Pollster Peter Hart read Gilligan's defeat at the hands of Rhodes as the finale of Gilligan's career. "I never saw him as a candidate after the 1974 race."[12] That view was sharply challenged by Gilligan's daughter Kathleen Sebelius, who pointed to the uncertain arc of her father's career: an upset election to Congress in 1964, defeat for reelection two years later, triumph over the "unbeatable" Frank Lausche only to fall short against William Saxbe that fall, then a convincing 1970 win of the governorship followed by an altogether surprising defeat. Given these ups and downs, she argued, the results of 1974 by no means should have been considered final.[13]

Gilligan agreed. As early as March 21, 1975, Gilligan received a fairly detailed memo from Bob Daley whose topic was "Campaign '76." That campaign was aimed at the U.S. Senate seat then held by Republican Robert Taft, whose term would end that year. (A Taft candidacy was not certain; in 1975, Taft took an eleven-week leave from office following a heart attack.) As for Gilligan's qualifications for office, Daley was not unduly modest, describing Gilligan as the "only honest, decent, compassionate, electable public figure with integrity and above-average intellectual ability in Ohio during the past thirty years, and probably longer."[14]

Gilligan had by this time already taken steps to secure an income and, what may have been equally important to him, intellectual collegiality. On January 29, barely two weeks after leaving office, he had announced the formation of John J. Gilligan Consultants, which would sell insurance and offer consulting advice from an office at 88 East Broad Street in Columbus—a literal hop, skip, and jump from the Statehouse. Bob Daley served as his partner in this enterprise, and Daley immediately undertook the course of study required to pass the state insurance examination. (Confirmation of his passing came from Harry V. Jump, Ohio's director of insurance, delivered on stationary perhaps ironically headed "James A. Rhodes, Governor." Mr. Jump's letter closed: "There are no particular catch-phrases or special messages I can give you as you start your career. In this respect, the Golden Rule is an excellent, if simplified, guideline."[15]) In truth, the enterprise was part insurance firm and part beachhead for any further possible Gilligan political initiatives.

Gilligan accepted a distinguished fellowship at the Woodrow Wilson International Center for Scholars in Washington, D.C. There he focused on issues in state and local government and undertook a book-length study of federal-state relations. In connection with his appointment to the Wilson Center, Jack and Katie Gilligan established a Washington residence on C Street, Northeast, in the city's comfortably settled Capitol Hill neighborhood.

Gilligan regularly returned to Ohio to keep his eye on things generally. Between visits, he was kept current on the Ohio political scene by Bob Daley, who was not shy about urging a Senate candidacy on Gilligan, the post many of Gilligan's friends and a fair number of his foes thought him best equipped for. On April 3, Daley sent Gilligan a detailed seven-page memo whose stated purpose was the formation of a Gilligan for Senate committee, "hopefully by May 1, 1975." The memo was a working document outlining ways in which Gilligan could keep himself in the public eye, distribute a monthly newsletter to major Ohio Democrats, and cultivate the press, among other steps. At one point, Daley urged that a "détente" be achieved with Ohio's new U.S. senator, John Glenn. The April 3 memo proposed an initial $10,000 be raised as seed money for the undertaking. Daley also reported some hesitating voices, quoting one as saying that "the question of the grand jury investigation of the payroll situation is a variable over which we have no control . . . Until this is clearer, we should not act."[16]

That grand jury investigation marked the messiest aftermath to the Gilligan administration, one not entirely vitiated by the fact that Gilligan was held personally blameless in the affair. In mid-February 1975, news reports and rumors were floating that in the all but final days of the Gilligan administration, people were added to the state payroll not to work state jobs but to assist with the recount.[17] By report, several additional state workers were "transferred" to Lieutenant Governor Richard Celeste to aid with his transition to office. According to the *Columbus Dispatch*, Celeste admitted that five members of his staff had been hired by other state agencies but had never appeared for work. This prompted Robert Netzley to suggest that Celeste "might now need some time to do some real soul searching about [his] future" and resign.[18]

The more serious allegation concerned state-paid workers working on the recount; their numbers were variously estimated from a dozen to forty. On February 19, Franklin County prosecutor George C. Smith announced he would open an investigation and present evidence to a local grand jury. With that announcement, State Auditor Thomas Ferguson, a Democrat, called off his own probe and rescinded subpoenas already issued to Jack Hansan, Jay Tepper, and Pete O'Grady. Columnist Hugh McDiarmid, often a Gilligan partisan, wrote that "there is substantial evidence that Democrats have done wrong."[19] Apparently, "forty or fifty dazed expatriates" from the Gilligan campaign "were spoon-fed onto the state payroll and that some of them either became total malingerers or were told to report for political work on the Gilligan recount effort."[20]

In mid-April, a Franklin County grand jury returned indictments against fourteen individuals for "theft by deception" because they had worked on the recount while being paid by the state.[21] Ten entered into plea bargains; each received a six-month sentence suspended on the condition that the compensation received from the state—which ranged from $665.60 to $1,374.80—was repaid. Three were convicted on grand theft. Further, a $5,000 fine was levied against the so-named Re-count Planning Group as the organizer of the deception. As perhaps consolation to Gilligan, the Franklin County prosecutor Smith stated there was "not one scintilla of evidence" that Gilligan knew the workers had not reported to state jobs.[22]

After receiving Daley's memo, Gilligan replied, saying that any action should be deferred for several months. Daley pressed. On April 9, he wrote Gilligan, "You told me once you had been advised [after his defeat] not to make for six months any decisions more important than what you were to have for lunch. We've passed five months and are coming up on six."[23] His letter carried the politically perti-nent news that "Howard Metzenbaum was working the tables at the Ohio Demo-cratic Party's dinner last Friday as if this were an election year."[24]

In early June, Gilligan invited Daley to a meeting in the Gilligan's Washington home to discuss a possible challenge to Taft.[25] In addition to Daley, those present included Jim Friedman, Mark Shields, Phil Moots, Peter Hart, and a few others—in short, much of what might be termed Gilligan's "brain trust." No hard decisions were reached.

Gilligan's decision was, in effect, made for him—first by Howard Metzenbaum and with subsequent finality by the Supreme Court of the United States. As Gil-ligan recalled, "Metzenbaum told me directly that there was no way he was going to step aside for me [for the Senate nomination]. If I got into the race, it would be over his dead or live body."[26] Gilligan long believed that any Democrat nomi-nated in a brawl of a spring primary stood little chance in the general election. As evidence, the tightly contested 1970 Senate primary between Metzenbaum and Glenn had ended in victory for Robert Taft. Further, on January 30, 1976, the U.S. Supreme Court crossed the Ts of Metzenbaum's candidacy when it ruled in *Buckley v. Valeo* that several sections of the Federal Campaign Act of 1971 were unconstitutional. Most pertinently, the high court stated that any given individ-ual was free to spend as much of his or her own money on behalf of his or her own candidacy as his or her checkbook would allow. And Howard Metzenbaum's checkbook was wide and deep.

With that, Jack Gilligan concluded that, in all likelihood, his political dream of a seat in the U.S. Senate would never be attained.

35

Washington, Again

With the demise of a possible Senate candidacy, 1976 became for Jack Gilligan perhaps his least active year politically in a quarter-century. Shortly before the Ohio primary in June, he endorsed the candidacy of former Georgia governor James Earl Carter. The endorsement was not of great consequence since, by June, Carter had the nomination all but wrapped up. Still, having endorsed Carter, Gilligan made a series of speeches on his behalf.

Gilligan had no particular expectations from a Carter victory, so he was quite surprised to receive a call from Cyrus Vance, Carter's designated secretary of state. Vance asked if Gilligan was planning to attend the Inaugural; Gilligan said no. Vance suggested that Gilligan reconsider, as there were matters Carter wished to discuss with him. (Gilligan and Carter knew each other moderately well from their shared attendance at various National Governors' Conference gatherings, where they had been doubles tennis partners. Assessing the president-elect's game, Gilligan said, "He scrambled around the court pretty quickly. Jimmy liked to win."[1])

Gilligan recalled, "Carter said he wanted me to be head of the Agency for International Development [AID]. It sort of shocked me. I had thought of half a dozen things he might have in mind, but foreign aid was not one of them. I said as much. I said I would serve any way I can, but I'm not sure I'm equipped for this."[2] Carter thought otherwise. Gilligan was formally sworn on March 30, 1977.

The U.S. Agency for International Development was something of an incongruity within the Washington bureaucratic scheme of things. AID had been established by President John Kennedy in 1961 to direct a fundamental geographic shift in American foreign assistance programs. Previously, American aid had flowed largely to the east and to Europe, as in the Marshall Plan; AID significantly redirected that aid to the south. As Kennedy wrote in his March 22, 1961, message to Congress:

We live at a very special moment in history. The whole southern half of the world—Latin America, Africa, the Middle East and Asia—are caught up in the adventures of asserting their independence and modernizing their old ways of life . . . The 1960s can be the crucial "decade of development"—the period when many less developed nations make the transition into self-sustained growth, the period in which an enlarged community of free, stable and self-reliant nations can reduce world tensions and inequality. Our job, in its largest sense, is to create a new partnership between the northern and southern halves of the world.[3]

AID was also a departure from the usual Washington administrative structure. The agency was not created by an act of Congress but by an executive order, which meant that the agency's administrator reported to the president "through" the secretary of state, suggesting that the AID administrator had some direct relationship with the president and a somewhat ambiguous relationship with the secretary of state. From its inception, AID had substantial funding. Kennedy sought and received $2.1 billion for fiscal year 1962.

At the time of Gilligan's appointment, AID was widely viewed as a deeply troubled agency. Much of that woe traced to the war in Vietnam. Lyndon Johnson, and then Richard Nixon, had used the agency to funnel aid to South Vietnam; one high-ranking AID official estimated that over half the agency's funds were going to that nation. In 1968, AID staffing peaked at 17,600; with U.S. disengagement from Southeast Asia, that had number plummeted by 1977 to 5,700. Of these, 3,700 were U.S. citizens, three-quarters of whom were posted in Washington. Given seniority rules, the reduction decimated the agency's lower ranks, leaving behind what the *New York Times* termed "one of the most top-heavy bureaucracies in Washington," with over half of its Foreign Service officers in the top three civil service grades.[4]

Second, the use of AID as backdoor financing of the war in Southeast Asia had alienated Congress, the source of the agency's funding. According to the *Times* article, "Congress has been profoundly disenchanted with foreign aid since the late 1960s, when it became a conduit for massive assistance to America's military allies in Southeast Asia."[5] Indeed, it was Gilligan's brief experience in Congress that had helped persuade President Carter that he might be the man to repair relations with the Hill.

Also, AID's reputation in Washington was not particularly good. Several months before Gilligan took office, the Brookings Institution produced a study recommending that the agency be abolished due to its "reputation for inefficiency, rigidity and slowness."[6] As evidence of this unwieldiness, the study blamed AID for "concentrating on small projects, subjecting each one to Congressional approval; requiring that modifications also be approved by Congressional committees; and testing each project according to a massive, sometimes inconsistent, and unweighted array of legislative criteria."[7] Asked to comment on the report, Gilligan with no enthusiasm observed that Congress was unlikely to surrender its oversight function.

Once in office, Gilligan encountered impressive problems with bookkeeping. As he later stated, "The agency had no idea how much money was being spent overseas. When I asked how much it cost to keep a person abroad, I was told $80,000, or maybe $100,000 or $120,000. They didn't even have an inventory of the millions of dollars in capital equipment and cash the agency had abroad."[8]

Pushing a positive perspective of AID was Hubert Humphrey, who, following his 1968 loss to Richard Nixon, had returned to the Senate with foreign assistance as one of his causes. He believed that all U.S. aid activities should be combined into a single agency, with that agency given a cabinet rank. At the time—and since—individual government departments administered foreign assistance programs piecemeal: for example, the Food for Peace program was part of the Department of Agriculture and relations with the World Bank were handled through the U.S. Treasury. As Gilligan observed, "All these primarily domestic agencies had their own foreign aid programs, which they operated as extensions of their domestic activities."[9] Further, Humphrey introduced legislation to support this change; legislation he believed had the backing of President Carter.

Foreign assistance had all the attraction that a new topic can hold for an intellectual. Gilligan said of his post, "There was a great need. It was possible to do some important things."[10] Further, he believed, money spent assisting what was then beginning to be called the "third world" might in the end, dollar for dollar, do more to provide for greater American security than military expenditures.

At the time, the $3.48 billion administered by AID fell into three categories: economic development assistance, humanitarian assistance (disaster relief), and "security supporting assistance," which was intended to "promote economic and political stability in countries whose well being [was regarded as] important to the United States." This rather vague-sounding category received three of every five AID dollars, with nearly two-thirds going to Israel and Egypt. On what might more commonly be thought of as assistance, the agency spent $515 million for food and nutritional programs, $167 million for population and planning, and $95 million for education and human resources.[11]

Given what Gilligan saw as the world's needs and of AID's charter to address them, there was much to be unhappy about given the agency's operation. He was unhappy with the level of aid to Israel and Egypt. He was also unhappy with the staff he had inherited. Alex Shakow, then a high-ranking AID official who later became a significant figure at the World Bank, observed dryly that Gilligan was "not remarkable for holding back on his views."[12] (When he had been ousted from office in Ohio, Gilligan acknowledged his tendency to make barbed comments that struck others as less amusing than he had intended.) He publicly described the AID staff as "over-aged, over-grade, over-paid, and over here"—the last sting suggesting they might be more useful in the field than riding a desk in Washington.[13] The remark was not so much untrue as insulting. According to report, one consequence of those comments was that Congressman Clement Zablocki (D-Wisconsin), chairman of the Foreign Affairs Committee, called Gilligan in and, in the words of one familiar with the situation, "took him to the woodshed."[14]

Gilligan devoted much of his early days at AID "selecting the staff first-hand."[15] He did this in concert with Jack Sullivan, who was somewhat on loan from Zablocki as Gilligan's right-hand man, and with Robert Noote, the agency's deputy administrator. Noote, a businessman-turned–public-servant and an avid collector of African art, possessed considerable administrative ability that Gilligan came to rely on. Gilligan judged the personnel effort a success: "As in any other bureaucratic setup that has been in business for awhile, the work becomes routine. Whatever energy people had when they came in, many of them are now sort of going through the motions. By introducing some people at various levels of the operation, we were able to put some new life into many of the people who were there."[16]

Bureaucracies are not particularly agile creatures, as Gilligan was to learn in his efforts to move AID staff from Washington to Africa, Asia, and Latin America. He was stymied by the fact that federal civil service and Foreign Service regulations protected employees from transfer. As did budgets. It cost three times as much to station someone overseas, and the money generally wasn't there. An article in the *Dayton Daily News* quoted Gilligan as saying, "We're losing people right now, the best we've got are throwing up their hands in despair and walking to private industry."[17]

The job had it compensations. High on Gilligan's list was residence in Washington, D.C. "We loved it. We had this great house, a lot of friends that we liked."[18] Katie Gilligan, who as First Lady of Ohio had often felt uncomfortably on display, particularly relished the freedom of their new home. Washington offered the cultural events that never made it to Ohio, the symphony and museums. Katie became a docent at the National Gallery of Art. And there was the welcoming mix of the city's international residents and a fair sprinkling of friends from Ohio, like Bill Geoghegan, Jack's old family friend from Cincinnati. The Gilligans regularly hosted dinner parties; Katie was now firmly established as a gourmet cook. The home they lived in had the distinction of being one of the few in the Capitol Hill neighborhood to have survived the burning of the city by the British in 1814. As a testament to its age, the house had no foundation; rather, it was supported by cedar posts.

Living on Capitol Hill, Gilligan often biked to his office in the Department of State building on C Street, Northwest. Once, stopped for a red light, he recognized the driver in the car adjacent as former Arkansas governor Dale Bumpers. He caught Bumpers's eye and, when the latter rolled down his window, Gilligan said, "I remember when you had a chauffeur." Not missing a beat, Bumpers replied, "And I remember when you had a car."[19]

Whatever the frustrations of the bureaucracy, Gilligan was an eloquent advocate for an increased role for U.S. foreign assistance. Jack Sullivan considered him a brilliant speaker and admired the fact that he wrote his own speeches. In one early article published in the Department of State *Bulletin*, August 15, 1977, Gilligan set forth a straightforward three-phase approach for U.S. development efforts: first, strengthen efforts to meet the needs of the world's poor; second, improve performance and efficiency of the UN; and, "to the extent the second could be achieved, then raise the level of the U.S. contribution to the UN and related activities."[20]

But to this he added what might be termed a distinctive Gilligan touch. The purpose of foreign aid was, he said, "not only closing the gap between the rich and poor nations but also between the rich and poor within nations." He urged that aid be focused directly on "poverty reduction" rather than on the large-scale projects and industrial expansion that had previously been emphasized.[21] In a subsequent article, he asserted that "early, rapid industrialization in many countries often also created a host of new problems. Millions of people moved from their peasant farms and villages to cities which were economically and socially unprepared to receive them, and without jobs, homes or food the newcomers became a turbulent, uprooted and increasingly desperate mass."[22]

Gilligan also wrote an article on "Women and Their Importance to the Third World" that appeared in the *Washington Post*. In the piece he said that Africa's escape from widespread poverty required a sharp drop in the continent's fertility rates, citing two prerequisites: first, fertility fell when better nutrition and health prompted couples to believe their offspring would survive to adulthood; second, fertility fell as education levels rose. He concluded: "The message is clear . . . if population growth rates are to be reduced . . . the education of the women in developing countries is an urgent imperative."[23]

He drew a sharp contrast between the postwar Marshall Plan aid to Europe and the current needs of the world's developing nations. Europe, he noted, had been physically devastated by war, but it retained much of its infrastructure of rails, ports, and factories; and, most important, it retained an educated populace that knew how to join together in effective organizational units. The southern hemisphere, Gilligan believed, had little of this. The Marshall Plan, he noted, had absorbed 3 percent of America's GNP; current efforts to aid areas with greater need were receiving only about 0.26 percent.

Gilligan understood that his principal audience was domestic. Speaking on December 5, 1977, in San Francisco to the Annual Congress of Cities, he noted that many of those present might be inclined to view "the director of AID as the proprietor of a large, international welfare program."[24] Actually, he said, he believed that he and the American city officials present in the audience were both "dealing with problems that directly affect the welfare, security and prosperity of the American people."[25] He noted, "Residents of the West Coast, more than most Americans, must recognize that if population growth in Mexico is not slowed and unemployment there is not reduced, the undocumented immigration we are now seeing is nothing compared to what we may have to face in the future."[26]

Gilligan was at times perhaps unwarrantedly optimistic. Writing in the *Christian Science Monitor*, he said, "I think that the developing countries who are interested in new access to international financial resources will commit themselves to meeting the minimum needs of their populations, and to distributing the benefits of development on an equitable basis, and to protecting the human rights of their populations, so that development can be self-sustaining"—a perhaps rather more sanguine view of third world governments than was justified.[27]

Gilligan traveled extensively, to thirty nations during his tenure. Primarily, he went to Africa. The late 1970s, he commented later, was a time of reasonable optimism on the continent: "There were instances where countries were showing real signs of hope; making progress in terms of nutrition and health care and education. It was a period of relative calm."[28] That calm did not last: "Shortly after that, one country after another had wars or insurrections; had power plays between tribes or groups of thugs."[29] Much of this, he added, was financed by European corporations that underwrote one faction or another in hopes of gaining effective control of some form of natural wealth—gold, diamonds, or timber. Gilligan noted, however, that "all the bad guys weren't white," that local corruption was endemic—"lots of people who were perfectly willing to skim whatever they could"—and it was a continuous task to keep AID personnel disentangled from such activity and in control of the local programs.[30] Still, Gilligan did place the brunt of the blame on Europeans and Americans: "From the fairly short time I was in it, I learned a lot, and a great deal of what I learned left me so angry with my own country because of various sins of omission and commission."[31]

At times, however, the sheer magnitude of the task seemed to overwhelm Gilligan. At one point, traveling through Ghana, he was advised to stop at a particular village that had been making considerable strides. Leaving town, the party, for some reason Gilligan could not recall, stopped at a cluster of shacks.

> I remember this one dwelling. No fireplace; just a scooped out area in the middle of the floor. The kitchen had a couple of clay pots sitting around the fire pit, and around the walls of the room were three or four piles of clothes or cloth, which were their beds. The couple had three children living with them; grade school age in our reckoning. Literally, the most sophisticated thing they had was the clay pot. They had a hatchet. I thought at the time: "This is rock bottom. What are we going to do about people who through no fault of their own are in this circumstance, people who love their children just as much as we love ours?"[32]

Gilligan's most consequential trip was in 1978 to India. At the time, the Carter administration wished to restore aid to India, which had been cut off years earlier, in part because of Secretary of State Henry Kissinger's preference for Pakistan. While India joined in the wish to have aid restored, politics and pride intervened. The U.S. Senate went on record that it would approve aid only if India requested it; India's position was that it would accept aid only if it was offered.

Gilligan, accompanied by Jack Sullivan, was dispatched to Asia. They stopped in Japan, where John and Katie Gilligan, who was traveling on that leg of the voyage, were disconcerted by a medium-grade earthquake. Then they flew on to the Philippines and, finally, India. Arriving, Gilligan and Sullivan were informed that they would have fifteen minutes—and not a moment longer—with the nation's prime minister, Morarji Desai. A chauffeured limousine collected them, delivered to the palace (somewhat surreptitiously, after dark), and ushered them in to the prime minister's office. To Sullivan's surprise and consternation, Gilligan raised the topic of the differing conceptions of the afterlife as presented by Christianity and Hinduism. Desai, as it happened, was an accomplished student of Buddhism and had an interest in Western religions.

Five of the precious fifteen allotted minutes passed in this not so much otherworldly as next-worldly discussion. Then ten minutes. At the twelve-minute mark, Sullivan recalled, he broke into a sweat. At that point, Gilligan asked Prime Minister Desai, "If we were to offer assistance, would you accept it?" To which replied, "If we were to accept it, would you offer it?" Both nodded in agreement. Sullivan was thrilled, because now he could return to Congress and report in good enough faith that India had requested aid.[33] The travelers made one more stop—in Nepal, where Gilligan and Sullivan attended Mass celebrated by a Jesuit priest, the vocation Gilligan had long since set aside.

Gilligan headed AID during the period in which Robert McNamara—often termed "the chief architect of the Vietnam War"—headed the World Bank. Because both were engaged in international development, they lunched periodically to share notes. McNamara, Gilligan said, "was a very bright guy, with vast experience. He was not a politician, not someone whose power was limited by the need to gather votes."[34] By the late 1970s, there was talk that McNamara had, on reflection, turned against the Vietnam enterprise. That there had been such an epiphany was unclear to Gilligan, who said it seemed to him that where Vietnam was concerned, McNamara's chief regret was that he couldn't get people to do things his way.[35]

In February 1978, *New York Times* reporter Ann Crittenden undertook a lengthy critique of Gilligan's first year of service. She noted that a recent survey of AID staff initiated by Gilligan showed strong dissatisfaction with his leadership; at the same time, she acknowledged that Gilligan was not getting much help from on high: "In spite of President Carter's promise last year to double foreign aid in the next five years the Administration request for AID programs for 1979—$3.8 billion—is less than the $4.1 billion the agency received in 1978 and far less than Mr. Gilligan had originally sought."[36] She noted that Gilligan had been directing much of his energy to establishing the fundamental managerial controls and accounting systems the agency had lacked at the time he took over. As a tangible symbol of this trend, she added, "AID managed to squeeze its Congressional budget request into three volumes this year, down from twenty last year."[37] Further, she reported that Gilligan had discharged the mission director in Kenya for living too lavishly and had halted the Food for Peace shipment to Ghana for six weeks when it appeared the food was going directly to the black market. Congressman Clarence Long (D-Maryland), chairman of the subcommittee on foreign operations, was quoted as saying, "Gilligan is the best AID administrator we've had in my fourteen years in Congress," then adding deflatedly: "That isn't saying much."[38]

Gilligan, for his part, was feeling that he and AID had all the protection of a duck in a shooting gallery. The agency had no constituency, no congressional committee looking out for it, no member of Congress aware that AID meant many jobs in their district. Gilligan commented, "A Congressman could draw some cheap applause by voting 'no' on an AID appropriation. There were no consequences for them."[39] Second, Gilligan lacked cover because he was an outsider. Though he had been governor of a major state, he had no foreign policy experience, no high-level administration experience, no powerful friends on Capitol Hill. The difference between Washington and Ohio, he observed, was like "the distinction between major league baseball and minor league baseball. Washington thought of itself as the major leagues."[40]

Also, the general public had a woeful misunderstanding of how foreign aid worked. People tended to greatly overestimate how much aid was given (the total rarely reached .3 percent of the GNP) and rarely understood that most aid did not travel very far. For example, money given to Country X to purchase tractors did not go to Country X but, instead, to a U.S. tractor maker—perhaps, a politically connected one—whose tractors were then sent abroad. The general public, Gilligan noted, was "not well aware that there was a lot of money to be made by being part of the pipeline."[41]

Hubert Humphrey's dream of an amalgamated foreign aid effort with cabinet rank died, for all practical purposes, along with that senator in early 1978. President Carter did, however, constitute the Development Coordination Committee (DCC), an interagency group charged with assessing the nation's foreign assistance programs and offering recommendations for action. He appointed Jack Gilligan its chair. Gilligan himself has become somewhat skeptical that much could be accomplished. First, even if all U.S. aid programs were combined, the resulting department would be dwarfed even by the small Department of Commerce. Second, no existing department that had a piece of the foreign aid pie was remotely inclined to let go of it, certainly not to score points with Jack Gilligan.

The DCC chairship did not prove a happy task. Essentially, Gilligan was out-ranked by everyone else in the room: Agriculture, Treasury, State, and other cabinet heads. Gilligan commented, "I don't care how small the pieces of the pie they had, there was nothing to their advantage in having it go someplace else—they'd lose jobs and positions. It was a cat and dog fight."[42] Gilligan regarded himself as simply outgunned: "Making the AID administrator chairman of the DCC was, in bureaucratic terms, like sending a boy to do a man's job. I was dealing with cabinet-level departments like Treasury, Agriculture, State, and the Office of Management and Budget. By these standards, AID is a little orphan in the storm."[43] Jack Sullivan quoted Gilligan as saying of his circumstance, "They want me to be part of the team, but they never give me the keys to the washroom."[44] Though his position was exposed and he lacked strong presidential backing, Gilligan was determined to remain. The *New York Times* quoted him as saying, "I'm not leaving until the guy kicks me out."[45]

For Gilligan, 1978 was saddened by the death of his irrepressible father, Harry Gilligan, a lively combination of funeral director, civic advocate, raconteur, and proud parent. The elder Gilligan supplied perhaps the best epitaph to his son's 1974 defeat: "What's the point of being Irish if you don't know the world is going to break your heart?"[46]

Gilligan's second year at AID was better. Alex Shakow praised Gilligan's efforts at implementing the congressionally mandated New Directions legislation, with its strong emphasis on poverty reduction. And the new management systems Gilligan had implemented were working well. As its head, Gilligan represented the agency before the various congressional committees that passed on its budget. Through personal lobbying, he said, "we got a better working relationship with the chairman of appropriations committee, which was helpful in getting the appropriation we got."[47] That appropriation—from the budget-conscious 95th Congress—was the largest in the agency's history. Also, slow progress was made in transferring staff overseas, where the number of AID professionals increased from 1,450 to 1,550. There were also successful steps in reducing paperwork, encouraging staff initiative at the local level, and getting overseas employees to maintain modest lifestyles.

Gilligan's own assessment as well was that things were running along relatively smoothly.

I told Katie one day [in late January 1979] that on that Saturday I was supposed to go in and have a talk with Secretary Vance.

She asked, "Why?"

He called my office and said he wanted to talk to me and said could I come over on Saturday.

She asked, "What's going on?" Was I going to be fired?

I said, "Of course not."

Well, I had a very brief discussion with Vance and came home and said to her that she had been right. He said the usual things about they were looking to make some change in direction and wanted to do this and that in a different direction. "If you'd like an embassy in Europe, we can set something up for you that you might enjoy more than what you are doing now. Let me know in a day or two what your decision is."[48]

There appears to be no very certain story as to why Gilligan was dismissed. His own view of the matter turns on his relationship with Carter. Unlike other presidents, Gilligan said, Carter actually read the detailed budget information sent to the Oval Office. Further, Carter established a policy whereby any agency head who felt they had been unfairly treated could appeal the decision over their superior directly to the president. In Gilligan's case, this involved some ambiguity: by AID charter, he reported "through" not "to" the secretary of state and may have felt some added freedom in taking matters directly to the president. Gilligan— "perhaps naively," he later said—several times sought to have President Carter overrule State's decisions. Worse, he several times won his argument.

Another view is that AID administrator John Gilligan and Deputy Secretary of State Warren Christopher (who did much of the actual administration while Secretary Cyrus Vance traveled abroad to conferences) had fundamentally divergent views of the purpose of foreign aid. Christopher, Gilligan said, did not "see a lot of value in working with these 'Banana Republics'; he was concerned with the world struggle with the Soviets."[49] In Gilligan's view, Christopher saw the purpose of aid being to reward friends and punish enemies: someone voted against you in the United Nations on Friday, the spigot was turned off the following Monday. This, Gilligan said, might work if what was involved was a commodity—one could readily halt the shipping of grain—but it was ruinous to development programs. If you are building a highway, he said, you have to keep at it.

There were other versions, too. *TIME* magazine accused Gilligan of empire building: "While Gilligan's sweeping managerial style won some praise in Congress, it undermined morale at AID. He antagonized the Departments of State, Treasury and Agriculture by stubbornly advocating that some of their foreign assistance activities be handed over, along with the Peace Corps, to a new super-agency that he presumably would head."[50] Perhaps the most insightful reason came from Richard Zimmerman and Robert Snyder of the *Cleveland Plain Dealer*: "Like Othello, a black in a white world, Gilligan was forever the outsider among the entrenched bureaucrats of the State Department. Not being a part of the 'old boy network' which has run the State Department since time immemorial, he could not recklessly and undiplomatically push through concepts, programs and changes that threatened the status quo."[51] The article include a quote from Mark Shields on the nature of the foreign policy establishment: "They have an absolute lack of respect for politicians."[52]

One very different but well-supported version of why Gilligan was dismissed turns on Texas Democratic congressman Charlie Wilson, best known for his promotion of military aid to the Afghans who were fighting against Soviet occupation. Wilson, so the story goes, was a college friend of the son of Anastasio Somoza, dictator of Nicaragua. Somoza, deeply disliked in the country's urban areas, tried to bolster support in the countryside by running improved programs there. Wilson wanted U.S. aid for the effort, but the "human rights people" at State fobbed him off. Wilson approached Warren Christopher, who reportedly said the problem was not the State Department's policy but AID—which took forever to do anything. Christopher then called Gilligan to say he would be hearing from Charlie Wilson on this—"back me up." When Wilson called, however, Gilligan reportedly said aid could be there tomorrow, thus undercutting Christopher. The congressman then called Christopher and raised hell.[53]

Gilligan's formal letter of resignation, dated January 31, 1979, called attention to what he regarded as some of the accomplishments of his tenure: "The bilateral assistance program of AID is, as Congress, OMB and GAO have readily and repeatedly acknowledged, much more tightly and efficiently managed than it was two years ago."[54] At the time of his resignation, he noted, the agency had fewer people in Washington and more in the field than at any time in its recent history; further, the "foreign assistance appropriations approved by the 95th Congress, in a political atmosphere that was quite unpropitious, were the highest ever." He further added that he "was pleased that not a breath of scandal" had touched the agency during his tenure.[55] His resignation was not effective until March 31, which meant he would represent AID in its forthcoming congressional budget hearings.

The following day, Secretary of State Cyrus Vance accepted Gilligan's resignation "with deep regret."[56] President Jimmy Carter expressed his own "deep regret" four days later.[57] Possibly, in government, "deep regret" is the only form of regret ever experienced. Vance's dismissal came with an offer of an embassy post somewhere. Indeed, Gilligan's personnel file contained the following fill-in-the-blank form:

> The President today appointed John J. Gilligan, administrator of the Agency for International Development, to _____.
> In making the appointment the President and Secretary emphasized the importance of _____.[58]

The blanks were never filled in. Gilligan admits he might have enjoyed being an ambassador (depending, of course, on the posting) but said that Katie had made it clear that she had no intention of him taking any position that would put them on the other side of the Atlantic from their children. Further, there was a certain matter of pride. Gilligan recalled, "I thought they were crazy: they are bouncing me and I'm supposed to work with these guys."[59]

It was already the case that the Gilligan children were scattered widely across the United States. Donald, following his father's defeat, had moved to Albany, New York, where he worked as a liaison between Governor Mario Cuomo and various state agencies on energy issues. Deciding he was "not a good fit for the bureaucratic world," Donald in 1977 left New York to found DMC Energy, Inc., in Massachusetts, a firm that installed energy-efficient systems, largely in private homes.[60] His and Betsy's first child, Hannah, was born in 1977 and James in 1979. Kathleen Gilligan Sebelius was living with her husband, Gary, in Topeka, Kansas, where she served as executive director for the Kansas Trial Lawyers Association and he was an attorney in private practice. John Gilligan took to heart the charge of his maternal father-in-law, Edward Dixon, judge and prominent Charterite, that "everybody should go to law school."[61] John did, after some hesitation, graduating from the University of California Berkeley School of Law in 1977. By 1979, he was working as a deputy public defender for Solano and Contra Costa counties in California. He and his wife, Megan, had one child, Dan, born in 1977. Ellen, the youngest, completed her education at the University of Colorado (where she had transferred from Boston College) and in 1979 was working with a nonprofit organization in Washington, D.C.

Gilligan emerged from his AID interlude with some reasonably favorable attention. On February 9, the *Washington Post* editorialized that "John Gilligan . . . wanted more money for his agency, a tighter focus on development as distinguished from political and military support, and a reorganization of all the government aid activities. The Carter administration decided on no extra money, no significant changes in the development-military-political mix and evidently, no boat-rocking reorganization." The *Post* added, "Development is shaping up as a major administration disappointment."[62] The *New York Times* editorialized: "Mr. Gilligan fought hard for the funds and structure needed for bilateral aid program. When the administration changed its priorities and lowered its sights, he fought harder—and now is being replaced."[63]

Disappointment was not universal, however. One AID employee, apparently still smarting from Gilligan's early comment, returned the formal announcement of Gilligan's departure, having added, "I'm glad your [*sic*] leaving. I think you are over-aged, over-graded and over here!"[64] Gilligan's successor at AID was Thomas Ehrlich, a Washington lawyer and former State Department official, who at the time was serving as president of the Legal Services Corporation.

Gilligan often stated that his life's ambition was to be a U.S. senator. The closest he had come was his single 1965–67 term in Congress. The AID post had brought him back to Washington, a city he loved for reasons beyond government. With his dismissal from AID, Gilligan, now fifty-eight, left federal service for good.

Gilligan received one other more-than-routine communication just as his tenure at AID was coming to an end. It came from the Reverend Theodore M. Hesburgh, president of the University of Notre Dame, who wrote to compliment Gilligan on a lecture Gilligan had recently given. Hesburgh said, "Somehow, through all the vagaries of life, I think the province of God moves surely and steadily. Believing that, I am sure the future will hold many importance tasks for you still to perform."[65] As things were to develop, Hesburgh was prepared to give life's vagaries a bit of a nudge.

36

Notre Dame, Again

For Jack Gilligan, his first reaction to his Saturday morning dismissal at the hands of Secretary of State Cyrus Vance was surprise; his subsequent and no more pleasant surprise was the realization that he was now unemployed. Gilligan rather tersely described his circumstance: "I was at loose ends."[1]

But he was not without associations—one of which was with Theodore Hesburgh. Hesburgh had been president of the University of Notre Dame since 1952, a quarter-century during which he had, in stages, transformed an institution best known for the ranking of its football team into one that laid fair claim to being the flagship institution of Catholic higher education in America. Several years Gilligan's senior, Hesburgh had been a rector at the university during Gilligan's undergraduate years, though they did not meet at the time. Paths did cross variously in later years, occasions that led Hesburgh to conclude that Gilligan would be a useful person for the university to have around.

In 1979, Gilligan recalled, "[Hesburgh] approached me soon after I left AID and asked would I be interested in coming to Notre Dame." Gilligan responded, "To do what?" Hesburgh replied, "We'll talk."[2] To Gilligan, Father Hesburgh was simply one of the world's "first-rate human beings, enormously gifted. He could charm the birds out of the trees—intelligent, serious, but not of a scholarly bent, and engaged in practically everything."[3] Possibly to sweeten the invitation, the University in May 1979 awarded Gilligan an honorary doctorate.

The idea of returning to his alma mater had considerable appeal to Gilligan. However, the idea of surrendering the cosmopolitanism of Washington, D.C., for the rather flat lands of South Bend, Indiana, offered less attraction to Katie Gilligan. Jack Gilligan recalled that when the couple went to South Bend for a predecision visit, they were met at the airport and driven around town by Father Ned Joyce, the school's executive vice president, with whom Gilligan rode in the front seat. Periodically, Gilligan said, he glanced at his wife riding in the back to ascertain her reaction: "She kept shaking her head, going 'No way. No way.'"[4] She was "quite opposed to the whole notion but loyally went along" (in part, perhaps, because no other employment was pending).[5] In time, she warmed to South Bend and worked to extend the couple's social circle. South Bend had neither the internationalism of Washington nor the deep family roots the Gilligans enjoyed in Cincinnati, but, like Cincinnati, it did have a river, the St. Joseph, along whose west bank Jack and Katie found a comfortable three-bedroom brick house several miles north of town.

Gilligan's formal return to Notre Dame came on October 21, 1979, when he was named to the Thomas J. White Chair of Law. His installation in that position came at a Red Mass celebrated by the Most Reverend Mark G. McGrath, the Archbishop of Panama. As part of the event, Gilligan presented an address, "Redeem the Time," which he began anecdotally by recalling his week-long freshman year attempt to join the football team. The team then had two enormous linemen, Lou Rymkus and Wally Zienba, who, Gilligan said, permanently established for him "the distinction between theoretical and practical knowledge."[6]

More seriously, he spoke of overpopulation, the costs of warfare, the interrelatedness of the world's major problems and the recent warning given by Pope John Paul II that young people, faced with these difficulties, attempted to escape into drugs, violence, cynicism, and indifference. Gilligan stated, "The first thing, therefore, that we can and must do for these young people, for their own sake as well as the sake of suffering humanity, is to require them to look closely at the full reality of the world that they live in, and to try to understand its meaning."[7] He quoted T. S. Eliot's reference to "a decent godless people" whose monument was "a thousand lost golf balls."[8] He also quoted Jacques Maritain, the French philosopher to whom Gilligan had been introduced as an undergraduate by Frank O'Malley: "In particular, the general paganization of our civilization has resulted in man's placing his hope in force alone and in the efficacy of hate, whereas in the eyes of an integral humanism a political ideal of justice and civic friendship, requiring political strength and technical equipment, but inspired by love, is alone able to direct the work of social regeneration."[9]

It was work, he closed, to which Notre Dame would contribute by bringing the processes of scholarship to bear on the nation's political life. And it was work for which the White Chair was an appropriate setting: as its founder, Thomas J. White, had stated, "Law schools today don't put enough emphasis on legal philosophy. Law students aren't exposed to Christian principles underlying our law."[10]

As a professor of law, Gilligan, somewhat incongruously, had less legal education than any of those he was teaching. He commented, "A degree in law is required to practice, but not to preach."[11] He told his students that while he was neither a lawyer nor a professor of political science, what he had to offer was "twenty-five years in the pits."[12] An article in the *Dayton Daily News* quoted an assistant law school dean as saying, "It helps a great deal to have someone on our staff who is familiar with the 'roar of the greasepaint and the smell of the crowd.'"[13] The article described Gilligan's teaching of the course Power and Policy in American Government, which "centered on the underpinnings of constitutional law, drawing parallels with the thought of St. Thomas Aquinas, and the practice of early monarchies [with] various side excursions into jurisprudence and consideration of the problems in development of a legal system for multi-tribal Nigeria."[14] One student was quoted as saying, "He was particularly good when he was talking about the committee system—how things really work, as opposed to how they are supposed to work."[15]

Brian Usher of the *Akron Beacon Journal* also visited South Bend to see how the man he had covered as a governor was faring in academia. He wrote: "The former Democratic governor strolled under the elms between the Morris Inn and the law school. His professorial presence was enhanced by a tweed coat and green tie sprinkled with small tennis rackets. A tweed cap perched on the familiar shocks of red hair, graying heavily at the temples. He was chuckling amiably with no hint of the once-famed 'arrogance' as governor."[16] As far as Usher could tell, Ohio's former chief executive had only one complaint: "Here I am in jock heaven with all these facilities and I've had tennis elbow for months."[17]

Though he taught law and politics, Gilligan all but entirely withdrew from active political participation. The national scene, he wrote in May 1980 to longtime associate Bob Daley, "continues to be depressing."[18] U.S. senator Edward Kennedy (D-Massachusetts) was challenging incumbent Jimmy Carter in that year's Democratic presidential primaries. Carter, Gilligan wrote, "seems utterly unable to get on top of things, and yet each fresh disaster seems to fuel a new electoral victory over Kennedy, who obviously isn't going anywhere, but doesn't know how to quit any more than he knew how to start."[19] Nor was he any happier with the manner in which his successor in Columbus, James Rhodes, was managing the public purse: "He plays the shell game with eight shells, whereas most sideshow operators use two or three."[20]

Gilligan was gone from Columbus, but he was hardly forgotten there. In January 1981, more than a hundred people—many of them veterans of the Gilligan administration—gathered in downtown Columbus to mark with speeches and fellowship the tenth anniversary of Jack Gilligan's inauguration as governor. Prior to the dinner, Gilligan told one reporter that he was "disappointed in seeing the country retreat in an attitude of fear and doubt."[21] That reporter was either sufficiently impressed or sufficiently nostalgic enough to write a column headlined "State Democrats Need a Leader and John Gilligan Is His Name."[22] Gilligan, while not a candidate for anything, was appreciative of the event. He wrote an associate of how "completely delighted both Katie and I were in the festivities of Saturday night . . . to see and spend some time with a lot of great people we haven't had the chance to see in far too many years."[23] Once inaugurated, the event was repeated generally at five-year intervals, carrying with it something of the spirit of a college reunion.

That same January, the Notre Dame School of Law combined three of its independent centers—the Center for Civil and Human Rights, which focused on scholarship and research; the Center for Constitutional Studies, which focused on public policy issues as they particularly affected independent institutions of higher education (and whose director was Phil Moots, former legislative liaison under Governor Gilligan); and the Thomas J. and Alberta White Center for Law, Government, and Human Rights, which, directed by Gilligan, aimed "to train lawyers for public service who have a Christian commitment"—into the Institute of Public Policy Research, which was placed under Gilligan's administrative direction.[24]

While Gilligan's efforts at the new institute were a full-time undertaking, his major work at Notre Dame was framed by the Catholic bishops' 1983 pastoral letter on peace. The letter, Gilligan wrote, "must have provided a severe jolt" to people, some Catholic educators included, who believed that service to God and to Caesar involved "quite separate patterns of thought and action."[25] Among other things, the bishops' letter stated: "We would urge every diocese and parish to implement balanced and objective educational programs to sensitize Christians at all age levels to issues of war and peace."[26] Among his own first actions, Gilligan designed the course The Nuclear Dilemma, in which faculty members from various departments addressed issues related to the nuclear arms race. Student interest was substantial; enrollment in the class had to be cut off at 200. This interest, Gilligan said, was driven less by the fear of war than by the nuclear arms buildup then occurring under President Ronald Reagan.

Prompted by the bishops' statement, Gilligan approached university president Theodore Hesburgh, saying that since Notre Dame regarded itself as the country's leading Catholic university, surely peace was an issue on which the university should take a lead. Hesburgh was fully receptive; he had spent fifteen years as the Vatican's representative to the International Atomic Energy Association, which was exploring peaceful purposes and uses of atomic energy. Hesburgh's urgency matched Gilligan's: nuclear arms, the Notre Dame president said, meant that "for the first time we had the power to destroy life on earth—not just the possibility, but the capability."[27]

As a first step, he assigned Gilligan a new position—the Frank O'Malley University Professor. To receive a chaired professorship named for his strongest influence at Notre Dame was highly gratifying to Gilligan. Hesburgh also made him a special assistant on matters of public policy. Hesburgh said, "I needed someone with experience and knowledge of the world."[28] The appointment made Gilligan the holder of one of Notre Dame's thirty-two endowed professorships. (Some indication of Hesburgh's influence on the institution was that Notre Dame had had no endowed professorships when he was appointed.)

Some early Gilligan activities in this role included moderating the five-part series "Search for Justice: Christianity and the American Economy," produced in August 1984 by a series of Catholic media organizations, and, several months later, a panel discussion in connection with a three-hour teleconference on World Food Day. More substantively, he gathered together eight or so Notre Dame faculty members from different disciplines to develop a curriculum for a program in peace studies. When Gilligan presented the outline to Hesburgh, he stressed that he doubted the program could survive as an outlier within the Notre Dame scheme of things; what was needed was a program endowment that would produce $500,000 a year, free and clear. Hesburgh endorsed the program outline and agreed to the financial requirement, however, he didn't have the money. He instructed Gilligan to pursue the planning, saying, Gilligan recalled, he "would see what [he] can do at the money end."[29]

Some while later, Father Hesburgh addressed an audience in San Diego on the need and requirements of world peace, stressing that peace could not occur without a tranquility of order. Following his talk, a woman from the audience came up and, without introducing herself, complimented his remarks and his efforts. One of Hesburgh's assistants urged him to make her acquaintance, telling him, "That is Joan Kroc." Hesburgh didn't know who she was but was told that she was the widow of the founder of McDonald's and was reportedly worth $1 billion. Hesburgh passed on the possibility to pursue Mrs. Kroc and her assets. Recalling the occasion, he said, "She seemed to be a woman who knew her own mind and was not going to be led."[30] Six months later, Joan Kroc called Hesburgh, commenting that she had never seen the Notre Dame campus. Hesburgh replied, "You can be here three hours after you get on your private plane."[31]

During her campus visit, she lunched with Hesburgh and Gilligan, who described the Peace Studies center they hoped to create at Notre Dame. Following lunch, as Gilligan drove her back to the airport, Joan Kroc asked, "What is the largest gift Notre Dame has ever received?" Gilligan replied that he did not know but imagined that she could top it if she wished.[32] Then Gilligan confessed to one small piece of curiosity. He told her that it had always been his impression that Ray Kroc was rather conservative. Joan Kroc acknowledged this, but added, "Ray never knew I voted for Kennedy."[33] Mrs. Kroc invited Gilligan to submit a proposal.

When that proposal arrived, Joan Kroc told Theodore Hesburgh that what the pending program most needed was a building. She said that she never made donations for buildings but that she might make an exception provided the building was named for Hesburgh. Hesburgh replied that as the university had recently named its major library in his honor and suggested, "Why not name it for Joan Kroc?" For two reasons, Mrs. Kroc replied—first, because she didn't want a building named for her, and, second, because it was her money. There would be a Hesburgh Center, she said, or a center financed by someone else. Hesburgh accepted Joan Kroc's $6 million to construct the Hesburgh Center for International Peace Studies and a second $6 million to provide the program's initial endowment. Joan Kroc's gifts to the Hesburgh Center during her lifetime totaled $20 million and, on her death, a bequest of $50 million in McDonald's stock.

On September 2, 1986, John Gilligan was named inaugural director of the Institute for International Peace Studies. Hesburgh said of the appointment: "Jack was the obvious choice as director; his heart was in it."[34] The new position entailed an administrative move: Gilligan became George N. Shuster University Professor to relieve him of the teaching requirements that had gone with the Frank O'Malley professorship.

Hesburgh, Gilligan noted, had one clear intention for the program: "With his usual inventive mind, one thing he stressed from the outset was that this program could not be just a group of Notre Dame faculty and students talking about peace; we'd have to have foreign students here."[35] The original hope was that half of the initial twenty students would be from other countries. Gilligan added, "Hesburgh said, 'We have to go recruit some people.' He had contacts everywhere. So the two of us did an around-the-world trip recruiting. We thought that, given the Soviet-American tensions, it was important to have some Russian students and faculty involved."[36]

In early 1987, the *Cincinnati Post* reported on the program's progress.

> Now, in a modest suite in the corner of the law school building Gilligan and his staff of four are creating a program that includes an undergraduate in peace studies, a course in President Reagan's "Space Defense Initiative"; and a peace course for Army Navy and Air Force ROTC students. "We have a very special obligation to those young people who are going to go out as professional military people. We think we need to analyze with them the kinds of moral problems which confront military leaders."[37] The reporter, Richard Gateau, presented a good portrait of Gilligan.

> [Gilligan] might seem at first glance much changed from the politically ambitious Jack Gilligan of 1953 to 1974. The lean, youthful, fast-moving Gilligan has given way to one who is fuller of face, one who moves at a more leisurely pace. His red hair is fading to gray along the temples, but the essence of the man, the Gilligan instinct for reforming society, is unchanged. And he's still competitive, even in play. The professor wore blood on the bridge of his generous Irish nose when he returned to his office late one recent afternoon. He explained to he had been wounded in a racquetball match with a campus colleague.[38]

In a *Cleveland Plain Dealer* interview published in early 1987, Gilligan stated his intention to remain with the peace program for another four years, until he reached the university's mandatory retirement age of seventy. He noted that he and Katie had barely returned to Cincinnati since he had left for the AID position in Washington; still, they regarded the city as their home: "I think it is the best place in the world to live. It's a great city, one of the best-kept secrets in the world, a marvelously civilized place to live."[39] After another four years of directing the program, Gilligan said, he would feel ready to turn the task over to somebody else. At that point, he added, "I think we'll move back to Cincinnati. My wife is counting the days."[40]

Across the decades and through various relocations, the Gilligans maintained their second home in Leland, which, during his Notre Dame years, remained the likeliest summer or holiday gathering spot for the expanding Gilligan clan. On June 29, 1987, Gilligan wrote to Bob Daley, "As you may guess, Katie and I and most of our family are in Leland, and while I will be in and out to some degree, I hope to spend a good part of the summer here."[41]

The entire brood was not on hand on the occasion. Donald was by then working as an independent energy consultant based in Massachusetts, developing the Army Facilities Energy Plan for the U.S. Army Corps of Engineers and executing business and marketing studies for Volkswagen AG Wolfsburg and the Federal Emergency Management Agency. He and Betsy had two offspring, Hannah and James, born 1977 and 1979, respectively. The previous year, Kathleen Gilligan Sebelius—living in Topeka with husband Keith, an attorney, and sons Ned and John, born 1982 and 1985, respectively—had decided to run for the Kansas legislature as, of course, a Democrat. She was elected in November 1986 to the first of four terms in the Kansas State Legislature.

Son John and his wife, Megan, returned to Ohio and Columbus in 1980, where their second son, Joe, was born in 1983. John worked for five years in the anti-trust enforcement and court of claims defense division of the Ohio attorney general's office before joining the major downtown law firm of Schottenstein, Zox, & Dunn, where he became a partner in 1988. Ellen, the youngest Gilligan, was living in Washington, D.C., where she worked with a series of nationally based nonprofit organizations.

Leland was a relatively unchanging refuge from the passage of time. In a note to Bob Daley, Jack Gilligan reported receiving an out-of-the-blue phone call from his one-time campaign media assistant, Jim Dunn, from whom he had not heard in years. Dunn, Gilligan said, had of late found himself reflecting on the assassination of Dr. Martin Luther King. This prompted Gilligan to write, "All of us seem to be in the same boat; we simply can't believe that those momentous events in our lives, which seemed to have happened the day before yesterday, really transpired twenty years ago. Now that has to be one of the sure signs of advancing age."[42]

Gilligan's thinking on peace issues reflected his experience at AID: "In some ways, AID had been an example of what not to do. I think there was a failure to develop progressively the kinds of programs at the recipient country level that would encourage peaceful development through shifting priorities from militaristic solutions."[43] Commonly, he said, the first form of assistance sought by "new nations with fractured economies" is armaments—and not entirely irrationally so.[44] "These nations were weak, militarily and otherwise, and needed some means to protect themselves against menaces foreign and domestic, and to have sufficient clout to be able to demonstrate that they could control the situation. Their arguments were not without merit: it was similar to the arguments you'd hear in America that the first thing we need to get on top of is 'law and order.'"[45]

But he recalled a pertinent AID experience, the May 1977 CIEC conference he had attended in Paris and which he wrote about in 1989 in a six-page letter to the Most Reverend William Keith Weigand, the bishop of Salt Lake City.

> After four days and nights of what is sometimes termed "the dialog of the deaf," in which all participants, speaking from prepared positions, volleyed and thundered over each other's heads, the entire American delegation was peremptorily summoned from the various conference rooms by the Secretary of State, at 2 a.m., [and] in a furious motorcade, with police motorcycle escort, we were driven across the sleeping city to the airport. The Secretary [Cyrus Vance], an eminently decent man, declared that he would never again, under any circumstances, subject himself and his people to the kind of abuse we had experienced during that conference. And he never did. After that Americans simply declined to discuss the subject in any formal conference setting.[46]

Gilligan noted that some of the offending talk had been Marxist, some Christian; but it was the talk about *justice* that baffled and infuriated the Americans and many representatives of developed countries. He described the apparently honest confusion and sense of unfairness that many ordinary decent people felt when asked to think about concepts like justice.

> In one sense, therefore, these good citizens who rail at the bishops for being "naive" about the real world have a point. When they demand that the bishops—and the philosophers and theologians—stick to their trade, and work out for the faithful the path to personal salvation, they are really complaining that they don't know how to put the two halves of their lives together. And, since they are immersed on a daily basis in the half that imposes its own set of standards and practices, the other half seems less real, and tends to wither away into an empty formalism.[47]

He added:

> One of the men at the board room table the other day made that point very explicitly, when he urged you and your fellow bishops to focus on preaching charity, which you might know something about, but to stay away from business and banking, about which you know little. Rarely if ever alluded to at that table by the bankers present was the concept of *justice*.[48]

Gilligan wondered aloud to Weigand how these bankers might react if a child in their own family was disabled or diseased—would they not wish some special provision be made? What the bankers and others needed to realize was that, for the Christian, there was only one family. What these bankers had not accepted was that "the teachings of Christ compel them to [adopt] practices that are more holistic, more humane, more rewarding. And that is the teaching mission of the Church."[49]

Gilligan was prepared to challenge the claim that those in government and business were life's "realists." In a 1990 letter to the *Chicago Tribune*, he took strenuous exception to the Reagan administration's policies toward Central America. "At precisely this magical moment in history of Western civilization," he wrote, referring to the recent fall of the Berlin Wall, "when millions of people were winning freedom and autonomy by nonviolent means, the government of the United States persists in trying to solve political and social problems with the application of military force. It is as though Vietnam never happened."[50]

He added a challenge of his own to issue:

> I want some of the self-styled realists who have controlled the foreign policies of this country for the past twenty-five years to tell me, and the rest of America, which would be the better investment of American dollars and energy: the continuation of the flow of hundreds of millions of dollars into the prolongation of the slaughter in El Salvador, Nicaragua, Panama and the other countries of Latin America, or the diversion of those same dollars to the rebuilding of the newly freed nations of Europe.[51]

In 1988, Gilligan was one of three Notre Dame alumni to receive the Reverend John J. Cavanaugh Award, which is "given to the graduate who has performed outstanding service in the field of local, state or national government and politics."[52] In 1990, he received the university's Reinhold Niebuhr Award, recognizing him as "ever a man of faith and reason, he centralized social justice and peace in his teaching, course development, and program structure. Leader of a vital campus institute, this chaired professor has created a climate where peace and justice thrive."[53]

In April 1991, the "Gilligan alumni" gathered again in Columbus in somewhat larger numbers to mark the twentieth anniversary of Gilligan's inauguration and his seventieth birthday. In a letter thanking those who organized the event and who attended, Jack Gilligan wrote that those who served in his gubernatorial administration had been "bound together by a common concern for the well-being of the entire community, and by a desire to use the powers of government to make things better for everyone and especially the poor, the weak and the dispossessed members of our society."[54] He expressed some uncertainty as to when all might meet again, but added, "Katie and I will be coming back to Cincinnati sometime in the next several months (and in broad daylight) and we hope that we will be able to see at least some of you more frequently than has been possible in the past several years."[55]

As Gilligan prepared to leave Notre Dame, a well-researched article in the *South Bend Tribune* assessed how far the field of peace studies had advanced. Day after day, it began, "people from all corners of the world meet at the University of Notre Dame to talk about the road of justice and peace. They come from Malaysia, Russia, Poland, Estonia, Kenya, China, England, Canada, and South Africa and, of course, the United States. They are the international scholars of Notre Dame's Institute for International Peace Studies."[56]

The article noted that when Notre Dame had founded its program, peace studies was limited to a "scattering of courses" offered at various institutions by individual college teachers. Now, it stated, hundreds of campuses were offering undergraduates a minor in peace studies; and twenty of these, including Notre Dame, offered master's degrees in the field. The Notre Dame program was thriving, it reported. The 1991 entering class had twenty openings: for these, it had received ninety-seven applications, including fifteen from the former Soviet Union and "one from a Buddhist monk in Katmandu."[57]

37

Cincinnati, Finally

With mandatory retirement from Notre Dame pending, Jack and Katie Gilligan needed to decide where they would live next. The Gilligans knew several couples who had retired to Florida; alternately, they considered settling in their home in Leland, which, while offering less beach and sun than Florida, held lengthy family associations, past and still to come. "But the more we talked about it," Jack Gilligan wrote Bob Daley, "the more we really wanted to live in Cincinnati."[1]

Cincinnati was a place from which Jack and Katie Gilligan had been all but absent in the twenty years since he had taken the oath of office as Ohio's governor. Some while after resettling in the city, Jack Gilligan reflected on the changes to the Queen City during his absence. Gilligan retained a sharp eye for the shortcomings of the city he loved.

In many respects, he said, "I felt like Rip van Winkle, awakening from a twenty-year nap."[2] The construction projects for which he and others on city council had sought funds three decades earlier had "transformed" the city's skyline, and the city's once-rural outskirts were mazes of subdivisions and shopping centers.[3] Yet, he wrote, "As I drove for hours through parts of Avondale and Walnut Hills and Price Hill and Over the Rhine and Mount Auburn, I was dismayed and saddened by the evident deterioration and abandonment of hundreds and hundreds of fine old homes."[4]

These homes, Gilligan said, had died of a disease, and the disease they had died of was poverty. He contended that the poor led lives little known by those who did not share them. "The lack of knowledge about the poor leads to a form of denial of the problem: if there are poor people in our society, there aren't very many and they aren't very poor, and their situation could easily be improved with a little initiative and hard work on their part"—statements that did more to comfort the comfortable than to aid the afflicted.[5] In the past decade, he said, the share of Cincinnatians living in poverty had doubled to 24 percent; two of every five schoolchildren lived in poverty. Poverty, Gilligan said, metastasized. The poor concentrated in given neighborhoods, where "their lack of disposable income becomes the economic equivalent of a tourniquet shutting off the life's blood of the community." Retail establishments close, public facilities suffer: "Economic and social gangrene sets in, and begins to spread."[6] To Gilligan, the lesson to be learned was simple, if not new: until the city's resources were directed at the circumstance of poverty, "I am afraid that our other efforts to keep Cincinnati as the most livable city in America are doomed to failure."[7]

By the time Gilligan delivered those remarks, he had acquired a podium from which to express himself. Shortly after his return to the city, the University of Cincinnati College of Law offered Gilligan an appointment as a part-time professor and organizer of a program on law and public policy. Drumming up support for the latter, Gilligan wrote to several dozen kindred spirits inviting ideas about a proposed seminar series "designed to open a dialogue between town and gown."[8] The program, he wrote, would stand at the crossroads of two facts:

> Today Americans are looking at a new world, a world filled with menace and with promise. Our society suddenly seems confronted with a wide range of problems that we don't know how even to describe, never mind solve—grinding economic recession; widespread bankruptcy in both the public and private sectors; the growing impotence of government at all levels; the evident failure of our educational and health care systems; the persistence of environmental pollution . . . [9]

Worst of all, he added, "we seem to have lost our ability to communicate with one another and we seem to have lost our sense of community."[10]

Gilligan had been influenced by Robert Bellah's book *The Good Society,* which argued that while Americans involved themselves in "an astounding number" of voluntary associations, this involvement did not produce a shared sense of what constituted the "public good." Rather, Gilligan quoted, "the conflicting demands of work, family, and community are sharply separated and often contradictory, a world of diverse, often hostile groups, interdependent in ways too complex for any individual to comprehend . . . In such circumstances, what positive meaning can public life have for the private individual?"[11]

Gilligan proposed addressing this question of public life through a seven-part seminar. Response was favorable. Gilligan lined up participants (sometimes tossing out the lure that the honoraria to be paid, while modest, might cover the cost of a drive to Cincinnati, depending on what fuel efficiency their vehicles offered), and in the fall of 1992, he gave the opening address of the first Civic Forum. The session drew two dozen participants—academics, local government figures, and others—for a week-long series of discussions on Policy, Politics and the Good Society. The audience was a mix of students and townspeople.

In his opening address, Gilligan contrasted the views of Alexis de Tocqueville, who visited Cincinnati in 1831 during his American tour, and those of Bellah. De

Tocqueville had found much to praise in the America's experiment with democracy but worried that "America seemed to recognize no moral authority as superior to the will of the majority" and wondered if such an approach "could actually work in times when national passion ran high"—an interesting anticipatory comment to the Civil War.[12] The French visitor added: "The principle of the Republics of antiquity was to sacrifice private interests to the public good. In that sense one could say that they were virtuous. The principle of this one seems to be to make private interests harmonize with the general interest. A sort of refined and intelligent selfishness seems to be the pivot on which the whole machine turns."[13]

Bellah, Gilligan noted, saw Americans as motivated by a belief in republican virtues, an espousal of certain biblical values, and a pragmatic utilitarianism—traditions he regarded as "not mutually reinforcing."[14] When, Gilligan said, a gap opened between what we profess and what we do, the resulting dissonance prompts a guilt that is commonly assuaged by cynicism—a cynicism which, quoting Bellah, Gilligan termed "the corrosive that eats away at the very fabric of society [in which] as a society, we espouse certain beliefs and standards, but the rewards of money, power and success seem to be reserved for those who actually live and work in accordance with other standards, or with no standards at all."[15] What was needed, Gilligan stressed, was that the community "try to resume the conversation . . . of these fundamental questions that, if left undiscussed, have a way of reducing our political dialogue to meaningless prattle."[16]

That first 1992 Civic Forum inaugurated a series, organized chiefly by Gilligan, of conversations on such subjects as the causes and effects of racial discrimination, poverty in Cincinnati, crime and punishment, the challenge of regionalism, the welfare of our children and other topics. It was quintessential Gilligan—the belief that informed dialog among community leaders would influence the thinking of the community, to its betterment.

Almost from the couple's return to Cincinnati, it was clear that Katie Gilligan was in declining health. The couple had first moved into a multilevel dwelling; but not long after, Katie became unable to manage its staircases with ease, and the two moved to a ground-floor apartment in Hyde Park. Katie's health had not been robust for some while; she suffered from an underlying and unrecognized immune-system deficiency related to the pituitary gland as well as congestive heart failure.

In 1995, Ellen Gilligan, with her husband, Charlie DeSandro, and sons Luke, born in 1993, and Carlo, born in 1994, moved back to Cincinnati from Washington, D.C., so that she could help with her mother's care. Ellen had made a career for herself in Washington with a series of major nonprofits that focused on resource development, program design, implementation, and management in nonprofit, philanthropic, and public sectors. Her own impressions of Cincinnati were strikingly like her father's: neighborhoods had diverged, growing either better or decidedly worse. The city generally was, in racial terms, much more segregated, both in housing and in personal association, than her own family's community in

Washington, D.C. Cincinnati, she said, spoke about race—or avoided speaking about race—"in ways that reminded her of the 1960s."[17]

The past, of course, is always with us, though on some occasions more self-consciously so. On October 29, 1994, John Joyce Gilligan joined with his fellow former governors, James Rhodes and Dick Celeste in a "Conversation Among Governors" panel discussion at Ohio Politics Day, a day-long conference held at the Ohio Historical Center in Columbus to address Ohio's postwar state government. It was a good-natured encounter. The *Columbus Dispatch* reported of Rhodes and Celeste: "The men who had faced each other in two gubernatorial elections talked about the sad fortunes of the Ohio State University football team."[18] Rhodes, then eighty-five, was something of the scamp of the occasion, claiming, "I'm retired—I don't pay much attention to politics," a remark that the *Dispatch* reported prompted "much skeptical laughter."[19] Asked to name the political figures he admired most, Rhodes somewhat surprisingly listed Franklin Roosevelt along with Dwight Eisenhower ("they got things done"); Celeste named former Connecticut governor Chester Bowles as his political mentor and Thomas Jefferson as his intellectual mentor. John Gilligan, to the surprise of no one who knew him, named Robert Kennedy.[20]

Two years later, Gilligan returned to Columbus for "A Capitol Revival," the rededication of the Ohio Statehouse following what Gilligan termed its "utterly magnificent" transformation from a one-time rabbit warren peopled by legislators grimly searching for their offices to a gem placed at the heart of the state's capital city.[21]

And there were less formal gatherings, including the 1996 Columbus reunion that drew more than a hundred friends and former members of the Gilligan administration to mark what simultaneously were the governor's seventy-fifth birthday and the twenty-fifth anniversary of his inauguration. As with the other similar such reunions, it was something of an "old home week"—James Friedman provided the introduction, Mark Shields talked on American politics, David Sweet moderated an "issues" forum that included Ira Whitman and Kenneth Gaver, and Peter Hart moderated a discussion of the media, politics, and pollsters. Gilligan, the speaker everyone had come to hear, did not disappoint. He spoke of the need to lure Americans away from a "consumerist" view of politics, a step necessary to the preservation of representative government: "The great disaster is the thrashing of the American system of government and its institutions [which] has increased the cynicism of the American people."[22] Mistrust of government, he said, was the reciprocal response to mistrust of the public by those who did the governing: "Do they really believe that the people will respond if they are not treated honestly, talked to honestly, and challenged to do their best?"[23]

Despite her poor health, Katie Gilligan was able to attend the reunion. It would be her last, however. On October 10, 1996, Katie Gilligan, age seventy-five, died at Cincinnati's Christ Hospital. The death record lists her occupation as "housewife/homemaker," which is true only if one appreciates how elastic that term can be.

Though often regarded as reticent and retiring, Katie Gilligan had been an enormous influence on her husband's work—as his enabler, looking to the home while he looked to politics, and then as a strong moral force in her own right, more inclined to reinforce than to damp down her husband's convictions. Possibly, her defining public act had been the 1967 letter she had written to the *Cincinnati Enquirer* after that newspaper had editorially criticized her son, John, for circulating a petition in support of Martin Luther King Jr. As noted, she was standing up for her son, standing up for her husband, and standing up for Dr. King.

Her funeral was held at St. Mary's Church on Cincinnati's Erie Avenue, the same church in which she and John Joyce Gilligan had been married fifty-one years previously. Father Theodore Hesburgh, president emeritus of Notre Dame University and a close friend, traveled from South Bend to officiate.

Now a widower, Gilligan had the comfort of seeing his children's careers and families grow. In 1998, Donald Gilligan left Conceco—a corporation he had cofounded in 1991 to supply back office analysis, design, construction, and financing services to major energy service companies and other services—to form the consulting firm Predicate, LLC, which provided management and marketing support services to major utilities and federal agencies. That same year, Kansas voters reelected Kathleen Gilligan Sebelius to a second four-year term as State Insurance Commissioner. Sebelius won the office in 1994, having pledged to reject contributions from the insurance industry. John Gilligan remained in Columbus at Schottenstein, Zox, & Dunn, where he was developing expertise in financial services and commercial litigation. And also in 1998, Ellen Gilligan joined the Cincinnati Foundation, becoming vice president for community investment, a post in which she was responsible for all aspects of the organization's charitable investments in the eight-county area it served.

Leland remained the Gilligan family's common ground, the likeliest gathering point in the warmer months. The calm of Lake Leelanau was mildly rippled in August 1999 when Jack Gilligan told his children that he was considering a return to elective politics. He had been approached by people dismayed at the poor performance and creaky financing of the Cincinnati public schools; they had suggested that he might be someone who could help set things to right. Gilligan, age seventy-eight, told his children that he was thinking of taking that advice—of running for a seat on the Cincinnati school board. Describing the scene in a note to Bob Daley, Gilligan wrote, "The four children were furious when I discussed the prospect with them at Leland. They think I am a nutty old man."[24]

Indeed, Ellen recalled, "My recollection is that we all told him he was crazy."[25] If, she added, her father wished to undertake public service, there were a dozen alternatives likely to prove more fruitful and satisfying. Kathleen pointed out the practical objections—he would be forced to do fund-raising, which he hated; many of his one-time strongest supporters were now dead; many voters were too young to remember his tenure as governor. Back in Cincinnati, Ellen Gilligan invited her father to dinner so that she could talk him out of the venture, but the next morning, she picked up the local newspaper and saw his announcement of candidacy. Word of his plan spread. Gilligan wrote Bob Daley that he'd received phone calls from Phil Moots and Bill Chavanne: "They seemed mystified, but generally supportive."[26]

Gilligan claimed nothing but the most rational of motives. His life, he noted, had been divided between politics and teaching—two interests that converged at public education. And public education was in trouble. He said, "I thought I would never see the day that the public school system in the United States, which was once among our proudest achievements, would be under concerted attack from all sides, as it is today."[27] He was concerned at the level of education being offered Ohio's children, concerned that the charter school movement and school vouchers would "bleed the system to the point where it is going to disappear." (This was an interesting comment coming from someone who had never attended public school.) This move was also a nod to his father, Harry Gilligan, who had repeatedly stressed that America and Cincinnati had sheltered and supported the Gilligan family, and so "we got to pay it back."[28]

A quarter-century since his last campaign, Gilligan made an active effort to win the seat. He stressed three themes: engage the public in the design and performance of the public schools; promote public awareness of why broad social changes required a different kind of public school; and increase understanding of how the state constitution influenced school funding. He drew an impressive range of endorsements—including the Hamilton County Democratic Party, Cincinnatians for Public Education, Cincinnati Federation of Teachers, Appalachian PAC, Cincinnati Women's Political Caucus, the American Federation of State, County and Municipal Employees, and the AFL-CIO. Just before Election Day, he wrote a friend that he felt good about the campaign, good that he had raised the issues that he had. The day before the election, he emailed Bob Daley: "The campaign is over and I am hiding away in my pad, enjoying the sunshine of the river and the quiet of the day."[29] Tuesday brought Gilligan a landslide victory. Six candidates had vied for three seats. Gilligan's vote total of 40,045 placed him well ahead of the 30,573 received by second-place finisher Rich Williams, a community planner, and the 29,616 total of Florence Newell, an associate professor of education at the University of Cincinnati.

During his campaign season, Jack Gilligan continued his almost daily attendance at St. Anthony's Catholic Church in the Madisonville neighborhood. He generally attended the 8:30 morning Mass and was therefore unaware that this same seat was often occupied at the 11:00 service by Dr. Susan Fremont. Susan Fremont had an eclectic background. Her Brittany-born father met her American mother while he was attending classes at Rensselaer Polytechnic Institute in Troy, New York; in 1951, the couple moved to Brazil, where her father pursued a variety of engineering and entrepreneurial activities. Susan was born there the following year, thus becoming the bearer of triple citizenship—French, Brazilian, and U.S. She returned to the United States as an infant, she recalled, "speaking toddler in three languages."[30]

She enrolled in Miami (of Ohio) University in 1970, intending to study geography. After graduation, she lived in Cincinnati and worked for an environmental nonprofit. Her life was redirected by a 1981 aircraft accident in which her brother was seriously injured in Colorado in a freak skydiving accident that killed seventeen people. She thereafter pointed her life toward health care. In 1981, Susan Fremont enrolled in a pre-nursing program at the University of Cincinnati, where she "fell in love with the life sciences" and, pursuing them seriously, received a doctorate in 1990.[31] She enrolled in medical school at the University of Toledo, the only state school willing to take a nearly-forty-year-old as a first-year student. After two years, she transferred to Wright State University near Dayton, where she received her medical degree. Despite an academic interest in oncology, she chose to pursue work as a family practitioner out of "a simple liking for patient contact."[32] In 1999 she joined a group practice with an office in Loveland.

Though raised Catholic, Susan had not been to church in thirty years. In 1999, she said, "There was, however, a softening in my doubts; I was starting to include prayer in my life."[33] She did not attend church, however, until a good friend invited her to hear her perform as a soloist at the 140th anniversary of St. Anthony's.[34] "I found everyone so friendly and nice," she recalled. "The church offered an odd familiarity that was not unpleasant. I had a nice feeling afterward of being part of the community."[35] She became a regular attendee.

Jack Gilligan and Susan Fremont's first encounter came in January 2000 when Susan's schedule forced her to attend the 8:30 Mass, at which Gilligan was present. A few weeks later, she exited the church after he did. She remembered that he was wearing a funny wool cap and a trench coat and that he leaned over to someone carrying a child, saying something about making sure the child was well bundled up. A few weeks later, after Mass, Gilligan invited her to join him for breakfast at a local establishment, the Echo, which he favored for its oatmeal.

These breakfasts became a routine. In these early courting days, she confessed that she had voted for James Rhodes in the 1974 election. By way of explanation, she said that she was twenty-two at the time, was living somewhat grumpily in Cincinnati, and was surrounded by people whose opinion of Rhodes was higher than that of Gilligan. She voted for Rhodes, she said, as an act of "this will serve you right."[35] (But she did vote for Gilligan in his 1999 school board race.) On hearing her confession, Gilligan's response was pragmatic: "In that case, you'll *have* to marry me."[36]

Gilligan's family was not without reservations about their father considering marriage to a woman thirty years his junior. Asked by one offspring how old the woman was, Gilligan replied that while Susan Fremont was not as old as his daughter Kathleen, she was older than his daughter Ellen. According to one newspaper account, Gilligan reminded his children that when each had brought their intended in to meet Jack and Katie, "Our only question was, 'Do you love each other?' Then do it."[37]

The couple was married September 30, 2000, at St. Anthony's Church in a ceremony officiated by Father Leonard Wenke. All the Gilligan offspring were present, as were both of Susan's parents and their respective second spouses. The reception was held at Cincinnati's Vernon Manor Hotel (a locale with some significance in Gilligan's life: it was where Jim Friedman had in 1967 persuaded him to challenge the incumbent Frank Lausche for the U.S. Senate).

The 1999 school board contest was the first time Jack Gilligan placed first in a Cincinnati municipal election in a career that began in 1953. In 1953, the electorate that gave him his first term on city council also turned down a renewal of the city's property tax, leaving a large hole in the municipal budget as the new councilman's first order of business. Similarly, the 1999 voters who placed Gilligan on the city's school board had rejected by a margin of 52–48 percent a 4.5 mil school tax renewal, leaving the school board with a resultant $20 million deficit.

School systems are resistant to change, Cincinnati's not least. Gilligan recalled of the teachers and staff he initially encountered that "a lot of them had a minimal interest in making any changes at all. They were drawing down a salary, doing what they were told to do by manuals and class schedules, and spending a lot of time talking to each other—bitching about the kids, colleagues, parents."[38] Morale, he felt, was low. "Yet I knew that among the teachers were a significant number of intelligent and good-hearted people."[39]

In truth, Gilligan often found the school board's meetings something of a trial; surprisingly little meeting time, he felt, was directed at the questions of how to improve school performance. Commonly, he said, two or three members were focused on pushing personal agendas that he saw as having little relevance to the district's needs and even less chance of passage. As a consequence, he said, personal contests and rivalries developed, which became obstacles to presenting a united front to the community. And though he was a four-decade supporter of labor unions, he at times found that positions taken by the local teachers union prompted an uncharacteristic irritation with unionism.

To a good extent, Gilligan attributed these difficulties to the simple fact that the schools were *public.* The Catholic schools (which he had attended), the Jewish community schools, and the military academies had in common a sense of vocation that was stronger and better rooted than that common to public schools. The educators he had experienced often came from religious orders: "They were not without blemish, but they seemed to share some broader image of what was possible, to see their work as a vocation, not a job."[40]

Broadly, Gilligan's effort on the school board was to find ways to focus the resources of the community on the schools. He became the board's leading advocate of community schools—that is, schools that are the organizing locus of their community, with afterschool programs for the students, social service offices, tutoring programs, and in-school police stations where "the kids could get to know the cops and the cops could get to know the kids somewhere other than out on the streets."[41] The idea grew in part from a 1990 Civic Forum report, "The Challenge of Child Development in a Changing Society." Gilligan became convinced that schools should be neighborhood learning centers, providing health care and other social services, life-long learning, and more. Such schools would draw on and thrive with community involvement. When he presented his idea to his fellow school board members, Gilligan said, "it was not a vision or an enthusiasm widely shared. They already had so much on their plate." And there were turf issues. Further, "it's hard to make a case for expanding the role of public schools when the district is classified by the state as being in an 'academic emergency.'"[42]

Gilligan was the only former governor in the nation to serve on a public school board. If experience in politics had taught him anything, it was the need to persevere. He worked at the idea of community schools through much of his four-year term. Rosa Blackwell, then deputy superintendent, recalled, "On the board, he was very diplomatic and reasoned in his approach, low key. Even as he moved about the community, he was very clear about what he wanted to have happen: the one very important need for the community was for the families and the community to connect with the schools, to enhance the schools through the community."[43]

He told the *Dayton Daily News* that he was committed to this issue "because education issues are the most important public policy debate of the day and symbolic of the divide between the haves and have-nots." The major problems of poor children, he said, traced to the fact that they "just didn't choose their parents very carefully."[44] One point to which he returned was that the current generation of students had little in common with their postwar counterparts. As he told *Cincinnati Enquirer* columnist Laura Pulfer, when he left Cincinnati in 1971, the city's public schools had 99,000 students—70 percent were white and 80 percent were from families "with a workingman's income or above." Now, the system has 41,000 students, with 70 percent African American and almost half from single-parent homes. It was, Gilligan said, "ridiculous to think we can run a school system like the one that worked fifty years ago."[45] He added that if one looked at proficiency scores, "what jumps off the page is that there are two worlds: a suburban world where children have all the comforts and resources they could have—soccer leagues and trips to the zoo—to support their education. You come to the inner city and you've got kids living right on the edge, with no resources. You have single parents or no parents."[46]

Late in Gilligan's first term on school board, Kathleen Sebelius took a further plunge into politics, standing for the position of governor of Kansas. She won handily, defeating her Republican opponent, Tim Shallenburger, by 7.5 percent—435,462

votes to 371,325. Her victory made her and her father the first father-daughter gubernatorial combination in the nation's history. (Several months before the election, Kathleen's husband, Gary, a longtime practicing attorney, was appointed to an
eight-year term as a U.S. magistrate judge in Kansas.)

In 2003, Gilligan stood for reelection to the Cincinnati school board. "We'd had
some minor successes," he said. "I was still interested and still hopeful."[47] He campaigned on the full implementation of the conversion to Neighborhood Learning
Centers, an effort to improve school district communication with the community,
and final approval of the teachers' evaluation/compensation contract. Once again,
Gilligan led the electoral field, as the three incumbents standing for office were
reelected.

Gilligan's proposed community schools were gaining traction. Following his
reelection, the *Cincinnati Enquirer* reported that he was "spearheading an initiative to convert nearly all of Cincinnati's public schools into community learning
centers. As the district renovates sixty-four of its schools, the buildings are being
designed to stay open past 3 P.M. and to house agencies and clinics to help families,
the elderly and neighborhoods six days a week."[48] The first such was the newly
constructed East End School scheduled to open in the fall of 2004 and designed to
include a health clinic, YMCA-run afterschool programs, and a police substation.

The school district had substantial financial resources to apply to these schools.
In May 2003, voters had approved $700 million in bonds for school construction
and reconstruction; this, combined with additional monies from the state and
funds already set aside by the district, brought the total available to over $1 bil-
lion. The money, said Rosa Blackwell, who was named superintendent in 2004, was
sorely needed. "Many of the school buildings were more than fifty years old, di-
lapidated. The public understood that students needed schools that were more than
safe, warm, and dry, but educational settings that would enhance their lives."[49] The
general idea, she said, was to build facilities that connected to communities: "We allowed members of the communities to have a voice, to meet with the architects on
how schools should be designed." This, Blackwell said, "led to an unbelievable number of meetings."[50] District staff met with parent and other groups in each neighborhood to see what activities the community sought and would support. Tutoring
was perhaps the most common request, along with afterschool activities to keep
students engaged until dinner time. Others wanted a mental health unit or a police
substation. And one group wanted space in which to teach ballroom dancing.

By the time Gilligan left the board in 2007, thirty schools—nearly half of the
city's total—were operating on versions of the plan he had proposed. He was not
successful in all things. Not all program coordinators were well selected, and he
was dismayed by the amount of administrative time and skill that was absorbed in
running the afterschool programs and the rapid turnover among those involved.
(Generally, once a given parent's child moved on to another school, the parent-

volunteer moved on as well.) Also, his hope that a merit pay plan would replace tenure and seniority rights went unrealized.

Jack Gilligan left the Cincinnati school board, but, like his previous retirement from Notre Dame and his subsequent retirement from the University of Cincinnati, this was rather more of a segue than a termination. Soon, he was back to teaching, this time in a program for those over age fifty-five coordinated by University of Cincinnati and offering an extensive list of offerings presented at fairly nominal cost. He taught several classes on government, noting, "I don't have a formally laid out course or series of lectures; I pick out related topics and try to provoke a conversation."[51] He said with some bemusement, "I am constantly—constantly—amazed how little people know about the government system under which they operate."[52]

Gilligan, in his eighties, had reached that phase of life when one is in some danger of becoming a public monument. Honors creep in. In 2004, the Charter Committee of Greater Cincinnati, possibly overlooking the vitriol it had dumped on Gilligan in 1959 when he chose the Democrats over the Charterites, bestowed on Gilligan its Twelfth Annual Charles P. Taft Civic Gumption Award. Likely, the warmer occasion came on April 1, 2006, when an "Eighty-Fifth Birthday Salute" to Gilligan was held at the Renaissance Hotel in Columbus. More than 400 people turned out to hear remarks from James Friedman, from Kathleen Gilligan Sebelius, Mark Shields, and Gilligan himself. Unable to attend due to illness, former Gilligan chief of staff Jack Hansan sent along a photo album that closed with a reproduction of a U.S. flag pin placed over "Gilligan for President, 1976." (That fall, Kathleen Sebelius—aided, likely, by her designation by *TIME* as one of the nation's five best governors—was reelected governor of Kansas by a seventeen-point margin over Republican Jim Barnett.

In 2008, the Cincinnati Chamber of Commerce bestowed on Gilligan its Greatest Living Cincinnatian Award for his work as a teacher, governor, and reformist. The award, according to the Chamber, goes to people who demonstrate "leadership, vision, tenacity and love of community."[53] Gilligan, characteristically, cited the influence of his father's strong belief in community service.

Jack Gilligan paid one further visit to the Governor's Mansion in Columbus, when in May 2008 he attended an evening reception hosted by Democratic governor Ted Strickland, an event held in association with the launching of the Gilligan Institute. The reception was followed by a breakfast at the Columbus Athletic Club, attended the following morning by more than 300 people. The two-day event was largely the work of the "usual suspects," with Jim Friedman as principal organizer and Mark Shields and Peter Hart as main presenters on a panel chaired by Kathleen Sebelius.

Interestingly, at that time both Governors Strickland and Sebelius were on various short lists as possible running mates with Barack Obama, whose nomination for president was growing increasingly likely. Sebelius had endorsed Obama, a step considered important in part because she was a Democrat successful on Republican turf and, further, because most high-ranking female officeholders were supporting U.S. senator Hillary Rodham Clinton.

With Obama's election, Kathleen Gilligan Sebelius was sounded out for a cabinet post, which she declined due to unresolved matters in Kansas. In his campaign, Obama had made clear that health care would be the central issue that his administration would pursue. Former Democratic Senate leader Tom Daschle was expected to be the administration's lead official in this area, but, following questions regarding nonpayment of taxes, Daschle withdrew himself from consideration. Shortly thereafter, Sebelius was asked if the Health and Human Services post were offered to her, would she accept it. After some consideration, she replied that she would—and the offer, its acceptance, and Senate confirmation followed.

On Friday, May 2, Jack Gilligan and Susan Fremont Gilligan joined Donald, John, and Ellen and various friends and associates—perhaps thirty in all—at the White House to witness the swearing-in of Secretary of Health and Human Services Kathleen Gilligan Sebelius. Gilligan recalled:

> We were taken to the Green Room first, in the White House. Then we went over to what they refer to as the Executive Dining Room, a big room. President Obama arrived, greeted everybody, shook hands all around, and made a little pitch for Kathleen's credentials. [Vice President] Joe Biden came in and gave her the oath of office. Obama was gracious and eloquent. He's a caution, that guy. Put him in any situation and he handles it perfectly, and he does it without any show of strain.[54]

The visit reminded Gilligan of just how deep his affection was for the nation's capital: "It's such an impressive place. I've often thought that if you're dealing with one of these Arab sheiks who is getting uppity, all you have to do is to walk them around Washington and the White House and ask them, 'Do you give up?'"[55]

Gilligan's other children prompted travel. In November 2009, Donald's daughter, Hannah, gave birth to Kathryn, presenting Jack Gilligan with his first great-grandchild and occasioning a visit by the Gilligans to Massachusetts to see all concerned. Donald had, since 2005, been president of the National Association of Energy Service Companies (NAESCO), a national advocate for energy efficiency programs and regulations at the state level. Among other activities, he was engaged in evaluating energy efficiency programs for the New York Public Service Commission and the California Public Utilities Commission.

In Columbus, John Gilligan remained with Schottenstein, Zox, & Dunn, where he had been repeatedly named one of the hundred best attorneys in Ohio and among the fifty best in Columbus.

In June 2010, Ellen Gilligan was named president and CEO of the Greater Milwaukee Foundation. That agency, founded in 1915, undertakes to play a leadership role in addressing the issues of the greater Milwaukee area and in providing individual donors with the means of creating personal charitable legacies that remain active after their lifetime.

In December 2010, son Donald was again the indirect cause for travel, as Jack and Susan traveled to Mexico for the wedding of Donald's son, Jamie.

Afterword

The first time I talked with former Ohio governor John Joyce Gilligan was in 1997, when I interviewed him for what became an article that appeared in *Ohio Magazine*. We met in his uncluttered office on what I believe was the fifth floor of the University of Cincinnati's school of law, where he was coordinating the Civic Forum program. When Gilligan was in his thirties and a Cincinnati city councilman, he was known for having something of a temper. By the time he became governor, temper had turned to exasperation. At the time of our interview, this had given way to what might be termed a sort of avuncular asperity. What had not changed was his commitment to activist government, his generalized faith in people (Republicans aside), and his appreciation for the type of stories of political skullduggery associated with Huey Long, Lyndon Johnson, and a long list of Ohioans.

After the interview, he kindly walked me to elevator and, while we awaited its arrival, searched his memory for a catchphrase from Garrison Keillor. Finding it, he offered me in parting: "Be well. Do good work. Keep in touch."[1]

Gilligan delivered the phrase somewhat as though he was setting an expectation. "Keep in touch" did not mean drop me a card from your next vacation spot; it meant, let me know what you have accomplished. And the tone suggested why so many in Gilligan's gubernatorial administration—particularly the young, bright, and optimistic—were reinforced in their desire to make something happen.

The last time I talked with John Joyce Gilligan in connection with this book was a messy December day, two weeks before Christmas 2010. The interview was at the Gilligan home on a street almost too small to have a name and tucked away near an impenetrable hedge in the nether reaches of Cincinnati's Clifton neighborhood. He and his second wife, Susan, had only recently moved back into this dwelling after having vacated it for some months while it was quite substantially rebuilt to make it more habitable for Gilligan, who was sharper of mind than nimble of foot.

His optimism was somewhat less in evidence that day. The previous month, the Ohio Democratic Party—the instrument for political advancement Gilligan had spent several decades building—had gotten slaughtered in the 2010 general election. Their losses rivaled those of the French at Agincourt—a governor, a senator, five congressmen, and more than enough state representatives to form both a glee club and a hockey team. But what more generally concerned him, he said, was the extent to which people in politics, people in both parties, did not know why they thought what they thought, assuming that they did think. Politicians of both parties, he said, were "talking baby talk to the public," that they were incapable of educating the public as to what needed to be done—a process he regarded as the politician's most important task.[2]

Looking to lighten the mood, I offhandedly asked the former governor if he had ever read the 1930s detective fiction of Dorothy Sayers. With an amused smile, he acknowledged that he had, "somewhere along the line." At one point, Sayers's detective-hero, Lord Peter Wimsey, observes to the woman of his intention how few people appear to intend anything one year to the next. John Joyce Gilligan, in contrast, was generally in the act of intending something. He had intended to be a Jesuit priest, until that vocation was displaced by the Second World War. He had intended to be a University of Chicago scholar, until family claims overrode the possibility. He had intended to help found a small Catholic liberal arts college, until the man he saw at the core of that undertaking withdrew.

Jack Gilligan did not reach politics until he was four intentions in, and this did not come until his early thirties. After nearly two decades of political success and occasional failure in the Cincinnati region, Gilligan was inaugurated as the sixty-second governor of the State of Ohio. It was a post he undertook with no shortage of intention—tax reform, education funding, environmental protection, aid to the mentally and physically disabled—intentions he pursued with sufficient success to support the judgment that though he was a one-term governor, he had fair claim to being Ohio's most important Democrat of the twentieth century.

Gilligan never outgrew having been an English teacher; his sense of language and of the grammatical was always acute. He inherited from a compelling professor at Notre Dame an understandable preference for Irish writers. Still, it seems appropriate to end this biography with some words from Walt Whitman, America's poet. Even though the lines quoted suggest a passivity that was not notably a part of Jack Gilligan's character, they do close with what he might wish his message to be.

I myself but write one or two indicative words for the future,
I but advance a moment only to wheel and hurry back in the darkness.

I am a man who, sauntering along without fully stopping, turns a
casual look upon you and then averts his face,
Leaving it to you to prove and define it,
Expecting the main things from you.[3]

Notes

1. MR. GILLIGAN

1. McFarland, *The Papers of Wilbur and Orville Wright*, 2:978.
2. Peirce and Keefe, *The Great Lake States of America*, 297.
3. Knepper, *Ohio and Its People*, 438.
4. Mark Shields, interviewed by author, July 7, 2009.
5. John J. Gilligan, interviewed by author, September 15, 2008.
6. John J. Gilligan, interviewed by author, August 31, 2009.
7. Mark Shields, speaking at Columbus Athletic Club, March 16, 2008.
8. David Broder, interviewed by author, April 27, 2009.
9. Bernstein, "The Accidental Governor," *Ohio Magazine*, October 1997, 39.
10. Kathleen Sebelius, interviewed by author, May 13, 2009.
11. Jack Beckman, interviewed by author, February 12, 2009.
12. Robert Tenenbaum, interviewed by author, July 1, 2009.
13. James Friedman, interviewed by author, December 26, 2009.
14. Charles Kurfess, interviewed by author, June 28, 2009.
15. Mark Shields, interviewed by author, January 7, 2009.
16. *New York Times*, December 1, 2008.
17. John J. Mahaney, interviewed by author, July 2, 2009.
18. Mark Shields, interviewed by author, January 7, 2009.
19. David Broder, interviewed by author, April 27, 2009.
20. Bernstein, "The Accidental Governor," 38.

2. BACKGROUND

1. *WPA Guide to Cincinnati: 1788–1943*, 38.
2. Ross, *American Family*, 8–9.
3. Bernstein, "The Pork Papers," 104.
4. *Columbia Encyclopedia*, 164.
5. *WPA Guide to Cincinnati 1788–1943*, 39.
6. Ibid., 43.
7. Letter in the possession of Judith Spraul-Schmidt, interviewed by author, September 19, 2008.
8. *WPA Guide to Cincinnati 1788–1943*, 69.
9. Knepper, *Ohio and Its People*, 414.

10. Lynch, *The Undertaking*, 88.

11. *WPA Guide to Cincinnati 1788–1943*, 39.

12. From the Gilligan Funeral Home's 1893 record book, manuscript collection, Cincinnati Historical Society.

13. Lynch, *The Undertaking*, 83.

14. John J. Gilligan, interviewed by author, February 9, 2009.

15. John J. Gilligan, interviewed by author, June 11, 2008.

16. Judith Spraul-Schmidt, interviewed by author, September 19, 2008.

17. John J. Gilligan, interviewed by author, September 15, 2008.

18. David Crowley, interviewed by author, September 15, 2008.

19. Michael Gilligan, interviewed by author, April 29, 2009.

20. John J. Gilligan, interviewed by author, June 11, 2008.

21. John J. Gilligan, interviewed by author, June 11, 2008.

22. Jeanne Derrick, interviewed by David Larson, undated interview [1972], 23. All transcripts and recordings from David Larson's interviews are found in the Ohio Historical Society.

23. Harry Gilligan, interviewed by David Larson, July 31, 1972, 5.

24. Harry Gilligan, interviewed by David Larson, July 31, 1972, 17.

3. JACK'S FAMILY

1. John J. Gilligan, interviewed by author, June 11, 2008.

2. John J. Gilligan, interviewed by author, June 11, 2008.

3. Jeanne Derrick, interviewed by David Larson, undated [1972], p. 12.

4. Michael Gilligan, interviewed by author, April 29, 2009.

5. John J. Gilligan, interviewed by author, June 11, 2008.

6. Jeanne Derrick, interviewed by David Larson, undated [1972], p. 11.

7. Jeanne Derrick, interviewed by David Larson, undated [1972], p. 11, 79.

8. Jeanne Derrick, interviewed by David Larson, undated [1972], p. 11, 23.

9. John J. Gilligan, interviewed by author, June 12, 2008.

10. Slayton, *Empire Statesman*, 308.

11. Michael Gilligan, interviewed by author, April 29, 2009.

12. Jeanne Derrick, interviewed by David Larson, undated [1972], p. 29.

13. Miller and Rhodes, "The Life and Times of the Old Cincinnati Ballparks," 32.

14. John J. Gilligan, interviewed by author, September 18, 2009.

15. John J. Gilligan, interviewed by author, June 9, 2008.

16. Michael Gilligan, interviewed by author, April 29, 2009.

17. John J. Gilligan, interviewed by author, September 18, 2009.

18. Jack Beckman, interviewed by author, February 12, 2009.

19. Jack Beckman, interviewed by author, February 12, 2009.

20. John J. Gilligan, interviewed by author, June 11, 2008.

21. Michael Gilligan, interviewed by author, April 29, 2009.

22. Jeanne Derrick, interviewed by David Larson, undated (1972?), p. 31.

23. Michael Gilligan, interviewed by author, April 29, 2009.

24. Michael Gilligan, interviewed by author, April 29, 2008.

25. John J. Gilligan, interviewed by author, June 12, 2008.

26. Jack Beckman, interviewed by author, February 12, 2009.

27. John J. Gilligan, interviewed by author, June 12, 2008.

28. John J. Gilligan, interviewed by author, June 11, 2008.

29. John J. Gilligan, interviewed by author, June 11, 2008.

4. NOTRE DAME

1. John J. Gilligan, interviewed by author, June 9, 2008.
2. John J. Gilligan, interviewed by author, June 9, 2008.
3. Meaney, *O'Malley of Notre Dame*, 1.
4. John J. Gilligan, interviewed by author, June 9, 2008.
5. "Education: Best Catholic Colleges."
6. John J. Gilligan, interviewed by author, June 12, 2008.
7. *The University of Notre Dame, 1842–1942* (yearbook), 19, University of Notre Dame Archives.
8. Ibid., 83.
9. Ibid.
10. John J. Gilligan, interviewed by author, June 9, 2008.
11. John J. Gilligan, interviewed by author, June 9, 2008.
12. John J. Gilligan, interviewed by author, June 9, 2008.
13. John J. Gilligan, interviewed by author, June 9, 2008.
14. Burns, *Being Catholic, Being American*, 21–22.
15. John J. Gilligan, interviewed by author, June 9, 2008.
16. John J. Gilligan, interviewed by author, June 9, 2008.
17. John J. Gilligan, interviewed by author, April 28, 2009.
18. John J. Gilligan, interviewed by author, April 28, 2009.
19. John J. Gilligan, interviewed by author, April 28, 2009.
20. John J. Gilligan, interviewed by author, April 28, 2009.
21. John J. Gilligan, interviewed by author, April 28, 2009.
22. Burns, *Being Catholic, Being American*, 58.
23. Ibid., 137.
24. Michael Gilligan, interviewed by author, April 29, 2009.
25. John J. Gilligan, interviewed by author, August 28, 2009.
26. John J. Gilligan, interviewed by author, June 9, 2008.
27. John J. Gilligan, interviewed by author, June 9, 2008.
28. Frank O'Malley Papers, University of Notre Dame Archives.
29. John J. Gilligan, interviewed by author, February 11, 2009.
30. John J. Gilligan, interviewed by author, June 9, 2008.
31. John J. Gilligan, interviewed by author, June 9, 2008.
32. John J. Gilligan, interviewed by author, June 9, 2008.
33. John J. Gilligan, interviewed by author, August 31, 2009.
34. *The University of Notre Dame, 1842–1942*, 150.
35. Ibid., 151.
36. Ibid.
37. Gilligan, "Who Has Tasted Bread."
38. Gilligan, "Inherit the Earth."
39. *The University of Notre Dame, 1842–1942*, preface.
40. Ibid.

5. TO D-DAY

1. Taft, *City Management*, 93.
2. John J. Gilligan, interviewed by author, August 31, 2009.
3. John J. Gilligan, interviewed by author, June 9, 2008.
4. John J. Gilligan, interviewed by author April 28, 2009.

5. John J. Gilligan, interviewed by author, June 9, 2008.
6. Billingsley, *The Emmons Saga*, 6.
7. John J. Gilligan, interviewed by author, June 9, 2008.
8. Alan Melamed, interviewed by author, December 22, 2008.
9. Billingsley, *The Emmons Saga*, 8.
10. Thomas Menaugh, interviewed by David Larson, July 29, 1974, p. 6.
11. John J. Gilligan, interviewed by author, June 9, 2008.
12. Billingsley, *The Emmons Saga*, 200.
13. John J. Gilligan, interviewed by author, June 9, 2008.
14. John J. Gilligan, interviewed by author, February 9, 2009.
15. John J. Gilligan, interviewed by author, August 31, 2009.
16. John J. Gilligan, interviewed by author, September 15, 2008.
17. John J. Gilligan, interviewed by author, June 9, 2008.
18. John J. Gilligan, interviewed by author, June 9, 2008.
19. John J. Gilligan, interviewed by author, June 9, 2008.
20. John J. Gilligan, interviewed by author, June 9, 2008.
21. Bliss, *In Search of Light*, 107.
22. Keegan, *The Second World War*, 381–82.
23. John J. Gilligan, interviewed by author, June 9, 2008.
24. Billingsley, *The Emmons Saga*, 240.
25. John J. Gilligan, interviewed by author, February 9, 2009.
26. John J. Gilligan, interviewed by author, February 9, 2009.
27. John J. Gilligan, interviewed by author, August 31, 2009.
28. John J. Gilligan, interviewed by author, April 28, 2009.
29. John J. Gilligan, interviewed by author, April 28, 2009.
30. John J. Gilligan, interviewed by author, June 9, 2009.
31. Gilligan, "Learning About Race in Cincinnati," 4.
32. John J. Gilligan, interviewed by author, June 9, 2008.
33. Gilligan, "Learning About Race in Cincinnati," 4.
34. John J. Gilligan, interviewed by author, June 11, 2008.

6. TO OKINAWA AND BACK

1. John J. Gilligan, interviewed by author, September 15, 2008.
2. John J. Gilligan, interviewed by author, September 15, 2008.
3. Billingsley, *The Emmons Saga*, 325.
4. John J. Gilligan, interviewed by author, September 15, 2008.
5. John J. Gilligan, interviewed by author, April 28, 2009.
6. John J. Gilligan, interviewed by author, September 15, 2008.
7. John J. Gilligan, interviewed by author, June 9, 2008.
8. Office of the Archivist, U.S. Navy.
9. John J. Gilligan, interviewed by author, June 9, 2008.
10. Billingsley, *The Emmons Saga*, 336.
11. Hastings, *Retribution*, 389.
12. Billingsley, *Emmons Saga*, 377.
13. John J. Gilligan, interviewed by author, August 28, 2009.
14. John J. Gilligan, interviewed by author, August 28, 2009.
15. John J. Gilligan, interviewed by author, August 28, 2009.
16. John J. Gilligan, interviewed by author, August 28, 2009.
17. John J. Gilligan, interviewed by author, February 9, 2009.

18. Jeanne Derrick, interviewed by David Larson, undated (1972), p. 28.
19. Michael Gilligan, interviewed by author, April 29, 2009.
20. John J. Gilligan, interviewed by author, September 15, 2008.
21. John J. Gilligan, interviewed by author, September 15, 2008.
22. John J. Gilligan, interviewed by author, September 15, 2008.
23. John J. Gilligan, interviewed by author, September 15, 2008.
24. John J. Gilligan, interviewed by author, February 9, 2009.
25. John J. Gilligan, interviewed by author, February 9, 2009.
26. John J. Gilligan, interviewed by author, June 9, 2009.
27. John J. Gilligan, interviewed by author, June 9, 2009.

7. XAVIER

1. John J. Gilligan, interviewed by author, February 9, 2009.
2. John J. Gilligan, interviewed by author, February 9, 2009.
3. Http://www.socialthought.uchicago/about/index.
4. John J. Gilligan, interviewed by author, February 9, 2009.
5. John J. Gilligan, interviewed by author, June 9, 2008.
6. John J. Gilligan, interviewed by author, June 12, 2008.
7. John J. Gilligan, interviewed by author, February 11, 2009.
8. John J. Gilligan, interviewed by author, June 9, 2008.
9. John J. Gilligan, interviewed by author, February 9, 2009.
10. John J. Gilligan, interviewed by author, February 9, 2009.
11. Michael Gilligan, interviewed by author, April 29, 2009.
12. Michael Gilligan, interviewed by author, April 29, 2009.
13. Fortin, *To See Great Wonders*, 194.
14. "New Faculty Join Xavier," *Xavier University News*, September 23, 1948.
15. John J. Gilligan, interviewed by author, September 15, 2008.
16. Fortin, *To See Great Wonders*, 210.
17. Zaidan, *Portraits of Power*, 110.
18. "The Athenaeum's Problem," *Xavier University News*, October 6, 1949.
19. Xavier University yearbook, 1949, Xavier University Archives.
20. Xavier University yearbook, 1949, Xavier University Archives.
21. "Famine Ends, Joy Reigns," *Xavier University News*, September 30, 1948.
22. John J. Gilligan, interviewed by author, June 9, 2008.
23. John J. Gilligan, interviewed by author, June 9, 2008.
24. Stan Herrlinger, "Vet-Teachers Warn Against Hasty Enlistments," *Xavier University News*, January 11, 1951.
25. "Fine O'Neill Drama Fills Auditorium to Rafters," ibid., April 1, 1951.
26. Meaney, *O'Malley of Notre Dame*, 141–46.
27. Ibid., 160.
28. President George H. W. Bush, "Remarks at the University of Notre Dame Commencement Ceremony in South Bend, Indiana," May 17, 1992, http://www.newinfo.ndedu.news/3779/remarks-by-president-bush-in-commencement-address.
29. John J. Gilligan, interviewed by author, September 15, 2008.
30. John J. Gilligan, interviewed by author, September 15, 2008.
31. John J. Gilligan, interviewed by author, June 10, 2008.
32. Davis, *The Politics of Honor*, 274.
33. Paul Welch, "Ike 'Selling Out,' Adlai Says," *Cincinnati Post*, October 3, 1952.

34. Charles O'Neil, "Thousands Turn out for Adlai," *Cincinnati Times-Star,* October 3, 1952.
35. John J. Gilligan, interviewed by author, June 10, 2008.

8. CHARTER POLITICS

1. Harry Gilligan, interviewed by David Larson, July 31, 1972, p. 12.
2. John J. Gilligan, interviewed by the author, September 15, 2008.
3. Donald Gilligan, interviewed by the author, October 13, 2009.
4. John J. Gilligan, interviewed by the author, June 12, 2008.
5. Miller, *Boss Cox's Cincinnati, 77.*
6. Fairfield, "Cincinnati Search for Order," 22.
7. Taft, *City Management,* 35.
8. Tichi, *Shifting Gears,* 67.
9. Taft, *City Management,* 57.
10. Ibid., 61.
11. Ibid., 59.
12. Ibid., 69.
13. Ibid.
14. Forest, "The Disestablishment of the Charter Committee," 35.
15. Ibid., 35.
16. Sidney Weil, interviewed by the author, September 18, 2008.
17. Miller, "Thinking, Politics, City Government," 27.
18. Ibid.
19. "Gilligan Is President of Charterite Board, Succeeds CP Taft," *Cincinnati Enquirer,* March 19, 1948.
20. "Harry J. Gilligan Quits Post as Head of Charter Party; Led Last Two Campaigns," *Cincinnati Enquirer,* December 7, 1949.

9. THE FIRST ELECTION

1. Miller and Tucker, "New Urban Politics."
2. John J. Gilligan, interviewed by author, June 9, 2008.
3. John J. Gilligan, interviewed by author, September 18, 2009.
4. John J. Gilligan, interviewed by author, September 11, 2009.
5. John J. Gilligan, interviewed by author, September 11, 2009.
6. "Funeral Home Is Purchased, Acquired by the 3 Sons of Harry J. Gilligan," *Cincinnati Times-Star,* November 24, 1953, 2.
7. John J. Gilligan, interviewed by the author, September 15, 2008.
8. John J. Gilligan, interviewed by the author, September 11, 2009.
9. John J. Gilligan, interviewed by author, September 11, 2009.
10. Gerckens, "The 'Trial' of Planning Director Sydney H. Williams," 46.
11. Ibid.
12. Ibid., 50.
13. "Planner Will Be Asked to Quit; Charterites Oppose Commission Action on Commie Charges," *Cincinnati Times-Star,* October 1, 1953, 1.
14. "Abuse of Public Trust," *Cincinnati Enquirer,* October 4, 1953.
15. Ibid.
16. David Larson, "Ohio's Fighting Liberal," 27.
17. Richard Guggenheim, interviewed by David Larson, September 16, 1974, p. 5.

18. Gerckens, "The 'Trial' of Planning Director Sydney H. Williams," 60.
19. John J. Gilligan, interviewed by author, September 11, 2009.
20. John J. Gilligan, interviewed by author, June 9, 2008.
21. Gilbert Sands, "FBI Report on Williams Is Bared," *Cincinnati Enquirer,* October 22, 1953, A7.
22. Advertisement: "Should Cincinnati Citizens Be Condemned Without Fair Trial?" *Cincinnati Times-Star,* October 26, 1953.
23. Advertisement: "Anti-Semitic, Anti-Negro, Anti-God," *Cincinnati Enquirer,* October 26, 1953, A12.
24. "City Council Race Stirs Cincinnati, *New York Times,* October 25, 1953.
25. John J. Gilligan, interviewed by author, June 9, 2008.
26. John J. Gilligan, interviewed by author, September 18, 2009.
27. John J. Gilligan, interviewed by author, September 18, 2009.
28. John J. Gilligan, interviewed by author, September 11, 2009.
29. John J. Gilligan, interviewed by author, September 11, 2009.
30. "City Earnings Tax Deadlocked 4–4–1," *Cincinnati Post,* January 12, 1954.
31. Ibid.
32. "A Compromise—Let's Face It," *Cincinnati Enquirer,* January 20, 1954.
33. "City Wage Tax Defeated in 5 To 4 Vote," ibid., February 4, 1954.
34. "City May Lay Off 600 Workers," *Cincinnati Times-Star,* February 4, 1954.
35. John J. Gilligan, interviewed by author, September 18, 2009.
36. John J. Gilligan, interviewed by author, September 15, 2008.
37. John J. Gilligan, interviewed by author, February 9, 2009.
38. "Gilligan May Quit Race For Mayor, End 'Silly Game,'" *Cincinnati Post,* November 8, 1954.
39. "The Impasse Ends," *Cincinnati Enquirer,* November 13, 1954.
40. Miller, *Suburb,* 11.
41. "Gilligan Urges Early Action for Improving Basin of City," *Cincinnati Enquirer,* June 29, 1955.
42. Ibid.
43. Kornbluh, *Lighting the Way,* 76.
44. Kersten, "Publicly Exposing Discrimination," 14.
45. Ibid., 17
46. Sidney Weil, interviewed by author, September 18, 2008.
47. "Fair Employment Bill Revisions Studied; Council Defeats FEPC," *Cincinnati Times-Star,* July 8, 1955.
48. Ibid.
49. Taft, *City Management,* 94.
50. John J. Gilligan, interviewed by author, June 9, 2008.
51. John J. Gilligan, interviewed by author, September 15, 2008.
52. "Gilligan Charges Fraud in Anti-PR Drive," *Cincinnati Post,* March 7, 1956.
53. "Council Bars Plan," *New York Times,* March 8, 1956.
54. "C. P. Taft Chosen Cincinnati Mayor, ibid., December 15, 1955.
55. John J. Gilligan, interviewed by author, September 15, 2008.
56. "G.O.P Plan Wins," *New York Times,* October 1, 1957.
57. "Whispering Campaign Against Berry," ibid., October 22, 1957.

10. THE DEMOCRATS STIR

1. David Broder, "Forty-Eight Freshmen Build Their Fences," *New York Times Sunday Magazine,* December 12, 1965.

2. Thomas Kircher (son), interviewed by author, September 29, 2009.

3. William Sheehan, interviewed by author, February 2, 2009.

4. Thomas Kircher (son), interviewed by author, September 29, 2009.

5. John J. Gilligan, interviewed by author, February 11, 2009.

6. Fenton, *Midwest Politics*, 126.

7. Ibid., 139.

8. John J. Gilligan, interviewed by author, June 10, 2008.

9. Peirce, *The Great Lake States of America*, 314.

10. Fenton, *Midwest Politics*, 117.

11. John J. Gilligan, interviewed by author, June 10, 2008.

12. John J. Gilligan, interviewed by author, June 10, 2008.

13. Pope Leo XIII, *Rerum Novarum: On the Condition of the Working Classes* (encyclical letter), May 15, 1891, http://www.vatican.va.holy_father/leo_13/encyclicals.

14. John J. Gilligan, interviewed by author, February 9, 2009.

15. Zimmerman, *Call Me Mike*, 129.

16. "Ohio Stage for Right-to-Work War," *Cincinnati Enquirer*, January 29, 1958.

17. William Sheehan, interviewed by author, February 10, 2009.

18. John J. Gilligan, interviewed by author, September 16, 2008.

19. John J. Gilligan, interviewed by author, June 10, 2008.

20. John J. Gilligan, interviewed by author, June 10, 2008.

21. Bill Kircher, "Unionism Is Pillar of Americanism," *Cincinnati Enquirer*, January 29, 1958.

22. John J. Gilligan, interviewed by author, June 10, 2008.

23. Larson, "Ohio's Fighting Liberal," 42.

24. Davies, *Defender of the Old Guard*, 200.

25. William Sheehan, interviewed by author, February 10, 2009.

26. "Ohio Station Sets Equal Time Pact," *New York Times*, October 26, 1958.

27. A. H. Raskin, "Right to Work Laws at Issue in Six States," ibid., October 28, 1958.

28. John J. Gilligan, interviewed by author, June 10, 2008.

29. Wayne Phillips. "DiSalle Elected Governor of Ohio," *New York Times*, November 5, 1958.

30. John J. Gilligan, interviewed by author, June 10, 2008.

31. John J. Gilligan, interviewed by author, June 10, 2008.

32. John J. Gilligan, interviewed by author, November 11, 2009.

33. John J. Gilligan, interviewed by author, November 11, 2009.

34. Sidney Weil, interviewed by author, September 18, 2008.

35. Michael Maloney, "Gilligan Set to Fight Breakup," *Cincinnati Enquirer*, January 3, 1959.

36. "Charterites Hold to Non-Partisanship in City Politics," *Cincinnati Enquirer*, January 14, 1959.

37. Ibid.

38. John Gilligan, correspondence to Fred Roth, February 12, 1959, box 173, Charles Phelps Taft Papers, Manuscript Division, Library of Congress.

39. John Gilligan, correspondence to Fred Roth, February 12, 1959, box 173, Charles Phelps Taft Papers.

40. John Gilligan, correspondence to Fred Roth, February 12, 1959, box 173, Charles Phelps Taft Papers.

41. Vincent Beckman, correspondence to Fred Roth, February 16, 1959, box 173, Charles Phelps Taft Papers.

42. Sidney Weil, interviewed by author, September 18, 2008.

43. John J. Gilligan, interviewed by author, September 17, 2008.

44. "Gilligan Sr. Quits Board of Charter," *Cincinnati Enquirer*, May 30, 1959.

45. Ibid.

46. Ibid.

47. All baseball-related comments from "Baseball Is Issue as 29 Bat for Council Seats," *Cincinnati Post and Times-Star*, October 15, 1959.

48. All development-related comments from "Develop Riverfront Yes Say 27 Candidates," ibid., October 13, 1959.

49. "Ike Reneged on Aid Program," *Cincinnati Enquirer*, July 10, 1959.

50. "I'll Eat My Hat if Garage is Built Under Square—Gilligan," *Cincinnati Post and Times-Star*, October 21, 1959.

51. Michael Maloney, "GOP Gets 5 Council Seats," *Cincinnati Post and Times-Star*, November 5, 1959.

52. Sidney Weil, interviewed by author, September 18, 2008.

53. Sidney Weil, interviewed by author, September 18, 2008.

11. URBAN RENEWAL

1. Kathleen Sebelius, interviewed by author, May 13, 2009.

2. John J. Gilligan, interviewed by author, December 30, 2009.

3. Judith Spraul-Schmidt, interviewed by author, September 19, 2008.

4. "A Familiar Look 5–2–2 Council," *Cincinnati Enquirer*, December 5, 1963.

5. Libby Lackman, "Councilman Gilligan Is Downright Unhappy with Downtown Planning . . . and He Says So," ibid., June 20, 1960.

6. Ibid.

7. Ibid.

8. Larson, "Ohio's Fighting Liberal," 60.

9. Eugene Ruehlmann, interviewed by author, May 3, 2010

10. "City Manager Government 'Misused,' Gilligan Charges," *Cincinnati Post and Times-Star*, December 6, 1961.

11. "Fiscal Policy of City is Target; Gilligan Asks Republicans to Turn Cash Control Over," *Cincinnati Enquirer*, December 27, 1962.

12. Eugene Ruehlmann, interviewed by author, May 3, 2010.

13. Eugene Ruehlmann, interviewed by author, May 3, 2010.

14. Eugene Ruehlmann, interviewed by author, May 3, 2010.

15. John J. Gilligan, interviewed by author, November 17, 2009.

16. John J. Gilligan, interviewed by author, September 15, 2008.

17. John J. Gilligan, interviewed by author, November 17, 2009.

18. Bob Otto, "Core Renewal 'A Must,' Experts Assert," *Cincinnati Enquirer*, April 3, 1962.

19. John J. Gilligan, interviewed by author, November 17, 2009.

20. "$100,000,000 Project Advanced by Cincinnati," *New York Times*, September 25, 1962.

21. Eugene Ruehlmann, interviewed by author, May 3, 2010.

22. Eugene Ruehlmann, interviewed by author, May 3, 2010.

23. Eugene Ruehlmann, interviewed by author, May 3, 2010.

24. John J. Gilligan, interviewed by author, June 10, 2008.

25. Eugene Ruehlmann, interviewed by author, May 3, 2010.

26. Eugene Ruehlmann, interviewed by author, May 3, 2010.

27. Larson. "Ohio's Fighting Liberal," 60–61.

28. John J. Gilligan, interviewed by author, September 15, 2008.

29. John J. Gilligan, interviewed by author, September 15, 2008.

30. "Landlords Blamed for Urban Decay," *Cincinnati Post and Times-Star*, March 27, 1961.

31. John J. Gilligan, interviewed by author, September 15, 2008.

32. John J. Gilligan, interviewed by author, September 15, 2008.

33. John J. Gilligan, interviewed by author, June 11, 2008.
34. John J. Gilligan, interviewed by author, June 11, 2008.
35. John J. Gilligan, interviewed by author, November 17, 2009.
36. John J. Gilligan, interviewed by author, November 17, 2009.
37. Gilligan, "Learning About Race in Cincinnati," 5.
38. Ibid., 7.
39. John J. Gilligan, interviewed by author, June 11, 2008.
40. John J. Gilligan, interviewed by author, June 11, 2008.
41. Ellen Gilligan, interviewed by author, September 16, 2008.
42. John J. Gilligan, interviewed by author, February 9, 2009.
43. Donald Gilligan, interviewed by author, October 13, 2009.
44. John P. Gilligan, interviewed by author, April 28, 2009.
45. John P. Gilligan, interviewed by author, April 28, 2009.
46. Kathleen Sebelius, interviewed by author, May 13, 2009.
47. Kathleen Sebelius, interviewed by author, May 13, 2009.
48. John P. Gilligan, interviewed by author, April 28, 2009.
49. Ellen Gilligan, interviewed by author, September 16, 2008.
50. Donald Gilligan, interviewed by author, October 13, 2009.
51. Kathleen Sebelius, interviewed by author, May 13, 2009.
52. John P. Gilligan, interviewed by author, April 28, 2009.
53. Ellen Gilligan, interviewed by author, May 13, 2009.
54. John P. Gilligan, interviewed by author, April 28, 2009.
55. Ellen Gilligan, interviewed by author, September 16, 2008.
56. Ellen Gilligan, interviewed by author, September 16, 2008.
57. Donald Gilligan, interviewed by author, October 13, 2009.
58. Ellen Gilligan, interviewed by author, September 16, 2008.
59. John P. Gilligan, interviewed by author, August 28, 2009.
60. Kathleen Sebelius, interviewed by author, May 13, 2009.
61. Ellen Gilligan, interviewed by author, September 16, 2008.
62. Ellen Gilligan, interviewed by author, September 16, 2008.
63. John P. Gilligan, interviewed by author, April 28, 2009.

12. "THE MIAMIS ARE EVERYWHERE"

1. "Gilligan Won't Run for Congress; May Quit Council at End of New 2-Year Term," *Cincinnati Post and Times-Star,* November 30, 1961.
2. John J. Gilligan, interviewed by author, February 9, 2009.
3. John J. Gilligan, interviewed by author, September 17, 2008.
4. John J. Gilligan, interviewed by author, February 9, 2009.
5. John Grupenhoff, interviewed by author, August 14, 2008.
6. "Gilligan Defeated; Taft Wins, Burying His Opponent," *Cincinnati Post and Times-Star,* May 9, 1962.
7. Untitled memorandum on AFL-CIO stationary, signed by Al Bilik, president, and William Sheehan, executive secretary-treasurer, Cincinnati AFL-CIO, box 1, John J. Gilligan Papers, Ohio Historical Society.
8. John J. Gilligan, interviewed by author, February 9, 2009.
9. John J. Gilligan, interviewed by author, February 9, 2009.
10. Sidney Weil, interviewed by author, September 18, 2008.
11. Wiethe citation, Xavier University Hall of Fame, http://www.goxavier.com/genrel/Wiethe_john00.html.

12. "UC Hall of Fame Taps Three," University of Cincinnati Press release, October 20, 1997.

13. Judith Spraul-Schmidt, interviewed by author, September 18, 2008.

14. Sidney Weil, interviewed by author, September 18, 2008.

15. John J. Gilligan, interviewed by author, June 10, 2008.

16. "Gilligan, Wiethe Split in Stormy Meeting of Dems," *Cincinnati Post and Times-Star,* May 22, 1962.

17. Sidney Weil, interviewed by author, September 18, 2008.

18. "Gilligan, Wiethe Split in Stormy Meeting of Dems," *Cincinnati Post and Times-Star,* May 22, 1962.

20. "Wiethe Resignation Pushed by Democratic Councilman," *Cincinnati Enquirer,* January 15, 1963.

21. Bill Kagler, "Group Forms to Oust Wiethe as Party Head," ibid., April 17, 1963.

22. "Wiethe Charges Power Lust Behind Move to Oust Him," ibid., April 18, 1963.

23. "Battle Lines Drawn; Wiethe Forces Plan to Change City Government Causes Stir," ibid., June 16, 1963.

24. "Gilligan Denies Negro was Refused Burial," ibid., October 17, 1963

25. State of Ohio Civil Rights Commission, "Public Accommodations Charge Affadavit," filed by James (Chaney) Alexander, October 29, 1963, 2.

26. Quoted in lawsuit filed in Court of Common Pleas, Hamilton County, Ohio: *John J. Gilligan v. P. W. Publishing Company, Inc., et al. Appellates,* 177 Ohio St. 159 (1964), 2.

27. John Wiethe statement released to the press, October 16, 1963.

28. Wiethe statement, October 16, 1963.

29. John J. Gilligan, interviewed by author, September 15, 2008.

30. John J. Gilligan, interviewed by author, September 15, 2008.

31. John J. Gilligan, interviewed by author, September 15, 2008.

32. Sidney Weil, interviewed by author, September 18, 2008.

33. "Wiethe Will Seek Re-Election in May," *Cincinnati Enquirer,* December 3, 1963.

34. John J. Gilligan, interviewed by author, June 10, 2008.

35. Sidney Weil, interviewed by author, September 18, 2008.

36. Jack Hansan, interviewed by author, August 7, 2008.

37. Jack Hansan, interviewed by author, August 7, 2008.

38. John J. Gilligan, interviewed by author, June 10, 2008.

39. Sidney Weil, interviewed by author, September 18, 2008.

40. Democrats United election brochure, courtesy of Sidney Weil.

41. Larson, "Ohio's Fighting Liberal," 57.

42. Kathleen Sebelius, interviewed by author, May 13, 2009.

43. Sidney Weil, interviewed by author, September 18, 2008.

44. Sidney Weil, interviewed by author, September 18, 2008.

45. John J. Gilligan, interviewed by author, June 10, 2008.

46. Sidney Weil, interviewed by author, September 18, 2008.

47. Sidney Weil, interviewed by author, September 18, 2008.

48. Sidney Weil, interviewed by author, September 18, 2008.

13. THE 1964 CAMPAIGN FOR CONGRESS

1. Ross, *An American Family,* 123.

2. John J. Gilligan, interviewed by author, June 10, 2008.

3. John J. Gilligan, interviewed by author, June 10, 2008.

4. John J. Gilligan, interviewed by author, June 10, 2008.

5. John J. Gilligan, interviewed by author, June 10, 2008.

6. John J. Gilligan, interviewed by author, June 10, 2008.
7. John J. Gilligan, interviewed by author, June 10, 2008.
8. Jack Hansan, interviewed by author, August 7, 2008.
9. Jack Hansan, interviewed by author, August 7, 2008.
10. Gilligan campaign memo, unsigned, July 15, 1964, box 64, Gilligan Papers.
11. Gilligan campaign memo, 3.
12. Gilligan campaign memo, 3.
13. Larson, "Ohio's Fighting Liberal," 72.
14. Ibid., 73.
15. John J. Gilligan, interviewed by author, June 10, 2008.
16. John J. Gilligan, interviewed by author, June 10, 2008.

14. THE GREAT SOCIETY CONGRESSMAN

1. Http://www.quotationsbook.com.quote.6877.
2. Mackenzie and Weisbrot, *The Liberal Hour,* 5.
3. John J. Gilligan, interviewed by author, June 10, 2008.
4. MacKenzie and Weisbrot, *The Liberal Hour,* 111.
5. Ibid., 104.
6. John J. Gilligan, interviewed by author, September 17, 2008.
7. Larson. "Ohio's Fighting Liberal," 76.
8. Ibid., 77.
9. John Grupenhoff, interviewed by author, August 14, 2008.
10. "New Congressman Faces Uncertain Prospects," *Cincinnati Post and Times-Star,* January 11, 1965.
11. Kathleen Sebelius, interviewed by author, May 13, 2009.
12. John P. Gilligan, interviewed by author, April 27, 2009.
13. Kathleen Sebelius, interviewed by author, May 13, 2009.
14. John J. Gilligan, interviewed by author, September 17, 2008.
15. John Grupenhoff, interviewed by author, August 14, 2008.
16. John Grupenhoff, interviewed by author, August 14, 2008.
17. John Grupenhoff, interviewed by author, August 14, 2008.
18. John Grupenhoff, interviewed by author, August 14, 2008.
19. Http://www.quotationspage.com/quotes/Alice_Roosevelt-Longworth/.
20. John J. Gilligan, interviewed by author, June 11, 2008.
21. "Remarks Supporting Congressman John J. Gilligan's Introduction of the 'Cold War GI Bill,'" *Congressional Record,* April 1, 1965 (no volume or issue number), box 177, Charles Phelps Taft Papers.
22. "Preserving the Taft-Hartley Act," *Congressional Record* 11, no. 84 (May 11, 1965), box 177, Charles Phelps Taft Papers.
23. Ibid.
24. Ibid.
25. John J. Gilligan, interviewed by author, June 10, 2008.
26. "The Address by President Johnson at Howard University," *Congressional Record* 111, no. 102 (June 7, 1965), box 177, Charles Phelps Taft Papers.
27. John Grupenhoff, interviewed by author, August 14, 2008.
28. John Grupenhoff, interviewed by author, August 14, 2008.
29. Ellen Gilligan, interviewed by author, September 16, 2008.
30. Ellen Gilligan, interviewed by author, September 16, 2008.
31. John J. Gilligan, interviewed by author, April 28, 2009.

32. John J. Gilligan, interviewed by author, April 28, 2009.
33. John Grupenhoff, interviewed by author, August 14, 2008.
34. John Grupenhoff, interviewed by author, August 14, 2008.
35. Congressman Gilligan, letter to constituent Margaret van Selle, April 27, 1965, box 63, Gilligan Papers.
36. Congressman Gilligan, letter to constituents Mr. and Mrs. Joseph Weinberger, August 25, 1965, box 63, Gilligan Papers.
37. Congressman Gilligan, letter to constituent Edward Coyne, December 16, 1965, box 63, Gilligan Papers.
38. John Grupenhoff, interviewed by author, August 14, 2008.
39. John J. Gilligan, interviewed by author, June 10, 2008.
40. John J. Gilligan, interviewed by author, June 10, 2008.
41. John J. Gilligan, interviewed by author, September 17, 2008.
42. "Report from Washington," newsletter no.1, p. 1, box 177, Charles Phelps Taft Papers.
43. "Report from Washington," newsletter no. 6, October 1966, p. 1, box 177, Charles Phelps Taft Papers.
44. "Report from Washington," newsletter no. 6.
45. Eugene Ruehlmann, interviewed by author, May 3, 2009.
46. John Grupenhoff, interviewed by author, August 14, 2008.
47. John J. Gilligan, interviewed by author, June 10, 2008.
48. John Grupenhoff, interviewed by author, August 14, 2008.
49. David Broder, interviewed by author, April 27, 2009.
50. "Forty-Eight Freshmen Build Their Fences," *New York Times Sunday Magazine*, December 12, 1965, 51.
51. Ibid.
52. Ibid.
53. Ibid., 100.
54. Ibid., 106.
55. Ibid., 107.
56. Ibid., 107.
57. John J. Gilligan, interviewed by author, September 15, 2008.
58. John J. Gilligan, interviewed by author, April 28, 2009.
59. "Report from Washington," newsletter no. 3, March 1966, p. 1, box 177, Charles Phelps Taft Papers.
60. "Report from Washington," newsletter no. 4, May 1966, p. 1, box 177, Charles Phelps Taft Papers.
61. "Report from Washington," newsletter no. 4.
62. John J. Gilligan, interviewed by author, June 10, 2008.
63. "Report from Washington," newsletter no. 5, August 1966, p. 2, box 177, Charles Phelps Taft Papers.
64. Report from Washington," newsletter no. 5.
65. Report from Washington," newsletter no. 5.
66. John J. Gilligan, interviewed by author, June 10, 2008.
67. John J. Gilligan, interviewed by author, June 10, 2008.
68. John J. Gilligan, interviewed by author, June 10, 2008.
69. John J. Gilligan, interviewed by author, June 10, 2008.
70. John J. Gilligan, interviewed by author, June 10, 2008.
71. Kathleen Sebelius, interviewed by author, May 13, 2009.
72. Kathleen Sebelius, interviewed by author, May 13, 2009.

73. Gilligan's statement from the *Congressional Record,* October 5, 1966, box 177, Charles Phelps Taft Papers.

74. Gilligan's statement from the *Congressional Record,* October 5, 1966.

15. DEFEAT

1. David Hess, "Taft Advantage Seen in Ohio Redistricting," *Christian Science Monitor,* November 7, 1966.

2. Ross, *An American Family,* 3.

3. Http://www.time.com/time/magazine/article/0,9171,798122,00.html

4. "Taft Jr. Upholds Family Tradition," *New York Times,* November 7, 1954.

5. David Broder, "Ohio GOP Is Trying That Name Again," *Washington Post,* September 25, 1966.

6. Ibid.

7. "The Great-Grandson Race."

8. Ibid.

9. Broder, "Ohio GOP Is Trying That Name Again."

10. "Why Won't Taft Jr., Debate Gilligan?" *The Chronicle: Cincinnati's Labor Newspaper,* October 5, 1966.

11. "The Great-Grandson Race."

12. Taft campaign leaflet, box 210, Charles Phelps Taft Papers.

13. "The Great-Grandson Race."

14. Gilligan undated campaign leaflet, with brief quotes from the *Cleveland Plain Dealer, Columbus Dispatch,* and *Washington Post,* box 211, Charles Phelps Taft Papers.

15. Broder, "Ohio GOP Is Trying That Name Again."

16. John Grupenhoff, interviewed by author, August 14, 2008.

17. John Grupenhoff, interviewed by author, August 14, 2008.

18. John Grupenhoff, interviewed by author, August 14, 2008.

19. John Grupenhoff, interviewed by author, August 14, 2008.

20. Taft campaign leaflet, box 210, Charles Phelps Taft Papers.

21. "Why We're for Taft," *Cincinnati Enquirer,* October 23, 1966.

22. Campaign letter signed by Charles Eisenstadt Jr., chairman, Citizens for Bob Taft, box 226, Charles Phelps Taft Papers.

23. Citizens for Bob Taft campaign letter.

24. John Gilligan to Charles Eisenhardt, October 25, 1966, box 226, Charles Phelps Taft Papers.

25. John J. Gilligan letter to Charles Phelps Taft, October 25, 1966, box 226, Charles Phelps Taft Papers.

26. David Jones, "House Rivals in Ohio Charge Bigotry," *New York Times,* November 7, 1966, 38.

27. Ad reprint, Gilligan campaign materials, Charles Phelps Taft Papers.

28. "The Great-Grandson Race."

29. David R. Jones, "House Rivals in Ohio Charge Bigotry," *New York Times,* November 8, 1966.

30. John Grupenhoff, interviewed by author, August 14, 2008.

31. Jack McDonald, "Campaign Directors Tell Why Taft Defeated Gilligan," *Cincinnati Enquirer,* November 16, 1966.

32. Larson, "Ohio's Fighting Liberal," 95.

33. Gilligan campaign materials, box 219, Charles Phelps Taft Papers.

34. Larson, "Ohio's Fighting Liberal," 96.
35. Ibid., 96.
36. Richard Guggenheim, interviewed by David Larson, September 16, 1974, p. 53.
37. Richard Guggenheim, interviewed by David Larson, September 16, 1974, p. 53.
38. Larson, "Ohio's Fighting Liberal," 96.
39. Mrs. John J. Gilligan, "Venomous, Unjust, Slanderous Editorial," *Cincinnati Enquirer,* December 8, 1966.
40. John J. Gilligan, interviewed by author, September 17, 2008.
41. Warren Wheat, "No Eye on Council—Gilligan," *Cincinnati Enquirer,* January 7, 1967.
42. Ibid.
43. Rowland Evans and Robert Novak, "Democrats Try Again to Purge Lausche," *Washington Post,* December 11, 1966.

16. FRANK LAUSCHE

1. Knepper, *Ohio and Its People,* 378.
2. Odenkirk, *Frank J. Lausche,* 105.
3. Usher, "The Lausche Era," 49.
4. Saxbe, *I've Seen the Elephant,* 46.
5. Odenkirk, *Frank Lausche,* 144.
6. Ibid., 164.
7. Usher, "The Lausche Era," 63.
8. Odenkirk, *Frank Lausche,* 340.
9. John J. Gilligan, interviewed by author, June 11, 2008.
10. John J. Gilligan, interviewed by author, June 11, 2008.

17. THE UNBEATABLE FOE

1. James Friedman, interviewed by author, December 26, 2008.
2. Zimmerman, "Rhodes's First Eight Years," 99.
3. Zimmerman, *Plain Dealing,* 9.
4. John J. Gilligan, interviewed by author, September 16, 2008.
5. Zaidan, *Portraits of Power,* 39.
6. John J. Gilligan, interviewed by author, February 9, 2009.
7. John J. Gilligan, interviewed by author, February 9, 2009.
8. John J. Gilligan, interviewed by author, February 9, 2009.
9. Fred Vierow, interviewed by author, October 4, 2010.
10. John J. Gilligan, interviewed by author, June 10, 2008.
11. James Friedman, interviewed by author, December 26, 2008.
12. John J. Gilligan, interviewed by author, June 11, 2008.
13. Tom Reynders, "Lausche Is Repudiated by Ohio Party Leaders in Bid for Reelection," *Toledo Blade,* January 12, 1968.
14. Larson, "Ohio's Fighting Liberal," 116.
15. Odenkirk, *Frank Lausche,* 351–52.
16. "In Character for Senator Lausche," *Cincinnati Enquirer,* January 15, 1968.
17. Ibid.
18. Odenkirk, *Frank Lausche,* 353.
19. Clingan Jackson, *Youngstown Vindicator,* January 14, 1968.
20. Ibid.
21. "Hays Blasts Dems, Praises Lausche," *Columbus Citizen-Journal,* January 16, 1968.

22. O. F. Knippenburg, "Demos Hopes Riding on Gilligan," *Dayton Daily News*, January 14, 1968.
23. John P. Gilligan, interviewed by author, April 28, 2009.
24. Peter Hart, interviewed by author, January 6, 2009.
25. Peter Hart, interviewed by author, January 6, 2009.
26. Chris Buchanan, interviewed by author, July 7, 2009.
27. Robert Daley, interviewed by author, December 29, 2008.
28. Gilligan campaign press release, February 6, 1966.
29. Gilligan campaign press release, March 21, 1968.
30. Robert Daley, interviewed by author, December 29, 2008.
31. Alan Melamed, interviewed by author, December 22, 2008.
32. Peter Hart, interviewed by author, January 6, 2009.
33. Robert Daley, interviewed by author, December 29, 2008.
34. James Friedman, interviewed by author, December 26, 2008.
35. James Friedman, interviewed by author, December 26, 2008.
36. James Friedman, interviewed by author, December 26, 2008.
37. Reynders, "Lausche Is Repudiated by Ohio Party Leaders."
38. Jack Hansan, interviewed by author, September 9, 2008.
39. Peter Hart, interviewed by author, January 6, 2009.
40. James McNaughton, "Ohio: A Lesson in Changing Politics," *New York Times*, May 5, 1968.
41. Ibid.
42. Odenkirk, *Frank Lausche*, 359.
43. Zaidan, *Portraits of Power*, 35.
44. Ibid.
45. Robert Daley, interviewed by author, December 29, 2008.
46. John J. Gilligan, interviewed by author, February 11, 2009.
47. Alan Melamed, interviewed by author, December 22, 2008.
48. Alan Melamed, interviewed by author, December 22, 2008.
49. James H. Bowman, "A Drumhead Court," *Ava Maria*, September 14, 1968, 16–22.
50. John J. Gilligan to Cincinnati City Councilmen, April 10, 1968, 2, box 3, Gilligan Papers.
51. Response addressed to John J. Gilligan, signed by five Cincinnati city councilmen, April 13, 1968, 2, box 3, Gilligan Papers.
52. Response by five Cincinnati city councilmen.
53. Eugene Ruehlmann, interviewed by author, May 3, 2010.
54. Eugene Ruehlmann, interviewed by author, May 3, 2010.
55. Eugene Ruehlmann, interviewed by author, May 3, 2010.
56. Mark Shields, interviewed by author, January 7, 2009.
57. Odenkirk, *Frank Lausche*, 354.
58. Zimmerman, *Plain Dealing*, 42.
59. Naughton, "Ohio."
60. Ibid.
61. Zaidan, *Portraits of Power*, 37.
62. Peter Hart, interviewed by author, January 6, 2009.
63. Joseph A. Luftus, "Labor in Ohio Making Major Drive to Oust Lausche," *New York Times*, May 6, 1968.
64. David Broder, "Lausche in Trouble," *Washington Post*, May 16, 1968.
65. Ibid.
66. Naughton, "Ohio."
67. Robert Daley, interviewed by author, December 29, 2008.
68. Ken W. Clawson, "Labor Strength Rises in Ohio, *Washington Post*, May 16, 1968.

18. THE SUMMER OF DISCONTENT

1. Abe Zaidan, "Ohio Gilligan: Hottest Politician," *New York Times,* May 16, 1968.

2. John J. Gilligan, interviewed by author, September 16, 2008.

3. John J. Gilligan, interviewed by author, September 16, 2008.

4. John J. Gilligan, interviewed by author, October 1, 2008.

5. John J. Gilligan, interviewed by author, September 16, 2008.

6. White, *Making of the President, 1968,* 174.

7. Peter Hart, interviewed by author, January 6, 2009.

8. John J. Gilligan, interviewed by author, October 10, 2008.

9. Mark Shields, interviewed by author, January 7, 2009.

10. Rowland Evans and Robert Novak, "Meany and Gilligan," *Washington Post,* May 26, 1968.

11. John J. Gilligan, interviewed by author, October 10, 2008.

12. John J. Gilligan, interviewed by author, October 10, 2008.

13. John J. Gilligan, interviewed by author, October 10, 2008.

14. John J. Gilligan, interviewed by author, February 9, 2009.

15. Gilligan campaign press release, June 12, 1968.

16. Gilligan campaign press release, June 12, 1968.

17. Phil Peloquin, interviewed by author, December 18, 2009.

18. Jim Dunn, interviewed by author, February 9, 2009.

19. John J. Gilligan, interviewed by author, October 11, 2008.

20. John J. Gilligan, interviewed by author, September 15, 2008.

21. John J. Gilligan, interviewed by author, September 15, 2008.

22. William Sheehan, interviewed by author, February 10, 2009.

23. Steven V. Roberts, "Humphrey Uses Pressure in Ohio," *New York Times,* August 15, 1968.

24. Ibid.

25. "Humphrey Denies Asking Labor to Cut Off Funds in Ohio Race," ibid., August 16, 1968.

26. Ibid.

27. John W. Finney, "Plank on Vietnam Devised by Doves," ibid., August 24, 1968.

28. John J. Gilligan, interviewed by author, September 15, 2008.

29. John J. Gilligan, interviewed by author, September 15, 2008.

30. William Geoghegan, interviewed by author, February 17, 2009.

31. Chester, Hodgson, and Page, *American Melodrama,* 535.

32. Ibid., 534.

33. Ibid., 553.

34. John J. Gilligan, interviewed by author, September 15, 2008.

35. William Geoghegan, interviewed by author, February 17, 2009.

36. Kathleen Sebelius, interviewed by author, May 13, 2009.

37. John J. Gilligan, interviewed by author, September 15, 2008.

38. John J. Gilligan, interviewed by author, September 15, 2008.

39. Text supplied by Jack Hansan.

40. David Broder, interviewed by author, April 27, 2009.

41. White, *Making of the President, 1968,* 298.

42. Chester, Hodgson, and Page, *American Melodrama,* 593.

43. Ibid., 603.

44. Kathleen Sebelius, interviewed by author, May 13, 2009.

45. John J. Gilligan, interviewed by author, September 15, 2008.

46. John J. Gilligan, interviewed by author, September 15, 2008.

47. Mark Shields, interviewed by author, January 7, 2009.

48. Mark Shields, interviewed by author, January 7, 2009.

49. Mark Shields, interviewed by author, January 7, 2009.

50. Robert Shipka, interviewed by author, October 29, 2009.

51. Robert Shipka, interviewed by author, October 29, 2009.

52. Robert Shipka, interviewed by author, October 29, 2009.

53. John J. Gilligan, interviewed by author, September 15, 2008.

54. John J. Gilligan, interviewed by author, September 15, 2008.

55. John J. Gilligan, interviewed by author, September 15, 2008.

56. Abe Zaidan, "Gilligan Seems Back in Fold for Ohio Bid," *Washington Post*, September 12, 1968.

19. "MY PURPOSE HOLDS"

1. Vincent Rakestraw, interviewed by author, December 11, 2009.

2. Vincent Rakestraw, interviewed by author, December 11, 2009.

3. Mark Shields, interviewed by author, January 7, 2009.

4. Mark Shields, interviewed by author, January 7, 2009.

5. Mark Shields, interviewed by author, January 7, 2009.

6. Peter Hart, interviewed by author, January 6, 2009.

7. James Friedman, interviewed by author, December 26, 2008.

8. Mark Shields, interviewed by author, January 7, 2009.

9. John J. Gilligan, interviewed by author, September 15, 2008.

10. Joseph A. Loftus, "Gilligan Ohio Bid Lagging in Funds," *New York Times*, September 15, 1968.

11. Ibid.

12. John J. Gilligan, interviewed by Gilligan, September 15, 2008.

13. Vivian Witkind Davis, interviewed by author, February 17, 2010.

14. Abe Zaidan, "Gilligan Seems Back in Fold for Ohio Bid," *Washington Post*, September 12, 1968.

15. John J. Gilligan, interviewed by author, September 15, 2008.

16. Rowland Evans and Robert Novak, "Gilligan Casts the Democratic Party, Labor Auxiliaries as Paper Tigers," *Washington Post*, October 10, 1968.

17. Vivian Witkind Davis, interviewed by author, February 17, 2010.

18. John Herbers, "Gilligan's Race in Ohio a Study in 'People's Politics," *New York Times*, October 22, 1968.

19. John J. Gilligan, interviewed by author, January 22, 2010.

20. Jack Hansan, interviewed by author, August 25, 2009.

21. John J. Gilligan, interviewed by author, January 21, 2010.

22. John J. Gilligan, interviewed by author, January 21, 2010.

23. Phil Peloquin, interviewed by author, December 18, 2009.

24. Phil Peloquin, interviewed by author, December 18, 2009.

25. Robert Daley, interviewed by author, December 29, 2008.

26. Robert Daley, interviewed by author, December 29, 2008.

27. Peter Hart, interviewed by author, January 6, 2009.

28. Peter Hart, interviewed by author, January 6, 2009.

29. Mark Shields, interviewed by author, January 7, 2009.

30. Mark Shields, interviewed by author, January 7, 2009.

31. John J. Gilligan, interviewed by author, September 15, 2008.

32. Saxbe, *I've Seen the Elephant*, 78.

33. Vincent Rakestraw, interviewed by author, December 11, 2009.

34. Robert Shipka, interviewed by author, October 30, 2009.

35. Robert Shipka, interviewed by author, October 30, 2009.
36. Vincent Rakestraw, interviewed by author, December 11, 2009.
37. Vincent Rakestraw, interviewed by author, December 11, 2009.
38. Saxbe, *I've Seen the Elephant,* 79.
39. Peter Hart, interviewed by author, January 6, 2009.
40. Wieck, "Wallace in Ohio."
41. John Herbers, "Gilligan's Race in Ohio a Study in 'People Politics,'" *New York Times,* October 22, 1968.
42. Wieck, "Wallace in Ohio."
43. Rowland Evans and Robert Novak, "Gilligan Casts the Democratic Party, Labor Auxiliaries as a Paper Tiger," *Washington Post,* October 10, 1968.
44. Jack Hansan, interviewed by author, September 9, 2009.
45. John Herbers, "Gilligan's Race in Ohio a Study in 'People's Politics,'" *New York Times,* October 22, 1968.
46. Ellen Gilligan, interviewed by author, September 16, 2008.
47. Kathleen Sebelius, interviewed by author, May 13, 2009.
48. Kathleen Sebelius, interviewed by author, May 13, 2009.
49. Donald Gilligan, interviewed by author, October 13, 2009.
50. CD recording, Cleveland City Club Debate, November 1, 1968.
51. Mark Shields, interviewed by author, January 7, 2009.
52. Vincent Rakestraw, interviewed by author, December 11, 2009.
53. CD recording, Cleveland City Club Debate, November 1, 1968. All quotes in discussion from this recording.
54. Saxbe, *I've Seen the Elephant,* 81.
55. Vincent Rakestraw, interviewed by author, December 11, 2009.
56. Saxbe, *I've Seen the Elephant,* 82.
57. Phil Peloquin, interviewed by author, December 18, 2009.
58. Ann Shields, interviewed by author, November 2, 2009.
59. Peter Hart, interviewed by author, January 6, 2009.
60. James Friedman, interviewed by author, December 26, 2008.
61. "Campaign Expense Reports Tell Ohio Election Story," *Dayton Daily News,* December 30, 1968.
62. John J. Gilligan, interviewed by author, January 21, 2010.
63. John J. Gilligan, interviewed by author, January 21, 2010.
64. Robert Shipka, interviewed by author, October 30, 2009.
65. Robert Shipka, interviewed by author, October 30, 2009.

20. SETTING SAIL FOR COLUMBUS

1. James Friedman, interviewed by author, December 26, 2008.
2. John J. Gilligan, untitled essay, January 8, 1969, 1, box 2, Gilligan Papers.
3. Gilligan essay, January 8, 1969.
4. Gilligan essay, January 8, 1969.
5. David Hess, "Ohio Democrats Face the Same Tasks," *Christian Science Monitor,* October 29, 1969.
6. Usher, "Ohio," 254.
7. Donald Gilligan, interviewed by author, October 13, 2009.
8. Kathleen Sebelius, interviewed by author, May 13, 2009.
9. Kathleen Sebelius, interviewed by author, May 13, 2009.
10. John J. Gilligan, interviewed by author, January 21, 2010.

11. John J. Gilligan, interviewed by author, January 21, 2010.

12. John J. Gilligan, interviewed by author, April 29, 2009.

13. John J. Gilligan, interviewed by author, April 29, 2009.

14. John J. Gilligan, interviewed by author, April 29, 2009.

15. John J. Gilligan, interviewed by author, April 29, 2009.

16. John J. Gilligan, interviewed by author, March 8, 2010.

17. John J. Gilligan, interviewed by author, March 8, 2010.

18. John J. Gilligan, interviewed by author, January 21, 2010.

19. John J. Gilligan, interviewed by author, January 21, 2010.

20. Mark Shields, interviewed by author, January 7, 2009.

21. Press release, Gilligan for Governor Campaign, December 18, 1969.

22. James Friedman, interviewed by David Larson, March 3, 1975, p. 36.

23. James Friedman, interviewed by David Larson, March 3, 1975, p. 39.

24. John J. Gilligan, interviewed by author, September 16, 2008.

25. John J. Gilligan, interviewed by author, September 16, 2008.

26. John J. Gilligan, interviewed by author, September 16, 2008.

27. Robert Tenenbaum, interviewed by author, July 1, 2009.

28. John J. Gilligan, interviewed by author, September 16, 2008.

29. CD recording, Cleveland City Club debate, April 3, 1970. All quotes in this discussion from this source.

30. James Friedman, interviewed by David Larson, March 3, 1975, p. 61.

31. Tom Wolfe, "One Giant Leap to Nowhere," *New York Times*, July 18, 2009.

32. Fenno, *The Presidential Odyssey of John Glenn*, 6.

33. Ibid., 11.

34. Ibid., 13.

35. Ibid., 14.

36. Diemer, *Fighting the Unbeatable Foe*, 11.

37. Nan Robertson, "TV Helped a Winner in Ohio," *New York Times*, May 9, 1970, 27.

38. Zimmerman, *Plain Dealing*, 47.

39. Ibid., 7.

40. Ibid.

41. Zimmerman, "Rhodes's First Eight Years," 90.

42. Ibid.

43. Ibid., 87.

44. Odenkirk, *Frank Lausche*, 219.

45. Peirce, *The Great Lake States of America*, 302.

46. Zimmerman, *Plain Dealing*, 10.

47. Ibid.

48. Ibid., 44.

49. Zaidan, *Portraits of Power*, 60.

50. Cayton, *Ohio*, 366.

51. Ibid., 367.

52. John J. Gilligan, interviewed by author, March 10, 2010.

53. Zimmerman, *Plain Dealing*, 10.

54. John J. Gilligan, victory statement, May 5, 1968.

21. THE 1970 CAMPAIGN

1. John J. Gilligan, interviewed by author, September 17, 2008.

2. John J. Gilligan, interviewed by author, September 17, 2008.

3. John McDonald, interviewed by David Larson, October 8, 1974, p. 9.

4. John McDonald, interviewed by David Larson, October 8, 1974, p. 8.

5. James Friedman, interviewed by David Larson, January 21, 1975, p. 82.

6. Harry J. Gilligan, correspondence to Jack Gilligan, October 12, 1970, box 95, Gilligan Papers.

7. Chris Buchanan, interviewed by author, July 7, 2009.

8. Chris Buchanan, interviewed by author, July 7, 2009.

9. Ann Shields, interviewed by author, November 2, 2009.

10. Ann Shields, interviewed by author, November 2, 2009.

11. Phil Peloquin, interviewed by author, December 18, 2009.

12. Phil Peloquin, interviewed by author, December 18, 2009.

13. John McDonald, interviewed by author, July 2, 2009.

14. Jack Davis, interviewed by author, February 17, 2010.

15. Jack Davis, interviewed by author, February 17, 2010.

16. Jack Davis, interviewed by author, February 17, 2010.

17. James Kaval, interviewed by author, August 11, 2010.

18. James Kaval, interviewed by author, August 11, 2010.

19. Alan Farkas, interviewed by author, January 4, 2010.

20. James Friedman, interviewed by David Larson, January 21, 1975, p. 70.

21. Donald Gilligan, interviewed by author, October 13, 2009.

22. Donald Gilligan, interviewed by author, October 13, 2009.

23. Mark Shields, interviewed by author, January 7, 2009.

24. Lee Leonard, interviewed by author, June 29, 2009.

25. Riffe, *Whatever's Fair*, 66.

26. Lee Leonard, interviewed by author, June 29, 2009.

27. Hugh McDiarmid, "The Gilligan Interlude," 114.

28. John J. Gilligan, interviewed by author, September 15, 2008.

29. Zimmerman, *Plain Dealing*, 49–50.

30. Jack Davis, interviewed by author, February 17, 2010.

31. Zimmerman, *Plain Dealing*, 48. Note that the sums mentioned are in 1970 dollars; to convert these to 2010 equivalents, multiply by about six.

32. Ibid.

33. "State GOP Must Act Decisively," *Cleveland Plain Dealer*, May 27, 1970.

34. "Herbert's Brave Defense Is Built on Flimsy Case," *Dayton Daily News*, May 30, 1970.

35. Lacy McCrary, "How Can They Sound So Innocently Amazed?" *Akron Beacon Journal*, May 31, 1970.

36. "Sues for Clarification on $4 million Ohio Loan," *Wall Street Journal*, June 16, 1970.

37. Gilligan campaign statement, September 24, 1970.

38. John Beavers, "Reconstructing a Republican Majority," unpublished manuscript, box 93, Gilligan Papers.

39. Beavers, "Reconstructing a Republican Majority," 52.

40. Rowland Evans and Robert Novak, "Ohio's a Republican Disaster Area," *Washington Post*, July 13, 1970.

41. Crable, "The Rhetorical Strategies of Governor John Joyce Gilligan in His 1970 Campaign," 40.

42. *Wall Street Journal*, October 23, 1970, quoted in Crable, "The Rhetorical Strategies," 10.

43. Haskell Short, "Governor Candidates Talk School Finances," *Cleveland Press*, August 31, 1970.

44. Ibid.

45. James Friedman, interviewed by David Larson, March 3, 1975, p. 67.

46. Robert Tenenbaum, interviewed by author, July 1, 2009.

47. Hugh McDiarmid, "Governor's Race Getting Roiled Up," *Dayton Journal Herald*, August 25, 1970.

48. Ibid.

49. Zimmerman, *Call Me Mike*, 55.

50. John J. Gilligan, interviewed by author, April 29, 2009.

51. Jim Fain, "Pray Mercy on Next Governor," *Dayton Daily News*, October 11, 1970.

52. "WHIO Says Gilligan Fails to Refute," *Dayton Journal Herald*, September 24, 1970.

53. "A JH Analysis: Advisor Spurs Cloud Drive," ibid., October 7, 1970.

54. Ibid.

55. Roger Cloud, speech, August 1970, Columbus, box 89, Gilligan Papers.

56. Roger Cloud, address, September 19, 1970, Ohio Fairgrounds, p. 5, box 89, Gilligan Papers.

57. Robert Tenenbaum, interviewed by author, July 1, 2009.

58. Crable, "The Rhetorical Strategies," 115.

59. John McDonald, interviewed by author, July 2, 2009.

60. Max Frankel, "Local Issues Blocking National Trend," *New York Times*, October 27, 1970.

61. Joseph Kraft, "Ohio Issues Clear Cut," *Washington Post*, October 20, A15.

62. David Broder, "Gains Seen for Most Parties," ibid., October 12, 1970.

63. James Naughton, "Gilligan Elected Governor of Ohio," *New York Times*, November 4, 1970.

64. William Batchelder, interviewed by author, February 19, 2010.

65. George Voinovich, interviewed by author, December 18, 2009.

22. OHIO ON THE VERGE

1. John J. Gilligan, interviewed by author, September 17, 2008.

2. O. F. Knippenburg, "Ohio to Have Hour's Surplus," *Dayton Daily News*, December 18, 1970, 4.

3. "Director's Comments," memo from Howard Collier, director of Finance, to Governor-elect John J. Gilligan, November 25, 1970, box 100, Gilligan Papers.

4. "Remarks by Governor-Elect John J. Gilligan to the Citizens Task Force on Tax Reform, Columbus, Ohio, December 17, 1970," reprinted in the "Citizens' Task Force on Tax Reform" report, February 15, 1971, State Library of Ohio.

5. John McDonald, interviewed by author, July 2, 2009.

6. John Mahaney, interviewed by author, July 2, 2009.

7. Stocker, "The Rough Road to Tax Reform," 11.

8. John J. Gilligan, interviewed by author, September 17, 2008.

9. John J. Gilligan, interviewed by author, September 17, 2008.

10. Ellen Gilligan, interviewed by author, September 16, 2008.

11. Kathleen Sebelius, interviewed by author, May 13, 2009.

12. Gold, *Democracy in Session*, 318–19.

13. Ibid., 319.

14. Ibid.

15. John Mahaney, interviewed by author, July 2, 2009.

16. John Johnson, interviewed by author, February 15, 2010.

17. Harry Meshel, interviewed by author, December 23, 2009.

18. Harry Meshel, interviewed by author, December 23, 2009.

19. Gold. *Democracy in Session*, 314.

20. William Chavanne, interviewed by author, February 10, 2009.

21. John Mahaney, interviewed by author, July 2, 2009.

22. Burke and Weld, "A Profile of State Government Taxation," 8.

23. Ibid., 14.

24. Ibid., 3.

25. Ibid., 18.

26. Ibid., 17.

27. Howard Huntzinger, "1.5% Flat Rate Tax by Counties Hinted," *Columbus Dispatch,* June 6, 1971.

28. Stocker, "The Rough Road to Tax Reform," 6.

29. Ibid., 6.

30. Ibid., 28.

23. SETTING UP SHOP

1. John J. Gilligan, interviewed by author, January 21, 2010.

2. Howard Hunzinger, "Gilligan Calls on Ohioans to 'Command,'" *Columbus Dispatch,* January 11, 1971.

3. Ibid.

4. Ibid.

5. Ibid., 2.

6. Ibid., 5.

7. Mark Shields, interviewed by author, January 7, 2009.

8. James Friedman, interview by author, July 1, 2009.

9. Robert Daley, interviewed by David Larson, January 31, 1974, p. 6.

10. John J. Gilligan, interviewed by author, March 19, 2010.

11. Lee Leonard, interviewed by author, August 29, 2009.

12. Lee Leonard, interviewed by author, August 29, 2009.

13. Robert Tenenbaum, interviewed by author, July 1, 2009.

14. James Friedman, interviewed by author, July I, 2009.

15. James Friedman, interviewed by author, July 1, 2009.

16. John J. Gilligan, interviewed by author, January 22, 2010.

17. John J. Gilligan, interviewed by author, January 22, 2010.

18. John J. Gilligan, interviewed by author, April 29, 2009.

19. John J. Gilligan, interviewed by author, January 22, 2010.

20. John McDonald, interviewed by David Larson, October 8, 1974, p. 50.

21. Lee Leonard, interviewed by author, June 29, 2009.

22. David Sweet, interviewed by author, January 15, 2010.

23. Office of the Governor-Elect, press release, December 29, 1970.

24. *Gongwer News Service Special Year-End Report* 48, no. 251 (December 30, 1970): 15.

25. John J. Gilligan, interviewed by author, September 17, 2008.

26. John J. Gilligan, interviewed by author, September 17, 2008.

27. John J. Gilligan, speech at Kent State University, December 8, 1970, Gilligan campaign release.

28. Speech at Kent State University, 2.

29. Speech at Kent State University, 3.

30. Speech at Kent State University, 3.

31. John J. Gilligan, interviewed by author, April 29, 2009.

32. Tom Menaugh, interviewed by David Larson, July 29, 1974, p. 29.

33. Tom Menaugh, interviewed by David Larson, July 29, 1974, p. 29.

34. John J. Gilligan, interviewed by author, September 17, 2008.

35. *Gongwer News Service Special Year-End Report* 49, no. 250 (December 31, 1971): 6.
36. John J. Gilligan, "State of the State" address, March 1, 1971.
37. "State of the State" 1971, 3.
38. "State of the State" 1971, 3.
39. "State of the State" 1971, 3.

24. ROUND 1: THE HOUSE

1. R. W. Apple Jr., "Ohio Governor Outlines High-Tax, High-Service Plan," *New York Times,* March 17, 1971.
2. Ibid.
3. Ibid.
4. Ibid.
5. "GOP Opposition to Gilligan Tax Plans Includes Question on School Needs," *Gongwer,* March 18, 1971.
6. John J. Gilligan, interviewed by author, September 17, 2008.
7. James Flannery, Cleveland City Club, April 23, 1971.
8. James Flannery, Cleveland City Club, April 23, 1971.
9. James Flannery, Cleveland City Club, April 23, 1971.
10. Stanley Aronoff, Cleveland City Club, April 23, 1971.
11. Stanley Aronoff, Cleveland City Club, April 23, 1971.
12. Stanley Aronoff, Cleveland City Club, April 23, 1971.
13. Stanley Aronoff, Cleveland City Club, April 23, 1971.
14. Stanley Aronoff, Cleveland City Club, April 23, 1971.
15. Stanley Aronoff, Cleveland City Club, April 23, 1971.
16. Charles Kurfess, interviewed by author, June 28, 2009.
17. Charles Kurfess, interviewed by author, June 28, 2009.
18. Charles Kurfess, interviewed by author, June 28, 2009.
19. Charles Kurfess, interviewed by author, June 28, 2009.
20. Gold, *Democracy in Session,* 259.
21. William Batchelder, interviewed by author, February 19, 2010.
22. George Voinovich, interviewed by author, December 18, 2009.
23. John J. Gilligan, interviewed by author, June 28, 2009.
24. John J. Gilligan, interviewed by author, June 28, 2009.
25. John J. Gilligan, interviewed by author, February 10, 2009.
26. Howard Huntzinger, "House Leaders Likely to Approve 1.5 or 1.75 Flat Rate County Tax," *Columbus Dispatch,* June 6, 1971.
27. John J. Gilligan, interviewed by author, September 17, 2008.
28. Keith McNamara, interviewed by author, December 22, 2009.
29. William Batchelder, interviewed by author, February 19, 2010.
30. William Batchelder, interviewed by author, February 19, 2010.
31. Charles Kurfess to Bruce Cable, April 22, 1971, Legislators' Files—Charles Kurfess, Ohio Historical Society.
32. Bill Chavanne, interviewed by author, February 16, 2010.
33. Bill Chavanne, interviewed by author, February 16, 2010.
34. "Gilligan Claims Republican Alternative Would Be Disastrous," *Columbus Dispatch,* May 18, 1971.
35. John Mahaney, interviewed by author, July 2, 2009.
36. John Mahaney, interviewed by author, July 2, 2009.
37. John J. Gilligan, interviewed by author, April 29, 2009.

38. John McDonald, interviewed by author, July 2, 2009.

39. William Chavanne, interviewed by author, February 16, 2010.

40. Hugh McDiarmid, "Tax Vote Delayed; Compromise Likely," *Dayton Journal Herald.* May 20, 1971.

41. Gene Jordan, "Brown Rips Gilligan on Income Tax Plan," *Columbus Dispatch,* May 20, 1971.

42. Ibid.

43. Charles Kurfess, letter to Governor Gilligan, May 28, 1971, Legislators' Files—Charles Kurfess.

44. Charles Kurfess to Governor Gilligan, May 28, 1971.

45. George Voinovich, interviewed by author, December 18, 2009.

46. George Voinovich, interviewed by author, December 18, 2009.

47. Lee Leonard, interviewed by author, June 29, 2009.

48. John Mahaney, interviewed by author, July 2, 2009.

49. John Mahaney, interviewed by author, July 2, 2009.

50. Keith McNamara, interviewed by author, December 22, 2009.

51. Huntzinger, "House Leaders Likely to Approve," 1A.

52. Ibid.

53. "Deadlocked Republicans Indicate Willingness to Compromise on Taxes," *Gongwer,* June 15, 1971.

54. "Interim Appropriations Bill May Hit Senate Floor Thursday," ibid.

55. "Senate Votes Operating Funds for July," ibid., June 24, 1971.

56. Ibid.

57. Lee Leonard, interviewed by author, June 29, 2009.

58. "Gilligan Looking to Senate for Tax Bill, Warns Against Further Deficit Financing," *Gongwer,* June 30, 1971.

59. "House to Receive Tax Bill Next Week but Democrats Express Unqualified Opposition," ibid., July 9, 1971.

60. "House Leadership Offers Tax 'Compromise' but Caucus Still Split," ibid., July 6, 1971.

61. David Lore, "Ohio Income Tax Plan in Hands of Senators," *Columbus Dispatch,* July 15, 1971.

62. Ibid.

63. "Gilligan's Support of Strip Mine Curbs Intensifies Ohio Dispute," *New York Times,* March 5, 1972.

64. Hill, "Social and Economic Implications of Strip Mining in Harrison County," 1, 8.

65. John J. Gilligan, interviewed by author, September 17, 2008.

66. John J. Gilligan, interviewed by author, September 17, 2008.

67. John J. Gilligan, interviewed by author, September 17, 2008.

68. John J. Gilligan, interviewed by author, September 17, 2008.

69. "Ohio Congressmen Urge Rigid Strip Mine Laws," *Dayton Daily News,* September 21, 1971.

70. Ibid.

71. John J. Gilligan, interviewer by author, September 17, 2008.

72. John J. Gilligan, interviewed by author, September 17, 2008.

73. John J. Gilligan, interviewed by author, September 17, 2008.

74. "Tough Ohio Strip Mine Bill Ready for House Action," *Dayton Daily News,* September 30, 1971.

75. "Governor Says Strip Mine Bill Not Perfect, but Urges Passage," *Gongwer,* October 21, 1971.

76. Richard Bragaw, "House Approves No-Amendment Strip Mine Bill 92–0," *Dayton Daily News,* October 29, 1971.

77. Ibid.
78. Office of Congressman John J. Gilligan, press release, reprinted from *Congressional Record,* April 8, 1965, box 214, Charles Phelps Taft Papers.
79. Richard Bragaw, "Appointment Plan Pushed Past GOP Complaints," *Dayton Daily News,* October 1, 1971.
80. John McDonald, interviewed by David Larson, October 17, 1974, p. 54.
81. John McDonald, interviewed by David Larson, October 17, 1974, p. 118.
82. John McDonald, interviewed by author, July 2, 2009.
83. Keith McNamara, interviewed by author, December 22, 2009.
84. Keith McNamara, interviewed by author, December 22, 2009.
85. Bill Chavanne, interviewed by author, February 16, 2010.
86. John McDonald, interviewed by David Larson, October 17, 1974, p. 126.
87. Chris Buchanan, interviewed by author, July 7, 2009.
88. Chris Buchanan, interviewed by author, July 7, 2009.
89. John McDonald, interviewed by interviewer, July 2, 2009.
90. John McDonald, interviewed by interviewer, July 2, 2009.
91. John McDonald, interviewed by author, July 2, 2009.
92. Chris Buchanan, interviewed by author, July 7, 2009.
93. Bill Chavanne, interviewed by author, February 16, 2010.
94. Bill Chavanne, interviewed by author, February 16, 2010.
95. John Johnson, interviewed by author, January 15, 2010.
96. John McDonald, interviewed by David Larson, October 17, 1974, p. 126.
97. John Thomas, "Local Politicians Jittery About Gilligan Re-Map Plans," *Dayton Daily News,* September 15, 1971.
98. Bill Chavanne, interviewed by author, May 3, 2010.
99. James Friedman, interviewed by author, July 1, 2009.
100. James Friedman, interviewed by author, July 1, 2009.
101. James Friedman, interviewed by author, July 1, 2009.
102. James Friedman, interviewed by author, July 1, 2009.
103. "State Remap Perils GOP Hold," *Cleveland Plain Dealer,* October 1, 1971.
104. Ibid.
105. Ibid.
106. Richard Bragaw, "Appointment Plan Pushed Past GOP Complaints," *Dayton Daily News,* October 1, 1971.
107. Lee Leonard, interviewed by author, June 29, 2009.
108. Howard Huntzinger, "Dem Official GOP Charge the Reapportionment Challenge is 'Friendly Suit,'" *Columbus Dispatch,* November 27, 1971, 1.
109. "Apportionment Plan to Be Reconsidered December 20," *Gongwer,* December 6, 1971.
110. Ibid.
111. William Batchelder, interviewed by author, February 19, 2010.
112. William Batchelder, interviewed by author, February 19, 2010.

25. ROUND 2: THE SENATE

1. John Mahaney, interviewed by author, July 2, 2009.
2. William Batchelder, interviewed by author, February 19, 2010.
3. John J. Gilligan, interviewed by author, June 11, 2008.
4. Zimmerman, *Plain Dealing,* 30.
5. Stanley Aronoff, interviewed by author, May 28, 2010.
6. Lee Leonard, interviewed by author, June 29, 2009.

7. John J. Gilligan, interviewed by author, April 29, 2009.

8. Alan Melamed, interviewed by author, December 22, 2008.

9. Stanley Aronoff, interviewed by author, May 28, 2010.

10. John Mc Donald, interviewed by author, July 2, 2009.

11. Hugh McDiarmid, interviewed by author, December 15, 2009.

12. McDiarmid, "The Gilligan Interlude," 115.

13. William Chavanne, interoffice memo to Governor Gilligan, August 4, 1971, courtesy of Phil Moots.

14. William Chavanne, interoffice memo to Governor Gilligan, August 4, 1971.

15. William Chavanne, interoffice memo to Governor Gilligan, August 4, 1971.

16. "Senate Leaders Ponder 'New Money' Spending Levels," *Gongwer,* August 10, 1971.

17. Ibid.

18. Howard Huntzinger, "Gilligan: No Chance Whatsoever of a Sales Tax Increase," *Columbus Dispatch,* August 20, 1971.

19. Letter from Theodore Gray and Michael Maloney to Governor Gilligan, August 13, 1971, p. 2, box 34, Gilligan Papers.

20. John McDonald, interviewed by author, July 2, 2009.

21. "Governor Says He Will Sign No More Interim Budgets," *Gongwer,* September 22, 1971.

22. George Embrey, "Saxbe, Taft Criticize Gilligan's Actions," *Columbus Dispatch,* September 22, 1971.

23. McDiarmid, "The Gilligan Interlude," 116.

24. John J. Gilligan, interviewed by author, April 29, 2009.

25. Ohio Democratic Newsletter, September 20, 1971.

26. "Meet Moved to Thursday for Remap," *Post Dispatch,* September 29, 1971.

27. Howard Huntzinger, "Grass-Cutting Called Not Funny by Gilligan," *Columbus Dispatch,* September 11, 1971.

28. Ned Stout, "Official Says Park Closings Unnecessary," ibid., September 12, 1971.

29. John McDonald, interviewed by author, July 2, 2009.

30. Press statement issued by Office of Charles Kurfess, Speaker of the House, October 22, 1971, courtesy of Phil Moots.

31. Robert Tenenbaum, interviewed by author, July 1, 2009.

32. Tom Menaugh, interviewed by David Larson, July 29, 1974, p. 39.

33. John McDonald, interviewed by author, January 2, 2009.

34. John Jones, interviewed by author, May 26, 2010.

35. John J. Gilligan, interviewed by author, April 29, 2009.

36. Keith McNamara, interviewed by author, December 22, 2009.

37. John J. Gilligan, speech, Cleveland City Club, December 1, 1972.

38. "Senate Will Dump Gilligan Income Tax," *Dayton Daily News,* September 8, 1971, 1.

39. John H. Gilligan, interviewed by David Larson, January 6, 1975, n.p.

40. John H. Gilligan, interviewed by David Larson, January 6, 1975, n.p.

41. David Lore "New Tax Idea is Cast Aside," *Columbus Dispatch,* September 14, 1971.

42. Ibid.

43. "Gilligan Urges Legislators 'To Join the Twentieth Century,'" *Gongwer,* September 14, 1971.

44. Ibid.

45. Ibid.

46. David Lore, "Senate 5 Continue Income Tax Support, with Misgivings," *Columbus Dispatch,* September 15, 1971.

47. David Lore, "Governors Says No to Interim Budgets," *Columbus Dispatch,* September 22, 1971.

48. "Dem Senators Parlay in German Village," ibid., September 22, 1971, 6A.

49. Richard Bragaw, "Income Tax Still Possible," *Dayton Daily News,* September 24, 1971, 11.

50. "Governor Says He Will Sign No More Interim Budgets," *Gongwer,* September 22, 1971.

51. Al Goldberg, "Sales Tax Vote Moves Nearer in Ohio Senate," *Toledo Blade,* September 23, 1971.

52. Al Goldberg, "Chances Appear Bleak for State Income Tax," ibid., September 22, 1971.

53. "Gilligan Smells Fight," *Dayton Daily News,* September 24, 1971.

54. Lee Leonard, interviewed by author, July 29, 2009.

55. David Lore, "Income Plan Pitched Out," *Columbus Dispatch,* September 26, 1971.

56. "Senate Passes Budget-Tax Bill," *Gongwer,* September 25, 1971.

57. "Gilligan Raps GOP Tax Plan," *Dayton Daily News,* September 27, 1971.

58. "House Renews Hunt for Tax Consensus," *Columbus Dispatch,* September 28, 1971.

59. Richard Bragaw, "Budget Panels Remains Split," *Dayton Daily News,* October 17, 1971.

60. Gold, *Democracy in Session,* 365.

61. Lee Leonard, interviewed by author, June 29, 2009.

62. Keith McNamara, interviewed by author, December 22, 2009.

63. Lee Leonard, interviewed by author, July 29, 2009.

64. Charles Kurfess, interviewed by author, June 28, 2009.

65. James Friedman, interviewed by author, December 26, 2009.

66. John J. Gilligan, interviewed by author, June 11, 2008.

67. Douglas W. Cray, "Tax Changes Pending in Four Big States," *New York Times,* October 10, 1971.

68. Ibid.

69. Ibid.

70. William K. Stevens, "School Tax Crisis Forcing Cutbacks," *New York Times,* December 14, 1971.

71. Ibid.

72. "Embarrassed Ohio Governor, a Democrat, Tangles with Labor on Income Tax," *New York Times,* October 7, 1971.

73. Ibid.

74. Ibid.

75. John J. Gilligan, interviewed by author, September 17, 2008.

76. Howard Huntzinger, "Gilligan Renews Push to Sell Income Tax," *Columbus Dispatch,* October 14, 1971.

77. Ibid.

78. Richard Bragaw, "Budget Panels Retains Split," *Dayton Daily News,* October 17, 1971.

79. Ibid.

80. "House Republicans Have Some Suggestions on Budget-Tax Bill," *Gongwer,* October 21, 1971.

81. Ibid.

82. Office of House Speaker Charles Kurfess, press release, October 22, 1971, Legislators' Files—Charles Kurfess.

83. Howard Huntzinger, "Assembly OK Expected on Income Tax," *Columbus Dispatch,* October 22, 1971.

84. Howard Huntzinger, "Senate Leaders Hope for Vote on Budget," *Columbus Dispatch,* October 28, 1971.

85. Richard Bragaw, "Late Night Work Taxing; Package Finally Ready?" *Dayton Daily News,* November 4, 1971.

86. Governor John J. Gilligan, correspondence to Democratic minority leader A. G. Lancione, November 4, 1971.

87. Charles Kurfess, interviewed by author, June 28, 2009.

88. Richard Bragaw, "GOP Tax Vote Slated Saturday," *Dayton Daily News,* November 12, 1971.

89. Ibid.

90. David Lore, "Senate Urged to Slow Down; Reconsider Income Tax Bill," *Columbus Dispatch,* November 14, 1971.

91. "GOP Income Tax Buried With Insults," *Dayton Daily News,* November 13, 1971.

92. Ibid.

93. McDiarmid, "The Gilligan Interlude," 116.

94. "Governor Hopeful on Budget Bill," *Columbus Dispatch,* November 15, 1971.

95. Richard Bragaw, "Tax Plan Shot Down," *Dayton Daily News,* November 23, 1971.

96. Ibid.

97. "Netzley Shedding No Tears," *Troy Daily News,* November 25, 1971.

98. "'Jack the Ripper' Gilligan," *Dayton Daily News,* November 15, 1971.

99. Ibid.

100. Ibid.

101. John Mahaney, interviewed by author, July 2, 2009.

102. John Johnson, interviewed by author, January 15, 2010.

103. Bob Tenenbaum, interviewed by author, July 1, 2009.

104. William Batchelder, interviewed by author, February 19, 2010.

105. John Mahaney, interviewed by author, July 2, 2009.

106. Lee Leonard, interviewed by author, June 29, 2009.

107. Stanley Aronoff, interviewed by author, May 28, 2010.

108. Stanley Aronoff, interviewed by author, May 28, 2010.

109. "Gilligan Agrees on Budget Cuts," *Dayton Daily News,* December 4, 1971, 2A.

110. John McDonald, interviewed by author, July 2, 2009.

111. "Tax Squeaks by Senate, Moves to House Battle," *Columbus Dispatch,* December 10, 1971, 1A.

112. Ibid., 22.

113. "House Adds Its Approval to Personal and Corporate Income Tax for Ohio," *Gongwer,* December 10, 1971.

114. Ibid.

115. Ibid.

116. Keith McNamara, interviewed by author, December 22, 2009.

117. Bob Tenenbaum, interviewed by author, July 1, 2009.

118. Stanley Aronoff, interviewed by author, May 28, 2010.

119. Gold, *Democracy in Session,* 443.

120. George Voinovich, interviewed by author, December 18, 2009.

121. John Mahaney, interviewed by author, July 2, 2009.

122. John Mahaney, interviewed by author, July 2, 2009.

26. THE HIGH POINT

1. John J. Gilligan, interviewed by author, March 8, 2010.

2. R. W. Apple Jr., "Governor of Ohio Will Back Muskie," *New York Times,* December 20, 1971.

3. "Gilligan Endorses Muskie Nomination," *Dayton Daily News,* December 22, 1971.

4. Ibid.

5. "Humphrey Raps Governor During Ohio Drive Kickoff," *Columbus Dispatch,* January 18, 1972.

6. Ibid.

7. "Republican Legislators Begin Drive to Repeal State Income Tax," *Gongwer*, January 7, 1972.

8. William Chavanne, interviewed by author, March 5, 2009.

9. John J. Gilligan, interviewed by author, April 29, 2009.

10. Riffe, *Whatever's Fair*, 49.

11. William Chavanne, interviewed by author, March 5, 2009.

12. William Chavanne, interviewed by author, March 5, 2009.

13. William Chavanne, interviewed by author, March 5, 2009.

14. William Chavanne, interviewed by author, March 5, 2009.

15. Jim Friedman, interviewed by author, July 1, 2009.

16. Larry Christman, interviewed by author, March 5, 2010.

17. Larry Christman, interviewed by author, March 5, 2010.

18. Larry Christman, interviewed by author, March 5, 2010.

19. Larry Christman, interviewed by author, March 5, 2010.

20. Larry Christman, interviewed by author, March 5, 2010.

21. Larry Christman, interviewed by author, March 5, 2010.

22. McDiarmid, "The Gilligan Interlude," 117.

23. "Gilligan Support of Strip Mining Curbs Intensifies Ohio Dispute," *New York Times*, March 5, 1972.

24. Chad Cochran, "Miners Accuse King of Selling Them Out," *Columbus Dispatch*, March 12, 1972.

25. Ibid.

26. "'High Wall' Furor Stalls Mine Bill," *Cleveland Plain Dealer*, March 10, 1972.

27. Harry Meshel, interviewed by author, December 23, 2009.

28. Harry Meshel, interviewed by author, December 23, 2009.

29. Robert J. Caldwell, "Strip Mine Bill Sent for Gilligan for Signature," *Columbus Dispatch*, April 7.

30. "Governor Gilligan Pledges Full Enforcement of Strip Mining Bill," *Gongwer*, April 10, 1972.

31. Ibid.

32. Robert Tenenbaum, interviewed by author, July 1, 2009.

33. John J. Gilligan, interviewed by author, March 19, 2010.

34. "Gilligan Seeks to Block GEM Crossing Plan," *Akron Beacon Journal*, April 6, 1972.

35. Lee Leonard, interviewed by author, June 29, 2009.

36. Hugh McDiarmid, "Gilligan Wields Big Broom; Ends up with Dust on Face," *Dayton Daily News*, May 9, 1972.

37. John J. Gilligan, interviewed by author, February 9, 2009.

38. John J. Gilligan, interviewed by David Larson, January 6, 1975, n.p.

39. "Hansan Made Gilligan's Chief of Staff," *Cincinnati Post*, May 4, 1972.

40. Robert Daley, interviewed by David Larson, January 31, 1974, p. 13.

41. Jack Hansan, interviewed by author, August 25, 2009.

42. Jack Hansan, interviewed by David Larson, February 9, 1974.

43. "Gilligan Makes Welfare Director His No. 2 Man," *Cleveland Plain Dealer*, May 4, 1972.

44. John McDonald, interviewed by author, July 2, 2009.

45. John McDonald, interviewed by author, July 2, 2009.

46. John McDonald, interviewed by author, July 2, 2009.

47. John McDonald, letter of resignation, May 16, 1972, box 43, Gilligan Papers.

48. McDonald resignation letter.

49. John Jones, interviewed by author, May 26, 2010.

50. Thomas Menaugh, interviewed by David Larson, July 29, 1974, p. 36.
51. Richard Guggenheim, interviewed by David Larson, September 16, 1974, p. 60.
52. Robert H. Snyder, "Two Expected to Quit High Posts on Gilligan Staff Over Shakeup," *Cleveland Plain Dealer*, May 6, 1972.
53. Robert Tenenbaum, interviewed by author, July 1, 2009.
54. John J. Gilligan, interviewed by author, February 9, 2009.
55. John J. Gilligan, interviewed by author, February 9, 2009.
56. James Friedman, interviewed by author, July 1, 2009.
57. Jack Hansan, interviewed by David Larson, February 4, 1974.
58. James Friedman, interviewed by author, July 1, 2009.
59. Patrick Leahy, interviewed by author, February 17, 2010.
60. James Friedman, interviewed by author, July 1, 2009.
61. Governor's office, press release, May 25, 1972.
62. Tom Menaugh, interviewed by David Larson, July 29, 1974, p. 46.
63. John McDonald, interviewed by author, July 2, 2009.
64. Jack Hansan, interviewed by author, August 25, 2009.
65. John J. Gilligan, interviewed by David Larson, January 6, 1975.
66. Ronald D. Clark, "Putting Gilligan's Staff Back Together Again," *Akron Beacon Journal*, September 10, 1972.
67. John J. Gilligan, interviewed by author, March 8, 2010.
68. R. W. Apple Jr., "Ohio Governor Dismayed at Muskie's Flagging Race," *New York Times*, April 12.
69. John J. Gilligan, interviewed by author, March 8, 2010.
70. Jack Davis, interviewed by author, February 17, 2010.
71. Dr. John W. Cashman to Pete O'Grady, May 23, 1972, Gilligan Papers.
72. James Friedman, interviewed by author, July 1, 2009.
73. John Olsen, interviewed by author, June 29, 2010.
74. John Olsen, interviewed by author, June 29, 2010.
75. John Olsen, interviewed by author, June 29, 2010.
76. John Olsen, interviewed by author, June 29, 2010.
77. John Olsen, interviewed by author, June 29, 2010.
78. Hugh McDiarmid, "The Fine Art of Political Lying," *Dayton Journal Herald*, October 21, 1974.
79. David Hopcraft, interviewed by author, May 16, 2008.
80. Lee Leonard, interviewed by author, July 29, 2009.
81. Editorial cartoon, *Columbus Dispatch*, June 6, 1971.
82. John J. Gilligan, interviewed by author, March 19, 2010.
83. John J. Gilligan, interviewed by author, March 19, 2010.
84. Robert Tenenbaum, interviewed by author, July 1, 2009.
85. "Governor of Ohio Gets TV Exposure," *New York Times*, May 14, 1972.
86. Lee Leonard, interviewed by author, June 29, 2009.
87. Lee Leonard, interviewed by author, June 29, 2009.
88. McDiarmid, "The Gilligan Interlude," 109.
89. Robert Tenenbaum, interviewed by author, July 1, 2009.
90. David Sweet, interviewed by author, January 15, 2010.
91. "GOP Leader Quietly Opposing Repeal," *Dayton Journal Herald*, May 26, 1972.
92. "Dear Fellow Republican," memo by E. W. Lampson, August 3, 1972.
93. William Batchelder, interviewed by author, February 19, 2010.
94. Robert Netzley, interviewed on WTVN-AM (Columbus), October 27, 1972, transcript courtesy of Phil Moots.

95. John J. Gilligan, interviewed by author, September 17, 2008.
96. John J. Gilligan, interviewed by author, September 17, 2008.
97. John J. Gilligan, interviewed by author, September 17, 2008.
98. John J. Gilligan, interviewed by author, September 17, 2008.
99. William Chavanne, interviewed by author, March 5, 2009.
100. Donald Pease to John C. McDonald, February 10, 1972.
101. Pease to McDonald, February 10, 1972; notation made on original.
102. John Jones, interviewed by author, May 26, 2010.
103. William Chavanne, interviewed by author, March 5, 2009.
104. William Chavanne, interviewed by author, March 5, 2009.
105. Governor John J. Gilligan, daily schedule, October 7, 1972.
106. "Don't Repeal Income Tax Says Maloney," *Cincinnati Post*, November 3, 1972, 11.
107. Ohioans for FAIR Taxation, press release, October 27, 1972.
108. Robert J. Caldwell, "Ohio C of C to Stay Neutral on Repeal," *Cleveland Plain Dealer*, November 1972.
109. Robert Netzley, press release, November 2, 1972.
110. "Hayes Backs Tax," *Cleveland Press*, November 4, 1972
111. Collection of 1972 repeal publicity, courtesy of Phil Moots.
112. David Lore, "Issue 2 Vote Baffles Unions," *Columbus Dispatch*, October 22, 1972, 21.
113. William Chavanne, interviewed by author, February 10, 2009.
114. William Chavanne, interviewed by author, February 10, 2009.
115. William Chavanne, interviewed by author, February 10, 2009.
116. "Netzley says 'Right to Vote' is Issue," *Cleveland Plain Dealer*, November 4, 1972.
117. "Repeal to Lose Big, Governor Predicts," ibid.
118. Ibid.
119. Haskell Short, "Tax Repeal Vote Likely to be Close," *Cleveland Press*, November 2, 1972.
120. John J. Gilligan, interviewed by author, September 17, 2008.
121. James Friedman, interviewed by author, July 1, 2009.
122. Stanley Aronoff, interviewed by author, May 28, 2010.
123. Stanley Aronoff, interviewed by author, May 28, 2010.
124. John J. Gilligan, interviewed by author, September 17, 2008.

27. THE PROGRESSIVE MOMENT

1. John J. Gilligan, interviewed by author, February 11, 2009.
2. John J. Gilligan, "State of the State" address, January 17, 1973, 7.
3. John J. Gilligan, interviewed by author, January 22, 2010.
4. John J. Gilligan, interviewed by author, January 22, 2010.
5. John J. Gilligan, interviewed by author, September 15, 2008.
6. John J. Gilligan, speaking at Cleveland City Club, December 1, 1972.

28. THE HUMANE ENVIRONMENT

1. David Lore, "Ohioans Are Exposed to Growing Mental Health Debate," *Columbus Dispatch*, October 19, 1969.
2. Ibid.
3. John J. Gilligan, interviewed by author, September 17, 2008.
4. John J. Gilligan, interviewed by author, April 29, 2009.
5. John J. Gilligan, interviewed by author, September 17, 2008.
6. John J. Gilligan, interviewed by author, September 17, 2008.

7. John J. Gilligan, interviewed by author, April 29, 2009.

8. "Overdue Action on Mental Health," *Dayton Daily News,* March 25, 1972.

9. Citizens' Task Force on Mental Health and Mental Retardation report, submitted September 9, 1971, State Library of Ohio.

10. Citizens' Task Force on Mental and Mental Retardation report.

11. John J. Gilligan, interviewed by author, September 17, 2009.

12. John J. Gilligan, interviewed by author, September 17, 2009.

13. John J. Gilligan, interviewed by author, January 22, 2010.

14. Kenneth Gaver, interviewed by author, October 19, 2010.

15. Kenneth Gaver, interviewed by author, October 19, 2010.

16. John J. Gilligan, interviewed by author, September 17, 2008.

17. John J. Gilligan, interviewed by author, April 29, 2009.

18. Kenneth Gaver, interviewed by author, October 19, 2010.

19. Kenneth Gaver, interviewed by author, October 19, 2010.

20. Kenneth Gaver, interviewed by author, October 19, 2010.

21. "Promise: An Information Handbook on Progress in Mental Health and Mental Retardation services in Ohio, 1970–1974," Ohio Department of Mental Health and Mental Retardation, June 1974, 4.

22. Kenneth Gaver, interviewed by author, October 19, 2010.

23. Gold, *Democracy in Session,* 313.

24. Gaver, interviewed by author, October 19, 2010.

25. John J. Gilligan, interviewed by author, February 9, 2009.

26. "Promise," 19.

27. Kenneth Gaver, interviewed by author, October 19, 2010.

28. Kenneth Gaver, interviewed by author, October 19, 2010.

29. Kenneth Gaver, interviewed by author, October 19, 2010.

30. Kenneth Gaver, interviewed by author, October 19, 2010.

31. John J. Gilligan, interviewed by author, September 17, 2008.

32. Kenneth Gaver, interviewed by author, October 19, 2010.

33. Kenneth Gaver, interviewed by author, October 19, 2010.

34. Kenneth Gaver, interviewed by author, October 19, 2010.

35. Kenneth Gaver, interviewed by author, October 19, 2010.

36. Denise Smith Ames, "Gilligan Ready to Go Back to School," *Cincinnati Enquirer,* December 21, 2003.

37. "Final Report of the Ohio Citizens' Task Force on Corrections," December 15, 1971, State Library of Ohio.

38. "Mail Censorship Eased in Revised Prison Policy," *Columbus Dispatch,* August 5, 1971.

39. "Prisoner Furlough Bill Signed," ibid., December 8, 1971.

40. "Gilligan: Ohio Spending $32 Million a Year to Maintain 'Human Powder Kegs,'" ibid., January 9, 1972.

41. Ibid.

42. Ned Stout, "Ohio Pen Demolition Forecast By Gilligan," ibid., January 18, 1973.

43. Don Matthews, "Task Force on Corrections Blast Lucasville," ibid., August 10, 1973.

44. "Governor Assures that Lucasville Prison Returning to Local Operation," *Gongwer,* August 8, 1973.

45. John J. Gilligan, interviewed by author, September 17, 2009.

29. THE PHYSICAL ENVIRONMENT

1. John J. Gilligan, interviewed by author, April 29, 2009.
2. *Science,* February 12, 1971, 536.
3. John J. Gilligan, interviewed by author, April 29, 2009.
4. John J. Gilligan, interviewed by author, September 17, 2008.
5. Zimmerman, *Plain Dealing,* 3.
6. "Report on the Citizens Task Force on Environmental Protection, State of Ohio," June 1971, 8, State Library of Ohio.
7. "Bipartisan Sponsorship on Gilligan's Environmental Bill," *Gongwer,* August 1, 1971.
8. Ibid.
9. Alan Farkas, interviewed by author, December 18, 2009.
10. Alan Farkas, interviewed by author, December 18, 2009.
11. Interoffice memo, Tom Menaugh to Jack Hansan, August 23, 1972.
12. Interoffice memo, John Hansan to William Nye, August 28, 1972.
13. Samuel Bleicher, January 13, 2010.
14. David Lore, "Environmental Protection Bill Finally Gets Moving," *Columbus Dispatch,* May 10, 1972.
15. Ibid.
16. Charles Kurfess, interviewed by author, June 28, 2009.
17. Charles Kurfess, interviewed by author, June 28, 2009.
18. Charles Kurfess, interviewed by author, June 28, 2009.
19. Alan Farkas, interviewed by author, December 18, 2009.
20. "House Gives up on EPA Bill Until July 6," *Gongwer,* June 20, 1972.
21. "Governor Names Director of EPA and Signs Bill," ibid., July 24, 1972.
22. Alan Farkas, interviewed by author, December 18, 2009.
23. Samuel Bleicher, interviewed by author, January 13, 2010.
24. Ira Whitman to Governor Gilligan, November 8, 1972, Inter-Office Communication, box 163, Gilligan Papers.
25. Whitman to Governor Gilligan, November 8, 1972.
26. Ira Whitman to Governor Gilligan, January 23, 1973, Inter-Office Communication, box 163, Gilligan Papers.
27. Ira Whitman, interviewed by author, May 20, 2010.
28. Ira Whitman, interviewed by author, May 20, 2010.
29. Samuel Bleicher, interviewed by author, January 13, 2010.
30. "EPA Concludes Removal Equipment Is Proven," *Columbus Dispatch,* May 12, 1973.
31. Ira Whitman, interviewed by author, May 20, 2010.
32. Ira Whitman, interviewed by author, May 20, 2010.
33. Ira Whitman, interviewed by author, May 20, 2010.
34. "A Little Easing Is Wise," *Akron Beacon Journal,* September 15, 1973.
35. Ibid.
36. "Senator Collins: Even His Enemies Love Him," *Dayton Daily News,* September 12, 1972.
37. "Pollution Order issued in Ohio City," *New York Times,* January 27, 1973.
38. "Air Pollution Alert Issued by Governor for Cleveland Area," *New York Times,* January 28, 1973.
39. David Templeton, "Steubenville Revealed Its Secrets in Historic Pollution Study," *Pittsburgh Post-Gazette,* December 15, 2010.
40. Ira Whitman, interviewed by author, May 20, 2010.
41. Ira Whitman, interviewed by author, May 20, 2010.

42. Ira Whitman, interviewed by author, May 20, 2010.

43. Samuel Bleicher, interviewed by author, January 13, 2010.

44. "S&T Schedules Costly Cleanup," *Youngstown Vindicator,* June 26, 1973.

45. Ira Whitman to Governor Gilligan, January 10, 1074, Governor's Newsletter, box 163, Gilligan Papers.

46. Samuel Bleicher, interviewed by author, January 13, 2010.

47. Jacobsen, "Anti-Pollution Backlash in Illinois," 39.

48. Ibid.

49. Ibid.

50. Ira Whitman, Governor's Newsletter, box 163, Gilligan Papers.

51. Whitman to Governor Gilligan, December 19, 1973.

52. Ira Whitman, "Industry Profits," memo distributed to Ohio EPA staff, August 1, 1974, box 163, Gilligan Papers.

53. Gold, *Democracy in Session,* 452.

54. Samuel Bleicher, interviewed by author, January 13, 2010.

55. Vivian Witkind Davis, interviewed by author, February 17, 2010.

56. Ira Whitman, interviewed by author, May 20, 2010.

57. Ira Whitman, interviewed by author, May 20, 2010.

58. Ira Whitman, interviewed by author, May 20, 2010.

59. Ira Whitman to Governor Gilligan, April 23, 1974, Governor's Newsletter, box 163, Gilligan Papers.

60. Ira Whitman, interviewed by author, May 20, 2010.

61. Ira Whitman, interviewed by author, May 20, 2010.

62. Samuel Bleicher, interviewed by author, January 13, 2010.

63. Samuel Bleicher, interviewed by author, January 13, 2010.

64. Samuel Bleicher, interviewed by author, January 13, 2010.

65. Samuel Bleicher, interviewed by author, January 13, 2010.

66. Ira Whitman, memo to Governor Gilligan, "Ohio's Future Environment: The Need for High Level Administrative Decisions," July 2, 1974, box 163, Gilligan Papers.

67. "Ohio's Future Environment."

68. "Ohio's Future Environment."

69. Samuel Bleicher, interviewed by author, January 13, 2010.

70. Samuel Bleicher, interviewed by author, January 13, 2010.

71. Ira Whitman, interviewed by author, May 20, 2010.

72. Ira Whitman, interviewed by author, May 20, 2010.

73. Ira Whitman, interviewed by author, May 20, 2010.

74. Ira Whitman, interviewed by author, May 20, 2010.

30. THE ECONOMIC ENVIRONMENT

1. David Sweet, interviewed by author, February 15, 2010.

2. David Sweet, interviewed by author, February 15, 2010.

3. David Sweet to James Friedman, "Revised Proposal for Governor's Task Force on Employment and Economic Expansion," August 3, 1971.

4. "Revised Proposal," 2.

5. "Revised Proposal."

6. Douglas W. Cray, "The Variance in Economic Growth," *New York Times,* November 28, 1971, F13.

7. David Sweet, interviewed by author, February 15, 2010.

8. David Sweet, interviewed by author, February 15, 2010.

9. Advertising supplement placed by Ohio Department of Economic and Community Development, *Fortune,* November 1972, 57.

10. Cray, "The Variance in Economic Growth."

11. Advertising supplement, *Fortune,* November 1972, 63–64.

12. Advertisement placed in various periodicals by the Ohio Department of Economic and Community Development.

13. "Ombudsman for Business," brochure published by Ohio Department of Economic and Community Development, 1972.

14. "Ombudsman for Business," 2.

15. "Business Has a Friend in Columbus," *Columbus Citizen Journal,* May 6, 1973.

16. David Sweet, interviewed by author, June 21, 2010.

17. Economic Development Council position paper, August 7, 1973.

18. Governor's office, "Governor's Business and Employment Council," press release, May 23, 1972.

19. "Governor's Business and Employment Council."

20. "Governor's Business and Employment Council."

21. W. R. Purcell Jr. to David Sweet, memorandum, September 5, 1972.

22. John J. Gilligan, remarks delivered to the Entrepreneurial Seminar, Ohio State University Fawcett Center for Tomorrow, September 9, 1972.

23. David Sweet to George S. Dively, May 16, 1973, courtesy of David Sweet.

24. Rubel, *Guide to Venture Capital Sources.*

25. Knepper, *Ohio and Its People,* 442.

26. David Sweet to Governor Gilligan, memorandum, "Let's Hear It For Ohio" month, January 22, 1973, courtesy of David Sweet.

27. David Sweet to John J. Gilligan, memorandum, September 6, 1973, courtesy of David Sweet.

28. David Sweet, "A State Planning Effort for Ohio," remarks delivered to the Ohio Planning Conference, Warren, April 26, 1971.

29. David Sweet, "The Regional Dilemma," remarks delivered to the County Commissioners' Association of Ohio, Toledo, June 1971.

30. "A Challenge for Ohio: The Need for State Planning and Service Regions," brochure published by the Ohio Department of Economic and Community Development, 1973, 15.

31. David Sweet, remarks to the Ohio Municipal League Convention, Cincinnati, September 1973.

32. "Regionalism: Freedom Lost," brochure published by the Ohio Campaign to Restore the Constitution, Inc., courtesy of David Sweet.

33. "Rhodes Challenges Regionalism," *Zanesville Times Recorder,* February 3, 1974.

34. David Sweet, interviewed by author, February 15, 2010.

35. David Sweet, interviewed by author, February 15, 2010.

36. David Larson, "Ohio's Fighting Liberal," 214.

37. John J. Gilligan, interviewed by author, February 9, 2009.

38. Knepper, *Ohio and Its People,* 437.

39. John J. Gilligan, interviewed by author, February 9, 2009.

31. THE POLITICAL ENVIRONMENT

1. John J. Gilligan, interviewed by author, September 12, 2009.

2. John J. Gilligan, interviewed by author, September 12, 2009.

3. John J. Gilligan, interviewed by author, September 12, 2009.

4. John J. Gilligan, interviewed by author, September 12, 2009.

5. John Joyce Gilligan, "State of the State" address, January 17, 1973, 2.

6. Barlett, *Familiar Quotations,* 455.

7. Pat Leahy, interviewed by author, February 17, 2010.

8. Jack Davis, interviewed by author, February 17, 2010.

9. Jack Davis, interviewed by author, February 17, 2010.

10. Chan Cochran, "Backer of Ethics Bill Assails 'Shakedowns,'" *Columbus Dispatch,* May 24, 1973.

11. John J. Gilligan, interviewed by author, September 17, 2008.

12. Patrick Sweeney, interviewed by author, February 16, 2010.

13. Patrick Sweeney, interviewed by author, February 16, 2010.

14. "Hovey Supports Ethics Measure," *Columbus Dispatch,* September 2, 1971, 3A.

15. Robert H. Snyder, "Gilligan, Sweeney, Gillmor Rate Praise," *Cleveland Plain Dealer,* September 2, 1973.

16. Harry Meshel, interviewed by author December 23, 2009.

17. Phil Moots, interviewed by author, January 19, 2010.

18. Phil Moots, interviewed by author, January 19, 2010.

19. Robert J. Caldwell, "Sweeping Ethics Bill Introduced by House," *Cleveland Plain Dealer,* January 11, 1973.

20. Ibid.

21. Ibid.

22. Harry Meshel, interviewed by author, December 23, 2009.

23. "Shaping Up Time," *Dayton Journal Herald,* January 19, 1973.

24. "Ban Conflicts for Public Officials," *Cleveland Plain Dealer,* January 17, 1973.

25. Chan Cochran, "Ohio House Panels OKs Ethics Bill," *Columbus Dispatch,* April 18, 1973.

26. "House Passed Code of Ethics Legislation Substantially Unchanged," *Gongwer,* May 2, 1973.

27. Patrick Sweeney, interviewed by author, February 16, 2010.

28. Patrick Sweeney, interviewed by author, February 16, 2010.

29. "House Passed Code of Ethics Legislation Substantially Unchanged."

30. Ibid.

31. "Ohio's New Ethics Law," *Cleveland Press,* August 29, 1973.

32. Chan Cochran, "Senate Passes Ethics Measure," *Columbus Dispatch,* July 28, 1973.

33. Ibid.

34. Ibid.

35. Patrick Sweeney, interviewed by author, February 16, 2010.

36. Andrew Alexander and Keith McKnight, "Ethics Bill: An Issue or Answer?" *Dayton Journal Herald,* August 27, 1973, 6.

37. Richard Celeste, interviewed by David Larson, undated, p. 42.

38. Richard Celeste, interviewed by David Larson, undated, p. 42.

39. Patrick Sweeney, interviewed by author, February 16, 2010.

40. Warren D. Wheat, "Ohio's Lawmakers Finally Vote for Ethics; But They Take a Big Step Backward," *Cincinnati Enquirer,* September 2, 1973.

41. "Ethics Law a Solid Gain, Even with Its Weaknesses," *Akron Beacon Journal,* September 2, 1973.

42. Memo from Robert Weinberger, Ohio tax office, to Bill Chavanne and Phil Moots, September 11, 1973, 3.

43. Correspondence, Bill Chavanne to Governor Gilligan, September 14, 1973.

44. "Governor Signs Code of Ethics Bill; Proclaims It a 'Landmark Effort,'" *Gongwer,* September 19, 1973.

45. Harry Meshel, interviewed by author, December 23, 2009.
46. Patrick Sweeney, interviewed by author, February 16, 2010.
47. Richard Celeste, interviewed by David Larson, pp. 44–45.
48. Richard Celeste, interviewed by David Larson, pp. 44–45.
49. Lee Leonard, interviewed by author, June 29, 2009.
50. Lee Leonard, interviewed by author, June 29, 2009.
51. Governor's office, press release, January 4, 1974.
52. Governor John Joyce Gilligan, "State of the State" address, January 15, 1974, 5.
53. "State of the State" 1974, 5.
54. Chan Cochran, "Campaign Finance Bill Passed by Ohio Senate," *Columbus Dispatch*, February 14, 1974.
55. Usher, "Ohio," 258.
56. Ibid., 259.
57. Ibid.
58. McDiarmid, "The Gilligan Interlude," 119.

32. THE SURE THING

1. John J. Gilligan, interviewed by author, April 29, 2009.
2. John J. Gilligan, interviewed by author, February 9, 2009.
3. John J. Gilligan, interviewed by author, February 9, 2009.
4. John J. Gilligan, interviewed by author, February 9, 2009.
5. Robert Daley, interviewed by David Larson, January 31, 1974, p. 11.
6. Max Brown, interviewed by author, January 20, 2010.
7. Max Brown, interviewed by author, January 20, 2010.
8. Discussed by John J. Gilligan with David Larson, August 2, 1974, pp. 376–80.
9. Discussed by John J. Gilligan with David Larson, August 2, 1974, p. 382.
10. Governor Gilligan's October 25, 1973, remarks to Democratic State Chairman, Louisville, Kentucky, reprinted by Ohio Democratic Party.
11. Gilligan remarks to Democratic State chairman, Louisville, Kentucky.
12. Gilligan, address to National Urban Coalition, June 1, 1973, 5.
13. Gilligan to National Urban Coalition, June 1, 1973, 6.
14. Gilligan to the Indiana Democratic Press Association, August 25, 1973, French Lick, 16.
15. David Broder, interviewed by author, April 27, 2009.
16. Clayton Fritchey, "Looking to the '76 Finals: Mondale v. Jackson," *Washington Post*, May 23, 1974.
17. Christopher Lydon, "Democratic Field Opens; Early Hopefuls See Gains," *New York Times*, September 24, 1974, 20.
18. Robert Daley, interviewed by David Larson, January 31, 1974, p. 23.
19. Mark Shields, interviewed by author, January 7, 2009.
20. Mark Shields, interviewed by author, January 7, 2009.
21. James Friedman, interviewed by author, February 16, 2010.
22. Robert Daley, interviewed by David Larson, p. 16.
23. Robert Daley, interviewed by David Larson, p. 16.
24. Robert Daley, interviewed by David Larson, p. 18.
25. James Friedman, interviewed by author, February 16, 2010.
26. Douglas Bailey, interviewed by author, August 3, 2010.
27. Robert Tenenbaum, interviewed by author, July 1, 2009.
28. Zaidan, *Profiles of Power*, 106.
29. Jauchius and Dudgeon, *Jim Rhodes' Big Win*, 40.

30. William Batchelder, interviewed by author, February 19, 2010.

31. Larson, "Ohio's Fighting Liberal," 230.

32. Saxbe, *I've Seen the Elephant,* 127.

33. John J. Gilligan, interviewed by author, February 9, 2009.

34. Max Brown, interviewed by author, January 20, 2010.

35. Diemer, *Fighting the Unbeatable Foe,* 85.

36. John Hansan to Governor John J. Gilligan, memo, September 10, 1973.

37. Hansan to John J. Gilligan, September 10, 1973.

38. Hansan to John J. Gilligan, September 10, 1973.

39. Jack Hansan, interviewed by author, August 25, 2009.

40. Jack Hansan, interviewed by author, August 25, 2009.

41. Tom Suddes, interviewed by author, July 10, 2008.

42. Fenno, *The Presidential Odyssey of John Glenn,* 17.

43. Ibid.

44. Ibid.

45. John J. Gilligan, interviewed by author, February 9, 2009.

46. Robert Tenenbaum, interviewed by author, July 1, 2009.

47. Robert Tenenbaum, interviewed by author, July 1, 2009.

48. Diemer, *Fighting the Unbeatable Foe,* 83.

49. Mark Shields, interviewed by author, January 7, 2009.

50. John McDonald, interviewed by author, July 2, 2009.

51. Robert Tenenbaum, interviewed by author, July 1, 2009.

52. Diemer, *Fighting the Unbeatable Foe,* 82.

53. John J. Gilligan, interviewed by author, February 9, 2009.

54. John J. Gilligan, interviewed by author, February 9, 2009.

55. John J. Gilligan, interviewed by author, February 9, 2009.

56. John J. Gilligan, interviewed by author, February 9, 2009.

57. Larson. "Ohio's Fighting Liberal," 223.

58. "Minimum Wage and Sex Discrimination Bills Pass House," *Gongwer,* June 28, 1973.

59. "Governor Signs Revised Workman's Compensation Bill into Law, Benefits to Increase," ibid., August 17, 1973.

60. Press release, Governor John J. Gilligan's office, September 6, 1973, 1.

61. Governor's office, press release, September 6, 1973.

62. "House Passes Abortion Standards after 'Grueling' Session," *Gongwer,* July 18, 1973.

63. Ibid.

64. "Gilligan Signs Cognovit Bill; Legislative Priority," ibid., August 21, 1973.

65. Ibid.

66. Ibid.

67. Richard Celeste, interviewed by David Larson, second segment, p. 1.

68. Robert Daley, interviewed by David Larson, January 31, 1974, 26.

69. John J. Gilligan, interviewed by author, March 19, 2010.

70. Peter T. Hart Research, Inc., to Jack Hansan, May 23, 1973, 16.

71. Peter T. Hart Research, Inc., to Jack Hansan, 16.

72. Peter T. Hart Research, Inc., to Jack Hansan, 16.

73. Peter T. Hart Research, Inc., to Jack Hansan, 16.

74. Peter T. Hart Research, Inc., to Jack Hansan, 16.

75. Jay Tepper, interviewed by author, June 23, 2010.

76. Alan Farkas, interviewed by author, December 15, 2009.

77. William Batchelder, interviewed by author, February 19, 2010.

78. Keith McNamara, interviewed by author, December 22, 2009.

79. Richard Celeste, interviewed by David Larson, second segment, p. 50.

80. John Johnson, interviewed by author, January 15, 2010.

81. John J. Gilligan, interviewed by David Larson, August 2, 1974, p. 395.

82. John J. Gilligan, interviewed by author, February 12, 2009.

83. John J. Gilligan, interviewed by author, February 12, 2009.

84. John McDonald, interviewed by author, July 2, 2009.

85. Phillip Moots, interviewed by author, January 19, 2010.

86. Max Brown, interviewed by author, January 20, 2010.

87. John J. Gilligan, interviewed by David Larson, p. 392.

88. Jack Hansan, interviewed by David Larson, February 4, 1974.

89. Jack Hansan, interviewed by David Larson, May 11, 1974.

90. Robert Tenenbaum, interviewed by author, July 1, 2009.

91. Robert Tenenbaum, interviewed by author, July 1, 2009.

92. "Metzenbaum Faces Glenn in Bitter Senate Primary," *New York Times*, March 11, 1974, 15.

93. Diemer, *Fighting the Unbeatable Foe*, 93.

94. Ibid., 94.

95. Jack Hansan, interviewed by David Larson, May 11, 1974.

96. Cohen, "The Rhetoric of Incumbency," 16.

97. Jauchius and Dudgeon, *Jim Rhodes' Big Win*, 43.

98. "Gilligan Is Victor in Labor Battle," *New York Times*, May 28, 1974, 26.

99. John J. Gilligan, interviewed by author, January 22, 2010.

100. John J. Gilligan, interviewed by author, January 22, 2010.

101. McDiarmid, "The Gilligan Interlude," 122.

102. "$80.5 Million Surplus Announced by Gilligan," *Columbus Dispatch*, July 9, 1974.

103. Robert Tenenbaum, interviewed by author, July 1, 2009.

104. McDiarmid, "The Gilligan Interlude," 122.

105. "Governor Gilligan Discloses That $80.5 Million Available for Spending," *Gongwer*, July 8, 1974.

106. John J. Gilligan, interviewed by author, February 9, 2009.

107. Donald Gilligan, interviewed by author, <<DATE>>.

108. Max Brown, interviewed by author, January 20, 2010.

109. Jauchius and Dudgeon, *Jim Rhodes' Big Win*, 58.

110. Ibid.

111. "Gilligan Attacked by Rhodes," *Columbus Dispatch*, August 24, 1974, 11.

112. Douglas Bailey, interviewed by author, August 3, 2010.

113. Jauchius and Dudgeon, *Jim Rhodes' Big Win*, 113.

114. Ibid.

115. Hugh McDiarmid, "Gilligan Seeks National Scene," *Dayton Journal Herald,* October 14, 1974, 1.

116. Gene Jordan, "Rhodes Predicts Victory; Attacks Gilligan's Record," *Columbus Dispatch,* October 18, 1974, 1A.

117. Abe Zaidan, *Portraits of Power,* 110.

118. Ibid., 109.

119. Ibid., 108.

120. "Let's Make Governor Rhodes Governor Again."

121. Robert H. Snyder, "Gilligan May Be Losing Steam," *Cleveland Plain Dealer,* October 13, 1974.

122. McDiarmid, "The Gilligan Interlude," 123.

123. Max Brown, interviewed by author, January 20, 2010.

124. Michael Ford, interviewed by author, October 19, 2010.

125. Michael Ford, interviewed by author, October 19, 2010.

126. Gene Jordan, "Gilligan Boiler Room Organization," *Columbus Evening Dispatch*, October 13, 1974, 1.

127. Michael Ford, interviewed by author, October 19, 2010.

128. Jauchius and Dudgeon, *Jim Rhodes' Big Win*, 111.

129. "The Next Governor of Ohio," *Cincinnati Enquirer*, October 20, 1974.

130. Ronald Clark, "Little Light at End of Ohio GOP Tunnel," *Akron Beacon Journal*, October 20, 1974.

131. Brian Usher, "Poll Gives Gilligan Shaky 6% Lead Over Rhodes," *Cleveland Plain Dealer*, May 15, 2008.

132. Brian Usher, interviewed by author, May 15, 2008.

133. Riffe, *Whatever's Fair*, 177.

134. Ibid.

135. "Labor Rallies Around Ticket," *Columbus Dispatch*, October 11, 1974, 22B.

136. Max Brown, Gilligan campaign memo to Ohio radio and television, October 15, 1976.

137. "Dem Labels Rhodes 'Political Swindler,'" *Columbus Dispatch*, October 12, 1974, 8.

138. Joseph D. Rice, "Governor to End Soft Sell; Rap Rhodes' Integrity Over Radio," *Cleveland Plain Dealer*, October 19, 1974.

139. "Rhodes Claims to Have Lacked Authority," *Akron Beacon Journal*, October 20, 1974.

140. Ibid.

141. Governor's office, press release, October 18, 1974.

142. "Jim Rhodes' Mental Lapse at Kent Defies Belief," *Akron Beacon Journal*, October 19, 1974.

143. Dick Feagler, "Gilligan Meets with Black Leaders," *Cleveland Plain Dealer*, October 22, 1974.

144. Cohen, "The Rhetoric of Incumbency," 60.

33. A LONG NIGHT, AND THE MORNING AFTER

1. Peter Hart, interviewed by author, January 6, 2009.

2. Peter Hart, interviewed by author, January 6, 2009.

3. Chris Buchanan, interviewed by author, July 7, 2009.

4. Robert Tenenbaum, interviewed by author, July 1, 2009.

5. Richard Celeste, interviewed by David Larson, p. 44.

6. Richard Celeste, interviewed by David Larson, p. 45.

7. Jauchius and Dudgeon, *Jim Rhodes' Big Win*, 128.

8. Vivian Witkind Davis, interviewed by author, May 2, 2011.

9. Jauchius and Dudgeon, *Jim Rhodes' Big Win*, 128.

10. Douglas Bailey, interviewed by author, August 3, 2010.

11. Robert Tenenbaum, interviewed by author, July 1, 2009.

12. Robert Tenenbaum, interviewed by author, July 1, 2009.

13. Cover art for Jauchius and Dudgeon, *Jim Rhodes' Big Win*.

14. Max Brown, interviewed by author, January 20, 2010.

15. William E. Farrell, "Rhodes Is Elected After He Concedes," *New York Times*, November 7, 1974, 33.

16. Jauchius and Dudgeon, *Jim Rhodes' Big Win*, 129.

17. Zimmerman, "Rhodes's First Eight Years," 128.

18. Larson, "Ohio's Fighting Liberal," 245.

19. Ellen Gilligan, interviewed by author, October 8, 2010.

20. Kathleen Sebelius, interviewed by author, October 7, 2010.

21. Robert Tenenbaum, interviewed by author, July 1, 2009.
22. William Geoghegan, interviewed by author, February 17, 2009.
23. Christopher Lydon, "Mistakes by Gilligan Are Blamed for Rhodes' Triumph in Ohio," *New York Times*, November 17, 1974.
24. McDiarmid, "The Gilligan Interlude," 124.
25. Ibid.
26. Ibid.
27. "Gilligan Confession," *Dayton Journal Herald*, November 23, 1974, 4.
28. Jim Fain, "'Humility' Theory of Gilligan's Loss," *Dayton Daily News*, November 12, 1974.
29. Kathleen Sebelius, interviewed by author, October 7, 2010.
30. Myra McPherson, "The Hero as Politician," *Washington Post*, January 12, 1975.
31. Ibid.
32. Robert Alan Cohen, "The Rhetoric of Incumbency," 73.
33. Ibid., 49.
34. Harry Meshel, interviewed by author, December 23, 2009.
35. Christopher Lydon, "Mistakes by Gilligans are Blamed for Rhodes' Triumph in Election in Ohio," 65.
36. George Voinovich, interviewed by author, December 18, 2009.
37. Gerald Austin, interviewed by David Larson, July 31, 1975, p. 37.
38. Richard Zimmerman, "Rhodes's First Eight Years," 127.
39. Ibid.
40. McDiarmid, "The Gilligan Interlude," 124.
41. "If All Had Voted," *Lorain Journal*, November 10, 1974.

34. DEPARTURE AND THE NEXT STEP

1. Robert Tenenbaum, interviewed by author, July 1, 2009.
2. Chris Buchanan, interviewed by author, July 7, 2009.
3. Chris Buchanan, interviewed by author, July 7, 2009.
4. Robert Tenenbaum, interviewed by author, July 1, 2009.
5. Robert Tenenbaum, interviewed by author, July 1, 2009.
6. John J. Gilligan, "State of the State" address, January 7, 1975.
7. "State of the State" 1975.
8. "Democrats Ram Through New Procedural Rules," *Columbus Dispatch*, January 7, 1975, 1A.
9. Gold, *Democracy in Session*, 327.
10. David Lore, "In Last Hours of Term, Governor Gilligan Signs Six Laws," *Columbus Dispatch*, January 12, 1975, 1A.
11. Gold, *Democracy in Session*, 327.
12. Peter Hart, interviewed by author, January 6, 2009.
13. Kathleen Sebelius, interviewed by author, October 7, 2010.
14. Robert Daley to John J. Gilligan, correspondence, March 21, 1975.
15. Correspondence, Harry V. Jump, Ohio Commissioner of Insurance, to Robert Daley, April 30, 1975.
16. Robert Daley to John J. Gilligan, memo, April 3, 1975.
17. Hugh McDiarmid, "Gilligan Failings Catch Up," *Dayton Journal Herald*, February 24, 1975.
18. "Netzley Urges Soul-Searching," *Columbus Evening Dispatch*, February 14, 1975.
19. Hugh McDiarmid, "Gilligan Failings Catch Up."

20. Ibid.

21. Brian Usher, "Ohio," 269.

22. Ibid.

23. Robert Daley to John J. Gilligan, April 9, 1975.

24. Robert Daley to John J. Gilligan, April 9, 1975.

25. John J. Gilligan to Robert Daley, June 5, 1976.

26. John J. Gilligan, interviewed by author, June 3, 2010.

35. WASHINGTON, AGAIN

1. John J. Gilligan, interviewed by author, February 11, 2009.

2. John J. Gilligan, interviewed by author, February 10, 2009.

3. President John F. Kennedy, "Message to Congress," March 22, 1961, http://www.presidency.ucsc.edu/ws/?pid=8545.

4. Ann Crittenden, "The Realpolitik of Foreign Aid," *New York Times,* February 26, 1978.

5. Ibid.

6. Susanna McBee, "Abolition of AID Is Recommended in Brookings Study," *Washington Post,* October 14, 1977.

7. Ibid.

8. Crittenden, "The Realpolitik of Foreign Aid."

9. John J. Gilligan, interviewed by author, February 11, 2009.

10. John J. Gilligan, interviewed by author, February 11, 2009.

11. Memorandum, James W. McCulla, director, Office of Public Affairs, USAID, December 1977.

12. Alex Shakow, interviewed by author, May 25, 2010.

13. Douglas Lowenstein, "After Year, Gilligan Struggling in Job," *Dayton Daily News,* February 26, 1978.

14. Alex Shakow, interviewed by author, May 25, 2010.

15. John J. Gilligan, interviewed by author, February 11, 2009.

16. John J. Gilligan, interviewed by author, February 11, 2009.

17. Lowenstein, "After Year, Gilligan Struggling in Job."

18. John J. Gilligan, interviewed by author, February 12, 2009.

19. John J. Gilligan, interviewed by author, February 11–12, 2009.

20. Gilligan, "United States Seeks Improved U.N. Programs to Meet Basic Needs of World's Poor," 204.

21. Ibid., 204–205.

22. Gilligan, "America's Stake in the Developing World," 689.

23. John J. Gilligan, "Women and Their Importance to the Third World," *Washington Post,* June 24, 1978.

24. "Remarks by John J. Gilligan," Fifty-Fourth Annual Congress of Cities, San Francisco, December 5, 1977.

25. "Remarks," 2.

26. "Remarks," 4.

27. John J. Gilligan, "Eliminating Poverty in Fifteen Years," *Christian Science Monitor,* July 14, 1977.

28. John J. Gilligan, interviewed by author, February 12, 2009.

29. John J. Gilligan, interviewed by author, February 12, 2009.

30. John J. Gilligan, interviewed by author, February 12, 2009.

31. John J. Gilligan, interviewed by author, February 12, 2009.

32. John J. Gilligan, interviewed by author, February 12, 2009.

33. Jack Sullivan, interviewed by author, November 5, 2010.
34. John J. Gilligan, interviewed by author, February 12, 2009.
35. John J. Gilligan, interviewed by author, February 12, 2009.
36. Crittenden, "The Realpolitik of Foreign Aid."
37. Ibid., 9.
38. Ibid.
39. John J. Gilligan, interviewed by author, February 11, 2009.
40. John J. Gilligan, interviewed by author, February 12, 2009.
41. John J. Gilligan, interviewed by author, February 12, 2009.
42. John J. Gilligan, interviewed by author, February 11, 2009.
43. John J. Gilligan, interviewed by author, February 11, 2009.
44. Jack Sullivan, interviewed by author, November 5, 2010.
45. Crittenden, "The Realpolitik of Foreign Aid."
46. Donald Gilligan, interviewed by author, October 13, 2009
47. John J. Gilligan, interviewed by author, February 12, 2009.
48. John J. Gilligan, interviewed by author, February 12, 2009.
49. John J. Gilligan, interviewed by author, February 12, 2009.
50. "Kicked Out: AID Chief Gilligan Goes," 19.
51. Richard G. Zimmerman and Robert H. Snyder, "Gilligan: Not Wisely, but Too Well," *Cleveland Plain Dealer,* February 2, 1979.
52. Ibid.
53. Jack Sullivan, interviewed by author, November 5, 2010.
54. John J. Gilligan to President Carter, letter of resignation, January 31, 1979, John J. Gilligan's personal files.
55. Letter of resignation.
56. Cyrus Vance to Jack Gilligan, letter, February 1, 1979, John J. Gilligan's personal files.
57. President Jimmy Carter to Jack Gilligan, letter, February 5, 1979, John J. Gilligan's personal files.
58. John J. Gilligan USAID personal files, John J. Gilligan's personal files.
59. John J. Gilligan, interviewed by author, February 12, 2009.
60. Donald Gilligan, interviewed by author, August 17, 2010.
61. John P. Gilligan, interviewed by author, April 28, 2009.
62. "Development Disappointment," *Washington Post,* February 9, 1979.
63. "John Gilligan's Departing Message," *New York Times,* February 14, 1979.
64. John J. Gilligan's personal file.
65. Rev. Theodore M. Hesburgh to John J. Gilligan, January 29, 1979, John J. Gilligan's personal files.

36. NOTRE DAME, AGAIN

1. John J. Gilligan, interviewed by author, August 17, 2010.
2. John J. Gilligan, interviewed by author, August 17, 2010.
3. John J. Gilligan, interviewed by author, August 17, 2010.
4. John J. Gilligan, interviewed by author, August 17, 2010.
5. John J. Gilligan, interviewed by author, August 17, 2010.
6. John J. Gilligan, "Redeem the Time," essay published by the University of Notre Dame, October 21, 1979, p. 3, Gilligan Collection, University of Notre Dame Archives.
7. Ibid., 12.
8. Ibid., 13.
9. Ibid., 14.

10. "The Campaign for Notre Dame," University of Notre Dame Archives.

11. McDiarmid, "The Gilligan Interlude," 125.

12. Dave Allbaugh, "University Professor's Lifestyle, Work Fit Gilligan Like Old Shoe," *Dayton Daily News*, February 11, 1980.

13. Ibid.

14. Ibid.

15. Ibid.

16. Brian Usher, "An Ex-Governor Finds Sanctuary," *Akron Beacon Journal*, June 7, 1981.

17. Ibid.

18. John J. Gilligan to Robert Daley, May 1, 1980.

19. John J. Gilligan to Robert Daley, May 1, 1980.

20. "Gilligan: Rhodes Runs Finances Like 'Shell Game,'" *Dayton Daily News*, December 17, 1980.

21. Jim Ripley, "State Democrats Need a Leader and John Gilligan Is His Name," *Dayton Daily News*, January 18, 1981.

22. Ibid.

23. John J. Gilligan to Robert Daley, January 14, 1981.

24. Press release, January 30, 1981, University of Notre Dame Archives.

25. Gilligan's course notes for The Nuclear Dilemma, University of Notre Dame, September 5, 1983.

26. Course notes.

27. Theodore Hesburgh, interviewed by author, November 23, 2010.

28. Theodore Hesburgh, interviewed by author, November 23, 2010.

29. John J. Gilligan, interviewed by author, November 18, 2010.

30. Theodore Hesburgh, interviewed by author, November 23, 2010.

31. Theodore Hesburgh, interviewed by author, November 23, 2010.

32. John J. Gilligan, interviewed by author, November 11, 2010.

33. John J. Gilligan, interviewed by author, November 11, 2010.

34. Theodore Hesburgh, interviewed by author, November 23, 2010.

35. John J. Gilligan, interviewed by author, August 17, 2010.

36. John J. Gilligan, interviewed by author, August 17, 2010.

37. Richard Gibeau, "Campaigning for Peace," *Cincinnati Post*, January 5, 1987.

38. Ibid.

39. "Peace Is Gilligan's Subject in Institute at Notre Dame," *Cleveland Plain Dealer*, January 11, 1987.

40. Ibid.

41. John J. Gilligan to Robert Daley, June 20, 1987.

42. John J. Gilligan to Robert Daley, April 11, 1988.

43. John J. Gilligan, interviewed by author, June 3, 2010.

44. John J. Gilligan, interviewed by author, June 3, 2010.

45. John J. Gilligan, interviewed by author, June 3, 2010.

46. John J. Gilligan to the Most Rev. William Keith Weigand, D.D., Bishop of Salt Lake City, April 25, 1989, 4.

47. John J. Gilligan to Weigand, April 25, 1989, 2.

48. John J. Gilligan to Weigand, April 25, 1989, 2.

49. John J. Gilligan to Weigand, April 25, 1989, 5.

50. John J. Gilligan letter, to *Chicago Tribune*, January 2, 1990.

51. Ibid.

52. Press release, December 1, 1987, University of Notre Dame Archives.

53. Award citation, 1990, University of Notre Dame Archives.

54. John J. Gilligan form letter to numerous event attendees, April 14, 1991.
55. Form letter, April 14, 1991.
56. Diane Stephen, "Peace Core," *South Bend Tribune,* March 10, 1991.
57. Ibid.

37. CINCINNATI, FINALLY

1. John J. Gilligan, correspondence to Bob Daley, December 21, 1971.
2. John J. Gilligan, "The Other Cincinnati," Seminar on the City, Union Terminal, Cincinnati, October 10, 1994, 1, as reported in *Cincinnati Enquirer,* October 12, 1994, C1.
3. Ibid., 2.
4. Ibid., 4
5. Ibid., 6.
6. Ibid., 9.
7. Ibid., 10.
8. John J. Gilligan to "interested parties," March 17, 1992.
9. John J. Gilligan to "interested parties."
10. John J. Gilligan to "interested parties."
11. John J. Gilligan to "interested parties."
12. John J. Gilligan, "A Search for Community."
13. Ibid., 105.
14. Ibid., 107.
15. Ibid., 108.
16. Ibid., 112.
17. Ellen Gilligan, interviewed by author, September 16, 2008.
18. Steve Stevens, "Ex-Governors Hold Own Talk Show," *Columbus Dispatch,* October 29, 1994.
19. Ibid.
20. Ibid.
21. Bernstein, "The Accidental Governor," 49.
22. Lee Leonard, "Gilligan Deplores Cynicism Trashing of American System," *Columbus Dispatch,* March 26, 1996.
23. Ibid.
24. John J. Gilligan to Robert Daley, August 21, 1999.
25. Ellen Gilligan, interviewed by author, September 27, 2010.
26. John J. Gilligan to Robert Daley, letter, August 21, 1999.
27. John J. Gilligan, interviewed by author, April 6, 2010.
28. John J. Gilligan, interviewed by author, April 6, 2010.
29. John J. Gilligan to Robert Daley, November 1, 1999.
30. Susan Gilligan, interviewed by author, September 24, 2009.
31. Susan Gilligan, interviewed by author, September 24, 2009.
32. Susan Gilligan, interviewed by author, September 24, 2009.
33. Susan Gilligan, interviewed by author, September 24, 2009.
34. Susan Gilligan, interviewed by author, September 24, 2009.
35. Susan Gilligan, interviewed by author, September 24, 2009.
36. John J. Gilligan, interviewed by author, September 24, 2009.
37. "Former Governor to Wed Physician," *Columbus Dispatch,* October 24, 2000.
38. John J. Gilligan, interviewed by author, April 6, 2010.
39. John J. Gilligan, interviewed by author, April 6, 2010.
40. John J. Gilligan, interviewed by author, April 6, 2010.

41. John J. Gilligan, interviewed by author, April 6, 2010.

42. John J. Gilligan, interviewed by author, April 6, 2010.

43. Rosa Blackwell, interviewed by author, August 22, 2010.

44. Ellen Belcher, "Ex-Gov. Gilligan's Job Not a Step Down," *Dayton Daily News,* July 23, 2000.

45. Linda Pulfer, "After 50 Years, What Makes Jack Gilligan Run?" *Cincinnati Enquirer,* September 23, 2003.

46. "Former Governor Still Helping Poor," *Dayton Daily News,* December 22, 2003.

47. John J. Gilligan, interviewed by author, April 6, 2010.

48. Denise Smith Amos, "Gilligan Ready to Go Back to School," *Cincinnati Enquirer,* December 21, 2003.

49. Rosa Blackwell, interviewed by author, August 22, 2010.

50. Rosa Blackwell, interviewed by author, August 22, 2010.

51. John J. Gilligan, interviewed by author, April 29, 2009.

52. John J. Gilligan, interviewed by author, April 29, 2009.

53. Award citation, Cincinnati USA Regional Chamber of Commerce, 2008.

54. John J. Gilligan, interviewed by author, May 8, 2009.

55. John J. Gilligan, interviewed by author, May 8, 2009.

AFTERWORD

1. Bernstein, "The Accidental Governor," 49.

2. John J. Gilligan, interviewed by author, December 15, 2010.

3. Walt Whitman, "Poets to Come."

A Note on Sources

This is substantially an interview-driven book, no interviews being remotely as important as those I conducted with John Joyce Gilligan in his Cincinnati homes. In sixty hours of conversation spread over thirty months, Governor Gilligan was unfailingly forthcoming, straightforward, amused, amusing, gracious, and opinionated. In addition, I interviewed nearly seventy-five other people, ranging from schoolboy acquaintances, family and friends, and political colleagues and supporters (and opponents) to the Reverend Theodore Hesburgh, with whom Gilligan had a vital relationship at the University of Notre Dame.

The John J. Gilligan Papers are housed at the Ohio Historical Society in Columbus. They comprise 439 cubic feet of material. More to the point, they include the papers of many members of Gilligan's gubernatorial administration—ranging from appointments secretary Robert Daley to chiefs of staff James Friedman, and Jack Hansan and perhaps a dozen others, not least among them Katie Gilligan.

In the 1970s, researcher David Larson undertook an extensive series of tape-recorded interviews with many members of the Gilligan administration and others. These recordings are housed at the Ohio Historical Society. Unfortunately, most of this material has never been transcribed, as the cost of doing so was too great. I have cited some of the transcribed material, including, and of particular value, the interviews with Harry Gilligan and Jeanne Gilligan Derrick.

The person of Charles Phelps Taft II bears an important relationship to the source material used in this biography. Charles Taft, the son of President William Howard Taft and uncle of Robert A. Taft, was a Cincinnati institution, serving no fewer than sixteen two-year terms on the city council. Happily, for the historian, Mr. Taft appears to have never thrown anything away. His family donated more than 200 boxes of his papers to the Library of Congress in Washington, D.C., which proved a valuable source on the activities of the Cincinnati City Council during Gilligan's service and on the 1966 electoral contest between Gilligan and Taft.

Several other individuals made papers of significant value available to the author. One is Robert Daley of Dayton, who joined Gilligan in 1968 as his traveling press secretary and who has remained close to the former governor ever since. The second is Phil Moots, an attorney in Columbus and one-time member of the Gilligan administration's inner circle. Mr. Moots had the foresight to save, and the graciousness to let me use, extensive papers related to the 1972 effort to repeal the newly passed state income tax and the 1973–74 efforts to enact state ethics legislation.

As governor, Gilligan commonly appointed citizens' task forces to study matters of interest to state government—taxes, higher education, mental health, prisons, and others. The reports by these bodies were made available to the author through the courtesy and cooperation of the State Library of Ohio in Columbus, Ohio.

Finally, there is no better concentrated source for the doings of the Ohio State Legislature than a brief, privately produced newsletter, universally referred to a *Gongwer,* which is issued every day the state legislature is in session. *Gongwer* is owned and edited by Alan Miller, who not only permitted the author to photocopy 1,000 pages of material from the years Gilligan was governor but insisted that that photocopying be done at *Gongwer*'s expense.

Bibliography

MANUSCRIPT COLLECTIONS AND ARCHIVAL SOURCES

Cincinnati Historical Society
Library of Congress, Washington, D.C.
Ohio Historical Society, Columbus
State Library of Ohio, Columbus
University of Notre Dame Archives, South Bend, Indiana
Xavier University Archives, Cincinnati, Ohio

PUBLISHED SECONDARY SOURCES

BOOKS

Alexander, Herbert E., ed. *Campaign Money: Reform and Reality in the States*. New York: Free Press, 1976.

Ashworth, William. *The Late Great Lakes: An Environmental History*. New York: Alfred A. Knopf, 1986.

Bartlett, John. *Familiar Quotations*. New York: Little, Brown, 1980.

Bergreen, Laurence. *Capone: The Man and the Era*. New York: Simon & Schuster, 1994.

Billingsley Edward Baxter. *The Emmons Saga: History of the USS Emmons*. Bloomington, IN: iUniverse, 2005.

Bliss, Edward Jr. *In Search of Light*. New York: Da Capo Press, 1963.

Burns, Robert E. *Being Catholic, Being American: The Notre Dame Story, 1934–1952*. South Bend, IN: University of Notre Dame Press, 2000.

Cayton, Andrew R. L. *Ohio: The History of a People*. Columbus: Ohio State University Press, 2002.

Chester, Lewis, Godfrey Hodgson, and Bruce Page. *American Melodrama: The Presidential Campaign of 1968*. New York: Viking Press, 1969.

Collett, Wallace T. *McCarthyism in Cincinnati: The Bettman-Collett Affair*. Rosemont, PA: Privately published, 2002.

Columbia Encyclopedia, 5th ed. New York: Houghton-Mifflin, 1993.

Curtin, Michael F. *Ohio Politics Almanac*. 2nd ed. Kent, OH: Kent State University Press, 2006.

Davies, Richard O. *Defender of the Old Guard: John Bricker and American Politics*. Columbus: Ohio State University Press, 1993.

Davis, Kenneth Sydney. *The Politics of Honor: A Biography of Adlai E. Stevenson*. New York: G. P. Putnam's Sons, 1957.

Dempsey, Dave. *On The Brink: The Great Lakes in the 20th Century*. East Lansing: Michigan State University Press, 1974.

Diemer, Tom. *Fighting the Unbeatable Foe: Howard Metzenbaum of Ohio, the Washington Years*. Kent, OH: Kent State University Press, 2008.

Dively, George S. *The Power of Professional Management*. New York: American Management Association, 1971.

Dudgeon, Tom. *Ohio's Governor of the Century: James A. Rhodes, Ohio Governor 1963–1971 and 1975–1983*. Privately published.

Fenno, Richard F. Jr. *The Presidential Odyssey of John Glenn*. Washington, DC: Congressional Quarterly Press, 1990.

Fenton, John H. *Midwest Politics*. New York: Holt, Rinehart & Winston, 1966.

Fortin, Roger A. *To See Great Wonders: A History of Xavier University, 1831–2006*. Scranton, PA: University of Scranton Press, 2006.

Gold, David M. *Democracy in Session: A History of the Ohio General Assembly*. Athens: Ohio University Press, 2009.

Gottlieb, Mark, and Diana Tittle. *America's Soapbox: 75 Years of Free Speaking at Cleveland's City Club*. Cleveland: Citizens Press, 1967.

Gould, Lewis L. *1968: The Election That Changed America*. American Way Series. Chicago: Ivan R. Dee, 1993.

Hastings, Max. *Retribution*. New York: Penguin Press, 2009.

Hesburgh, Theodore M., with Jerry Reedy. *God, Country, Notre Dame: The Autobiography of Theodore M. Hesburgh*. New York: Doubleday, 1990.

Jauchius, R. Dean, and Thomas H. Dudgeon. *Jim Rhodes' Big Win*. Columbus, OH: PoliCom, 1978.

Keegan, John. *The Second World War*. New York: Penguin, 2005.

Knepper, George. *Ohio and Its People*. Bicentennial Edition. Kent, OH: Kent State University Press, 2003.

Kornbluh, Andrea Tuttle. *Lighting the Way: The Women's City Club of Cincinnati*. Cincinnati: Young & Klein, 1986.

Lamis, Alexander P., and Brian Usher, eds. *Ohio Politics*. 2nd ed. Kent, OH: Kent State University Press, 2007.

Lynch, Thomas. *The Undertaking: Life Studies from the Dismal Trade*. New York: W.W. Norton, 1997.

Mackenzie, G. Calvin, and Robert Weisbrot. *The Liberal Hour: Washington and the Politics of Change in the 1960s*. New York: Penguin Press, 2008.

Mailer, Norman. *Miami and the Siege of Chicago*. New York: New York Review Books, 1968.

Mandall, Betty Reid, ed. *Welfare in America: Controlling the "Dangerous Classes."* Englewood Cliffs, NJ: Prentice-Hall, 1975.

McCarthy, Eugene. *Up 'Til Now: A Memoir*. New York: Harcourt, Brace, Jovanovich, 1987.

McDiarmid, Hugh. "The Gilligan Interlude, 1971–1975." In Lamis and Usher, *Ohio Politics*, 109–125.

McFarland, Marvin W. *The Papers of Wilbur and Orville Wright*. Vol. 2. New York: McGraw-Hill, 1953.

Meaney, John M. *O'Malley of Notre Dame*. South Bend, IN: University of Notre Dame Press, 1991.

Miller, Zane L. *Boss Cox's Cincinnati: Urban Politics in the Progressive Era*. New York: Oxford University Press, 1968.

———. *Suburb: Neighborhood and Community in Forest Park, Ohio, 1935–1976.* Knoxville: University of Tennessee Press, 1981.

———. *Visions of Place: The City, Neighborhoods, Suburbs and Cincinnati's Clifton.* Columbus: Ohio State University Press, 2001.

Miller, Zane L., and Bruce Tucker. "New Urban Politics: Planning and Development in Cincinnati, 1954–1988." In *Snow Belt Cities: Metropolitan Politics in the Northeast and Midwest Since World War II.* Ed. Richard M. Bernard. Bloomington: Indiana University Press, 1990.

Mowbray, A. Q. *The Thumb on the Scale: or, The Supermarket Shell Game.* Philadelphia: J. B. Lippincott, 1967.

Odenkirk, James E. *Frank J. Lausche: Ohio's Great Political Maverick.* Wilmington, OH: Orange Frazer Press, 2005.

Peirce, Neal R., and John Keefe. *The Great Lake States of America.* New York: W. W. Norton, 1980.

———. *The Megastates of America: People, Politics and Power in the Ten Great States.* New York: W. W. Norton, 1972.

Rhodes, James A. *Alternative to a Decadent Society.* Indianapolis: Howard W. Sams, 1969.

Rhodes, James A., and Dean Jauchius. *The Court-Martial of Commodore Perry.* Indianapolis: Bobbs-Merrill, 1961.

Riffe, Vernal K. Jr. *Whatever's Fair: The Political Autobiography of Ohio House Speaker Vern Riffe.* Kent, OH: Kent State University Press, 2007.

Rodenhauser, Paul, ed. *Mental Health Care Administration: A Guide for Practitioners.* Ann Arbor: University of Michigan Press, 2000.

Ross, Ishbel. *An American Family: The Tafts, 1678–1964.* Cleveland: World, 1964.

Rubel, Stanley S. *Guide to Venture Capital Sources.* New York: Capital Publishing, 1973.

Russell, Francis. *The Shadow of Blooming Grove: Warren G. Harding and His Times.* New York: McGraw-Hill, 1968.

Saxbe, William B., with Peter D. Franklin. *I've Seen the Elephant: An Autobiography.* Kent, OH: Kent State University Press, 2000.

Schmuhl, Robert P. *The University of Notre Dame: A Contemporary Portrait.* South Bend, IN: University of Notre Dame Press, 1986.

Slayton, Robert A. *The Empire Statesman: The Rise of Redemption of Al Smith.* New York: Free Press, 2001.

Stokes, Carl B. *Promises of Power.* New York: Simon & Schuster, 1973.

Stradling, David. *Cincinnati: From River City to Highway Metropolis.* Charleston, SC: Arcadia, 2003.

Sundquist, James L. *Dynamics of the Party System: Alignment and Realignment of Political Parties in the United States.* Washington, DC: Brookings Institution, 1983.

Taft, Charles P. *City Management: The Cincinnati Experiment.* New York: Farrar & Reinhart, 1933.

Tichi, Cecelia. *Shifting Gears: Technology, Literature, and Culture in Modernist America.* Chapel Hill: University of North Carolina Press, 1987.

Usher, Brian. "The Lausche Era: 1945–1957." In Lamis and Usher, *Ohio Politics,* 45–68.

———. "Ohio: A Tale of Two Parties." In *Campaign Money: Reform and Reality in the States.* Ed. Herbert E. Alexander. New York: Free Press, 1976. 252–276.

White, Theodore. *The Making of the President, 1968.* New York: Atheneum, 1969.

WPA Guide to Cincinnati, 1788–1943. Cincinnati: Cincinnati Historical Society, 1987.

Zaidan, Abe, with John C. Green. *Portraits of Power: Ohio and National Politics 1964–2004.* Akron, OH: University of Akron Press, 2007.

Zimmerman, Richard G. *Call Me Mike: A Political Biography of Michael V. DiSalle.* Kent, OH: Kent State University Press, 2003.
———. *Plain Dealing: Ohio Politics and Journalism Viewed from the Press Gallery.* Kent, OH: Kent State University Press, 2006.
———. "Rhodes's First Eight Years, 1963–1971." In Lamis and Usher, *Ohio Politics,* 85–108.

JOURNAL AND MAGAZINE ARTICLES
Bernstein, Mark. "The Accidental Governor." *Ohio Magazine* 20 (October 1997): 44–49.
"Education: Best Catholic Colleges." TIME, February 9, 1962.
Fairfield, John. "Cincinnati Search for Order." *Queen City Heritage* 48 (Summer 1990): 15–26.
Forest, Frank. "The Disestablishment of the Charter Committee." *Cincinnati Historical Society Bulletin* (Spring 1975): 35.
Gale, Oliver M. "The Queen City Cub: The First Hundred Years." *Cincinnati Historical Society Bulletin* (Winter 1974).
Gerckens, Laurence C. "The 'Trial' of Sydney M. Williams." *Queen City Heritage* 46 (Winter 1988): 45–64.
Gilligan, John J. "America's Stake in the Developing World." *Department of State Bulletin,* November 14, 1977.
———. "Inherit the Earth." *Scrip,* August 1942.
———. "Learning About Race in Cincinnati." *Queen City Heritage* 52 (Fall 1994): 3–8.
———. "A Search for Community: The Problem of Governance in a Democratic Society." *University of Cincinnati Law Review* 62 (Summer 1993).
———. "United States Seeks Improved U.N. Programs to Meet Basic Needs of World's Poor." *Department of State Bulletin,* August 15, 1977.
———. "Who Has Tasted Bread." *Scrip,* May 1942.
"The Great-Grandson Race." TIME, October 21, 1966.
Jacobsen, Sally. "Anti-Pollution Backlash in Illinois: Can a Tough Protection Program Survive." *Science and Public Affairs* 30 (January 1974): 39–44.
Kersten, Andrew E. "Publicly Exposing Discrimination: The 1945 FEPC Hearings in Cincinnati." *Queen City Heritage* 52 (Fall 1994): 9–22.
"Kicked Out: AID Chief Gilligan Goes." TIME, February 12, 1979.
Miller, Zane L. "Thinking, Politics, City Government: Charter Reform in Cincinnati, 1890s-1990s." *Queen City Heritage* 55 (Winter 1997): 24–37.
Miller, Richard, and Gregory Rhodes. "The Life and Times of the Old Cincinnati Ballparks." *Queen City Heritage* 46 (Summer 1988): 25–41.
Spraul, Judith. "Cultural Boosterism: The Construction of Music Hall." *Cincinnati Historical Society Bulletin* 34 (Fall 1976): 189–203.
Wieck, Paul. "Wallace in Ohio—Who Will Get Him?" *New Republic,* October 5, 1968.

UNPUBLISHED REPORTS, DISSERTATIONS, AND THESES
Burke, John F. Jr., and Eric A. Weld Jr. "A Profile of State Government Taxation and Revenue for Ohio, 1968." Institute of Urban Studies, Cleveland State University, 1969.
Burnham, Robert A. "'Pulling Together' for Pluralism, Politics, Planning and Government in Cincinnati, 1924–1959." PhD dissertation. University of Cincinnati, 1990.
Cohen, Robert Alan. "The Rhetoric of Incumbency in Ohio Governor John J. Gilligan's 1974 Campaign for Re-Election." Master's thesis. Ohio State University, 1975.
Coil, William Russell. "'New Deal Republican'—James A. Rhodes and the Transformation of the Republican Party, 1933–1983." PhD dissertation. Ohio State University, 2005.

Crable, Richard Ellsworth. "The Rhetorical Strategies of Governor John Joyce Gilligan in His 1970 Campaign." Master's thesis. Ohio State University, 1971.

Davis, John Emmeus. "In the Interest of Property: Group Formation and Inter-Group Conflict in the Residential Urban Neighborhood." PhD dissertation. Cornell University, 1996.

Governor's Office Research. "Administrative Achievements Handbook." September 19, 1972. State Library of Ohio.

"Governor's Task Force on Health Care: Final Report." December 1973. State Library of Ohio.

Guckian, Jacqueline Sue. Ohio Environmental Protection Agency internship report. Miami University, 2007.

Hill, Jack. "Social and Economic Implications of Strip Mining in Harrison County." Ohio State University, 1965.

Larson, David. "Ohio's Fighting Liberal." PhD dissertation. Ohio State University, 1982.

Mitchell, Lawrence Frederick. "The Evolution of the Cincinnati Central Business District and Riverfront: An Historical and Architectural Approach, 1900–1989." University of Cincinnati, 1998.

Nguyen, Vinh Huu. "Population Redistribution within the Cincinnati Metropolitan Area, 1970–1990." PhD dissertation. University of Cincinnati, 2002.

Ohio Legislative Service Commission. "Comparative State Strip Mining and Reclamation Laws." Report No. 67. 1965. State Library of Ohio.

Stocker, Frederick D. "The Rough Road to Tax Reform: The Ohio Experience." Ohio State University, 1972.

"Transportation Advisory Committee Report to Honorable John J. Gilligan, Governor of Ohio." January 1972. State Library of Ohio.

NEWSPAPERS

Akron Beacon Journal
Christian Science Monitor
The Chronicle: Cincinnati's Labor Newspaper
Cincinnati Enquirer
Cincinnati Post
Cincinnati Post and Times-Star
Cincinnati Times-Star
Cleveland Plain Dealer
Cleveland Press
Columbus Citizen-Journal
Columbus Dispatch
Dayton Daily News
Dayton Journal Herald
Gongwer

Lorain Journal
New York Times
New York Times Sunday Magazine
Pittsburgh Post-Gazette
South Bend Tribune
Toledo Blade
Troy Daily News
Wall Street Journal
Washington Post
Xavier University News
Youngstown Vindicator
Zanesville Times Recorder

Index

Abel, I. W., 157
Abercrombie, Gene, 224, 236, 286
Adler, Mortimer, 29
Affluent Society, The (Galbraith), 128
AFL-CIO: Gilligan's U.S. Senate race and, 157–58, 163, 168–69; Gilligan U.S. Congress race and, 111, 112; on Ohio income tax, 246, 249, 266
Agnew, Spiro, 346
Alexander, James, 116–17
Alsop, Joseph, 217–18
American Can Company, 80
American Electric Power (AEP), 322
Ames, Van Meter, 74
Anderson, John, 141
Anderson, Wendell, 269
Andrews, John, 266, 296
Apple, R. W., Jr., 241, 278–79, 291
Aronoff, Stanley, 226, 242–43, 260–61, 274–75, 276, 301
Askew, Reuben, 351
Athenaeum (Xavier University), 58
Austin, Gerald, 386

Baetke, F. W. Waldemar, 42
Bailey, Doug, 371, 377, 381, 386
Baldwin, James, 196
Barkan, Al, 157, 175
Barnett, Jim, 427
Bartunek, Joseph, 268
Batchelder, William: ethics legislation and, 344; Gilligan's gubernatorial race (1970) and, 220; Netzley and, 296; redistricting and, 258; tax reform and, 244, 245, 260, 274, 277; views on Gilligan, 363; views on Rhodes, 354–55; as youngest Ohio legislator, 226
Battisti, Frank, 258
Bayh, Birch, 248, 352
Beavers, John H., 209, 213, 216
Bechtold, John, 259

Beckman, Father Jack, 22–23, 24, 114
Beckman, Vincent ("Vince"), 78, 79, 83, 93, 94, 96, 112, 114, 118, 120–21
Bellah, Robert, 418–19
Benton, William, 177
Bentsen, Lloyd, 372
Bernardin, Joseph (archbishop of Cincinnati), 60
Berry, Bill, 171
Berry, Ted, 76–77, 79, 80–83, 93, 105, 106, 117, 118, 119, 124
Bettman, Henry, 72–74, 75
Biden, Joe, 428
Bingle, Anne, 209, 212, 223
Black, Hugo, 131
Blackwell, Rosa, 425, 426
Blaine, James G., 65
Blair, Bill, 319
Bleicher, Samuel ("Sam"), 320–22, 325, 327, 328, 329
Bliss, Ray C., 87–89, 218
Boggs, Hale, 129, 175, 176, 178
Boggs, Robert, 298
Booth, Junius Brutus, 10
Bowles, Chester, 420
Branigan, Julia (Joyce), 16–17
Bricker, John, 86, 87, 89, 90, 91, 203, 229
Broban, Harry, 214
Broder, Ann, 139
Broder, David, 4, 7, 137–39, 145, 155, 178, 220, 352
Brown, John, 247, 261, 273, 389, 390
Brown, Max, 290, 303, 351, 356, 364, 369–70, 373, 376, 381
Brown, Paul, 200, 214, 215
Brown, Ted W., 217, 295–96, 296, 379, 388, 390
Brown, Thomas, 31
Brown, William J., 310, 367, 390
Brown, William K., 367
Buchanan, Christopher, 160, 210, 221, 254–55, 257, 380, 388, 389–90
Bumpers, Dale, 397

Burke, John F., Jr., 228–29, 230
Burton, Harold, 86
Bush, George W., 60
Butterfield, Alexander, 355

Cadell, Pat, 199
Cain, Harry, 16, 18
Calabrese, Anthony ("Tony"): characterization of, 6, 228, 235; Gilligan's views on, 288, 355, 361, 367; as Ohio Senate minority leader, 253–54, 260–61, 267–68, 270, 273, 276, 303, 344
Calhoun, John, 144
Carlson, Chester, 335
Carrier, Maria, 278
Carson, Rachel, 128
Carter, Jimmy, 6, 351, 352, 394–96, 400–401, 403–5, 409
Cash, Al, 70
Cashman, John, 291
Castell, Ron, 336
Catholic Interracial Council, 105
Catholicism: Catholic immigration to Cincinnati, 9, 11, 15–17; Gilligan's religious beliefs and, 20, 32–33, 107–8, 112–13; Jesuit order, 22–23, 33, 57–58; *Rerum Novarum*, 88–89; Vatican II, 112–13. *See also individual names of Catholic institutions*
Cayton, Andrew, 207
Cecile, Robert, 242
Celebrezze, Frank, 390
Celebrezze, James, 256
Celeste, Richard ("Dick"), 218, 303, 345, 346, 361, 363, 367, 380, 386, 392, 420
Charter Party: Democratic Party and, 92–96; Gilligan as city council member, 70–83; history of, 63–69
Chavanne, Bill: as assistant legislative liaison, 227–28, 245–47; ethics legislation and, 345; Gilligan's Cincinnati school board election, 422; Gilligan's gubernatorial reelection bid (1974) and, 363; as *Gongwer* reporter, 233; redistricting and, 254–57, 297–98; tax reform and, 261, 273, 280–83, 300–301
Chavez, Cesar, 84, 385
Christ College, 59–60
Christman, Larry, 282, 283
Christopher, Warren, 403–4
Cincinnati, Ohio: Charter Party history and, 63–69; Gilligan as city council member, 70–83; 166; immigration to, 9–10, 12–13, 15–17; Ohio River flood (1937), 23; race relations, 15, 43, 419–20; school board, 421–22, 424–27; trade in, 8–10; urban renewal, 97–109
Cincinnati College, 9
Cincinnati Enquirer, characterization of, 69
Cincinnatus Association, 65–69
citizens task forces, created by Gilligan, 308, 314, 318

Clark, Blair, 175
Clark, Ronald, 375
Clay, Henry, 144
Cleveland Regional Sewer District (CRSD), 327–28
Clinton, Hillary Rodham, 427–28
Cloud, Clifford ("Kip"), 213, 218
Cloud, Roger, 198, 200–201, 208, 209, 210, 212–20, 244, 381
Coffey, Ronald, 236
Cohen, Benjamin, 134
Cohen, Robert Alan, 364–65, 384–85
Cohen, Wilbur, 131
Cold War GI Bill, 132
Coles, Robert, 276
College of Law, University of Cincinnati, 418
Collett, Wallace, 72–74, 75
Collier, Howard, 222, 230, 243, 298–99
Collins, Philip, 99, 112, 115, 116, 117
Committee on Social Thought, University of Chicago, 54–55
Conlon, Tom, Sr., 124
Conners, Donald Dennis, 34
Cook, Howard, 274
Cooper, Benjamin J., 236, 314
Cooper, Bennett, 315
Corey, Paul A., 236, 286, 340
Cox, Archibald, 355
Cox, George Barnstable, 64–66
Cox, James, 2
Coyne, Edward, 135
Craddick, Father, 26
Crittenden, Ann, 400
Crofters, 213–16
Crosby, Bing, 37
Crosley, Powel, 24, 95
Crowley, Pat, 72
Cruze, Chester, 318
Cummings, Roger Sullivan, 27, 36–37

Daley, Robert ("Bob"): on administration infighting, 351, 353; as assistant to governor, 297, 303; Gilligan's gubernatorial campaign (1970), 209; Gilligan's gubernatorial reelection bid (1974) and, 361, 380, 382, 391–92, 393; Gilligan's post-political career and, 409, 413, 417, 421–22; Gilligan's U.S. Senate race and, 161, 162, 163, 164–65, 174, 185, 190; Glenn-Metzenbaum rivalry and, 358; as governor's appointments secretary, 232–33; Hansan and, 287, 290, 309; as press secretary, 139
Daschle, Tom, 428
Daveney, Kathy, 209
David, A. D., 133
Davis, Jack, 211, 213–14, 291
Davis, Jacob ("Jake"), 223, 239
Davis, Walt, 163
Dead Man's Corner (saloon), 64–65

Deardourff, John, 371
DeCourcy, Joseph, 94
Del Corso, Sylvester, 238, 376
Democratic Party: in Cincinnati, 11; Democratic National Committee (DNC) and Shields, 198; Gilligan's alliance with, 84–96; Stevenson candidacy, 61–62. *See also individual names of politicians*
Democrats United, 115–20
Dennis, Max, 274
Derrick, Jeanne. *See* Gilligan, Jeanne (sister)
Derringer, Paul, 24
Desai, Morarji, 400
DeSandro, Carlo, 419
DeSandro, Charlie, 419
DeSandro, Luke, 419
DeShetler, Kenneth, 237
de Tocqueville, Alexis, 418–19
Dewey, Thomas, 86
Dickens, Charles, 8, 9, 12
Diemer, Tom, 358
DiPaolo, Roger, 182
DiSalle, Michael ("Mike"), 90–91, 110–12, 130, 205, 207, 210, 294, 307, 363
Dively, George S., 333, 334–35
Dixon, Donald, 50, 56
Dixon, Edward T., 36, 39, 54–55, 67, 72, 107, 405
Dixon, Mary Kathryn ("Katie"). *See* Gilligan, Mary Kathryn ("Katie") Dixon (wife)
Dolbey, Dorothy, 78–79, 94–95, 96
Donahey, Gertrude, 367, 390
Donahue, Gerald, 214
Duchin, Peter, 232
Duncan, Robert, 141
Dunn, James "Jim," 174, 183, 294, 413
Dunn, Patrick J., 169
Dutton, Fred, 175, 176
Duveneck, Frank, 11

Eckert, Henry, 286
Edwards, Don, 130
Ehrlich, Thomas, 405
Ehrlichman, John, 355
Eisenhardt, Charles, Jr., 148
Eisenhower, Dwight David, 40, 61–62, 64, 82–83, 86, 95, 144, 420
Elliott, Ross T., 48–49
Elston, Charles, 123
English, William, 11
Ensign, William J., 237
environmental issues: Environmental Protection Agency (EPA) (Ohio), 319–29; reform during Gilligan's tenure, 317–29; strip mining, 250–52, 283–86
Ervin, Sam, 355
Essex, Martin W., 263, 299
Evans, Rowland, 150, 172, 184, 188, 216

Fain, Jim, 218, 384
Fair Employment Practices Commission (FEPC) (Cincinnati), 80–81
Fairfield, John, 65
Farkas, Alan, 212, 319, 320–21, 362
Farrell, James, 52
Federal Communications Commission, 91
Fenno, Richard, 202, 356, 357
Fenton, John H., 86, 152
Ferguson, Thomas, Sr. ("Jumping Joe"), 6, 217–18, 220, 253–54, 290, 340, 392
Flannery, James, 242, 248, 271
Fleming, Arthur, 86
Ford, Michael, 365, 370, 374, 375
Foss, Eugene N., II, 45, 48
Frank, Barney, 155
Frankel, Max, 220
Fremont, Susan. *See* Gilligan, Susan Fremont (second wife)
Friedman, Bernard, 314, 315
Friedman, James ("Jim"): as chief of staff, 232, 233, 234, 235, 238, 239; dismissal of, 286–91; economic reform, 330, 331; environmental reform and, 319; ethics legislation and, 347; Gilligan Institute, 427; Gilligan's gubernatorial race (1970) and, 195, 198, 199, 200, 209, 210, 211, 218; Gilligan's gubernatorial reelection bid (1974) and, 282, 286, 288–92, 301, 350–51, 353, 358, 386, 393; Gilligan's post-political career and, 420, 424; Gilligan's U.S. Senate race and, 139, 155, 156, 157, 160, 162–63, 167, 173, 182, 183, 188, 192, 193; as governor's administration counsel, 223; presidential race (1972) and, 278, 279; tax reform and, 247, 249, 254, 256, 257, 258, 264, 268–69
Friedrich, Carl J., 29
Fritchey, Clayton, 352
Fry, Charles, 255, 259, 340, 354

Gaffin, Ira, 254
Galbraith, John Kenneth, 128, 344
Gamble, James, 9
Garfield, James, 11
Garnes, William E., 236, 286
Garth, David, 199, 210, 364
Gateau, Richard, 412
Gaver, Kenneth ("Ken"), 288, 308–9, 310–13, 420
Geoghegan, Susan, 130, 223
Geoghegan, William ("Bill"), 22, 28, 70–72, 129, 163, 173, 175, 176–77, 382–83, 397
GI Bills, 56–57, 132
Gibson, James Slater, 347
Gilligan, Andrew (uncle), 15
Gilligan, Betsy Tarlin (daughter-in-law), 274, 405, 413
Gilligan, Blanche Joyce (mother), 16–17, 18, 19–20, 23, 36, 54–55, 108, 109, 129, 361
Gilligan, Dan (grandson), 405

Gilligan, Donald (son): biographical information, 56, 106, 107, 108, 109; career of, 196–97, 225, 405, 413, 428; education of, 155; father's political career and, 134, 142, 188, 189, 212, 369; father's run for Cincinnati school board, 421; marriage and family of, 274, 429

Gilligan, Ellen (daughter): biographical information, 58, 106, 107, 108–9; career of, 405, 413, 419–20, 423; education of, 196, 224–25; family of, 428; father's political career and, 130, 134, 167, 177, 179, 188, 370, 382; on father's run for Cincinnati school board, 421–22

Gilligan, Frank (brother), 18, 19, 20, 22, 23–24, 28, 50, 55, 56, 71, 109

Gilligan, Hannah (granddaughter), 405, 413, 428

Gilligan, Harry, Jr. ("Michael," "Mike") (brother), 18, 19, 20, 21, 22, 23–24, 28, 31, 50, 51, 55, 56, 71, 109

Gilligan, Harry (father): biographical information, 14, 16, 17, 18, 19, 20, 21–22, 23, 26, 36, 39, 50; Cincinnati's Charter Party and, 63–64, 67, 68–69, 75, 94; death of, 402; son's early career and, 51, 54–55, 56; son's political career and, 71–72, 108–9, 126, 188, 210, 211; views on Cincinnati, 422; wife's death and, 361

Gilligan, James (grandson), 405, 413

Gilligan, Jamie (granddaughter), 429

Gilligan, Jeanne (sister), 18–19, 20, 23, 50, 108, 109, 198

Gilligan, Joe (grandson), 413

Gilligan, John (grandfather), 15, 16, 22, 63

Gilligan, John Joyce ("Jack"): academic posts of, 54–62, 74, 75, 197, 407–16, 418; childhood of, 12–17, 18–25; on Cincinnati City Council, 70–83, 84–96, 97–109, 110–21; on Cincinnati school board, 421–22, 424–27; early career ambitions of, 33, 54–55, 59–60; education of, 18–19, 22–25, 26–35, 36, 54–62, 56, 57–61; gubernatorial administration of, 286–91 (see also individual names of administration members); gubernatorial career, newly elected, 222–30, 231–40; gubernatorial race (1970) and, 195–208, 209–21; gubernatorial race (1974) and, 350–78, 379–87, 388–93; homes of, 18–19, 21–22, 58, 106, 108–9, 196, 222, 223–25, 391, 408, 417, 419, 430; insurance business of, 155, 195, 197; legacy of, 1–7, 409, 427, 430–31; marriage (first) of, 36, 52–53 (see also Gilligan, Mary Kathryn ["Katie"] Dixon [wife]); marriage (second) of, 6, 422–24, 428–29, 430; military service of, 29–31, 33–35, 34–35, 36–44, 45–53; New York Times Sunday Magazine on, 4, 137–39; presidential elections and involvement by, 61–62, 170–80, 278–79, 284, 287, 291–92, 300–301; religious beliefs of, 20, 32–33, 107–8, 112–13; U.S. Congressional career of, 110, 120–21, 122–26, 127–42, 143–50; U.S. Senate race, 150, 151–54, 155–69, 195; at U.S. AID,

394–406; at Woodrow Wilson International Center for Scholars, 391

Gilligan, John Patrick (son): biographical information, 58, 106, 107, 108, 109; career of, 223–24, 225, 405; education of, 155; family of, 413, 428; father's political career and, 118, 130, 134, 142, 159, 165, 187, 377; on father's run for Cincinnati school board, 421; military service of, 197

Gilligan, Kathleen (daughter). See Sebelius, Kathleen Gilligan (Gilligan's daughter)

Gilligan, Mame Cain (grandmother), 16

Gilligan, Mary Kathryn ("Katie") Dixon (wife): biographical information, 50, 67; career of, 39; death of, 6, 419–20; husband's City Council career and, 71, 76, 90, 97, 106, 107–8, 117; husband's Congressional career and, 126, 130, 134, 139, 150; husband's early career and, 54, 55–56; husband's gubernatorial campaigns and, 196, 379–80, 383, 386; husband's post-political career and, 391, 397, 400, 402–3, 404–5, 407–8, 409, 412–13, 415–16, 417; husband's U.S. Senate race and, 159, 177; legacy of, 421; marriage of, 4, 36, 39, 52–53; as Ohio First Lady, 222, 223–24, 294, 309

Gilligan, Megan (daughter-in-law), 405, 413

Gilligan, Patrick (great-grandfather), 12, 15–16, 143

Gilligan, Susan Fremont (second wife), 6, 422–24, 428–29, 430

Gilligan Funeral Home: Barrere Funeral Home acquired by, 71; Jack Gilligan's work at, 54–55, 56; origins of, 12–14, 17, 20; Wiethe and, 116–17

Gilligan Institute, 427

Ginsberg, David, 176

Glenn, John, 193–94, 197–99, 201–3, 208, 318, 356–59, 361, 365–67, 375, 384, 392, 393

Gold, David, 227, 244, 277, 390

Goldstein, Harold, 78

Goldwater, Barry, 125, 126

Good Society, The (Bellah), 414–19

Gordon, Alice, 130

Gore, Al, Sr., 178

Governor's Business and Employment Council (Ohio), 333–35

grand jury investigation, gubernatorial recount (Ohio, 1974) and, 392–93

Grant, Ulysses S., 143

Gray, Theodore ("Ted"), 260, 261, 262, 274–75, 284, 303

Great Society, 128–29, 130, 133–34, 195

Griffey, Ken, Jr., 97

Griffin, Jack, 44

Griffin, Jim, 180

Griffin, John, 48

Griffith, Sidney, 214

Groban, Harry, 214

Gruen, Victor, 101

Grupenhoff, John, 111–12, 129–30, 131–32, 133–34, 135, 137, 146–47, 149
Guggenheim, Charles, 167, 203, 364, 373–74
Guggenheim, Polly, 120
Guggenheim, Richard E. ("Dick"), 74, 110, 112, 114, 120, 149–50, 237, 288
Gurian, Waldemar, 29–30, 31, 35

Haas, Arthur, 29
Haldeman, H. R., 355
Hall, Frank A.B., 68
Hall, John, 272, 282
Hall, Tony, 348, 367, 379
Hancock, Winfield, 11
Hanna, Marcus Alonzo, 86
Hanna Amendment, 86
Hansan, Jack: as chief of staff, 299, 300, 303; economic reform, 335; Friedman and, 289, 290–91; Gilligan Institute, 427; Gilligan's Congressional career and, 119, 129, 147; Gilligan's gubernatorial reelection bid (1974), 350, 351, 353, 356–57, 361, 365, 367, 368, 369, 370, 373–74, 375, 386; Gilligan's U.S. Senate race and, 160, 163, 168, 177, 182, 183, 184–85, 186, 188, 193; grand jury investigation and, 392; McDonald and, 288; Muskie and, 287; at RFK's funeral, 174; as welfare director, 235, 275, 286
Harding, Warren G., 61–62, 227
Hare Proportional Representation (PR) (voting system), 68, 81–83
Hargenow, Bob, 262–63
Harrington, Michael, 128
Harris, Fred, 198
Harris, Lou, 87, 160, 165
Hart, Peter: Friedman and, 291; Gilligan Institute, 427; Gilligan's gubernatorial campaigns and, 199, 350–51, 362, 369, 379, 380, 391; Gilligan's post-political career and, 393, 420; Gilligan's U.S. Senate race and, 3, 160, 162, 163–64, 165, 167, 171, 182, 183, 185, 187, 193; Muskie and, 278
Harvard University, 197
Harvey, Fred, 232
Hatch, Ralph, 283, 285
Hayes, Wayne ("Woody"), 251, 299–300, 302
Haynsworth, Clement, 355
Hearnes, Warren, 178
Henri, Robert, 11
Herbers, John, 220
Herbert, John D., 214, 215, 216, 218
Herbert, John T., 344–45
Hermens, Ferdinand Alois, 29
Hesburgh, Father Theodore M., 406, 407, 410–12, 421
Hesburgh Center for International Peace Studies, University of Notre Dame, 411
Hess, David, 196
Hill, Jack, 250
Hill, Lydia, 130
Hinzelman, Slim, 211

Hitler, Adolf, 29
Hodge, Leondres, 116
Hoffa, James ("Jimmy"), 85, 92
Holcomb, David, 256, 273
Hollister, John, 123
Hoover, Herbert, 20
Hopcraft, David, 214, 293, 352–53
Hopkins, Gerard Manley, 59
Hovey, Hal, 235, 239, 246, 248, 262, 265, 286, 287, 298–99, 330, 341
Hughes, Martin J., 237
Humphrey, Hubert, 141, 170, 172, 175–77, 179, 181–82, 184, 187–89, 192, 243, 279, 291, 396, 401
Humphreys, George, 86
Hutchins, Robert Maynard, 54
Hyde Park Country Club, 15, 19, 90, 106, 107
Hynicka, Rodolph, 65

"Inherit the Earth" (Gilligan), 35
International Bakery and Confectionary union, 85
Interstate Highway System, impact on urban areas, 103–4

Jackson, Henry ("Scoop"), 291, 352, 372
Jacobsen, Sally, 325
James, Troy, 256, 301
Jamison Funeral Home, 116
Jauchius, R. Dean, 370
Jefferson, Thomas, 420
Joe (trusty), 224
John Paul II (pope), 408
Johnson, John, 227, 248, 255–56, 274, 363
Johnson, Lyndon: characteristics of, 135–36, 137; Cold War GI Bill, 132; Congressional elections (1966) and, 149; Gilligan's Congressional campaign and, 124, 125, 126; Gilligan's U.S. Senate race and, 159–60, 165, 183, 189–90; Great Society and, 128–29, 133–34; on mental health and retardation, 131; 1968 presidential race and, 172, 174, 175, 176–77, 178, 179, 180; 1964 presidential race, 143; Vietnam War and, 140–42, 146
Johnston, David, 226
Jones, John, 234, 264, 286, 288, 297
Jordan, Albert ("Al"), 77, 78–79, 80–81, 82
Jordan (trusty), 224
Joyce, Blanche. See Gilligan, Blanche Joyce (mother)
Joyce, Father Francis ("Frank"), 17, 18, 52
Joyce, Father Ned, 407
Joyce, Julia Branigan, 16–17
Joyce, Patrick, 16–17
Jump, Harry V., 391

Kaval, James, 211–12
Keegan, John, 41
Kellogg, Wilbur R., 73
Kempe, Margery, 56
Kennedy, Edward ("Ted"), 147, 183, 352, 409, 411
Kennedy, Ethel, 170, 171

Kennedy, John Fitzgerald, 112, 113, 117, 125, 126, 127, 135, 136, 170–71, 173, 394–95
Kennedy, Richard D., 111–12
Kennedy, Robert F., 146–47, 157, 170–76, 178, 185, 190, 420
Kennedy Institute of Politics, Harvard University, 197
Kent State University, 1970 shootings, 207–8
Kerns, George, 276
Kerwin, Mike, 153
Kiefer, Patricia, 124
Kilpatrick, Bishop, 270
King, Frank, 246, 261–62, 266, 270, 272, 283–84, 300, 368, 370
King, Martin Luther, Jr., 159, 165, 178, 192, 203, 413, 421
Kirby, Charles John, 34
Kirby, James C., Jr., 347
Kircher, Bill, 84–85, 88, 90, 105, 111, 112, 126, 157, 175
Kircher, Tom, 85
Kissinger, Henry, 400
Kleindienst, Richard, 355
Knepper, George, 2, 11, 151, 335
Knippenburg, O. F., 159
Kosydar, Robert J., 237
Kovacik, Steve, 182–83, 199, 366–67
Kraft, Joseph, 220
Kroc, Joan, 411
Kroc, Ray, 411
Kroger Corporation, 223
Kurfess, Charles: environmental reform and, 320; ethics legislation and, 342; Gilligan's gubernatorial reelection bid (1974), 354; mental health reform and, 311; as minority leader, 303; tax reform and, 5–6, 243–49, 257, 263, 267, 268, 271, 272, 276–77

labor unions: Gilligan on Cincinnati City Council and, 84–92; Gilligan's gubernatorial reelection bid (1974) and, 385; Gilligan's U.S. Senate race and, 157–59, 161, 163, 165, 167–69; on Ohio income tax, 246, 249, 265, 266; Taft-Hartley Act, 88, 91, 132–33, 135, 153. See also individual names of labor unions and labor leaders
La Follette, Robert, 144
Lake Erie, environmental issues of, 317, 326–29
Lampson, E. W., 296, 347
Lancione, A. G., 248, 249, 288, 303, 343, 358
Larson, David ("Dave"), 102, 285–86, 367
Latta, Alexander, 10
Lausche, Frank: characteristics of, 87, 151–54; Gilligan's inauguration and, 234; Gilligan's U.S. Senate race and, 150, 155–69, 170, 172, 181–82, 193–94; popularity of, 289, 382; Rhodes and, 205; Rhodes's challenge to, 229; Stevenson and, 62
Lazar, Nancy Brown, 372, 384
Leahy, Pat, 290
Lee (trusty), 224

Lehman, Henry, 218, 225, 257, 360
Leonard, Lee, 213, 233, 247, 249, 257, 260, 267, 274–75, 293, 295, 346
Leonard, William J., 114
Leo XIII (pope), 88–89
Licavoli, Thomas ("Yonnie"), 207
Liddy, G. Gordon, 355
Lima (Ohio) State Hospital, 310, 311
Limehouse, Harry ("Buck"), 218–19
Lincoln, Abraham, 10, 63
Lindbergh, Charles, 30
Lippmann, Walter, 66, 352
Lodge, Henry Cabot, 140–41
Lombardi, Ernie, 24
Long, Clarence, 401
Longnecker, Roy, 243
Longworth, Alice Roosevelt, 4, 122–23, 132
Longworth, Nicholas, 4, 19, 122–23
Lore, David, 300, 306–7
Love, Rodney, 149
Lowenstein, Allard, 187
Lucasville (Ohio) prison, 315–16
Lucey, Pat, 173, 269, 351
Luken, James ("Jim"), 92, 112, 115
Lukens, Donald, 200, 263
Lydon, Christopher, 349, 352
Lyman, Luther, Jr., 207
Lynch, Thomas, 12, 14

Mahaney, John ("Johnno"), 223, 227, 246, 247, 274, 277
Maher, Richard L., 168
Mallory, William ("Bill"), 165, 303
Maloney, Michael ("Mike"), 259, 261–62, 267, 273, 274, 298, 348, 389, 391
Mankiewicz, Frank, 175
Marcy, William Learned, 340
Marietta Coal Company, 252
Marsh, Milan, 368
McCarthy, Eugene, 159–60, 165, 170, 172, 175, 179–80, 183, 188–89, 211
McCord, James W., 355
McCormack, Blanche, 129
McCormack, John, 129, 140, 141
McCormack, Tim, 282
McDiarmid, Hugh, 217, 261, 262, 293, 373, 381, 392
McDonald, Jack (writer), 149
McDonald, John (Gilligan aide): austerity measures and, 262, 263, 264; environmental reform and, 285; Gilligan administration reassignments and, 286–88, 290, 297; Gilligan's gubernatorial campaign (1970) and, 211, 215, 220; Gilligan's gubernatorial reelection bid (1974), 358, 363, 364; King and, 261; as liaison to state legislature, 233, 235, 236, 238, 239; mental health reform and, 308; redistricting and, 253, 254, 255, 256, 280–81; state welfare office and, 275; tax reform and, 223, 245, 246–47, 273
McElroy, John, 207, 222, 233–34, 258, 289

McElroy, Mark, 199, 200
McElroy, Neil, 64, 86
McGee, Gale, 178
McGough, Kent B., 348–49, 374–75
McGovern, George, 135, 180, 248, 279, 280, 297, 298, 300, 301, 303
McGrath, Mark G., 408
McGuffey, William Holmes, 9
McGuire, James F., 57
McKinley, William, 86
McMahon, Francis E., 30
McNamara, Keith, 245, 247, 254, 264, 268, 275, 276, 363
McNamara, Robert, 400
Meany, George, 172
Meeker, David, 299, 359
Melamed, Alan, 160, 161, 162, 165, 239
Menaugh, Thomas ("Tom"), 38, 41, 49, 220, 223, 232–33, 235, 238–39, 264, 286–88, 290
Meshel, Harry, 227, 276, 284, 342–43, 344, 346, 385
Metzenbaum, Howard, 163, 186, 193–94, 197–99, 201–3, 208, 220, 356–59, 361, 365, 366, 384, 393
Meyer, Rabbi Isaac, 10
Miami Society, 114
Miller, Ray T., 151–52
Miller, Zane, 10, 64, 65, 68, 70
Mitchell, George, 278
Mitchell, John, 355
Mitchell, Lawrence Frederick, 97
Moeller, Walter, 149
Mondale, Walter, 352, 372
Moore, George, 108
Moorhous, Margaret, 130, 137
Moots, Phil, 290, 303, 342, 349, 364, 393, 410, 422
Morrison, Toni, 104
Morse, Wayne, 135, 175
Moss, Bob, 211–12
Mottl, Ron, 273
Moyer, "Jimmy," 124
Mueller, James, 267–68, 267–68 or 267
Murdock, Norman, 273, 303
Murrow, Edward R., 40–41
Music Hall (Cincinnati), 11
Muskie, Ed, 178, 278–79, 284, 287, 291–92

National Education Association, 269–70
National Labor Relations Board (NLRB), 133
Naughton, James, 164, 168
Nef, John U., 54
Neil House Hotel, 227
Neipp, Morton, 156, 157, 158
Ness, Elliot, 152
Netzley, Robert ("Bob"), 241, 245, 249, 257, 259, 263, 271, 273–74, 276, 277, 296, 299, 300, 392
Neustadt, Richard, 276
Newell, Florence, 422
Newman, Bruce L., 237
New York Times Sunday Magazine, 4, 137–39
Nicolozakes, George, 252

Nixon, Richard M.: Cambodia and, 207; environmental record, 327; Gilligan's Congressional race (1964) and, 126; Gilligan's gubernatorial race (1970) and, 195, 196, 207, 218; Gilligan's U.S. Senate race and, 183, 187, 188–89, 192; Gilligan's views on, 303–4, 352, 361–62, 369–70; presidential campaign (1972), 280, 291, 300, 301, 354; U.S. AID and, 395, 396; Watergate and, 355–56
Nolan, James D., 367
Noote, Robert, 397
Norris, Alan, 241, 258, 303
Novak, Robert, 150, 172, 184, 188, 216
Nye, William B. ("Bill"), 237, 294, 299, 319

Obama, Barack, 427–28
Obie (trusty), 224
O'Brien, Jack A., 30, 31
Ocasek, Oliver, 266, 276, 318, 389, 390
Odenkirk, James, 164, 167
O'Donnell, Kenneth, 170, 175, 178
Ogilvie, Richard, 325
O'Grady, Eugene ("Pete"), 156–57, 170, 196, 236, 286, 291, 358, 361, 369, 370, 374, 380, 386, 392
O'Hara, John F., 29
Ohio Bond Commission, 155–56, 157
Ohio Council of Retail Merchants, 245–46
Ohio Department of Economic and Community Development, 330, 334
Ohio Department of Mental Hygiene and Corrections, 294, 304–5, 306–16
Ohio Department of Natural Resources (ODNR), 319
Ohio Education Association (OEA), 245–46, 272, 273
Ohio Environmental Protection Agency (EPA), 319–29. See also environmental issues
Ohio Farm Bureau, 245–46, 273
Ohio General Assembly: governor's biennia and, 302–3; on income tax, 241–50, 252, 256, 257, 272, 276; 1972 elections and, 279–83, 300–301; redistricting of (1971), 217, 252–59, 279; redistricting of (1974/1975), 389–90; on strip mining, 250–52. See also individual names of representatives
Ohio National Guard, Kent State University 1970 shootings and, 207–8
Ohio Retail Merchants Association, 223, 273
Ohio Senate: characterization of, 259–61; 1972 elections and, 279–83, 300–301; Ohio austerity measures and, 262–65, 384; on strip mining, 283–86; tax reform and, 259, 261–62, 265–77. See also individual names of senators
Oliver, Jack, 257
Olsen, John, 292–93
O'Malley, Francis J. ("Frank"): Christ College plans of, 59–60; on Gilligan's early career, 54; at Gilligan's wedding, 52–53; at Notre Dame, 26–27, 30–32, 33, 35, 57

O'Neill, C. William, 89, 90, 91, 231
Orth, Patricia, 130
Ostrovsky, Leonard, 257
Other America, The (Harrington), 128

Pease, Donald ("Don"), 263, 288, 297
Peirce, Neil, 87, 206
Pell, Claiborne, 175
Peloquin, Phil, 173–74, 183, 185, 192, 211
Perk, Ralph, Jr., 256
Petrie, Bruce, 347
pinball games, in Cincinnati bars, 78
Polcar, Gertrude, 247
Powell, Jody, 352
Presser, Jack ("Jackie"), 85, 385
Presser, William ("Big Bill"), 186
prison reform, in Ohio, 314–16
Procter, William, 9
Procter & Gamble, 9, 101, 139
Pulfer, Laura, 425
Purcell, W. R., Jr., 334, 335
Pyle, Ernie, 49

Quilter, Barney, 303, 360

race relations: in Cincinnati, 15, 43, 419–20;
    Cincinnati's Charter Party on, 64, 68, 80–83;
    Gilligan on civil rights initiative (1966), 148;
    Gilligan's gubernatorial reelection bid (1974)
    and, 385; in 1960's Washington, D.C., 127–28,
    130; Ohio General Assembly and, 256–57; ur-
    ban renewal and, 103–6; Wiethe and, 116–17;
    World War II military and, 43–44
Raines, Robert A., 347
Rakestraw, Vince, 181, 186, 192
Raskin, A. H., 91
Rauh, Joe, 175
Rawson, Barbara, 347
Ray, James Earl, 165
Rayburn, Sam, 136
Reagan, Ronald, 153, 220, 269, 410, 412, 415
Reardon, Jack, 63
Reconstructing a Republican Majority (Beavers), 209
Reds (Cincinnati), 10, 20–21, 95–96
Reichel, Richard, 248
Rerum Novarum, 88–89
Rhodes, Helen, 222, 223–24, 379, 380
Rhodes, James A. ("Jim"): biographical infor-
    mation, 204; characteristics of, 293, 295;
    economic policy, 330, 331, 333, 337–38; en-
    vironmental policy, 317–18, 327; Gilligan's
    gubernatorial race (1970) and, 201, 203–8,
    210, 212, 213, 214, 219, 222; Gilligan's inaugura-
    tion and, 233–35, 236, 240; gubernatorial race
    (1966), 143, 149; gubernatorial race (1974), 277,
    354–55, 362, 364–65, 367–78, 379–87, 388–91,
    407; Ohio Bond Commission, 155–56, 157; as
    Ohio state auditor, 112; records destroyed by,
    339; tax policy, 229–30, 246, 298–99

Rich, Carl D., 77, 78–79, 123, 125–26, 130, 382
Richards, Earl, 327
Richardson, Elliot, 355
Richley, J. Phillip, 236, 285, 286, 299
Riffe, Vern, 213, 247, 281, 303, 346, 375–76
Right-to-Work, Inc., 88
right-to-work (RTW) initiative, 88–92
Rivers, Father Clarence, 105
Roberts, Gordon, 242
Rockefeller, John D., 326
Rockefeller, Nelson, 204, 210, 350
Rogers, Archibald, 101
Roosevelt, Alice. *See* Longworth, Alice Roosevelt
Roosevelt, Franklin Delano, 11, 29, 30, 38, 63, 86,
    123, 128, 134, 152, 298, 420
Roosevelt, Theodore, 4, 122–23
Ross, Ishbel, 143
Ross, Ray, 266, 300
Roth, Fred, 93–94
Rubin, Carl, 149
Ruehlmann, Eugene, 94, 99, 101–2, 137, 166
Rymkus, Lou, 34, 408

St. Jaeger College, 16
St. Xavier High School, 22–25
Samuels, Helen, 275
Sauter, William, 155
Saxbe, Ardath ("Dolly"), 169, 192
Saxbe, William Bart ("Bill"): Gilligan's guberna-
    torial race (1970) and, 214, 216, 391; Gilligan's
    gubernatorial reelection bid (1974), 350,
    355–56, 357, 359, 365, 382, 384; Gilligan's U.S.
    Senate race against, 169, 180, 181–82, 183,
    186–87, 189–92, 193, 195; Lausche and, 152;
    Ohio gubernatorial race (1970) and, 199, 203;
    redistricting and, 253
Sayler, Milton, 143
Schaefer, Laurie Lea, 335–36
Scherer, Gordon, 123, 296
Schleiden, Jim, 211–12
Scrip (Notre Dame), 34–35
Seasongood, Murray, 66
Sebelius, Gary, 388–89, 405, 426
Sebelius, John, 413
Sebelius, Kathleen Gilligan (Gilligan's daughter):
    biographical information, 56, 97, 106, 107,
    108, 109; early career of, 225, 405; educa-
    tion of, 155, 165, 197; father's political career
    and, 120, 124, 130, 134, 142, 177, 179, 188–89,
    382, 384, 391; on father's remarriage, 423; on
    father's run for Cincinnati school board,
    421–22; as Kansas governor, 425–26; in
    Kansas legislature, 413; marriage and family
    of, 388–89, 413; as U.S. Health and Human
    Services secretary, 427–28
Sebelius, Keith, 388–89, 413
Sebelius, Ned, 413
Seiberling, John, 251
Seltzer, Louis B., 152

Sensenbrenner, Jack, 264
Shakow, Alex, 396, 402
Shallenburger, Tim, 425–26
Shapiro, Josephine, 115
Shaul, Dennis ("Denny"), 199, 209, 286, 358
Shaw, Robert, 261
Shawk, Abel, 10
Sheehan, William ("Bill"), 89, 90–91, 111, 175
Sherrill, Clarence, 67
Shields, Ann, 173, 182, 183, 193, 199, 209, 211
Shields, Mark: Gilligan Institute, 427; Gilligan's
    gubernatorial race (1970) and, 198, 199, 200,
    209, 211, 212, 218, 220, 232, 234–35, 238; Gil-
    ligan's gubernatorial reelection bid (1974),
    350–51, 353, 358, 366, 369, 379, 386; Gilligan's
    post-political career and, 393, 420; Gilligan's
    U.S. Senate race and, 3, 172, 173, 179–80, 182,
    183, 185, 189, 192; Ohio's Washington, D.C., of-
    fice headed by, 278–79, 291; redistricting and,
    254–55; on U.S. AID, 404; views on Gilligan, 4
Shipka, Bob, 180, 186, 194
Short, Haskell ("Mr. Small"), 293
Shriver, Sargent, 147, 298
Shump, Joe, 286
Sigall, Herschel, 272
Silent Spring (Carson), 128
Sindell, Steven, 377
Sinton, Annie. See Taft, Annie Sinton
Sive, Leonard, 116
Slagle, Gene, 344
Smith, Al, 20
Smith, George C., 392, 393
Smith, Reverend Alvin Duane, 275
Smith, Warren, 368
Snyder, Robert, 403
Sommer, Joseph, 286
Somoza, Anastasio, 404
Sorenson, Ted, 170, 175, 178
Souder, Bill, 195
Speck, Sam, 284
Spraul, Tom, 112, 115, 116
Spraul-Schmidt, Judith, 15, 98, 114
Springer, Gerald ("Jerry"), 238
Staab, Charles, 139
Steinbeck, John, 1–2
Steubenville (Ohio), air quality of, 323
Stevenson, Adlai, 60–62, 70, 173, 352–53
Stewart, Dana, 238
Stewart, James Garfield, 152
Stewart, Potter, 74, 81, 86
Stockdale, Robert E., 252, 273
Stocker, Frederick D., 223, 229–30
Stokes, Carl, 189, 193–94, 204
Stokes, Louis, 189
Straus, Robert, 352–53
Strickland, Ted, 427
Suddes, Tom, 357
Sulligan, Jack, 161–62, 180, 340–41

Sullivan, Jack, 397, 398, 400, 402
Sullivan, Jimmy, 114
Sullivan, Richard, 31
Sullivant, John T., 12
Sutton, Mrs. William, 13
Swanbeck, Ethel, 245
Sweeney, Patrick, 276, 341, 342, 344–45, 346
Sweeney, Robert, 199, 200
Sweet, David, 235, 237, 276, 279, 288, 295, 322,
    330–38, 420

Taft, Alphonso, 143–44
Taft, Annie Sinton, 143, 144
Taft, Charles Phelps, 67, 81, 82, 83, 89, 90, 93–94,
    96, 101, 117, 118, 139, 143, 144, 148
Taft, Helen, 144
Taft, Hulbert, 144
Taft, Robert A. ("Bob") Jr.: biographical infor-
    mation, 143–44, 214, 220, 371, 391, 393; Con-
    gressional races of, 111, 112, 139–40, 143–50;
    Ohio gubernatorial race (1970) and, 197, 201,
    203, 206–7, 208
Taft, Robert Alfonso, 61, 64, 67, 86, 87, 144
Taft, William Howard ("Bill"), 67, 122–23, 143–
    44, 266, 271, 273
Taft-Flannery bill (Ohio), 272, 273, 274
Taft-Hartley Act, 88, 91, 132–33, 135, 153
Tarlin, Betsy. See Gilligan, Betsy Tarlin (daughter-
    in-law)
tax reform (Ohio): Gilligan on, as Cincinnati
    city council member, 76–77; Gilligan on, as
    governor, 228–30; Gilligan on, as gubernato-
    rial candidate (1970), 200, 217; income tax
    passed by voters, 295–301; Ohio House on,
    241–50, 252, 256, 257, 272, 276; Ohio Senate
    on, 259, 261–62, 265–77; sales tax, 217, 230,
    239, 245–46, 262, 264, 266–67, 270, 272–74;
    school tax levy, 223, 386, 424
Teamsters, 85, 92, 186, 385
Teeter, Robert, 181
Teheran Conference, 38
Tenenbaum, Judy, 380
Tenenbaum, Robert ("Bob"): austerity measures
    and, 264; Chavanne and, 257; environmental
    issues and, 285; Friedman and, 289; Gilli-
    gan's gubernatorial race (1970) and, 199, 209,
    217, 219; Gilligan's gubernatorial reelection
    bid (1974), 354, 358, 366, 369, 380–82; press
    secretary role of, 223, 232, 233, 294, 295, 388;
    on Taft-Flannery bill, 272; tax reform and,
    274, 276
Tepper, Jay, 267, 268, 275, 290, 303, 362, 369, 392
Thomas, Lowell, 23
Thomas J. and Alberta White Center for Law,
    Government, and Human Rights, University
    of Notre Dame, 410
Thornberry, Homer, 130
Thurber, James, 225

Tillson, Brad, 387
Times-Star (Cincinnati), characteristics of, 62
Tipps, Paul, 283
Tracy, Roger, 220
Truman, Harry, 84–85, 91, 124, 140, 153
Truth-in-Packaging, 139–40
Tulley, Joseph, 250, 259, 296
Tunney, John, 291–92
Turner, Richmond K., 46
Turner, Robin, 214, 215, 216, 218
TV Beeper, 294
Twachtman, John Henry, 11

Udall, Morris ("Mo"), 372
United Auto Workers, 87, 266, 271, 273
United Farm Workers, 84, 385
University of Chicago, 54–55
University of Cincinnati, 56, 418
University of Notre Dame, 26–35, 57, 407–16
U.S. Agency for International Development (AID), 394–406
U.S. Department of Health and Human Services, 427–28
Usher, Brian, 196, 347, 352, 373, 375, 409
USS Emmons, 37–44, 45–53
USS Iowa, 38
USS Rodman, 40, 45–53

Valiquette, Marigene, 344
Vance, Cyrus, 394, 402–3, 404, 407, 414
Vander Meer, Johnny, 24
Vanelli, Frank, 158
van Selle, Margaret, 134
Victoroff, Victor M., 308
Vietnam War: Gilligan's U.S. Senate race and, 159–60, 167, 181, 182, 183–84, 186, 188, 191; Johnson administration, 134–35, 140–42; Kent State University 1970 shootings and, 207–8; 1968 presidential race and, 174–80
"Vision of Margery Kempe, The" (Gilligan), 56
Voinovich, George, 220, 226, 244, 247, 277, 281–82, 385
Voting Rights Act, 133

Wagner, Edward ("Ed"), 124, 129–30, 131, 156, 160, 163
Waldvogel, Edward M., 78
Walker, Dan, 179, 325
Walker, Thomas, 130
Wallace, George, 178, 187, 192, 291
Walnut Hills High School (Cincinnati), 38
Warburg, Paul, 337
Wargo, John P., 252
Warren, Earl, 131
Watergate, 355–56
Webster, Daniel, 144
Weigand, Most Reverend William Keith (bishop of Salt Lake City), 414, 415

Weil, Sidney, 61, 67, 80, 92, 93, 96, 114, 115, 117, 118, 119, 120, 121
Weisenborn, Clara, 256
Weisert, David, 246
Weld, Edric A., Jr., 228–29, 230
Welsh, Bill, 176
Wenke, Leonard, 424
Westmoreland, William, 140–41, 160
Whealon, W. J., 316
Wheat, Warren, 150, 216, 345
White, Byron ("Whizzer"), 113
White, Theodore, 171, 178
White, Thomas J., 408
Whitman, Ira L., 318–22, 324–30, 420
"Who Has Tasted Bread" (Gilligan), 35
Wiethe, John A. ("Socko"), 96, 113–21, 126, 182, 198
Wilkowski, Arthur, 360
Williams, Rich, 422
Williams, Sydney, 72–75, 76
Williamson, C. R., 42
Wilson, Charles (cabinet member, Eisenhower administration), 86
Wilson, Charlie (Texas Congressman), 404
Wilson, Nancy, 232
Wilson, Woodrow, 63
Wing, George, 124
Winn-Dixie Stores, 133
Wirtz, W. William, 147
Witkind, Vivian, 183, 184, 327
Wolfe, Tom, 201
Women's City Club (Cincinnati), 80–81
Woodrow Wilson International Center for Scholars, 391
Woolf, Virginia, 225
Working Review Committee (Cincinnati), 101
World War II: African Americans in military, 43–44; D-Day, 40–43; Okinawa invasion, 45–53; race issues, 43–44; Teheran Conference, 38; veterans of, and Johnson administration, 132
Wright, Wilbur, 1
Wylie, Chalmers, 203

Xavier University, 16, 54–62, 74, 190, 218–19

Young, Stephen A., 6, 91, 126, 139, 193, 197, 201, 202, 203
Youngstown Sheet & Tube, 324

Zablocki, Clement, 396–97
Zahm, John Augustine, 27
Zaidan, Abe, 156, 164, 180, 184, 293, 372
Zienba, Wally, 408
Zimba, Wally, 34
Zimmerman, Richard, 203, 208, 213, 214, 260, 317–18, 403